Family in Transition

Family in Transition

Rethinking Marriage, Sexuality, Child Rearing, and Family Organization

Arlene S. Skolnick
Jerome H. Skolnick
University of California, Berkeley

Little, Brown and Company   *Boston*

For Michael and Alexander

Preface

Probably never before in history have people in any one society held such widely differing opinions about the family as in America today. Some believe that the nuclear family—mama, papa, and the children—is a "biological phenomenon . . . as rooted in organic and physiological structures as insect societies."* At the opposite extreme are those who believe that a taste for family life is something that any sophisticated person naturally outgrows, like a taste for ice cream and sticky sweets. In the middle are those who believe that mother and child are the basic human couple, with the male only a fleeting and almost dispensable presence; and those who see man and woman as central and children as only an afterthought. Although there is rough correlation between age and conservatism in family matters, outward styles can be misleading: a hip exterior can hide the heart of a true believer in biological destiny, whereas a suit and tie can cover the epicene tastes of a Roman emperor and a belief in the obsolescence of all family ties.

This book is addressed mainly to those who hold conventional assumptions about the necessity of the nuclear family, the inherent nature of male and female sex-role differences, and the unchangeability of human nature. We would hope that even the most sophisticated would find some interest in the issues we raise, but our purpose is to do for the family what some poets have described as the main aim of poetic art: to make the familiar seem strange. Philosophers have often remarked on how we stop noticing things that are always before our eyes, but perceive strangeness only in deviations from the familiar. Thus we often ask:

Why did couple X get divorced, rather than why does couple Y stay together?

Why are women protesting, rather than why have they accepted an inferior status for so long?

*Weston Labarre, *The Human Animal* (Chicago: Univ. of Chicago Press, 1954), p. 104.

Why is he or she a homosexual, rather than how did that "normal" person come to identify with one sex and want erotic relations with the other?

Why do people live in communes, rather than why do they live in isolated houses in the suburbs?

Why was that child beaten or driven schizophrenic, rather than what goes on behind the closed doors of the "average" family?

Why do they rebel, rather than why do they "behave themselves" in schools and jobs that oppress and bore them?

What harm comes to children from mothers who work, rather than how are children harmed by long hours in the total power of their mothers, out of sight of any other eyes?

Besides familiarity, our knowledge of the family is obscured by two other sets of blinders: secrecy and sacredness. To a remarkable degree, the social-scientific study of the family has respected these taboos, and has done little more than confirm the conventional mystique of family life.

Our challenge to the conventional views, popular and professional, is divided into four parts. After the overview of our perspective on the family, developed in the Introduction, we present a number of conceptions of the family in the relevant scholarly disciplines. In the second part, we examine theories and data on sexuality and sex roles. Part 3 deals with the politics of socialization, from the point of view of both parent and child. In the last part, we present the variety of family forms existing in the United States today, as well as experimental forms of the family.

Finally, we should answer the question we have often been asked in informal discussions: Is this an "anti-family" book, and, if so, how do we justify our own nuclear family life? Our answer is that this book is not anti-family; rather, it challenges an ideology of the nuclear-family which implies that there is only one best way for people to live their lives, and that alternative arrangements must be sick or evil. Certainly, we value a lasting love relationship as a fine and rare achievement, yet we question whether the nuclear family provides the only setting for developing such a relationship. We also question an ideology of the family which asserts, as one prominent psychiatrist recently stated, that the monogamous family provides the perfect environment for child development. Whether or not there really are perfect families is beside the point. As John Stuart Mill pointed out, it is misleading to judge social institutions such as political despotism and the family in terms of their purportedly best examples. We must also consider the abuses of power that an institution permits and encourages. Finally, we have suggested that the isolated nuclear-family characteristic of industrial society may prove to be only an unstable, transitional stage of the family between two kinds of wider sociability—an early one built on kinship ties, and a later one, only now emerging, based on ties of common interest or community.

In developing this book we have discussed our ideas with a number of friends who have helped with critical comments and suggestions for readings. They include: Menachim Amir; Howard S. Becker; John Gagnon; Alvin Gouldner; Arlie Hochschild; Joachim and Ulla Israel; Berl and Suzie Kutchinsky; David Matza; Sheldon L. Messinger; Anthony Platt; Gertrude and Philip Selznick; June Tapp. We are extremely grateful for the research assistance of Steven Brick, Audrey McCool, and Richard Spieglman, as well as the secretarial help of Judy Dahle and Emily Knapp.

Arlene S. Skolnick
Jerome H. Skolnick

Berkeley
February, 1971

Contents

x

PART 3 / THE POLITICS OF CHILD REARING
Introduction, 302

PART 4 / THE POLITICS OF HOUSEHOLD AND LIFE STYLE
Introduction, 389

Family in Transition

Rethinking the Family

While gathering materials for this book we came across the following items in newspapers and magazines:

—A feature newspaper article about the effects of longevity on marriages, questioning whether twenty-year-olds can realistically make marriage contracts that will remain emotionally valid fifty years hence.

—An editorial in a prestigious science journal urging that the population explosion makes parenthood a privilege rather than a right, and that women must be educated to seek careers other than multiple motherhood. If such inducements as community child-care facilities and tax rewards for *not* having children fail to reduce the birthrate, the author suggests sterilization.

—An article in the parent and child department of the *New York Times* Sunday Magazine listing thirteen wrong reasons for having children, including the desire for immortality and the couple's parents' desires for grandchildren. (The prospective grandparents are advised to find fulfillment instead in a more active sex life.) The article asserts that child rearing is so demanding of time, effort, and talent that very few can really be good at it, especially people who are ambitious in their work.

—An article in the Sunday entertainment section of a newspaper on the large number of movies about troubled marriage; it is now almost a Hollywood cliché to portray marriage as unhappy, particularly if the partners are middle-aged and affluent.

—A series of articles in a major West Coast newspaper on homosexuals as a minority group, in which homosexuals, male and female, present the case for viewing homosexuality as a valid way of life. Included in this way of life are homosexual marriage and the bringing up of children.

A content analysis of the mass media during the past few years would reveal other challenges to conventional views on sex, marriage, and family, such as communal living and women's liberation. No one needs to be told how restrictions on sexual themes in movies, books, and stage plays have been dramatically loosened. Even a U.S. Government commission

1

on pornography, expected by its sponsors to "do something" about changing morals in this area, was rather undisturbed by the social effects of
obscenity and pornography.

Some see changes in sex and family life as frightening evidence that society is falling apart, that we are descending into anarchy and barbarism;
others feel that a time of genuine liberation may be coming. Understandably, students turn to social-science books and courses for enlightenment.
They are likely to be disappointed. They will repeatedly encounter affirmations of stability—affirmations that few changes in family and sex life are
occurring, and further, that no change is possible in the basic form of the
family.

The following excerpts typify social-science conclusions of stability in
the family:

> . . . Each new generation smiles with amusement at the courtship
> patterns of the preceding generation, and each generation of parents
> looks with some consternation on the innovations introduced by its
> children. In this way, intergenerational change calls attention to itself
> so that our interests are focussed on the differences. . . . The similarity
> from one generation to the next is ignored. . . . Yet studies of attitudes
> and behavior covering all the generations of the century show only rel-
> atively minor changes in basic patterns between contiguous genera-
> tions. Each generation introduces some new twist on an old theme:
> Statistical averages change slightly: A few more girls have intercourse
> with their fiancés before marriage, men get married a fraction of a
> year younger on the average, a few more couples practice contracep-
> tion, a few more women are employed in outside jobs. . . .[1]

> . . . The popular notion that America is undergoing a sexual "revo-
> lution" is a myth. The belief that our more permissive sexual code is a
> sign of a general breakdown of morality is also a myth.[2]

> . . . The available data indicate that since World War II, there has
> not been a mass retreat from chastity standards among the advantaged
> groups. . . .[3]

Having learned that there is no sexual revolution, the student may not be
surprised if told there is no generation gap, and that the divorce rate,
though in some places approximating the marriage rate, indicates little instability in the institution of marriage.

Some social scientists do see significant changes in contemporary behavior and values, most notably Margaret Mead, Philip Slater, and Robert
Lifton. Yet in reading through what often seemed like endless piles of
books and articles on marriage, the family, and sexuality, we were struck
by the uniformity and strenuousness of the efforts to seek out regularity
and to deny and rationalize change. On each key issue—the sexual revolution, the generation gap, the impact of divorce on the institution of

marriage—the writers in question seize upon one aspect of a complicated situation that *may* show continuity with the past, and disregard what may be genuinely novel.

With regard to divorce, for example, some writers argue that marriage is no less an imposing social institution than it used to be: more people are getting married more times than ever; in other words, there are fewer people who never marry, and more multiple marriages. Thus marriage is even more important than it ever was, because people are trying very hard to find compatible mates, rather than remain with unsatisfactory ones.

But the argument misses the point about marriage as a normative institution; it has lost its taken-for-granted, lifelong quality. In a sense, the Catholic view of marriage had a kind of emotional if not a doctrinal validity for most people until recently, and *this* is what has changed. The possibility of divorce is an unspoken but significant part of marriage vows today. And as one writer suggests, both partners remain permanently available on the marriage market until death do them part.' Thus the ground rules of marriage have changed so much that there are articles in women's magazines warning against getting divorced too easily. One author, a marriage counselor, wrote of a number of instances of arguments escalating into divorce threats, even into actual divorce, without either partner really wanting to go that far. The main point about marriage now is that it seems to possess an unprecedented fragility, no matter how many times people marry and remarry.

The Sexual Revolution and the Generation Gap

Similarly, many sociologists argue that a sexual revolution is not taking place: behavior, it is said, has not really changed all that much since the 1920s; it is just that people have become more open about their behavior. There are two difficulties with this argument. First, it often assumes that projections of the future are soundly made on the basis of prior regularities. For example, several writers have argued that Kinsey found little change in behavior among women born in 1920-1929, as compared to their mothers. On the basis of that finding, it is assumed that regularities will continue for girls born 1945-1955. Second, even if behavior were to remain the same, and only attitudes changed, that would be extraordinary in itself. Hypocrisy, La Rochefoucauld noted, is the homage that vice renders to virtue. Previous generations of secret swingers connived in upholding the puritanical definitions of morality.

The argument against the existence of a "generation gap" is based on the fact that working-class youths and those not going to college tend to be conventional, nonrebellious, and generally unlike the young who capture the headlines. Again, it may well be true that there is a "silent majority" among noncollege youth; still it is precisely those youths in whom the society has made the greatest investment, the ones ordinarily destined to run the nation's corporations, laboratories, law firms, universities, and the government itself, who are the most alienated.

Moral Contexts and Plausible Deviance

Moreover, arguments back and forth about numbers—how many student militants there are, how many college girls are having intercourse with how many men, how many homosexuals there are—obscure a vital point; namely, behavior is a form of communication where the same act can have different meanings according to its moral context. Thus an unmarried girl's affair with a man may be seen by her and others in a context of sin and remorse—as in the standard confession magazine story. This expression of deviance serves to reinforce conventional morality. Alternatively, the "deviants" may not actually adhere to conventional standards, but still respect them outwardly by keeping variant behavior discreet. This second approach undermines conventional morality, but does not really challenge it. Furthermore, the "deviant" sexuality is carried out under conditions of pluralistic ignorance; each violator wonders if he is the only one ever to have acted this way. The third alternative is to defy conventional standards openly, as happens when college girls live openly with young men, unwed movie actresses publicize their pregnancies, homosexuals picket in support of gay liberation, or women's liberationists denounce marriage and advocate masturbation.

The open violation of conventional norms, and the publicity lavished on famous violators by the media, affects even the most conservative elements of society. As Sumner[5] pointed out long ago, much of the force of moral rules rests in their being taken for granted, in the unthinkability of their being questioned, and in the assumption, sometimes unconscious, that terrible consequences will follow their violation. The failure of public sinners to suffer either guilt or the wrath of God further undermines the authority of the rules. Furthermore, once a rule becomes the subject of debate, no matter how the debate comes out, it can scarcely maintain its sacred character. The more sexual norms are discussed, the more life becomes both eroticized and politicized.

Consider, for example, the girl who wishes to follow a highly traditional life style—playing the sorority-girl role her mother played twenty-odd years before, and marrying and having babies as quickly as possible. She can no longer play the traditional role in the traditional way—as the unquestioned and inevitable progression of life's stages. Rather, each step of the way involves a conscious choice among competing values. She has to justify, if only to herself, a defense of her motives and behavior to counter the arguments of "the other side." The burden of proof has shifted from those who would depart from the conventional and has come to be shared by those who would maintain the status quo.

Although the open flaunting of unconventional behavior in the name of alternative standards is perhaps the most dramatically different feature of the present time, social change may occur even in the absence of large numbers of new recruits to the "deviant" ranks. As Gagnon and Simon comment:

> . . . significant social change does not come about only when there have been changes in overt behavior patterns. The moment of change may simply be the point at which new forms of behavior appear plausible. An example of this phenomenon of the increased plausibility of a behavior without behavioral change is the current status of homosexuality as a public topic. There is no evidence that there has been a growth in the proportion of the population with homosexual preferences. . . . [The homosexual] still faces the risks of arrest, conviction, or imprisonment, and the more frequent costs of rejection by friends, family, or loss of employment.
>
> Nevertheless, in recent years homosexuality has become one of the standard fares on the frontiers of the American cultural scene. . . .[6]

The notion of *plausibility* suggests that whether or not there has been revolutionary change in the family, sex, and child-rearing behavior, such change now appears possible to increasingly large numbers of people, especially young people.

Familiarity and the Family

Just as *plausibility* opens the mind's eye to fresh possibilities of experimentation and acceptance, so does *familiarity* tend to close off inquiry. In relations between people familiarity is said to breed contempt; in society, familiarity is more likely to breed not only acceptance, but the demand for more of the same. As Chomsky observes, it is all too easy for the familiar to be transformed into the "natural."

> One difficulty in the psychological sciences lies in the familiarity of the phenomena with which they deal. A certain intellectual effort is required to see how such phenomena can pose serious problems or call for intricate explanatory theories. One is inclined to take them for granted as necessary or somehow "natural."[7]

Here, Chomsky was speaking of language, but the same point may be made of the study of the family; it too remains hidden from us because we are so familiar with it. We ask questions only about departures from the expected norms, not the norms themselves. For example, as Hoffman argues:

> Virtually all the literature on homosexuality is marred by the failure of its authors to take account of the fact that heterosexuality is just as much a problematic situation for the student of human behavior as is homosexuality. The only reason it does not seem to us a problem is because we take its existence for granted. However, we should know enough about science by now to realize that it is just those questions we take for granted that are the ones, when properly asked, which would open up new areas of scientific exploration.[8]

Our major criticism of the field of the family, therefore, and here we include much of the professional literature as well as texts and readers directed to students, is its failure to consider how problematic and controversial the concepts and issues pertaining to the family really are. Conventional family patterns are projected backward and forward in time, without allowing for the possibility that there has been, and could be, change. A rather gentle critique of the "textbook world of family sociology" is offered by Rodman:

> It is with pleasure that I note that college level textbooks are, on the whole, rather free of one-sided interpretations that merely stress the contemporary mores, without any attempt to assess the data objectively . . . but what is generally lacking . . . is a treatment of the whole issue of varying interpretations, so that students, even though they are not being misinformed by the text they are using, will be prepared to recognize misinformation and biased interpretations that are presented to them elsewhere.[9]

Rodman lists a number of these issues which ought explicitly to be handled as controversies rather than as accepted doctrine:

> Are interfaith marriages the problem or is it organized religion and its demands that is the problem? Are "illegitimacy," "desertion," and "common law" unions *problems* of the lower class, or are they *solutions* of the lower class to more basic problems? Do we take the fact that there are few interracial marriages and few fulltime career women to indicate that these matters are somehow against human nature and therefore best to avoid? Or do we take these as indicative of cultural obstacles that should be removed?
> . . . Are the findings of role differentiations between the sexes sufficient ground for continuing to advocate a traditional system of such differentiation?[10]

We would add the following to the list of issues about which alternatives ought to be posed:

1. Is there any relevance to human marriage and family life today to be found in studies of animal mating and child rearing?

2. Does the population explosion and the biological revolution—the control of heredity, the possibility of transferring a fertilized egg from one womb to another, or to a test tube—mean the end of marriage and the family as institutions?

3. Are there any natural, inherent limitations on the design of human communities and families? Most writers on the subject of utopian communities and other experimental forms of the family assume that these are doomed to failure. They seem to discount the role of social pressures from the larger community, the prior cultural conditioning of the inhabitants, and other factors that might make such communities vulnerable to disintegration, rather than destined to fail because of "human nature."

The Nuclear Family Model

Why have these questions not been asked? Surely, the model of the family on which most scholars in the field build their research offers a heavy clue to the answer. For this model is astonishingly similar to the conventional ideas about the family held by the lay person. If we ask why this should be so, the answer must be found in the fundamental, usually unstated, assumptions about nature, human nature, and society that every social scientist brings to his work. Here we come to a paradox about social science: while there is a popular stereotype that social scientists tend to be liberal politically, and this may be true of their voting records, their work is, on the whole, profoundly conservative in its broader social implications. Freud's work is the most clear-cut example of this paradox. While to the average person Freud and psychoanalysis stand for uninhibited sex, Freud's teachings and most of the psychoanalytic movement have reinforced conventional morality and sex roles in almost every way. Further, the Freudian doctrine of an instinctually dark side of human nature makes any real social change seem an impossible dream. Similar points may be made about sociology and anthropology; while they seem to be radical in their attempts to understand and explain exotic cultures and subcultures, there is a conservative thrust in their tendency to justify existing institutions and practices. In fact, it has been persuasively argued that one cannot understand the history of anthropology and sociology in the past half-century unless one realizes that the major figures in these fields were carrying on a vehement but often unacknowledged argument against nineteenth-century socialism, particularly Marxism.[11, 12]

Here, then, are the main tenets of the dominant model of the family, as it emerges in the writings of social scientists:

1. The nuclear family—a man, a woman, and their children—is universally found in every human society, past, present, and future.

2. The nuclear family is the building block of society. Larger groupings—the extended family, the clan, the society—are combinations of nuclear families.

3. The nuclear family is based on a clear-cut, biologically structured division of labor between men and women, with the man playing the "instrumental" role of breadwinner, provider, and protector, and the woman playing the "expressive" role of housekeeper and emotional mainstay.

4. A major "function" of the family is to socialize children; that is, to tame their impulses and instill values, skills, and desires necessary to run the society.

5. Unusual family structures, such as mother and children, or the experimental commune, are regarded as deviant by the participants, as well as the rest of the society, and are fundamentally unstable and unworkable.

Anthropology and the Nuclear Family

This view of the family—with the nuclear unit occupying a central position—was first enunciated in anthropology in the works of Westermarck, Lowie, and Malinowski, and given its most classic expression by Murdock:

> The nuclear family is a universal social grouping. Whether as the sole prevailing form of the family or as the basic unit from which more complex familial forms are compounded, it exists as a distinct and strongly functional group in known society. No exception . . . has come to light in the 250 representative cultures surveyed for the present study, which thus corroborates the conclusion of Lowie. "It does not matter whether marital relations are permanent or temporary; whether conditions are complicated by the addition of members not included in *our* family circle: the one fact stands out beyond all others that everywhere the husband, wife, and immature children constitute a unit apart from the remainder of the community."[13]

Most anthropologists today do not go along with the idea of the universality of the nuclear family; it is becoming a dead issue in that field. The study of complex systems of kinship, which is a central concern in anthropology, is hindered rather than helped by assuming that the nuclear family is the basic unit. Rather, it appears that brothers and sisters are.[14]

Certain biologists and physical anthropologists stress the *evolutionary* importance of the nuclear family. Desmond Morris's best-selling book, *The Naked Ape,* has popularized one version of this view, based on the notion of the "killer ape": the idea that early man evolved out of apehood by becoming a carnivorous hunter. Hunting is seen not just as a way of getting food to eat, but rather as ". . . the master behavior pattern of the human species."[15] The nuclear family was one of the main products of the hunt:

> . . . a nuclear family—a minimal unit of father, mother, and children—may not have existed in early periods. The family among hunters and gatherers is based on strong sexual complementarity, men being primarily hunters and women carriers of wood and water, seed collectors, camp keepers, and child tenders. . . . Hunting . . . gives men a distinctive and important subsistence role and was presumably the principal factor that created the nuclear family. If the early hominids were not hunters, their family may have been matrifocal in that it consisted of females and immature offspring. Food collecting, as far as we know, does not create a sexual division of labor, for it is carried out by both sexes in the same way.[16]

Steward, author of the foregoing quote, says also that the nuclear family and its accompanying sexual division of labor are best understood as cultural, learned adaptations to the hunting way of life, rather than as inherent and "natural." But most students of prehistoric man also believe that the side effects of hunting—aggressiveness and the tendency to run in packs in men, gentleness and domesticity in women, plus a host of other human traits, were programmed into man's genes during the course of evolution. These genes will press for expression. Thus, today man's aggressive instincts are expressed in masculine occupations and in war, and women's place in the home preordained by genetic preferences for domesticity.

Psychoanalytic Theory and the Nuclear Family

Psychoanalytic theory has been even more emphatic in asserting the necessity and inevitability of the nuclear family:

> . . . More than any other influence, psychoanalytic psychology has, during the last generation, made us aware of two crucial things. First is the fundamental importance for the individual personality of the process of growing up in the intimacies of the family. Not only is mental illness to a large, though by no means exclusive, extent generated in the relations of a child to members of his family, but normal personality development is highly contingent on the proper combination of influences operating in the family situation. . . .[17]

Some psychoanalytic writers have gone even further than this; they see the family as the creator not only of the child's personality, but of most of the realities of social life. Everything in society outside of the family—religion, government, art—is only another, disguised form of the family:

> The family is the very root of all specifically human behaviors and institutions. Law is the codification and reprojection of the introjected fiats of the fathers, the lawgivers, the judges, and the kings. The State is the geographically rather than blood-based institution expressing our struggle to find both power and justice in the governing of men within the synthetic paradigm of the family. Morality is a precipitate of the oedipal predicament in man, a peace-making between superego, ego,

and id. Religion is a yearning for rapport with the divine father. . . .
Art itself is an oedipal rebellion against the real.[18]

Sociology and the Nuclear Family

Borrowing from anthropology and from psychoanalysis, the prestigious
functionalist school of sociology, under Parsons and his students, has made
of the nuclear family the keystone institution in the arch supporting society. To understand this sociological approach to the family, we must
spend some time in discussing the role of the structural-functional school
in sociology. It has been argued that functional analysis is nothing more
than the basic operating procedure of any social scientist—he looks at
aspects of social life and tries to figure out how they are related, what their
causes and effects are, etc. This is both true and misleading. Lumping all
social scientists together as analysts of social functions obscures the differences between them.

> The contrast between different kinds of sociocultural theories is not
> built around the question of whether sociocultural systems have parts
> which are integrated with or affected by other parts, but rather, which
> parts, and how often, and with what kind of effect, and for how long?
> In this sense we may distinguish the functionalism of Radcliffe-Brown
> from the functionalism of Boas from the functionalism of Marx, etc.
> To cut through the verbiage [we must ask] . . . how does a particular
> theoretician propose to explain observable cultural differences and sim-
> ilarities? If he is to provide any explanation at all, he must sooner or
> later commit himself to the assumption that he is dealing with systems
> —i.e., sets of causally related variables. What we want to know, what
> we must know is why he emphasizes certain sets of variables rather
> than others.[19]

The kind of functionalism that we and other critics have in mind is
properly called structural functionalism, and follows a line of descent from
Durkheim through Malinowski, Radcliffe-Brown, to Parsons and his
students. This genealogy is extensively documented in Gouldner.[20]

The points to remember about the structural-functional school are these:

1. Its statements pertain to a universal, timeless present—as in the idea
that the nuclear family has existed everywhere since time immemorial.
Accordingly, it raises generalizations into universal laws. For instance,
leading functionalists argue that social stratification or inequality is an inherent, necessary feature of society. Marx said the same thing about the
past in the first sentence of the Communist Manifesto, "The history of all
past society is the history of class struggle . . ."—but he obviously conceived
of the possibility of change. Or consider Malinowski on fatherhood and
legitimacy:

> . . . The most important moral and legal rule concerning the physio-
> logical side of kinship is that no child should be brought into the
> world without a man—and one man at that—assuming the role of
> sociological father, that is, guardian and protector, the male link between
> the child and the rest of the community.
>
> I think this generalization amounts to a universal sociological law
> and as such I have called it in some of my previous writings *The
> Principle of Legitimacy.*[21]

Similar points have been made by functionalists about sex roles. It is the
extra step, the timelessness, the denial of the possibility of exception or of
change, the elevation of description to a level of absolute and inevitable
principle that critics of functionalism are most likely to question.

2. Functionalism is based on an organismic metaphor, in which society
is analyzed as if it were an individual biological organism. Features of social structure—such as relationships between particular relatives, the practice of prostitution, sex roles, rituals—are assumed to act like bodily organs
in carrying out vital social functions.

Analogies and models often help scientific thinking. But the organismic
metaphor in social science probably creates more issues than it resolves. It
especially does so by begging the question of the *necessity* of particular
features of society. Nobody, in fact, can ever see a "society" as a whole,
as they can a frog or a horse, and agree as to where the head is and where
the tail. Thus there is always a question whether to cast the nuclear family
in the vital role of heart or brain, or as an appendage of other more vital
systems—for example, the unilineal kinship principle.

If a social institution is as necessary to society as the liver is to the
body, it would be dangerous to change it or remove it. By ignoring alternatives to contemporary social structures, functionalism tends to assume
that things *must* be as they are, especially in the area of familial and sexual
statuses and roles. By implying, without arguing the point, that the fundamental goal of society is the same as that of an individual organism—
surviving and maintaining a steady state—the organismic metaphor is
politically conservative. (It is true that the organismic metaphor is sometimes used by social critics who suggest society is "sick," but this view is not
as prevalent or as influential as the functionalist view of society as a healthy
organism.)

3. Functionalism argues that social structure is determined by society's
needs, rather than by social history. Ultimately, it says, social structure is
determined by social functions rather than technological and economic
conditions or political action. Thus, features of society from vagrancy to
voting may be explained by social functions, rather than social conditions
and power relations. Suffrage rights, for example, might be explained on
the basis of the functional needs of a democratizing society, rather than as

the result of political organization and action. So functionalism depoliti-
cizes history by interpreting outcomes as arising out of some putative need,
rather than as the result of social conflict.

4. Functionalism interprets every feature of society in terms of its contribution to social order, stability, and continuity. Thus, the family is the
functional institution par excellence. It not only provides society with new
bodies as the old ones wear out, but duplicates the class system—this function is usually called social placement—and provides society with the
manpower it "needs," making people *want* to do what the social system
happens to require.

History and the Nuclear Family

Obviously, the nuclear family model is not wrong in a literal sense, as
was the idea that the earth was the center of the solar system. The main
problem with the nuclear family model is intellectual; it influences thinking
in certain directions or, more precisely, it impedes us from considering
alternative interpretations.

In looking at exotic cultures, the model leads us to assume that because
one can find parents and their children in every society, their ideas and
feelings about family life must also be like ours. In our own society, the
nuclear model defines what is normal and natural both for research and
"therapy," and subtly influences our thinking to regard deviations from the
nuclear model as sick or perverse or immoral. Birdwhistell describes the
intellectual influence of the nuclear family model as follows:

> Statistics are made of units derived from this model, anecdotes are
> collected, and formalistic abstractions are derived from it. . . . Idealistic
> models can be dangerous when professionals who are empowered by
> the society to manipulate the lives of their fellows are encaptured by
> such models. The marriage counselor, the social worker, the psychia-
> trist, or the family doctor, if he unquestionably accepts the ideal
> model of the family as "healthy," has no recourse but to direct his cli-
> entele toward unreality or toward passive or "philosophical" accept-
> ance of their failures in familial relationships.[22]

Yet the detailed study of the actual relations between men, women,
and children during specific periods in Western history undermines the
concept of a universal, timeless, functional nuclear family. For example,
Kessen's history of the field of child study observes:

> Perhaps the most persistent single note in the history of the child is
> the reluctance of mothers to suckle their babies. The running war be-
> tween the mother, who does not want to nurse, and the philosopher-
> psychologists, who insist she must, stretches over two thousand years;
> the redundancy of the argument and its slow but discernible develop-

ment form a model—and a somewhat amusing one—for the history of
child study.[23]

At a more general level, Philippe Aries and other historians have convincingly defended the thesis that the concepts of childhood and of the nuclear family are relatively recent inventions. Aries begins by making a
crucial distinction between the family as an invariant physical reality, and
the *idea* of the family, which is susceptible to change:

> . . . have we any right to talk of a history of the family? Is the family
> . . . any more subject to history than instinct is? It is possible to
> argue that it is not, and maintain that the family partakes of the im-
> mobility of the species. It is no doubt true that since the beginning of
> the human race men have built homes and begot children . . .
>
> On the other hand, the great demographic revolution from the
> eighteenth to the twentieth century [the reduction of deathrates from
> infectious diseases] has revealed to us considerable possibilities of
> change in structures hitherto believed to be invariable because they
> were biological. The adoption of contraceptive measures has brought
> about both quantitative and qualitative changes in the family. How-
> ever, it is not so much the family as a reality that is our subject here as
> the family as an idea. True, men and women will always go on loving
> one another, will always go on having children, . . . and will always go
> on guiding the first steps of those children. That is not the question at
> issue. The point is that the ideas entertained about these relations may
> be dissimilar at moments separated by lengthy periods of time.[24]

Aries argues that the idea of "childhood" as having a "particular nature" different from adults, and requiring special institutions, did not exist
before the Middle Ages:

> In medieval society, the idea of childhood did not exist; this is not
> to suggest that children were neglected, forsaken, or despised. The
> idea of childhood is not to be confused with affection for children: it
> corresponds to an awareness of the particular nature of childhood,
> that particular nature which distinguishes the child from the adult,
> even the young adult. In medieval society this awareness was lacking.
> That is why, as soon as the child could live without the constant solici-
> tude of his mother, his nanny, his cradle-rocker, he belonged to adult
> society. The infant who was too fragile as yet to take part in the life
> of adults "did not count."[25]

The reason the infant "did not count" was the grim statistical probability
that he would soon be dead: before 1750, the odds in London were three
to one against a child living until the age of five.[26] During those centuries
parents could not indulge in the tender feelings toward infants that we
take for granted.

What came before the nuclear family, according to Aries, was a general
sociability in which people lived "on top of one another" in all-purpose

rooms where they ate, slept, danced, worked, and received visitors, all at the same time. Privacy did not exist, and was invented along with childhood and the family.

> The movement of collective life carried along in a single torrent all ages and classes, leaving nobody any time for solitude and privacy. In these crowded collective existences, there was no room for a private sector. The family fulfilled a function: it ensured the transmission of life, property, and names, but it did not penetrate very far into human sensibility. Myths such as courtly and precious love denigrated marriage, while realities such as the apprenticeship of children loosened the emotional bonds between parents and children.[27]

The work of Aries, Richard Sennett,[28] and other demographic historians demonstrates the useful insights that can be gained when the family is taken out of the historical void of functionalism and the search for universals, and placed into an historical context where it can be studied as something that changes in response to changing social, technological, and ecological conditions. We now turn to some work in sociology that attempts to carry out this kind of analysis.

The Conjugal Family and Industrialism

In sociology, the most extensive analysis of the nuclear family as an historical phenomenon rather than an eternal constant is provided by William Goode.[29] Goode concludes, after surveying data from around the world, that in every country in which there is modernization, industrialization, and urbanization, traditional family patterns are giving way to the familiar Western nuclear or, as he prefers to call it, conjugal pattern. (There is some confusion in the literature as to the distinction between the "nuclear" family and the "conjugal" family; we are using "nuclear" to mean the ideal, timeless, building-block view.)

According to Goode then, the conjugal family is one end of a dimension, the other end of which is a large kinship group—an extended family, or a matrilineal or patrilineal group in primitive societies. The large kin groups at one end of the continuum may differ from each other considerably, but conjugal families are alike. The change from large kin group to conjugal family consists of the following:

1. Most, but not all, ties and obligations based on kinship disappear.
2. Marriages are undertaken through love and relatively free choice, rather than through arrangement.
3. Dowry and bride-price disappear.
4. Marrriages between kin become less common.
5. Authority of parents over children and husbands over wives diminishes.

6. Equality between the sexes increases, and the legal system tends to equalize inheritance among all children.

There is a "peculiar fit" between the conjugal family pattern and the needs of an industrializing economy. How this "peculiar fit" comes about has become the subject of disagreement. Previous writers—for example, Ogburn, Engels—saw technology as a prime cause of family arrangements, but Goode sees technology, family patterns, and ideology as independent converging forces. As he writes:

> . . . The ideology of the conjugal family has generally entered a country before any substantial industrialization has taken place, and has the same effect as the equally radical ideology of economic progress by which so many countries have recently come to guide their decisions. . . .
> . . . Indeed, the ideology which stresses industrial expansion and the material good it brings, and the ideology that urges freedom from old restrictions in family life, are closely tied. They are likely to enter in a less developed country at about the same time. Their connection can be seen in the apparent harmony between the conjugal system and the needs of an industrial system. The rough empirical observation that whenever a country moves toward industrialization its family system begins to move towards some type of conjugal system suggests that in important ways a family system may hinder or facilitate industrialization.[30]

It is not necessary to agree with Goode that conjugal ideology is a prime mover in history to see how readily industrialism and the conjugal family fit together. When kin ties are diminished couples can move where jobs are, jobs can be granted on a merit basis rather than on family connections, and the breadwinners who need not share with extended kinfolk may work harder. Finally, the conjugal family may provide support against emotional stress created by the industrial system.

Goode's analysis, however, is limited since it confines itself to one segment of a continuum that may be extended back into the past and forward into the future. Winch and Blumberg carry Goode's analysis back into the past, or as they prefer to put it, toward the simple end of a scale of societal complexity. Noting that the nuclear family is found among the Eskimo and other peoples who live by hunting and gathering, they suggest that the nuclear family occurs:

> . . . not only under industrialism, but under simple subsistence conditions as well. The extended family, on the other hand, is found mainly in societies in the middle of the scale of technological development, that is, in agricultural societies in which there is a reliable food supply, little geographic mobility, a demand for the family as a unit of labor, and familial ownership of land.[31]

They also question the idea that all around the world, and within every society, all families are coming to resemble Goode's model of the conjugal unit: mother, father, and children, with reduced but not completely vanished ties with immediate kin. They recognize Goode's valuable contribution in placing the conjugal unit back into history and relating it to broader social conditions; yet they argue that his ideas hang too close to the ideal image of the nuclear family of functional theory, and too far from social reality:

> . . . we propose that the dimensions of familism in developing and developed societies be made the subject of empirical inquiry, rather than a deductive typological conclusion. For example, in contrast to the single nuclear family form implied by Goode's hypothesis of convergence, we shall consider evidence from one highly developed country, the United States, to the effect that at least three types of family can be distinguished.[32]

Accordingly, they distinguish the isolated nuclear family, the nuclear family embedded in a network of extended kin, and the mother-child family. Family type turns out to be highly related to ethnicity: the isolated nuclear family is most common among white Protestants, the extended family is most common among Jews and Italians, and the mother-child family among blacks. The effects of ethnicity on family type can in turn be explained by: variations among ethnic groups in social class; time since migration to this country, and occupational traditions—for example, family ties among people who were peasants in the old country are more disrupted by migration than are ties between people who were storekeepers or otherwise in trade.

We are not directly concerned here with the content of the foregoing research, but rather with the approach to the family it exemplifies: it is empirical, and it is willing to explore rather than explain away variation. Moreover, it relates these variations to meaningful sociological dimensions, rather than reducing them to biological or functional constants. This research is limited, however, in that it extends Goode's analysis back into the past, but, like his, seems to assume that industrialism is the last stop in technical history.

A deeper understanding of the family is to be gained, we think, by extending this analysis in two directions. The first is to analyze the family as a social problem. The second is to extend the line of societal and technological development against which the form of the family is plotted.

The Family as a Social Problem

Analysis of the nuclear family as a social problem suggests more than a long list of unhappy conditions: these have always been seen as problems *of* the family: divorce, broken homes, mental illness, juvenile delinquency.

But these problems are usually seen as standing apart from the family, as forms of illness or evil feeding upon it, yet essentially different. We propose to analyze the social problems of the nuclear family not as alien growths, but as arising out of the very structure of the nuclear family itself.

The analysis of the institution itself as a social problem constitutes one of the fundamental differences between writers on social problems.

> All writers on social problems agree that things qualify as "prob-lems" only when it is felt that something can be done about them. And much of the conflict between approaches to social problems can be reduced to differences in their understanding of those which among contemporary conditions are needless impositions of human suffering, and which are fundamental facts basic to social existence, elements of the human condition about which nothing can be done. To speak of something as a "problem" is to bring it out of the realm of the inevita-ble or the tacitly accepted, take away its "sacred" character, and sug-gest that it need not be the way it is.[33]

Goode comes close to analyzing the family as a social problem, but he nonetheless celebrates the conjugal family as part of the great sweep of human progress and takes for granted its continued viability as an ideal norm and reality for most people. Still, Goode writes uneasily about the conjugal family. Between the lines of his book, one can discern the shad-owy presence of another book that could be called "the tragedy of the family." Every so often, he breaks away from the detached stance of the scientific observer to speak with emotion about his findings. His conclusions reveal profound ambivalence. On the one hand, he sees the conjugal family's break from the bonds of kinship as a great victory for human freedom:

> . . . I welcome the great changes now taking place, and not because it might be a more efficient instrument of industrialization, for that is irrelevant in my personal scheme. Rather, I see in it and in the indus-trial system that accompanies it the hope of greater freedom: from the domination of elders, from caste and racial restrictions, from class ri-gidities. Freedom is *for* something as well: the unleashing of personal potentials, the right to love, to equality in the family, to the establish-ment of a new marriage when the old has failed. I see the world revo-lution in family patterns as part of a still more important revolution that is sweeping the world in our time, the aspiration on the part of billions of people to have the right for the first time to *choose* for themselves—an aspiration that has toppled governments both old and new, and societies and social movements.[34]

On the other hand, he does not believe "for a moment" that human happiness has been increased by the conjugal system's replacement of the older system. And he offers an analysis of the human costs of both indus-trialism and the conjugal family, which, although scattered throughout the book, and presented with the cool neutrality of an engineer describing stresses in the structure of a bridge, is as devastating a critique of Western capitalist society as has been made by a Marxist, or women's liberationist, or antitechnology counterculturist.

The first and most obvious "cost" of the conjugal as opposed to the extended family system is to the elders. Viewed as a power struggle, the rise of the conjugal system is a victory of youth over age. Under the new system age means less rather than more power, authority, and relevance. Years of experience make one obsolescent rather than wise . . . "although the older systems weighed heavily upon the young and upon women, the elders did, in fact, have more wisdom, and the young in time grew older and took their place in the community. . . ."[35]

But, as the analysis unfolds in the course of the book, it turns out that the very beneficiaries of the new system are also its victims. Take, for example, the young man, now freed to pursue his talents wherever they may lead. According to Goode, the industrial system, based on competition and achievement, creates great psychological tension. Security and satisfaction in work are almost impossible, no matter whether a man is janitor of the building or president of the corporation:

> The modern technological system is psychologically burdensome on the individual because it demands an unremitting discipline. . . . Lower level jobs give little pleasure to most people. However, in higher level professional, managerial, and creative positions, the standards of performance are not only high but are often without clearly stated limits. The individual is under considerable pressure to perform better than he is able.
>
> The conjugal family again integrates with such a system by its emphasis on emotionality, especially in the relationship of husband and wife. . . . Of course, the family cannot succeed in this task, but at least the technological system has no moral responsibility for it and can generally ignore the problem in its work demands.[36]

Goode does not explicitly explain why the family cannot succeed in providing emotional solace, although his writings emphasize the pressures of the competitive system, with limitless aspirations built in for the male; and the pressure of the housewife role on the female. Recall Goode's emphasis on the ideological values embodied in the conjugal system, as opposed to the traditional system: freedom, individualism, sexual equality. Ironically, the woman is liberated from the extended family only to find that her domestic burdens are increased rather than lightened.

> The modern woman is given little relief from child care, which is typically handed over to one person, the wife, rather than to several women, some of them elders, who are part of the family unit in the more extended systems. . . . Even the substantial development of labor saving devices and technology has not lightened labor in the modern

United States home, contrary to both advertising in women's magazines and the stereotyped notions of Europeans. Most of these devices
merely raise the standards for cleanliness and repairs, and allow the
housewife to turn out more "domestic production" each day. Every
study of the time allocation of mothers shows that housewives work
extremely long hours.[37]

If there is a peculiar fit between industrial work and the conjugal family,
there is a peculiar lack of fit between domestic work and the conjugal
family: any kind of economic analysis would suggest that such tasks as
child care, meal preparation, and clothes washing make more sense as
communal work rather than as the reduplicated tasks of isolated individuals.

Although Goode acknowledges that these strains in the conjugal system
may lead to changes, he does not think that these will be coming very
soon, and does not give much thought to what they might be like.

> . . . in the age-old war between the sexes and between generations,
> the entrance of the new ideology of the family plays a crucial role. . . .
> However, we do not believe that any family system now in operation,
> or likely to emerge in the next generation, will grant full equality to
> women, although throughout the world the general position of women
> will improve greatly. . . . We believe that it is possible to develop a soci-
> ety in which this could happen, but not without radical reorganization
> of the social structure. The family base on which all societies rest at
> present requires that much of the daily work of the house and children
> be handed over to women. Doubtless men can do this nearly as well,
> but they have shown no eagerness to assume these tasks, and families
> continue to rear their daughters to take only a modest degree of inter-
> est in fulltime careers. . . .[38]

Goode's analysis of the role of women under the conjugal system is re-
freshingly free of the biological cant that is usually presented as sociological analysis of sex roles. He argues that what perpetuates the system is
men's lack of eagerness to assume women's tasks and the continuing socialization of children into "proper" sex roles, rather than biological predesti-
nation. Yet, while analyzing strains in the man's and woman's role, Goode
tends to overlook the third corner of the nuclear triangle, the children. The
possibility that children may also be victimized by the nuclear family is
considered neither by Goode nor by very many other family sociologists.
He notes only that in the shift from the extended family to the conjugal
form, the mother is left alone with the children most of the time. Only the
disadvantages from the woman's point of view are considered, and these not
very deeply.

Power and Powerlessness in the Nuclear Family

The role of the child in the nuclear family shows how a sentimentalized
model of an institution can obscure and distort perceptions of reality. Senti-

mentalization leads most child-rearing researchers and most family writers to concentrate almost exclusively on the mother-child relation.[39] Moreover, the sentimental model of the nuclear family fosters a set of myths of the nuclear family: that the least powerful are the most indulged; that benefits are distributed in largest abundance to the children, next most generously to women, and least of all to men; that because the nuclear family is assigned by tradition and social theory the job of nurturing, protecting, and socializing children, that it actually carries out these tasks well; that all women are primarily mothers, and all mothers are good mothers; and, finally, that departures from the usual child-rearing patterns—for example, day-care centers or communal arrangements such as the kibbutzim in Israel—will harm children. The assumption is that the child can only lose in such a shift in care, that he must be moving from a loving home, where his mother fulfills all his needs, to one in which he will be emotionally, if not physically, deprived. For example, Dr. Abram Kardiner has recently argued, "You can't pay anyone to love your child. The monogamous family is the perfect environment for child development, for the incubation of feelings. I think you're dealing with dynamite when you toy with it."[40]

A few observers have seen the fallacy in this idealization of family life. In 1858 Herbert Spencer noted:

> The current assumption respecting family government, as respecting national government, is that the virtues are with the rulers and the vices with the ruled. Judging by educational theories, men and women are entirely transfigured in their relations to offspring. The citizens we do business with, the people we meet in the world, we know to be very imperfect creatures. In the daily scandals, in the quarrels of friends, in bankruptcy disclosures, in lawsuits, in police reports, we have constantly thrust before us the pervading selfishness, dishonesty, brutality. Yet when we criticize nursery management and canvass the misbehavior of juveniles, we habitually take for granted that these culpable persons are free from moral delinquency in the treatment of boys and girls.[41]

Today, even though parents are often blamed for the sins of the children, rather than the other way around, as in Spencer's day, his analysis still holds: people who in one context may be seen as morally or emotionally deficient are somehow transfigured when they become parents. This is best illustrated by the teachings of psychoanalysis. Psychoanalysis is correctly known for placing the blame for children's problems squarely on the shoulders of parents. As one writer recently put it, Freudian theory implies there is nothing "guaranteed" about psychosexual development—everything depends on "what the parents do, how they do it, how often they do it, or what they don't do."[42] Along with the idea of children as fragile beings whose entire futures are determined by the first three to five years of experience, psychoanalysis advanced the idea that many, if not most, parents are unable to meet these needs because of their own personality problems. Further, psychoanalysts argued that personality problems are not easily solved by will power or admonition, but only yield, if at all, to long-term psychoanalytic treatment. While this analysis should have led logically to demands for "a new society or perhaps different organic ancestors,"[43] psychoanalysis has paradoxically argued in the strongest possible terms that the conjugal family is the best place in which to bring up children, and further, that young children should not be deprived of their mothers and homes even temporarily, as for example, if mother were to work or children to attend day-care centers. That such separation could be defined, at least in some cases, as rescuing the children is an idea totally alien to the classic psychoanalytic world view.

In order to see this possibility, it is necessary to break away from the timeless, eternal, conflict-free model of the family and consider what happens to children when the nuclear family becomes isolated from the larger sociability of the extended family or the medieval town. Aries writes:

> Family and school together removed the child from adult society. The school shut up a childhood which had hitherto been free within an increasingly severe disciplinary system . . . the solicitude of family, church, moralists, and administrators deprived the child of the freedom he had hitherto enjoyed among adults. It inflicted upon him the birch, the prison cell—in a word, the punishments usually reserved for convicts from the lowest strata of society. But this severity was the expression of a very different feeling from the old indifference: an obsessive love which was to dominate society from the eighteenth century on.[44]

Perhaps the surest key to understanding the problems of the nuclear family is the concept of power—in particular the power of parents over children, which is enhanced by isolation. About a hundred years ago, John Stuart Mill argued that the power of the Victorian husband and father was comparable to that of a political despot. The family "is a school of willfullness, overbearingness, self-indulgence, and a double-dyed and idealized selfishness, of which sacrifice itself is only a particular form,"[45] a school of despotism, in which the virtues of despotism, but also its vices, are largely nourished."[46] Mill's point is not that men are evil, but that any situation of power and privilege that is based on one's status at birth potentially leads to the corruption of the privileged and the abuse of the dominated. Today the popular image of the husband as a hen-pecked Dagwood Bumstead has replaced the Victorian brute Mill was denouncing, typified by Bill Sykes the woman-murderer in *Oliver Twist,* although the more subtle effects of sexual inequality, which Mill also dissected, remain with us. As far as children are concerned, however, Bill Sykes and Fagan and other Dickensian child-abusers, male and female, live on today.

The Child as Victim

We are accustomed to think now that children are society's darlings, that this is the century of the child, and so forth. There is the joke about the man who never tasted white chicken meat because when he was a child, his parents got it, and when he grew up, his children got it. If this joke reveals how contemporary children are indulged, it also expresses the resentment of adults toward children. Whether indulgence or resentment dominates the parent-child relationship, it is a fact that within the privacy of the nuclear family home the young child is in the objective position of being a prisoner: all activities—eating, playing, sleeping—are under the total control of a single authority, empowered by the state to employ corporal punishment to enforce his rules, however arbitrary these may seem to the child. Nor is there any provision for appealing to a higher authority.

If this seems a rather extreme and legalistic interpretation, consider the phenomenon called "the battered-child syndrome," which is defined as

> Non-accidental physical attack or physical injury, including minimal or fatal injury, inflicted on children by persons caring for them.[47]

Everyone has read of some of the more spectacular incidents of child abuse in the papers, and we need not elaborate on gruesome details. One's first reaction to such incidents is to apply the deviance paradigm: to define these as extreme acts, mercifully rare, carried out by deranged, bizarre, or otherwise disreputable people. In other words, a phenomenon quite apart from the normal life of society.

This was also the way in which the researchers who studied the problem approached it at first. Rather than dealing with an isolated phenomenon, however, they came to see that they were dealing with the tip of an iceberg: the part above water was easy to see and identify, the tens of thousands of children severely battered or killed yearly in the United States,[48] but it was hard to figure out where to draw a line at the "milder" end of the continuum that did not take in practically all of the rest of "normal society."

> Physical punishment is an accepted form of reprimand in our society. A rigid definition for a battered child, therefore, cannot be determined. . . .[49]

One of the leading studies of the battered-child syndrome[50] took as its sample the parents of infants and children under three who had been significantly abused by their parents, short of direct murder. Although these people's attacks on their children had come to the attention of hospitals, doctors, or the police, they were on the whole a rather random cross section of the population. There was nothing to set these parents off as a group in such terms as social class, occupation, IQ, urban-rural residence.

Neither did the researchers find any particular psychopathology or character type. What they did find was a pattern of child rearing that was only an exaggeration of the normal one. These parents had a curious sense of righteousness:

> From early infancy the children of abusing parents are expected to show exemplary behavior and a respectful, submissive, thoughtful attitude toward adult authority and society.[51]

One man said of his sixteen-month-old son:

> "He knows what I mean and understands it when I say 'come here.' If he doesn't come immediately, I go and give him a gentle tug on the ear to remind him of what he's supposed to do." In the hospital it was found that Johnny's ear was lacerated and partially torn away from his head.[52]

The researchers conclude:

> There seems to be an unbroken spectrum of parental action toward children ranging from the breaking of bones and the fracturing of skulls through severe bruising, through severe spanking and on to mild "reminder" pats on the bottom. To be aware of this, one has only to look at the families of one's friends and neighbors, to look and listen to the parent-child interactions at the playground and the supermarket, or even to recall how one raised one's own children or how one was raised oneself. The amount of yelling, scolding, slapping, punching, hitting, and yanking acted out by parents on very small children is almost shocking. Hence, we have felt that in dealing with the abused child we are not observing an isolated, unique phenomenon, but only the extreme form of what we would call a pattern or style of child rearing quite prevalent in our culture.[53]

We suggest that the problem is not that parents are bad and children are good, but rather, in Lord Acton's by now clichéd words, "power corrupts and absolute power corrupts absolutely." The nuclear family, especially in its more isolated version, gives parents nearly absolute power over children. Jules Henry states the problem succinctly as follows:

> . . . Pinched off alone in one's own house, shielded from critical eyes, one can be as irrational as one pleases with one's children as long as severe damage does not attract the attention of the police.
> . . . there is minimal *social regulation* of parent-child relations in our culture; this is, above all, what makes lethal child care practices possible. In a primitive culture . . . or in large households, where many people can see what a mother is doing and where deviation looses

critical, interested tongues, it is impossible for a parent to do as he or she pleases with his children. In a literal sense, the baby is often not even one's own in such societies, but belongs to a lineage, clan, or household—a community—having a real investment in the baby.[54]

Mothering

If the mythology of the nuclear family tends to place child-beaters out in the moral limbo reserved for sex fiends and other "degenerates," while denying the danger to children from ordinary parents, it also exaggerates in an opposite but perhaps equal direction another threat to children, that of maternal "deprivation."

The first studies of children placed in institutions early in life revealed many cases of irreparable emotional, intellectual, and, in some cases, physical damage. The concept of maternal deprivation passed into the popular lore on child rearing to mean that any separation from the mother must have devastating effects on the child. All separations, no matter how long they lasted, for what reasons, and without regard to what happened to the child in the interim, tended to be lumped together.[55] Thus the child sent into the hospital to have his appendix removed was put in the same category as the child who was sent to Grandma for a week while his parents went on vacation. Later, more careful researchers tended to cast doubt on the early idea that "maternal deprivation" was a simple unitary phenomenon. Recent research has emphasized the need for environmental stimulation as well as loving care and has shown that even within the confines of an institution, infants' development can be normalized and even accelerated by providing them with interesting sights and playthings.[56] The need of children for interesting playthings and environments is usually slighted, however, in comparison with emphasis on the need for maternal child rearing. One of the consequences has been large-scale inattention, especially by psychoanalytically oriented child-rearing specialists, to the possibilities of enriching children's lives through day-care centers, supervised playgrounds, and similar institutions which relieve the strain of both parenthood and childhood.

Further evidence on the effects of nuclear-family isolation and the total environment was found in a cross-cultural study of child rearing.[57] In comparing mothers and children in six cultures, this study found that the households in a New England suburb, called Orchardtown, were much more isolated than in the five other, more primitive societies. It also found that, in general, mothers in isolated households tended to be more hostile to children than in those where other women were around. Further, the Orchardtown mothers entertained a host of beliefs, which they put into practice, concerning children's needs for much sleep and outdoor play, for independence and settling fights by themselves, which were absent in the other cultures, and which the investigators felt were best explained by the mothers' needs for relief from the unremitting burdens of child care.

The authors confess that after spending ten years with their data, they have come to radically different conclusions from the ones they started out with: most studies see parental behavior as reflecting either parental beliefs and theories, or else the parents' unconscious motives and anxieties. But this study showed:

> . . . the pressures impinging on the growing child are much more
> . . . by-products of the horde of apparently irrelevant considerations
> that impinge upon the parents. These considerations of household
> composition, size of family, work load, etc., determine the time and
> energy that mothers have available to care for children. They deter-
> mine the range and content of mother-child relations. . . .
> All this seems very obvious once it has been said, . . . but these
> forces have been ignored in many studies. . . . Further, we contend that
> not only have important variables been neglected, but also the causal
> factors behind child-training practices have been misinterpreted. . . .
> Beatrice Whiting . . . suggests that child-rearing practices are
> based . . . upon "certain conditions in the natural and social environ-
> ment" . . . these practices, arising from necessities that do not pertain
> to children, are rationalized and justified by a structure of beliefs and
> values designed to support them. This interpretation holds that the be-
> liefs do not produce the practices, rather, the practices precede and
> necessitate the beliefs. We agree with Mrs. Whiting's point of view.
> The Rajput mother's contention that the fate of her child is written on
> his forehead reflects her inability to mold her child's fate in a society
> based on caste. The belief of the Orchardtown mother that her chil-
> dren should play out in the fresh air, and then retire early and get
> plenty of sleep, supports her need for some relief from constant child
> care.[58]

To which we might add that the whole set of beliefs constituting the nu-clear-family model reflect the realities of child rearing under industrial capitalism.

The psychological effects within the family of parents setting up rules supposedly for the benefit of the children, but which are actually based on their own needs or on some other circumstance, have been studied at great length by the psychiatrist R. D. Laing. Starting with the study of schi-zophrenics and their families, Laing comes to the conclusion that there is a "politics of experience" in every family, "normal" as well as schizophrenic. At issue is a political or power struggle over whose experience is to be val-idated, or defined as real. For example, parents may promise a child a trip to an amusement park, and then, finding that for some reason it is in-convenient to go, may say to the child, "You don't really want to go there anyway." Similarly, "bedtime problems" may be defined as a conflict of two perceptions of reality: the child's that he isn't sleepy, and the adult's perception that the child really needs his sleep and, besides, we need some peace and quiet around here. It is interesting to note that sleep problems are the leading pediatric complaint of recent years, in contrast to the eating problems of earlier generations. Given the Laingian analysis, it is easy to see why they have proved to be so intractable.

The Family in the Future

Our analysis of the strains within the nuclear family has suggested that we look beyond the walls of the household to what is happening in the world outside in order to understand family relations. Goode has done this by examining the effects of industrialism. But the social order of industrialism, with which the nuclear family had a "peculiar fit," is, in the more advanced countries, already giving way to a new stage of economic development.

There is no agreed-upon name for this stage—post-industrial, post-modern, cybernetic, technotronic have been put forth by different writers.[59] While there is disagreement about labeling and measuring these changes, there does seem to be agreement about a vaguely conceived set of changes that transform an industrial society into a post-industrial one. These may be listed as follows:

1. Societal complexity increases—there is a greater division of labor, or more specialized occupations requiring specialized training.
2. Per capita energy consumption increases.
3. Automation replaces human labor in industry and in clerical jobs.
4. Affluence replaces scarcity; problems of distribution and consumption replace problems of production.
5. Urbanization increases.
6. Electronic media and modern transportation increase communication, break down time and distance barriers—emergence of a "world community."
7. The pace of social change accelerates.
8. Learning and knowledge become major growth industries.
9. Scientific and technological advances lead to increasing obsolescence of existing knowledge.

The "world-wide revolt of youth,"[60] the rise of a counter or underground or psychedelic culture, can be interpreted not only as a revolt against the technological order, but, ironically, as an adaptive response to the new technology, one that will supply it with the manpower it needs, in the same way as the nuclear family processed the human raw material for industrialism.

The increasing pace of social change has the most serious implications for family life. The problem is experienced most directly in the feeling that one generation's knowledge and perspectives are irrelevant for the next. The central problem of socialization today is not how society can ensure that the culture and skills of the older generation will be passed on to the children, but rather, how the burden of obsolescent knowledge can be kept from interfering with necessary changes. How can children be taught in a way that will not close their minds against further knowledge? How, in short, can human beings remain childlike all their lives in their curiosity and openness to new experience? We are suggesting that "adulthood" may be an obsolete stage of life in the post-industrial era.

Philippe Aries, as we have seen, has argued that childhood as a separate stage in life is a relatively recent cultural invention; childhood seems to be a by-product of a way of life in which all available hands do not have to work at making a living. Thus, in primitive hunting and farming societies, in medieval times, in farm families and lower-class families today, children go directly from toddlerhood into adult work roles; childhood as a long, leisurely "time-out" from real life work, in which one learns skills that will not be used until some distant future, does not exist. A group of elderly, white, working-class widows recalled this way of life for a young sociologist studying the aged:

> The mother set her young toddlers to work, feeding the rabbits, geese, and chickens, hanging out clothes on the line or barbed wire, or ironing clothes with an iron heated on the stove. The older children learned to quilt and darn . . . to refill gas lanterns . . . to grind the coffee, to stoke the fire, to can the vegetables for winter, to retrieve a pail of milk hung in the well to keep cool. . . . And they passed on the same skills to younger siblings. . . .
> As older children, a quarter of the widows worked in the fields or factories. One woman recalled picking her first bag of cotton, before the era of child labor laws, when she was five. . . . Play was something you did in between tasks. . . .[61]

These working children, according to the anthropologists and psychologists who have studied them, do not seem to have the "typical" childish traits of curiosity or imagination. Like the children in medieval paintings, they are miniature adults.

The greatest differentiation between adults and children seems to occur at a level of societal development where the children's labors are not needed, and where adult roles demand long apprenticeships, either on the job or at school. The age at which adulthood supposedly begins has been steadily moving up, defined not by biology, but by the social requirements for the adult role. The first shift moved the line from childhood to puberty; for many eras in Western history, the teens were a time for beginning work and family life. School typically ended with the completion, if one went that far, of grammar school. The next development was the invention of adolescence as the stage of life between childhood and adulthood, a period which has come to take up more and more years of the life span, as education has continued to lengthen. It is difficult to state at what age, in the United States today, adolescence ends. Perhaps thirty, as in the expression "never trust anyone over. . . ." If we grant that we are not talking about a biological event, what can we take to be the line of demarcation between adolescence and adulthood? An irrevocable commitment to a career, a life style? A final solution to the problem of identity, and a commitment never to change? A commitment to a marriage that will be regarded as final come what may?

If adulthood is defined as the end of growth and learning, then it is clear that an adult is someone by definition obsolete in a time of rapid social change. Society might come to be organized into "horizontal" layers of people the same age, with little contact between the different age groups, rather than the "vertical" grouping of people of different ages in the family. The study of aging mentioned earlier makes the following interpretation of how the aged fit into the total society:

> The country as a whole has "aged"; the proportion of those aged 0–14 has steadily declined since 1900 and the proportion of those over 65 has increased. . . . *more* generations are *alive* . . . in 1960 than was true in 1900. The biological "turnover" has slowed down. . . .
>
> Thus, while there is a premium on flexibility, the extension of life, and the unprecedented co-existence of three and four generations, tends to forestall flexibility. Mannheim remarked in his essay on "The Question of Generations" that if birth and death were not natural facts, we would have to "invent" them. I suggest that a functional equivalent to death *has* been devised in the sibling model of relationship . . . dividing society into layers of time (which) immunizes the young, and cuts them adrift from the old. The family, which as traditionally fostered, crosses generational ties, is on the decline. And as it declines, the sibling bond emerges. Thus, the equalitarian, nonauthoritarian character of American life . . . can be cast in a new light, as a mechanism which retains social flexibility, thus simulating the biological death which science has postponed.[62]

Perhaps the generations need not, however, be as rigidly stratified as geological layers. Sex and generation are not matters of biology and chronology only, as we have argued before. There is another possible pattern for the relations of the generations; comparing this generation of parents with the immigrants who came to America from Europe and had to learn new ways from their children, Margaret Mead writes:

> . . . the freeing of men's imagination from the past depends, I believe, on the development of a new kind of communication with those

who are most deeply involved with the future—the young who were
born in a new world. That is, it depends on the direct participation of
those who, up to now, have not had access to power and whose nature
those in power cannot fully imagine. In the past, in cofigurational cultures, the elders were gradually cut off from limiting the future of
their children. Now, as I see it, the development of prefigurational
cultures will depend on the existence of a continuing dialogue in
which the young, free to act on their own initiative, can lead their
elders in the direction of the unknown.[63]

In other words, this image of the future is one in which children and
adults are again like each other, as under subsistence conditions, but this
time the model person is the child rather than the adult. There is nothing
shocking or unprecedented about this: culture heroes of creative achievement—poets, artists, scientific geniuses—have always retained a kind of
childishness. A bit of data from the study of primate evolution would perhaps not be inappropriate here: the line of development that led to man
was associated with a trend toward infantilization or neoteny, that is, as one
progresses up from monkeys, through apes to man, the adults of each species retain infantile behavioral and physical traits for longer periods into
adulthood.[64] The adaptive significance of this was to preclude too early
specialization, to extend the period during which learning is possible.

We cannot confidently predict the future of the family. We have already indicated the present strains generated by the nuclear family in an
era of industrialism, and we see no easing of these strains in a post-industrial age. Not only is the nuclear family a faultily constructed piece of social engineering, but it also, in the long run, contains the seeds of its own
destruction. As Birdwhistell points out, the nuclear family dies while the
extended or interdependent family may remain immortal. That is, when a
child of a nuclear family grows up he

> . . . must break away from his original family to gain independence.
> In so doing, he establishes a unit which, as it accomplishes its pur-
> poses, inevitably moves towards its own—and his—death.[65]

In terms of day-to-day life, this means that the nuclear family, like the
crew of a spaceship, is highly vulnerable to disruption by the departure or
sickness of one of its members, while in the extended family, someone is
usually there to take over.

The functional problem of the family today is the recreation of extended family relationships without kinship. It is virtually impossible to restore
irrational ties of blood when the traditional social and economic conditions
that made them meaningful no longer exist. Besides, it would be undesirable to do so. As Goode so eloquently argued, the conjugal family stands
for equality, individuality, and freedom. The problem is one of maintain-

ing these values while recreating the kind of social solidarity that exists in the extended family, or the medieval village described by Aries. Two groups in our society have already begun to build this form of solidarity: the old and the young. The old in their retirement villages and the young in their crash pads and communes have much in common. The fact that one group has had this form of life thrust on it, while the other has chosen it, should not obscure the similarities between them. They are both living out post-industrial, post-Protestant ethic, post-nuclear family lives during a time of social and technological transition.

If there is anything to be said with some degree of assurance, it is that the future will probably see family arrangements at least as varied and colorful as those at present. Barring some sort of massive state interference, there is unlikely to be one family pattern which everyone will automatically follow on pain of being labeled deviant, in the manner of the nuclear family. There will probably be families, there will be couples, there will be communes, homosexuals, some homosexual marriages, there will be many free individuals, men and women, who choose to spend their lives, or part of them, outside of families. The "sacred" nuclear model, as we have seen, has obscured the history of the diversity of family life—that there have been such societies as that of imperial Rome, where the family was not something everyone had, and groups, such as the early Christians, where men and women lived together communally, on the basis of mutual love, or agape. Shakespeare, we think, had the last word on the future of the family:

> *There are more things in heaven and earth, Horatio,*
> *Than are dreamt of in your philosophy.*
> *O brave new world, that has such people in it.*

References

1. J. R. Udry, *The Social Context of Marriage* (Philadelphia: Lippincott, 1966), pp. 25–26.

2. I. L. Reiss, "How and Why America's Sex Standards Are Changing," in J. H. Gagnon and William Simon, *The Sexual Scene* (Chicago: Aldine, 1970), pp. 43–58.

3. H. Pope and D. Knudsen, "Premarital Sex Norms, The Family and Social Change," *Journal of Marriage and Family*, August 1965, pp. 314–323.

4. See B. Farber, *Family Organization and Interaction* (San Francisco: Chandler, 1964).

5. See W. G. Sumner, *Folkways* (New York: Mentor, New American Library, 1960) (first published in 1907).

6. J. H. Gagnon and W. Simon, *The Sexual Scene* (Chicago: TRANS-action Books, Aldine, 1970), pp. 10–12.

7. N. Chomsky, *Language and Mind* (New York: Harcourt, Brace and World, 1968), p. 21.

8. M. Hoffman, *The Gay World* (New York: Basic Books, 1968; Bantam Books, 1969), p. 30.

9. H. Rodman, "The Textbook World of Family Sociology," *Social Problems,* 12, 1965, p. 449.

10. *Ibid.,* p. 450.

11. M. Harris, *The Rise of Anthropological Theory* (New York: Crowell, 1968).

12. A. Gouldner, *The Coming Crisis in Western Sociology* (New York: Basic Books, 1970).

13. G. P. Murdock, "On the Universality of the Nuclear Family," *Social Structure* (New York: Macmillan, 1949), pp. 1–11.

14. See R. Fox, *Kinship and Marriage* (Baltimore: Penguin Books, 1967).

15. W. S. Laughlin, "Hunting: An Integrating Biobehavior System and Its Evolutionary Importance," in R. B. Lee and I. DeVore (eds.), *Man the Hunter* (Chicago: Aldine, 1968), pp. 304–321.

16. J. H. Steward, "Causal Factors and Processes in the Evolution of Prefarming Societies," in R. B. Lee and I. DeVore (eds.), *Man the Hunter* (Chicago: Aldine, 1968), pp. 321–335.

17. T. Parsons, "The Normal American Family," in Farber, Mustachi, and Wilson (eds.), *Man and Civilization: The Family's Search for Survival* (New York: McGraw-Hill, 1965), pp. 31–50.

18. W. La Barre, "Family and Symbol," in W. Munsterburger (ed.), *Psychoanalysis and Culture: Essays in Honor of Geza Roheim* (New York: International Universities Press, 1951), pp. 156–167.

19. Harris, *op. cit.*

20. Gouldner, *op. cit.*

21. B. Malinowski, "Parenthood, the Basis of Social Structure," in R. Coser (ed.), *The Family, Its Structure and Functions* (New York: St. Martin's Press, 1964), pp. 3–18.

22. R. L. Birdwhistell, "The American Family: Some Perspectives," *Psychiatry,* **29,** 1966, pp. 203–212.

23. W. Kessen, *The Child* (New York: Wiley, 1965), pp. 1–2.

24. P. Aries, *Centuries of Childhood* (New York: Random House, Vintage Books, 1962), p. 9.

25. *Ibid.,* p. 128.

26. Kessen, *op. cit.,* p. 8.

27. Aries, *op. cit.,* p. 491.

28. R. Sennett, *The Uses of Disorder, Personal Identity, and City Life* (New York: Knopf, 1970).

29. See W. Goode, *World Revolution and Family Patterns* (New York: Free Press of Glencoe, 1963).

30. W. Goode, "The Role of the Family in Industrialization," in R. F. Winch and L. W. Goodman (eds.), *Selected Studies in Marriage and the Family* (New York: Holt, Rinehart and Winston, 1960), p. 65.

31. R. F. Winch and R. L. Blumberg, "Societal Complexity and Familial Organization," in R. F. Winch and L. W. Goodman (eds.), *Selected Studies in Marriage and the Family* (New York: Holt, Rinehart and Winston, 1960), p. 92.

32. Winch and Blumberg, *ibid.,* p. 3.

33. J. H. Skolnick and E. Currie, *Crisis in American Institutions* (Boston: Little, Brown, 1970), p. 15.

34. W. Goode, *World Revolution and Family Patterns, op. cit.,* p. 380.

35. *Ibid.,* p. 379.

36. *Ibid.,* p. 14.

37. *Ibid.,* p. 15.

38. *Ibid.,* p. 373.

39. See E. E. LeMasters, *Parents in Modern America* (Homewood, Ill.: Dorsey, 1970).

40. *Newsweek,* March 23, 1970, p. 75.

41. H. Spencer, *Essays on Education* (New York: Dutton, 1946), p. 87.

42. LeMasters, *op. cit.*, p. 44.

43. *Ibid.*, p. 45.

44. Aries, *op. cit.*, p. 413.

45. J. Mill, *On Liberty, etc., Three Essays* (London: Oxford, 1912), pp. 66–67.

46. *Ibid.*, p. 88.

47. D. G. Gil, "Incidence of Child Abuse and Demographic Characteristics of Persons Involved," in R. E. Helfer and C. H. Kempe (eds.), *The Battered Child* (Chicago: Univ. of Chicago Press, 1968).

48. *Ibid.*, p. vii.

49. *Casebook and Proceedings: Seminar on the Battered Child Syndrome*, Jan. 21, 1965, State Dept. of Social Welfare, Topeka, Kans.

50. B. F. Steele and C. B. Pollock, "A Psychiatric Study of Parents Who Abuse Infants and Small Children," in R. E. Helfer and C. H. Kempe (eds.), *The Battered Child* (Chicago: Univ. of Chicago Press, 1968).

51. *Ibid.*, p. 110.

52. *Ibid.*

53. *Ibid.*, p. 104.

54. J. Henry, *Culture Against Man* (New York: Random House, 1963), p. 332.

55. L. Yarrow, "Maternal Deprivation: Toward an Empirical and Conceptual Re-evaluation," *Psych. Bull.*, 58, 1961, pp. 459–490.

56. B. L. White, "An Experimental Approach to the Effects of Experience on Early Human Behavior," in J. P. Hill (ed.), *Minn. Sympos. Child Psychol.* (Minneapolis: Univ. of Minn. Press, I, 1967), pp. 201–226.

57. L. Minturn, W. E. Lambert, et al., *Mothers of Six Cultures* (New York: Wiley, 1964), pp. 291–292.

58. *Ibid.*, pp. 291–292.

59. See V. Kavolis, "Post-modern Man," *Social Problems*, XVII, 1970, pp. 435–437; Daniel Bell (ed.), *Toward the Year 2000* (Boston: Houghton Mifflin, 1968, book version of special issue of *Daedalus*, Summer 1967); Norman Birnbaum, "Is There a Post-industrial Revolution?" *Social Policy*, July-August 1970, pp. 3–13; Alvin Toffler, *Future Shock* (New York: Random House, 1970).

60. M. Mead, *Culture and Commitment* (Garden City, N.Y.: Doubleday, 1970), pp. 93–94.

61. A. Hochschild, unpublished ms., Sociology Dept., University of California at Santa Cruz, 1970.

62. *Ibid.*

63. Mead, *loc. cit.*

64. W. A. Mason, "Early Social Deprivation in the Non-human Primates: Implications for Human Behavior," in D. C. Glass (ed.), *Environmental Influences* (New York: Rockefeller Univ. Press and Russell Sage Foundation, 1968), pp. 70–101.

65. Birdwhistell, *op. cit.*

1

Conceptions
of the Family

33

Introduction

Scholarship and the Family

The study of the family does not fit neatly within the boundaries of any single scholarly field; genetics, physiology, archeology, anthropology, sociology, and psychology all touch upon it. Religious and ethical authorities also claim a stake in the family. In addition, troubled individuals and families generate therapeutic demands on family scholarship. In short, the study of the family is interdisciplinary, controversial, and meaningful for social policy and practices.

Interdisciplinary subjects present certain characteristic problems. First, there is the problem of each discipline's differing assumptions and views of the world. Such perspectives may not directly transfer into another field. For example, biologists and physically oriented anthropologists tend to analyze human affairs in terms of individual instincts; for them, society is a shadowy presence, serving mainly as the setting for biologically motivated individual action. Sociologists and cultural anthropologists, by contrast, usually perceive the individual as an actor playing a role written by culture and society; according to this view, the individual has no wholly autonomous thoughts and impulses. An important school of psychologists sees man neither as passive recipient of social pressure nor as a creature driven by powerful lusts, but as an information processor trying to make sense of his environment. There is no easy way of reconciling such perspectives. Scientific paradigms—characteristic ways of looking at the world—determine not only what answers will be found, but what questions will be asked.

There is a further problem with the family as an interdisciplinary field —it demands competence in more than one subject. At a time when competent scholars find it difficult to master even one corner of a field—say the terminology of kinship, or the physiology of sexual arousal—intellectual demands on students of the family become vast. Although writers on the family confront many issues, their professional competence is usually limited. Thus a biologist may cite articles in psychology to support a position, without comprehending the tentativeness with which psychologists regard the researcher and his work. Similarly, a psychologist or sociologist may draw upon controversial medical studies. Professional competence means more than the ability to read technical journals; it includes informal knowledge—being "turned in" to verbal understandings and evaluations of

34

research validity. Usually, a major theory or line of research is more heavily questioned in its own field than outsiders realize.

Prehistory

The distinction between tentativeness of research and the assertiveness of popular writings is illustrated by research on the prehistoric origins of the human family. Washburn and his associates have hypothesized a series of causal links relating hunting, brain size, dependency of the human infant, upright posture, tool use, and language to forms of human social organization, particularly the family. In the selection by Washburn and DeVore the theory is presented rather tentatively, in accord with scientific norms. Within the field of anthropology, Washburn's theory was and is the subject of numerous debates, particularly regarding the contention (not found in the present selection) that when man was a hunter, he was genetically programmed to be aggressive, and hence is innately driven to warfare.

Washburn's theory, however, has been introduced to the public through the more sensationalized and exaggerated versions of Desmond Morris, Robert Ardrey, and Lionel Tiger. These writers take the most speculative and controversial aspects of the theory—the idea of man as a killer ape born with implacable instincts to make war on his fellows, seize and defend territory, and exclude and dominate females—and raise these aspects to the level of established scientific fact. Further, on the basis of these alleged facts they construct analyses of social problems and recommend political solutions.

Besides the characteristic ideology of each field of study, there is the personal ideology each individual brings to the study of the family. No one can approach the subject without assumptions and preferences about reality, human nature, the social and political order—for example, the necessity of the nuclear family, the insatiability of human drives, the scarcity of goods, the fragility of society, and so on. This section is not a comprehensive review of the approaches taken to the family by the fields mentioned—obviously, to do so would require an entire volume, at least. Nor have we been able to give equal weight to both sides of each issue: for example, we do not include psychoanalytic arguments about the biological immutability of sex differences and the family, found in the work of Freud, or the most prominent advocate of the psychoanalytic determinants of the universal nuclear family, Weston LaBarre. (There is a review, however, of Freud's ideas concerning femininity in the Marmor article in Part 2.)

In addition to considerations of space, we omitted these selections because we felt that the more conventional sides of the issues are easily found in other texts, as well as in the minds of readers. Thus it would be more useful to present viewpoints challenging established ideas.

Anthropology

The anthropology selections question the universality of the nuclear family and conventional Western sex role differences. Margaret Mead's article is from her classic study of sex differences in three South Pacific societies. Each society held a conception of male and female temperament that varied from the familiar: in one society both sexes fitted the stereotype of a maternal person in Western culture; in another, both sexes were expected to be tough, aggressive, and competitive; and in the third, Western sex role temperaments were reversed, with men being gentle and passive, and women aggressive.

The article by Richard Adams develops the theme of diverse possibilities by arguing that the nuclear family model and the search for universal functions are misleading guides to the study of the family. The theoretical analysis of the family should begin, according to Adams, with the study of the dyads that compose the family: mother-father, mother-child, father-child. According to his view, the nuclear family is a complex arrangement of dyads, rather less significant than each of its components. The nuclear family may successfully fulfill the functions ascribed to it, but the reverse assumption that other social forms can never fulfill these functions is unjustified.

Like Murdock and his followers, Lévi-Strauss finds the nuclear family almost everywhere, but he explains its existence on grounds different from that of the usual nuclear family theorist. His analysis proceeds from several paradoxes: one is, if there is no biological necessity for the nuclear family, why does the nuclear family exist almost everywhere, except in certain specialized and sophisticated societies? Another is, every society seems to have a sexual division of labor, so why is there no sure way to predict what tasks will be assigned to which sex? And third, why is marriage (almost) always based on sexual union, when marriage often has little to do with sexual gratification? Lévi-Strauss argues that these paradoxes arise from erroneous attempts to explain the family on grounds of psychological feelings between men and women and parents and children; he prefers to interpret each conjugal family as an exchange between two other families, one providing a man, the other a woman. The nuclear family is thus an arbitrarily conceived social organization linking families in a chain of such reciprocal exchanges. Lévi-Strauss argues that man's evolutionary survival as a species depended on cultural development, and that cultural development required that people form social bonds with other people besides their immediate blood kin. Thus the incest taboo had the important effect of linking up families into wider social organizations. Similarly, the division of labor between the sexes promotes marriage by making men and women dependent on each other. The family, he argues, is a somewhat arbitrary, but necessary linking mechanism. In a sense, if it did not exist, something like it would have to be invented. We should mention that Lévi-Strauss's analysis of the incest taboo is by no means the last word on the subject. The origin and nature of the incest taboo is a subject that will continue to be discussed by many.

New discoveries in biology may lead to a revolutionary break with the reproductive and family patterns of the past. One writer has described the significance of these new discoveries as follows:

> The architecture of our morality and the structure of our tradition rest solidly upon the foundation of reproductive biology. The study and practice of obstetrics and gynecology, begun in earnest not much more than a half century ago, constitute one of the younger branches of medical science. But the generations that lived on earth before the onset of these investigations and discoveries, though they were ignorant of the precise mechanisms, understood the basic and hitherto unarguable facts: that a man and a woman must unite sexually in order to produce a child; that the child somehow begins to develop, on its own and in secret—inaccessible except for whatever mysterious interchanges take place between itself and its mother—for the long, dark, quiet months before it is ejected from its snug place into the shock of life outside; that the helpless mammal that is a human infant requires an unusually prolonged period of parental protection and training before it can cope on even a minimal basis with either its physical or its cultural environment.
>
> All this being so, and assuming that human beings in even a relatively primitive state would instinctively want to insure the perpetuation of their kind, it was inevitable that certain sets of conventions would evolve. Thus grew our social institutions of marriage and the family, buttressed by religion, law, politics, philosophy, education, commerce, literature, and the arts—an interdependent edifice of formidable dimensions, endowed by its creators with an aura of self-evident immutability. But in the sciences, even in the life sciences, perpetuity has a way of turning out to be not so perpetual after all.[1]

Not only does the new biology raise the possibility of babies conceived and developed in test tubes, transplanted from one womb to another, and sired by the sperm of long-dead geniuses, but it also raises the possibility of genetic engineering—the manufacture of new types of human beings—perhaps with heads and brains twice as large as usual, as Francis Crick has suggested. One can foresee a time when present concerns with sexual morality will seem trivial compared to moral questions about the proper use of genetic engineering. The article by Etzioni spells out some of the social implications that might follow the introduction of one of its less dramatic forms—the control of sex—and raises questions about the ethical responsibilities of scientists for the social effects of their innovations.

Social History

The final section presents articles already described at length in the introduction: Aries' analysis of the transition between the medieval and the modern family; Goode's analysis of the peculiar fit between industrialism and the conjugal family; Winch and Blumberg's analysis of the societal correlates of family forms. In addition, there is the description by Marx of family life under the factory system—a grim reality that contrasted with the romantic mystification of family life during the Victorian era.

Reference

1. A. Rosenfeld, *The Second Genesis* (Englewood Cliffs, N.J.: Prentice-Hall, 1969), pp. 104–105.

Chapter 1

Biology, Culture, and the Family

The Social Behavior of Baboons and Early Man

Sherwood L. Washburn and Irven DeVore

Mother-Child Relations

The motor development of the newborn baboon baby is more advanced than that of the human infant and enables the baby to cling to the mother. The baby baboon may be helped a little on the first day or two, but a quadruped that must walk several miles every day cannot use its hands to carry its infant. Bipedal locomotion is essential to the human mother-child relationship; mothers who cannot carry things cannot carry babies. The psychological consequences of the change from the monkey pattern to the human are profound. Bowlby has described the mental defects arising from deficient maternal care in man. He says that the first six postnatal months are the most important in man. In a baboon the comparable developmental stages are *in utero*, and, when the baby baboon is born, it has the reflexes and motor development that enable it to help determine its own relationship to the mother. In the baboon, species-specific behavior is guaranteed by pre- and postnatal events that are very different from those of man. The helpless human infant is exposed to maternal whim, custom, or vagary in a way that is true of no other primate.

At least a part of this momentous change in the role of the mother can be detected in the fossil record. Clearly the reason man must be born in such an immature state is that the pelvis will not permit the birth of a larger head. Selection that favored larger brains also had to favor earlier

From Sherwood L. Washburn and Irven De Vore, "The Social Behavior of Baboons and Early Man," in S. L. Washburn (ed.), *Social Life of Early Man* (Chicago: Aldine, 1961), pp. 96–100. References cited in the original have been deleted.

birth, but earlier births were impossible unless the mother was already bipedal and able to hold the baby. The fossil record shows that the australopithecines were bipeds with ape-size brains. Their young could easily have been born with brains that were 40–50 percent as large as the adult size and with a motor development comparable to that of a monkey or ape, which would have allowed the baby to hold on to the mother. Although it may have begun at this time, it would not be necessary to postulate the human mother-child relationship among the australopithecines. But, with the large-brained men of the Middle Pleistocene, a human kind of mother-child relationship must have been established. Their larger brains required both that the infant be born earlier and that it be carried and cared for by a bipedal mother.

In the infants of monkeys and apes the great toe is very important in holding the mother. In newborn Old World monkeys the foot is specialized to hold the mother's hair. The great toe may be abducted to a degree impossible later on; the ankle is bent so that the foot faces inward, and the tarsal region is relatively elongated. In man bipedal locomotion makes this kind of adaptation impossible. This is another line of evidence showing that the human mother must have taken more responsibility for holding the baby. If the australopithecine foot was fully evolved for bipedal locomotion, the australopithecine mother must have held the baby more than is the case among monkeys or apes. This would have prepared the way for the great change in mother-child relations that was necessitated by the evolution of the large brain.

Sexual Behavior

Among baboons the female cycle averages around thirty-four days and oestrus lasts approximately a week. In the beginning of oestrus the female mates with juvenile males and the less dominant adults. She actively solicits the attention of the males and may mate with several in close succession. In the later part of oestrus, the female forms temporary consort relationships with the dominant adult males. These consort pairings may last a matter of hours or days and usually dissolve peacefully. However, fighting may occur if a male tries to break up the consort pair. A full description of the complicated sex life is given elsewhere by DeVore, but the pattern is similar to that of the *Rhesus macaque*.

The baboon's pattern of mating differs from the human family in that no lasting male-female relationship is established, and there are no economic ties or other social controls. Oestrus disrupts all other social relations; the female leaves her preference group and her infant (if she has one) to form a temporary consortship with a male. Her position within the troop is altered both by her oestrus and by the status of the male with which she is paired. We can see no way that oestrus behavior could be combined with the care of an infant that is still economically dependent upon the mother. The physiology of the human female has become radically modified, with the endocrine control of behavior being greatly reduced. The apparent difference between the sociosexual behavior of man and monkey has been minimized by the use of the words "family," "harem," and "jealousy" to describe the behavior of monkeys and apes. Actually, oestrus, multiple mates, and no economic responsibility present a pattern that is fundamentally different from that of man.

The origin of the human family pattern presents three problems: (1) the evolution of a helpless, slow-growing human infant, (2) loss of oestrus, and (3) the male's role as an economic provider. It has already been shown that the human mother-child relationship must evolve after bipedalism and together with large brains; that is, by the Middle Pleistocene. At the moment, there seems to be no direct evidence on the time of the loss of oestrus, but we may speculate that this occurred early, together with bipedalism and a lengthening of the period of infant dependency. It has already been suggested that oestrus is incompatible with continuing child care. By the same token, it can be argued that prolonged receptivity in the female was necessary before a lasting male-female relationship of the human type could be formed. In this view, oestrus is associated with rotating mateship; the family, with noncyclical receptivity.* The male's role as an economic provider had certainly appeared by the Middle Pleistocene, when men were killing large animals. Hunting large animals was probably based on cooperation, and the band must have shared in the eating.

By the Middle Pleistocene there is direct evidence of hunting and indirect evidence for cooperation, division of labor, and sharing of food. This human pattern differs on each of these points from that of baboons, who do not hunt, share, or cooperate, and where there is no sexual division of economic activity.

We are tempted to date human notions of range and territory from the same time. Earlier, we indicated that baboons do not defend a territory, but occupy a small range. However, we have seen baboons drive vervets from fruit trees. The sources of vegetable food are normally so widespread that the overlapping of ranges does not appear serious, but with the hunting of large animals the matter is entirely different. If strangers hunt game, or

*The gibbon troop is composed of an adult male, adult female, and their young. This grouping bears a superficial resemblance to the human family, but it is produced by an entirely different mechanism. Except for a mating pair, adult gibbons are extremely antagonistic. This adult antagonism is a primitive species-spacing mechanism, comparable to that in tree shrews and some lemurs.

even disturb it, scaring it from its normal routes, the plans of the local hunters are ruined. Hunting man requires a large area free from the interference of other hunters. When man became a hunter, his relation to the land changed from one in which a small range was adequate to one that demanded a large territory. Hunting large animals made children and females economically dependent. A young baboon receives no food from other members of the troop, and, once it is weaned, it is economically independent, but in a band of hunters children are dependent on adults for a substantial portion of their food. So the relation of the human child to adults differs from that of the monkey in two ways: it is more dependent both physically and economically.

Economic Dependence

The relation of the infant monkey or ape to its mother is guaranteed by biology—by the infant's reflexes and the mother's drives and physiology. A close mother-child relationship lasts only as long as lactation. No such direct biological bonds bind the human mother to her older children, or the human father to his offspring. Although female monkeys appear to learn part of their maternal behavior patterns, and older juvenile females hold and carry infants before they have any of their own, the role of learning, culture, and custom in determining the care of the young is vastly greater in man than in any nonhuman primate. In the evolution of society, the most important rules are those that guarantee economic survival to the dependent young. Human females and their young are efficient gatherers, so the crucial customs are those that guarantee the services of a hunter to a woman and her children. That the resulting family bonds are much more than sexual is shown by the fact that custom in contemporary hunter-gatherer groups provides that new families may be formed only around males who have proved themselves as economic providers. The maturing human male is dependent upon the adult males not only for food but for years of instruction in the techniques of hunting. The human male matures sexually from about twelve to fourteen years, but he reaches full and physical maturity much later, from about eighteen to twenty. The wide variety of customs that insure this delay in social maturity all have the same biological function: to delay the production of children until the male can provide for them. As Schultz has outlined, biological maturation in the monkeys, and even more in the apes, is delayed in comparison to that in other mammals. This biological delay in development is greatest in man, and a considerable social delay, determined by custom, is added to the biological.

The economic advantages of delaying the formation of a new family until the male was a fully efficient, proved provider, however, would be largely nullified if delayed marriage was not accompanied by the incest tabu. From a biological point of view, father-daughter mating amounts to taking a second wife, regardless of economic considerations. Brother-sister mating adds babies without adding an economically responsible, fully socially mature male. It is probably impossible to encourage the sexuality of the young male in mother-son relations while at the same time prohibiting other sexuality in the family.

In addition to creating within the family economic conditions that favored exogamy, hunting as a major activity may have reinforced this tendency by bringing about a new type of relationship between bands. The exclusive control of a hunting territory can be efficiently maintained only with the mutual consent of neighboring bands; excessive fighting over territorial borders both disturbs game and dissipates the energy of the hunters. The exchange of mates between neighboring groups helps to insure friendly relations with them because it disperses persons with close emotional ties among many groups and over a large area. By contrast, the baboon troop is a self-sufficient, closed social system with no supralocal affiliations.

It cannot be proved, of course, that incest prohibitions and exogamous matings arose in the Middle Pleistocene, but it can be shown that the conditions that made such regulation advantageous arose at that time. All data suggest that the killing of large animals is a task for adult men and that, once hunting became important to the group, children had to depend upon adults for many years. Both by increasing the importance of the male as provider and by making control of a hunting area essential, large-scale hunting activity created conditions that favored exogamous mating. The offspring of *Australopithecus* may have been just as independent as those of a chimpanzee, but the children of Ternifine or Peking man depended upon the hunting of adult males, and their survival depended upon the relations between the young and the hunters. It is impossible to date the beginning of the human family or of the incest tabu, but the conditions that made these institutions advantageous in the evolution of the species are concomitant with the hunting of large animals.

Sex and Temperament in Three Primitive Societies

Margaret Mead

We have now considered in detail the approved personalities of each sex among three primitive peoples. We found the Arapesh—both men and women—displaying a personality that, out of our historically limited preoccupations, we would call maternal in its parental aspects, and feminine in its sexual aspects. We found men, as well as women, trained to be cooperative, unaggressive, responsive to the needs and demands of others. We found no idea that sex was a powerful driving force either for men or for women. In marked contrast to these attitudes, we found among the Mundugumor that both men and women developed as ruthless, aggressive, positively sexed individuals, with the maternal cherishing aspects of personality at a minimum. Both men and women approximated to a personality type that we in our culture would find only in an undisciplined and very violent male. Neither the Arapesh nor the Mundugumor profit by a contrast between the sexes; the Arapesh ideal is the mild, responsive man married to the mild, responsive woman; the Mundugumor ideal is the violent aggressive man married to the violent aggressive woman. In the third tribe, the Tchambuli, we found a genuine reversal of the sex attitudes of our own culture, with the woman the dominant, impersonal, managing partner, the man the less responsible and the emotionally dependent person. These three situations suggest, then, a very definite conclusion. If those temperamental attitudes which we have traditionally regarded as feminine—such as passivity, responsiveness, and a willingness to cherish children—can so easily be set up as the masculine pattern in one tribe, and in another be outlawed for the majority of women as well as for the majority of men, we no longer have any basis for regarding such aspects of behavior as sex-linked. And this conclusion becomes even stronger when we consider the actual reversal in Tchambuli of the position of dominance of the two sexes, in spite of the existence of formal patrilineal institutions.

The material suggests that we may say that many, if not all, of the personality traits which we have called masculine or feminine are as lightly linked to sex as are the clothing, the manners, and the form of head-dress that a society at a given period assigns to either sex. When we consider

From Margaret Mead, *Sex and Temperament in Three Primitive Societies* (New York: Morrow, 1939; Mentor Books, 1950), pp. 279–288.

the behavior of the typical Arapesh man or woman as contrasted with the behavior of the typical Mundugumor man or woman, the evidence is overwhelmingly in favor of the strength of social conditioning. In no other way can we account for the almost complete uniformity with which Arapesh children develop into contented, passive, secure persons, while Mundugumor children develop as characteristically into violent, aggressive, insecure persons. Only to the impact of the whole of the integrated culture upon the growing child can we lay the formation of the contrasting types. There is no other explanation of race, or diet, or selection that can be adduced to explain them. We are forced to conclude that human nature is almost unbelievably malleable, responding accurately and contrastingly to contrasting cultural conditions. The differences between individuals who are members of different cultures, like the differences between individuals within a culture, are almost entirely to be laid to differences in conditioning, especially during early childhood, and the form of this conditioning is culturally determined. Standardized personality differences between the sexes are of this order, cultural creations to which each generation, male and female, is trained to conform. There remains, however, the problem of the origin of these socially standardized differences.

While the basic importance of social conditioning is still imperfectly recognized—not only in lay thought, but even by the scientist specifically concerned with such matters—to go beyond it and consider the possible influence of variations in hereditary equipment is a hazardous matter. The following pages will read very differently to one who has made a part of his thinking a recognition of the whole amazing mechanism of cultural conditioning—who has really accepted the fact that the same infant could be developed into a full participant in any one of these three cultures—than they will read to one who still believes that the minutiae of cultural behavior are carried in the individual germ plasm. If it is said, therefore, that when we have grasped the full significance of the malleability of the human organism and the preponderant importance of cultural conditioning, there are still further problems to solve, it must be remembered that these problems come *after* such a comprehension of the force of conditioning; they cannot precede it. The forces that make children born among the Arapesh grow up into typical Arapesh personalities are entirely social, and any discussion of the variations which do occur must be looked at against this social background.

With this warning firmly in mind, we can ask a further question. Granting the malleability of human nature, whence arise the differences between the standardized personalities that different cultures decree for all of their members, or which one culture decrees for the members of one sex as contrasted with the members of the opposite sex? If such differences are culturally created, as this material would most strongly suggest that they are, if the new-born child can be shaped with equal ease into an unaggressive Arapesh or an aggressive Mundugumor, why do these striking contrasts occur at all? If the clues to the different personalities decreed for men and women in Tchambuli do not lie in the physical constitution of the two sexes—an assumption that we must reject both for the Tchambuli and for our own society—where can we find the clues upon which the Tchambuli, the Arapesh, the Mundugumor, have built? Cultures are man-made, they are built of human materials; they are diverse but comparable structures within which human beings can attain full human stature. Upon what have they built their diversities?

We recognize that a homogeneous culture committed in all of its gravest institutions and slight usages to a cooperative, unaggressive course can bend every child to that emphasis, some to a perfect accord with it, the majority to an easy acceptance, while only a few deviants fail to receive the cultural imprint. To consider such traits as aggressiveness or passivity to be sex-linked is not possible in the light of the facts. Have such traits, then, as aggressiveness or passivity, pride or humility, objectivity or a preoccupation with personal relationships, an easy response to the needs of the young and the weak or a hostility to the young and weak, a tendency to initiate sex relations or merely to respond to the dictates of a situation or another person's advances—have these traits any basis in temperament at all? Are they potentialities of all human temperaments that can be developed by different kinds of social conditioning and which will not appear if the necessary conditioning is absent?

When we ask this question we shift our emphasis. If we ask why an Arapesh man or an Arapesh woman shows the kind of personality that we have considered in the first section of this book, the answer is: Because of the Arapesh culture, because of the intricate, elaborate, and unfailing fashion in which a culture is able to shape each new-born child to the cultural image. And if we ask the same question about a Mundugumor man or woman, or about a Tchambuli man as compared with a Tchambuli woman, the answer is the same kind. They display the personalities that are peculiar to the cultures in which they were born and educated. Our attention has been on the differences between Arapesh men and women as a group and Mundugumor men and women as a group. It is as if we had represented the Arapesh personality by a soft yellow, the Mundugumor by a deep red, while the Tchambuli female personality was deep orange, and that of the Tchambuli male, pale green. But if we now ask whence came the original direction in each culture, so that one now shows yellow, another red, the third orange and green by sex, then we must peer more closely. And leaning closer to the picture, it is as if behind the bright consistent yellow of the Arapesh, and the deep equally consistent red of the Mundugumor, behind the orange and green that are Tchambuli, we found in each case the delicate, just discernible outlines of the whole spectrum, differently overlaid in each case by the monotone which covers it. This spectrum is the range of individual differences which lie back of the so much more conspicuous cultural emphases, and it is to this that we must turn to find the explanation of cultural inspiration, of the source from which each culture has drawn.

There appears to be about the same range of basic temperamental variation among the Arapesh and among the Mundugumor, although the violent man is a misfit in the first society and a leader in the second. If human nature were completely homogeneous raw material, lacking specific drives and characterized by no important constitutional differences between individuals, then individuals who display personality traits so antithetical to the social pressure should not reappear in societies of such differing emphases. If the variations between individuals were to be set down to accidents in the genetic process, the same accidents should not be repeated with similar frequency in strikingly different cultures, with strongly contrasting methods of education.

But because this same relative distribution of individual differences does appear in culture after culture, in spite of the divergences between the cultures, it seems pertinent to offer a hypothesis to explain upon what basis the personalities of men and women have been differently standardized so often in the history of the human race. This hypothesis is an extension of that advanced by Ruth Benedict in her *Patterns of Culture*. Let us assume that there are definite temperamental differences between human beings which if not entirely hereditary at least are established on a hereditary base very soon after birth. (Further than this we cannot at present narrow the matter.) These differences finally embodied in the character structure of adults, then, are the clues from which culture works, selecting one temperament, or a combination of related and congruent types, as desirable, and embodying this choice in every thread of the social fabric—in the care of the young child, the games the children play, the songs the people sing, the structure of political organization, the religious observance, the art and the philosophy.

Some primitive societies have had the time and the robustness to revamp all of their institutions to fit one extreme type, and to develop educational techniques which will ensure that the majority of each generation will show a personality congruent with this extreme emphasis. Other societies have pursued a less definitive course, selecting their models not from the most extreme, most highly differentiated individuals, but from the less marked types. In such societies the approved personality is less pronounced, and the culture often contains the types of inconsistencies that many human beings display also; one institution may be adjusted to the uses of pride, another to a casual humility that is congruent neither with pride nor with inverted pride. Such societies, which have taken the more usual and less sharply defined types as models, often show also a less definitely patterned social structure. The culture of such societies may be likened to a house the decoration of which has been formed by no definite and precise taste, no exclusive emphasis upon dignity or comfort or pretentiousness or beauty, but in which a little of each effect has been included.

Alternatively, a culture may take its clues not from one temperament, but from several temperaments. But instead of mixing together into an inconsistent hotchpotch the choices and emphases of different temperaments, or blending them together into a smooth but not particularly distinguished whole, it may isolate each type by making it the basis for the approved social personality for an age group, a sex group, a caste group, or an occupational group. In this way society becomes not a monotone with a few discrepant patches of an intrusive color, but a mosaic, with different groups displaying different personality traits. Such specializations as these may be based upon any facet of human endowment—different intellectual abilities, different artistic abilities, different emotional traits. So the Samoans decree that all young people must show the personality trait of unaggressiveness and punish with opprobrium the aggressive child who displays traits regarded as appropriate only in titled middle-aged men. In societies based upon elaborate ideas of rank, members of the aristocracy will be permitted, even compelled, to display a pride, a sensitivity to insult, that would be deprecated as inappropriate in members of the plebeian class. So also in professional groups or in religious sects some temperamental traits are selected and institutionalized, and taught to each new member who enters the profession or sect. Thus the physician learns the bedside manner, which is the natural behavior of some temperaments and the standard behavior of the general practitioner in the medical profession; the Quaker learns at least the outward behavior and the rudiments of meditation, the capacity for which is not necessarily an innate characteristic of many of the members of the Society of Friends.

So it is with the social personalities of the two sexes. The traits that occur in some members of each sex are specially assigned to one sex, and disallowed in the other. The history of the social definition of sex differences is filled with such arbitrary arrangements in the intellectual and artistic field, but because of the assumed congruence between physiological sex and emotional endowment we have been less able to recognize that a similar arbitrary selection is being made among emotional traits also. We have assumed that because it is convenient for a mother to wish to care for her child, this is a trait with which women have been more generously endowed by a carefully teleological process of evolution. We have assumed that because men have hunted, an activity requiring enterprise, bravery, and initiative, they have been endowed with these useful attitudes as part of their sex temperament.

Societies have made these assumptions both overtly and implicitly. If a society insists that warfare is the major occupation for the male sex, it is therefore insisting that all male children display bravery and pugnacity. Even if the insistence upon the differential bravery of men and women is not made articulate, the difference in occupation makes this point implicitly. When, however, a society goes further and defines men as brave and women as timorous, when men are forbidden to show fear and women are indulged in the most flagrant display of fear, a more explicit element enters in. Bravery, hatred of any weakness, of flinching before pain or danger— this attitude which is so strong a component of *some human* temperaments has been selected as the key to masculine behavior. The easy unashamed display of fear or suffering that is congenial to a different temperament has been made the key to feminine behavior.

Originally two variations of human temperament, a hatred of fear or willingness to display fear, they have been socially translated into inalienable aspects of the personalitites of the two sexes. And to that defined sex personality every child will be educated, if a boy, to suppress fear, if a girl, to show it. If there has been no social selection in regard to this trait, the proud temperament that is repelled by any betrayal of feeling will display itself, regardless of sex, by keeping a stiff upper lip. Without an express prohibition of such behavior the expressive unashamed man or woman will weep, or comment upon fear or suffering. Such attitudes, strongly marked in certain temperaments, may by social selection be standardized for everyone, or outlawed for everyone, or ignored by society, or made the exclusive and approved behavior of one sex only.

Neither the Arapesh nor the Mundugumor have made any attitude specific for one sex. All of the energies of the culture have gone toward the creation of a single human type, regardless of class, age, or sex. There is no division into age classes for which different motives or different moral attitudes are regarded as suitable. There is no class of seers or mediums who stand apart drawing inspiration from psychological sources not available to the majority of the people. The Mundugumor have, it is true, made one aribtrary selection, in that they recognize artistic ability only among individuals born with the cord about their necks, and firmly deny the happy exercise of artistic ability to those less unusually born. The Arapesh boy with a tinea infection has been socially selected to be a disgruntled, antisocial individual, and the society forces upon sunny cooperative children cursed with this affliction a final approximation to the behavior appropriate to a pariah. With these two exceptions no emotional role is forced upon an individual because of birth or accident. As there is no idea of rank which declares that some are of high estate and some of low, so there is no idea of sex difference which delcares that one sex must feel differently from the other. One possible imaginative social construct, the attribution of different personalities to different members of the community classified into sex, age, or caste groups, is lacking.

When we turn however to the Tchambuli, we find a situation that while bizarre in one respect, seems nevertheless more intelligible in another. The Tchambuli have at least made the point of sex difference; they have used the obvious fact of sex as an organizing point for the formation of social personality, even though they seem to us to have reversed the normal picture. While there is reason to believe that not every Tchambuli woman is born with a dominating, organizing, administrative temperament, actively sexed and willing to initiate sex relations, possessive, definite, robust, practical, and impersonal in outlook, still most Tchambuli girls grow up to display these traits. And while there is definite evidence to show that all Tchambuli men are not, by native endowment, the delicate responsive actors of a play staged for the women's benefit, still most Tchambuli boys manifest this coquettish play-acting personality most of the time. Because the Tchambuli formulation of sex attitudes contradicts our usual premises, we can see clearly that Tchambuli culture has arbitrarily permitted certain human traits to women, and allotted others, equally arbitrarily, to men.

The Family | *Claude Lévi-Strauss*

The word *family* is so plain, the kind of reality to which it refers is so close to daily experience that one may expect to be confronted in this chapter with a simple situation. Anthropologists, however, are a strange breed; they like to make even the "familiar" look mysterious and complicated. As a matter of fact, the comparative study of the family among many different peoples has given rise to some of the most bitter arguments in the whole history of anthropological thought and probably to its more spectacular reversal.

From Claude Lévi-Strauss, "The Family," in Harry L. Shapiro (ed.), *Man, Culture, and Society* (New York: Oxford Univ. Press, 1956), pp. 142–170.

During the second half of the nineteenth century and the beginning of the twentieth, anthropologists were working under the influence of biological evolutionism. They were trying to organize their data so that the institutions of the simpler people would correspond to an early stage of the evolution of mankind, while our own institutions were related to the more advanced or developed forms. And since, among ourselves, the family founded on monogamic marriage was considered as the most praiseworthy and cherished institution, it was immediately inferred that savage societies —equated for the purpose with the societies of man at the beginning of its existence—could only have something of a different type. Therefore, facts were distorted and misinterpreted; even more, fanciful "early" stages of evolution were invented, such as "group marriage" and "promiscuity" to account for the period when man was still so barbarous that he could not possibly conceive of the niceties of the social life it is the privilege of civilized man to enjoy. Every custom different from our own was carefully selected as a vestige of an older type of social organization.

This way of approaching the problem became obsolete when the accumulation of data made obvious the following fact: the kind of family featured in modern civilization by monogamous marriage, independent establishment of the young couple, warm relationship between parents and offspring, etc., while not always easy to recognize behind the complicated network of strange customs and institutions of savage peoples, is at least conspicuous among those which seem to have remained on—or returned to—the simplest cultural level. Tribes like the Andamanese of the Indian Ocean Andaman Islands, the Fuegians of the southernmost tip of South America, the Nambikwara of central Brazil, and the Bushmen of South Africa—to quote only a few examples—live in small, semi-nomadic bands; they have little or no political organization and their technological level is very low since, in some of them at least, there is no knowledge of weaving, pot-making, and even sometimes hut-building. Thus, the only social structure worth speaking of among them is the family, mostly monogamous. The observer working in the field has no trouble identifying the married couples, closely associated by sentimental bonds and economic cooperation as well as by the rearing of children born from their union.

There are two ways of interpreting this preeminence of the family at both ends of the scale of development of human societies. Some writers have claimed that the simpler peoples may be considered as a remnant of what can be looked at as a "golden age," prior to the submission of mankind to the hardships and perversities of civilization; thus, man would have known in that early stage the bliss of monogamic family only to forgo it later until its more recent Christian rediscovery. The general trend, however, except for the so-called Vienna school, has been that more and more anthropologists have become convinced that familial life is present practically everywhere in human societies, even in those with sexual and educational customs very remote from our own. Thus, after they had claimed for about fifty years that the family, as modern societies knew it, could only be a recent development and the outcome of a slow and long-lasting evolution, anthropologists now lean toward the opposite conviction, i.e., that the family, consisting of a more or less durable union, socially approved, of a man, a woman, and their children, is a universal phenomenon, present in each and every type of society.

These extreme positions, however, suffer equally from oversimplification. It is well known that, in very rare cases, family bonds cannot be claimed to exist. A telling example comes from the Nayar, a very large group living on the Malabar coast of India. In former times, the warlike type of life of the Nayar men did not allow them to found a family. Marriage was a purely symbolical ceremony which did not result in a permanent tie between a man and a woman. As a matter of fact, married women were permitted to have as many lovers as they wished. Children belonged exclusively to the mother line, and familial as well as land authority was exercised not by the ephemeral husband but by the wife's brothers. Since land was cultivated by an inferior caste, subservient to the Nayar, a woman's brothers were as completely free as their sister's temporary husband or lovers to devote themselves to military activities.

Now, the case of the Nayar has been frequently misunderstood. In the first place, they cannot be considered as a vestige of a primitive kind of social organization which could have been very general, in the past, among mankind. Quite to the contrary: the Nayar exhibit an extremely specialized and elaborate type of social structure and from that point of view, they do not prove very much.

On the other hand, there is little doubt that the Nayar represent an extreme form of a tendency which is far more frequent in human societies than is generally acknowledged.

There are a large number of human societies which, although they did not go quite as far as the Nayar in denying recognition to the family as a social unit, have nevertheless limited this recognition by their simultaneous admission of patterns of a different type. For instance, the Masai and the Chagga, both of them African tribes, did recognize the family as a social unit. However, and for the same reason as among the Nayar, this was not true for the younger class of adult men who were dedicated to warlike activities and consequently were not allowed to marry and found a family. They used to live in regimental organizations and were permitted, during that period, to have promiscuous relations with the younger class of adult girls. Thus, among these peoples, the family did exist side by side with a promiscuous, nonfamilial type of relations between the sexes.

For different reasons, the same type of dual pattern prevailed among the Boróro and several other tribes of central Brazil, the Muria, and other tribes of India and Assam, etc. All the known instances could be arranged in such a way as to make the Nayar appear only as the more consistent, systematic, and logically extreme case of a situation which may eventually reappear, at least in embryonic form, in modern society.

This was well shown in the case of Nazi Germany, where a similar cleavage was beginning to appear in the family unit: on the one hand, the men dedicated to political and warlike activities, with a great deal of freedom resulting from their exalted position; and on the other hand, women with their "3K" functional assignment: *Küche, Kirche, Kinder,* i.e., kitchen, church, and children. One might very well conceive that, had the same trend been maintained for several centuries, this clear-cut division of functions between men and women, together with the accompanying differentiation of their respective status, could very well have led to a type of social organization where the family unit would receive as little recognition as among the Nayar.

During recent years anthropologists have taken great pains to show that, even among people who practice wife-lending, either periodically in religious ceremonies or on a statutory basis (as where men are permitted to enter into a kind of institutional friendship entailing wife-lending among members), these customs should not be interpreted as survivals of "group marriage" since they exist side by side with, and even imply, recognition of the family. It is true enough that, in order to be allowed to lend one's wife, one should first get one. However, if we consider the case of some Australian tribes as the Wunambal of the northwestern part of the continent, a man who would not lend his wife to her other potential husbands during ceremonies would be considered as "very greedy," i.e., trying to keep for himself a privilege intended by the social group to be shared between numerous persons equally entitled to it. And since that attitude toward sexual access to a woman existed along with the official dogma that men have no part in physiological procreation (therefore doubly denying any kind of bond between the husband and his wife's children), the family becomes an economic grouping where man brings the products of his hunt and the woman those of her collecting and gathering. Anthropologists, who claim that this economic unit built upon a "give and take" principle is a proof of the existence of the family even among the lowest savages, are certainly on no sounder basis than those who maintain that such a kind of family has little else in common than the word used to designate it with the family as it has been observed elsewhere.

The same relativistic approach is advisable in respect to the polygamous family. The word polygamy, it should be recalled, refers to polygyny, that is, a system where a man is entitled to several wives, as well as to polyandry, which is the complementary system where several husbands share one wife.

Now it is true that in many observed cases, polygamous families are nothing else than a combination of several monogamous families, although the same person plays the part of several spouses. For instance, in some tribes of Bantu Africa, each wife lives in a separate hut with her children, and the only difference with the monogamous family results from the fact that the same man plays the part of husband to all his wives. There are other instances, however, where the situation is not so clear. Among the Tupi-Kawahib of central Brazil, a chief may marry several women who may be sisters, or even a mother and her daughters by former marriage; the children are raised together by the women, who do not seem to mind very much whether they nurse their own children or not; also, the chief willingly lends his wives to his younger brothers, his court officers, or to visitors. Here we have not only a combination of polygyny and polyandry, but the mix-up is increased even more by the fact that the co-wives may be united by close consanguineous ties prior to their marrying the same man. In a case which this writer witnessed, a mother and daughter, married to one man, were together taking care of children who were, at the same time, stepchildren to one woman and, according to case, either grandchild or stepbrother to the other.

As to polyandry proper, it may sometimes take extreme forms, as among the Toda where several men, usually brothers, share one wife, the legitimate father of the children being the one who has performed a special ceremony and who remains legal father of all the children to be born until another husband decides to assume the right of fathership by the same process. In Tibet and Nepal, polyandry seems to be explained by occupational factors of the same type as those already stated for the Nayar: for men living a semi-nomadic existence as guides and bearers, polyandry provides a good chance that there will be, at all times, at least one husband at hand to take care of the homestead.

If the legal, economic, and sentimental identity of the family can be maintained even in a polygynous or a polyandrous setup, it is not sure that the same would be true when polyandry exists side by side with polygyny. As we have already seen, this was to some extent the case among the Tupi-Kawahib, since polygynous marriages existed, at least as a chief's privilege, in combination with an elaborate system of wife-lending to younger brothers, helpers, and visitors from different tribes. Here one might argue that the bond between a woman and her legal husband was more different in degree than in kind from a gamut of other bonds which could be arranged in order of decreasing strength: from rightful, semi-permanent lovers to occasional ones. However, even in that case, the chil-

dren's status was defined by the legal marriage, not by the other types of
unions.

We come closer to the so-called "group marriage" when we consider
the modern evolution of the Toda during the nineteenth century. They
had originally a polyandrous system, which was made possible through the
custom of female infanticide. When this was prohibited by the British administration, thus restoring the natural sex ratio, the Toda continued to
practice polyandry; but now instead of several brothers sharing one wife, it
became possible for them to marry several. As in the case of the Nayar,
the types of organization which seem remotest to the conjugal family do
not occur in the more savage and archaic societies but in the relatively recent and extremely sophisticated forms of social development.

Therefore, it becomes apparent why the problem of the family should
not be approached in a dogmatic way. As a matter of fact, this is one of
the more elusive questions in the whole field of social organization. Of the
type of organization which prevailed in the early stages of mankind, we
know very little, since the remnants of man during the Upper Paleolithic
Period of about 50,000 years ago consist principally of skeletal fragments
and stone implements which provide only a minimum of information on
social customs and laws. On the other hand, when we consider the wide
diversity of human societies which have been observed since, let us say,
Herodotus' time until present days, the only thing which can be said is as
follows: monogamic, conjugal family is fairly frequent. Wherever it seems
to be superseded by different types of organizations, this generally happens
in very specialized and sophisticated societies and not, as was previously
expected, in the crudest and simplest types. Moreover, the few instances
of nonconjugal family (even in its polygamous form) establish beyond
doubt that the high frequency of the conjugal type of social grouping does
not derive from a universal necessity. It is at least conceivable that a perfectly stable and durable society could exist without it. Hence the difficult
problem: if there is no natural law making the family universal, how can
we explain why it is found practically everywhere?

In order to try to solve the problem, let us try first to define the family,
not by integrating the numerous factual observations made in different
societies nor even by limiting ourselves to the prevailing situation among us,
but by building up an ideal model of what we have in mind when we use
the word *family*. It would then seem that this word serves to designate a
social group offering at least three characteristics: (1) it finds its origin in
marriage; (2) it consists in husband, wife, and children born out of their wedlock, though it can be conceived that other relatives may find their place
close to that nuclear group; and (3) the family members are united together
by (a) legal bonds, (b) economic, religious, and other kinds of rights and

obligations, (c) a precise network of sexual rights and prohibitions, and a varying and diversified amount of psychological feelings such as love, affection, respect, awe, etc. We will now proceed to a close examination of several aspects in the light of the available data.

As we have already noticed, marriage may be monogamous or polygamous. It should be pointed out immediately that the first kind is not only more frequently found than the second, but even much more than a cursory inventory of human societies would lead to believe. Among the so-called polygamous societies, there are undoubtedly a substantial number which are authentically so; but many others make a strong difference between the "first" wife who is the only true one, endowed with the full right attached to the marital status, while the other ones are sometimes little more than official concubines. Besides, in all polygamous societies, the privilege of having several wives is actually enjoyed by a small minority only. This is easily understandable, since the number of men and women in any random grouping is approximately the same with a normal balance of about 110 to 100 to the advantage of either sex. In order to make polygamy possible, there are definite conditions which have to be met: either children of a given sex are voluntarily destroyed (a custom known to exist in a few rare cases, such as female infanticide among the Toda already referred to), or special circumstances account for a different life expectancy for members of both sexes, as among the Eskimo and some Australian tribes where many men used to die young because their occupations— whale-hunting in one case, warfare in the other—were especially dangerous. Or else we have to look for a strongly hierarchical social system, where a given class: ancients, priests and sorcerers, rich men, etc., is powerful enough to monopolize with impunity more than their share of the womenfolk at the expense of the younger or the poorer people. As a matter of fact, we know of societies—mostly in Africa—where one has to be rich to get many wives (since there is a bride-price to pay), but where at the same time the increase in wives is a means to increase wealth, since female work has a definite economic value. However, it is clear that the systematic practice of polygamy is automatically limited by the change of structure it is likely to bring up in the society.

Therefore, it is not necessary to wonder a great deal about the predominance of monogamic marriage in human societies. That monogamy is not inscribed in the nature of man is sufficiently evidenced by the fact that polygamy exists in widely different forms and in many types of societies; on the other hand, the prevalence of monogamy results from the fact that, unless special conditions are voluntarily or involuntarily brought about, there is, normally, about just one woman available for each man. In modern societies, moral, religious, and economic reasons have officialized monogamous marriage (a rule which is in actual practice breached by such different means as premarital freedom, prostitution, and adultery). But in societies which are on a much lower cultural level and where there is no prejudice against polygamy, and even where polygamy may be actually permitted or desired, the same result can be brought about by the lack of social or economic differentiation, so that each man has neither the means, nor the power, to obtain more than one wife and where, consequently, everybody is obliged to make a virtue of necessity.

If there are many different types of marriage to be observed in human societies—whether monogamous or polygamous, and in the last case, polygynous, polyandrous, or both; and whether by exchange, purchase, free choice or imposed by the family, etc.—the striking fact is that everywhere a distinction exists between marriage, i.e., a legal, group-sanctioned bond between a man and a woman, and the type of permanent or temporary union resulting either from violence or consent alone. This group intervention may be a notable or a slight one, it does not matter. The important thing is that every society has some way to operate a distinction between free unions and legitimate ones. There are several levels at which that distinction is made.

In the first place, nearly all societies grant a very high rating to the married status. Wherever age-grades exist, either in an institutional way or as noncrystallized forms of grouping, some connection is established between the younger adolescent group and bachelorhood, less young and married without children, and adulthood with full rights, the latter going usually on par with the birth of the first child. This threefold distinction was recognized not only among many primitive tribes but also in peasant western Europe, if only for the purpose of feasts and ceremonies, as late as the early twentieth century.

What is even more striking is the true feeling of repulsion which most societies have toward bachelorhood. Generally speaking it can be said that, among the so-called primitive tribes, there are no bachelors, simply for the reason that they could not survive. One of the strongest field recollections of this writer was his meeting, among the Boróro of central Brazil, a man about thirty years old: unclean, ill-fed, sad, and lonesome. When asked if the man were seriously ill, the natives' answer came as a shock: what was wrong with him?—nothing at all, he was just a bachelor. And true enough, in a society where labor is systematically shared between man and woman and where only the married status permits the man to benefit from the fruits of woman's work, including delousing, body painting, and hair-plucking as well as vegetable food and cooked food (since the Boróro woman tills the soil and makes pots), a bachelor is really only half a human being.

This is true of the bachelor and also, to a lesser extent, of a couple without children. Indeed they can make a living, but there are many societies where a childless man (or woman) never reaches full status within the group, or else, beyond the group, in this all-important society which is made up of dead relatives and where one can only expect recognition as ancestor through the cult, rendered to him or her by one's descendants. Conversely, an orphan finds himself in the same dejected condition as a bachelor. As a matter of fact, both terms provide sometimes the strongest insults existing in the native vocabulary. Bachelors and orphans can even be merged together with cripples and witches, as if their conditions were the outcome of some kind of supernatural malediction.

The interest shown by the group in the marriage of its members can be directly expressed, as it is the case among us where prospective spouses, if they are of marriageable age, have first to get a license and then to secure the services of an acknowledged representative of the group to celebrate their union. Although this direct relationship between the individuals, on the one hand, and the group as a whole, on the other, is known at least sporadically in other societies, it is by no means a frequent case. It is almost a universal feature of marriage that it is originated, not by the individuals but by the groups concerned (families, lineage, clans, etc.), and that it binds the groups before and above the individuals. Two kinds of reasons bring about this result: on the one hand, the paramount importance of being married tends to make parents, even in very simple societies, start early to worry about obtaining a suitable mate for their offspring and this, accordingly, may lead to children being promised to each other from infancy. But above all, we are confronted here with that strange paradox to which we shall have to return later on, namely, that although marriage gives birth to the family, it is the family, or rather families, which produce marriage as the main legal device at their disposal to establish an alliance between themselves. As New Guinea natives put it, the real purpose of getting married is not so much to obtain a wife but to secure brothers-in-law. If marriage takes place between groups rather than individuals, a large number of strange customs become immediately clearer. For instance, we understand why in some parts of Africa, where descent follows the father's line, marriage becomes final only when the woman has given birth to a male child, thus fulfilling its function of maintaining her husband's lineage. The so-called *levirate* and *sororate* should be explained in the light of the same principle: if marriage is binding between two groups to which the spouses belong there can be without contradiction a replacement of one spouse by his brothers or by her sisters. When the husband dies, the levirate provides that his unmarried brothers have a preferential claim on his widow (or, as it is sometimes differently put, share in their deceased brother's duty to support his wife and children), while the sororate permits a man to marry preferentially in polygamous marriage his wife's sisters, or—when marriage is monogamous—to get a sister to replace the wife in case the latter remains childless, has to be divorced on account of bad conduct, or dies. But whatever the way in which the collectivity expresses its interest in the marriage of its members, whether through the authority vested in strong consanguineous groups, or more directly, through the intervention of the State, it remains true that marriage is not, is never, and cannot be a private business.

We have to look for cases as extreme as the Nayar, already described, to find societies where there is not, at least, a temporary *de facto* union of the husband, wife, and their children. But we should be careful to note that, while such a group among us constitutes the family and is given legal recognition, this is by no means the case in a large number of human societies. Indeed, there is a maternal instinct which compels the mother to care for her children and makes her find a deep satisfaction in exercising those activities, and there are also psychological drives which explain that a man may feel warmly toward the offspring of a woman with whom he is living, and the development of which he is witnessing step by step, even if he does not believe (as is the case among the tribes who are said to disclaim physiological paternity) that he had any actual part in their procreation. Some societies strive to reinforce these convergent feelings: the famous *couvade,* the custom according to which a man is made to share in the inabilities (either natural or socially imposed) of the woman in confinement, has been explained by some as an attempt to build up a welded unit out of these otherwise not too homogeneous materials.

The great majority of societies, however, do not show a very active interest in a kind of grouping which, to some of them at least (including our own), appears so important. Here too, it is the groups which are important, not the temporary aggregate of the individual representatives of the group. For instance, many societies are interested in clearly establishing the relations of the offspring with the father's group on the one hand, and with the mother's group on the other, but they do it by differentiating strongly the two kinds of relationships. Territorial rights may be inherited through one line, and religious privileges and obligations through the other. Or else, status from one side, magical techniques from the other. Innumerable examples could be given from Africa, Australia, America, etc. To limit oneself to just one, it is striking to compare the minute care with which the Hopi Indians of Arizona traced different types of legal and religious rights to the father's and to the mother's lines, while the frequency of divorce made the family so unstable that many fathers did not actually share the same house as their children, since houses were women's properties and, from the legal point of view, children followed the mother's line.

This brittleness of the conjugal family, which is so common among the so-called primitive peoples, does not prevent them from giving some value to conjugal faithfulness and parental attachment. However, these are moral norms and they should be contrasted strongly with the legal rules which in many cases only acknowledge formally the relationship of the children with either the father's or the mother's lines or, when both lines are formally recognized, do so for wholly different types of rights and/or obligations. Extreme cases have been recorded such as the Emerillon, a small tribe of French Guiana now reduced to about fifty persons. Here, according to recent informants, marriage is so unstable that, during a life-time, everybody has a good chance to get married to everybody of the opposite sex and the tribe is said to use special names for children, showing from which one of at least eight consecutive marriages they may be the offspring. This is probably a recent development which should be explained on the one hand by the smallness of the tribe and, on the other, by the unstable conditions under which it has lived for the past century. However, it shows that conditions may exist where the conjugal family is hardly recognizable.

Instability accounts for the above examples; but some others may stem from quite opposite considerations. In most of contemporary India and in many parts of western and eastern Europe, sometimes as late as the nine-teenth century, the basic social unit was constituted by a type of family which should be described as *domestic* rather than *conjugal*: ownership of the land and of the homestead, parental authority and economic leadership were vested in the eldest living ascendant, or in the community of brothers issued from the same ascendant. In the Russian *bratsvo*, the south-Slavic *zadruga*, the French *maisnie*, the family actually consisted of the elder or the surviving brothers, together with their wives, married sons with their wives and unmarried daughters, and so on down to the great-grandchil-dren. Such large groups, which could sometimes include several dozen persons living and working under a common authority, have been desig-nated as *joint families* or *extended families*. Both terms are useful but misleading, since they imply that these large units are made up of small conjugal families. As we have already seen, while it is true that the conju-gal family limited to mother and children is practically universal, since it is based on the physiological and psychological dependency which exists between them at least for a certain time, and that the conjugal family consisting of husband, wife, and children is almost as frequent for psycho-logical and economical reasons which should be added to those previously mentioned, the historical process which has led among ourselves to the legal recognition of the conjugal family is a very complex one: it has been brought about only in part through an increasing awareness of a natural situation. But there is little doubt that, to a very large extent, it has resulted from the narrowing down to a group, as small as can be, the legal standing of which, in the past of our institutions, was vested for centuries on very large groups. In the last instance, one would not be wrong in disallowing the terms joint family and extended family. Indeed, it is rather the conjugal family which deserves the name of: *restricted family*.

We have just seen that, when the family is given a small functional value, it tends to disappear even below the level of the conjugal type. On the contrary, when the family has a great functional value, it becomes actualized much above that level. Our would-be universal conjugal family, then, corresponds more to an unstable equilibrium between extremes than to a permanent and everlasting need coming from the deepest requirements of human nature.

To complete the picture, we have finally to consider cases where the conjugal family differs from our own, not so much on account of a different amount of functional value, but rather because its functional value is conceived in a way qualitatively different from our own conceptions.

As will be seen later on, there are many peoples for whom the kind of spouse one should marry is much more important than the kind of match they will make together. These people are ready to accept unions which to us would seem not only unbelievable, but in direct contradiction with the aims and purposes of setting up a family. For instance, the Siberian Chukchee were not in the least abhorrent to the marriage of a mature girl of let us say about twenty, with a baby-husband two or three years old. Then, the young woman, herself a mother by an authorized lover, would nurse together her own child and her little husband. Like the North American Mohave, who had the opposite custom of a man marrying a baby girl and caring for her until she became old enough to fulfill her conjugal duties, such marriages were thought of as very strong ones, since the natural feelings between husband and wife would be reinforced by the recollection of the parental care bestowed by one of the spouses on the other. These are by no means exceptional cases to be explained by extraordinary mental abnormalities. Examples could be brought together from other parts of the world: South America, both highland and tropical, New Guinea, etc.

As a matter of fact, the examples just given still respect, to some extent, the duality of sexes which we feel is a requirement of marriage and raising a family. But in several parts of Africa, women of high rank were allowed to marry other women and have them bear children through the services of unacknowledged male lovers, the noble woman being then entitled to become the "father" of her children and to transmit to them, according to the prevalent father's right, her own name, status, and wealth. Finally, there are the cases, certainly less striking, where the conjugal family was considered necessary to procreate the children but not to raise them, since each family did endeavor to retain somebody else's children (if possible of a higher status) to raise them while their own children were similarly retained (sometimes before they were born) by another family. This happened in some parts of Polynesia, while "fosterage," i.e., the custom whereby a son was sent to be raised by his mother's brother, was a common practice on the Northwest Coast of America as well as in European feudal society.

During the course of centuries we have become accustomed to Christian morality, which considers marriage and setting up a family as the only way to prevent sexual gratification from being sinful. That connection has been shown to exist elsewhere in a few scattered instances; but it is by no means frequent. Among most people, marriage has very little to do with the satisfaction of the sexual urge, since the social setup provides for many opportunities which can be not only external to marriage, but even contradictory to it. For instance, among the Muria of Bastar, in central India, when puberty comes, boys and girls are sent to live together in communal huts where they enjoy a great deal of sexual freedom, but after a few years of such leeway they get married according to the rule that no former adolescent lovers should be permitted to unite. Then, in a rather small village, each man is married to a wife whom he has known during his younger years as his present neighbor's (or neighbors') lover.

On the other hand, if sexual considerations are not paramount for marriage purposes, economic necessities are found everywhere in the first place. We have already shown that what makes marriage a fundamental need in tribal societies is the division of labor between the sexes.

Like the form of the family, the division of labor stems more from social and cultural considerations than from natural ones. Truly, in every human group, women give birth to children and take care of them, and men rather have as their specialty hunting and warlike activities. Even there, though, we have ambiguous cases: of course men never give birth to babies, but in many societies, as we have seen with the couvade, they are made to act as if they did. And there is a great deal of difference between the Nambikwara father nursing his baby and cleaning it when it soils itself, and the European nobleman of not long ago to whom his children were formally presented from time to time, being otherwise confined to the women's quarters until the boys were old enough to be taught riding and fencing. Conversely, the young concubines of the Nambikwara chieftain disdain domestic activities and prefer to share in their husband's adventurous expeditions. It is by no means unlikely that a similar custom, prevailing among other South American tribes, where a special class of women, half wantons and half helpers, did not marry, but accompanied the men on the warpath, is at the origin of the famous legend of the Amazons.

When we turn to activities less basic than child-rearing and war-making, it becomes still more difficult to discern rules governing the division of labor between the sexes. The Boróro women till the soil while among the Zuñi this is a man's work; according to tribe, hut-building, pot-making, weaving, may be incumbent upon either sex. Therefore, we should be careful to distinguish the *fact* of the division of labor between the sexes which is practically universal, from the *way* according to which different tasks are attributed to one or the other sex, where we should recognize the same paramount influence of cultural factors, let us say the same *artificiality* which presides over the organization of the family itself.

Here, again, we are confronted with the same question we have already met with: if the natural reasons which could explain the division of labor between the sexes do not seem to play a decisive part, as soon as we leave the solid ground of women's biological specialization in the production of children, why does it exist at all? The very fact that it varies endlessly according to the society selected for consideration shows that, as for the family itself, it is the mere fact of its existence which is mysteriously required, the form under which it comes to exist being utterly irrelevant, at least from the point of view of any natural necessity. However, after having considered the different aspects of the problem, we are now in a position to perceive some common features which may bring us nearer to an answer than we were at the beginning of this chapter. Since family appears to us as a positive social reality, perhaps the only positive social reality, we are prone to define it exclusively by its positive characteristics. Now it should be pointed out that whenever we have tried to show what the family is, at the same time we were implying what it is not, and the negative aspects may be as important as the others. To return to the division of labor we were just discussing, when it is stated that one sex must perform certain tasks, this also means that the other sex is forbidden to do them. In that light, the sexual division of labor is nothing else than a device to institute a reciprocal state of dependency between the sexes.

The same thing may be said of the sexual side of the family life. Even if it is not true, as we have shown, that the family can be explained on sexual grounds, since for many tribes, sexual life and the family are by no means as closely connected as our moral norms would make them, there is a negative aspect which is much more important: the structure of the family, always and everywhere, makes certain types of sexual connections impossible, or at least wrong.

Indeed, the limitations may vary to a great extent according to the culture under consideration. In ancient Russia, there was a custom known as *snokatchestvo* whereby a father was entitled to a sexual privilege over his son's young wife; a symmetrical custom has been mentioned in some part of southeastern Asia where the persons implied are the sister's son and his mother's brother's wife. We ourselves do not object to a man marrying his wife's sister, a practice which English law still considered incestuous in the mid-nineteenth century. What remains true is that every known society, past or present, proclaims that if the husband-wife relationship, to which, as just seen, some others may eventually be added, implies sexual rights, there are other relationships equally derived from the familial structure, which make sexual connections inconceivable, sinful, or legally punishable. The universal prohibition of incest specifies, as a general rule, that people considered as parents and children, or brother and sister, even if only by name, cannot have sexual relations and even less marry each other. In some recorded instances—such as ancient Egypt, pre-Columbian Peru, also some African, southeast Asian, and Polynesian kingdoms —incest was defined far less strictly than elsewhere. Even there, however, the rule existed, since incest was limited to a minority group, the ruling class (with the exception of, perhaps, ancient Egypt where it may have been more common); on the other hand, not every kind of close relatives were permitted as spouse: for instance it was the half-sister, the full-one being excluded; or, if the full-sister was allowed, then it should be the elder sister, the younger one remaining incestuous.

The space at our disposal is too short to demonstrate that, in this case as previously, there is no natural ground for the custom. Geneticists have shown that while consanguineous marriages are likely to bring ill effects in a society which has consistently avoided them in the past, the danger would be much smaller if the prohibition had never existed, since this would have given ample opportunity for the harmful hereditary characters to become apparent and be automatically eliminated through selection: as a matter of fact, this is the way breeders improve the quality of their subjects. Therefore, the dangers of consanguineous marriages are the outcome of the incest prohibition rather than actually explaining it. Furthermore, since very many primitive peoples do not share our belief in biological harm resulting from consanguineous marriages, but have entirely different theories, the reason should be sought elsewhere, in a way more consistent with the opinions generally held by mankind as a whole.

The true explanation should be looked for in a completely opposite direction, and what has been said concerning the sexual division of labor may help us to grasp it. This has been explained as a device to make the sexes mutually dependent on social and economic grounds, thus establishing clearly that marriage is better than celibacy. Now, exactly in the same way that the principle of sexual division of labor establishes a mutual dependency between the sexes, compelling them thereby to perpetuate themselves and to found a family, the prohibition of incest establishes a mutual dependency between families, compelling them, in order to perpetuate themselves, to give rise to new families. It is through a strange oversight that the similarity of the two processes is generally overlooked on account of the use of terms as dissimilar as *division,* on the one hand, and *prohibition* on the other. We could easily have emphasized only the negative aspect of the division of labor by calling it a prohibition of tasks; and conversely, outlined the positive aspect of incest-prohibition by calling it the principle of division of marriageable rights between families. For incest-prohibition simply states that families (however they should be defined) can only marry between each other and that they cannot marry inside themselves.

We now understand why it is so wrong to try to explain the family on the purely natural grounds of procreation, motherly instinct, and psychological feelings between man and woman and between father and children. None of these would be sufficient to give rise to a family, and for a reason simple enough: for the whole of mankind, the absolute requirement for the creation of a family is the previous existence of two other families, one ready to provide a man, the other one a woman, who will through their marriage start a third one, and so on indefinitely. To put it in other words: what makes man really different from the animal is that, in mankind, a family could not exist if there were no society; i.e., a plurality of families ready to acknowledge that there are other links than consanguineous ones, and that the natural process of filiation can only be carried on through the social process of affinity.

How this interdependency of families has become recognized is another problem which we are in no position to solve because there is no reason to believe that man, since he emerged from his animal state, has not enjoyed a basic form of social organization, which, as regards the fundamental principles, could not be essentially different from our own. Indeed, it will never be sufficiently emphasized that, if social organization had a beginning, this could only have consisted in the incest prohibition since, as we have just shown, the incest prohibition is, in fact, a kind of remodeling of the biological conditions of mating and procreation (which know no rule, as can be seen from observing animal life), compelling them to become perpetuated only in an artificial framework of taboos and obligations. It is there, and only there, that we find a passage from nature to culture, from animal to human life, and that we are in a position to understand the very essence of their articulation.

As Taylor has shown almost a century ago, the ultimate explanation is probably that mankind has understood very early that, in order to free itself from a wild struggle for existence, it was confronted with the very simple choice of "either marrying-out or being killed-out." The alternative was between biological families living in juxtaposition and endeavoring to remain closed, self-perpetuating units, overridden by their fears, hatreds, and ignorances, and the systematic establishment, through the incest prohibition, of links of intermarriage between them, thus succeeding to build, out of the artificial bonds of affinity, a true human society, despite, and even in contradiction with, the isolating influence of consanguinity. Therefore we may better understand how it came to be that, while we still do not know exactly what the family is, we are well aware of the prerequisites and the practical rules which define its conditions of perpetuation.

The so-called primitive peoples have, for that purpose, very simple and clever rules which the tremendous increase in size and fluidity of modern society makes it sometimes difficult for us to understand.

In order to insure that families will not become closed and that they will not constitute progressively as many self-sufficient units, we satisfy ourselves with forbidding marriage between near relatives. The amount of social contacts which any given individual is likely to maintain outside his or her own family is great enough to afford a good probability that, on the average, the hundreds of thousands of families constituting at any given moment a modern society will not be permitted to "freeze," if one may say so. On the contrary, the greatest possible freedom for the choice of a mate (submitted to the only condition that the choice has to be made outside the restricted family) insures that these families will be kept in a continuous flow and that a satisfactory process of continuous "mix-up" through intermarriage will prevail among them, thus making for a homogeneous and well-blended social fabric.

Conditions are quite different in the so-called primitive societies: there, the global figure of the population is a small one, although it may vary from a few dozen up to several thousands. Besides, social fluidity is low and it is not likely that many people will have a chance to get acquainted with others, during their lifetime, except within the limits of the village, hunting territory, etc., though it is true that many tribes have tried to organize occasions for wider contacts, for instance, during feasts, tribal ceremonies, etc. Even in such cases, however, the chances are limited to the tribal group, since most primitive peoples consider that the tribe is a kind of wide family, and that the frontiers of mankind stop together with the tribal bonds themselves.

Given such conditions, it is still possible to insure the blending of families into a well-united society by using procedures similar to our own, i.e., a mere prohibition of marriage between relatives without any kind of positive prescriptions as to where and whom one should correctly marry. Experience shows, however, that this is only possible in small societies under the condition that the diminutive size of the group and the lack of social mobility be compensated by widening to a considerable extent the range of prohibited degrees. It is not only one's sister or daughter that, under such circumstances, one should not marry, but any women with whom blood relationship may be traced, even in the remotest possible way. Very small groups with a low cultural level and a loose political and social organization, such as some desert tribes of North and South America, provide us with examples of that solution.

However, the great majority of primitive peoples have devised another method to solve the problem. Instead of confining themselves to a statistical process, relying on the probability that certain interdictions being set up, a satisfactory equilibrium of exchanges between the biological families will spontaneously result, they have preferred to invent rules which every individual and family should follow carefully, and from which a given form of blending, experimentally conceived of as satisfactory, is bound to arise.

Whenever this takes place, the entire field of kinship becomes a kind of complicated game, the kinship terminology being used to distribute all the members of the group into different categories, the rule being that the category of the parents defines either directly or indirectly the category of the children, and that, according to the categories in which they are placed, the members of the group may or may not get married. The study of these rules of kinship and marriage has provided modern anthropology with one of its more difficult and complicated chapters. Apparently ignorant and savage peoples have been able to devise fantastically clever codes which sometimes require, in order to understand their workings and effects, some of the best logical and even mathematical minds available in modern civilization. Therefore, we will limit ourselves to explaining the crudest principles which are the more frequently met with.

One of these is, undoubtedly, the so-called rule of cross-cousin marriage, which has been taken up by innumerable tribes all over the world. This is a complex system according to which collateral relatives are divided into two basic categories: "parallel" collaterals, when the relationship can be traced through two siblings of the same sex, and "cross" collaterals, when the relationship is traced through two siblings of opposite sex. For instance, my paternal uncle is a parallel relative and so is my maternal aunt; while the maternal uncle on the one hand, the paternal aunt on the other, are cross-relatives. In the same way, cousins who trace their relationship through two brothers or two sisters, are parallel-cousins; and those who are connected through a brother and a sister are cross-cousins. In the generation of the nephews, if I am a man, my brother's children will be my parallel-nephews while my sister's children are my cross-nephews.

Now, the startling fact about this distinction is that practically all the tribes which make it claim that parallel relatives are the same thing as the closest ones on the same generation level: my father's brother is a "father," my mother's sister a "mother"; my parallel-cousins are like brothers and sisters to me; and my parallel-nephews like children. Marriage with any of these would be incestuous and is consequently forbidden. On the other hand, cross-relatives are designated by special terms of their own, and it is among them that one should preferably find a mate. This is true to the extent that quite frequently, there is only one word to mean both "cross-cousin" and "spouse." What can be the reason for this claim, exactly similar among hundreds of different tribes in Africa, America, Asia, Oceania, that one should not marry, under any pretense, a father's brother's daughter, since that would amount to marrying one's sister, while the best conceivable spouse consists of a mother's brother's daughter, namely a relative who, on purely biological grounds, is exactly as close as the former?

There are even tribes which go a step further in these refinements. Some think that it is not cross-cousins who should marry, but only cross-cousins once removed (i.e., children of cross-cousins); others, and this is by far the most frequent case, are not satisfied with the simple distinction between cross- and parallel-cousins; they subdivide the cross-cousins themselves into marriageable and nonmarriageable ones. For instance, although a mother's brother's daughter is, according to the above definitions, a cross-cousin in the same sense as a father's sister's daughter, there are in India, living side by side, tribes which believe that one of them, only different according to case, makes a suitable spouse, death being preferable to the sin of marrying the other.

All these distinctions (to which others could be added) are fantastic at first sight because they cannot be explained on biological or psychological grounds. But, if we keep in mind what has been explained in the preceding section, i.e., that all the marriage prohibitions have as their only purpose to establish a mutual dependency between the biological families, or, to put it in stronger terms, that marriage rules express the refusal, on the part of society, to admit the exclusive existence of the biological family, then everything becomes clear. For all these complicated sets of rules and distinctions are nothing but the outcome of the processes according to which, in a given society, families are set up against each other for the purpose of playing the game of matrimony.

Let us consider briefly the rules of the game. Since societies try to maintain their identity in the course of time, there should be first a rule fixing the status of the children in respect to that of their parents. The simplest possible rule to that end, and by far the most frequently adopted, is the generally called rule of *unilineal descent*, namely that children get the same status of either their father (patrilineal descent) or their mother (matrilineal descent). It can also be decided that the status of both the father and the mother are taken into consideration, and that they should be combined to define a third category in which the children will be put. For instance, a child of a father belonging to the status A and of a mother belonging to the status B, would himself belong to a status C; and the status will be D if it is the father who is B and the mother who is A. Then, C and D will marry together and procreate children either A or B according to the sex orientation, and so on indefinitely. Everybody with some leisure time may devise rules of this kind, and it will be surprising indeed if some tribe, at least, cannot be found where each rule is actually being applied.

The rule of descent being defined, the second question is to know in how many exogamous groups the society in consideration is being divided. An exogamous group is one inside of which intermarriage is forbidden and which, consequently, requires at least another exogamous group with whom it may exchange its sons and/or daughters for marriage purposes. Among ourselves, there are as many exogamous groups as restricted families, that is, an extremely high number, and it is this high number which allows us to rely on probability. In primitive societies, however, the figure is usually much smaller, on the one hand because the group itself is a small one, and on the other hand because the familial ties go much further than is the case among us.

Our first hypothesis will be the simpler one: that of unilineal descent and of two exogamous groups, A and B. Then, the only solution will be that men of A marry women of B, and men of B marry women of A. A typical case will be that of two men, respectively A and B, exchanging their sisters so that each one may get a wife. The reader has just to take a pencil and a sheet of paper to build up the theoretical genealogy which will be the outcome of such a set-up. Whatever the rule of descent, siblings and parallel-cousins will always fall in the same category, while cross-cousins of whatever kind will fall in opposite categories. Therefore, only cross-cousins (if we are playing the game with 2 to 4 groups) or children of cross-cousins (if we are playing with 8 groups, for 6 provide an intermediary case) will meet the initial rule that spouses should belong to opposite groups.

So far, we have considered groups tied up in pairs: 2, 4, 6, 8. They can only come in even numbers. What, now, if the society is made up of an odd number of exchanging groups? With the preceding rule, there will be a group which will remain alone by itself, without a partner with whom to set up an exchange relationship. Hence, the need for additional rules which can be of use whatever the number of elements, either even or odd.

There are two ways to meet the difficulty. Exchange can either remain simultaneous and become indirect, or remain direct at the expense of becoming consecutive. The first type will be when group A gives its daughters as wives to group B, B to C, C to D, D to n . . . and finally n to A. When the cycle is completed, every group has given a woman and has received one, though it has not given to the same group as that from which it has received. In that case, pencil and paper will show that parallel-cousins always fall in one's own group, the same as brothers and sisters, and cannot consequently be married according to rule. As to cross-cousins, a new distinction will appear: the female cross-cousin on the mother's side (i.e., the mother's brother's daughter) will always fall in the marriageable group (A to B, B to C, etc.), while that on the father's side (father's sister's daughter) will fall in the opposite group (that is, the one to which my group gives wives, but from which it does not receive any: B to A, C to B, etc.).

The alternative would be to keep the exchange direct, though in consecutive generations: for instance, A receives a wife from B, and returns to A the daughter born from that marriage to become the spouse of a man A of the following generation. If we keep our groups arranged in a series: A, B, C, D, n . . . , the general set-up will be, then, that any group, let us say C, at one generation gives to D and receives from B; at the following generation, C repays B and gets its own return from D, and so on indefinitely. Here again the patient reader will find out that cross-cousins are being distinguished in two categories, but this time in a reverse way: for a man, the correct mate will always be the father's sister's daughter, the mother's brother's daughter being always in the "wrong" category.

These are the simplest cases. All over the world there are still kinship systems and marriage rules for which no satisfactory interpretation has as yet been brought forward; such are the Ambrym system in the New Hebrides, the Murngin of northwestern Australia, and the whole North American complex known as the Crow-Omaha kinship system. It is fairly certain that to explain these and other sets of rules, however, one will have to proceed as we have shown here, namely to interpret kinship systems and marriage rules as embodying the rule of that very special kind of game which consists, for consanguineous groups of men, in exchanging women among themselves, that is, building up new families with the pieces of earlier ones, which should be shattered for that purpose.

The female reader, who may be shocked to see womankind treated as a commodity submitted to transactions between male operators, can easily find comfort in the assurance that the rules of the game would remain unchanged should it be decided to consider the men as being exchanged by women's groups. As a matter of fact, some very few societies, of a highly developed matrilineal type, have to a limited extent attempted to express things that way. And both sexes can be comforted from a still different (but in that case slightly more complicated) formulation of the game, whereby it would be said that consanguineous groups consisting of both men and women are engaged in exchanging together bonds of relationships.

The important conclusion to be kept in mind is that the restricted family can neither be said to be the element of the social group, nor can it be claimed to result from it. Rather, the social group can only become established in contradistinction, and to some extent in compliance, with the family, since in order to maintain the society through time, women should procreate children, benefit from male protection while they are engaged in confinement and nursing, and, since precise sets of rules are needed, to perpetuate throughout the generations the basic pattern of the social fabric. However, the primary social concern regarding the family is not to protect or enhance it: it is rather an attitude of diffidence, a denial of its right to exist either in isolation or permanently; restricted families are only permitted to live for a limited period of time, either long or short according to case, but under the strict condition that their component parts be ceaselessly displaced, loaned, borrowed, given away, or returned, so that new restricted families may be endlessly created or made to vanish. Thus, the relation between the social group as a whole and the restricted families which seem to constitute it is not a static one, like that of a wall to the bricks it is built with. It is rather a dynamic process of tension and opposition with an equilibrium point extremely difficult to find, its exact position being submitted to endless variations from time to time and from society to society. But the word of the Scriptures: "You will leave your father and mother" provides the iron rule for the establishment and functioning of any society.

Society belongs to the realm of culture, while the family is the emanation, on the social level, of those natural requirements without which there could be no society and indeed no mankind. As a philosopher of the sixteenth century has said, man can only overcome nature by complying with its laws. Therefore, society has to give the family some amount of recognition. And it is not so surprising that, as geographers have also noticed with respect to the use of natural land resources, the greatest amount of compliance with the natural laws is likely to be found at both extremes of the cultural scale: among the simpler peoples as well as among the more highly civilized. Indeed, the first ones are not in a position to afford paying the price of too great a departure, while the second have already suffered from enough mistakes to understand that compliance is the best policy. This explains why, as we have already noticed, the small, relatively stable, monogamic restricted family seems to be given greater recognition, both among the more primitive peoples and in modern societies, than in what may be called (for the sake of the argument) the intermediate levels. However, this is nothing more than a slight shift of the equilibrium point between nature and culture, and does not affect the general picture given in this chapter. When one travels slowly and with great effort, halts should be long and frequent. And when one is given the possibility to travel often and fast, he or she should also, though for different reasons, expect to stop and rest frequently. The more roads there are, the more crossings there are likely to be. Social life imposes on the consanguineous stocks of mankind an incessant traveling back and forth, and family life is little else than the expression of the need to slacken the pace at the crossroads and to take a chance to rest. But the orders are to keep on marching. And society can no more be said to consist of families than a journey is made up of the stopovers which break it down into discontinuous stages. They are at the same time its condition and its negation.

An Inquiry into the Nature of the Family

Richard N. Adams

The Universal Functions Approach

Murdock's Multiple-Function Approach

Murdock's major reasons for seeing the nuclear family as a universal and inevitable phenomenon are that it was present in all the societies in his original sample for *Social Structure* (1949), and that logically it seemed to him that the family fulfilled a number of functions better than any other conceivable agency. The four functions he regards as primary (although he would doubtless allow others for any specific society) are "fundamental to human social life—the sexual, the economic, the reproductive, and the educational." Murdock is quite explicit in saying that "Agencies or relationships outside of the family may, to be sure, share in the fulfillment of any of these functions, but they never supplant the family." The immediate issue that arises from Murdock's propositions is whether in fact other agencies have not frequently taken over the functions that he regards as being uniquely served by the nuclear family. In reading Murdock, one gathers that he is referring not only to the presence of a nuclear family in all societies, but also to its pervasiveness among household groups in all

From Richard N. Adams, "An Inquiry into the Nature of the Family," in Dole and Carneiro (eds.), *Essays in the Science of Culture* (New York: Crowell, 1960), pp. 35–49. References cited in the original have been deleted.

societies. The implication is that its absence is considered by him to be an abnormal situation. When he says that "no society . . . has succeeded in finding an adequate substitute for the nuclear family, to which it might transfer these functions," one cannot help concluding that almost everyone in all societies must therefore rely on the nuclear family to fulfill these functions.

The cases cited earlier make it clear that large segments of some contemporary societies do not have functioning nuclear families, and that the nonnuclear family segments cannot fruitfully be cast aside as "abnormal" or "disorganized," but are regular, viable, family units in a regular, functioning society. With respect to the four functions listed by Murdock, we simply find that other social agents do in fact take over the functions for extended periods; precisely who may do it varies from one society to another. The educational function may be taken care of by the mother, other relatives, chums, schools, and so on. The rationale that a male child must have a resident father in order to learn to be a man does not hold in fact. The economic function may be handled by the mother and the children as they grow older; to this can be added grandparents, brothers, and other relatives who help either regularly or periodically. And, of course, the sexual function is handled well by other married men, boarders, visitors, friends, and so forth. The reproductive function does not need the father's presence; a midwife is more useful. While there is no denying the social necessity of the functions that Murdock has delineated, there is evidence that some families can achieve them without the presence of someone identified as a "father-husband."

Parsons' Dual-Function Approach

In a recent collection of papers Talcott Parsons has expressed the opinion that the multiple-functions approach is not adequate to explain the basic necessity of the nuclear family. In its place, he offers another functional explanation. There are, he feels, two functions, and two functions only, that are necessary everywhere and account for the universal presence of the nuclear family. One of these concerns, which Murdock calls the "educational," is namely the necessity of providing socialization of the child. The other (not on Murdock's list, but again he probably would not deny its potential importance) consists of the constant development and balancing of the adult personality which is achieved because of the constant interaction between spouses. Parsons singles out this second function as being of particular importance in explaining the restrengthening of the American (U.S.A.) nuclear family today.

Since Parsons proposes these two functions as being essential everywhere, any documented instance in which they are not operative should be sufficient to cast doubt on his thesis. Such an instance is provided by R. T. Smith's detailed study of the British Guiana Negro family. While Smith would hold that the nuclear family does have universality in the sense that all the statuses therein are recognized, he makes it clear in his study that some households remain with women as heads for extended periods, often for the greater part of the adult life of the woman concerned. He adds, furthermore, that even when men are attached to the household, it is precisely during this period that the "men spend a considerable amount of time working away from home and they do not take any significant part in the daily life of the household. . . . There are no tasks allotted to a man in his role as husband-father beyond seeing that the house is kept in good repair, and providing food and clothing for his spouse and the children." The function of sociopsychological integration assigned by Parsons to the husband-wife relationship would have considerable difficulty operating if the husband were absent most of the time. The specific functions that Smith assigns to the husband-father are economic. Parsons' argument for the universality of the nuclear family is basically no stronger than that of Murdock since the functions delineated by both can be taken care of by other agents in the society, or by other members of the family.

The fundamental weakness in Murdock's and Parsons' points of view is that they take functions that may be "imperatives," "universal functions," or "basic prerequisites" for a society, and try to correlate them with functions that are fulfilled by the nuclear family. Since it is mistakenly believed that the nuclear family form is found everywhere, that is, a universal, it must therefore be correlated with some universal requirement of human society. It is correct that there are social prerequisites, and that the nuclear family has numerous functions; but to correlate the two is a deduction that is not empirically supported.

A Structural Approach

Another approach to the problem of the significance of the woman-headed household and maternal-dyad families is taken up in Smith's study. Following the lead of his mentor, Meyer Fortes, Smith regards the family as something to be studied empirically and within a temporal as well as spatial framework and not a hard-shelled cell that forms the building unit of all kin-based social structure. Unlike Murdock and Parsons, Smith has approached the family from the point of view of the ethnographer and not the ethnologist or comparative sociologist, and studied a society where the dyad family and woman-headed households are normal. Much of Smith's work is of interest, but we will concentrate here on some major propositions referring to the woman-headed households.

Smith reports that the woman-headed household in British Guiana Negro society almost always goes through a stage during which there is a man attached to it. A family starts in a nuclear form, and later develops into the maternal dyad form when the man leaves. Smith goes on to propose that there is a basic "matrifocal" quality in the familial relations so that it is relatively easy for a family to be reduced to the maternal dyad type; the husband-wife relationship and the father-child relationship are much less important than is the mother-child relationship. The weak character of the husband-father role is related to a situation in the general social structure in British Guiana. General social status is conferred through ascribed membership in an ethnic-class group. The specific occupation of the husband, in the lower class, confers no prestige, and hence the children have nothing to gain from their fathers in this matter. This is made more obvious by comparing the lower class Negroes with members of the higher class. In the latter, the occupation of the father is of importance for the general social status of the entire family, and the father is considered an indispensable part of the family. Smith correlates the presence of the woman-headed household with a social status system in which the father can achieve no superior status.

Smith's work provides an important structural analysis of the significance of the woman-headed household and shows that the maternal dyad can and does exist effectively in spite of the theoretical positions of Murdock and Parsons. Parsons, who had access to Smith's study prior to the preparation of his own paper, failed to see the full implications of the Guiana material. The fact that the Guiana family may include a man long enough to get a household institutionalized in the local society and to undertake the procreation of children, does not mean that the man is present to fulfill either of the functions that Parsons tries to hold as being "root functions" that "must be found wherever there is a family or kinship system at all. . . ."

The Elemental Family Units: Dyads and Nucleus

In rejecting the propositions advanced by Parsons and Murdock in favor of a structural approach, their position concerning the elemental importance of the nuclear family is also cast into doubt. If "functions" do not explain the absence of the nuclear family in some situations, they can hardly be called upon to support the claim of universality for that form. No matter how fruitful this position has been in reference to other problems in social structure, we must seek an alternative view here.

The nuclear family comprises three sets of relationship that are identifiable as dyads. There is the relationship based on coitus between a man and a woman, and which may be identified as the sexual dyad until or unless it is recognized as a marital union, in which case it becomes a conjugal dyad. There is, second, the maternal dyad, composed of mother and child, that presumably begins at the time of conception but is not of great social significance as a dyad until parturition. And third, there is the paternal dyad, between father and child, that is identified specifically because of the relationship established by the sexual or conjugal dyad. Both the sexual and conjugal dyad, on the one hand, and the maternal on the other, have clear-cut correlates in biological activity. The paternal does not. So no matter what importance it may hold in a given society, at the present level of analysis it must be looked upon as a dyadic relationship of a different order; it exists not by virtue of a biological correlate, but by virtue of other dyads. Once given these dyads (all three, the sexual-conjugal, maternal, and paternal) there are important economic functions that may be assigned them. Infant dependency through nursing is, after all, an economic relationship as well as a biological one. But the economic cooperation and interdependency that may be assigned beyond this level is clearly a socially defined activity with no immediate biological correlates.

If we reject the idea that the nuclear family is the fundamental "atom" in the social "molecule," or the irreducible unit of human kin organization, and take initially the two dyads with biological correlates as two distinct components which must each be present at certain times, but not necessarily always or simultaneously, we will be approaching a view of the elements of social organization which is less biased by contemporary social system philosophy. If we allow that the nuclear family is not the minimum model for the building of subsequent structures, then we can see that it is basically, as Lowie partially suggested, an unstable combination of two simpler elements, each of which is also unstable and temporal. This allows us to look at more complex forms without the bias of assuming the nuclear family always to be present, and to seek excuses for its absence. There is a significance to be attached to the nuclear as well as the dyad forms, but it is distinctive. The conjugal or sexual dyad is particularly significant because it is the reproductive unit of the society; the maternal dyad is the temporal link between successive generations of adult dyads. While theoretically the two kinds of dyads can operate independently at all times, the society would be a sadly disjointed affair were they to do so. Their combination into a nuclear family provides generational relationships for all concerned. Since such combinations can be a short-lived activity for the individuals involved, and actually may occupy only a limited time, most people are theoretically available most of the time to focus on the dyadic relationships.

The reason that human societies have supported the nuclear family in such abundance can be found at the level of social analysis. Like all animals, human beings live not only in families, but in larger aggregates which, following general usage, can generically be called *communities*. A community cannot maintain stability and continuity solely with such unstable and temporal forms as dyads for elemental units. Seen from this point of view, the nuclear family becomes one combination that, if on nothing more than a random basis, must inevitably occur from time to time. It is the simplest way of joining the two dyads. Since the mother is the only adult in the maternal dyad, and the wife is the only female in the sexual dyad, they can be jointed most readily by identifying the wife with the mother. Once this identification is made, the nuclear unit is created and can fulfill many potential functions. But while its occurrence is inevitable, its continuation is by no means inevitable because each of the dyads alone can also fulfill some functions, and there are, in addition, presumably other societal agents that can also fulfill them. The nuclear family therefore becomes only *one of the ways* the community maintains itself. For some functions and under some circumstances, individuals may be effective agents; for others the elemental dyads are more efficient; for yet others the nuclear family may serve, and still others find other kinds of groups more useful. There are, in short, *alternative* ways in which the basic kin units can be used and combined for continued maintenance of the community.

The social universals of human society are not, then, as has been held by many students, the nuclear family and the community, but rather the community and the two dyads. The nuclear family is, in a sense, a structural by-product of the nature of the dyads, but one which is almost inevitable, even if for the briefest period. However, beyond these, the dyads may be subject to a variety of combinations to further the continuity of the community. The case described by Spiro as existing in the *kibbutz,* and the details of the woman-headed households of the British Guiana Negroes described by Smith should not be interpreted as being exceptions to a principle of nuclear family universality, but as positive illustrations of how dyads may and do operate outside of the nuclear family.

Before turning to the final points of the paper, we should deal briefly with other possible dyadic forms. Two candidates for basic forms are the paternal and sibling dyads. The appearance of a paternal dyad, as was mentioned earlier, is a result of the joining of the maternal and sexual dyads in the easiest way they can be joined. It is a logical derivative, a potential focus of social emphasis and available for further combinations itself. The sibling dyad is logically somewhat similar, being a derivative of the joining of two maternal dyads through the presence of a common mother. Again, once created it serves as a potential focus of emphasis and can combine with other dyads. While logically other dyads can be derived through further combinations, it is not within the scope of this essay to take the next step, and begin a logical and exhaustive construction of the possible combinations and derivative combinations of dyads, triads, quads and so on. It seems reasonable, however, to assume that such an analysis would lead us far in the creation of models of social structure, and offer insight into the actual forms that kin groups take in human society.*

It should not be thought that the concept of the dyad in social structure has gone unnoticed in social anthropology. Its significance, however, has usually been in descriptive terms rather than as an analytical tool. A. R. Radcliffe-Brown, certainly a pioneer in structural studies, pointed out on a number of occasions that the basic elements of social structure were dyadic:

> I regard as a part of the social structure all social relations of person to person. For example, the kinship structure of any society consists of a number of such dyadic relations, as between a father and son, or a mother's brother and his sister's son. In an Australian tribe the whole social structure is based on a network of such relations of person to person, established through genealogical connections.

But Radcliffe-Brown's view was somewhat different from that proposed here, as he also held that, "The unit of structure from which a kinship system is built up is the group which I call an 'elementary family,' consisting of a man and his wife and their child or children, whether they are living together or not." The nuclear family, as a constellation of statuses, served as the central block although, unlike Murdock and Parsons, Radcliffe-Brown did not hold that this unit must everywhere exist.

While Radcliffe-Brown saw in the "elementary family" three kinds of social relationships, "that between parent and child, that between children of the same parents (siblings), and that between husband and wife as parents of the same child or children," he did not expressly project these as potential analytical units that could themselves be examined apart from the nuclear family context and considered as distinctive building blocks. On the other hand, Radcliffe-Brown did, in his principles of "the unity of the sibling group" and "the unity of the lineage," recognize the theoretical significance of a society's placing emphasis upon a given set of relationships that, in terms of the present discussion, we would see as a "sibling dyad" and either the maternal or paternal dyad. He did not carry it farther at the time of the essay in question to include the husband-wife dyad as also being a potential center of emphasis, nor did he distinguish between other maternal and paternal relations.

The Woman-Headed Household and the Total Society

The thesis presented by Smith concerning the reasons for the appearance of the woman-headed household provides an analysis that on the surface fits well into the present argument. Over a single life cycle of Guiana Ne-

---

* Analysis based on triadic and quadic relations has already been started in communications research.

groes the sexual or conjugal dyad tends to come into play strongly only at limited periods—for procreation and for support of the woman with infant. As a woman becomes free of dependent infants, the conjugal relation can and often does disappear or change its character. This dyad is weak because the members are part of an ethnically distinct, lower-class community in which there is no status differentiation possible between males, and hence, little that one man can offer a family or son over what another can offer. According to this analysis we would expect to find similar developments in other similar situations. However, the data from Latin America do not support the extension of the analysis. Three examples will indicate the nature of the variations.

The first involves a comparison of the Guatemalan Indians and neighboring Ladinos. The former have predominantly nuclear families while the latter have a significantly high proportion of woman-headed households. The populations involved hold comparable positions within the total social structure, but the Indians in particular are similar to the Guiana Negroes in being a lower-class ethnic group within which the status of the father does not necessarily give status to the son. There is some variation in this matter, and a situation comparable to that of the Guiana Negroes is to be found less among the more traditional Indians than among the more acculturated ones. Among both Indians and Ladinos some segments of the population work on plantations, some live in independent villages, and some are part-time subsistence farmers and part-time laborers. Both have the same general concept of land tenure, and both live within the same general national context. But, it will be remembered, in the predominantly Indian departments the percentage of households with women as heads is considerably lower than that of the Ladino departments.

Although Indians and Ladinos live under similar conditions, the Ladino family is much closer to the model Smith sets up for the British Guiana Negroes than is the Mayan Indian family. The difference lies in what Smith has referred to in the Guiana situation as the "marginal nature of the husband-father role" that gives rise to a "matrifocal system of domestic relations and household groupings." Shifting the theoretical focus from the structure of the family to the values associated with it is in one sense a shorthand method of indicating that somewhere the structure, in spite of overtly similar conditions, is different. Thus, presumably the Indians have within the structure of their total community certain features which stress the father-husband role, but they are not necessarily the same features whose absence causes the weak role in the Guiana Negro situation.

Smith reports another case in a later paper in which he says that the East Indian residents of British Guiana (like the Guatemalan Mayan Indians) have retained a strong father-husband role in spite of the similarity to the Negroes in their general circumstances. "Quite apart from their historical derivation the ideal patterns of [East] Indian culture and family life have themselves become an object of value in distinguishing Indians from their nearest neighbors in the ethnic status system, the Negroes." If Smith is interpreting his Guiana data and I my Guatemalan material correctly, the reasons behind women-headed households among the Guiana Negroes are relative to the structure of the particular society. Values associated with one phase or aspect of the social structural system may in fact conflict with or contradict values stemming from or associated with other aspects. Thus in many Guatemalan Indian situations, where the population works on coffee plantations, the nuclear family is not sustained through variable social status derived from the father, but is important economically. During the five or six months of harvest, the wife also brings in a significant income through picking coffee. This means that a man with a wife has access to a larger income than one without a wife.

Societies, in which families exist, offer many faces, and the form a specific family takes must integrate with as much of the total system as possible. Total systems are complex and seldom completely self-integrated, so some aspects will be more significant for the family form of some parts of the population, while other aspects prove to be more important for others. There is thus room for variation in the form a family may take simply because different families may be answering to different structural features.

The last case involves the Guiana Negroes and the Ladinos themselves, both societies in which two distinctive forms of the family appear within a similar total structural situation. Smith reported, and the censuses for Central America show, that within these populations there are variations in the degree to which the woman-headed household occurs. If Smith's argument with respect to the relation between the dyadic Negro household and the total system is valid, we must then account for the presence of some continuous nuclear families. The answer here is probably the same as that just discussed. Within the total structure, there is room for variation, and we must assume that in spite of the structural features appearing to be the same, we are not identifying those features which the different family forms are answering to.

The evidence from the present cases does not provide us with a clear enough picture to delineate with precision why some families go one way and some go another. It is here that we must rest our case simply by preferring to place our confidence in the structural approach to solve the issue as over and against the "universal functions" preferred by other writers. We need to seek out facts pertaining to a number of situations:

1. We need to delineate the types of structural aspects which can differentially affect family forms within a single class or ethnic societal group, or both.

2. Given this, we need then to establish the principles which will hold for such relationships within any society.

Summary and Conclusions

The preceding discussion has been exploratory, working on the hypothesis-building level. The following summary remarks are made in the light of the same approach.

1. The concept of "functions" as being activities necessary to the maintenance of the species, society, or individual personality is one which is not satisfactory to explain the various forms that the family may have in a given society. The economic, sexual, reproductive, and educational functions as outlined by Murdock, or the socialization and adult-personality-maintaining functions of Parsons may be taken care of by the nuclear family under some circumstances and not under others. We cannot agree with Parsons that there are "root functions" everywhere associated with the nuclear family. If there are such things, they would probably be better identified in terms of the community and the dyads. The search for universal functions has unfortunately become an activity not unlike the continuing search for human instinct: it is not that there are none, but that it is misleading unless it is correlated with structure.

2. A theoretical analysis of the human family must not start with the assumption that the nuclear family is a basic cell or atom, but rather that there are two distinct dyadic relations that go into the formation of the nuclear family as well as into other family forms. While the concept of the nuclear family is doubtless useful for many kinds of social analysis, the fact that it fails in analyzing some family forms means we must look further. A full understanding of family form requires an analysis beginning with dyads. With this kind of approach, it may well prove that the nuclear family has not had the extensive ramifications which have been attributed to it heretofore. By adding other dyads, we are in a position to reanalyze kin and family structure as well as to pursue more analytically the nature of intrafamilial and other interpersonal relationships. It has been recognized that the nuclear family, as found among apes and men, is essentially a very primitive form. It is not surprising to find that man's culture elaborates on the dyadic possibilities of the family, and produces forms intricate and fantastic.

3. Smith's work among the British Guiana Negroes gives us a most important insight into the structural correlates of the woman-headed household in that society. It leads us to the next step, which is to seek the structural correlates which will explain why woman-headed households sometimes appear and sometimes do not within apparently a single structural system. One step in this explanation is to have recourse to the theoretical

position that the other aspects of the total social structure may be working adversely to those which are producing a nuclear or a dyadic emphasis. The emphasis thus placed, however, must have structural correlates, even if they are merely reflective of some structural aspect that is about to disappear. In this case we need more research into the exact nature of form and structure relationships, both in a synchronic and a diachronic context.

4. The final general position to be derived from the preceding discussion is that it is neither necessary nor valid to attempt to find a single normal structural form for the family within a society. That there *may* be only one is possible; but the assumption that there *can* be only one is unfruitful. The conviction that there is only one right way is older than social science, but it continues to make itself felt today. Many sociologists and anthropologists have regarded the woman-headed household as an abnormal, incomplete, or disorganized form of the family. This has contributed to the argument that the nuclear family is an indispensable, basic, stable, family type, and that its absence must therefore represent a breakdown. If we accept the notion, however, that the basic relational elements of the family are dyadic, and that the nuclear family is a more complex arrangement but one which is probably even less significant temporally than its dyad components, then we are in a position to see women-headed households as alternative or secondary norms rather than forms of disorganization. The assertion that the nuclear family successfully fulfills certain functions is perfectly valid. But the reverse assertion that other social forms can never suitably fulfill these functions is both empirically and theoretically invalid.

The denial of this reverse assertion is also important for our approach to other cultural forms. The search for a fundamental cell or building block of kin organization leads not only to a misplaced emphasis on the nuclear family, but towards a biased approach in the study of the entire family system. As Goodenough has pointed out with respect to residence, there are ethnographic ways of seeing things, and there are ethnological ways of seeing the same things. Just as the desire to discover cross-cultural regularities has led to forcing an ethnological straight jacket on a society's residence rules, so it has led to misleading assumptions concerning the identification of the nuclear family as the minimum structural form of family organization. If we look into other aspects of culture, it seems likely that we should assume that all cultural forms are alternatives (in the Lintonian sense) until a given form can be demonstrated to be universal by the ethnographers. To assume that a form, because it is a variant, is abnormal, is to evade the task before us. The first job of science is, after all, to study what *is*, not what might, or could, or should be.

Sex Control, Science, and Society

Amitai Etzioni

Using various techniques developed as a result of fertility research, scientists are experimenting with the possibility of sex control, the ability to determine whether a newborn infant will be a male or a female. So far, they have reported considerable success in their experiments with frogs and rabbits, whereas the success of experiments with human sperm appears to be quite limited, and the few optimistic reports seem to be unconfirmed. Before this new scientific potentiality becomes a reality, several important questions must be considered. What would be the societal consequences of sex control? If they are, on balance, undesirable, can sex control be presented without curbing the freedoms essential for scientific work? The scientific ethics already impose some restraints on research to safeguard the welfare and privacy of the researched population. Sex control, however, might affect the whole society. Are there any circumstances under which the societal well-being justifies some limitation on the freedom of research? These questions apply, of course, to many other areas of scientific inquiry, such as work on the biological code and the experimental use of behavior and thought-modifying drugs. Sex control provides a useful opportunity for discussion of these issues because it presents a relatively "low-key" problem. Success seems fairly remote, and, as we shall see, the deleterious effects of widespread sex control would probably not be very great.

Societal Use of Sex Control

If a simple and safe method of sex control were available, there would probably be no difficulty in finding the investors to promote it because there is a mass-market potential. The demand for the new freedom to choose seems well established. Couples have preferences on whether they want boys or girls. In many cultures boys provide an economic advantage (as workhorses) or a form of old-age insurance (where the state has not established it). Girls in many cultures are a liability; a dowry which may be a sizable economic burden must be provided to marry them off. (A working-class American who has to provide for the weddings of three or

From Amitai Etzioni, "Sex Control, Science, and Society," *Science*, September 13, 1968, pp. 1107–1112. References cited in the original have been deleted.

four daughters may appreciate the problem.) In other cultures, girls are profitably sold. In our own culture, prestige differences are attached to the sex of one's children, which seem to vary among ethnic groups and classes.

Our expectations as to what use sex control might be put to in our society are not a matter of idle speculation. Findings on sex preferences are based on both direct "soft" and indirect "hard" evidence. For soft evidence, we have data on preferences parents expressed in terms of the number of boys and girls to be conceived in a hypothetical situation in which parents would have a choice in the matter. Winston studied 55 upperclassmen, recording anonymously their desire for marriage and children. Fifty-two expected to be married some day; all but one of these desired children; expectations of two or three children were common. In total, 86 boys were desired as compared to 52 girls, which amounts to a 65 percent greater demand for males than for females.

A second study of attitudes, this one conducted on an Indianapolis sample, in 1941, found similar preferences for boys. Here, while about half of the parents had no preferences (52.8 percent of the wives and 42.3 percent of the husbands), and whereas the wives with a preference tended to favor having about as many boys as girls (21.8 percent to 25.4 percent), many more husbands wished for boys (47.7 percent as compared to 9.9 percent).

Such expressions of preference are not necessarily good indicators of actual behavior. Hence of particular interest is "hard" evidence, of what parents actually did—in the limited area of choice they already have: the sex composition of the family at the point they decided to stop having children. Many other and more powerful factors affect a couple's decision to curb further births, and the sex composition of their children is one of them. That is, if a couple has three girls and it strongly desires a boy, this is one reason it will try "once more." By comparing the number of families which had only or mainly girls and "tried once more" to those which had only or mainly boys, we gain some data as to which is considered a less desirable condition. A somewhat different line was followed in an early study. Winston studied 5466 completed families and found that there were 8329 males born alive as compared to 7434 females, which gives a sex ratio at birth of 112.0. The sex ratio of the last child, which is of course much more indicative, was 117.4 (2952 males to 2514 females). That is, significantly more families stopped having children after they had a boy than after they had a girl.

The actual preference for boys, once sex control is available, is likely to be larger than these studies suggest for the following reasons. Attitudes, especially where there is no actual choice, reflect what people believe they ought to believe in, which, in our culture, is equality of the sexes. To prefer to produce boys is lower class and discriminatory. Many middle-class parents might entertain such preferences but be either unaware of them or unwilling to express them to an interviewer, especially since at present there is no possibility of determining whether a child will be a boy or a girl.

Also, in the situations studied so far, attempts to change the sex composition of a family involved having more children than the couple wanted, and the chances of achieving the desired composition were 50 percent or lower. Thus, for instance, if parents wanted, let us say, three children including at least one boy, and they had tried three times and were blessed with girls, they would now desire a boy strongly enough to overcome whatever resistance they had to having additional children before they would try again. This is much less practical than taking a medication which is, let us say, 99.8 percent effective and having the number of children you actually want and are able to support. That is, sex control by a medication is to be expected to be significantly more widely practiced than conceiving more children and gambling on what their sex will be.

Finally, and most importantly, such decisions are not made in the abstract, but affected by the social milieu. For instance, in small *kibbutzim* many more children used to be born in October and November each year than any other months because the community used to consider it undesirable for the children to enter classes in the middle of the school year, which in Israel begins after the high holidays, in October. Similarly, sex control—even if it were taboo or unpopular at first—could become quite widely practiced once it became fashionable.

In the following discussion we bend over backward by assuming that actual behavior would reveal a smaller preference than the existing data and preceding analysis would lead one to expect. We shall assume only a 7 percent difference between the number of boys and girls to be born alive due to sex control, coming on top of the 51.25 to 48.75 existing biological pattern, thus making for 54.75 boys to 45.25 girls, or a surplus of 9.5 boys out of every hundred. This would amount to a surplus of 357,234 in the United States, if sex control were practiced in a 1965-like population.

The extent to which such a sex imbalance will cause societal dislocations is in part a matter of the degree to which the effect will be cumulative. It is one thing to have an unbalanced baby crop one year, and quite another to produce such a crop several years in a row. Accumulation would reduce the extent to which girl shortages can be overcome by one age group raiding older and younger ones.

Some demographers seem to believe in an invisible hand (as it once was popular to expect in economics), and suggest that overproduction of boys will increase the value of girls and hence increase their production, until a balance is attained under controlled conditions which will be similar to the natural one. We need not repeat here the reasons such invisible arrangements frequently do not work; the fact is they simply cannot be relied upon, as recurrent economic crises in pre-Keynesian days, or overpopulation, show.

Second, one ought to note the deep-seated roots of the boy-favoring factors. Although there is no complete agreement on what these factors are, and there is little research, we do know that they are difficult and slow to change. For instance, Winston argued that mothers prefer boys as a substitute for their own fathers, out of search for security or Freudian considerations. Fathers prefer boys because boys can more readily achieve success in our society (and in most others). Neither of these factors is likely to change rapidly if the percentage of boys born increases a few percentage points. We do not need to turn to alarmist conclusions, but we ought to consider what the societal effects of sex control might be under conditions of relatively small imbalance which, as we see it, will cause a significant (although not necessarily very high) male surplus, and a surplus which will be cumulative.

Societal Consequences

In exploring what the societal consequences may be, we again need not rely on the speculation of what such a society would be like; we have much experience and some data on societies whose sex ratio was thrown off balance by war or immigration. For example, in 1960 New York City had 343,470 more females than males, a surplus of 68,366 in the 20- to 34-age category alone.

We note, first, that most forms of social behavior are sex correlated, and hence that changes in sex composition are very likely to affect most aspects of social life. For instance, women read more books, see more plays, and in general consume more culture than men in the contemporary United States. Also, women attend church more often and are typically charged with the moral education of children. Males, by contrast, account for a much higher proportion of crime than females. A significant and cumulative male surplus will thus produce a society with some of the rougher features of a frontier town. And, it should be noted, the diminution of the number of agents of moral education and the increase in the number of criminals would accentuate already existing tendencies which point in these directions, thus magnifying social problems which are already overburdening our society.

Interracial and interclass tensions are likely to be intensified because some groups, lower classes and minorities specifically, seem to be more male oriented than the rest of the society. Hence while the sex imbalance in a society-wide average may be only a few percentage points, that of some groups is likely to be much higher. This may produce an especially high boy surplus in lower status groups. These extra boys would seek girls in higher status groups (or in some other religious group than their own)—in which they also will be scarce.

On the lighter side, men vote systematically and significantly more Democratic than women; as the Republican party has been losing consistently in the number of supporters over the last generation anyhow, another 5-point loss could undermine the two-party system to a point where Democratic control would be uninterrupted. (It is already the norm, with Republicans having occupied the White House for 8 years over the last 36.) Other forms of imbalance which cannot be predicted are to be expected. "All social life is affected by the proportions of the sexes. Wherever there exists a considerable predominance of one sex over the other, in point of numbers, there is less prospect of a well-ordered social life." "Unbalanced numbers inexorably produce unbalanced behavior."

Society would be very unlikely to collapse even if the sex ratio were to be much more seriously imbalanced than we expect. Societies are surprisingly flexible and adaptive entities. When asked what would be expected to happen if sex control were available on a mass basis, Davis, the well-known demographer, stated that some delay in the age of marriage of the male, some rise in prostitution and in homosexuality, and some increase in the number of males who will never marry are likely to result. Thus, all of the "costs" that would be generated by sex control will probably not be charged against one societal sector, that is, would not entail only, let us say, a sharp rise in prostitution, but would be distributed among several sectors and would therefore be more readily absorbed. An informal examination of the situation in the U.S.S.R. and Germany after World War II (sex ratio was 77.7 in the latter), as well as Israel in early immigration periods, supports Davis' nonalarmist position. We must ask, though, are the costs justified? The dangers are not apocalyptical; but are they worth the gains to be made?

A Balance of Values

We deliberately chose a low-key example of the effects of science on society. One can provide much more dramatic ones; for example, the invention of new "psychedelic" drugs whose damage to genes will become known only much later (LSD was reported to have such effects), drugs which cripple the fetus (which has already occurred with the marketing of thalidomide), and the attempts to control birth with devices which may produce cancer (early versions of the intrauterine device were held to have such an effect). But let us stay with a finding which generates only relatively small amounts of human misery, relatively well distributed among various sectors, so as not to severely undermine society but only add, maybe only marginally, to the considerable social problems we already face. Let us assume that we only add to the unhappiness of seven out of every 100 born (what we consider minimum imbalance to be generated), who will not find mates and will have to avail themselves of prostitution, homosexuality, or be condemned to enforced bachelorhood. (If you know someone who is desperate to be married but cannot find a mate, this discussion will be less abstract for you; now multiply this by 357,234 per annum.) Actually, to be fair, one must subtract from the unhappiness that sex control almost surely will produce, the joy it will bring to parents who will be able to order the sex of their children; but as of now, this is for most, not an intensely felt need, and it seems a much smaller joy compared to the sorrows of the unmatable mates.

We already recognize some rights of human guinea pigs. Their safety and privacy are not to be violated even if this means delaying the progress of science. The "rest" of the society, those who are not the subjects of research, and who are nowadays as much affected as those in the laboratory, have been accorded fewer rights. Theoretically, new knowledge, the basis of new devices and drugs, is not supposed to leave the inner circles of science before its safety has been tested on animals or volunteers, and in some instances approved by a government agency, mainly the Federal Drug Administration. But as the case of lysergic acid diethylamide (LSD) shows, the trip from reporting of a finding in a scientific journal to the bloodstream of thousands of citizens may be an extremely short one. The transition did take quite a number of years, from the days in 1943 when Hoffman, one of the two men who synthesized LSD-25 at Sandoz Research Laboratories, first felt its hallucenogenic effect, until the early 1960's, when it "spilled" into illicit campus use. (The trip from legitimate research, its use at Harvard, to illicit unsupervised use was much shorter.) The point is that no additional technologies had to be developed; the distance from the chemical formula to illicit composition required in effect no additional steps.

More generally, Western civilization, ever since the invention of the steam engine, has proceeded on the assumption that society must adjust to new technologies. This is a central meaning of what we refer to when we speak about an industrial revolution; we think about a society being transformed and not just a new technology being introduced into a society which continues to sustain its prior values and institutions. Although the results are not an unmixed blessing (for instance, pollution and traffic casualties), on balance the benefits in terms of gains in standards of living and life expectancy much outweigh the costs. (Whether the same gains could be made with fewer costs if society would more effectively guide its transformation and technology inputs, is a question less often discussed.) Nevertheless we must ask, especially with the advent of nuclear arms, if we can expect such a favorable balance in the future. We are aware that single innovations may literally blow up societies or civilization; we must also realize that the rate of social changes required by the accelerating stream of technological innovations, each less dramatic by itself, may supersede the rate at which society can absorb. Could we not regulate to some extent the pace and impact of the technological inputs and select among them without, by every such act, killing the goose that lays the golden eggs?

Chapter 2

Social Organization
and the Family

From the Medieval
to the Modern Family

Philippe Aries

The story outlined here strikes one as that of the triumph of the modern family over other types of human relationship which hindered its development. The more man lived in the street or in communities dedicated to work, pleasure or prayer, the more these communities monopolized not only his time but his mind. If, on the other hand, his relations with fellow workers, neighbors and relatives did not weigh so heavily on him, then the concept of family feeling took the place of the other concepts of loyalty and service and became predominant or even exclusive. The progress of the concept of the family followed the progress of private life, of domesticity. For a long time the conditions of everyday life did not allow the essential withdrawal by the household from the outside world. One of the great obstacles was doubtless the departure of the children when they were sent away to serve their apprenticeship, and their replacement by little strangers. But the return of the children, after the institution of the school, and the emotional consequences of this tightening of the family bonds were still not enough to create the modern family and its strong inner life; the general sociability of old, which was incompatible with it, remained virtually intact. An equilibrium was established in the seventeenth century between the centrifugal or social forces and the centripetal or family forces which was not destined to survive the progress of domesticity.

We have seen in the preceding pages the rise of these centripetal forces. Let us now study the resistance of the centrifugal forces, the survival of a stubborn sociability.

The historians have already stressed the survival late into the seventeenth century of relationships which had previously been neglected. The monarchical centralization achieved by Richelieu and Louis XIV was more political than social. If it succeeded in crushing the political powers competing with the crown, it left the social influences intact. Seventeenth-century society in France was made up of graded clienteles in which the little men mixed with the greatest. The formation of these groups called for a whole network of daily contacts, involving an unimaginable number of calls, conversations, meetings and exchanges. Material success, social conventions and collective amusements were not separate activities as they are today, any more than professional life, private life and social life were separate functions. The main thing was to maintain social relations with the whole of the group into which one had been born, and to better one's position by skilful use of this network of relations. To make a success of life was not to make a fortune, or at least that was of secondary importance; it was above all to win a more honourable standing in a society whose members all saw one another, heard one another and met one another nearly every day. When the French translator of Laurens Gracian (1645) suggested that the future "Hero" should find an *emploi plausible,* he did not mean what we would now call a good job, but "one which was performed in sight of everybody and to the satisfaction of all." The art of succeeding was the art of being agreeable in society. That was how Balthazar Castiglione's courtier saw it in the sixteenth century: "This is in my opinion the most fitting way of paying court for a nobleman living at a princely court, by which he may render perfect service in all reasonable matters in order to acquire the favour of some and the praise of others." A man's future depended entirely on his "reputation." "It seems to me that there is another thing which adds to or detracts from a man's reputation, and that is his choice of the friends with whom he must maintain constant and close relations."

Since everything depended on social relations, one is bound to wonder where people met. They still often met outside, in the street. Not only by chance, because towns were comparatively small, but also because certain streets or squares were promenades where at certain hours one met one's friends, as one does today in Mediterranean towns. The teeming crowds of the Corso or the Piazza Major were to be found in squares which are now deserted or crossed by pedestrians who, even when they loiter, are unknown to one another. The present-day tourist finds it hard to recognize the Place Bellecour at Lyons in this description of it given by an Italian traveler of 1664, the Abbé Locatelli:

> Men and women were walking about arm in arm, holding one another as one holds a child. . . . A woman gave her arm to two men, a man his arm to two women. Unaccustomed as we were to these manners [the good priest came from Bologna where people were more reserved than in Lyons], we thought we had entered a brothel. . . . I noticed how gay they all were, and at the entrance to the promenade, I saw them take each other by the arm, which they held bent like the handle of a basket, and they walked about in this way.

The surprise felt by this seventeenth-century Bolognese at the sight of this laughing population walking about arm in arm is the same as that which we experience today when we mingle with an Italian crowd.

People met in the street; where did they forgather? In nineteenth-century France, and modern France too, the men often gather together in the café. Contemporary French society remains unintelligible unless one recognizes the importance of the café: it is the only meeting-place which is accessible at any time, as regular as a habit. The English equivalent is the "public house" or pub. The society of the sixteenth and seventeenth centuries was a society without a café or pub: the tavern was a place of ill repute reserved for criminals, prostitutes, soldiers, students on the spree, down-and-outs, and adventurers of every sort—it was not frequented by decent people, whatever their station in life. There were no other public places except private houses, or at least certain private houses: the big houses in either the town or country.

What do we mean by a big house? Something very different from the meaning we would give today to the same expression. A house today is said to be big in relation to the density of its population. A big house is always a house with few people in it. As soon as the population density rises, people say that they are beginning to feel cramped for room, and the house, comparatively speaking, is no longer as big as it was. In the seventeenth century, and also in the fifteenth and sixteenth centuries, a big house was always crowded, with more people in it than in little houses. This is an important point, which emerges from all the investigations into density of population made by demographic historians.

The population of Aix-en-Provence at the end of the seventeenth century has been studied by means of the capitation register of 1695. In the light of these analyses, a sharp contrast can be seen between the poor, densely populated districts and the rich, less populated districts: the former had little houses with few people in each house, the latter big houses crowded with people. Some houses contained three or fewer than three occupants, while others contained twenty-five people (two masters, six children, seventeen servants) or seventeen people (two masters, eight children, seven servants).

This contrast was not peculiar to the seventeenth century or to Provence. A recent article on Carpentras in the middle of the fifteenth century gives the same impression. Twenty-three families of notabilities comprised one hundred and seventy-seven people, or 7.7 people to each house; 17.4 percent of the population lived in houses containing more than eight people. One noble had twenty-five people in his house. The cathedral architect lived with fourteen other people. It is a delicate matter to draw conclusions about the birth rate from these figures. But they show clearly that the houses of the rich sheltered, apart from the family proper, a whole population of servants, employees, clerics, clerks, shopkeepers, apprentices and so on. That was the case from the fifteenth to the seventeenth century in the greater part of Western Europe. The houses in question were big houses, with several rooms on each floor and several windows overlooking the street, courtyard or garden. Taken by themselves they formed a veritable social group. Beside these big, crowded houses there were tiny houses containing only married couples and probably just a few of their children, the youngest. In the towns, these were houses such as are still to be found here and there in the old districts, houses with only one or two windows on each floor. According to Paul Masson, it seems that the house with two windows was considered at Marseilles to be an improvement on the house with one window: "The apartments on each floor are composed of two rooms, one overlooking the street, the other overlooking a narrow space separating the backs of these houses from those of the next street." Often the two windows lighted only one room. Thus there were only one or two rooms in these urban lodgings. In the country, the little houses had no more than that, and when there were two rooms, one of them was reserved for the animals. They were obviously shelters for sleeping and sometimes (not always) eating. These little houses fulfilled no social function. They could not even serve as homes for families. The housing crisis after the Second World War has taught us something of the effect of housing on the family. Admittedly people were not as sensitive about promiscuity under the ancien regime. But there has to be a certain amount of space or family life is impossible, and the concept of the family cannot take shape or develop. We may conclude that these poor, badly housed people felt a commonplace love for little children —that elementary form of the concept of childhood—but were ignorant of the more complex and more modern forms of the concept of the family. It is certain that the young must have left at a very early age these single rooms which we would call hovels, either to move into other hovels—two brothers together, or husband and wife—or to live as apprentices, servants or clerks in the big houses of the local notabilities.

In these big houses, neither palaces, nor yet mansions, we find the cultural setting of a concept of childhood and the family. Here we collected all the observations which have gone to the making of this book. The first modern family is that of these notabilities. It is that family which is depicted in the abundant family iconography of the mid-seventeenth century, the engravings of Abraham Bosse, the portraits of Philippe de Champaigne, the scenes by the Dutch painters. It is for that family that the moralist pedagogues wrote their treatises, that more and more colleges were founded. For that family, that is to say for the whole group it formed, a group which comprised, apart from the conjugal family, not other relatives (this type of patriarchal family was clearly very rare) or at the very most bachelor brothers, but a houseful of servants, friends and protégés.

The big house fulfilled a public function. In that society without a café or a "public house," it was the only place where friends, clients, relatives and protégés could meet and talk. To the servants, clerics and clerks who lived there permanently, one must add the constant flow of visitors. The latter apparently gave little thought to the hours and were never shown the door, for the seventeenth-century pedagogues considered that the frequency and the time of these visits made a regular timetable, especially for meals, quite impossible. They regarded this irregularity as sufficiently harmful for children's education to justify sending them to college, in spite of the moral dangers of school life. The constant coming and going of visitors distracted children from their work. In short, visits gave the impression of being a positive occupation, which governed the life of the household and even dictated its mealtimes.

These visits were not simply friendly or social: they were also professional; but little or no distinction was made between these categories. A lawyer's clients were also his friends and both were his debtors. There were no professional premises, either for the judge or the merchant or the banker or the business man. Everything was done in the same rooms where he lived with his family.

Now these rooms were no more equipped for domestic work than they were for professional purposes. They communicated with one another, and the richest houses had galleries on the floor where the family lived. On the other floors the rooms were smaller, but just as dependent on one another. None had a special function, except the kitchen, and even then the cooking was often done in the hearth of the biggest room. Kitchen facilities in the towns did not allow of many refinements, and when there were guests, dishes were bought ready-cooked from the nearest caterer.

When Hortensius, Francion's master, wanted to entertain some friends, he told his servant: "Go and ask my neighbour the tavern-keeper to send me some of his best wine together with a roast. Now he said this because as it was already very late, and seeing that the latest to arrive had brought a hurdy-gurdy, he realized that he would have to offer supper to all the people in his room." Francion went out with the servant. At the tavern-keeper's, "we found nothing to suit us and we just bought some wine. We decided to go to the cook-shop on the Petit Pont. The servant bought a capon, and as he also wanted a sirloin of beef, went into all the cook-shops to see if he could find a good one."

People lived in general-purpose rooms. They ate in them, but not at special tables: the "dining table" did not exist, and at mealtimes people set up folding trestle tables, covering them with a cloth, as can be seen from Abraham Bosse's engravings. In the middle of the fifteenth century the humanist architect Alberti, very much a *laudator temporis acti,* recalled the manners of his childhood: "When we were young . . . the wife would send her husband a little jug of wine and something to eat with his bread; she dined at home and the men in the workshop." He must not be taken literally, for this custom was still common in many artisan and peasants homes at the time he was writing. But he contrasted this simple custom with urban usage at the time: "the table put up twice a day as for a solemn banquet." In other words, it was a collapsible table, like so many pieces of furniture in the early seventeenth century.

In the same rooms where they ate, people slept, danced, worked and received visitors. Engravings show the bed next to a dumbwaiter loaded with silverware, or in the corner of a room in which people are eating. A picture by P. Codde (1636) shows a dance: at the far end of the room in which the mummers are dancing, one can make out a bed with the curtains around it drawn. For a long time the beds too were collapsible. It fell to the apprentices or pages to put them up when company was expected. The author of *Le Chastel de joyeuse destinée* congratulates the youths "dressed in the livery of France" on their agility at setting up beds. As late as the early seventeenth century Heroard wrote in his diary on March 12th, 1606: "Once he [the future Louis XIII] had dressed, he helped to undo his bed." March 14th, 1606: "Taken to the Queen's apartments, he was lodged in the King's bedchamber [the King was away fighting] and helped to take his wooden bed round to the Queen: Mme de Montglat installed her bed there to sleep there." On September 8th, 1608, just before setting out for Saint-Germain, "he amused himself by undoing his bed himself, impatient to leave." Already, however, beds had become less mobile. Alberti, in his regrets for the good old days, wrote: "I remember . . . seeing our most notable citizens, when they went off to the country, taking their beds and their kitchen utensils with them, and bringing them back on their return. Now the furniture of a single room is bigger and more expensive than that of a whole house used to be on a wedding day." This transformation of the collapsible bed into a permanent piece of furniture undoubtedly marks an advance in domesticity. The ornamental bed, surrounded by curtains, was promptly seized upon by artists to illustrate the themes of private life: the room in which husband and wife came together, in which mothers gave birth, in which old men died, and also in which the lonely meditated. But the room containing the bed was not a bedroom because of that. It remained a public place. Consequently the bed had to be fitted with curtains which could be opened or drawn at will, so as to defend its occupants' privacy. For one rarely slept alone, but either with one's husband or wife or else with other people of one's own sex.

Since the bed was independent of the room in which it stood, there could be several in the same room, often one in each corner. Bussy-Rabutin tells how one day, in the course of a campaign, a girl frightened by the troops asked him for protection and hospitality: "I finally told my servants to give her one of the four beds in my room."

It is easy to imagine the promiscuity which reigned in these rooms where nobody could be alone, which one had to cross to reach any of the communicating rooms, where several couples and several groups of boys or girls slept together (not to speak of the servants, of whom at least some must have slept beside their masters, setting up beds which were still collapsible in the room or just outside the door), in which people forgathered to have their meals, to receive their friends or clients, and sometimes to give alms to beggars. One can understand why, whenever a census was taken, the houses of notabilities were always more crowded than the little one-room or two-room apartments of ordinary folk. One has to regard these families, for all that they were giving birth to the modern concept of the family, not as refuges from the invasion of the world but as the centres of a populous society, the focal points of a crowded social life. Around them were established concentric circles of relations, increasingly loose towards the periphery: circles of relatives, friends, clients, protégés, debtors, etc.

At the heart of this complex network was the resident group of the children and the servants. The progress of the concept of childhood in the course of the sixteenth and seventeenth centuries and the moralists' mistrust of the servants had not yet succeeded in breaking up that group. It was as if it were the living, noisy heart of the big house. Countless engravings show us children with servants who themselves were often very young. For example Lagniet's illustrations of a book of proverbs—a little servant is shown playing with the child of the house who is only just start-

ing to walk. The same familiarity must have existed in poorer families between artisans and labourers and their young apprentices. There was not a
great age difference between the children of a big house and the servants,
who were usually engaged very young and some of whom were foster-
brothers of members of the family. The Book of Common Prayer of 1549
made it the duty of heads of houses to supervise the religious instruction of
all the children in their house, that is to say, of all the "children, servants
and 'prentices." The servants and apprentices were placed on the same
footing as the children of the family. They all played together at the same
games. "The abbé's lackey, playing like a little dog with sweet little Jac-
quine, threw her on the ground just now, breaking her arm and dislocating
her wrist. The screams she gave were quite terrifying." So wrote Mme. de
Sévigné, who seemed to find this all very amusing.

Sons of houses went on performing domestic functions in the seventeenth century which associated them with the servants' world, particularly
waiting at table. They carved the meat, carried the countless dishes in the
French-style service which has now gone out of fashion and which consisted of offering several dishes at once, and poured out the wine, carrying
glasses or filling them. The manuals of etiquette devoted a long chapter to
the subject of waiting at table, and genre pictures often showed children
performing this service. The idea of service had not yet been degraded.
One nearly always "belonged" to somebody. The handbooks of the type
of *The Courtier* advised the *gentilhomme particulier* or minor noble to
choose his master well and try to win his favour. Society still appeared as
a network of "dependencies." Whence a certain difficulty in distinguishing
between honorable services and mercenary services reserved for the me-
nials: this difficulty still existed in the seventeenth century, although the
servants were henceforth placed on the same footing as the despised manual workers. There still remained between masters and servants something
which went beyond respect for a contract or exploitation by an employer:
an existential bond which did not exclude brutality on the one hand and
cunning on the other, but which resulted from an almost perpetual community of life. Witness the terms used by moralists to denote the duties of
a father: "The duties of a good father can be placed under three principal
heads: his first duty is to *control his wife,* the second to *bring up his children,* and the last to *govern his servants.*" "Solomon gives us some very
judicious advice on this point, which contains all a Master's duties to his
servants. There are three things, he says, which they must not lack:
bread, work, and scoldings. Bread because it is their right; work because
it is their lot; scoldings and punishment because they are our interest."
"There would be very few servants who behaved badly, if they were fed
properly and paid their wages regularly." But wages were not paid as they

are today. Listen to Coustel: prodigal parents "place themselves in a position where they are unable to *reward their servants,* to satisfy their creditors, or to help the poor, as is their duty." Or Bordelon: "There are reciprocal duties between servants and masters. For their services and their submission, give them *compassion and financial reward."* A servant was not paid, he was rewarded: a master's relationship with his servant was not based on justice but on patronage and pity, the same feeling that people had for children. This feeling has never found better expression than in Don Quixote's thoughts when he awakens and considers the sleeping Sancho: "Sleep, you have no worries. You have committed the responsibility for your person to my shoulders; it is a burden which nature and tradition have imposed on those who have servants. The valet sleeps while the master sits up, wondering how to *feed him, improve him and do good to him.* Fear (of a bad harvest, etc.) does not affect the servant, but only the master, who must support during sterility and famine him who served him during fertility and abundance." The familiarity which this personal relationship produced can be seen in Molière's comedies, in the language of the maidservants and valets when they are speaking of their masters. In those rooms intended for no special purpose, where people ate, slept and received visitors, the servants never left their masters: in the *Caquet de l'accouchée,* dialogues between a woman who had just had a child and her visitors, the maidservant joined quite naturally in the conversation. This was not only true of the middle class, but of the nobility as well. "Madame la Princesse [de Condé]," writes Mme. de Sévigné, "having conceived an affection some time ago for a footman of hers called Duval, the latter was foolish enough to show signs of impatience at the kindness which she also showed young Rabutin, who had been her page." They started a fight in front of the princess. "Rabutin drew his sword to punish him, *Duval drew his too,* and the princess, stepping between them to separate them, was slightly wounded in the breast."

This familiarity was undoubtedly beginning to disappear from adult relationships, and the moralists most concerned to ensure good treatment for servants also advised the greatest reserve when dealing with them: "Speak very little to your servants." But the old familiarity remained between servants and children or youths. The latter had played since infancy with the little lackeys, some of whom were personally attached to them and sometimes served them at college; a genuine friendship could arise between them. Molière's valets and the valet in Corneille's *Menteur* are well known. But a forgotten stage valet, the one in Larivey's *Les Écoliers,* expresses the feeling he has for his master with a more sincere emotion: "I was brought up with him and I love him more than any other living person."

The historians taught us long ago that the King was never left alone.

But in fact, until the end of the seventeenth century, nobody was ever left alone. The density of social life made isolation virtually impossible, and people who managed to shut themselves up in a room for some time were regarded as exceptional characters: relations between peers, relations between people of the same class but dependent on one another, relations between masters and servants—these everyday relations never left a man by himself. This sociability had for a long time hindered the formation of the concept of the family, because of the lack of privacy. The development in the sixteenth and seventeenth centuries of a new emotional relationship, or at least a newly conceived relationship, between parents and children, did not destroy the old sociability. The consciousness of childhood and the family postulated zones of physical and moral intimacy which had not existed before. Yet, to begin with, it adapted itself to constant promiscuity. The combination of a traditional sociability and a new awareness of the family was to be found only in certain families, families of country or city notabilities, both nobles and commoners, peasants and artisans. The houses of these notabilities became centres of social life around which there gravitated a whole complex little world. This equilibrium between family and society was not destined to survive the evolution of manners and the new progress of domesticity.

In the eighteenth century, the family began to hold society at a distance, to push it back beyond a steadily extending zone of private life. The organization of the house altered in conformity with this new desire to keep the world at bay. It became the modern type of house, with rooms which were independent because they opened on to a corridor. While they still communicated with each other, people were no longer obliged to go through them all to pass from one to another. It has been said that comfort dates from this period; it was born at the same time as domesticity, privacy and isolation, and it was one of the manifestations of these phenomena. There were no longer beds all over the house. The beds were confined to the bedrooms, which were furnished on either side of the alcove with cupboards and nooks fitted out with new toilette and hygienic equipment. In France and Italy the word *chambre* began to be used in opposition to the word *salle*—they had hitherto been more or less synonymous; the *chambre* denoted the room in which one slept, the *salle* the room in which one received visitors and ate: the *salon* and the *salle à manger, the caméra* and the *sala da pranza.* In England the word "room" was kept for all these functions, but a prefix was added to give precision: the dining room, the bedroom, etc.

This specialization of the rooms, in the middle class and nobility to begin with, was certainly one of the greatest changes in everyday life. It

satisfied a new desire for isolation. In these more private dwellings, the
servants no longer left the out-of-the-way quarters which were allotted to
them—except in the houses of princes of the blood, where the old manners
endured. Sébastien Mercier noted as a recent innovation the habit of ringing for the maidservant. Bells were arranged in such a way that they could
summon servants from a distance, whereas they had previously been capable of arousing attention only in the room in which they were rung. Nothing could be more characteristic of the new desire to keep the servants at a
distance and also to defend oneself against intruders. It was no longer
good form in the late eighteenth century to call on a friend or acquaintance
at any time of day and without warning. Either one had days when one
was "at home," or else "people send each other cards by their servants."
"The post also takes care of vists. . . . The letter-box delivers cards; nothing is easier, nobody is visible, everyone has the decency to close his
door."

The use of "cards" and "days" was not an isolated phenomenon. The
old code of manners was an art of living in public and together. The new
code of manners emphasized the need to respect the privacy of others.
The moral stress had been moved. Sébastien Mercier was quick to observe
this change: "Present-day custom has cut short all ceremonies and only a
provincial stands on ceremony now." Meals were shortened too: "They
are much shorter, and it is not at table that people talk freely and tell
amusing stories," but in the *salon,* the room to which people withdraw: the
"drawing room." "People are no longer in a hurry to drink, no longer tor-
ment their guests in order to prove that they know how to entertain, no
longer ask you to sing [the old concerts over dessert of the sixteenth and
seventeenth centuries]." "People have abandoned those foolish and ridiculous customs so familiar to our ancestors, unhappy proselytes of an
embarrassing and annoying tradition *which they called correct."* "Not a
moment's rest: people tried to outdo each other in politeness before the
meal and during the meal with pedantic stubbornness, and the experts on
etiquette applauded these puerile combats." "Of all those stupid old customs, that of blessing someone who sneezes is the only one that has lasted
down to the present day." "We leave it to the cobbler and the tailor to
give each other the sincere or hypocritical accolade which was still usual in
polite society forty years ago." "Only the *petit bourgeois* now employs
those tiresome manners and futile attentions which he still imagines to
be correct and which are intolerably irksome to people who are used to
society life."

The rearrangement of the house and the reform of manners left more
room for private life; and this was taken up by a family reduced to parents
and children, a family from which servants, clients and friends were ex-

cluded. General de Martange's letters to his wife between 1760 and 1780 enable us to gauge the progress made by a concept of the family which had become identical with that of the nineteenth and early twentieth centuries. The family had invaded people's correspondence and doubtless their conversations and preoccupations too.

The old forms of address such as "Madame" had disappeared. Martange addressed his wife as "dear *maman*" or "my dear love," "my dear child," "my dear little one." The husband called his wife by the same name that his children gave her: *maman*. His correspondence with his wife was full of details about the children, their health and their behavior. They were referred to by nickname: Minette and Coco. This increasingly widespread use of nicknames corresponded to a greater familiarity and also to a desire to address one another differently from strangers, and thus to emphasize by a sort of hermetic language the solidarity of parents and children and the distance separating them from other people.

When the father was away, he kept himself informed of all the little details of everyday life, which he took very seriously. He waited impatiently for letters: "I beg you, my dear little one, to write just a few words." "Scold Mlle. Minette for me for so far neglecting to write to me." He spoke of the joy of seeing his family again very soon: "I look forward to being with you once more in our poor little home, and I should like no responsibility better than that of arranging your room and making our stay pleasant and comfortable." Here we already have the modern taste for domesticity, contrasting the house, the object of enthusiastic pottering, with the outside world.

In this correspondence, questions of health and hygiene occupied an important place. Hitherto people had worried about serious illnesses, but they had not shown this constant solicitude, they had not bothered about a cold, a minor ailment: physical life had not been regarded as so important. "I should be so unhappy if I had no news about your health and that of my little girls." "Although what you tell me about the poor health which you and my poor little girls are enjoying is not as comforting as a father's heart might wish . . ." "I am not very happy about what you tell me about our little boy's pains and loss of appetite. I cannot recommend you too earnestly, dear child, to procure some Narbonne honey for both him and Xavière, and to rub their gums with it when they are in pain." This was the anxiety of parents over their children's teething troubles: it could have interested a few old women in Mme. de Sévigné's time, but it had not hitherto been given the honours of a place in a staff officer's correspondence. "My daughters' colds worry me. . . . But it seems to me that the weather finally took a turn for the better this morning." Vaccination against smallpox was discussed then as inoculation against poliomyelitis is today. "I leave it to you to see to Xavière's vaccination, and the sooner the better, because everybody is satisfied with the vaccination." He advised his wife to drink "Sedlitz water," "the salts of the same name," and lemonade, and also to mix vinegar or brandy with her water, to guard against infection.

One of the girls had got married in Germany. In a letter to her "dear sweet *maman*" of January 14th, 1781, she explained her long silence: "First of all the two youngest had whooping-cough for two months, so badly that every time they coughed they went purple in the face and the blood came bubbling out of their nostrils. After that illness, my little girl and Xavier caught the worst brain fever you could imagine." The doctors had given up hope of saving Xavier: "The poor child suffered all it is possible to suffer." However, in the end he was saved: "Thanks to the Supreme Being, all three have been returned to me." Nobody would now dare to seek consolation for losing a child in the hope of having another, as parents could have admitted doing only a century before. The child was irreplaceable, his death irreparable. And the mother found happiness in the midst of her children, who no longer belonged to an intermediary region between existence and nonexistence: "The company of my little ones is my sole delight." Here we see the connection between the progress of the concept of childhood and the progress of hygiene, between concern for the child and concern for his health, another form of the link between attitudes to life and attitudes to death.

Considerable attention was also paid to the children's education, the importance of which was fully recognized: "Above all I urge you not to waste a minute that can be given to the children's education; double or treble their lessons every day, especially to teach them how to stand, walk and eat" (an echo of the old manuals of etiquette). The three children had a tutor: "Let the three children profit by his tuition and let the two girls in particular learn how to stand and walk. If M. H. can give them grace, he can consider himself a clever master."

Martange ran into financial difficulties. He dreaded the consequences: "The sorrow of being unable to give them the education I would have wished has given me some bitter moments of reflection." Whatever happened, the "master's" fees had to be paid. We are a long way here from the laments of the moralists of the 1660s, who complained that schoolmasters were not paid because people did not realize the importance of their work. "I should sell my last shirt, if I had nothing else, to see my children on the same level as all the others of their age and rank. They must not be brought into the world to humiliate us with their ignorance and behaviour. I think of nothing else, my dear, but of repairing my fortune to ensure their happiness, but if they wish to ensure mine, they must work hard and not waste time." Martange was worried when his children were vaccinated, in case "the time taken by vaccination is lost by their masters." "Use your stay in town to give them a little of that education which my (financial) misfortunes have so far prevented us from obtaining for them."

Health and education: these would henceforth be the chief preoccupations of all parents. One cannot help being struck by the extremely modern tone of this correspondence. In spite of the two centuries which separate us, it is closer to us than to Mme. de Sévigné, who lived only a century earlier. In Mme. de Sévigné, apart from the maternal solicitude of a good grandmother, what appears above all, at odd moments in her life, is an amused interest in the caprices of childhood, what I have called the first attitude to childhood, the "coddling" attitude. This attitude is almost entirely absent from Martange. He treats everything much more seriously. His is already the gravity of the nineteenth century, applied to both little things and big: Victorian gravity. In the seventeenth century, when he was not a subject of amusement, the child was the instrument of matrimonial and professional speculation designed to improve the family's position in society. This idea is relegated to the background in Martange: his interest in education seems much more disinterested. Here children as they really are, and the family as it really is, with its everyday joys and sorrows, have emerged from an elementary routine to reach the brightest zones of consciousness. This group of parents and children, happy in their solitude and indifferent to the rest of society, is no longer the seventeenth-century family, open to the obtrusive world of friends, clients and servants: it is the modern family.

One of the most striking characteristics of this family is the concern to maintain equality between the children. We have seen that the moralists of the second half of the seventeenth century gave timid support to this equality, chiefly because favouring the eldest son often drove the younger children into false religious vocations, but also because they were ahead of their times and foresaw the future conditions of family life. We have seen from their writings how conscious they were of going against public opinion. Henceforth, from the end of the eighteenth century on, inequality between the children of one family would be considered an intolerable injustice. It was manners, and not the Civil Code or the Revolution which abolished the law of primogeniture. The families of France would reject it out of hand when the Ultras of the Restoration restored it, inspired by a new concept of the family which they incorrectly attributed to the ancien regime: "Out of twenty well-to-do families," Villèle wrote to Polignac on October 31st, 1824, "there is scarcely one which uses the power to favour the eldest or some other child. The bonds of subordination have been loosened everywhere to such an extent that in the family, the father considers himself obliged to humour his children."

Between the end of the Middle Ages and the seventeenth century, the child had won a place beside his parents to which he could not lay claim at a time when it was customary to entrust him to strangers. This return of the children to the home was a great event: it gave the seventeenth-century family its principal characteristic, which distinguished it from the medieval family. The child became an indispensable element of everyday life, and his parents worried about his education, his career, his future. He was not yet the pivot of the whole system, but he had become a much more important character. Yet this seventeenth-century family was not the modern family: it was distinguished from the latter by the enormous mass of sociability which it retained. Where the family existed, that is to say in the big houses, it was a centre of social relations, the capital of a little complex and graduated society under the command of the paterfamilias.

The modern family, on the contrary, cuts itself off from the world and opposes to society the isolated group of parents and children. All the energy of the group is expended on helping the children to rise in the world, individually and without any collective ambition: the children rather than the family.

This evolution from the medieval family to the seventeenth-century family and then to the modern family was limited for a long time to the nobles, the middle class, the richer artisans and the richer laborers. In the early nineteenth century, a large part of the population, the biggest and poorest section, was still living like the medieval families, with the children separated from their parents. The idea of the house or the home did not exist for them. The concept of the home is another aspect of the concept of the family. Between the eighteenth century and the present day, the concept of the family changed hardly at all. It remained as we saw it in the town and country middle classes of the eighteenth century. On the other hand, it extended more and more to other social strata. In England in the late eighteenth century, agricultural laborers tended to set up house on their own, instead of lodging with their employers, and the decline of apprenticeship in industry made possible earlier marriages and larger families. Late marriage, the precariousness of work, the difficulty of finding lodgings, the mobility of journeyman labor and the continuation of the traditions of apprenticeship, were so many obstacles to the ideal way of middle-class family life, so many obstacles which the evolution of manners would gradually remove. Family life finally embraced nearly the whole of society, to such an extent that people have forgotten its aristocratic and middle-class origins.

On Family Life
Under the Factory System

Karl Marx

In so far as machinery dispenses with muscular power, it becomes a means of employing laborers of slight muscular strength, and those whose bodily development is incomplete, but whose limbs are all the more supple. The labor of women and children was, therefore, the first thing sought for by capitalists who used machinery. That mighty substitute for labor and laborers was forthwith changed into a means for increasing the number of wage laborers by enrolling, under the direct sway of capital, every member of the workman's family, without distinction of age or sex. Compulsory work for the capitalist usurped the place, not only of the children's play but also of free labor at home within moderate limits for the support of the family.

The value of labor power was determined, not only by the labor time necessary to maintain the individual adult laborer but also by that necessary to maintain his family. Machinery, by throwing every member of that family on to the labor market, spreads the value of the man's labor power over his whole family. It thus depreciates his labor power. To purchase the labor power of a family of four workers may, perhaps, cost more than it formerly did to purchase the labor power of the head of the family, but in return, four days' labor takes the place of one, and their price falls in proportion to the excess of the surplus labor of four over the surplus labor of one. In order that the family may live, four people must now, not only labor, but expend surplus labor for the capitalist. Thus we see, that machinery, while augmenting the human material that forms the principal object of capital's exploiting power, at the same time raises the degree of exploitation.

Machinery also revolutionizes out and out the contract between the laborer and the capitalist, which formally fixes their mutual relations. Taking the exchange of commodities as our basis, our first assumption was that capitalist and laborer met as free persons, as independent owners of commodities; the one possessing money and means of production, the other labor power. But now the capitalist buys children and young persons under age. Previously, the workman sold his own labor power, which he

From Karl Marx, *Capital* (New York: Modern Library, original copyright 1906 by Charles H. Kerr), pp. 431–440. References cited in the original have been deleted.

disposed of nominally as a free agent. Now he sells wife and child. He has become a slave dealer. The demand for children's labor often resembles in form the inquiries for negro slaves, such as were formerly to be read among the advertisements in American journals. "My attention," says an English factory inspector, "was drawn to an advertisement in the local paper of one of the most important manufacturing towns of my district, of which the following is a copy: Wanted, 12 to 20 young persons, not younger than what can pass for 13 years. Wages, 4 shillings a week. Apply &c." The phrase "what can pass for 13 years," has reference to the fact, that by the Factory Act, children under 13 years may work only 6 hours. A surgeon officially appointed must certify their age. The manufacturer, therefore, asks for children who look as if they were already 13 years old. The decrease, often by leaps and bounds in the number of children under 13 years employed in factories, a decrease that is shown in an astonishing manner by the English statistics of the last 20 years, was for the most part, according to the evidence of the factory inspectors themselves, the work of the certifying surgeons, who overstated the age of the children, agreeably to the capitalist's greed for exploitation, and the sordid trafficking needs of the parents. In the notorious district of Bethnal Green, a public market is held every Monday and Tuesday morning, where children of both sexes from 9 years of age upwards, hire themselves out to the silk manufacturers. "The usual terms are 1s. 8d. a week (this belongs to the parents) and '2d. for myself and tea.' The contract is binding only for the week. The scene and language while this market is going on are quite disgraceful." It has also occurred in England, that women have taken "children from the workhouse and let any one have them out for 2s. 6d. a week." In spite of legislation, the number of boys sold in Great Britain by their parents to act as live chimney-sweeping machines (although there exist plenty of machines to replace them) exceeds 2000. The revolution effected by machinery in the judicial relations between the buyer and the seller of labor power, causing the transaction as a whole to lose the appearance of a contract between free persons, afforded the English Parliament an excuse, founded on judicial principles, for the interference of the state with factories. Whenever the law limits the labor of children to 6 hours in industries not before interfered with, the complaints of the manufacturers are always renewed. They allege that numbers of the parents withdraw their children from the industry brought under the act, in order to sell them where "freedom of labor" still rules, i.e., where children under 13 years are compelled to work like grown-up people, and therefore can be got rid of at a higher price. But since capital is by nature a leveller, since it exacts in every sphere of production equality in the conditions of the exploitation of labor, the limitation by law of children's labor, in one branch of industry, becomes the cause of its limitation in others.

We have already alluded to the physical deterioration as well of the children and young persons as of the women, whom machinery, first directly in the factories that shoot up on its bases, and then indirectly in all the remaining branches of industry, subjects to the exploitation of capital. In this place, therefore, we dwell only on one point, the enormous mortality, during the first few years of their life, of the children of the operatives. In sixteen of the registration districts into which England is divided, there are, for every 100,000 children alive under the age of one year, only 9000 deaths in the year on an average (in one district only 7047); in 24 districts the deaths are over 10,000, but under 11,000; in 39 districts over 11,000, but under 12,000; in 48 districts over 12,000, but under 13,000; in 22 districts over 20,000; in 25 districts over 21,000; in 17 over 22,000; in 11 over 23,000; in Hoo, Wolverhampton, Ashton-under-Lyne, and Preston, over 24,000; in Nottingham, Stockport, and Bradford, over 25,000; in Wisbeach, 26,000; and in Manchester, 26,125. As was shown by an official medical inquiry in the year 1861, the high death rates are, apart from local causes, principally due to the employment of the mothers away from their homes, and to the neglect and maltreatment consequent on her absence, such as, amongst others, insufficient nourishment, unsuitable food, and dosing with opiates; beside this, there arises an unnatural estrangement between mother and child, and as a consequence intentional starving and poisoning of the children. In those agricultural districts, "where a minimum in the employment of women exists, the death rate is on the other hand very low." The Inquiry Commission of 1861 led, however, to the unexpected result, that in some purely agricultural districts bordering on the North Sea, the death rate of children under one year old almost equaled that of the worst factory districts. Dr. Julian Hunter was therefore commissioned to investigate this phenomenon on the spot. His report is incorporated with the "Sixth Report on Public Health." Up to that time it was supposed, that the children were decimated by malaria, and other diseases peculiar to low-lying and marshy districts. But the inquiry showed the very opposite, namely, that the same cause which drove away malaria, the conversion of the land, from a morass in winter and a scanty pasture in summer, into fruitful corn land, created the exceptional death rate of the infants. The 70 medical men, whom Dr. Hunter examined in that district, were "wonderfully in accord" on this point. In fact, the revolution in the mode of cultivation had led to the introduction of the industrial system. Married women, who work in gangs along with boys and girls, are, for a stipulated sum of money, placed at the disposal of the farmer, by a man called "the undertaker," who contracts for the whole gang. "These gangs will sometimes travel many miles from their own village; they are to be met morning and evening on the roads, dressed in short petticoats, with suitable coats and boots, and sometimes trousers, looking wonderfully strong and healthy, but tainted with a customary immorality, and heedless of the fatal results which their love of this busy and independent life is bringing on their unfortunate offspring who are pining at home." Every phenomenon of the factory districts is here reproduced, including, but to a greater extent, ill-disguised infanticide, and dosing children with opiates. "My knowledge of such evils," says Dr. Simon, the medical officer of the Privy Council and editor in chief of the Reports on Public Health, "may excuse the profound misgiving with which I regard any large industrial employment of adult women." "Happy indeed," exclaims Mr. Baker, the factory inspector, in his official report, "happy indeed will it be for the manufacturing districts of England, when every married woman having a family is prohibited from working in any textile works at all."

The moral degradation caused by the capitalistic exploitation of women and children has been so exhaustively depicted by F. Engels in his "Lage der Arbeitenden Klasse Englands," and other writers, that I need only mention the subject in this place. But the intellectual desolation, artificial-ly produced by converting immature human beings into mere machines for the fabrication of surplus value, a state of mind clearly distinguishable from that natural ignorance which keeps the mind fallow without destroy-ing its capacity for development, its natural fertility, this desolation finally compelled even the English Parliament to make elementary education a compulsory condition to the "productive" employment of children under 14 years, in every industry subject to the Factory Acts. The spirit of capi-talist production stands out clearly in the ludicrous wording of the so-called education clauses in the Factory Acts, in the absence of an administrative machinery, an absence that again makes the compulsion illusory, in the opposition of the manufacturers themselves to these education clauses, and in the tricks and dodges they put in practice for evading them. "For this the legislature is alone to blame, by having passed a delusive law, which, while it would seem to provide that the children employed in fac-tories shall be *educated,* contains no enactment by which that professed end can be secured. It provides nothing more than that the children shall on certain days of the week, and for a certain number of hours (three) in each day, be inclosed within the four walls of a place called a school, and that the employer of the child shall receive weekly a certificate to that ef-fect signed by a person designated by the subscriber as a schoolmaster or schoolmistress." Previous to the passing of the amended Factory Act, 1844, it happened, not unfrequently, that the certificate of attendance at school were signed by the schoolmaster or schoolmistress with a cross, as they themselves were unable to write. "On one occasion, on visiting a place called a school, from which certificates of school attendance had been issued, I was so struck with the ignorance of the master, that I said to him:

"Pray, sir, can you read?" His reply was: "Aye, summat!" and as a justification of his right to grant certificates, he added: "At any rate, I am before my scholars." The inspectors, when the Bill of 1844 was in preparation, did not fail to represent the disgraceful state of the places called schools, certificates from which they were obliged to admit as a compliance with the laws, but they were successful only in obtaining thus much, that since the passing of the Act of 1844, the figures in the school certificate must be filled up in the handwriting of the schoolmaster, who must also sign his Christian and surname in full." Sir John Kincaid, factory inspector for Scotland, relates experiences of the same kind. "The first school we visited was kept by a Mrs. Ann Killin. Upon asking her to spell her name, she straightway made a mistake, by beginning with the letter C, but correcting herself immediately, she said her name began with a K. On looking at her signature, however, in the school certificate books, I noticed that she spelt it in various ways, while her handwriting left no doubt as to her unfitness to teach. She herself also acknowledged that she could not keep the register. . . . In a second school I found the schoolroom 15 feet long, and 10 feet wide, and counted in this space 75 children, who were gabbling something unintelligible." But it is not only in the miserable places above referred to that the children obtained certificates of school attendance without having received instruction of any value, for in many schools where there is a competent teacher, his efforts are of little avail from the distracting crowd of children of all ages, from infants of 3 years old and upwards; his livelihood, miserable at the best, depending on the pence received from the greatest number of children whom it is possible to cram into the space. To this is to be added scanty school furniture, deficiency of books, and other materials for teaching, and the depressing effect upon the poor children themselves of a close, noisome atmosphere. I have been in many schools, where I have seen rows of children doing absolutely nothing; and this is certified as school attendance, and, in statistical returns, such children are set down as being educated." In Scotland the manufacturers try all they can to do without the children that are obliged to attend school. "It requires no further argument to prove that the educational clauses of the Factory Act, being held in such disfavor among mill owners tend in a great measure to exclude that class of children alike from the employment and the benefit of education contemplated by this Act." Horribly grotesque does this appear in print works, which are regulated by a special Act. By that Act, "every child, before being employed in a print work must have attended school for at least 30 days, and not less than 150 hours, during the six months immediately preceding such first day of employment, and during the continuance of its employment in the print works, it must attend for a like period of 30 days, and 150 hours during every successive period of six months. . . . The attendance at school must be between 8 a.m., and 6 p.m. No attendance of less than 2½ hours, nor more than 5 hours on any one day, shall be reckoned as part of the 150 hours. Under ordinary circumstances the children attend school morning and afternoon for 30 days, for at least 5 hours each day, and upon the expiration of the 30 days, the statutory total of 150 hours having been attained, having, in their language, made up their book, they return to the print work, where they continue until the six months have expired, when another instalment of school attendance becomes due, and they again seek the school until the book is again made up. . . . Many boys having attended school for the required number of hours, when they return to school after the expiration of their six months' work in the print work, are in the same condition as when they first attended school as print-work boys, that they have lost all they gained by their previous school attendance. . . . In other print works the children's attendance at school is made to depend altogether upon the exigencies of the work in the establishment. The requisite number of hours is made up each six months, by instalments consisting of from three to five hours at a time, spreading over, perhaps, the whole six months. . . . For instance, the attendance on one day might be from 8 to 11 a.m., on another day from 1 p.m. to 4 p.m., and the child might not appear at school again for several days, when it would attend from 3 p.m. to 6 p.m.; then it might attend for 3 or 4 days consecutively, or for a week, then it would not appear in school for 3 weeks or a month, after that upon some odd days at some odd hours when the operative who employed it chose to spare it; and thus the child was, as it were, buffeted from school to work, from work to school, until the tale of 150 hours was told."

By the excessive addition of women and children to the ranks of the workers, machinery at last breaks down the resistance which the male operatives in the manufacturing period continued to oppose to the despotism of capital.

World Revolution and Family Patterns

William J. Goode

Idealization of the Recent Past: The United States

In order to weigh the extent and type of changes now taking place in family systems in various parts of the world, it is necessary to examine the recent past; otherwise no trends can be seen. We then usually discover only idealized or stereotyped descriptions of family systems of a generation ago. We must correct such stereotypes in order to measure present-day trends.

In another context, I labeled this stereotype of the United States family of the past, when *praised,* "the classical family of Western nostalgia." It is a pretty picture of life down on grandma's farm. There are lots of happy children, and many kinfolk live together in a large rambling house. Everyone works hard. Most of the food to be eaten during the winter is grown, preserved, and stored on the farm. The family members repair their own equipment, and in general the household is economically self-sufficient. The family has many functions; it is the source of economic stability and religious, educational, and vocational training. Father is stern and reserved, and has the final decision in all important matters. Life is difficult, but harmonious because everyone knows his task and carries it out. All boys and girls marry, and marry young. Young people, especially the girls, are likely to be virginal at marriage and faithful afterward. Though the parents do not arrange their children's marriages, the elders do have the right to reject a suitor and have a strong hand in the final decision. After marriage, the couple lives hamoniously, either near the boy's parents or with them, for the couple is slated to inherit the farm. No one divorces.

Those who believe we are seeing progress rather than retrogression often accept the same stereotype but describe the past in words of different emotional effect. We have progressed, they say, from the arbitrary power of elders toward personal freedom for the young, from cold marriages based on economic arrangements to unions based on the youngsters' right of choice, from rigidly maintained class barriers between children to an open class system, from the subjugation of the wife to equalitarianism and

From William J. Goode, *World Revolution and Family Patterns* (New York: Free Press of Glencoe, 1963), pp. 6–17. References cited in the original have been deleted.

companionship in marriage, and from the repression of children's emotions to permissiveness.

Like most stereotypes, that of the classical family of Western nostalgia leads us astray. When we penetrate the confusing mists of recent history we find few examples of this "classical" family. Grandma's farm was not economically self-sufficient. Few families stayed together as large aggregations of kinfolk. Most houses were small, not large. We now *see* more large old houses than small ones; they survived longer because they were likely to have been better constructed. The one-room cabins rotted away. True enough, divorce was rare, but we have no evidence that families were generally happy. Indeed, we find, as in so many other pictures of the glowing past, that in each past generation people write of a period *still* more remote, *their* grandparents' generation, when things really were much better.

If, then, the stereotype of the United States and Western family is partially incorrect, we may suppose stereotypes of other past family systems to be similarly in error. We shall, therefore, describe current changes in family patterns while ascertaining, where possible, what the patterns of the recent past were.

The Conjugal Family as an Ideal Type

As now used by family analysts, the term "conjugal family" is technically an *ideal type*; it also represents an ideal. The concept was not developed from a summary or from the empirical study of actual United States urban family behavior; it is a *theoretical* construction, derived from intuition and observation, in which several crucial variables have been combined to form a hypothetical structural harmony. Such a conceptual structure may be used as a measure and model in examining real time trends or contemporary patterns. In the ensuing discussion, we shall try to separate the fundamental from the more derivative variables in this construction.

As a concept, the conjugal family is also an *ideal* in that when analysts refer to its spread they mean that an increasing number of people view some of its characteristics as *proper* and legitimate, no matter how reality may run counter to the ideal. Thus, although parents in the United States agree that they *should* not play an important role in their children's choice of spouse, they actually do. Relatives *should* not interfere in each other's family affairs, but in a large (if unknown) percentage of cases they do. Since, however, this ideal aspect of the conjugal family is also part of the total reality, significant for changes in family patterns, we shall comment on it later as an ideology.

The most important characteristic of the ideal typical construction of the conjugal family is the relative exclusion of a wide range of affinal and blood relatives from its everyday affairs: There is no great extension of the kin network. Many other traits may be derived theoretically from this one variable. Thus, the couple cannot count on a large number of kinfolk for help, just as these kin cannot call upon the couple for services. Neither couple nor kinfolk have many *rights* with respect to the other, and so the reciprocal *obligations* are few. In turn, by an obvious sociological principle, the couple has few moral controls over their extended kin, and these have few controls over the couple.

The locality of the couple's household will no longer be greatly determined by their kin since kinship ties are weak. The couple will have a "neolocal" residence, i.e., they will establish a new household when they marry. This in turn reinforces their relative independence, because it lowers the frequency of social interaction with their kin.

The choice of mate is freer than in other systems, because the bases upon which marriage is built are different: The kin have no strong rights or financial interest in the matter. Adjustment is primarily between husband and wife, not between the incoming spouse and his or her in-law group. The courtship system is therefore ideally based, and, at the final decision stage, empirically as well, on the mutual attraction between the two youngsters.

All courtship systems are market or exchange systems. They differ from one another with respect to *who* does the buying and selling, which characteristics are more or less valuable in that market, and how open or explicit the bargaining is. In a conjugal family system mutual attraction in both courtship and marriage acquires a higher value. Nevertheless, the elders do not entirely lose control. Youngsters are likely to marry only those with whom they fall in love, and they fall in love only with the people they meet. Thus, the focus of parental controls is on who is allowed to meet whom at parties, in the school and neighborhood, and so on.

When such a system begins to emerge in a society, the age at marriage is likely to change because the goals of marriage change, but whether it will rise or fall cannot be predicted from the characteristics mentioned so far. In a conjugal system, the youngsters must now be old enough to take care of themselves; i.e., they must be as old as the economic system forces them to be in order to be independent at marriage. (Alternative solutions also arise: Some middle-class youngsters may marry upon the promise of support from their parents, while they complete their education.) Thus, if the economic system changes its base, e.g., from agriculture to industry, the age at marriage may change. The couple decides the number of children they will have on the basis of their own needs, not those of a large kin group, and contraception, abortion, or infanticide may be used to control this number. Whether fertility will be high or low cannot, however, be deduced from these conjugal traits. Under some economic systems—for example, frontier agriculture—the couple may actually need a large number of children.

This system is bilineal or, to use Max Gluckman's term, multilineal: The two kin lines are of nearly equal importance, because neither has great weight. Neolocality and the relative freedom from control by an extended kin network prevent the maintenance or formation of a powerful lineage system, which is necessary if one line is to be dominant over the other.

Since the larger kin group can no longer be counted on for emotional sustenance, and since the marriage is based on mutual attraction, the small marital unit is the main place where the emotional input-output balance of the individual husband and wife is maintained, where their psychic wounds can be salved or healed. At least there is no other place where they can go. Thus, the emotions within this unit are likely to be intense, and the relationship between husband and wife may well be intrinsically unstable, depending as it does on affection. Consequently, the divorce rate is likely to be high. Remarriage is likely because there is no larger kin unit to absorb the children and no unit to prevent the spouses from re-entering the free marriage market.

Finally, the couple and children do recognize some extended kin, but the husband recognizes a somewhat different set of kindred than does his wife, since they began in different families. And the children view as important a somewhat different set of kindred than do their parents: the parents look back a generation greater in depth than do the children, and perhaps a greater distance outward because they have had an adult lifetime in which to come to know more kin. That is, each individual takes into account a somewhat different set of kindred, though most of them are the same for all within the same nuclear unit.

The foregoing sketch is an ideal typical construction and thus must be compared with the reality of both behavior *and* ideal in those societies which are thought to have conjugal family patterns. To my knowledge, no such test has been made. Very likely, the *ideals* of a large proportion of United States families fit this construction very well. Some parts of the construction also fit the *behavior* of a considerable, but unknown, fraction of United States families—e.g., the emphasis on emotionality within the family, the free choice of spouse, and neolocality, bilineality, and instability of the individual family. On the other hand, data from both England and the United States indicate that even in lower-class urban families, where the extension of kin ties might be thought to be shorter (following the ideal type), many kin ties are active. We shall examine this in later chapters. No one has measured the intensity and extensiveness of kin ties in a range of societies in order to ascertain how Western family patterns compare in these respects. It is quite possible that those countries thought to be closest to the conjugal pattern do in fact have a less extended kin network.

Nevertheless, the ideal type conflicts sharply with reality *and* theory in one important respect. Theoretical considerations suggest that, without the application of political pressure, the family *cannot* be as limited in its kin network as the ideal typical construction suggests. Both common observation and theory coincide to suggest that: (1) grandparent-grandchild ties are still relatively intense and (2) emotional ties among siblings are also strong. Consequently (3), parents-in-law interact relatively frequently with their children-in-law, and (4) married people have frequent contacts with their brothers- or sisters-in-law. It follows, then, that (5) children maintain contacts, at least during their earlier years, with their uncles and aunts, as well as with their first cousins. Without question, of all types of "visiting" and "social occasions," the most common, even in the urban United States, is "visiting with relatives."

If no active ties are maintained with the categories of kin mentioned above, the family feels that some explanation is called for, and pleads some excuse ("They live too far away," or "We've never got along well").

In addition, perhaps most families have *some tie* with one or more relatives still further away in the kin network. Those noted above seem to be linked to the nuclear family in an inescapable way; it is difficult to ignore or reject any of them without simultaneously rejecting a fellow member of *one's own* nuclear family. The child can not ignore his uncle without hurting one of his own parents, and reciprocally. A girl may not neglect her sister-in-law without impairing her relationship with her brother. Of course, brother and sister may combine against their own spouses, and social interaction may continue even under an impaired relationship. Cousins are dragged along by their parents, who are siblings and siblings-in-law to one another. The extension of the family network to this point, then, seems determined by the emotional ties within the nuclear family unit itself. To reduce the unit to the nuclear family would require coercive restriction of these ties between siblings or between parents, as the Chinese commune has attempted to do.

The "Fit" Between the Conjugal Family and the Modern Industrial System

The argument as to whether political and economic variables, or the reverse, generally determine family patterns seems theoretically empty. Rather, we must establish any determinate relations (whichever direction the causal effect) among any particular family variables and the variables of other institutional orders—not a simple task. Even the relation between the conjugal family and industrialization is not yet entirely clear. The common hypothesis—that the conjugal form of the family emerges when a culture is invaded by industrialization and urbinization—is an undeveloped observation which neglects three issues: (1) the theoretical harmony or "fit" between this ideal typical form of the family and industrialization; (2) the empirical harmony or fit between industrialization and any actual system; and (3) the effects upon the family of the modern (or recent past) organizational and industrial system i.e., how the factors in the system influence the family.

At present, only the first of these can be treated adequately. The second has been dealt with primarily by researchers who have analyzed a peasant or primitive culture with reference to the problem of labor supply, and who suggest that family systems *other* than the conjugal one do not adequately answer the demands of an expanding industrial system. Malinowski asserted, for example, that although young Trobriander men could earn more by working on plantations than by growing yams, they preferred to grow yams because this activity was defined as required for their family roles. Similarly, a head tax was necessary to force young men to leave their families to work in the South African mines. Men's objections to women leaving the home for outside jobs have limited the labor supply in various parts of the world, especially in Islamic areas. On the other hand, within conjugal or quasi conjugal systems such as those in the West, the strains between family patterns and industrial requirements have only rarely been charted empirically.

This last task would require far more ingenious research designs than have been so far utilized. It requires that the exact points of impact between family and industrial organization be located and the degree of impact measured. Succeeding chapters will devote some attention to this problem. Specific decisions or choices need to be analyzed, in which both family and industrial variables are involved.

Nevertheless, if we are to achieve a better understanding of world changes in family systems, it may help if we can correct the theoretical analyses of the first problem, the fit between the ideal typical form of the conjugal family and industrialization. It seems possible to do this through some reference to common observations about both United States and European family patterns.

Let us consider first the demands of industrialization, which is the crucial element in the complex types of change now occurring in even remote parts of the world. Although bureaucratization may occur without industrialization (witness China), and so may urbanization (for example, Dahomey, Tokugawa Japan), neither occurs without some rise in a society's technological level, and certainly the modern system of industry never occurs without *both* urbanization and bureaucratization.

The prime social characteristic of modern industrial enterprise is that the individual is ideally given a job on the basis of his ability to fulfill its demands, and that this achievement is evaluated universalistically; the same standards apply *to all who hold the same job*. His link with the job is functionally specific; in other words, the enterprise cannot require behavior of him which is not relevant to getting the job done.

Being achievement-based, an industrial society is necessarily open-class, requiring both geographical and social mobility. Men must be permitted to rise or fall depending on their performance. Moreover, in the industrial system, jobs based on ownership and exploitation of land (and thus on inheritance) become numerically less significant, again permitting considerable geographical mobility so that individuals are free to move about in the labor market. The neolocality of the conjugal system correspondingly frees the individual from ties to the specific geographical location where his parental family lives.

The conjugal family's relationship to class mobility is rather complex. Current formulations, based on ancient wisdom, assert that by limiting the extensiveness of the kin network, the individual is less hampered by his family in rising upward in the job structure. Presumably, this means that he owes less to his kin and so can allocate his resources of money and time solely to further his career; perhaps he may also more freely change his style of life, his mode of dress and speech, in order to adjust to a new class position without criticism from his kin. On the other hand, an industrial system pays less attention to what the individual does off the job, so that family and job are structurally somewhat more separated than in other systems. Consequently, one might reason that differential social or occupational mobility (as among siblings or cousins) would not affect kin ties. Yet the emotional ties within the conjugal system are intense, compared to other systems, so that even though there are fewer relatives, the weight of kin relationships to be carried upward by the mobile individual might be equivalent to that in a system with more, but less intense, ties.

An alternative view must also be considered. Under some circumstances the kin network actually contributes greatly to the individual's mobility, and "social capillarity" as a process (that is, that individual rises highest who is burdened with least kin) moves fewer people upward than does a well-integrated kin network. A brief theoretical sketch of this alternative view also throws light on the supposed "adjustment" between the needs of the small conjugal family and those of a modern industrial system.

First, in the modern industrial system, the middle and upper strata are by definition more "successful" in the obvious sense that they own it, dominate it, occupy its highest positions, and direct its future. One must concede that they are "well adjusted" to the modern industrial society. Paradoxically, their kin pattern is in fact *less* close to the ideal typical form of the conjugal family than is the family behavior of the lower strata. The upper strata recognize the widest extension of kin, maintain most control to give and receive help from one another.

Consequently, the lower strata's freedom from kin is like their "freedom" to sell their labor in an open market. They are less encumbered by the weight of kin when they are able to move upward, but they also get less help from their kin. Like English peasants, who from the sixteenth to eighteenth centuries were gradually "freed" from the land by the enclosure movement, or nineteenth-century workers, who were "freed" from their tools by the development of machinery, the lower strata have fewer family ties, less family stability, and enjoy less family-based economic and material security. The lower-class family pattern is indeed most "integrated" with the industrial system but mainly in the sense that the individual is forced to enter its labor market with far less family support—his family *does not prevent industry from using him for its own goals.* He may move where the system needs him, hopefully where his best opportunity lies, but he *must* also fit the demands of the system, since no extended kin network will interest itself greatly in his fate. The job demands of the industrial system move the individual about, making it difficult for him to keep his kin ties active; and because his kin are also in the lower strata he has little to lose by relinquishing those ties. In short, lower-strata families are most likely to be "conjugal" and to serve the needs of the industrial system; this system may not, however, serve the needs of that family pattern. This means that when industrialization begins, it is the lower-class family that loses least by participating in it and that lower-class family patterns are the first to change in the society.

We might speculatively infer further that *now,* a century after the first great impact of industrialization of the lower-class family in the Western urban world, family patterns of Western middle and upper classes may be changing more rapidly than those of the lower. (Whether rural changes may not be occurring equally rapidly cannot be deduced from these inferences.) However, although this inference may be empirically correct, the available data demand a more cautious inference: Whether or not the middle and upper strata *are* now changing more rapidly in the Western world, they *do* have more resources with which to resist certain of the industrial system's undermining pressures (e.g., capital with which to support their youngsters through a long professional training) and a considerable interest in resisting them because their existing kin network is more active and useful. We would suppose, then, that in an industrializing process both the peasants and primitives are forced to adjust their family patterns to the demands of industrial enterprise more swiftly, and see less to lose in the adjustment. By contrast, the middle and upper strata are better able to utilize the new opportunities of industrialization by relinquishing their kin ties more slowly, so that these changes will occur only in a later phase of industrialization, such as the United States is now undergoing.

Continuing now with our analysis of the "fit" of the conjugal family to industrial needs; the more limited conjugal kin network opens mobility channels somewhat by limiting the "closure" of class strata. In general, rigid class boundaries can be maintained partly by the integration of kin bonds against the "outsider" through family controls. When the network of each family is smaller, the families of an upper stratum are less integrated, the web of kin less tightly woven, and entrance into the stratum easier. Since the industrial system requires relatively free mobility, this characteristic of the conjugal pattern fits the needs of that system. This general principle also holds for classical China, where an empirically different system prevailed. A successful family would normally expand over generations, but thereby have insufficient resources to maintain so many at a high social rank. That is, the reciprocal exchanges necessary for tightness and closure of the kin system could be kept up only by a few individual families in the total network. If all the families in the network shared alike as kinsmen (which did not happen), the entire network would lose social rank. If the few well-to-do families helped their kin only minimally, and maintained ties with other upper stratum families, the integration of the stratum was kept intact and the stratification system was not threatened.

The modern technological system is psychologically burdensome on the individual because it demands an unremitting discipline. To the extent that evaluation is based on achievement and universalism, the individual gets little emotional security from his work. Some individuals, of course, obtain considerable pleasure from it, and every study of job satisfaction shows that in positions offering higher prestige and salaries a higher proportion of people are satisfied with their work and would choose that job if they had to do it again. Lower level jobs give little pleasure to most people. However, in higher level professional, managerial, and creative positions the standards of performance are not only high but are often without clearly stated limits. The individual is under considerable pressure to perform better than he is able.

The conjugal family again integrates with such a system by its emphasis on emotionality, especially in the relationship of husband and wife. It has the task of restoring the input-output emotional balance of individualism in such a job structure. This is so even for lower strata jobs where the demands for performance are kept within limits by an understood quota but where, by contrast with upper strata jobs, there is less intrinsic job satisfaction. Of course, the family cannot fully succeed in this task, but at least the technological system has no moral responsibility for it and can generally ignore the problem in its work demands.

Bilateral in pattern, this family system does not maintain a lineage. It does not concentrate family land or wealth in the hands of one son through whom the property would descend, or even in the hands of one sex. Dispersal of inheritance keeps the class system fluid. Daughters as well as sons will share as heirs, and a common legal change in the West is toward equal inheritance by all children (as is already the situation generally in the United States). Relatively equal advantages are given to all the sons, and although even United States families do not invest so heavily in daughters as in sons (more boys than girls complete college), the differences in training the two sexes are much less than in other family systems. Consequently, a greater proportion of all children are given the opportunity to develop their talents to fit the manifold opportunities of a complex technological and bureaucratic structure.

The conjugal system also specifies the status obligations of each member in much less *detail* than does an extended family system, in which entrepreneurial, leadership, or production tasks are assigned by family position. Consequently, wider individual variations in family role performance are permitted, to enable members to fit the range of possible demands by the industrial system as well as by other members of the family.

Since the young adult is ideally expected to make his own choice of spouse and the young couple is expected to be economically independent, the conjugal system, by extending the adolescent phase of development, permits a long period of tutelage. For example, it is expected that the individual should be grown up before marrying. Note, however, that it is not the family itself that gives this extended tutelage, but public, impersonal agencies, such as schools, military units, and corporations, which ideally ignore family origin and measure the individual by his achievement and talent. This pattern permits the individual to obtain a longer period of training, to make a freer choice of his career, and to avoid the economic encumbrance of marriage until he has fitted himself into the industrial system. Thus, the needs of the industrial system are once more served by the conjugal family pattern.

The *different* adjustment of families in *different* classes to the industrial system emphasizes the *independence* of the two sets of variables, the familial and the industrial, as well as the presence of some "disharmonies" between the two. Further points where the two do not adjust fully may be noted here. The modern woman is given little relief from child care, which is typically handed over to one person, the wife, rather than to several women, some of them elders, who are part of the family unit in more extended systems. Adjustments in modes of child care, which seem to accompany industrialization, are in part a result of the decline of a family tradition handed down from older women to the younger. With the weakening of ties with the older generation younger women depend increasingly on the published opinions of experts as a guide for child-rearing practices.

Even the substantial development of labor-saving devices and technology has not lightened labor in the modern United States home, contrary to both advertising in women's magazines and the stereotyped notions of Europeans. Most of these devices merely raise the standards for cleanliness and repairs, and allow the housewife to turn out more "domestic production" each day. Every study of the time allocation of mothers shows that housewives work extremely long hours. For those who have assumed otherwise, let me remind them that the washing machine brings back into the home a job that an earlier generation delegated to lower-class labor or the laundry; that the vacuum cleaner merely raises standards without substantially speeding up work; that the electric sewing machine is exactly analogous to the washing machine. On the other hand, the organized activities of children have become so complex, and the number of objects in the house so numerous, that even the middle-class housewife must spend much of her time in essentially administrative activities when she is not laboring with her hands. Marx, commenting on John Stuart Mill's doubt that mechanical inventions had lightened man's toil, asserted that lightened toil was not the *aim* of the capitalist use (for the modern scene, read "industrial use") of machinery. While one might quarrel with Marx's concept of *deliberate* aim, it remains true that it is difficult to release even well-trained women from their household tasks, and especially from their emotional tasks; there is no one to substitute for that labor, unless new agencies such as communal nurseries are created. In addition, since the amount of work is great and there is presumptive equality of husband and wife, the husband generally has to step in to help after work, which in turn diverts some of his energy from his occupation.

Ignoring the question of feasibility of additional time, it also remains true that for women, the roles of wife and mother are their central obligations. For this reason, and because there is no one else who can be given the care of house and children, over the past half-century in the United States, women have not become much more "career-minded" than they were, and polling evidence suggests that a similar conclusion may be applied to Europe. Even though an increasing percentage of women in the

United States are in the labor force, as in some countries of Europe, there has been over the past few decades (in the United States) only a very slight increase in the proportion of mothers of small children who are in the labor force, and these are predominantly in the lower income groups, where the economic pressure to work is great. Much of the recent great increase in female participation in the United States labor force has been concentrated in the older age groups. Toward the higher economic strata generally, a lower proportion of women work.

Unlike men, women do not as yet think of job-holding as a *career*, as a necessary and intrinsic part of their destiny. From 1910 to 1950 in the United States, while the conjugal family was spreading beyond the city, the proportion of women in the established professions did not change greatly. The number of women physicians increased from 6 percent to 6.1 percent. In dentistry, the proportion decreased slightly. In law, engineering, architecture, and the ministry, the increase was substantial, but in none did the proportion rise above 4.1 percent. In college teaching there was a slight increase, so that women constituted 23.2 percent of the total in 1958, as compared with 19.8 percent in 1899-1900. The proportion of college-educated women who have gone into the established professions has dropped during the past half-century, although of course the percentage of women has increased substantially within a range of technical or semiprofessional jobs in the natural sciences. Clearly, the "needs" of industrialization are not in easy adjustment with the role obligations of women.

Societal Complexity and Familial Organization

Robert F. Winch and
Rae Lesser Blumberg

In his book *World Revolution and Family Patterns,* William J. Goode has concluded that as the nations of the world become industrialized and urbanized, their familial systems are converging on what he calls the con-

From R. F. Winch and R. L. Blumberg, "Societal Complexity and Familial Organization," in *Selected Studies in Marriage and the Family* (New York: Holt, Rinehart and Winston, 1953), 3rd ed., pp. 70–92. References cited in the original have been deleted.

jugal family system. With this book Goode has achieved a synthesis of a generation of sociological dialogue about the direction of trends in familial organization.

The round of thesis might be entitled "the withering away of the family." An early salvo in this round was fired by Wirth, who viewed the city as freeing the individual from the "kinship group characteristic of the country." Seeing a similar process but evaluating it more dourly was Zimmerman, for whom the contemporaneous American family was "atomistic," meaning that it exerted minimum influence over the behavior of the individual. To Parsons the emerging familial form was isolated and nuclear, although the precise meaning of the former adjective has been variously interpreted. Linton concurred by remarking the "extreme degeneration" of the extended family, "the increasing anonymity of individuals and conjugal family groups," and the decrease of sanctions to prevent marital dissolutions.

Antithesis was the product of a set of revisionists employing a generally more limited—but empirically based—frame of reference: Sussman, Greer, Sharp and Axelrod, Bell and Boat, Townsend, Young and Willmott, Firth and Djamour, Litwak, Haller, Key, Mitchell, Rogers and Leichter, and Leichter and Mitchell. These investigators emphasized the extent to which U.S. and British urban families of the working and middle classes were *not* isolated. On the contrary, they found that these families, although nuclear, engaged in considerable interaction with other related nuclear families, and that this interaction not only constituted a considerable proportion of the off-the-job social life of the family members but also provided instrumental aid in illness and other episodes of need and crisis.

Actually, the revisionists never did join issues with Wirth, Zimmerman, Parsons, or Linton, who seemed to be asserting or implying that the family —generally the urban middle-class family of the United States—was less enmeshed in a network of the extended family than was the familial form from which it was evolving, be that a rural (perhaps peasant) family or, in the case of Zimmerman, the tribal family of Homeric Greece. What the revisionists actually refuted was something the former authors never asserted—although their imprecise diction may have justified the interpretation—that the urban nuclear family was *absolutely* isolated from kinsmen.

Goode then provided the synthesis by integrating the foregoing crosscurrents into a cogent formulation. Noting the diversity of familial types in traditional societies—patrilineal or matrilineal or other, polygamous or monogamous, extended or not—Goode proposed that coordinate with the trend of societies toward modernization, industrialization, and urbanization, there is a convergence of these diverse traditional familial forms onto what he calls the "conjugal family."

It is our judgment that Goode's thesis is an insightful conclusion drawn from fragmentary and intransigent data. The next step in constructing the sociology of the family, we believe, should be to pose and to try to answer two important questions.

1. *Under which conditions does the nuclear family occur?* Goode notes that the conjugal family is found in technologically simple societies, such as the Eskimo, as well as in urban, industrial Western ones. But by defining the conjugal family in terms of the fading away of a series of preexisting familial prerogatives, Goode places the conjugal family of primitive societies beyond the reach of his conceptual framework. Accordingly he cannot address the general question of the occurrence of the small family—whether it be called the nuclear or the conjugal family.

2. *Under which conditions and in which respects does the nuclear family vary in societies where it is embedded in the social and cultural pattern?* Goode explores only one factor, socioeconomic status, as a source of variation in familism *within* societies. Otherwise he tends to present conjugal familism as an ideal type—a virtually undifferentiated end-state. On the *Day of Convergence*, it would seem, all families will have become non-isolated nuclear units.

In this paper we propose to build upon Goode's formulation so as to make possible at least a preliminary examination of these two important questions.

To explore the first question, we suggest replacing Goode's term "world revolution" with the concept we shall call "societal complexity." This shift in concept removes the necessity of concentrating almost exclusively on the world's headlong rush into industrialization, urbanization, and modernization, for the substitution permits the ahistorical ordering of all known human societies along a dimension representing degree of organizational complexity, structural differentiation, and technological "development." The immediate benefit is that we are able to scrutinize the entire spectrum of societies from simple to complex and then to hypothesize that societal complexity is curvilinearly related to nuclear familism.

To explore the second question, no change of terminology is needed. Instead, we propose that the dimensions of familism in developing and developed societies be made the subject of empirical inquiry rather than a deductive typological conclusion. For example, in contrast to the single nuclear family form implied by Goode's hypothesis of convergence, we shall consider evidence from one highly developed country, the United States, to the effect that at least three types of family can be distinguished. Similarly, this approach permits the incorporation of findings suggesting that degree of familism in industrial societies is a function of a variety of other variables beyond variation in social class, especially migration and ethnicity.

Some Observations on Goode's Study

By using a wide range of data Goode has corrected some of the more fanciful errors of his predecessors in the "thesis round." For example, in noting that the Eskimo as well as industrial societies have a small-family pattern Goode has dispelled the myth that all non-modern societies have elaborate kinship systems. He points out that the masses of even the most prototypically traditional societies have lived in small, conjugal households—a consequence of the poverty and high mortality rates suffered by the masses in such societies. Goode also emphasizes that in both traditional and modern societies the greatest degree of extended familism is encountered among the higher socioeconomic strata. (In this connection, the contribution of Sjoberg as another puncturer of myths deserves mention. He writes that the extended family occupying a house bursting with kin has *not* been, in Wirth's phrase, "the kinship group characteristic of the country," but a phenomenon of the elite in traditional societies, and the *urban* elite at that.)

Our Thesis

We have asserted that Goode's framework of "world revolution" has led to a penetrating hypothesis of the convergence of diverse familial patterns onto what he calls the conjugal form. We shall undertake to give further development to this idea. To account for all the available evidence—including some presented by Goode—it seems advisable to conceptualize a dimension of societal complexity. For the moment we shall regard this term as a primitive and define it in a subsequent section. If we think of societies arrayed along this dimension from the very simplest at the left end to the most highly developed at the right, we find that Goode has concentrated on the right side, that is, on that part of the continuum ranging from relatively complex traditional societies to highly complex industrial, urban societies. It is over this range that Goode finds a convergence of diverse traditional family forms onto the modern conjugal family.

We have posed two questions that lead into terrain beyond that mapped by Goode's hypothesis of convergence: (1) under which conditions does nuclear familism (or the pattern of the small family) occur, and (2) under which conditions does nuclear familism vary within societies?

To analyze question (1) we shall define and discuss societal complexity as well as familial structure and familial functions. Before undertaking the analysis it is advisable for us to indicate that although we shall speak of independent and dependent variables, we do not believe that there exists among the variables we shall consider any invariant causal sequence. Goode has argued too forcefully on the negative side for unidirectional causation to be credible in the present state of our knowledge. We shall consider the intriguing study by Nimkoff and Middleton, which not only supports the curvilinear hypothesis but also seems to specify conditions under which the small-family pattern arises.

With respect to question (2) we shall relate the findings of Nimkoff and Middleton to findings that American family patterns covary with migration, rural-urban residence, ethnicity, and occupation. Finally we shall probe more deeply into variation in familism within relatively complex societies by considering the triangular relationships between "female power," "familial complexity," and some of the intrasocietal variables that covary with familial complexity, such as socioeconomic status.

Some Remarks on One Dependent Variable: Familial Structure

It is our view that the literature on the sociology of the family suffers from the failure to make one important distinction—that between household and family. Taking account of the fact that household refers to people living together whether related or not, and family refers to relatives whether or not living together, we shall speak of the domestic family when we wish to denote related persons living together. With this distinction in mind let us consider some definitions.

Social system: a social group with two or more differentiated social positions; the positions of a social system and the relationships among them specify its structure.

Social position: "a location in a social structure which is associated with a set of social norms."

Family: a social system whose structure is specified by familial positions and whose basic societal function is replacement.

Nuclear family: a social system consisting of the three following familial positions: husband-father, wife-mother, and offspring-sibling, in which the last mentioned is an unmarried minor.

It should be noted that:

(a) there may be more than one incumbent of each position, that is, there may be a polyandrous nuclear family (more than one incumbent in the position of husband-father), a polygynous nuclear family (more than one incumbent in the position of wife-mother), and of course a nuclear family including two or more children;

(b) where these positions are considered two at a time and with respect to the connecting relationship (for example, the marital relationship of husband and wife), we speak of a dyad of the nuclear family;

(c) there are exactly three dyads in the nuclear family—husband-wife, mother-offspring, and father-offspring; of course we could mention more if we were to distinguish more positions, such as brother, sister, older brother, younger sister, senior wife, and so forth.

Incomplete nuclear family: a social system including incumbents in only one or two of the three nuclear positions. Among the types of incomplete nuclear family are:

(a) a mother and her child(ren),

(b) a marital couple with no children, and

(c) a set of siblings.

Of course a social system consisting of one or more incumbents in each of the three nuclear positions may be spoken of as a "complete nuclear family."

Extended family: a social system consisting of two or more familial positions, at least one dyad of which is *not* a nuclear dyad. An example would be a complete nuclear family plus the paternal uncle of the husband-father. Inclusion in the system of the father of the husband-father would also constitute an extended family since the definition of the nuclear family limits the generations to two—one adult and one minor. It should be noted that:

(a) unlike the nuclear family, the extended family does not have a fixed number of specifiable positions;

(b) the extended family must include at least one non-nuclear dyad; and

(c) of course a system involving two or more related nuclear families is an extended family.

Domestic family: a set of persons related to each other by blood, marriage, or adoption, and residing in a common dwelling unit. As defined, "domestic" is a purely ecological term and denotes no systemic relationship among family members, whereas the terms "nuclear" and "extended" are purely systemic and denote no ecological relationship among the members. Of course we may combine ecological and systemic adjectives to make such a phrase as "complete nuclear domestic family."

Some Remarks on Another Dependent Variable:
Familial Functions

Many writers have proposed activities that members of an autonomous and independent social system must carry out in order to assure the survival of that system. Under the rubric of basic societal functions, Winch has proposed the following five categories of activities as constituting such a set: reproductive, economic, political, socializing-educational, and religious. In general these activities may be carried on in a variety of structural contexts. (Of course the reproductive function is an exception since its legitimate fulfillment is the monopoly of the nuclear family.) Thus in a subsistence economy it is frequently the case that the family—extended or nuclear—is the unit of production, of distribution, and of consumption; in such a setting the economy is not differentiated from the family. In highly developed societies we are accustomed to the presence of a variety of economically specialized organizations that may be viewed at the analytic level as collectively comprising a specialized economic structure of the society.

Very simple, undifferentiated societies tend to be organized on the basis of kinship. This means that the family has not only the function of reproduction but also the other four mentioned above, with the consequence that the head of a family is not only a progenitor but also an economic leader, political leader, teacher, and priest.

Because of its basic societal function—reproduction—and its structure, Winch reasons that the family, especially the nuclear family, has two derived functions. From its function of providing human replacements comes the necessity to provide each new arrival with an identity and a position in the society. For this he proposes the phrase "position-conferring" function. Because the family, and again especially the nuclear family, is a relatively small and usually solidary group, it frequently also has the function of constituting an emotional haven—a site for the mutual enjoyment of personal and collective triumphs and the assuaging of emotional bruises. For this function Winch proposes the term "emotional gratification."

Homans has noted that the term function has been used in two quite different senses. First, the term has been used to refer to consequences of activities that contribute to the survival of social systems as systems, and second, to consequences of activities that meet the need of individuals. Winch has attempted to integrate both of these uses into a single Janus-faced concept of function as both system-serving and individual-serving.

With respect to the individual-serving aspects of functions, it can be argued that the consequences of functions can be viewed as resources, that these resources—when cathected—become rewards, and hence that one who exercises control over resources has the potential capability to influence the behavior of others.

Cutting across the group-serving versus individual-serving distinction is the question as to whether each function is more instrumental or more expressive. Since some conceptual utility of this distinction will presently be suggested, we propose the schema below:

	Functions that are primarily	
	INSTRUMENTAL	EXPRESSIVE
Basic Societal Functions	Reproductive Economic Political *Educational	Religious *Socializing
Derived Familial Functions	Position-conferring	Emotionally gratifying

* Here the socializing-educational function is divided into components proposed to be primarily instrumental and primarily expressive.

Extended Familism: A Functional Variable

A social system is understood to have a structure and functions. To the degree that it is completely functional, it is an autonomous and independent social system. Since systems vary in this regard, it is useful to conceptualize a gradient of functionality ranging from those functions carried out by such a self-sufficient social system to a state of complete functionlessness, at which point the system ceases to exist. In particular, it is useful to think of extended families in this way since they differ considerably from each other in functionality. Moreover, a single family may vary in functionality over time. These considerations lead to the following definition:

Extended familism: the gradient of functionality of the kin network as reckoned from a single nuclear family.

From time to time we may use the phrase "extended familism" to emphasize the functionality of the extended kin network or the phrase "nuclear familism" to emphasize the relative absence of the functionality of the extended kin network.

Some Difficulties in Conceptualizing

The "world revolution" remarked by Goode involves industrialization, urbanization, social change, modernization, Westernization, and decolonialization. Even though each of these concepts is at least partially independent of the others at both the empirical and analytical levels and even though each has its distinct bibliography, still many writers subsume most or all of the processes named under one or another of these terms. This state of affairs has had two consequences. First, each concept tends in use to become a catch-all. Second, attempts to define such terms precisely give rise to outcries that the resulting formulation is time-bound or culture-bound or otherwise unsuitable.

In view of the foregoing, it is not surprising that there is little consensus about how to measure the "world revolution." One school sees the heart of the matter in the degree to which nonhuman power has superseded human power, and some of its members accordingly adopt as their index the number of kilowatt hours consumed per capita per annum. But to students of urbanization who must incorporate into their conceptual framework the cases of Thebes and Timbuktu as well as Tokyo, the world did not begin with Thomas Alva Edison.

Shevky and Bell have offered the concept of the "scale of the society" as a way of thinking about our independent variable. To the anthropologically oriented formulation of the Wilsons, from whom they got the term, Shevky and Bell added the ideas of Colin Clark on the shifts from primary to secondary to tertiary industry and some of the concepts underlying Wirth's view of urbanism: size, density and heterogeneity. Through an analysis to ascertain underlying dimensions of U.S. census data and the construction of some indexes, Shevky and Bell sought to build a logical bridge between readily available data and the concepts of Wirth, Clark, and the Wilsons. Despite the underlying concept of a continuum of societal scale, however, the operations of social area analysis seem to be mainly appropriate for the urban populations of societies at the extreme industrial end of the scale of complexity.

In the face of all the diffuseness of concepts and dissensus about measurement there does seem to be agreement on a vaguely conceived but generally accepted set of changes that transform tribal, or traditional, societies to whatever it is we are trying to denote when we talk of "developed societies." The idea that societies develop from simple to complex states has been recognized for some time. Herbert Spencer's formulation of societal evolution is one example; others are the polar ideal types of Tönnies (*Gemeinschaft-Gesellschaft*) and Durkheim (*solidarité mécanique-solidarité organique*) as well as Redfield's more recent idea of the folk-urban continuum. Attempts to operationalize a continuum of societal complexity can be traced back to Hobhouse, Wheeler and Ginsberg in 1915 and the more recent efforts of Naroll and of Freeman and Winch in 1956 and 1957 respectively. Naroll constructed his "social development index" from data on 30 preliterate societies, and Freeman and Winch used a sample of 48 societies to establish a scale of societal complexity up to the emergence of written language.

Societal Complexity and Societal Differentiation:
Static and Dynamic Candidates for the Independent Variable

Until we are better able to comprehend exactly what societal development and its various partial synonyms denote, we believe it is prudent to move along to what seems to be the most relevant and most immediate consequence of that process—societal complexity, and its dynamic counterpart, societal differentiation.

Implied in the concept of societal complexity is a model of social change. Social organization—whether a society or a business—becomes more complex by growing from a simple, homogeneous system to one that is differentiated and includes specialized subsystems. Central to the process by which a simple society develops is the fact that at the concrete level the number of (differentiated) social positions in the society increases. For example, at the simplest level a boy's father would serve also as his priest, teacher, and so forth. As specialized occupations of priest and teacher arise in such a society, as these new social positions develop, the boy comes to attend to three different persons instead of one. And of course in highly developed societies the number of occupations runs into the thousands. This process is spoken of as societal differentiation; its product, or static counterpart, is known as societal complexity. When conceived as broadly as possible, division of labor seems to be equivalent to societal complexity.

Evidence from the left side of the continuum of societal complexity converges on the finding that differentiation from the very simple folk society occurs in a more or less patterned sequence. In their sample drawn from the Cross-cultural Survey and the Human Relations Area Files, Freeman and Winch found that emergence of the occupations of priest and teacher seems generally to occur after the development of a money economy and recognizable government but before the emergence of bureaucrats or of a written language.

There is no need to conclude that a social system will always change in the direction of greater complexity. When the process becomes clearly understood, it seems likely that the explanation will assert that one necessary condition for societal differentiation to occur is an increase in resources. For example, a surplus must be available to support a priest or a teacher. On the other hand, when resources become scarce, as in a disaster, the complexity of the social system affected can be expected to diminish.

The Nimkoff-Middleton Study

Now let us consider the perspective of societal complexity and see how it contributes to the analysis of (1) the emergence of either the nuclear or the extended familial system and (2) sources of variation in familism within societies.

Using evidence overwhelmingly drawn from the "simpler" (or left) side of the continuum of societal complexity, Nimkoff and Middleton have tested the hypothesis of a correlation between type of subsistence pattern and type of familial system. The evidence is drawn from the 549 of the 565 cultures in Murdock's "World Ethnographic Sample" (WES) that could be coded on these two variables. Coding for type of subsistence was with respect to Murdock's categories as to the presence or absence, and the importance of, such subsistence activities as hunting and gathering, fishing, animal husbandry and agriculture. Type of familial system was dichotomized into independent and extended.

A relationship emerged: peoples at the least complex level of subsistence—hunting and gathering—almost without exception have independent familial systems, whereas extended familism was almost universally encountered among societies on a more complex level of subsistence—sedentary agriculture with part-time herding.

Continuing their secondary analysis, Nimkoff and Middleton isolated four factors that appear to influence type of familial system through their association with type of subsistence: (1) abundance and stability of the food supply; (2) degree of demand for the family as a unit of labor; (3) the amount of geographic mobility involved in subsistence activities, and (4) the amount and nature of property. The first of these factors can be considered to be the most important in the sense that the only deviant cases of extended familism among hunting and gathering peoples occurred among those whose food supplies were unusually plentiful and regular for that type of subsistence, and also in the sense that, statistically speaking, food supply "explained" the correlations between the other three factors and type of familism. In short, a relatively ample and regular food supply, high use of the family as a laboring unit, low necessity for geographic mobility with respect to subsistence, and strongly developed concepts of property (especially land) as owned collectively rather than individually were associated with the maximum probability of extended familism, and of course the reverse conditions were associated with familism of the independent-conjugal-nuclear type.

One other factor emerged as important: in societies complex enough to have stratification (which presupposes an assured food supply and the concept of property), this factor was positively correlated with extended familism even when type of subsistence was held constant.

Having concluded that type of subsistence, type of familial property and degree of stratification are related to type of familial system among the simpler societies in the WES, Nimkoff and Middleton extrapolated beyond their data and proposed that some of the same relationships should hold among the modern industrial societies. In the latter type of society there are a low demand for the family as the unit of labor (since individuals are hired for cash on achievement criteria) and a high degree of geographic mobility in the pursuit of subsistence (the hunter pursues his game; the industrial worker or bureaucrat, his job). To be sure, the concept of property is more highly developed among the modern practitioners of nuclear familism, but Nimkoff and Middleton suggested that the shift from both or either group-owned land to land individually acquired or to disposable cash makes for the easier emergence of nuclear familism.

From these considerations it seems to follow that there is a curvilinear relationship between societal complexity (as measured by type of subsistence) and familial complexity, as follows: at the simplest level of subsistence (hunting and gathering) there is a nuclear family system; at the intermediate level of subsistence (sedentary agriculture and herding) there is an extended family system; and with the industrial type of economy there is a nuclear family system.

Although the results of Nimkoff and Middleton are highly suggestive and theoretically plausible, it is premature to conclude that they have isolated the "conditions under which" the nuclear familial system emerges. Their method does not yield a causal chain, and the data themselves must be scrutinized for sources of bias.

As we have noted, the Nimkoff-Middleton study is based upon data drawn from ethnographies concerning 549 of the 565 societies in Murdock's WES. Most of the other studies of societal complexity that have been cited here are based on the WES or an early version of the WES (both or either the Cross-cultural Survey or the Human Relations Area Files) or on some modification of one of these data banks. Since this remark can be applied to the studies by Naroll, Freeman-Winch, Freeman, and Tatje-Naroll, it follows that these studies have a considerable number of societies and ethnographic sources in common. For this reason it is necessary to conclude that these different studies can not be regarded as independent studies of the same or similar hypotheses. Rather similarities of results between studies can be thought of as registering alternate forms of reliability in the sense of measuring degree of equivalence of variations on a basically common technique.

Another important qualification to keep in mind in interpreting these results is that these studies of societal complexity have been secondary analyses. That is, the social scientists who have performed these studies have been using data that were not gathered for this purpose, nor indeed were the data coded with this purpose in mind. Of course all data must be coded before quantitative analysis can be undertaken. The difficulty with secondary analysis is that the user of the data often does not know the rules that were followed in coding the data; hence he cannot know which information has been included and which excluded. With respect to the WES, however, the situation is unusually good since Murdock has specified in considerable detail a set of 15 variables that have been coded and since Sawyer and LeVine have factor-analyzed intercorrelations among these variables. Of the nine factors extracted by Sawyer and LeVine, the first four were Murdock's "basic types of economy": agriculture, animal husbandry, fishing, and hunting and gathering. The next four factors related to variations in the familial system: nuclear family household, patrilineality, matrilineality, and cross-cousin marriage. The final factor was that of social stratification.

The results of the Sawyer-LeVine study do not indicate that there is anything spurious about the correlations reported by Nimkoff-Middleton. What these results do indicate, however, is that since other information was not included, it was not possible to find any other type of correlation, for example, that the nature of the value system or of the religious organization might have any influence either on the level of subsistence or on familial complexity.

A final comment on the methodology of our problem is that the measures of societal complexity based on the WES or some derivative of it cover mainly the left side and not the full range of complexity. With such a measure, therefore, it is not possible to test a general hypothesis about societal complexity.

The Winch-Greer-Blumberg Studies

In presenting the findings of these studies, we are addressing our second question, which concerns the factors involved in *intra*societal variation in nuclear familism. In this discussion we shall confine our attention to one advanced, industrial society—the United States. We shall present evidence relating to the dimensions of ethnicity, migration, and rural-urban residence, as well as socioeconomic status.

In a sample drawn from an upper-middle-class suburb of Chicago, ethnicity (as indexed by religious preference) was found to be the strongest predictor of the degree of extended familism: Jews had more kin in the Chicago area, they interacted with more of their kin and did so more frequently, and they exchanged more goods and services with their relatives (that is, had more functional interaction with them) than did the Catholics and Protestants. Because all of the respondents in this study lived in two adjacent census tracts in a single suburb, there was little variation in socioeconomic status. Although migration correlated considerably with familism (nonmigrants were most familistic) and although Jews were much less likely to be migrants than were Catholics or Protestants, still Jews were more familistic than the others when migratory status was held constant.

In a somewhat parallel study using a probability sample of the state of Wisconsin, ethnicity, migration, and residence (rural versus urban) all had some predictive power with respect to extended familism. Catholics and Lutherans were more familistic than "other Protestants," but the degree of correlation was considerably less than in the suburban study, and it disappeared when one or both spouses were migrants. In general, socioeconomic status proved to be a very weak predictor of extended familism, but one index of it—occupation of the husband—was about as strong as ethnicity. And as with ethnicity, controlling for migratory status wiped out the relationship between occupation and familism except among migrant couples.

Some parallels can be drawn between the variables proving significant in the foregoing two studies and the four factors that emerged in the Nimkoff-Middleton analysis of the simpler societies of the WES:

1. *Migration* emerged in all of these studies: the degree of extended familism was lower among those who were geographically mobile. Nimkoff and Middleton report that for the simpler societies, mobility was completely related to type of economy. Technical difficulties have prevented our making a parallel determination for the two American studies.

2. *Property in the form of land* was associated with extended familism among the societies of the WES. In Wisconsin the degree of extended familism was higher among rural than among urban nuclear families. Although we do not have data on this point, it seems plausible that land ownership might be more common among rural than urban residents.

3. *Family as a unit of labor* correlated with extended familism in the Nimkoff-Middleton study. In the suburban study it was discovered that those families wherein the father had ever been associated in a family business were likely to be high in extended familism. It would seem that the rural families of Wisconsin—at least to the extent that they are farmers—would also make some use of their families as workers, and it will be recalled that the rural families were more extended-familistic on the average than were the urban families. It is consistent with this presentation that among farm families and among those where the head had been in a family business, the high scores on extended familism were especially high on functionality—their exchange of goods and services with kinfolk.

Toward the simpler end of the scale of societal complexity, it appears that the factors just noted—spatial immobility, collectively owned property, and family labor—are indicative of the higher level of subsistence (plow agriculture) rather than the lower (hunting and gathering). At the more complex end of the scale, it seems that we have found some segments of the population (namely Jews) that show these traits considerably more than others (namely "other Protestants") and also show the greatest degree of extended familism.

Now have we any grounds for believing that these Midwesterners who happen to be from different ethnic categories are at different points along the continuum of societal complexity? One of the most intriguing aspects of the Nimkoff-Middleton analysis is the manner in which they relate all the factors correlated with familism to their measure of societal complexity. Let us see if we can perform a parallel operation with ethnicity.

Even though ethnic heterogeneity is not a necessary concomitant of a high degree of societal complexity—witness Scandinavia—it tends to increase positively with complexity. (Note its frequent use as an index of urbanism.) But not all the diverse ethnic categories found in a complex society have originated there. In this fact lies the relation between ethnicity and complexity. Each ethnic category enters the scene from some particular niche with respect to complexity. For each ethnic category the question to be asked is: were they formerly hunters, peasants, cash-crop farmers, tradesmen, or bureaucrats?

With respect to migrants to the United States, it should not seem strange that Polish Jews, who were shopkeepers well acquainted with the ways of a money economy and the necessity of literacy, should advance faster than Polish Catholics who were peasants and migrated to the United States at the same time. If it is true that the level of familism is currently higher among Polish Jews than among Polish Catholics, this may at first seem puzzling since it might be expected that the immigrant Catholic peasants originally had the extended family systems typical of sedentary agriculturists. But as Pius Okigbo documents with reference to West Africa, where control over land is the basis of familial authority, the extended family structure can be severely upset by the loss or economic eclipse of this authority. It is easier for an immigrant trader than an immigrant peasant to reestablish himself in his old subsistence pursuit so as to provide continuing opportunities for family members. The immigrant entrepreneur is more likely to retain more of the family organization built up around his traditional mode of subsistence than is the peasant who left the authority basis of his family system behind in the "ould sod." This reasoning suggests two hypotheses:

1. The amount of change in the familial system of incoming ethnic categories is positively related to the amount of change in type of subsistence.

2. The rate of advancement of incoming ethnic categories is positively related to the complexity level of their original type of subsistence.

From this reasoning it follows that, with number of generations since migration held constant, even (and perhaps especially) when socioeconomic status is controlled, we should expect categories of peasant origin to show less extended familism than categories of trade origin. (It should be noted that exceptions to these predictions are made for people of peasant origin who become farmers in this country.) To the extent that Greeks, Armenians, Lebanese, Syrians, and so forth resemble the Jews in coming from a trade-based type of subsistence (that is, level of societal complexity) and are able to move into trade in their new environment, their rate of socioeconomic advance and maintenance of networks of extended kin should outstrip contemporaneous cohorts of peasant origin. We should expect the Greeks to be like the Jews in having relatively high proportions of veterans of family businesses, lower proportions in the nomadic bureaucratic occupations, and highly functional rather than merely large kin networks.

To this point our assertions have concerned members of ethnic categories arriving in this country at roughly the same time. The crest of the wave of Jewish immigration arrived at least a quarter of a century after the peak of Christian migration from Europe. The Christians' greater time in this country has allowed more opportunity to disperse, and hence we should expect them to have fewer extended kin nearby.

Societal Complexity, Familial Complexity, and Female Power

We have proposed that the relation between societal complexity and familial complexity (or extended familism) is curvilinear. That is, if we should plot scale of societal complexity on an abscissa and degree of extended familism on an ordinate, the resulting curve would have a tail at either end of the distribution and an intermediate hump. Accordingly, highly developed societies would be registering relatively low extended familism. One element in the decline in extended familism in complex societies is frequently a reduction in economic functionality. Since so much of the male's daily acitivity is instrumental (especially economic) in nature, men tend to lose interest in the family when it ceases to function as an economic organization. We should not be surprised to find, then, that as instrumental functions decline within the family, the maintenance of kin ties becomes a feminine task.

Because of the biological fact that only women bear and nurse children, there is a tendency for societies to define the duties of women as less mobile, as pertaining more to home and hearth, and thus it seems plausible that in the more highly developed societies there should be less differentiation among women than among men. As the occupations of men become more diverse, they cease to have as much in common as before, and here we can see one basis for kin-keeping to become a woman's activity. If Parsons and Bales are right in linking instrumental roles to men and expressive roles to women, and if, as seems to be the case from the evidence on the sequences of societal differentiation, instrumental functions tend to leave the family at a faster rate than do expressive functions, this would be another pressure for women to take over the kin-keeping activities.

These theoretical deductions are consistent with Clignet's observation that in contemporary Africa, as in other parts of the world, the less functional kin affiliations are, "the more familial ties will be maintained by women rather than by men." Clignet goes on to remark that "the severance of such ties is usually more threatening for the former than for the latter." In the context of intergenerational solidarity Sweetser has studied the same phenomenon, and she concludes:

> Intergenerational solidarity follows the line of male succession in instrumental tasks; when the latter disappears, matrilineal solidarity between generations becomes the rule. We have a society in which kin can rarely be of use to men in their daily business, while kin can be of considerable use to women in their daily business.

Among the simplest societies one may speak of the median instrumental functionality of women; among the most complex societies there is of course much differentiation, and hence one should relate the instrumental functionality of women to such variables as social class, rural versus urban residence, employment outside the home, and so forth. When several of these many factors making for differentiation act in combination, the effect may be even more pronounced. Accordingly, it is not surprising that the extreme case of female familial power appears to occur most strikingly within societies in the upper rather than the lower sectors of the continuum of societal complexity. Let us proceed from this reasoning in an attempt to illuminate the "matrifocal family."

The Mother-Child Incomplete Nuclear Family

Recently—since the cauldron containing the long-simmering American problems of poverty, discrimination and race reached a raging boil in the sixties, and particularly since the publication of the document popularly known as "the Moynihan Report"—one type of family has been hotly discussed and frequently bemoaned in the United States. This type of family consists of a woman and her children with no permanently resident husband-father; it may include other members, particularly the maternal grandmother of the children. Its current notoriety stems from the fact that in this country it occurs in greatest proportion among urban, lower-class Negroes. But this mother-child incomplete nuclear family is also common among certain sectors of the lower classes in many Latin American and Caribbean countries, and far from rare among urban, lower-class whites in the United States.

Furthermore, despite the fact that the Caribbean islanders, British Guianans and Americans most likely to live in such families are black, an explanation based on ethnicity, "West African origins" or caste is inadequate. For in Guatemala, female-headed families are more common among Spanish-American *ladinos* than among Mayan Indians, the local lower-class ethnic group; and in the U. S. itself, while 47 percent of urban Negro families with incomes under $3,000 are headed by females, so are 38 percent of their white counterparts.

What is needed is the delineation of the structural features common to all of these instances of mother-centered families. As Adams points out, given the evidence that large segments of some contemporary societies manifest this type of family, it is better sociology to regard it as one among a set of family types, each of which calls for explanation, than to regard it as "abnormal" or "disorganized" and thereby to relegate it to "social pathology." Accordingly, after discussing some of the dimensions of the mother-child dyadic family among U. S. Negroes, we shall seek to extract those factors apparently making for its appearance in other settings as well.

The one factor that seems to impress observers of the black ghetto scene as most critical is the economic status of the average lower-class man: low, marginal, and insecure. It is a commonplace that, relatively speaking, Negro women have been better off with the opportunity for regular, even though poorly paid, employment. Failing that, they have experienced easier access to public assistance for their families.

Less well known, however, are the following two relevant empirical generalizations:

1. Marital stability tends to be greater in the more economically advantaged strata of societies.
2. The higher the economic level of the family, the greater on the average is the marital dominance of the husband.

Given that the Negro lower-class male is at the bottom of the economic spectrum in American society, the second proposition above predicts that he will frequently exhibit minimum—probably negative—marital dominance, and this is what we find. Ethnographic accounts of Negro life in the slums indicate that many of the women tend to show very little respect for Negro men. During periods of unemployment, moreover, a husband is frequently treated by his wife as having no claim upon her loyalty, her company, or indeed even the use of their common facilities. Not only is the woman responsible for running the household but frequently for providing its stable economic support.

Relatively speaking, then, the role performance of the ghetto black woman is often markedly more competent than is the man's. In the sense that the woman keeps the family running and the man is supererogatory, there is a functional basis for female dominance, low respect for males, and fragile marriages.

Matrilineal Extension of the Mother-Child Incomplete Nuclear Family into a Particular Form of Extended Family

Ethnographic accounts of the lower-class urban black family indicate that frequently (but we cannot be sure just how frequently) the maternal grandmother socializes and nurtures her grandchildren and runs the house while the young mother provides the funds through her employment. It appears that such a three-generational matrilineal family is not uncommon, whether or not they all live in a common dwelling unit.

Ethnographies such as Rainwater's give some indication as to the way in which boys and girls are prepared for this kind of family. In the black ghettos it appears that neither boys nor girls develop very high expectations of marriage—either with respect to its stability or the gratifications to be derived from it. From the middle-class point of view another element in underplaying marriage is that it seems not to have much significance as a *rite de passage* to mark the achievement of adult status. Rather it appears that for the girl adulthood comes upon her becoming a mother for the first time, and for the boy when he has fathered his first child. When a girl becomes premaritally pregnant, it is frequently assumed that she will stay at home and that her mother (or parents if she also has a resident father) will assume responsibility for her child. Rainwater further reports that at this time it is typical for the girl's mother to care for the child and for the girl to become more active socially with her peer group and more active sexually as well.

To the writers' knowledge it is not possible from presently available data to tell whether or not the mother-child family of black ghetto usually includes the maternal grandmother. The reason is that the data of the U. S. Bureau of the Census do not shed light directly on familial structure. If a maternal grandmother lives in the next apartment to her daughter and the latter's children, the grandmother is not a part of the mother-child family in the bookkeeping of the Census, no matter how active the grandmother may be in keeping the family running. What is critical here is that members of a family living in two or more separate dwelling units may interact with each other in a sufficiently functional manner to constitute a single familial social system, and yet such a family would not be recorded as such by the Census.

Nevertheless, with respect to the three-generational households actually counted by the Census, they are reported as being twice as common among nonwhites as among whites—9.2 percent versus 4.5 percent—in husband-wife households, and three times as common among nonwhites—3.1 percent versus 1.0 percent—in other than husband-wife households. It must be emphasized that even should there exist an equal number of three-generational families who happen *not* to reside in the same household, this would not raise the percentage of matriarchal families to anything approaching a norm among either blacks or whites.

Common Elements Underlying Mother-Child Incomplete Nuclear Families

1. *Poverty.* In all the societies where mother-centered families have been documented, they are apparently most characteristic of the lower class.

2. *Class-related marital characteristics.* In general, we know that:

(a) Women who have worked outside the home tend to have more domestic power than those who haven't.

(b) Lower-class women are more likely to be in the labor force; the difference is especially pronounced when there are small children at home.

(c) As mentioned above, a study based on data from Detroit reports that the lower the economic level of the family, the less on the average is the marital dominance of the husband.

(d) Also as noted, marital stability in a number of societies is inversely related to socioeconomic status.

3. *Subsistence-complexity factors.* Poverty is not enough. Some lower-class groups seem virtually "immune" to this form of the family, while among others it is rampant:

(a) We have noted that the mother-child dyadic family is more common among poor *urban* Americans than among poor *rural* Americans. Its higher association with urban populations is also documented by Adams for Central America.

(b) Where the family is the unit of labor, mother-centered families are infrequent.

(c) Where the individual is the unit of labor, mother-centered families are most likely where the woman is less economically marginal than the man. As discussed above, Negro males of the urban lower class are most likely to fall into this unenviable situation in the U. S. But again let us stress that this factor is not unique to American ghettos. Indeed, the generally vulnerable position of the male entering the industrial economy at its bottom level has been noted by many writers. For example, Smelser, in his analysis of the Industrial Revolution and family disorganization in England, has pointed out that at certain stages wives and children were more likely to be steadily employed than adult males.

4. *Biological factors.* Everywhere, the biological tie is closer between mother and child than between father and child.

As we try to integrate these considerations, the following picture emerges: In more complex societies the family tends to show a relatively low degree of extended familism. More analytically, the family has simple organization and a low level of instrumental functionality. As instrumental functionality has been leaving the family, it has become less vital, less rewarding and less interesting to men; they have a smaller stake in it. At the lower-class level, husbands tend to have the least domestic power relative to their wives. At this level again, in the urban setting, men show the highest proportions of being economically more marginal than wives. For these reasons there is little to bind such a man to such a woman. Since the mother-child tie is stronger than the father-child bond, it is the biologically given, the mother-child dyad, that survives while the marital tie has little payoff for either spouse and is correspondingly fragile. Thus, under the conditions we have enumerated, we encounter the maximum incidence of the lowest existing level of family structure, and the apogee of "female power."

Three Familial Types in the United States

Focusing now on the U. S., we find we have described three types of family that may be found in this country. Of course these types are not clearly set off from each other, but rather they will be found to blur into each other. Moreover, no claim is made that these three exhaust the set of familial types in American society. With these qualifications the three familial types that have been considered are as follows:

1. *A nuclear family embedded in a network of extended kin.* Among the segments of population considered, this type seems to be more characteristic of Jews than of the others. If the presence of 12 or more households of extended kin in the metropolitan area be used as a criterion of "high" extended familism, our sample of suburban Jews showed 78 per-

cent of its households having high extended familism, compared with 35 percent for Catholics and 24 percent for Protestants.

2. *An isolated nuclear family.* This type occurs most frequently among white Protestants although within this category it accounts for probably no more than one out of every four families (28 percent in the suburban sample and 22 percent in the "other Protestant" category of the Wisconsin sample reported no kin in the locality). Our data do not reveal the frequency of this type among Negroes.

3. *A mother-child nuclear family, sometimes with matrilineal extension.* It appears that this form is more widely known among poor urban blacks than in other segments of American society although even there it is not clear that it is a majority pattern. As has been pointed out, it is not clear in which proportion of poor Negro urban families with a female head the maternal grandmother is actually a functioning member. Moreover, although this type is proportionately most frequent among the poor black urban segment of the population, it does appear of course in other segments as well.

Are there other types? There may be; we cannot be sure. The dimensions of analysis used here are two: (a) completeness versus incompleteness of the nuclear family, and (b) isolation of the nuclear family versus extended familism. It would appear that the Italian-American family as described by Campisi would fit into our type 1 (along with the Jews). But it is conceivable that we could use other variables (including complexity-subsistence factors) for the analysis and emerge with different types. This is clearly a matter for further research.

But more importantly, it should be cross-cultural research. In this manner, complexity factors could be related to more precise studies of variations in familial structure and function, opening up an important new dimension for sociological investigation.

Summary

Goode's formulation that around the world societies are developing small-family systems has inspired us to question the prospect that there is a single emerging familial form and to look for correlates of familial variation. To do this, we have proposed that the independent variable be conceptualized as societal complexity and that (although we are not the first to remark it) familial complexity is a curvilinear function of societal complexity. Very simple and very developed societies show the pattern of the nuclear family, whereas societies of intermediate complexity show the pattern of the extended family. From intersocietal data it appears that the existence of the extended family is associated with a reliable food supply, a demand for the family as a unit of labor, little geographic mobility in subsistence activities, and the collective (familial) ownership of land. It is important to remember that the data supporting these relationships—those of the World Ethnographic Sample—have been shorn of information about institutional contexts other than family and economy, and accordingly cannot show other societal structures covarying with type of family.

Using two dimensions of analysis—degree of isolation of the nuclear family, and its completeness versus incompleteness—we have proposed the existence of three familial types in the United States: isolated nuclear, nonisolated nuclear, and mother-child nuclear (sometimes with matrilineal extension). It was found that degree of isolation varied with migration, socioeconomic status, urban versus rural residence and ethnicity. With respect to ethnicity, the Protestants showed the greatest, and the Jews the least proportions of isolated families, and it was proposed that familial types of ethnic categories varied with their level of societal complexity at the time of their entry into a society and with the amount of change in their type of subsistence. The mother-child incomplete nuclear family— found in highest proportion in the black urban ghetto—is associated with poverty, greater economic marginality of the man than of the woman, and low instrumental functionality of the nuclear family as a unit.

On the basis of published studies and our own work we have extended Goode's synthesis both intersocietally and intrasocietally. As with his work, however, our paper has had to rely upon fragmentary data, and hence there is an urgent need for research to give greater empirical support to these propositions.

2

The Politics
of Sex and Marriage

145

Introduction

Sexual Politics

Some readers may wonder why we use the term "politics" in discussing sexuality, sex roles, and marriage. Kate Millett suggests:

> The answer depends on how one defines politics. . . . The term "politics" shall refer to power-structured relationships, arrangements whereby one group of persons is controlled by another . . . it may be imperative that we give some attention to defining a theory of politics which treats of power relationships on grounds less conventional than those to which we are accustomed.[1]

The argument of Kate Millett's *Sexual Politics* is that the history of relations between men and women is like the history of relations between different races, classes, and castes. In each instance one group, defined by birth, rules over members of another group, also defined by birth. Thus partriarchy—the rule of men over women—must be placed alongside feudalism, despotism, slavery, aristocracy, and racism. When such power arrangements are in force, they appear natural and inevitable, and alternatives to them unthinkable. Therefore forms of domination are usually justified in terms of biological necessity, irrevocable instincts, and inherent inferiority. In approaching the study of either the physical or the social relations between the sexes, it is important to understand how male dominance may have influenced both popular and professional conceptions of femininity, masculinity, and sexuality.

The conventional idea of sexuality, a view reinforced by Freudian theory, defines sex as a powerful biological drive continually struggling for gratification against restraints imposed by civilization. The notion of sexual instincts also implies a kind of innate knowledge: that a person intuitively knows his own identity as male or female; that he knows how to act accordingly, and that he is attracted to the "proper" sex object—a person of the opposite gender. In other words, the view of sex as biological drive pure and simple implies "that sexuality has a magical ability, possessed by no other capacity, that allows biological drives to be expressed directly in psychological and social behaviors."[2]

147

Biology and Sex

We are not asserting that biology has nothing to do with sexuality, but rather that the role of biological factors is less direct and more complicated than the idea of instinct implies. That sex is not a simple biological drive is evident from a number of facts. First, some men and women can live with little or no sexual experience without showing evidence of strain or compensation.[3] Further, as Ford and Beach note, in both man and the primates, sexual behavior may be performed in the service of needs other than those of sex—for example, as a sign of dominance or submission.

Those who believe in sex as largely biological emphasize the role of hormones in sexual arousal and capacity. Actually, however, as Ford and Beach point out, the dominant fact with regard to human sexuality is the evolutionary trend away from hormonal control over sexual behavior and toward control by the higher centers of the brain—in other words, control by learning and by symbolic, social meaning. Further, studies of the actual effects of hormones reveal that there is no simple relation between the amount of sex hormones in a person's blood and erotic arousal; that is, high arousal is possible at low levels of the hormones, and high levels need not necessarily lead to arousal. The research emphasizes the importance of psychological factors in erotic arousal.[4]

Even more striking evidence of the independence of sexual identity and activity from biological determinants comes from studies of hermaphrodites and other "sex errors of the body." A program of research into the psychological effects of such errors has been carried out by John Money and his associates.[5,6,7,8] Although the papers of this group of researchers are for the most part too technical to include here, their findings are highly pertinent to the present discussion. Their most significant conclusion is that the sense of gender identity—I am a boy, or I am a girl—is a product of social learning, rather than of anatomy and physiology. Indeed, a person without male genitalia can have a sense of maleness; and a person possessing a penis, testes, and scrotum can possess a female identity.

Money and the Hampsons delineate nine levels or aspects of maleness-femaleness, six physiological and three psychological. Physiological aspects of sex identity go beyond appearance of external genitals to include chromosomes, gonads, hormones before birth and at adolescence, and internal accessory organs. Psychological levels include sex of assignment and rearing, sex identity, and sex preference. Errors—that is, inconsistencies—can occur between any of these levels. For example, a child may be born with what appears to be a normal set of male or female external genitals, and to be raised accordingly, only to discover later on, perhaps at adolescence, that he or she is genetically and internally a member of the opposite sex. Inconsistencies can also occur within the levels—for example, babies may be born with both ovaries and testes, or with external genitals so ambiguous as to make sex determination impossible. Before tests were invented that tell whether newborns are chromosomally male or female, doctors would arbitrarily assign ambiguous-looking infants to one sex or the other. Money et al studied several adults assigned at birth to the wrong gender. Unless treated as freaks, they seemed well adjusted in their assigned sex.

Money's ultimate conclusion is that *every* child is "psychosexually neutral" at birth. Life experiences rather than physiology will determine whether the individual sees himself and acts like a "normal" male, a "normal" female, a homosexual (a person who prefers to have erotic relations with his or her own sex), or a transsexual (one who actually sees himself or herself as a member of the opposite sex, but with a mistaken anatomy). Moreover, learned gender identity has a powerful psychological impact, and is rarely unlearned. Money compares the process to imprinting in birds. Thus, people who identify with the "wrong" gender typically prefer surgery to relearning as the means of bringing about consistency between physiology and psychosocial sex identity. The selection by Garfinkle is a study of one such transsexual case, a male with a female identity who became a "female" surgically. It provides insight into the way in which such a person develops a view of self and body, and also into the complexity of what we commonly assume to be "normal" sexuality.

Kohlberg's article provides detailed understanding of how a child learns gender identity. The process, as explained by Money and associates and by Kohlberg, consists of "cognitive rehearsal." At about the time the child is learning to talk—eighteen months or so—it is also learning to label itself and others as male or female. Thus begins a lifelong accumulation of memories and fantasies in which the appropriate roles are acted out. The learning is very gradual, and changes with the child's stage of thinking— that is, young children may think that one's sexual identity is something that can change, like one's age. Kohlberg also shows that genital anatomy plays a surprisingly small part in young children's thinking about sex differences. Haircuts and social role differences, such as the fact that males are policemen and firemen, are more impressive to childish minds. In short, learning to be male or female seems to be a process of learning the rules, both explicit and implicit, defining sex roles.

The idea of sex as a social role is further developed by Mary McIntosh, who argues that the current idea of homosexuality as a "condition" is wrongly held, resulting from ethnocentric bias. Relying on anthropological and historical evidence, she shows that the homosexual role does not exist in all societies, and where it does, it is not always the same as in modern

Western societies. Moreover, in contemporary society, much homosexual behavior occurs outside the recognized role, and the distinction between homosexual and heterosexual is often difficult to draw.

While much of sex-role learning has to do with obvious behavioral differences—the kinds of feminine movements and attitudes Garfinkle's transsexual subject tried so hard to mimic—there are many subtle differences as well. Eleanor Maccoby has analyzed some of the child-rearing sources of women's lesser intellectual performance in adult life. Aside from the gross kind of instruction that "if you act too smart, you will have trouble getting a husband," Maccoby suggests that girls are taught passivity and dependence. This inhibits women from being more creative later on, and handicaps them in dealing with such abstract subjects as mathematics. Both creativity and competence in mathematics require a psychological ability called analytic thinking: the ability to work alone, to turn one's back on conventional opinions and the more obvious solutions to problems, and to strike out in new directions. This ability, according to Maccoby, seems to go along with child-rearing experiences that stress independence, assertiveness, competitiveness—in other words, the kinds of qualities parents usually push in boys and discourage in girls. Women who are creative or mathematically talented turn out to have been tomboys, or unusually close to their fathers, or unusually distant from their mothers. Further, while the girl's upbringing turns her away from intellectual mastery, thinking in terms of a career, and so forth, she is always being turned toward love and marriage as a full-time career. Thus the answer to the question "Why is there no woman Shakespeare, Bach, or Picasso?" is that women have been trained to think of themselves as the wife or mother of a genius, rather than of being one themselves.

Sexual Activity

The article by Susan Lydon on female orgasm offers another illustration of how social and cultural definitions can influence biological facts. The first and most obvious point about the study of sexuality, male and female, is that until quite recently, such investigation was considered almost as improper for the scientist as for anybody else. The second important point is that many of the pioneers who first challenged the taboos against sex research and writing succeeded only in replacing ignorance with misinformation. Thus, most people used to believe, and many still do, that normal women do not have sexual feelings at all, and certainly nothing comparable to the orgasm in males.

Later, under the influence of psychoanalysis and certain other writers, such as Van de Velde, sophisticated people came to believe that women were indeed capable of sexual arousal and climax, and that the normal female response was the exact counterpart of the male's: the same sexual acts that resulted in the male orgasm should lead to a simultaneous vaginal orgasm in the woman. The fact that the majority of women appeared incapable of having orgasms in the prescribed way was attributed by Freud and his followers to frigidity: the woman had either totally repressed all sexual feeling, or else she had neurotically failed to transfer her sexual sensitivity from the clitoris to the vagina. Susan Lydon's article reviews the recent Masters and Johnson findings which disproved Freud's transfer theory and the notion of two different kinds of female orgasm. Physiologically the focus of all female orgasms is the clitoris.

It is impossible to estimate the amount of mischief in the form of comic or tragic misunderstanding between couples stirred up by such misguided expertise as the mythical vaginal and simultaneous orgasm. Sexual experience is still so private. One can envision vast midnight armies of frustrated women, and of men whose sense of sexual competence has been damaged by their failure to "make the earth move" for their partner.

It is no wonder Susan Lydon and others question whether the sex manuals cause more harm than enlightenment. A more elaborate critique of marriage manuals is found in the article by Lewis and Brissett. Americans, they feel, are basically puritanical, and must justify sex as a leisure-time activity. The manuals provide such justification by setting standards of performance appropriate to the office or factory: the orgasm is an achievement dependent on careful scheduling, arduous preparation in the form of reading as well as foreplay, and the expenditure of much effort and delay of gratification.

Perhaps this view, however, casts the marriage manual too much in the role of brake and not enough as spur. The concern with sex technique may not mean only that people are trying to legitimize sexual impulses, but rather are seeking to discover or rediscover impulses repressed by years of antisensual socialization. Also they may be desperately seeking valid information about sexual potential and technique. Even the Masters and Johnson work leaves many questions unanswered and raises new ones.

One such issue is the nature of female sexual capacity and inclination. A group of Negro streetcorner men advanced the following theories (as reported by Elliot Liebow):

> . . . when the question arose as to whether women have as much dog in them as men, the men were less sure of their answers and disagreed among themselves. One said that women have as much dog in them as men but that a good woman also has a lot of pride and that's what keeps her from acting the same way men do. Another said that women have less dog in them, hence their more conservative sexual behavior. A third opinion held that women had more dog than men but that this was obscured by the double standard which inhibited

women's freedom of action. And still another held that some women
have less dog than men, some more, and that this accounted for the
division of women into "good" and "bad."[9]

A similar range of opinion may be found among more scholarly
theorists. Thus Masters and Johnson have demonstrated that women have
greater orgasmic capacity than men. Dr. Mary Jane Sherfey has explored
the implications of the Masters and Johnson finding.[10] She argues that the
"natural" sexual encounter dictated by female sexuality is polyandry—
intercourse with many partners one right after the other. She argues further,
as do certain other women's liberationists, that patriarchy has repressed
women's sexuality, and that unrepressed women would be naturally inclined to have much sex with many partners. An opposing radical point
of view, presented by Engels and also such women's liberation writers as
Shulamith Firestone, argues that the true mode of human sexuality is the
conventional female pattern—that is, a stable relationship with one person.
Engels was a firm believer in love, as the selection here shows. He felt that
if marriages were based on "individual sex love" rather than bourgeois
considerations of class and status, monogamy would naturally prevail.
(The reader should be aware that the evolutionary sequence from group
marriage to monogamy which Engels describes has been discredited by
contemporary anthropologists.)

There is no clear radical stance regarding sexuality and sex role differences. Radicals vary from advocating celibacy to advocating promiscuity,
from an exaggeration to a denial of sex differences. Yet the selections by
Bertrand Russell, Morton Hunt (in Part 4), as well as others in this book,
suggest that the sexual behavior of both men and women actually lies somewhere between stereotypical conceptions of "male promiscuity" and "female
faithfulness." "Male" and "female" are simply not powerful analytic
categories.

Neither is marriage. One of the most famous sentences in world literature
is probably the one with which Tolstoy opened *Anna Karenina:* "Happy
families are all alike, but each unhappy family is unhappy in its own way."
The article by Cuber and Harroff suggests that Tolstoy was wrong: there
are at least five ways that marriages can be happy, or at least happy in their
lack of happiness. Some marriages may thrive on constant arguments,
some on the dead embers of past love, some on convenient partnerships
that never had much passion in them, while some achieve the great or total
involvement that corresponds more closely to the romantic ideal of the
happy marriage.

As people and society have become more complicated and differentiated,
marriage has become more fragile. Bertrand Russell's analysis of marriage,
written in 1929, is thoroughly contemporary. As the erotic potential of the
world outside marriage has increased, marriage partners find themselves

overtly or covertly rewriting their marriage contracts. We deal with some of the ways in which people have revised marriage in the analysis of experimental and "deviant" forms of the family in Part 4. In neither place, however, have we been able to capture all of the facets of a very complicated, changing picture.

Sexual Freedom and Women's Liberation

A glimpse into the near future of sex in the United States is provided by Moskin's article on Sweden as a contraceptive society. The Scandinavian nations provide a model for what happens in countries culturally similar to the United States when traditional sexual mores are liberalized. The results bear little resemblance to the apocalyptic visions predicted by the conservative imagination. As Malinowski pointed out some years ago, the puritanical traditions of Western culture have placed too great an emphasis on sexual restraints as the basis for family life and even civilization. Relaxing these restraints need not mean the end of marriage, parenthood, and social stability. When not bent into devious channels by repression, sexuality seems to be a rather self-regulating appetite rather than an insatiable lust that will override any obstacle in its path.

The relationship between sexual freedom and sexual equality, however, is not simple. As Juliet Mitchell points out, sexual freedom is only one of several factors that have to be taken into account in assessing the status of women in a given society. For equality to prevail, there must be, she argues: economic independence for women, including the right to equal work itself as well as equal pay for doing the same job as a man; full voluntary control over reproduction; the provision of responsible assistance in the socialization of children; and sexual freedom, including the absence of separate standards for judging sexual behavior in men and women. Also, we might add that, whenever necessary domestic chores are defined as degrading dirty work and as exclusively the province of women, there can be no sex equality.

Some of these innovations require drastic change in the daily lives of most people. But there are two obstacles to equality which may be overcome without revolutionary change in daily life. These are first, women's legal status, especially laws prohibiting abortion, which mean, in effect, that either a woman must bear a child against her will or submit to the dangers of an illegal operation; and second, the legacy of influential ideas concerning women's inherent inferiority, the most notable of which is Freud's work, which has had enormous influence over the past fifty years on both professionals and lay people. The articles by Robert Hall and Judd Marmor deal, respectively, with these issues.

We would like to have included more on male roles but, unfortunately, there is practically no literature to be drawn upon. Some writers have made passing comments on one or another aspect of masculinity: for example, John Stuart Mill has written of how the little boy is corrupted by his sultanlike assurance that he is superior to his mother and sisters just by being male. A psychologist who has studied sex-role development in children describes socialization into the male role as a process of learning how not to be female, thus implying that denigration of women is built into definitions of masculinity.[11] Philip Slater has criticized those who argue that women are better off at home than in the careerist rat race for not going on to argue that men also should have the opportunity to stay home rather than devote their lives to meaningless jobs.[12] Another psychologist has tried to explain men's dying at a younger age than women in terms of lethal aspects of the male role—the fact that men are unable to get relief from stress because they are taught to suppress rather than express their emotions in order not to appear weak.[13] In sum, if the female predicament is that she is not allowed to transcend her biological "destiny," the male has his own set of difficulties in being obliged to do so.

References

1. Kate Millett, *Sexual Politics* (Garden City, N.Y.: Doubleday, 1970), pp. 23–24.
2. See J. H. Simon and William Gagnon, *The Sexual Scene* (Chicago: Trans-action Books, Aldine, 1970).
3. *Ibid.*
4. John Money, "Sex Hormones and Other Variables in Human Eroticism," in William C. Young (ed.), *Sex and Internal Secretions,* 3rd ed., Vol. II (Baltimore: Williams and Wilkins, 1961), pp. 1383–1400.
5. John L. and Joan Hampson, "The Ontogenesis of Sexual Behavior in Man," in William C. Young (ed.), *Sex and Internal Secretions,* 3rd ed., Vol. II (Baltimore: Williams and Wilkins, 1961), pp. 1401–1432.
6. Money, *op. cit.*
7. See John Money, *Sex Research: New Developments* (New York: Holt, Rinehart and Winston, 1965).
8. Robert J. Stoller, *Sex and Gender* (New York: Science House, 1968).
9. Elliot Liebow, *Tally's Corner* (Boston: Little, Brown, 1966–1967), p. 122.
10. Mary Jane Sherfey, "The Evolution and Nature of Female Sexuality in Relation to Psychoanalytic Theory," *The Journal of American Psychoanalytic Association,* Vol. 14, pp. 28–128, 1966.
11. Walter Emmerich, "Parental Identification in Young Children," *Genet. Psychol. Monogr.,* 1959, 60, pp. 257–308.
12. Philip Slater, *The Pursuit of Loneliness* (Boston: Beacon Press, 1970).
13. Sidney M. Jourard, "Some Lethal Aspects of the Male Role," in *The Transparent Self,* Van Nostrand Insight Book No. 17 (Princeton, N. J.: Van Nostrand, 1964).

Chapter 3

The Meaning
of Sexual Behavior

Human Sexual Behavior
in Perspective

Clellan S. Ford and
Frank A. Beach

One essential way of looking at [human sexual behavior] involves the achievement of a cross-cultural perspective. Only in this manner can the behavior of men and women in any given society be compared and contrasted with that of peoples belonging to quite different societies. The results of our cross-cultural analysis emphasize the important fact that the members of no one society can safely be regarded as "representative" of the human race as a whole. Although there are many cross-cultural similarities there are also many differences between societies. Both of these must be recognized and interpreted before it is possible to formulate a valid and comprehensive description of human sexuality.

A second perspective . . . derives from comparisons between human beings and lower animals. This evolutionary or zoological kind of analysis has revealed the existence of certain common elements in the sexual behavior of many species, including *Homo sapiens*. Man is far from unique in his patterns of sexual behavior. Many of the behavioral items occurring in various human societies are equally characteristic of apes, monkeys, and even lower mammals. Taken together, these broadly distributed types of sexual response may be said to constitute a basic mammalian pattern. Some sexual practices are engaged in only by the human animal. Behavioral differences between man and all other animals are due to two classes of factors. The first comprises the multitude of biological changes that

From Clellan S. Ford and Frank A. Beach, "Human Sexual Behavior in Perspective," in *Patterns of Sexual Behavior* (New York: Harper, 1951), pp. 250-267.

have occurred in the course of human evolution. The second encompasses the profound modifications that every society imposes upon the inherited tendencies of its members.

The third perspective that we have endeavored to develop centers about the relationship between sexual behavior and physiology. Sexual reactions are in part an expression of deep-rooted urges and needs, and the behavior through which these find expression is organized by the physical machinery of the body. The structural and functional capacities of the nervous and muscular systems determine the kinds of behavior that can occur, and, in addition, incline the individual toward certain activities and against others. The chemistry of the blood is particularly important. The presence or absence of certain glandular secretions has far-reaching effects upon susceptibility to sexual arousal and capacity for sexual performance. The chief value of a physiological perspective on human sexual life is that it affords an explanation for many of the differences and similarities between our own and other species.

Evolutionary Changes in the Biology of Sexual Behavior

In most lower animals sexual behavior tends to occur only when fertilization can take place. With relatively few exceptions, the courtship and mating activities of most mammals are tied very closely to reproduction of the species. This obviously is not the case for men and women. On the contrary, in all human societies sexual relations serve a variety of nonreproductive functions. The apparent magnitude of this difference has so impressed many writers that they regard human sexual activities as entirely different from the reproductive responses of all other living creatures.

This view is quite incorrect. Its fallacious nature is at once apparent when one examines the behavior of those animal species whose evolutionary status most closely approximates our own. The infrahuman primates are known to indulge in sexual intercourse under conditions in which such relations cannot possibly result in fertilization. For example, female chimpanzees sometimes offer themselves to the male during the infertile phases of their menstrual cycle. Proffered coitus may be employed to divert an impending attack or to induce the male to share some desired object such as a bit of food. Monkeys are less apt than apes to engage in coitus when the female is infertile but they do so occasionally. Mammals below the primates on the evolutionary scale appear to restrict their copulatory activities to the times when the female is capable of conceiving. One sees, then, evidence for an evolutionary change from strict periodicity of sexual behavior in the female to relative absence of such behavioral rhythms. This change is not an abrupt one. Instead it is progressive, with lower mammals representing one extreme, human beings the other, and infrahuman primates in an intermediate position between the two.

Importance of the Gonadal Hormones

Part of the explanation for the differences between animal species lies in the nature of the physiological factors that control sexual activity. The ease with which erotic arousal occurs and the vigor with which it is expressed depend in part upon the individual's physiological condition. The tendency of men and women to indulge in sexual experiences may be strongly affected by the current state of nourishment, freedom from debilitating disease, chemical composition of the blood, and a variety of other bodily factors. This is equally true of lower animals. There are, however, important physiological differences between species. The most obvious and impressive difference between the physiological control of sexual behavior in human beings and other animals lies in the relative importance of the gonadal or sex hormones.

It is a general rule that females of lower mammalian species are sexually stimulating to the male and are willing to mate with him only when their ovaries are secreting large amounts of estrogenic hormone. In the nonpregnant female this condition obtains only when the ovaries contain ripe eggs and, therefore, when the female can become pregnant as a result of intercourse. Animals that are sexually immature or are past the breeding age, and those from which the ovaries have been removed, do not under ordinary circumstances show any sexual activity. In such cases the ovarian hormones are absent, or are present only in very low concentrations. It is entirely feasible to induce sexual behavior in the immature, the ovariectomized, or the aged female of these species by injecting ovarian hormones. Such treatment does not render the animal fertile but causes her temporarily to behave as if she were so.

The sexual activities of monkeys and apes differ from those of lower mammals in that the female's receptivity is less rigidly controlled by blood chemistry. The independence of feminine eroticism from hormonal domination is far from complete, however. It is quite clear, for example, that female chimpanzees are maximally receptive and exciting to the male during that phase of the menstrual cycle when ovulation is imminent, when coitus can result in pregnancy, and when the estrogenic ovarian hormone is being secreted in large quantities. But, as was noted before, some females occasionally invite and accept the male's sexual attentions during other phases of the cycle. Furthermore, female apes from whom the ovaries have been removed sometimes demonstrate a low but recognizable degree of sexual responsiveness. Although distinctly limited, this partial independence of feminine sexual behavior from hormonal support sets the infrahuman primate apart from lower mammals and represents a step toward the much more pronounced freedom that characterizes the human species.

The human female appears capable of marked sexual excitability without the physiological stimulation provided by the ovarian hormones. She may be sexually aroused before puberty and after menopause. Very often the surgical removal of the ovaries has no effect upon the enjoyment of sexual relations. When this operation does depress responsiveness, the change can often be shown to depend upon some other factors, not directly upon the withdrawal of ovarian hormones.

The dependence of men upon testicular hormone for sexual ability is also less marked than that of males of many lower mammalian species. There is evidence to suggest that at least some eunuchs experience sexual arousal and retain the ability to copulate for many years after loss of the reproductive glands. There are other cases in which castration or failure of the testes to develop is accompanied by a decrease in sexual responsiveness and activity. And in some cases desire and capacity can be revived if the missing hormone is supplied by injection. Since replacement therapy is not always effective it is apparent that nonhormonal influences play a major role in regulating the sexuality of men as well as women.

Like some human castrates, the male chimpanzee may continue to show active sexual behavior for years after loss of the testes. But most of the lower animals that have been examined cease to display signs of intense sexual arousal shortly after their reproductive glands have been removed; their sexual performance can be restored if the appropriate hormone is injected at regular intervals. The evolutionary picture is less clear and complete for the male than for the female, but such evidence as is available suggests that a comparable change has taken place in both sexes. For males of species that are relatively low on the mammalian scale, testicular hormone is essential to normal sexual vigor. This hormone is obviously less important for coital behavior in the case of some higher animals, particularly for apes and human beings.

Importance of the Cerebral Cortex

The progressive reduction in hormonal control of sexual behavior is best understood in its relation to another series of evolutionary changes. These are changes in the size and complexity of certain parts of the brain. The most recently evolved part of the nervous system is the cerebral cortex. This structure is absent from the brains of fishes, rudimentary in reptiles, and well developed only in the mammals. In the lowest mammals the cortex is not highly differentiated and constitutes less than one-quarter of the volume of the entire brain. In monkeys and apes the cortex is much larger and is clearly differentiated into a number of complex areas. Ninety percent of the adult human brain consists of cortical substance, and this mass of nervous tissue is elaborately subdivided into hundreds of different nuclei and tracts, each serving certain functions and all acting together in integrated fashion to produce unified adaptive behavior.

As the cortex has grown in size and complexity its control over behavior has increased. The degree to which cortical activities influence most of the organism's daily responses is lowest in rodents, more marked in carnivores, pronounced in monkeys and apes, and most extreme in the human species. Sexual impulses and responses are no exception to this generalization. We suggest that the evolutionary decrease in the importance of gonadal hormones for sexual behavior reflects a compensatory increase in the degree of control exerted over such activities by the cortex of the brain.

Another consequence of these variations in the structure of the brain deserves special emphasis. In very general fashion it is correct to state that members of the mammalian species that possess a very large and complexly organized cerebral cortex are more susceptible to the effects of learning and personal experience than are other kinds of animals with a simpler and smaller cortex. It is to be expected, therefore, that a high degree of cortical development will be associated with more variable behavior and with more easily modified inherited behavioral tendencies. Because all complex human behavior is heavily dependent upon cortical processes, it is automatically open to modification through the influences of previous experience. This explains why, in human beings more than in any other sepcies, sexuality is structured and patterned by learning.

Some Consequences of Man's Mammalian Heritage

Up to this point we have concerned ourselves primarily with differences between man and other animals, but of equal significance are the various points of similarity that reflect the evolutionary heritage of *Homo sapiens*. As we have said, these are sufficiently numerous and important to justify the concept of a basic mammalian pattern of sexual behavior, certain elements of which persist in human beings. Many of these separate items have been pointed out in preceding chapters and only a few need be reviewed here.

Sex Play in Childhood

Three generalizations can be made with respect to this topic: First, that early sex play occurs in many species other than our own. Second, that the frequency, variety, and completeness of prepubertal sexual reaction tends to increase from the lower mammals to the higher. And third, that species differences in the amount of such behavior are directly related to the physiological differences we have just discussed.

The cross-cultural evidence clearly reveals a universal human tendency for sexual responses to appear in the immature person long before he or she is capable of fertile coitus. Impulses of this nature are condoned and encouraged in some societies, strictly forbidden and punished in others. But regardless of the cultural ideal with respect to sex play in childhood, the underlying drive toward such activity constitutes one feature of the heredity of the human species.

Many years before they are fertile, male and female apes and monkeys indulge in a variety of sexual games which include attempts at heterosexual union. This form of infantile play is no less natural for the young primate than are the chasing, wrestling, and mock fighting that consume much of his waking life. Furthermore, these tendencies are not confined to primates. Although immature females of infraprimate species rarely show the adult mating response, very young males often engage in incomplete coital attempts with other individuals of their own age. This behavior may appear as soon as the young animal is physically capable of performing the necessary responses. For example, some animals such as the sheep are able to stand and walk shortly after birth, and sexual mounting appears in the first few days of life.

Self-Stimulation

Manipulation and stimulation of one's own sexual organs is another item that can be classified as basically mammalian. From the evolutionary point of view this kind of behavior seems to stem from the universal tendency of lower mammals to clean their genitalia by licking and manipulating them with the feet or mouth. Such behavior on the part of such animals as rats and cats cannot be classified as a deliberate attempt at self-excitation. Nevertheless, close observation of the animal's behavior strongly suggests that the resultant sensations have a sexually exciting quality.

In some infrahuman primates, genital manipulation assumes a frankly sexual character and is classifiable as masturbation. Immature and adult apes and monkeys occasionally indulge in stimulation of their own genitalia, and some adult males habitually induce ejaculation by masturbating. It is of considerable importance that this type of behavior is much less common in female primates of infrahuman species. Although a few mature female chimpanzees have been seen to masturbate, this is relatively rare.

Masturbation by captive primates has long been recognized, but most observers have considered the behavior an unnatural response produced by the artificial conditions of cage life. Recently, however, it has been found that self-stimulation is practiced by at least some male monkeys in their native habitat despite ample opportunity for coitus with receptive females. For lower primates, therefore, masturbation does not appear to be an unnatural or abnormal form of sexual activity.

Different human societies maintain widely divergent attitudes toward self-masturbation. Some social codes enforce different rules depending upon the age of the individual involved. There are people who condone or even encourage masturbation during childhood, whereas some other societies condemn this form of sexual expression for all individuals from infancy onward. Almost all human groups subject adult masturbation to negative sanctions ranging from mild ridicule to severe punishment. It should be added, however, that regardless of social condemnation, at least some adults in all or nearly all the societies in our sample appear to practice it. In every society self-stimulation seems to be less common among women than among men, and, as was noted earlier, a comparable sex difference is seen in infrahuman primates. The zoological and the cross-cultural evidence leads us to conclude that the tendency toward self-stimulation should be classified as one more item in the basic mammalian sexual repertoire and that masturbation is more likely to occur in the male than in the female.

Homosexual Behavior

Homosexual behavior is never the predominant type of activity for adults in any of the societies covered by this book. Heterosexual coitus is the dominant sexual activity for the majority of the adults in every society. But some homosexual behavior occurs in nearly all the societies comprising our sample. It is generally more common in men than in women. The apparent universality of this form of sexual activity might be due to some equally widespread social influence that tends to force a portion of every group into homosexual alliances. Certain social factors probably do incline certain individuals toward homosexuality, but the phenomenon cannot be understood solely in such terms.

Social codes differ markedly in their treatment of liaisons between members of the same sex. At one extreme are societies such as our own that forbid and punish any homosexual relationship in individuals of any age and of either sex. There are, in contrast, other peoples who are tolerant of homosexual play in childhood but disapprove of the same behavior on the part of adults. Still a third group of societies actively enforces homosexual relations upon all its male members. This is true, however, only for a given age group, and it is usually associated with puberty ceremonials. A number of cultures make special provisions for the adult male homosexual, according him a position of dignity and importance and permitting him to live as the "wife" of some other man.

Our cross-cultural comparisons suggest three generalizations concerning homosexual behavior in human beings: First, there is a wide divergence of social attitudes toward this kind of activity. Second, no matter how a particular society may treat homosexuality, the behavior is very likely to occur in at least a few individuals. Third, males seem more likely to engage in homosexual activity than do females. In order to interpret these facts it is necessary to see their relationships to the zoological and physiological data.

Homosexual behavior is not uncommon among males and females of several infrahuman primate species. Immature monkeys and apes indulge in a variety of homosexual games which include manipulation of the genitals of a like-sexed partner and may even involve attempts at homosexual coitus. Such relationships tend to occur less frequently after puberty, but in some cases an adult individual may form an enduring homosexual liaison with an immature member of his own sex. It is significant that in other primates, as in human beings, homosexuality is less prevalent among females than among males. It is also important to note the absence of any evidence to justify classifying this behavior exclusively as a substitute for heterosexual relations. Adult male monkeys with ample opportunity for heterosexual intercourse may nevertheless indulge in homosexual relations with younger males. And in some cases the same individual will carry on hetero- and homosexual alliances concurrently.

Male and female mammals belonging to infraprimate species sometimes display mating responses typical of the opposite sex. Adult females often mount other females in masculine fashion, and the females that are thus mounted react as they would to a male. Under certain circumstances males attempt to copulate with males, and occasionally the one thus approached will react in the manner of a receptive female. Such observations reveal the bisexuality of the physiological mechanisms for mammalian mating behavior. Even in such species as the rat or rabbit, the neuromuscular basis for feminine responses is present in males as well as females, and the normal female's physiological capacities include the ability to react as would the male. Temporary inversions of the sexual role are due in these species not to an underlying physical abnormality in the individual but to the nature of the external stimulus situation.

It is our belief that a comparable though much more complex condition obtains in human beings. It seems probable that all men and women possess an inherited capacity for erotic responsiveness to a wide range of stimuli. Tendencies leading to sexual relations with individuals of the same sex are probably not as strong as those leading to heterosexual relations. But the important fact is that all societies enforce some modification of the individual's genetically determined impulses, with the result that the preferred type of behavior is strongly influenced by experience.

Men and women who are totally lacking in any conscious homosexual leanings are as much a product of cultural conditioning as are the exclusive homosexuals who find heterosexual relations distasteful and unsatisfying. Both extremes represent movement away from the original, intermediate condition which includes the capacity for both forms of sexual expression. In a restrictive society such as our own a large proportion of the population learns not to respond to or even to recognize homosexual stimuli and may eventually become in fact unable to do so. At the same time a certain minority group, also through the process of learning, becomes highly if not exclusively sensitive to the erotic attractions of a like-sexed partner. Physical or physiological peculiarities that hamper the formation of heterosexual habits may incline certain individuals to a homosexual existence. But human homosexuality is not basically a product of hormonal imbalance or "perverted" heredity. It is the product of the fundamental mammalian heritage of general sexual responsiveness as modified under the impact of experience.

Types of Foreplay

Comparisons between man and lower animals make it clear that many elements in the human heterosexual coital pattern are directly determined by species heredity. For example, the male's erection and ejaculation are basic reflexes present in all mammals. Similarly, the tendency to respond to rhythmic stimulation of the genitals with thrusting movement of the pelvic region is a fundamental reaction in the mammalian repertoire.

Somewhat less apparent is the evolutionary generality of several types of behavioral interactions that tend to occur just before heterosexual coitus. For instance, investigation and consequent stimulation of the feminine genitalia by the male are a universal response in all mammals. The manner in which such stimulation is achieved varies from species to species and depends in large measure upon the effector equipment of the animal involved. Application of the male's tongue, teeth, and lips to the vulva and clitoris is extremely common. The forefeet or hands are employed in the same fashion by males of several species. The behavior seems to be investigatory as far as the male is concerned, but the female's bodily responses make it obvious that she is sexually excited by the resultant stimulation.

In all animal species for which adequate knowledge is available, males exhibit much more of this kind of behavior than do females. Nevertheless, females of many if not all species do occasionally investigate and therefore stimulate the sexual organs of the male. This is most likely to occur when the female is sexually aroused and the male is sluggish or slow to respond to her coital invitations.

Some amount of precoital stimulation occurs in nearly every society of which we have record. In certain cases, as in the Ponapeans, the techniques involved are elaborate, involving use not only of the hands but of the mouth as well. There are a few societies which disapprove of any form of genital stimulation except that derived from coitus, but these are rare. Within American society the individual's social stratum partially determines his or her tendency to practice or permit precoital caressing of the sexual organs. Men and women on lower social levels are less likely to indulge in these forms of foreplay than are individuals belonging to a higher socioeducational level. When such behavior is engaged in, it may be mutual or unilateral; but if only one of the partners stimulates the other, the active individual is almost always the male. This is true not only for our own society but also for the vast majority of the remaining ones in our sample. And, as has been pointed out, the same generalizations extend to other animals as well.

Another very common type of prelude to copulation is grooming behavior. This type of activity is characteristic of many human societies and appears in much the same form in every infrahuman primate species that has been studied. In some peoples sexual arousal and expression are enhanced by moderately painful stimulation. Among the Trukese, the Siriono, and certain other tribes, scratching, biting, and hair pulling form a regular part of the coital pattern. Similarly, in several species of lower animals aggressive or assaultive behavior is characteristically incorporated into the mating relationship. One interesting difference between human beings and lower animals is that sexually receptive females of subhuman species rarely bite or otherwise injure the male. Even though, as in the baboon or macaque monkey, the male may severely wound the female, she remains receptive and does not retaliate. But we have found no human society in which such a unilateral relationship exists. On the contrary, if the cultural stereotype of foreplay involves biting or scratching, both partners show this behavior.

The biological functions of preliminaries to intercourse in lower animals are evident. They tend to increase the degree of excitement in both sexes and also to synchronize the behavior of the pair. In this manner foreplay increases the probability of fertile intercourse. Man's capacity for responding to symbolic stimuli such as those involved in language has to some extent reduced the biological necessity for direct physical stimulation prior to copulation, but unless social conditioning imposes inhibitions upon active foreplay it is very likely to occur. And when it does appear it often takes essentially the same forms seen in other mammals and has essentially the same behavioral results.

Man the Learning Animal

We have said that evolution of the human brain has endowed man with a greater ability to learn from experience than is present in any other animal species. It would, of course, be a mistake to conclude that lower animals cannot learn. In this respect, as in so many others, the human species differs from other mammals more in degree than in kind. The role of learning in sexual behavior varies from species to species in two ways. There are differences in the degree to which learning is necessary for successful coitus, and there are differences in the extent to which learning can suppress, redirect, or otherwise modify the inherited sexual tendencies of the individual.

Learning and practice are apparently not essential for fertile mating in the few species of lower animals that have been carefully studied. If male rats are reared in complete isolation they are nevertheless capable of copulating effectively the first time they are placed with a receptive female. No practice or experimentation is necessary. The behavior is what is ordinarily called "instinctive." This does not mean, however, that experience cannot affect sexual behavior in male rodents. On the contrary, an individual that has repeatedly been presented with receptive females in a particular cage, pen, or experimental room tends to become sexually excited whenever he is returned to the same setting. Under such circumstances sexual attempts may be directed toward any other animal encountered in that particular environment. And conversely, the male may fail to respond sexually to receptive females encountered in surroundings in which he has previously experienced pain or frustration.

Experience and learning appear to be much more important in the sexual performance of the primates. At least some, and perhaps all, male chimpanzees have to learn how to copulate. Adult apes lacking any copulatory experience respond to the receptive female with evident sexual excitement, but they appear to be incapable of carrying out the bodily adjustments necessary for coitus. Their response to the female's sexual invitation is awkward, poorly organized, and inadequately directed. Only after several years of practice and experimentation do male apes of this species become capable of effective and well-integrated coital behavior.

As a result of experimentation some chimpanzees develop highly individualistic methods of mating. For example, the usual method of coitus consists of the male mounting the stooping female from the rear; but some male apes acquire a preference for intercourse in which they remain seated on the ground and the female reclines upon their thighs.

In addition to shaping the physical reactions involved in intercourse, learning exerts other effects upon the sexual habits of infrahuman primates. It contributes to the formation of personal preferences and tastes in sexual matters. Although they occasionally show some selective tendencies, potent males of most of the lower mammalian species will copulate readily with any female who is receptive; and females in estrus are equally undiscriminating. This is much less true as far as monkeys and apes are concerned. Some male chimpanzees show a distinct preference for certain feminine partners and are reluctant or unwilling to copulate with others. Females of these species also tend to seek the company of some potential partners and to ignore or avoid others.

We interpret the increased importance of learning in primates as being due primarily to the evolutionary advance in brain structure and the partial release from rigid hormonal control. From what has already been said concerning the physiological changes associated with human evolution, it might be expected that in our own species learning would have the most marked and far-reaching effects upon sexual activities. This expectation is amply verified by the facts. Human sexuality is affected by experience in two ways: First, the kinds of stimulation and the types of situations that become capable of evoking sexual excitement are determined in a large measure by learning. Second, the overt behavior through which this excitement is expressed depends largely upon the individual's previous experience.

Human beings can learn without tutelage. That is to say, they can learn by trial and error in much the same fashion as a rat learns to traverse a maze or a cat to open a puzzle box. And to a certain degree, unguided trial-and-error learning may influence the development of the individual's sexual patterns. But this is exceptional. By far most of what people learn to feel and to do in the realm of sex is learned from or with other individuals. Human learning, in other words, customarily occurs in a social context. For this reason the impact of learning upon human sexuality is best understood within the frame of reference provided by the society of which the individual is a member.

Man the Social Animal

Human infants are always born into extensive social groups, or societies. And the things that children and adults learn are governed to a considerable extent by the social structure and culture of their societies. Every society has accumulated, over centuries of experience, preferential ways of behaving, habits and codes that are transmitted from one generation to the next. Each new member of the society finds pressures brought to bear upon him to behave in the traditional manner, to conform to custom. Cultural precepts define for the individual when and where it is proper to behave in a certain manner, and they even specify the types of activities in which he may engage. In a word, the culture provides, through the habits of its members, the major learning conditions for the maturing individual.

The social structure and culture of a society have special significance with respect to sexual behavior. The position occupied by the individual in the social group carries with it definitions of the sexual activities expected of him. Some of these definitions are taken so seriously that severe punishment awaits the person who fails to perform his role in the traditionally accepted manner. Other rules are regarded more lightly, and the individual who varies his behavior may run only the risk of ridicule. But in any case cultural pressure is constantly exerted on all members of any society to express their sexual impulses in socially accepted fashion.

Intercultural Similarities Produced by Learning

There are many general similarities between human cultures in respect to sexual behavior. Some of these cultural universals cannot be explained solely in terms of the species heredity. Instead, they seem to be the products of common learning experience on the part of the members of all societies. An outstanding example is seen in the universal prohibition against primary incest.

Animals of infrahuman species freely interbreed with their own offspring, parents, and siblings. And in human beings consanguinity is no barrier to erotic attractiveness. Analyses of the fantasies and dreams of people in our own and many other societies plainly reveal the existence of unconscious sexual desires directed toward offspring, parents, and siblings. One must therefore look to social learning rather than to biological factors for an interpretation of incest taboos. The tentative explanation which we have offered involves the assumption that such taboos have arisen and persisted during societal evolution because they serve as a protective device against disintegration of the nuclear family—disintegration which would result if intrafamilial sexual jealousies and conflicts were not held at a minimum. We do not suppose that this device has been rationally conceived and instituted. On the contrary, it seems best understood as a product of natural selection. Societies lacking this protective regulation could not long endure. Survival of the larger social group depends too heavily upon preservation of its basic unit, the nuclear family. It is true that close inbreeding sometimes has biologically unfortunate or maladaptive consequences. And it might be surmised that this in itself would result in the eventual extinction of any society that failed to forbid incestuous relations. However, the evidence in this direction is scant, and it seems to us that the universality of incest taboos is more adequately explained on social-psychological grounds.

Another illustration of the way in which learning and societal evolution may produce widespread channelization of sexual impulses is the almost universal prohibition against intercourse with a menstruating woman. There is no evidence to suggest that these restrictions rest upon a biologically controlled absence of desire for sexual stimulation or capacity to respond to it on the part of either the woman or the man. On the contrary, the taboo appears to reflect common attitudes toward menstrual blood as a substance somehow associated with disease or physical injury.

Intercultural Differences Produced by Learning

Socially controlled learning is responsible not only for a number of intercultural similarities but also for many of the differences that exist between societies. It is generally agreed that all human races belong to the same species. They will, therefore, possess essentially the same species heredity. Whether or not there are important genetic differences between races—differences directly affecting behavior—is a matter of some dispute. However, no one has suggested, and we do not believe, that members of separate societies are sufficiently different genetically so that the variations in their sexual codes and habits can be explained on the basis of heredity. It follows, then, that marked intersocietal variations in such matters must be referable to differences in the cultural modification of inherited sexual impulses.

The full extent to which social forces can influence the behavior of the individual is not immediately obvious. It should be apparent that the attitude of members of a given society toward masturbation or toward homosexuality will be shaped to a large degree by early training. The result is that many members of our own society, for instance, look upon such phenomena with loathing and disgust and tend to classify the behavior as "abnormal" or "perverted." But the Keraki of New Guinea regard a man as "abnormal" if he abstains from homosexual relations prior to marriage. The importance of learning and culture in the formation of attitudes toward various sexual practices becomes fairly obvious after the evidence is reviewed and reflected upon, but there are still other effects that are less likely to be recognized. For example, various aspects of the heterosexual relationship are also influenced by training.

Certain elements in the coital pattern appear to be so completely reflexive that their control by voluntary means might seem impossible, but in fact some of them are powerfully affected by experience. One of these is the occurrence of man's ejaculation within a relatively short time after the penis has entered the vagina. Data presented in Chapter II indicate that for the majority of men in our society, ejaculation and orgasm occur within two minutes or less after the beginning of intercourse. Among the Marquesans, in contrast, the habitual copulatory pattern involves reservatus, and every man learns early in life to control his ejaculatory reflexes in such a manner as to permit maintenance of an erection and continuation of coitus for as long as the woman desires.

Both the tendency to incorporate painful stimulation in the culturally accepted pattern of precoital play and the type of response to such stimulation are strongly influenced by learning. From early life the Siriono or the Trobriand man or woman has learned to associate sexual excitement with the experience of being scratched or bitten. Accordingly, such sensations acquire erotic value and are subjectively experienced as pleasantly stimulating. Most members of other societies in which love-making lacks such aggressive components are likely to find physical pain a deterrent to sexual arousal and satisfaction.

Social learning and experience powerfully affect the extent to which a man or woman adopts and enjoys a passive or an active role in the sexual relationship. We have pointed out that in every infrahuman species the distribution of sexual initiative is bilateral. Both the male and the female may extend the sexual invitation and both have an active share in the continuation of the relationship until coitus is completed. The wide divergence between different human societies in this regard is probably due, not to biological differences between males and females, but to the lifelong effects of early training.

The societies that severely restrict adolescent and preadolescent sex play, those that enjoin girls to be modest, retiring, and submissive, appear to produce adult women that are incapable or at least unwilling to be sexually aggressive. The feminine products of such cultural training are likely to remain relatively inactive even during marital intercourse. And, quite often, they do not experience clear-cut sexual orgasm. In contrast, the societies which permit or encourage early sex play usually allow females a greater degree of freedom in seeking sexual contacts. Under such circumstances the sexual performance of the mature woman seems to be characterized by a certain degree of aggression, to include definite and vigorous activity, and to result regularly in complete and satisfactory orgasm.

Individual Differences Produced by Learning

Personal experience, operating through learning, is one important source
of variation in the sexual practices followed by different members of the
same society. We have noted, for instance, that at least a small proportion
of every society engages in homosexual behavior even though the social
code may strongly condemn such activities. It is our opinion, as expressed
earlier in this chapter, that the occurrence of exclusive homosexuality in
the face of severe disapproval is due primarily to learning rather than to
constitutional factors. In other words, men and women who are exclusively homosexual become so because of personal experience rather than because of some imperative, inherited urge. Of equal importance is the point
that total absence of any conscious response to homoseuxal stimuli probably reflects the inhibiting effects of social conditioning.

The amount and kinds of foreplay which the individual finds satisfying
and stimulating depend in part upon learning. Some American women are
sexually aroused if the partner manipulates the vulva and clitoris before
coitus, whereas other individuals find the same techniques unpleasant.
These individual differences might be due in part to variations in the sensitivity of the organs involved, but we consider it much more likely that
learned attitudes toward this type of behavior play the major role in determining its effects.

The ability of a man to perform the coital act depends not solely upon
his physical condition, but also upon emotional attitudes toward the general subject of sex and toward the particular feminine partner involved. As a
result of personal experience, some men become unable to achieve and
maintain an erection or to reach climax under certain conditions, although
they may be potent in other circumstances. The feminine orgasm is an
especially sensitive indicator of experience. Many women have to learn to
recognize orgasm when it occurs; and others, as a result of learned inhibitions, may go through life without ever experiencing a satisfactory sexual
climax.

A Final Word

If we have achieved our original objective, the reader of this book will
have gained an appreciation of the necessity of viewing sexual behavior in
broad perspective, and of interpreting the habits of any particular group of
human beings in terms of the broad background provided by the cross-
cultural and cross-species evidence. The pressing need for some such
frame of reference is particularly obvious in a society such as our own
which, until quite recently, has refused to deal with sexuality in objective
terms. The traditional reserve with respect to sexual matters has, with a

few notable exceptions, inhibited American scientists almost as strongly as laymen. This book is addressed, therefore, to all serious students of human behavior, be they professional specialists or otherwise.

It is most regrettable that an area of inquiry having such fundamental importance in both its practical and its theoretical aspects should have been so inadequately studied and so incompletely understood. Hesitancy to attack basic problems in this field cannot today be excused on grounds of public disapproval or moral censorship. Intelligent people everywhere are eager for information that will help them to understand their own sexual lives and those of their associates. This information must be gathered and interpreted by social and biological scientists.

It is our hope that the present volume will serve as a useful step toward the development of a sound understanding of the sexual behavior of human beings as it is affected by their evolutionary heritage and by the conditions imposed upon them by their social environment.

Understanding Orgasm | Susan Lydon

Tiresias, who had been both man and woman, was asked, as Ovid's legend goes, to mediate in a dispute between Jove and Juno as to which sex got more pleasure from lovemaking. Tiresias unhesitatingly answered that women did. Yet in the intervening 2000 years between Ovid's time and our own, a mythology has been built up which not only holds the opposite to be true, but has made this belief an unswerving ideology dictating the quality of relations between the sexes. Women's sexuality, defined by men to benefit men, has been downgraded and perverted, repressed and channeled, denied and abused until women themselves, thoroughly convinced of their sexual inferiority to men, would probably be dumbfounded to learn that there is scientific proof that Tiresias was indeed right.

The myth was codified by Freud as much as anyone else. In *Three Essays on the Theory of Sexuality,* Freud formulated his basic ideas concerning feminine sexuality: for little girls, the leading erogenous zone in their bodies is the clitoris; in order for the transition to womanhood to be successful, the clitoris must abandon its sexual primacy to the vagina; women in whom this transition has not been complete remain clitorally-oriented, or "sexually anaesthetic," and "psychosexually immature." In the context

From Susan Lydon, "Understanding Orgasm," *Ramparts,* December 14–28, 1968.

of Freud's total psychoanalytic view of women—that they are not whole human beings but mutilated males who long all their lives for a penis and must struggle to reconcile themselves to its lack—the requirement of a transfer of erotic sensation from clitoris to vagina became a prima facie case for their inevitable sexual inferiority. In Freud's logic, those who struggle to become what they are not must be inferior to that to which they aspire.

Freud admitted near the end of his life that his knowledge of women was inadequate. "If you want to know more about femininity, you must interrogate your own experience, or turn to the poets, or wait until science can give you more profound and more coherent information," he said; he also hoped the female psychoanalysts who followed him would be able to find out more. But the post-Freudians adhered rigidly to the doctrine of the master, and, as with most of his work, what Freud hoped would be taken as a thesis for future study became instead a kind of canon law.

While the neo-Freudians haggled over the correct reading of the Freudian bible, watered-down Freudianism was wending its way into the cultural mythology via Broadway plays, novels, popular magazines, social scientists, marriage counselors and experts of various kinds who found it useful in projecting desired images of woman. The superiority of the vaginal over the clitoral orgasm was particularly useful as a theory, since it provided a convenient basis for categorization: clitoral women were deemed immature, neurotic, bitchy, and masculine; women who had vaginal orgasms were maternal, feminine, mature, and normal. Though frigidity should technically be defined as total inability to achieve orgasm, the orthodox Freudians (and pseudo-Freudians) preferred to define it as inability to achieve vaginal orgasm, by which definition, in 1944, Edmond Bergler adjudged between 70 and 80 percent of all women frigid. The clitoral vs. vaginal debate raged hot and heavy among the sexologists—Kinsey's writings stressed the importance of the clitoris to female orgasm and contradicted Bergler's statistics—but it became clear that there was something indispensable to society in the Freudian view which allowed it to remain unchallenged in the public consciousness.

In 1966, Dr. William H. Masters and Mrs. Virginia E. Johnson published *Human Sexual Response,* a massive clinical study of the physiology of sex. Briefly and simply, the Masters and Johnson conclusions about the female orgasm, based on observation of and interviews with 487 women, were these:

1. That the dichotomy of vaginal and clitoral orgasms is entirely false. Anatomically, all orgasms are centered in the clitoris, whether they result from direct manual pressure applied to the clitoris, indirect pressure resulting from the thrusting of penis during intercourse, or generalized sexual stimulation of other erogenous zones like the breasts.

2. That women are naturally multiorgasmic; that is, if a woman is immediately stimulated following orgasm, she is likely to experience several orgasms in rapid succession. This is not an exceptional occurrence, but one of which most women are capable.

3. That while women's orgasms do not vary in kind, they vary in intensity. The most intense orgasms experienced by the research subjects were by masturbatory manual stimulation, followed in intensity by manual stimulation by the partner; the least intense orgasms were experienced during intercourse.

4. That there is an "infinite variety in female sexual response" as regards intensity and duration of orgasms.

To anyone acquainted with the body of existing knowledge of feminine sexuality, the Masters and Johnson findings were truly revolutionary and liberating in the extent to which they demolished the established myths. Yet two years after the study was published, it seems hardly to have made any impact at all. Certainly it is not for lack of information that the myths persist; *Human Sexual Response,* despite its weighty scientific language, was an immediate best seller, and popular paperbacks explicated it to millions of people in simpler language and at a cheaper price. The myths remain because a male-dominated American culture has a vested interest in their continuance.

Before Masters and Johnson, men defined feminine sexuality in a way as favorable to themselves as possible. If woman's pleasure was obtained through the vagina, then she was totally dependent on the man's erect penis to achieve orgasm; she would receive her satisfaction only as a concomitant of man's seeking his. With the clitoral orgasm, woman's sexual pleasure was independent of the male's, and she could seek her satisfaction as aggressively as the man sought his, a prospect which didn't appeal to too many men. The definition of feminine sexuality as normally vaginal, in other words, was a part of keeping women down, of making them sexually as well as economically, socially, and politically subservient.

In retrospect, particularly with the additional perspective of our own times, Freud's theory of feminine sexuality appears an historical rationalization for the realities of Victorian society. A prisoner of the Victorian ethos, Freud had to play the paterfamilias. Freud's analysis implied that woman's low status had not been conferred upon her by men, but by God, who created her without a penis.

The superiority of the vaginal orgasm seems almost a demoniac determination on Freud's part to complete the Victorians' repression of feminine eroticism, to stigmatize the remaining vestiges of pleasure felt by women and thus make them unacceptable to the women themselves. For there were still women whose sexuality hadn't been completely destroyed, as evidenced by one Dr. Isaac Brown Baker, a surgeon who performed numerous clitoridectomies on women to prevent the sexual excitement which, he was convinced, caused "insanities," "catalepsy," "hysteria," "epilepsy," and other diseases. The Victorians needed to repress sexuality for the success of Western industrialized society; in particular, the total repression of woman's sexuality was crucial to ensure her subjugation. So the Victorians honored only that aspect of sexuality which was necessary to the survival of the species—the male ejaculation; made women submissive to sex by creating a mystique of the sanctity of motherhood; and, supported by Freud, passed on to us the heritage of the double standard.

When Kinsey laid to rest the part of the double standard that maintained women got no pleasure at all from sex, everyone cried out that there was a sexual revolution afoot. But such talk, as usual, was deceptive. Morality, outside the marriage bed, remained the same, and children were socialized as though Kinsey had never described what they would be like when they grew up. Boys were taught that they should get their sex where they could find it, "go as far" as they could. On the old assumption that women were asexual creatures, girls were taught that since they needed sex less than boys did, it was up to them to impose sexual restraints. In whatever sex education adolescents did manage to receive, they were told that men had penises and women vaginas; the existence of the clitoris was not mentioned, and *pleasure* in sex was never discussed at all.

Adolescent boys growing up begging for sexual crumbs from girls frightened for their "reputations"—a situation that remains unchanged to this day—hardly constitutes the vanguard of a sexual revolution. However, the marriage manual craze that followed Kinsey assumed that a lifetime of psychological destruction could, with the aid of a little booklet, be abandoned after marriage, and that husband and wife should be able to make sure that the wife was not robbed of her sexual birthright to orgasm, just so long as it was *vaginal* (though the marriage manuals did rather reluctantly admit that since the clitoris was the most sexually sensitive organ in the female body, a little clitoral stimulation was in order), and so long as their orgasms were *simultaneous.*

The effect of the marriage manuals of course ran counter to their ostensible purpose. Under the guise of frankness and sexual liberation, they dictated prudery and restraint. Sex was made so mechanized, detached, and intellectual that it was robbed of its sensuality. Man became a spectator of his own sexual experience. And the marriage manuals put new pressure on women. The swing was from repression to preoccupation with the orgasm. Men took the marriage manuals to mean that their sexuality would be enhanced by bringing women to orgasm and, again coopting feminine sexuality for their own ends, they put pressure on women to perform. The marriage manuals' endorsement of the desirability of vaginal orgasm insured that women would be asked not only, "Did you come?" but also, "Did you conform to Freud's conception of a psychosexually mature woman, and thereby validate my masculinity?"

Appearances notwithstanding, the age-old taboos against conversation about personal sexual experience haven't yet been broken down. This reticence has allowed the mind-manipulators of the media to create myths of sexual supermen and superwomen. So the bed becomes a competitive arena, where men and women measure themselves against these mythical rivals, while simultaneously trying to live up to the ecstasies promised them by the marriage manuals and the fantasies of the media ("If the earth doesn't move for me, I must be missing something"). Our society has made sex a sport, with its record-breakers, its judges, its rules, and its spectators.

As anthropologists have shown, woman's sexual response is culturally conditioned; historically, women defer to whatever model of their sexuality is offered them by men. So the sad thing for women is that they have participated in the destruction of their own eroticism. Women have helped make the vaginal orgasm into a status symbol in a male-dictated system of values. A woman would now perceive her preference for clitoral orgasm as a "secret shame," ignominious in the eyes of other women as well as those of men. This internalization can be seen in literature: Mary McCarthy and Doris Lessing's writings on orgasm do not differ substantially from Ernest Hemingway's, and Simone de Beauvoir, in *The Second Sex,* refers to vaginal orgasm as the only "normal satisfaction."

One factor that has made this possible is that female sexuality is subtle and delicate, conditioned as much by the emotions as by physiology and sociology. Masters and Johnson proved that the orgasm experienced during intercourse, the misnamed vaginal orgasm, did not differ *anatomically* from the clitoral orgasm. But this should not be seen as their most significant contribution to the sexual emancipation of women. A difference remains in the *subjective* experience of orgasm during intercourse and orgasm apart from intercourse. In the complex of emotional factors affecting feminine sexuality, there is a whole panoply of pleasures: the pleasure of being penetrated and filled by a man, the pleasure of sexual communication, the pleasure of affording a man his orgasm, the erotic pleasure that exists even when sex is not terminated by orgasmic release. Masters and Johnson's real contribution was to show this "infinite variety in female sexual response"; that one experience is not better than another, but merely different.

There is no doubt that Masters and Johnson were fully aware of the implications of their study to the sexual liberation of women. As they wrote, "With orgasmic physiology established, the human female now has an undeniable opportunity to develop realistically her own sexual response levels." Two years later this statement seems naive and entirely too optimistic. Certainly the sexual problems of our society will never be solved until there is real and unfeigned equality between men and women. This idea is usually misconstrued: sexual liberation for women is wrongly understood to mean that women will adopt all the forms of masculine sexuality. As in the whole issue of women's liberation, that's really not the point. Women don't aspire to imitate the mistakes of men in sexual matters, to view sexual experiences as conquest and ego-enhancement, to use other people to serve their own ends. But if the Masters and Johnson material is allowed to filter into the public consciousness, hopefully to replace the enshrined Freudian myths, then woman at long last will be allowed to take the first step toward her emancipation: to define and enjoy the forms of her own sexuality.

Sex as Work: A Study of Avocational Counseling

Lionel S. Lewis and
Dennis Brissett

It is commonly accepted that America is a society of leisure. The society is said to have shifted from one of production to one of consumption. The American of today spends little time working; he has a great deal of time to play.

With this surfeit of leisure, Americans have been called upon to engage in forms of consumption quite unknown to their inner-directed predecessors. There exist extensive opportunities for play, but little knowledge of how to conduct oneself in this play. As Riesman has remarked, "To bring the individual into unfrightening contact with the new range of opportunities in consumption often requires some guides and signposts." Knowing how to play has become problematic; it is something the individual must learn. He must, in a word, be socialized into the art of play.

Faced with this necessary socialization, the consuming American seeks out persons to teach him how to play. Very often this involves engaging the services of avocational counselors. The term avocational counseling ". . . describe[s] the activities undertaken by a number of relatively rapidly

From Lionel S. Lewis and Dennis Brissett, "Sex as Work: A Study of Avocational Counseling," *Social Problems,* 1967 (Vol. 15, no. 1), pp. 8–17. References cited in the original have been deleted.

growing professions in the United States, including travel agents, hotel men, resort directors, sports teachers and coaches, teachers of the arts, including dancing teachers, and so on." Each of the various counselors supplies the American public with advice on play and leisure. The advice of one such group of counselors is the subject matter of this paper.

Quite recently, Nelson Foote has observed that sex, since it is becoming increasingly dissociated from procreation, is becoming more and more a kind of play activity. He states that "the view that sex is fun can . . . hardly be called the invention of immoralists; it is every man's discovery." The arena of consumption is extended to include the realm of man's sexual activity, and the avocational counselor finds himself a place advising people on the vicissitudes of sex as play.

Concomitant with this increasing amount of leisure time, and the attendant problem of learning how to play, it has been observed that the play of most Americans has become a laborious kind of play. "Fun, in its rather unique American form, is grim resolve. . . . We are as determined about the pursuit of fun as a desert-wandering traveler is about the search for water. . . ." Consumption, to most Americans, has become a job. Like work, play has become a duty to be performed. This interpretation is supported by the emergence of what Wolfenstein has labeled a "fun morality." Here "play tends to be measured by standards of achievement previously applicable only to work . . . at play, no less than at work, one asks: 'Am I doing as well as I should?' " Consumption very definitely has become production.

It is the purpose of this paper to examine the product of the avocational counselors of marital sex and to inquire as to their depiction of man's sexual behavior. If it is true that play is becoming work in the mass society, it might be necessary to amend Foote's notion of the character of sexual play. In focusing on how marital sex is handled by these avocational counselors, we will show how sex, an area of behavior usually not thought of as involving work, has been treated as such. We will emphasize how general work themes are presented as an essential part of sexual relations, and how the public is advised to prepare for sex just as they are advised to prepare for a job.

Marriage Manuals

The avocational counselors of sex with the widest audience are those who write what are frequently referred to as marriage manuals. These manuals are designed to explain all aspects of the sexual side of marriage. Their distribution is wide: many are in paperback and are readily available in drug stores; many can be found in multiple copies in public and university libraries; and some are distributed by facilities which offer services in sex, fertility, and contraception, such as planned parenthood clinics.

Fifteen manuals were selected from a listing of almost fifty for analysis in this study. They are listed in Appendix A [omitted]. The first criterion for using a manual was wide circulation. This was determined by number of printings and number of copies sold. For example, one volume in 1965 was in its forty-fifth printing and had sold more than one-half million copies in the United States; a second was in its forty-eighth printing and had sold almost six hundred thousand; a third was in its thirtieth printing and has "been read by" two million eight hundred thousand; and a fourth advertises on its cover "over a million and a half copies in print." Other criteria were that the book be still read and available. The fifteen volumes ranged from fourteen-page pamphlets to full-sized, indexed, hard-bound books.

Each manual was read by both authors, and principal themes were recorded. Notes were taken, compared, and classified. Only material about whose meaning both authors agreed was utilized in drawing conclusions about the themes in a book.

Working at Sex

Marital sex, as depicted by the marriage manuals, is an activity permeated with qualities of work. One need not even read these books, but need only look at the titles or the chapter headings to draw this conclusion. Thus, we have books titled *The Sex Technique in Marriage, Modern Sex Techniques, Ideal Marriage: Its Physiology and Technique.* There are also chapters titled "How to Manage the Sex Act," "Principles and Techniques of Intercourse," "The Fourth Key to Soundly Satisfying Sex: A Controlled Sexual Crescendo."

From the outset, as we begin to read the books, we are warned not to treat sex frivolously, indeed not to play at sex:

> An ardent spur-of-the-moment tumble sounds very romantic. . . .
> However, ineptly arranged intercourse leaves the clothes you had no
> chance to shed in a shambles, your plans for the evening shot, your
> birth control program incomplete, and your future sex play under considerable better-be-careful-or-we'll-wind-up-in-bed-again restraint.

In other words, marital sex should not be an impromptu performance.

Moreover, sex should not be approached with a casual mien. Rather, we are counseled, sexual relations, at least good sexual relations, are a goal to be laboriously achieved. It is agreed that "satisfactory intercourse is the basis for happy marriage." However, it is added, "It does not occur automatically but must be striven for." In the plain talk of the avocational counselor, "Sexual relations are something to be worked at and developed."

This work and its development are portrayed as a taxing kind of endeavor; as behavior involving, indeed requiring, a good deal of effort. That sex involves effort is a pervasive theme in the fifteen manuals. From the start one is advised to direct his effort to satisfying his or her mate so that mutual climax is achieved, sexual activity is continual, and one's partner is not ignored after climax. Thus, we are told:

> Remember, *couple* effort for *couple* satisfaction! That's the key to well-paced, harmonious sex play.

Certain positions of intercourse are also seen as particularly taxing, in fact so taxing that certain categories of people are advised not to use them. One author, in discussing a particularly laborious position, remarks that "This is no position for a couple of grandparents, no matter how healthy and vigorous they are for their age, for it takes both effort and determination." Quite obviously, certain kinds of marital sex are reserved only for those persons who are "in condition."

The female is particularly cautioned to work at sex, for being naturally sexual seems a trait ascribed only to the male. The affinity of sex to her other work activities is here made clear: "Sex is too important for any wife to give it less call upon her energy than cooking, laundry, and a dozen other activities." To the housewife's burden is added yet another chore.

Even the one manual that takes great pains to depict sex as sport, injects the work theme. It is pointed out that

> You certainly can [strive and strain at having a climax]—just as you can . . . help yourself to focus on a complex musical symphony. . . . Just as you strive to enjoy a party, when you begin by having a dull time at it. Sex is often something to be worked and strained at—as an artist works and strains at his painting or sculpture.

Sex, then, is considered a kind of work; moreover, a very essential form of labor. Regular sexual activity is said, for instance, to contribute to "physical and mental health," and to lead to *"spiritual unity."* In the majestic functionalist tradition, "A happy, healthy sex life is vital to wholesome family life, which in turn is fundamental to the welfare of the community and of society." Marital sex, most assuredly, is the cornerstone of humanity, but not any kind of marital sex—only that which leads to orgasm. "It is the orgasm that is so essential to the health and happiness of the couple. . . ."

Indeed it is the orgasm which may be said to be the *product* of marital sexual relations. It is the *raison d'être* for sexual contact, and this orgasm is no mean achievement. In fact,

> Orgasm occasionally may be the movement of ecstasy when two people together soar along a Milky Way among stars all their own. This moment is the high mountaintop of love of which the poets sing,

on which the two together become a full orchestra playing a fortissimo of a glorious symphony.

In masculine, and somewhat more antiseptic terms, "ejaculation is the aim, the summit and the end of the sexual act." Woe be to the couple who fail to produce this state, as there are dire consequences for the unsuccessful, particularly for the woman.

> When the wife does not secure an orgasm, she is left at a high peak of sexual tension. If this failure to release tension becomes a regular thing, she may develop an aversion to starting any sex play that might lead to such frustrations. . . . Repeated disappointments may lead to headache, nervousness, sleeplessness, and other unhappy symptoms of maladjustment.

So important is it to reach orgasm, to have a product, that all the other sexual activities of marriage are seen as merely prosaic ingredients or decorative packaging of the product.

In fact, orgasm as a product is so essential that its occasion is not necessarily confined to the actual act of intercourse, at least for the women. Numerous counselors indicate that it may be necessary for the man to induce orgasm in the woman during afterplay. "A woman who has built up a head of passion which her husband was unable to requite deserves a further push to climax through intensive genital caress. . . ." Particularly in the early years of marriage, before the husband has learned to pace his orgasm, he may have to rely on the knack of digital manipulation. In one author's imagery, "Sometimes it may be necessary for the husband to withdraw and continue the stimulation of his wife by a rhythmic fondling of clitoris and vulva until orgasm is attained."

The central importance of experiencing orgasm has led many of the authors to de-emphasize the traditional organs of intercourse. The male penis (member) is particularly belittled. It is considered "only one of the instruments creating sensation in the female, and its greatest value lies as a mental stimulant and organ of reproduction, not as a necessary medium of her sexual pleasure." The same author adds, ". . . the disillusioning fact remains that the forefinger is a most useful asset in man's contact with the opposite sex. . . ." Furthermore, this useful phallic symbol should be directed primarily to the woman's seat of sensation, the clitoris. Only a man who is ignorant of his job directs his digital attention to the vulva, the female organ that permits conventional union.

One must often deny himself immediate pleasure when manufacturing the orgasm. One author, in referring to an efficient technique to attain orgasm, states that: "Unfortunately, some men do not care for this position. This, however, should be of little importance to an adequate lover, since his emotions are the less important of the two." Likewise, the woman may have to force herself in order to reach orgasm, even though she may not desire the activity which precedes it. It is specified that "If you conscientiously work at being available, you may ultimately find the feminine role quite satisfying even in the absence of ardor or desire." The work ethic of the sexual side of marriage, then, is one resting quite elaborately on what has been referred to as the "cult of the orgasm."

Still, one cannot easily perform one's job; its intricacies must first be mastered. After all, ". . . there is considerably more in the sexual relationship than . . . at first thought." "Remember that complete development of couple skills and adaptations takes literally years." There is a great deal to be learned. One author talks of eight steps "in order to facilitate sexual arousal and lead, finally, to satisfactory orgasm" and of seven "techniques which she and her mate may employ to help her attain full climax."

All of this requires a good deal of mastery, a mastery that is necessary if the sex relationship is not to undergo "job turnover." Firstly, in the fact of incompetence, the marriage partner may, at times, turn to auto-eroticism. One author stipulates that "There cannot be a shadow of a doubt that faulty technique, or a total lack of it on the man's part, drives thousands of wives to masturbation as their sole means of gratification." Moreover, if sexual skills are not acquired, the husband or wife may seek out new partners for sexual activity. The woman is admonished that adequate sexual relations will keep a man from "The Other Woman. . . ." The male also must be proficient in sexual encounters for "it is the male's habit of treating . . . [sexual relationships] as such [mechanically] which causes much dissatisfaction and may ultimately drive the wife to someone who takes it more seriously."

Learning Sex: Passive and Active

Marital sex is said to necessitate a good deal of preparation if it is to be efficiently performed. In one author's words, "This (complete satisfaction) cannot be achieved without study, practice, frank and open discussion. . . ." This overall preparation seems to involve both a passive and an active phase. The passive phase seems most related to an acquisition of information previous to engaging in sexual, at least marital sexual, relations. The active phase best refers to the training, one might say on-the-job training, that the married couple receive in the sexual conduct of wedlock.

The matter of passive preparation receives a great deal of attention from the avocational counselors. Thirteen of the fifteen books call attention to the necessity of reading, studying, and discussing the various facets of sexual relationships. After listing a number of these activities, one author advises that "If the two of them have through reading acquired a decent vocabulary and a general understanding of the fundamental facts listed above, they will in all likelihood be able to find their way to happiness." Another counselor cites the extreme importance of reciprocal communication by noting that ". . . the vital problem . . . must be solved through intelligent, practical, codified, and instructive discussion. . . ." The general purpose of all this learning is, of course, to dispel ignorance, as ignorance is said to lead to "mistakes at work," and such cannot be tolerated. The learning of the other partner's physiology is particularly emphasized, most counselors devoting at least one chapter and a profusion of illustrations to relieve the ignorance of the marriage partners. One author, however, quite obviously feels that words and pictures are insufficient. Presenting a sketch of the woman's genitals, he asserts that "It should be studied; on the bridal night . . . the husband should compare the diagram with his wife's genital region. . . ."

Together with learning physiology, the various manuals also stress the critical importance of learning the methodology of marital sex. Sexual compatibility seems not a matter of following one's natural proclivities, but rather "The technique of the sexual relation has to be learned in order to develop a satisfactory sex life." One must know one's job if one is to be successful at it. Not surprisingly, to like one's job also requires a learning experience, particularly for the woman. As one book scientifically asserts:

> There is a striking consensus of opinion among serious specialists (both men and women) that the average woman of our time and clime must *learn* to develop specific sexual enjoyment, and only gradually attains to the orgasm in coitus. . . . They [women] have to *learn how* to feel both voluptuous pleasure and actual orgasm.

In summary, then, passive learning involves the mastering of physiology and techniques. By the desexualized female of the marriage manuals, the fine art of emotional experience and expression is also acquired. And the naturally inept male must learn, for

> If the husband understands in even a general way the sexual nature and equipment of his wife, he need not give the slightest offense to her through ignorant blundering.

This learning process, according to most of the manuals, eventually becomes subject to the actual experience of matrimonial sex. The marriage bed here becomes a "training" and "proving" ground. Again, wives seem particularly disadvantaged: "Their husbands have to be their guides." However, generally the training experience is a mutual activity. As one author suggests in his discussion of the various positions for coitus,

> In brief, the position to be used is not dictated by a code of behavior

but should be selected as the one most acceptable to you and your mate. To find this you will examine your own tastes and physical conformations. By deliberate application of the trial-and-error method you will discover for yourselves which is most desirable for you both.

In training, rigorous testing and practice is a must. In the words of one manual "experimentation will be required to learn the various responses within one's own body as well as those to be expected from one's beloved . . . ," and also, "After a variable time of practice, husband and wife may both reach climax, and may do so at the same time."

Both the husband and wife must engage in a kind of "muscular control" training if the sex act is to be efficiently performed. The woman's plight during intercourse is picturesquely portrayed with the following advice. "You can generally contract these muscles by trying to squeeze with the vagina itself . . . perhaps by pretending that you are trying to pick up marbles with it." Fortunately, the man is able to practice muscular control at times other than during intercourse. Indeed, the man, unlike the woman, is permitted to engage in activities not normally related to sexual behavior while he is training. It is advised that "You can snap the muscles [at the base of the penile shaft] a few times while you are driving your car or sitting in an office or any place you happen to think of it. . . ." The practice field, at least for the male, is enlarged.

In general, then, a careful learning and a studied training program are necessary conditions for the proper performance of marital sex. As seems abundantly true of all sectors of work, " 'Nature' is not enough. . . . Man must pay for a higher and more complex nervous system by study, training, and conscious effort. . . ."

The Job Schedule

As in most work activities, the activity of marital sex is a highly scheduled kind of performance. There is first of all a specification of phases or stages in the actual conduct of the sex act. Although there is disagreement here, some authors indicating four or five distinct phases, the consensus of the counselors seems to be that "Sexual intercourse, when satisfactorily performed, consists of three stages, only one of which is the sex act proper."

The sexual act therefore is a scheduled act and the participants are instructed to follow this schedule. "All three stages have to be fitted into this time. None of them must be missed and none prolonged to the exclusion of others." Practice and study is said to insure the proper passage from one phase to another. Moreover, to guarantee that none of the phases will be excluded, it is necessary to engage in relations only when the sexual partners have a sizable amount of time during which they will not be dis-traced: ". . . husbands and wives should rarely presume to begin loveplay that may lead to coitus unless they can have an hour free from interrup-tions." Even then, however, the couple must be careful, for there is an optimal time to spend on each particular phase. For instance, "Foreplay should never last less than fifteen minutes even though a woman may be sufficiently aroused in five." Likewise, the epilogue to orgasm should be of sufficient duration to permit the proper recession of passion.

Given this schedule of activity, the marriage manuals take great pains to describe the various activities required at each particular phase. It is cautioned, for instance, that "all contact with the female genital region . . . should be kept at an absolute minimum" during foreplay. The man is warned furthermore to "refrain from any excessive activity involving the penis" if he wishes to sustain foreplay. Regarding afterplay, the advice is the same; the partners must not permit themselves "any further genital stimulation."

The "job specification" is most explicit, however, when describing the actual act of intercourse. It is particularly during this stage that the sexual partners must strain to maintain control over their emotions. Innumerable lists of "necessary activities" are found in the various manuals. The ade-quate lovers should not permit themselves to deviate from these activities. Sometimes, in fact, the male is instructed to pause in midaction, in order to ascertain his relative progress:

> After the penis has been inserted to its full length into the vagina, it is usually best for the husband to rest a bit before allowing himself to make the instinctive in-and-out movements which usually follow. He needs first to make sure that his wife is comfortable, that the penis is not pushing too hard against the rear wall of the vagina, and that she is as ready as he to proceed with these movements.

Techniques

The "labor of love" espoused by the avocational counselors is one whose culmination is importantly based on the proper use of sexual tech-nique. In fact, ". . . *miserable failure results from ignorance of technique.*" Indeed "no sex relationship will have permanent value unless technique is mastered. . . ." Thirteen of the fifteen books devote considerable space to familiarizing the reader with the techniques of sexual activity. These dis-cussions for the most part involve enumerating the various positions of intercourse, but also include techniques to induce, to prolong, to elevate, and to minimize passion. Many times the depiction of particular coital posi-tions takes on a bizarre, almost geometric, aura. In one such position "The woman lies on her back, lifts her legs at right angles to her body from the hips, and rests them on the man's shoulders; thus she is, so to speak, doubly cleft by the man who lies upon her and inserts his phallus; she enfolds both his genital member and his neck and head. At the same time the woman's spine in the lumbar region is flexed at a sharp angle. . . ." Often, however, the mastery of sexual technique seems to involve little more than being able to keep one's legs untangled, ". . . when the woman straightens her right leg, the man, leaving his right leg between both of hers, puts his left one outside her right, and rolls over onto his left side facing her."

At times, in order to make love adequately, it is required of the participants that they supplement their technique with special equipment. Some of this equipment, such as lubricating jellies, pillows, and birth control paraphernalia, is simple and commonplace. Others are as simple but not as common, such as chairs, foot-high stools, and beds with footboards or footrails. Some, like aphrodisiacs, hot cushions, medicated (carbonic acid) baths, and sitz baths, border on the exotic. Still others actually seem to detract from the pleasure of intercourse. In this vein would be the rings of sponge rubber which are slipped over the penis to control depth of penetration and the various devices which make the male less sensitive, such as condoms and a local anesthetic applied to the glans.

This equipment that minimizes stimulation, while not particularly inviting, might be said to give greater pleasure than still other techniques that are suggested to add variety to the sex life. The latter, in fact, seem cruelly painful. For instance,

> . . . both partners tend to use their teeth, and in so doing there is naught abnormal, morbid or perverse. Can the same be said of the real love-bite that breaks the skin and draws blood? Up to a certain degree—yes.

Indeed, a certain amount of aggression should be commonplace.

> . . . both of them can and do exult in a certain degree of male aggression and dominance. . . . Hence, the sharp gripping and pinching of the woman's arms and nates.

At times, the authors seem to go so far as to indicate that the proper performance of the sex act almost requires the use of techniques that create discomfort. The element of irksomeness becomes an almost necessary ingredient of the conduct of marital sex.

Concluding Remarks

The kinds of impressions assembled here seem to support the notion that play, at least sexual play in marriage, has indeed been permeated with dimensions of a work ethic. The play of marital sex is presented by the counselors quite definitely as work.

This paradox, play as work, may be said to be an almost logical outcome of the peculiar condition of American society. First of all, it seems that in America, most individuals are faced with the problems of justifying and dignifying their play. In times past, leisure was something earned, a prize that was achieved through work. In the present era, it might be said that leisure is something ascribed or assumed. Indeed, as Riesman and Bloomberg have noted, "leisure, which was once a residual compensation for the tribulations of work, may become what workers recover from at work."

The American must justify his play. It is our thesis that he has done this by transforming his play into work. This is not to say that he has disguised his play as work; it is instead to propose that his play has become work. To consume is, in most cases, to produce. Through this transformation of play, the dignity of consumption is seemingly established; it is now work, and work is felt to carry with it a certain inherent dignity. The individual now is morally free to consume, and moreover free to seek out persons to teach him how to consume, for learning how to play is simply learning how to do one's job in society.

This transformation of play into work has been attended by another phenomenon that is also quite unique to contemporary American society. Given the fact that work has always been valued in American society, a cult of efficiency has developed. As a consequence, the productive forces in America have become very efficient, and an abundance of consumer goods have been created. So that such goods will be consumed, Americans have been socialized into being extremely consumption oriented. As Jules Henry has noted, the impulse controls of most Americans have been destroyed. The achievement of a state of general satisfaction has become a societal goal. To experience pleasure is almost a societal dictum.

Thus there seem to be two antagnostic forces operating in American society. On the one hand, there is an emphasis on work and, on the other hand, there is an emphasis on attaining maximum pleasure. These two themes were recurrent in the fifteen manuals which we read, and as one writer put it:

> . . . it may well be that the whole level of sexual enjoyment for both partners can be stepped up and greatly enriched if the man is able to exercise a greater degree of deliberation and management.

It was as if the avocational counselors were trying to solve a dilemma for their audience by reminding them to both "let themselves go" while cautioning them that they should "work at this." If sex be play, it most assuredly is a peculiar kind of play.

Sweden:
The Contraceptive Society

J. Robert Moskin

The Swedes are curious about their own sexuality. They feel a mite uneasy about their reputation for free-swinging love. But behind their unease, one smells pride; they know it's true.

Now, they have completed an official survey of their sexual behavior, knowledge, and attitudes—the first ever to examine the sex life of a whole nation. It confirms some of the things people have been saying and springs some surprises.

The Royal Commission on Sex Education, which ordered the study, is acutely aware that inside Sweden, its findings will anger both extremes: the bluenosed traditionalists and bishops of the Lutheran Church as well as the enthusiasts for sex without limits and rules. No one in Sweden is much concerned about the outside world's reactions, except perhaps as they may affect Sweden's blonde-and-bust tourism.

Actually, to outsiders—especially Americans and others in modern, affluent Western societies—this study reveals the shape of their sexual future. The prime causes of the changes in Swedish sexual morality are very much with us too: modern contraceptives are cutting drastically the likelihood of unwanted pregnancies; the welfare state is softening the consequences of such accidents; and a growing faith in romantic love is providing the rationale for sex outside marriage.

The new study is titled ambiguously *On Sexual Life in Sweden*. Prof. Hans L. Zetterberg, who directed the survey, wanted to call it *The Contraceptive Society*. He concludes that, above all, contraception makes possible present Swedish sex activity and attitudes. Until just before World War II, it was illegal to discuss or sell contraceptives in the country. Today, they are easily obtainable in stores and even sidewalk machines, and a young girl can keep herself in pills for a dollar a month. Zetterberg says this makes all the difference.

Surprisingly, Zetterberg is to be found not in Stockholm, where he was born, but in Columbus, Ohio, where he is, at 41, the chairman of the Department of Sociology of Ohio State University. He got his master's degree at the University of Minnesota and taught at Columbia for a decade before

From J. Robert Moskin, "The New Contraceptive Society," *Look,* February 4, 1969, pp. 50–53.

going to Ohio State. The Royal Commission chose him to run the study because he is a respected theoretical sociologist who never got enmeshed in the battles over sex that have been fought in Sweden ever since national compulsory sex education was introduced in 1956. In addition, Zetterberg is the co-owner with his brother of the Gallup-like Swedish Institute of Opinion Research, which made the survey for the Royal Commission.

The Commission was created to settle the continuing controversies over sex education. It is wrestling with three main questions: Are teachers adequately prepared to teach about sex? Should schoolchildren be taught about contraception? What should the schools say about sexual morality, particularly intercourse before marriage?

The report now being made public is the first of several that will seek to replace guesses, accusations, and myths with more scientific truth. Other studies will analyze the knowledge and attitudes of both teachers and students. The Commission hopes finally to announce its recommendations by the end of next year.

This survey has taken more than a year to complete. Interviewers questioned a representative sample of 1,952 Swedes, who also filled out a secret, anonymous questionnaire dealing with the more intimate aspects of their sexual experience.

The study differs radically from the pioneering investigations of Dr. Alfred C. Kinsey, who, Zetterberg says, "counted orgasms, basically." This study is built on a representative population sample, rather than on volunteers such as Kinsey used, and is much broader in its sociological interests and range of questions. Although the survey covered subjects like abortions, masturbation, and intercourse positions, most of these findings are not included in the report. Zetterberg credits Dr. Paul H. Gebhard, director of the Institute for Sex Research, which Kinsey founded at Indiana University, with having helped him on the methodology of his study. In Stockholm, Carl Gustaf Boëthius, the secretary of the Royal Commission, calls the result "the finest investigation ever made of sexual behavior and attitudes of a whole people, made by modern sociological methods."

The study lays bare the new sexual morality of the affluent West. For example, the researchers determined that during the one month in 1967 when the interviews were conducted, there were 9.7 million intercourses in Sweden, resulting in 8,800 births. Therefore, they conclude, in The Contraceptive Society there is one birth for roughly every 1,100 intercourses. The effect of modern birth-control methods is clearly overwhelming.

The study finds that the young are having sex relations with more persons and starting a sex life earlier than their parents. Says Zetterberg, "The younger generation knows sexually as many or more people than their parents, which is one reason why they speak with authority." For men above 30 years, the mean is seven sex partners; for younger men (21 to 30), with fewer years for sex relations, the mean is already eight.

The age of the onset of sex relations declined about a year between 1920 and 1950, and the decline is continuing. Those who are now 21 to 25 began sex relations at the median age of 16.9 years.

In the whole population, ages 18 to 60, 57 percent of the men and 44 percent of the women began sex relations before they were 18; 85 percent of the men and 82 percent of the women, before they were 20. The survey also proves that once sex activity starts, it tends to continue. The great majority had their second intercourse within five weeks after their first experience.

The study shows that the better educated delay the start of sex relations, but eventually catch up and have more sex partners than the less educated. It also confirms that young people start sex later when their parents set up simple controls, establishing hours by which they have to be home and asking whom they were out with.

Some experts had related the prevalence of premarital relations to the age at which marriage begins—five years later, on the average, than in the United States. But the survey surprised them; the age of marriage has actually been declining faster than the age of the beginning of sex relations.

Ninety-three percent of all Swedes accept sex relations between persons who are engaged or "going steady." Ninety-eight percent of the married population had intercourse before marriage. Only 20 percent of the married women now over 30 waited until their wedding, and only 9 percent of those under 30. There is, suggests Zetterberg, considerable hypocrisy in the older generation. Only among those who had religious parents and are themselves active in church was there a significantly higher percentage of virgins at marriage.

Today, the survey shows, almost half the brides in Sweden are pregnant at their weddings. The chief reason: Couples who are living together—in a society where premarital sex relations are accepted and fidelity is expected—need to formalize their relationship only when a child is expected. In Sweden, where every tenth child is born outside marriage, 99 percent of the population feel children of unwed parents should have all the rights of those born in wedlock; and 98 percent want unmarried mothers to have all the rights of married mothers. The majority of women want free abortions provided by the official health-care system.

"In our modern times, this new type of living in the sexual field has come to stay," says Boëthius. "The new type of living is that premarital sex relations are so common, and young people in most Western countries regard this as all right."

In certain respects, the study found that the double standard does persist. The majority of men have had as many as five sex partners, while the majority of women, only one or two. Only 18 percent of the married men have not had intercourse with anyone but their first partner, while 45 percent of the married women have not. More persons would permit men to have premarital experience than women. And more women accept the idea of a double standard than do men.

Probably the most significant shift revealed by the study deals with how society seeks to control sexual activity and attitudes.

In the past, society regulated sex by taboos, fear, inhibitions, emotional restraints, and silence. "Our society has traditionally controlled sex by limiting knowledge. Those with the traditional morality know less, want others to know less, and want to know less themselves," says Zetterberg. "This is why sex education has become so controversial. Knowledge was a form of social control. Now, with contraception, we have another form of social control of the consequences, rather than the programmatic limitation of sex knowledge."

This suggests that to control the undesirable consequences of sex, a society had better have one or the other—taboos or knowledge about contraception. And the evidence is that taboos no longer work in a society with a welfare economy and a contraception technology.

Today, 77 percent of the young men and 63 percent of those over 30 use modern forms of contraception. Says Zetterberg: "It is a new morality that one should use contraception unless you want to beget children—this is taken very seriously."

Those who feel they are in love can have intercourse without marriage; 85 percent of all Swedes believe this. Since only those involved can determine whether they are in love or not, this means that the individual, not society, decides when intercourse is permissible.

But the survey also reveals a strong sense of commitment to the sex partner—in marriage and out. The overwhelming majority believe that promiscuity is wrong. Says Zetterberg: "The idea that this [new morality] generates a free-for-all doesn't work. It becomes a code of honor. This is the code of honor emerging in The Contraceptive Society: you don't hurt a *good* established relationship." Of all Swedes, 77 percent feel this way.

"Marriage is no total solution," says Boëthius. "In marriage, thousands of people are hurting each other terribly. We always have such problems, both inside marriage and outside marriage." And he adds, "What was immoral 100 years ago may not be immoral today."

The survey finds that marital infidelity has not increased among the younger generation. The incidence of extramarital sex relations is very low; 95 percent of all married Swedes say they have not had extramarital relations within a year. This does not mean, of course, that they have never had them. And 93 percent say they disapprove of extramarital sex. Occasional infidelity is forgiven, the study indicates, by the majority of those with a consistent sex relationship in or outside marriage. Zetterberg emphasizes that premarital relations clearly do not mean that the participants will necessarily have extramarital relations later on.

In essence, the survey pictures a society in which premarital sex is approved, but the constancy of a good relationship is respected. Zetterberg says, "It looks like the nature of the beast. One wants to preserve the good thing one has."

He adds: "I was surprised at some results—mostly at the solidity and faithfulness of the typical Swede. It does not fit the image of Sweden propagated abroad. You wonder if a study of this kind will have a harmful effect on the tourist trade."

Dr. Maj-Briht Bergström-Walan, an internationally known school psychologist and member of the Royal Commission, shares Zetterberg's reaction. She says, "The trend I was a little surprised at was the conservative attitude that it is almost necessary for persons to be true when they have a stable sex relationship with another person."

Swedes are leading a highly satisfactory sex life, the study shows. The great majority are content. Sixty percent call their experience "satisfactory," and 24 percent regard it as "wonderful."

The survey also learned something about preferences. Those who had their last intercourse with a steady partner were more satisfied than those with a temporary partner. (There was not a single case of a "most-recent intercourse" with a prostitute.) Those in love were more satisfied than those who were not in love. When both partners took the initiative, they were more satisfied than when only one did. Those who used contraceptives reported more satisfaction than those who did not. Those who talked together during lovemaking and those who left on some light were more satisfied than those who were silent and in the dark. "Sexual intercourse may be seen as a kind of human communication," says Zetterberg.

Overall, most people in the study want more intercourse than they presently have. Even the older population is sexually active; among the 55-60 age group, 58 percent had intercourse at least once during the previous month.

The vast majority of Swedes, according to the survey, want their schools to give sex instruction; 5 percent are hesitant or don't know, and only 9 percent oppose sex education. But one third of the schoolchildren failed to receive such instruction. Many teachers and schools still avoid it.

Those who had received sex instruction in school knew a little more about the subject than those who did not—but not much more. The report concludes that the schools cannot be first on the scene with knowledge about sex, but they can integrate information received from friends, parents, the press, books—and correct misinformation.

The school sex-education program was found to have little effect on morality and attitudes; these depend on personal characteristics, not on a few hours of classroom instruction. Sex morality is anchored in the society. Zetterberg compares sex education to cheering for a football team in front of a television set: "It doesn't have much effect."

Dr. Preben Hertoft, who recently published a study of the sexual behavior of young Danish males, is even more emphatic:

> It doesn't do any good for school to say this is good and that is not good. The school has no influence on the sexual behavior of the children. That depends on other things—what they have seen in their homes, psychological things. The home is a very, very big factor. If children see their parents live a calm sexual life, that is more important than what a teacher says.

He adds,

> You have to tell children some people have sex without love. You have to tell them how it is. I don't think it's good if a boy thinks his father is an angel. It is better if he knows his father is human.

There is a substantial split in the kind of sex education desired by those under 24 years and those who are older. In general, young people reject the official guidelines for the Swedish school program, which preaches abstinence before marriage; they want to choose their moral standards for themselves. Says Bergström-Walan, "We should never teach morality, but we should present different attitudes. We should talk about the Pope. We should talk about free love—if there is free love. We should help young people think."

Only 4 percent of those under 24 and 20 percent of those above want abstinence taught by the schools. Thirty-three percent of those under 24 and 47 percent of those above want the schools to teach all ethical views but to recommend abstinence. But 60 percent of those under 24 and 31 percent of those above want the schools to teach all views and let the students decide. Only 3 percent of those under 24 and 2 percent of those above want the schools to recommend a free sexual morality for the teenage years.

The Swedish Student Organization (SECO) has formed its own Sex Education Committee, which wants sex education to start earlier, be improved, and be separated from religious teaching. Says Stefan Westergren, 22, the Committee's head, "It shouldn't be the teachers' morality or someone else's. It should teach all the moralities that exist in the society and let the students decide."

Mrs. Birgitta Linnér, marriage counselor and author of *Sex and Society in Sweden,* says,

> The parents' generation is more conservative than the young people. So it's dangerous to take up the values of the parents and not the young people. They have to solve their own sex problems without the older generation—and they do it. I feel it's a risk that the United States will take up the same wrong views we had. Teachers knew lots of young people were having sex life without marriage. It wasn't a realistic program. I'm scared now the United States will make the same mistake.

"Sex education," Zetterberg is convinced,

> is a means by which society can shift its control of the consequences of sex from taboo and fear to reliance on contraception. We have found a better way for limiting the consequences of sex. The vehicle for this is sex education.

The survey specifically punctuates two myths: The official sex-education syllabus urges teachers to warn youngsters against mixing drinking and dancing because the combination will lead to sex relations. But the survey shows that only 1 percent had mixed dancing and alcohol before their first intercourse. The study also refuted the idea that contraception is not used until after the first intercourse: 56 percent of those under 30 used contraceptives the first time. Such findings are likely to influence the Royal Commission's recommendations about sex education.

"The welfare state has taken over many economic responsibilities of the parents. We are all becoming that kind of society," concludes Zetterberg.

> It seems Sweden is some years ahead of us here. You can spot trends that may have a chance to become dominant in other countries. In sex education, there are some local programs that are very good, but most of the United States has nothing.

He ends his report with this statement:

> The Contraceptive Society is now here and can be pushed back as little as the industrialized society and the automobile. We must therefore educate and legislate to make it as functional as possible and as free from injustices as possible.

Zetterberg admits he did not feel this way when he started the study. He felt then that sex relations are a private matter; now, he is convinced the government must share the responsibilities in a modern society. He says,

> We have introduced a major social change, relying on contraception rather than prohibitions. This sneaked up on us. It contains some frictions and some conceivable injustices. We will have to face up to them.

Chapter 4

Male/Female
Status, Role, and Temperament

Primate Studies and Sex Differences

Sally Linton

If we want to get to the heart of male/female sex differences, we must be able to separate the biological from the learned (sociocultural). Comparing cultures can only take us so far—there are human possibilities which *no* culture that we know of has yet instituted. Because we don't find a particular behavior in any culture now or in the past does not mean the behavior is impossible. If we can imagine it, it is possible. So comparing sex roles in various cultures does not give us anything approaching a total picture of the potentialities of either males or females. Since in most cultures we find females subservient to males, it is often assumed that there is a biological or physiological basis for this. Anthropologists, ethnologists, and psychologists have recently turned to primate studies as a way of finding out the "truth" about sex differences. They have done this in two ways: first by observing the natural behavior of nonhuman primates in the wild, and second by tampering with the balance of male and female hormones in the animals and then observing their behavior.

On the *first* point, it has been observed that male monkeys and apes seem to be more aggressive than females. They initiate, and participate in, more rough-and-tumble, dominance-type interactions. The females show more interest in infants, try to hold them, care for them, etc. From this sort of observation some researchers have concluded that aggressiveness and nurturance are biologically-based characteristics of males and females respectively, in all primates both human and nonhuman. This is an extreme-

From Sally Linton, "Primate Studies and Sex Differences," *Women: A Journal of Liberation,* Summer 1970, pp. 43–44.

ly poor use of the evidence; it is both anthropomorphic and ethnocentric. The major factor which is being overlooked is that these primates under observation *live in a social group.* Animal behaviorists have been emphasizing for years the importance of the social group, and the extent to which most primate behavior is *learned.* It is inexcusable to emphasize the importance of this learned behavior in all other contexts, and to ignore it when considering sex-role behavior. Monkey and ape socialization must begin as early as it does in humans. Has any observer of primate behavior in the wild investigated the following questions: How soon does the mother recognize the sex of her newborn infant? How does she recognize it—by smell, by the sight of genital organs? Does she treat male and female infants differently once she has recognized their sex? How soon do other members of the troop recognize the infant's sex? Do they react differently to males and females? When the infant first moves into peer-group interactions, what sexual distinctions are applied?

Surely monkeys and apes can tell a male from a female at a fairly early age. To the human observer the animals all look alike at first, but familiarity soon brings recognition of each animal as an individual, and as male or female. If a human is able to make observations such as more aggressiveness in the males, more nurturance in the females, we must assume that the primates under observation can distinguish between the sexes at least as well! At some point the primate social group begins to train its members for their adult roles, including their sexual roles. To my knowledge, no researcher has ever raised any of the above questions. They have simply observed male/female differences in behavior, *in a social group,* and gone on to make completely unwarranted assumptions about biology.

There is evidence (from the Japanese studies) that the offspring of less dominant animals are much less likely to grow up to be dominant themselves. In other words, they begin to *learn submissiveness* at an early age. If this is true, there is a very strong basis for inferring that they also learn their sex roles at an early age. In Harlow's experiments monkeys raised in isolation were unable to perform properly as adults. Those who were isolated from adult monkeys but allowed contact with a peer group did much better. Were the typical male/female behavior differences noted in these peer groups? The question was never asked. It has often been observed that female primates who did not receive the proper socialization, or who are isolated from others of their kind, make very poor mothers. They tend to reject the infant, fail to care for it properly, sometimes deliberately kill it when it does not simply die from neglect. This has usually been taken as a sign of pathology, because of course any "normal" primate mother cares for her infant. What has never been suggested in this context is that the nurturing female role is *socially learned,* and that without this social learning it is perfectly natural for the female primate to fail to care for her infant. It is not natural (instinctive) for her, any more than for a human female, to be nurturing unless she has been taught this behavior by her social group.

In sum, the observation of primate behavior in the wild which has been done so far gives us no sort of argument for the "instinctive" or biological nature of observed differences in male/female sex-role behavior.

The *second* sort of "biological" evidence comes from experiments where the balance of sex hormones was tampered with. It was observed, for instance, that when female monkeys were shot full of male hormones they became more aggressive. This has been taken as evidence to "prove" that males are naturally (instinctively) more aggressive and females more passive. All it actually proves is that females with an overabundance of male hormones act more aggressively. Our suspicions should be aroused when we note that this aggression occurs only in *specific social situations* where it is proper for male monkeys to be aggressive. These females have *not* been made into males, they cannot scientifically be compared to normal males—they are animals with a disturbed and unusual hormone balance. It is to be expected that their behavior would change. We know that humans with unbalanced hormones also tend to behave in unusual ways. We do not know exactly how monkeys distinguish between males and females, although smell is certainly important. We might hypothesize that the hormone balance affects smell, so that the injected females begin to smell more like males. If this is the case, then their social group would treat them as males, and they would accordingly be differentially socialized. This has never been investigated. When looked at closely this biological "proof" of sex differences also withers away.

It seems to me that all these rather desperate attempts to prove from biology that human males are naturally aggressive, while human females are naturally passive and nurturing, are ethnocentric strivings designed to find scientific support for a status quo which is now being threatened. It is obvious that if any large number of females in our culture reject the submissive, dependent, nurturing role they have traditionally played, massive social upheaval will follow. This is beginning to happen already, and many members of our culture (both male and female) do not wish to face the implications or the consequences of this sort of social change. So attempts are made to prove "scientifically" and "biologically" that females are naturally destined to be passive and dependent. To approach any topic with such massive preconception and bias contradicts the ideals (though not always the practice) of scientific investigation. On a subject such as male/female differences, which is both scientifically and humanly important, every effort should be made to recognize and eliminate our cultural biases from the research design and from the interpretation of results.

Even if it could be demonstrated that there is a biological predisposition for the sorts of male/female differences discussed above, it would mean very little in modern society. Many biological tendencies are overcome by cultural and social conditioning—that is part of being human. Most of our "instinctive" behavior is under cortical control. We may want to have sexual intercourse with almost every individual of the opposite sex we see; we may want to kill the person who makes us angry; but we don't do thsee things. We behave, in other words, in "unbiological" ways. Any argument from biological fact to cultural necessity must be made with extreme care. The discovery of a biological predisposition is one thing: what we choose to do about it culturally is another. Because someone is stronger than I, does that mean I must let him beat me up? To limit female options in our society because of some sort of biological or pseudo-biological argument is to fail to understand the nature of human life, of our society, culture *and* biology.

"Passing" as a Woman: A study of Sex Change | *Harold Garfinkle*

Agnes

Agnes appeared at the Department of Psychiatry at U.C.L.A. in October, 1958, where she had been referred to Dr. Robert J. Stoller by a private physician in Los Angeles to whom Agnes had in turn been referred by her physician in her home town, Northwestern City. Agnes was a nineteen-year-old, white, single girl, who was at the time self-supporting and working as a typist for a local insurance company. Her father was a machinist who died when Agnes was a child. Her mother supported a family of four children, of whom Agnes was the youngest, with occasional and semi-skilled work in an aircraft plant. Agnes said that she was raised as a Catholic but has not taken Communion for the past three years. She said of herself that she no longer believed in God.

Agnes' appearance was convincingly female. She was tall, slim, with a very female shape. Her measurements were 38-25-38. She had long, fine dark-blonde hair, a young face with pretty features, a peaches-and-cream complexion, no facial hair, subtly plucked eyebrows, and no makeup ex-

From Harold Garfinkle, "Agnes," in *Studies in Ethnomethodology* (Englewood Cliffs, N. J.: Prentice-Hall, 1967), pp. 118–133.

cept for lipstick. At the time of her first appearance she was dressed in a tight sweater which marked off her thin shoulders, ample breasts, and narrow waist. Her feet and hands, though somewhat larger than usual for a woman, were in no way remarkable in this respect. Her usual manner of dress did not distinguish her from a typical girl of her age and class. There was nothing garish or exhibitionistic in her attire, nor was there any hint of poor taste or that she was ill at ease in her clothing, as is seen so frequently in transvestites and in women with disturbances in sexual identification. Her voice, pitched at an alto level, was soft, and her delivery had the occasional lisp similar to that affected by feminine-appearing male homosexuals. Her manner was appropriately feminine with a slight awkwardness that is typical of middle adolescence.

Details of her medical, physical, and endocrinological characteristics have been reported elsewhere [reference deleted]. To summarize her medical, physical, and endocrinological characteristics, prior to any surgical procedures she appeared as a person with feminine body contours and hair pattern. She had large, well-developed breasts coexisting with the normal external genitalia of a male. An abdominal laparotomy and pelvic and adrenal exploration, performed two years before she was first seen at U.C.L.A., revealed no uterus or ovaries, no evidence of any vestigial female apparatus nor any abnormal tissue mass in the abdomen, retroperitoneal area, or pelvis. Bilateral testicular biopsy showed some atrophy of the testes. A large number of laboratory tests on blood and urine as well as X-ray examinations of the chest and skull were all within normal limits. A buccal smear and skin biopsy revealed a negative (male) chromatin pattern. There was some evidence of a urethral smear showing cellular cornification suggestive of moderately high estrogenic (female hormone) activity.

Agnes was born a boy with normal-appearing male genitals. A birth certificate was issued for a male and she was appropriately named. Until the age of seventeen she was recognized by everyone to be a boy. In the biography furnished to us over many hours of conversations, the male role was both consistently and insistently described as a difficult one and poorly managed. Her accounts exaggerated the evidences of her natural femininity and suppressed evidences of masculinity. Secondary feminine sex characteristics developed at puberty. According to her account, grammar-school years were at least tolerable whereas the three years of high school were stressful in the extreme. At the age of seventeen, at the end of her junior year of high school, she refused to return to complete the senior year. This was in June, 1956. After considerable planning, rehearsals, dieting to "make myself pretty," and similar preparations, she left her home town in August, 1956, for a month's visit with a grandmother in

Midwest City. At the end of the month's visit, according to plan, she left her grandmother's house without leaving word of her whereabouts, and in a downtown hotel changed to feminine attire with the hope of finding a job in that city. For various reasons she felt unable to carry through with the plan of remaining in Midwest City and after phoning her mother returned home on the evening of the change. In the fall of 1956, she entered a hospital in her home town for examinations and the exploratory laparotomy which was done under the supervision of her private physician. During the fall of 1956 and following her hospitalization, she continued her schooling with the help of a tutor that had been provided under her mother's arrangement with the public-school system. She chafed under this as a resented confinement. In December, 1956, the tutor was dismissed and Agnes got a job as a typist in a small factory on the outskirts of town. She continued with this job until August, 1957, when, accompanied by girl-friends, she came to Los Angeles. She lived in Long Beach with a girl-friend and worked in downtown Los Angeles in a small insurance office. In December, 1957, she and her roommate moved into downtown Los Angeles "to be close to our work." In February, 1958, she met her boy-friend Bill, and in April, 1958, to be closer to him, moved to the San Fernando Valley. She quit her job in March, 1958, and was out of work at the time that she moved to the Valley. After a succession of crises with her boyfriend she returned to her home town in April, 1958, to see her previous physician for the purpose of obtaining a letter from him "explaining" Agnes' condition to her boyfriend. This letter was deliberately written by her physician in a general manner so as to mask the actual character of the difficulty. The boyfriend found this only temporarily satisfactory. His increasing insistence upon intercourse and plans for marriage, which Agnes frustrated, produced a series of increasingly severe quarrels. In June, 1958, Agnes disclosed her actual condition to her boyfriend and the affair continued on this basis. In November, 1958, Agnes was seen for the first time at U.C.L.A. Regular conversations at weekly intervals were held until August, 1959. In March, 1959, a castration operation was performed at U.C.L.A. in which the penis and scrotum were skinned, the penis and testes amputated, and the skin of the amputated penis used for a vagina while labia were constructed from the skin of the scrotum.

During this period Agnes was seen regularly by Dr. Robert J. Stoller, psychiatrist and psychoanalyst, Dr. Alexander Rosen, a psychologist, and by me. Approximately thirty-five hours of conversations that I had with her were tape-recorded. My remarks in this paper are based upon transcriptions of these materials and upon materials collected by Stoller and Rosen with whom the work was done collaboratively.

Agnes, the Natural, Normal Female

Agnes had an abiding practical preoccupation with competent female sexuality. The nature of her concerns, as well as the incongruity that such an abiding concern presents to "common sense," permits us to describe, preliminarily at least, the strange features that the population of legitimately sexed persons exhibit as *objective* features from the point of view of persons who are able to take their own normally sexed status for granted. For such members perceived environments of sexed persons are populated with natural males, natural females, and persons who stand in moral contrast with them, i.e., incompetent, criminal, sick, and sinful. *Agnes agreed with normals in her subscription to this definition of a real world of sexed persons, and treated it, as do they, as a matter of objective, institutionalized facts, i.e.,* moral facts.

Agnes vehemently insisted that she was, and was to be treated as, a natural, normal female. The following is a preliminary list of properties of "natural, normally sexed persons" as cultural objects. Intended as an anthropological paraphrasing of members' beliefs, these properties are to be read with the use of the invariable prefix, "From the standpoint of an adult member of our society, . . ." Examples are furnished in the first two properties.

1. From the standpoint of an adult member of our society, the perceived environment of "normally sexed persons" is populated by two sexes and only two sexes, "male" and "female."

2. From the standpoint of an adult member of our society, the population of normal persons is a morally dichotomized population. The question of its existence is decided as a matter of motivated compliance with this population as a legitimate order. It is not decided as a matter of biological, medical, urological, sociological, psychiatric, or psychological fact. The question of its existence is instead decided by consulting both the likelihood that compliance to this legitimate order can be enforced and the conditions that determine this likelihood.

3. The adult member includes himself in this environment and counts himself as one or the other not only as a condition of his self-respect, but as a condition whereby the exercise of his rights to live without excessive risks and interference from others are routinely enforceable.

4. The members of the normal population, for him the *bona fide* members of that population, are essentially, originally, in the first place, always have been and always will be, once and for all, in the final analysis, either "male" or "female."

5. Certain insignia are regarded by normals as essential in their identi-

fying function,* whereas other qualities, actions, relationships, and the like are treated as transient, temporary, accidental, circumstantial, and the rest. For normals the possession of a penis by a male and a vagina by a female are essential insignia. Appropriate feelings, activities, membership obligations, and the like are attributed to persons who possess penises and vaginas. (However, the possession of a penis or a vagina as a biological event is to be distinguished from the possession of one or the other or both as a cultural event. The differences between biological and cultural penises and vaginas as socially employed evidences of "natural sexuality" will be commented on at greater length below.)

6. The recognition of either male or female is made by normals for new members not only at the point of their first appearance, e.g., the neonate, but even before. It extends as well to the entire ancestry and to posterity. The recognition is not changed by the death of the member.†

7. For normals, the presence in the environment of sexed objects has the feature of "a natural matter of fact." This naturalness carries along with it, as a constituent part of its meaning, the sense of its being right and correct, i.e., morally proper that it be that way. Because it is a natural matter of fact, for the members of our society there are only *natural* males and *natural* females. The good society for the member is composed only of persons who are either one sex or the other. Hence the *bona-fide* member of the society, within what he subscribes to as well as what he expects others to subscribe to as committed beliefs about "natural matters of fact" regarding distributions of sexed persons in the society, finds the claims of the sciences like zoology, biology, and psychiatry strange. These sciences argue that decisions about sexuality are problematic matters. The normal finds it strange and difficult to lend credence to "scientific" distributions of *both* male and female characteristics among persons, or a procedure for deciding sexuality which adds up lists of male and female characteristics and takes the excess as the criterion of the member's sex, or the practice of using the first three years of training to decide sexuality, or the provision for the presence in the familiar society of males who have vaginas and females who have penises.

This "common sense" characterization is in no way limited to nonprofessional opinion. For example, a leading member of a prominent department of psychiatry in this country commented after hearing about the case,

* For example, the board of health officer in Midwest City where Agnes was born, when he refused to approve Agnes' application for a change of birth certificate, was supposed to have agreed that "in the final analysis" the capacity to perform the male reproductive function settled Agnes' sex.

† These properties need to be reviewed by considering actual cases that vary them along one or another "parameter" of recognition: deities, for one example; and war combatants whose genitals were destroyed as part of heroic mortal wounds, etc.

"I don't see why one needs to pay that much interest to such cases. She is after all a very rare occurrence. These persons are after all freaks of nature." We could not have solicited a more commonsense formula. A measure of the extent of the member's commitment to the moral order of sexual types would consist of the reluctance to lend credence to a characterization that departed from the "natural facts of life." As we shall see below, in many different ways Agnes taught us as well, though unwittingly, the institutionally motivated character of this reluctance.

I have stressed several times that for the *bona-fide* member "normal" means "in accordance with the mores." Sexuality as a natural fact of life means therefore sexuality as a natural and *moral* fact of life. The member's willingness, therefore, to treat normal sexuality as an object of theoretical interest requires, in deciding for himself the real nature of sexed persons, that he suspend the relevance of his institutionally routinized practical circumstances. We find, however, that the normal member does *not* treat sexuality, his own or others', as a matter of mere theoretic interest, whereas this is in principle the limit of our investigative interest in the phenomenon of normal sexuality as it is in other sciences as well. The normal also treats the sexed character of persons populating his everyday environment as a quality that is "decided by *nature*." This quality, once the member's "nature" decided it, holds thereafter irrespective of time, occasion, circumstance, or considerations of practical advantage. The person's membership as a normally sexed member, male or female, has the characteristic of, and is treated by the normal as, remaining invariant throughout that person's biography and throughout his future lifetime and beyond. His sexual membership remains unchanged through any imputed actual and potential lifetime. To use Parsons' phrasing, it is "invariant to all exigencies."

8. From the standpoint of the normal member, if one examines the population of sexed persons at one time counting the presence of males and females, and at a later time examines the population again, no transfers will have occurred from one sex status to the other except for those transfers that are ceremonially permitted.

Our society prohibits willful or random movements from one sex status to the other. It insists that such transfers be accompanied by the well-known controls that accompany masquerading, play-acting, party behavior, convention behavior, spying, and the like. Such changes are treated both by those making the changes as well as those observing them in others as limited both by the clock as well as by occasions and practical circumstances. The person is expected "after the play" to "stop acting." On the way home from the party the person may be reminded that the party "is over," and that he should conduct himself like the person he "really is." Such admonitions as a "first line of social control" make up commonly encountered sanctions whereby persons are reminded to act in accordance with expected attitudes, appearances, affiliations, dress, style of life, round of life, and the like that are assigned by the major institutions. In our society these consist prominently of occupational and kinship arrangements with their intended obligatory statuses. Their importance is this: that persons are held to compliance with them regardless of their desires, i.e., "whether they like it or not." From the standpoint of the normal, changes of the population's composition can be accomplished by the paths only of birth, death, and migration.

Agnes was all too aware that an alternative path had been traveled, that it was traveled with negligible frequency, and that the transfer was harshly punishable. Like Agnes, the normal knows that there are persons who make the change but he, as did she, counts such persons as freaks, unusual, or bizarre. Characteristically he finds the change itself difficult to "understand" and urges either punishment or medical remedy. Agnes did not depart from this point of view* even though her sex was for her a matter of willful election between available alternatives. This knowledge was accompanied by a burdensome necessity for justifying the election. The election consisted of choosing to live as the normally sexed person that she had always been.

Agnes subscribed to this description of a real world even though there were for her in that world persons, among whom she included herself, who had made the change from one sex to the other. Her early history stood in contrast for her to what she was nevertheless convinced about as to her normal sexuality. In seeking a change of birth certificate, Agnes treated the change as the correction of an original error committed by persons who were ignorant of the "true facts."

Agnes held the conviction that there are not many people who could be told what she had done and who "will really understand." Hence, for Agnes an otherwise important common understanding with others had the troublesome feature that does not occur for normals, particularly where the dichotomy of sex types is concerned; namely, Agnes was unable to exercise the assumption that her circumstances, as they appeared to her, would appear in a more or less identical way to her interactional partners, were they to exchange places. We might refer to this as the existence of a problematic "community of understandings" by and about sexed persons treating each other's sex as known in common and taken for granted by them.

9. In the cultural environments of normally sexed persons, males have

* Nevertheless, further information is needed comparing Agnes with normals with respect to the possibility that normals are more accepting of willful election than she was. For example, several lay persons who were told about her case expressed considerable sympathy. They found as the thing to be sympathetic about that she should have had to have been confronted with the election in the first place.

penises and females have vaginas. From the point of view of a normal member, wherever there are cases of males with vaginas and females with penises there are persons who, though they may be difficult to classify, must nevertheless be in principle classifiable and must be counted as members of one camp or the other. Agnes subscribed to this view too as a natural fact of life, even though this same population included at least one female with a penis, i.e., herself, and following the operation included a female with a man-made vagina. It included others as well that she had learned of through her readings and contacts with physicians both in her home town and in Los Angeles. According to her account all others besides herself were personally unknown to her.

10. That Agnes could insist on her membership in the natural population of sexed persons even though she was, prior to the operation, a female with a penis and, following the operation, a female with a man-made vagina, suggests another important property of a naturally sexed person. When we compare Agnes' beliefs not only with those of normals but with what normals believe about persons whose genitals for one reason or another change in appearance, or suffer damage or loss, through aging, disease, injuries, or surgery, we observe that it is not that normals and Agnes insist upon the possession of a vagina by females (we consider now only the case of the normal female; the identical argument holds for males). They insist upon the possession of *either* a vagina that nature made *or* a vagina that *should have been there all along,* i.e., the *legitimate* possession. The legitimately possessed vagina is the object of interest. *It is the vagina the person is entitled to.* Although "nature" is a preferred and *bona-fide* source of entitlement, surgeons are as well if they repair a natural error, i.e., if they serve as nature's agents to provide "what nature meant to be there." Not *just this* vagina but *just this* vagina as the case of the *real thing.* In the identical way that for a member of a language community a linguistic utterance is a case of a word-in-the-language, or for a game player a move is a move-in-the-game, the genitals that serve the normal member as insignia of normally sexed membership consist of penises-and-vaginas-in-the-moral-order-of-sexed-persons. (I am speaking descriptively. I propose these "essences" as attributions that members find in their environments. To avoid any misunderstandings, I would like to stress that I am talking data. I am not arguing platonic realism as a philosophy of social science.)

Agnes' experiences with a female cousin, sister-in-law, and aunt may illuminate this property. In the course of commenting on what she characterized as her cousin's "jealousy" when a male visitor to her brother's home who had not met either one clearly preferred Agnes to her cousin who was approximately the same age, Agnes commented on her cousin's change in attitude from one in which she was favorable to Agnes before the trip to Midwest City but showed strong disapproval afterward. According to Agnes' comments, Agnes felt that her cousin thought of Agnes as a fake, not a real woman. Agnes said of her cousin that the cousin felt that Agnes was a rival. (The portrayed rivalry was reciprocally felt, for Agnes said that she found it hard to "get her out of my mind.") Similarly for Agnes' sister-in-law, a mild disapproval on the sister-in-law's part prior to the Midwest City trip changed to open hostility upon Agnes' return. Agnes attributed this to the sister-in-law's resentment that Agnes was hardly the person to compare herself to the sister-in-law in affairs of proper domestic and marital conduct. By comparison with these rivals, Agnes commented on the dramatic change on the part of the elderly aunt who accompanied her mother to Los Angeles to care for Agnes during her convalescence from the castration operation. Agnes characterized the aunt as a natural female with no questions about it. The aunt, said Agnes, reflected the attitude of other family members. This attitude, said Agnes, was one of general acceptance prior to the trip to Midwest City, consternation and severe disapproval after the return, and relieved acceptance and treatment of her as a "real female after all" (Agnes' quotation of the aunt's remark) following the operation and during our conversations while the aunt was in Los Angeles. The point: in each case the object of interest was not the possession of the penis or of the man-made vagina, but, in the case of the cousin and sister-in-law, Agnes' penis was *prima facie* contradictory of Agnes' claims, by her other appearances, to possess the real thing. In the case of the aunt, although the vagina was man-made it *was* a case of the real thing since it was what she was now seen to have been entitled to all along. Both the aunt and the mother were strongly impressed by the fact that the operation had been done at all "in this country." That the physicians at the U.C.L.A. Medical Center by their actions reconstructed and validated Agnes' claim to her status as a natural female needs, of course, to be stressed.

Some additional features of Agnes as the natural female require mention.
Not only did Agnes directly express the claim "I have always been a girl," but it was advanced by the device of a remarkably idealized biography in which evidences of her original femininity were exaggerated while evidences of a mixture of characteristics, let alone clear-cut evidences of a male upbringing, were rigorously suppressed. The child Agnes of Agnes' accounts did not like to play rough games like baseball; her *"biggest"* problem was having to play boys' games; Agnes was more or less considered a sissy; Agnes was always the littlest one; Agnes played with dolls and cooked mud patty cakes for her brother; Agnes helped her mother

with the household duties; Agnes doesn't remember what kinds of gifts she received from her father when she was a child. I once asked Agnes if she had lined up with the boys in public school. Her startled and angry reply was, "Lining up with the boys for what!" When I told her I was thinking of lining up in dancing class or lining up for physical examinations at school, Agnes said, "Lining up never came up." I asked her if medical examinations with boys never happened. She agreed, "That's right, they never happened." We came to refer to her presentation of the 120 percent female. Not only in her accounts, but at times in her conversations with me, Agnes was the coy, sexually innocent, fun-loving, passive, receptive, "young thing." As a kind of dialectical counterpart to the 120 percent male who, she said, when we first started to talk, and repeated through eight stressful weeks following the operation when postoperative complications had subsided and the recalcitrant vagina was finally turning out to be the thing the physicians had promised, "wouldn't have been interested in me at all if I was abnormal." The penis that was possessed by the natural female was, repeatedly and under recurrent questioning, an accidental appendage used for the sole purpose of passing urine. The penis of Agnes' accounts had never been erect; she was never curious about it; it was never scrutinized by her or by others; it never entered into games with other children; it never moved "voluntarily"; it was never a source of pleasurable feelings; it had always been an accidental appendage stuck on by a cruel trick of fate. When it was amputated and Agnes was asked now that her penis and scrotum were gone what did she think of the penis and scrotum that were gone, her answer was that she did not feel it was necessary to give it any more thought than one would give to having had a painful wart that had been removed.

Agnes frequently called my attention to her lack of a biography that was appropriate to the fact that she was accepted by others and most particularly by her boyfriend as a girl. Agnes talked of the seventeen-year gap in her life and indicated that her present female character was assigned by others a continuous history as a female that extended to the time of her birth. She pointed out that only since the time that she made the change had she been able to establish a female biography of experiences which she and others could draw on as a precedent in managing present appearances and circumstances. She lacked a proper biography to serve as an historico-prospective context for managing current situations. For others, and most particularly with her boyfriend, an all-along female corresponded to the anticipations that she encouraged with her boyfriend. Two years of accumulating memories presented her a chronic source for a series of crises about which more will be spoken below when I discuss her passing occasions and her management devices.

Another feature of the normal natural female was found in Agnes' portrayal of and insistence upon her lifelong desire to be the thing that she had always known she was. Within her portrayals, her desires came essentially from mysterious and unknown sources, and withstood all vicissitudes posed by an ignorant environment that attempted to force, though unsuccessfully, an arbitrary line of departure from a normal course of development. Agnes stressed repeatedly, "I've always wanted to be a girl; I have always felt like a girl; and I have always been a girl but a mistaken environment forced the other thing on me." On many occasions of our conversations she was asked how she accounted for the desire that withstood environmental exigencies. Her replies invariably elaborated the theme, "There's no explaining it."

Given Agnes' subscription to the normal's distinction between the normal natural male and the normal natural female, there was less ambiguity for Agnes in distinguishing between herself as either a male or a female than there was in distinguishing between herself as a natural female and a male homosexual. The very extensiveness of the exaggerations of her feminine biography, of the masculinity of her boyfriend, of her anaesthetized penis, and the like, furnish the feature continually insisted upon: an identification which is consistently feminine. Much of the instrumental realism that she directed to the management of her chosen sexual status was concerned with so managing her circumstances as to avoid what she treated as a mistaken and degrading identity. Confounding the two were matters of objectively assessable error, ignorance, and injustice on the parts of others. Those of her defenses which cost her dearly in effectiveness and reality orientation were directed to keeping the distance between her natural normal femininity and male homosexuals in repair. Time after time in the course of our meetings when I directed the conversation to homosexuals and transvestites, Agnes had a great deal of difficulty simultaneously managing her fascination for the topic and the great anxiety that the conversation seemed to generate. The picture she would present then was that of a mild depression. Her answers would become impoverished. Occasionally her voice would break as she denied knowledge of this or that. There was a repeated insistence that she was in no way comparable. "I'm not like them," she would continually insist. "In high school I steered clear of boys that acted like sissies . . . anyone with an abnormal problem I would completely shy away from them and go to the point of being insulting just enough to get around them . . . I didn't want to feel noticed talking to them because somebody might relate them to me. I didn't want to be classified with them."

Just as normals frequently will be at a loss to understand "why a person would do that," i.e., engage in homosexual activities or dress as a member of the opposite sex, so did Agnes display the same lack of "understanding" for such behavior, although her accounts characteristically were delivered with flattened affect and never indignation. When she was invited by me to compare herself with homosexuals and transvestites, she found the comparison repulsive. Although she wanted to know more, when I proposed that a transvestite who was being seen by another researcher was interested in talking with her, she refused to have any contact with him. Nor would she consider talking with any of the other patients that I mentioned to her who we were seeing who had experiences similar to hers. When I told her that a group of about seventeen persons in San Francisco who had either received or were planning to have a castration operation were interested in meeting and exchanging experiences with persons with similar problems, Agnes said that she could not imagine what they would have to talk with her about and insisted that she was in no way any concern of theirs.

As we have seen, she insisted that her male genitals were a trick of fate, a personal misfortune, an accident, above all "it was beyond my control," whose presence she never accepted. She treated her genitals as an abnormal growth. Ocassionally she would speak of them as a tumor. With genitals ruled out as essential signs of her femininity, and needing essential and natural signs of female sexuality, she counted instead the lifelong desire to be a female and her prominent breasts. Her self-described feminine feelings, behavior, choices of companions, and the like were never portrayed as matters of decision or choice but were treated as *given* as a natural fact. As they were displayed in her accounts, their natural exercise would have been displayed from the beginning, she insisted, were it not for a misdirecting, frustrating, misunderstanding environment.

Before all she counted her breasts as essential insignia. On several occasions in our conversations she expressed the relief and joy she felt when she noticed at the age of twelve that her breasts were starting to develop. She said that she kept this discovery from her mother and siblings because "it was none of their business." It was clear from her later remarks that she meant by this that she feared that they would regard the development of the breasts as a medical abnormality and because of her age and incompetence might decide, regardless of and contrary to her wishes and to what she felt that she could have enforced upon them, that she receive medical attention and thereby risk their loss. She took particular pride in the size of her breasts, as she did in her measurements. Prior to the operation she was fearful that "the doctors at U.C.L.A." would decide among themselves, and without consulting her, and at the time of the operation, that the remedy for her condition consisted in amputating her breasts instead of her penis and scrotum. Following the operation, because of endocrinological changes and for other reasons, she lost weight. Her breasts became smaller; her chest measurement dropped from 38 to 35. The distress that she showed was sufficiently apparent to have been considered by us as one of the factors making up a short-lived but severe postoperative depression. When the Department of Endocrinology and Urology had finished their medical work, but before the operation, she permitted herself a mild optimism which she kept under heavy check by the continual reminder that the decision was no longer in her hands, and by reminding herself, me, Stoller, and Rosen that on prior occasions, most particularly after examinations in her home town, after permitting herself great optimism, she had been left with "nothing but encouragement. Just words." When she was told to report to the U.C.L.A. Medical Center and that the decision had been made to amputate the penis and make an artificial vagina for her, she spoke of the decision with great relief. She spoke of the medical decision as an authoritative vindication of her claims to her natural femininity. Even the complications following the operation furnished episodes of pleasurable vindication. For example, following the operation she developed a mild urethral drip for which she had been advised by the physician to wear a Kotex pad. When I observed rather pleasantly that this was certainly a new experience for her, she laughed and was obviously pleased and flattered.

There were many occasions when my attentions flattered her with respect to her femininity; for example, holding her arm while I guided her across the street; having lunch with her at the Medical Center; offering to hang up her coat; relieving her of her handbag; holding the automobile door for her while she entered; being solicitous for her comfort before I closed the auto door and took my own seat behind the wheel. At times like this her behavior reminded me that being female for her was like having been given a wonderful gift. It was on such occasions that she most clearly displayed the characteristics of the "120 percent female." At such times she acted like a recent and enthusiastic initiate into the sorority of her heart's desire.

Changing Patterns
of Femininity

Judd Marmor

There is probably no area in Freud's writings more fraught with theoretical and clinical contradictions than his pronouncements concerning
feminine psychophysiology. In what follows, I shall examine these pronouncements in the light of certain developments and changes in the behavioral patterns of twentieth-century women, with some consideration to
the impact of these changes on the institution of Western marriage.

The exact nature of the relationship of primitive man and woman is
shrouded in conjecture (the popular fantasy pictures a masterful caveman
dragging his willing and passively inert mate along the ground by her
hair). We know, however, that since recorded history there has been no
fixed pattern to this relationship. There is evidence to suggest that in most
primitive nomadic communal societies, family descent was reckoned
through the mothers (probably for the obvious reason that maternity, in
contrast to paternity, could not be doubted), and clans were consequently
organized along matrilineal lines. With the evolution of agriculture, and
the gradual development of private property, the transfer of property from
father to son became a paramount socioeconomic factor, and families
began to be organized along patrilineal lines. The risk of false paternity
was protected against by the development of the institution of wifely chas-
tity, and gradually woman began to occupy a more and more subordinate
role as a sexual chattel of man.

However, there has not been a straight line of social evolutionary development in the relationship between the sexes. The social status of
woman has changed at various times both within the same society and in
different societies. Thus, in ancient Greece up to the reign of Cecrops,
families were matrilineal; women enjoyed considerable status and voted
with men in the popular assembly. Yet subsequently, in the Platonic era,
the position of the woman in the family became a degraded and depreciated one, and she was strictly confined to the home, without political or economic rights. There were important social and economic factors involved
in these shifting vicissitudes, but they are beyond the purview of this
chapter.

From Judd Marmor, "Changing Patterns of Femininity: Psychoanalytic Implications," in S. Rosenbaum and S. Alger (eds.), *The Marriage Relationship: Psychoanalytic Perspectives* (New York: Basic Books, 1968), pp. 31–44. References cited in
the original have been deleted.

The Emancipation of Modern Woman

What concerns us more directly here is that in American and European history, up to the end of the eighteenth century, woman's position, for the most part, was distinctly subordinate to that of man. She was totally dependent upon him economically, had no vote and relatively few legal rights, and was denied access to formal education. Early in the nineteenth century, however, in the wake of the egalitarian spirit set into motion by the American and French revolutions and of the sociological changes engendered by the Industrial Revolution, women in England and America began, for the first time in modern history, to assert their prerogatives in relationship to men. Nevertheless, it was almost a hundred years before they obtained the right to vote and began to move toward fuller equality before the law. Even now, in the second half of the twentieth century, there are many states of the Union in which such equivalence does not exist; and the constitutional amendment on equal rights for men and women has repeatedly failed to pass Congress. Despite this, the decades since 1920 have seen remarkable changes in the status of women throughout the world. They are able to vote in most countries where voting franchises exist, to enter many professions previously reserved for men, and to move out of the confines of the home into the broader arena of social, cultural, and political life.

However, even within our lifetime there has been a discernible ebb and flow to this pattern. The "feminine revolt" that was so manifest in the twenties through the forties seems to have given way to the "feminine mystique" of the fifties. Where after World War I women were struggling to get out of the home, the current trend seems to be back to the home. A smaller percentage of college graduates today are women than were thirty years ago, and American women constitute a smaller proportion of the professional world today than they did then. (By contrast, women in some Eastern European countries have more than doubled their representation in professional occupations.)

The reasons for this apparent recession in the revolutionary upsurge of women in America are complex. Some classical Freudians would argue that the entire feminine revolution was essentially a neurotic outbreak of "penis envy" and that what we are now witnessing is a healthy return to "normal" patterns of femininity. Such a statement, however, merely attaches value-laden labels to the phenomenon without really explaining it. Indeed, there are those who claim that the post-World War II popularity of Freudian theory in America has been in itself a potent factor in "pushing" American women back toward a more subordinate and passive role. While this view may have some validity, it seems more likely that certain broad socioeconomic factors have been involved, notably the gradual increase of automation and the pressure from men to push women out of the shrinking labor market except in those areas traditionally reserved for them (domestic work, secretarial and teaching positions, retail selling, and so forth). Friedan suggests that an additional factor may have been the increased awareness of American business and merchandising executives that "women will buy more things if they are kept in the under-used, nameless-yearning, energy-to-get-rid-of-state of being housewives."

Nonetheless, the increased emancipation of women that began in the twenties has left an important imprint on the relationship between the sexes that deserves our further consideration.

Changing Male-Female Relationships

What are some of the changes that have taken place? By and large there has been a considerable relaxation of the social and sexual restrictions placed upon female children born after World War I. Little girls are now allowed to play more vigorously and competitively, with resultant greater muscular strength and athletic capability. During the preadolescent and adolescent years, contacts between the sexes have become freer, and adolescent as well as preadolescent petting occurs with much greater frequency than in previous decades. This increased freedom, both socially and sexually, has led to a higher degree of sophistication and self-confidence in young girls. This, combined with the earlier physiological maturation curves of most girls, tends to give them a considerable degree of relative dominance and mastery over boys of similar age levels, particularly during the adolescent years. Post-World War I mores have also accorded women greater freedom in taking the initiative in reaching out to men both socially and sexually, and as a result much feminine assertiveness that would have been dampened or totally inhibited by the convention of earlier eras has been enabled to flourish. Many other time-hallowed conventions have also changed. For example, it is no longer considered "unfeminine" for women to wear slacks, wear short hair, or smoke cigarettes. Indeed, we are beginning to see evidences that before too long women will also be smoking cigars and pipes without loss of feminine status.

These changing conventions have been reflected in current patterns of marital relationships also. Women have tended to become more dominant in the home, in an interpersonal sense. Discipline, once the exclusive domain of the father, has been increasingly delegated to the mother. Indeed, in many homes it is now father rather than mother to whom the children turn for redress from discipline or as the "soft touch." Similarly, women are playing a more important role in family decision-making. The popular joke that wives make all the minor decisions (those concerning the family), while husbands make all the major ones (those concerning inter-national relations), is a reflection of this shift in family dominance.

Another important indication of this shift in marital equilibrium has been the increasing emphasis upon female orgasm. In the Victorian era, "it was considered unfeminine for a woman to acknowledge or display sexual feelings of any kind, even in the conjugal relationship." Now a sig-nificant proportion of women express their sexual desires quite openly and engage in the sexual act not as passive recipients but as active participants, indeed often taking the initiative in arousing the man. Sexual intercourse now is expected to culminate in orgasm for the woman no less than for the man, and failure to achieve orgasm is generally as disappointing to the woman as it would be to the man.

The changing status of women has had noteworthy reverberations out-side the home also. The percentage of women in the American labor force (excluding the actual war years) has slowly but steadily increased in the past forty years. According to Bureau of Labor statistics for 1962, 24 million, or just over one-third of all working people for that year, were women.

Thirty-six percent of all women were working women. Of these 24 million working women, moreover, less than 25 percent were single, and slightly over 20 percent were widowed, divorced, or separated. The re-maining 56 percent, 13½ million working women, were married and liv-ing with their husbands. These figures indicate that American women are assuming an increasingly important economic role in the family, not merely as the primary spenders of the family income, but also as wage earners. An additional factor in this growing economic importance is the fact that many women outlive their husbands and end up controlling their estates.

Because it is generally easier for Negro women to obtain work than it is for their husbands, the Negro woman in America is often the *only* wage earner in the family, and the Negro family therefore tends to be matri-archal, with the father occupying a depreciated status position. Although these effects are easily recognized in the Negro family, the corresponding, more subtle consequences in the white American family as a result of the economic factors described above are less easily recognizable but no less real.

Women who are not in the labor force also occupy a different psycho-logical position than do men. The man who does not work in our society is apt to be left with a loss of identity and severe impairment of his morale; he generally becomes either depressed or apathetic, or aggressively anti-social. The nonworking wife, however, still retains a meaningful identity as a wife and mother. She is thus able to use her leisure time more construc-tively. Increasing numbers of middle-class wives attend adult-education classes, read books, and participate in various artistic and creative activities. The result is that while many working husbands become progressively narrower in their areas of interest and knowledge, their wives become the chief purveyors of cultural and aesthetic interests in and outside the home. These factors tend also to increase the relative importance of the mother in the family vis-à-vis the father, and their effects upon the identifications formed by children in the family can be of great significance. It is possible, for example, that they play a part in the increasing incidence of homosexuality in modern society; a common thread in the histories of many homosexuals is the identification with the "more cultured and aesthetically oriented mother."

The progressive technological development of society in the coming decades can be expected to have continuing important effects on the relations between the sexes. Not only does the increase in automation mean that women will become more and more able to do "men's jobs," but also the sharp decline in total jobs available is bound to mean an enormous increment in leisure time for both sexes, with profound changes in family relationships.

Psychoanalytic Implications

The classical psychoanalytic position on women as outlined by Freud is too well known to require detailing here. Its salient features, however, can be outlined briefly as follows:

1. *Anatomy is fate.* The basic nature of woman is determined by her anatomy; most importantly by her discovery that she does not possess a penis.

2. *Penis envy.* All female children naturally envy males for having penises, and the desire for a penis is a universal fact of normal feminine psychology, only partially compensated for by giving birth to a male child. Helene Deutsch asserts that penis envy is a natural consequence of the fact that the clitoris actually is "an inferior organ" in terms of its capacity to provide libidinal gratification, as well as for its lack of "the forward thrusting, penetrating qualities of the penis."

3. *Masochism and passivity.* These are outgrowths of normal feminine developments and are natural and essential components of healthy femininity.

4. *Faulty superego development.* Due to the fact that the feminine castration complex (precipitated by the little girl's discovery that she has no penis) pushed the little girl *away* from her mother *into* an Oedipal attachment for her father, the little girl has greater difficulty than the boy in resolving the Oedipal complex. Consequently, she tends to develop a de-

fective superego (because the latter presumably comes into being only as the "heir" of the repressed Oedipal complex). The result in women, according to Freud, is an inadequate sense of justice, a predisposition to envy, weaker social interests, and a lesser capacity for sublimation.

Let us now consider these formulations in the light of contemporary knowledge.

1. *"Anatomy is fate."* That the anatomical differences between the sexes must inevitably be reflected in some personality differences, regardless of variations in cultural patterns, would seem to be almost axiomatic. Differences in body image, in the experience of menstruation at puberty, in the subsequent monthly cyclical variations of endocrine function, and in the experiences of sexual intercourse, pregnancy, childbirth, and menopause are all aspects of bodily sensation and function that are uniquely different for the woman as compared to the man; and in the biological-environmental interaction that leads to personality formation, these *must* result in significant personality variances between the sexes. To deny this, and to argue, as some strongly oriented feminists have done, that personality differences between the sexes have *nothing* to do with biological differences but are *totally* a reflection of cultural factors is to miss the mark no less than do those who have overemphasized the importance of the biological factor. The fact is that only by taking into consideration *both* the biological differences between the sexes *and* the variations in cultural reactions to these differences—that is, the *field situation*—can the personality similarities and dissimilarities between men and women, at any given time and place, be fully understood.

Even as sophisticated an observer as Erik Erikson tends to fall into the error of trying to derive some of woman's psychological characteristics *solely* from her anatomical structure. In his recent, beautifully written "Inner and Outer Space: Reflections on Womanhood," he advances the thesis that women are prone to be more concerned with "inner-space" as compared to men's greater preoccupation with "outer-space," and this is somehow due to "the existence of a *productive inner-bodily space* safely set in the center of female form and carriage." He presents as evidence for this conclusion the fact that in a study of 150 boys and 150 girls, aged ten to twelve, in which they were asked to construct a "scene" with toys on a table, two-thirds of the girls constructed *peaceful interior* scenes, while two-thirds of the boys constructed *aggressive exterior* scenes, or else structures with protruding walls. One need not question the accuracy of Erikson's observations to raise serious doubts concerning his conclusions that these differences derive somehow only from the anatomical differences between the sexes. What about the enormous multitude of acculturation factors—the toys, the games, the adult expectations, and so forth—that have played a part in shaping the fantasies, the perceptions, and the activities of these ten- to twelve-year-old children? Erikson himself notes that in almost one-third of the subjects the girls constructed "male" configurations and the boys constructed "female" configurations. Obviously these were the results of experiential, not anatomical, variations. The point, simply, is that to attempt to derive such differences solely from anatomical or physiological considerations inevitably results in oversimplifications. One must always take into consideration the interaction between these factors and the experiences they encounter in the environment—in time, place, family, and culture.

2. *"Penis envy."* It is, for example, a massive oversimplification to assume, as Freud did, that the lack of a penis must inevitably be considered as a defect by the female child, in all times and cultures. Clara Thompson and others have quite correctly pointed out that the phenomenon of "penis envy" that Freud observed and described in his women patients was not a universal feminine occurrence but was related to the "culturally underprivileged" position that these women occupied. That this is so is confirmed by what has been happening to this phenomenon as the position of Western women has changed in the past four decades. Not only is it manifesting itself with much lesser intensity than it used to, but more and more psychoanalysts report that they do not even always find evidences of it. Meanwhile, another manifestation has begun to make its appearance with increasing frequency, a phenomenon in men which has been variously described as breast envy, womb envy, and woman envy, and which is derived from men's supposed jealousy of women's ability to bear and suckle children. In the past, when such a reaction was encountered in men, it was assumed to be deeply neurotic, but now it is beginning to be described as a more "universal" phenomenon. But how is it possible that a clinical genius like Freud would have failed to recognize such a common aspect of male psychology? The answer, of course, is that it was *not* a frequent occurrence in his time, and has become so only as a consequence of the shifting equilibrium between the sexes. The fact is that womb envy, like penis envy, can only be understood by taking into consideration the total field situation in which it appears. The presence or absence of a penis may be regarded by the developing child as an asset *or* a deficit depending on the nature of the cues that he or she is getting from the environment. When a society places greater value on the birth of a son than on that of a daughter, children in the family become aware of this in a myriad subtle ways; the same is true when little boys are accorded greater freedom of movement and play, and when fathers are accorded greater respect and deference than mothers. In such a society little girls, and later women, will

inevitably manifest many indications of penis envy, while indications of woman envy in men will be relatively rare. On the other hand, when these conditions no longer hold true, or become reversed (as has begun to happen in Western society in recent decades), *then we can expect to find that unconscious manifestations of penis envy will begin to diminish, and those of woman envy will begin to increase.*

A male patient of mine—not a homosexual—grew up as the only boy and youngest child in a family of three children. The father was a relatively weak and incompetent person in contrast to the mother, who was a warm, competent, and dominant individual. The two older sisters were also extremely effective and assertive children. Little wonder that my patient recalled as a child strongly wishing he were a girl, and fantasying that the front of his body was smooth and penis-less just like his sisters'! *For his milieu,* his envy reaction was no less "normal" than the penis envy of the little girl who grows up in a male-centered environment.

In this connection, Helene Deutsch's dismissal of the clitoris as "an inferior organ" in terms of its capability to provide libidinal gratification is a remarkable example of culturally influenced amblyopia, coming as it does from a woman. The actual fact, as Dickinson has pointed out, is that although

> the female organ is minute compared with the male organ . . . the size
> of its nerves . . . and nerve endings . . . compare strikingly with the
> same provision for the male. Indeed . . . the glans of the clitoris is de-
> monstrably richer in nerves than the male glans, for the two stems of
> the dorsalis clitoridis are relatively three to four times as large as the
> equivalent nerves of the penis. . . .

Little wonder that this "inferior organ" enables the orgastically potent female often to have multiple orgasms to every single orgasm of the male!

More recently, in the most definitive article to date on female sexuality in the psychoanalytic literature, Sherfey, leaning heavily on the unprecedented and significant research findings of Masters and Johnson, puts the finishing touch to the myth of clitoral inferiority. Not only is clitoral stimulation capable of producing multiple orgasms to an extent unknown in men (as many as twenty to fifty consecutive orgasms have been recorded within the span of an hour!), but also the average orgastic response in women is generally more prolonged than that of men and just as intense in terms of their muscular capacities.

3. *"Masochism and passivity."* The assumption that normal men are naturally dominant and aggressive, while normal women are naturally submissive and masochistic, is another myth that the changing patterns of relationship between the sexes have begun to dispel. Even the biological evidence has never justified these conclusions. It is well known that among

lower animals the female of the species can be fully as vicious and aggressive as the male, while dominance per se, as biologists have long recognized, is not a simple sex-linked trait but depends on a number of variables, including relative size and strength, motivation, previous experiences, social setting, and so forth.

A variant of this, the effort to justify this myth on the basis of the differences in roles in sexual intercourse, similarly fails to stand up under careful analysis. The common argument advanced here is that in the sexual act it is the male who must be the penetrator, while the woman is merely the recipient, and that the aggressivity of the male and the passivity of the female naturally follow from this. The error here lies in confusing a *behavioral* phenomenon with a *motivational* one. A male can be a passive and submissive penetrator, while a female can be an aggressive and dominant recipient, in the sexual act. Indeed, recent researches indicate that the female genital apparatus during orgasm is extremely active. Receptivity and passivity are not synonymous. It is a striking commentary on the power of a cultural prejudice that both male and female classical Freudians have always assumed that the vagina, as a hollow organ, *had* to be a passive receptacle, although they came to no such conclusions about either the mouth or the anus. "Oral" and "anal" aggression were readily recognized, but the same theoreticians, caught in the meshes of an unconscious common prejudice, were unable to see that, under certain conditions, the vagina too could be an aggressively seeking, grasping, holding, or expulsive organ. The analogy between the mouth and the vagina has, of course, been recognized unconsciously by many males in the symbolism of the "dentate vagina," but most psychoanalysts have tended merely to dismiss this as a neurotic construction, without recognizing the important kernel of truth that it contains.

An additional refutation of the myth of "normal feminine masochism" is that women who are passive and submissive in relation to men are *less* apt to be orgastically potent than those who are more assertive, self-confident, and dominant.

It may be argued by some that one cannot ignore the impact of fantasy on character formation and that the sexual fantasies of men and women are inevitably different: the male adolescent's fantasies deal with penetration; the female's with presumably anxious fears of being penetrated, and deflorated. The experience of periodic menstruation with its bleeding also is supposed to contribute in some way to an inevitable masochistic inclination in women as compared to men. Perhaps. But here too I must caution that the psychological impact of what appear to be simple biological events in men cannot ever be divorced from their sociocultural context. Fantasies of being penetrated *may or may not* be associated with anxiety or masochistic implications. The little girl, relatively early in her life, under conflict-free circumstances, experiences the insertion of objects (or her finger) into her vagina as a pleasurable, not a painful, experience. It is man, not woman, who assumes that to experience such penetration is painful and therefore masochistic. The fact that so many women in our culture are indeed apprehensive about their first sexual experience is not a biological inevitablility but the result of a puritanical culture which in its effort to maintain a completely artificial sexual morality fills little children, and particularly little girls, with fears of sex as something dirty, sinful, and even dangerous. Even the bleeding of menstruation need not necessarily be anxiety-provoking. I have known a number of adolescent girls—and I am sure there are many—who welcomed their first menstrual period with tremendous elation and excitement and could not wait to tell their parents and friends that at last they had achieved the visible evidence of maturity. The fantasies and self-images of men and women are indeed different— and inevitably so, for both biological and cultural reasons—but these differences do not necessarily lead to sex-linked patterns of masochism or sadism.

4. *"Faulty superego development."* Nowhere does the cultural bias inherent in Freud's views about the nature of women become more apparent than in his bland assumption that women have less adequate superegos than men. (One is reminded of Professor Higgins's plaintive cry in *My Fair Lady:* "Why can't women be like men?" Certainly no objective mid-twentieth-century American behavioral scientist would seriously argue any longer that women inherently have a lesser sense of justice, a greater disposition to envy, weaker social interests, or a lesser capacity for sublimation than men. The record of women in England and America in the past four decades on behalf of social justice and human brotherhood compares more than favorably with that of men.

It is important to note, however, that Freud's views on women were not merely an outgrowth of his position as a nineteenth-century middle European male; they flowed quite logically from his theory about superego development. If they were in error, as they obviously were, his theory of superego development must also be fallacious. It simply cannot be that the development of the superego results only from the resolution of the Oedipus complex, as classical psychoanalytic theory has long held. This is not the place to enter into a detailed dissertation on how the personality phenomenon that Freud designated as superego comes into being, but suffice it to say that it is obviously an acculturation phenomenon that develops from the child's gradual incorporation of the do's and don't's from its environment—beginning from the time the child is first able to comprehend the significance of such interdictions. The impact of this acculturation process is felt by girls as fully and as early as it is by boys. Indeed, the evidence is that since, culturally, little girls are expected to be better behaved than little boys, the pressure of this process is *greater* upon girls than upon boys. As a result, as might be anticipated, females in our culture, at least in their early years, are apt to show evidence of *better* superego development than do males—the very reverse of Freud's theoretical assumption.

The Problem of Gender Role

Actually, much of what we have been talking about in this essay revolves around the problem of what modern social psychologists would call "gender role"—that is, what is considered "masculine" or "feminine" behavior. The fact is that gender-role patterns have varied widely in different times and in different cultures. As Opler has put it:

> A Navajo Indian may be a he-man, a gambler, and a philanderer while dressing in bright blouses adorned with jeweled belts, necklaces, and bracelets. French courtiers in the retinues of effete monarchs were equally philanderers, though rouged, powdered, and bedecked with fine lace. The Andaman Islanders like to have the man sit on his wife's lap in fond greetings, and friends and relatives, of the same or opposite sex, greet one another in the same manner after absences, crying in the affected manner of the mid-Victorian woman. Like the Ute, they value premarital sexual experimentation and sexual prowess and technique in any later life period. Obviously, the style of social and sexual behavior is something of an amalgam and is culturally influenced.

Gender role and gender identity, although generally related to the biological sex of a child, actually are not shaped by biological factors but by cultural ones. Once the child's biological ascription is settled, a myriad of culturally defined cues begin to be presented to the developing infant which are designed to shape its gender identity to its assigned sex. Little girls are handled more gently than little boys, are given different toys to play with, are expected to be quieter and cleaner, are spoken to in different tones, and are addressed in different terms. The little girl who wheedles is spoken of fondly as a "charmer" and a "coquette"; the little boy is told to stop being a baby and to act like a man. The little girl's clothes and hairdos are noticed, complimented, and fussed over. Not so the little boy's; he is more apt to be praised for his agility and courage. The girl is expected to help with "inside" chores (cleaning up, doing dishes); the boy, with "outside" ones (shoveling snow, mowing the lawn). So powerful are these acculturation processes that, as the Hampsons have demonstrated, in certain cases of pseudo-hermaphroditism in which the child's biological sex is mistaken for that of the opposite sex, the incorrect gender identity becomes so powerfully established by the age of two or three that it becomes psychologically destructive to the child to try to change it.

What is important to our present thesis, however, is not that this acculturation occurs, but that, as we have seen, its *content* can and does change. What we have been observing in recent decades is a gradual change in certain female gender-role patterns that have previously been traditional in Western culture.

The implications of these changing patterns extend beyond psychoanalytic theory to psychoanalytic therapy. Erich Fromm once observed that a psychoanalyst's value system would profoundly affect how he would treat a female patient who presented the problem of Nora in Ibsen's *Doll House*. If he held to classical psychoanalytical views concerning femininity, he would focus his interpretations upon her "penis envy" and her rejection of the "normal" feminine goals of wifehood and motherhood. On the other hand, if he were a feminist, he would, instead, focus upon her "healthy" rebellion against her husband's infantilization of her and would encourage her move out of the home as a laudable effort at self-realization. Still another alternative to these two extremes exists, however. One need not assume that motherhood and a fulfilling life in the outside world are incompatible, any more than fatherhood and such a life. In contrast to men, however, who are *expected* to combine these two aspects of life, women have alternatives now; they may or may not choose to combine them, and the choice is theirs. The task of the analyst is to help them make this choice, freely, without guilt, and in relationship to the realities of their specific life situations.

A Cognitive-Developmental Analysis of Sex-Role Concepts

Lawrence Kohlberg

Oddly enough, our approach to the problems of sexual development starts directly with neither biology nor culture, but with cognition. In this chapter we shall elaborate and document a theory which assumes that

Abridged from Lawrence Kohlberg, "A Cognitive-Developmental Analysis of Children's Sex-Role Concepts and Attitudes," in Eleanor E. Maccoby (ed.), *The Development of Sex Differences* (Stanford: Stanford Univ. Press, 1966), pp. 82–98. References cited in the original have been deleted.

basic sexual attitudes are not patterned directly by either biological instincts or arbitrary cultural norms, but by the child's cognitive organization
of his social world along sex-role dimensions. Recent research evidence
suggests that there are important "natural" components involved in the
patterning of children's sex-role attitudes, since many aspects of sex-role
attitudes appear to be universal across cultures and family structures, and
to originate relatively early in the child's development. This patterning of
sex-role attitudes is essentially "cognitive" in that it is rooted in the child's
concepts of physical things—the bodies of himself and of others—concepts
which he relates in turn to a social order that makes functional use of sex
categories in quite culturally universal ways. It is not the child's biological
instincts, but rather his cognitive organization of social-role concepts
around universal physical dimensions, which accounts for the existence of
universals in sex-role attitudes.

While we are talking about cognitive organization, and universals common to all children in sexual cognitions, we must take into account the fact
that basic modes of cognitive organization change with age. As Piaget and
his followers have documented in depth and detail, the child's basic cognitive organization of the physical world undergoes radical transformations
with age development. So, too, do the child's conceptions of his social
world. We shall review research findings which suggest that not only do
young children's sex-role attitudes have universal aspects, but also that
these attitudes change radically with age development. These age changes
do not seem to be the result of age-graded sex-role socialization, but rather to be "natural" changes resulting from general trends of cognitive-social
development. There is little reason to accept Freud's and Gesell and Ilg's
view that these age changes are directly related to the maturation of the
body or of body instincts. Instead, we shall review evidence suggesting
that these trends are the result of general experience-linked changes in
modes of cognition. Sex-role concepts and attitudes change with age in
universal ways because of universal age changes in basic modes of cognitive organization. Increasing evidence from studies in the Piaget tradition
suggests culturally universal developmental shifts in conceptualizations of
physical objects. Because children's sex-role concepts are essentially defined in universal physical, or body, terms, these concepts, too, undergo
universal developmental changes. As an example, recent research indicates that children develop a conception of themselves as having an un-
changeable sexual identity at the same age and through the same processes
that they develop conceptions of the invariable identity of physical objects.

The basic claim of theories of sexual instinct like Freud's libido theory
is that the basic patterning of sexual attitudes is instinctual and "natural"
in its origins, but that the expressions of these patterns are eventually

channeled, distorted, or influenced by cultural forces. In contrast, social-learning theories of sex-role development, such as Walter Mischel's in this volume, see the patterning of sexual attitudes as a reflection of the patterning, or sex-typing, of the culture.

In contrast to either of these views, we see the child's social and sexual attitudes neither as direct reflections of cultural patterns nor as direct reflections of innate structures. Both research results and clinical observation indicate that much of the young child's thinking about sex roles is radically different from the adult's. His physical concepts of anatomical differences, birth, sexual relations, etc., are quite different, as are his concepts of the social attributes and values of males and females. Following Piaget's argument concerning physical concepts, we shall contend that these differences are due not to ignorance or inadequate teaching patterns, but to qualitative differences between the structure of the child's thought and the adult's. The child's sex-role concepts are the result of the child's active structuring of his own experience; they are not passive products of social training.

It appears to us that this interactional point of view best fits the clinical data on sexual psychopathology and its relationship to early experience. Ever since Freud's classic statement, it has been recognized that sexual abnormalities are incomprehensible if one assumes that there is a single innate or "normal" pattern of sexuality. As David Hamburg's chapter in this volume indicates, there is clear evidence that hormonal and genetic factors influence the level of sexual arousal, but there is no clear evidence that these factors determine the patterning of sexuality, i.e., its aims and objects. Money and Hampson find that hermaphrodites who are chromosomally and hormonally of one sex lead normal sex lives patterned in terms of the opposite sex if they have been reared as a member of that sex.

At first, this and other evidence seems to support the social-learning assumption that basic sexual attitudes are directly patterned by cultural expectations and reinforcement. However, it is extremely difficult to account for recurrent forms of adult sexual psychopathology in terms of the general mechanisms of social reinforcement or modeling, since abnormal sex-role behaviors are obviously highly resistant to both cultural expectations and social reinforcement. It was this double-edged problem of sexual psychopathology that led Freud to postulate that there are innate "abnormal" or deviant instinctual sexual patterns which unfold in early childhood, and which can be fixated through childhood experience. On the one hand, therefore, it is clear that human sexual behavior is not the product of a strict and fixed instinct, or there would be no sexual psychopathology. On the other hand, it is just as clear that sexual behavior is not simply culturally patterned, or there would be no recurrent and resistant forms of sexual psychopathology in cultures and families that strongly disapprove of them.

Freud's notions of definite and instinctively patterned sexual stages have not stood up well in the face of direct psychological observations of children, although such observations clearly suggest infantile sexual interests, concerns, and pleasures in various body zones. However, in modified forms the notion that an experience at a critical period in the unfolding of instinctive patterns can affect subsequent attitudes and behaviors has received considerable support from animal and clinical research. In ground-nesting birds, early exposure to a moving object leads to imprinting, not only of following responses but of later sexual ones. Money, Hampson, and Hampson report critical-period phenomena which suggest that there is something like sexual imprinting in humans. They suggest that the development of normal adult sexual behavior is contingent on having been socially assigned to a given sex before the age of three or four. Hermaphrodites assigned at birth to one sex because of external genital characteristics have sometimes been reassigned later to the other sex, so that their social sex identity will be more consistent with their internal sex characteristics. Money and Hampson report that if this is done before age three to four, the child's later sexual adjustment is normal. If it is done after this age, real maladjustment seems to result. Money and Hampson use the term imprinting to describe this critical-age-period phenomenon in sex-role attitudes, since it is obviously not the result of the usual social reinforcement mechanisms, which are in principle reversible. The critical-period phenomena described by Money and Hampson are, however, obviously not genuine imprinting phenomena. As observed in birds, imprinting takes place at a very early period through exposure to a definite object. In contrast, the "imprinting" described by Money and Hampson occurs throughout the first three or four years, and is not the result of exposure to a definite object. Instead it is the fixation of an "abstract" self-concept or identity. Rearing a person as a member of one sex rather than the other does not mean that there will be a difference in exposure to parents or other love objects; there will be, however, a difference in labeling of the self. Such labeling is perhaps irreversible because basic cognitive categorizations are irreversible. After a certain point, social reinforcement cannot readily reverse or change basic categorizations of constancies in the child's physical world, though such reinforcement can readily change categorizations at earlier cognitive stages before constancies are stabilized. In a similar way the child aged two to four is very uncertain of the constancy of his sexual identity, and the label "boy" is for him as arbitrary as the label "Johnny." Once his sexual identity has been cognitively stabilized in the Money and Hampson "critical period," it must become extremely difficult to change it by social sex-role reassignment.

In general, then, our theory accepts the notion that there are important linkages between childhood experiences and adult psychopathology. It does so without postulating either biologically based critical periods or biologically patterned childhood sexual instincts. Instead, these linkages are explained in terms of the cognitive distortions characteristic of childhood sexual concepts, distortions which may become "fixated" by certain interpersonal experiences that stabilize distorted conceptions of body interactions and body feelings.

Our stress upon the cognitive basis of sex-role attitudes and their development does not mean that we are shifting our attention away from the motivational and emotional aspects of sex-role attitudes. We shall argue, however, that motivational aspects of sex-role development are best understood in terms of a theory of the self and of identification that rests on general competence, effectance, and self-regard motives, rather than upon infantile sexual drives or attachment and dependency motivations unique to the early parent-child relationship. The child's sexual identity is maintained by a motivated adaptation to physical-social reality and by the need to preserve a stable and positive self-image. We shall argue that motives to love and identify with parental models in the critical childhood years derive primarily from the child's adaptation to this reality and from his self-maintaining motives, rather than from fixed instincts or primary drives. Accordingly, sexual identifications with parents are primarily derivatives of the child's basic sexual identity and his self-maintaining motives— not the reverse, which is what psychoanalysis and social-learning theories have held. Our chapter, then, will start with fundamental concepts and findings on the development of the child's basic sex-role concepts and sex-role identity, and will move on to a consideration of how this identity determines the development of parent identifications.

Sex-Role Identity as a Product of Cognitive Growth

The Money and Hampson data suggest to us the following points: (1) Gender identity, i.e., cognitive self-categorization as "boy" or "girl," is the critical and basic organizer of sex-role attitudes. (2) This "gender identity" results from a basic, simple cognitive judgment made early in development. Once made, this categorization is relatively irreversible and is maintained by basic physical-reality judgments, regardless of the vicissitudes of social reinforcements, parent identifications, etc. Claiming that a simple gender self-categorization organizes sex-role attitudes, we can postulate the following: (3) Basic self-categorizations determine basic valuings. Once the boy has stably categorized himself as male, he then values positively those objects and acts consistent with his gender identity. This assumption that there are tendencies toward cognitive consistency which lead to the formation of values consistent with self-conceptual cognitive judgments has been elaborated and documented by "clinical" self-theorists (Rogers, Lecky, Kelly) and by "experimental" cognitive-balance theorists (Festinger, Osgood and Tannenbaum, Newcomb, Rosenberg).

Our view of the importance of gender identity in psychosexual development is not shared by many social-learning theorists, including Walter Mischel. In Mischel's view, sex-typed behavior and attitudes are acquired through social rewards that follow sex-appropriate responses made by the child or by a relevant model. The social-learning syllogism is: "I want rewards, I am rewarded for doing boy things, therefore I want to be a boy." In contrast, a cognitive theory assumes this sequence: "I am a boy, therefore I want to do boy things, therefore the opportunity to do boy things (and to gain approval for doing them) is rewarding."

The Money and Hampson "critical period" data suggest that by age five children have a stable gender identity which determines the value—rather than being primarily instrumental in the achievement—of many social rewards. . . .

Gender identity is perhaps the most stable of all social identities. If an American adult is asked what social class he belongs to, he is very often "objectively" incorrect; and if he is asked whether he is a Jew or a German or a Catholic or a Californian, he may be uncertain and engage in a long discussion of the criteria for being placed in these categories. The only category of social identity that is as basic and clear as gender is age, but age, unlike gender, continually changes. As we know, children lie to themselves and others in order to appear older, and middle-aged women lie to themselves and others in order to appear younger.

Even though the psychology of adult personality may take gender identity for granted, the genesis of this identity is still of great interest for developmental psychology. We have pointed out that adult gender identity is a basic cognitive reality judgment, and not a derivative of social rewards, parent identifications, or sexual identifications. At the same time, however, this gender identity had to develop. As we shall now attempt to demonstrate, the reality judgment "I really am and always will be a boy (or girl)" is the result of a cognitive development which is quite independent of variations in social sex-role training, and which is central to the development of other aspects of sex-role attitudes.

Obviously, this process begins with the child's hearing and learning the verbal labels "boy" and "girl." The child's verbal learning of his own gender label occurs quite early, usually sometime late in the second year of life. Gesell et al. report that two-thirds to three-fourths of 3-year-olds answered correctly the question "Are you a little girl or a little boy?" while the majority of 2½-year-olds did not answer it correctly. At this early age, however, correct self-labeling does not imply correct self-classification in a general physical category. The label "boy" may be a name just like the name "Johnny." The child may recognize that there are other boys in the world, just as there may be other Johnnies, but this recognition need not imply a basic criterion for determining who is a boy any more than it does for determining who is a Johnny; nor does it necessarily imply that everyone in the world is either a boy or a girl, or a Johnny or a non-Johnny. In the second year, the child learns that "boy" is a name which may be applied to others, and he may even experience a vague pleasurable "identification" in such common labeling. But this extension of the label does not imply the ability to make categorizations. A 2½-year-old boy, Tommy, observed by the writer, would go around the family circle saying, "I'm boy," "Daddy boy," "Mommy boy," "Joey (brother) boy." After correction he eliminated his mother from the list, but did not label people outside the family correctly.

In the third year of life then, the child seems to know his own sex label, and to generalize it unsystematically to others on the basis of a loose cluster of physical characteristics. Rabban reports that about two-thirds of a group of sixty middle-class and working-class children aged thirty to forty-one months (with an average age of three years) were able to reply correctly to the questions "Which doll looks most like you?" and "Is it (the doll) a boy or a girl?" Such generalization of a correct self-label to a doll did not, however, imply generally correct discrimination of the sex of the doll. Rabban reports that only about half of his three-year-old group was able to label correctly six dolls (father, mother, two boys, two girls) as "boy" or "girl." By age four almost all of Rabban's children labeled themselves and the dolls correctly. By four, children tend to label gender by some general physical criteria, primarily clothing and hair-style.

The findings discussed so far merely suggest that children learn gender self-labeling early (age two to three), and in the next two years learn to label others correctly according to conventional cues. Obviously there is more to the development of a stable gender identity than this. Investigations of this "more" have started from two points of view: the psychoanalytic and the cognitive-developmental. Both recognize that the young child's use of gender concepts is confused, and that correct and stable gender identification depends upon the child's ability to classify a physical object, the body. Both agree that the development of a stable gender identification is an important psychosexual developmental task, but disagree about how this development takes place: the psychoanalytic view stresses the interaction between the child's wishes and the adult's provision or denial of anatomical information in this development, whereas the cognitive-developmental view holds that the child's difficulties in establishing gender definition closely parallel his difficulties in establishing stable definitions of physical concepts in general, and that the former are resolved as the latter are. While both theories point to a number of important developments in gender-identity concepts, the central focus of both is upon the constancy of gender identity. The child's gender identity can provide a stable organizer of the child's psychosexual attitudes only when he is categorically certain of its unchangeability.

The fact that the young child is not certain of the constancy of gender identity before the age of five to six has been demonstrated by Kohlberg. In the course of this study, children of four to eight were asked whether a pictured girl could be a boy if she wanted to, or if she played boy games, or if she wore a boy's haircut or clothes. Most four-year-olds said that she could be a boy if she wanted to, or if she wore the appropriate haircut or clothes. By age six to seven, most children were quite certain that a girl could not be a boy regardless of changes in appearance or behavior. These findings correspond to more anecdotal observations. The following comments were made by Jimmy, just turning four, to his 4½-year-old friend Johnny:

> *Johnny:* I'm going to be an airplane builder when I grow up.
> *Jimmy:* When I grow up, I'll be a Mommy.
> *Johnny:* No, you can't be a Mommy. You have to be a Daddy.
> *Jimmy:* No, I'm going to be a Mommy.
> *Johnny:* No, you're not a girl, you can't be a Mommy.
> *Jimmy:* Yes, I can.

Among other difficulties, it would seem that Jimmy does not recognize that the category "male" applies to both boys and fathers, and that while age changes occur, gender changes do not. As another example, Philip (aged three years, ten months) told his mother, "When you grow up to be a Daddy, you can have a bicycle, too (like his father)."

Rabban found that the majority of his three-year-olds did not correctly use generalized sex labels, and did not reply correctly to the question "When you grow up, would you like to be a mamma or a daddy?" In contrast, 97 percent of his five-year-olds replied correctly. In light of findings discussed later, it is likely that the change in responses to questions of desired future identity primarily reflects cognitive stabilization of sex-role categories rather than changes in role preference.

From the cognitive-developmental point of view, the stabilization of gender-identity concepts is only one aspect of the general stabilization of constancies of physical objects that takes place between the years three and seven. The development of such conceptual constancies has been discussed by Piaget in terms of the conservation of physical-object properties under apparent changes. Piaget and his followers have demonstrated that children below the age of six to seven do not view physical objects as retaining an invariable mass, number, weight, length, etc., when the perceptual configuration in which the objects appear varies. While Piaget has only considered and studied conceptual constancies involving conservation of an object's quantity along some dimension, it appears that qualitative constancies of category or generic identity develop in the same period and in parallel fashion. Thus a majority of four-year-old children said that a pictured cat could be a dog if it wanted to, or if its whiskers were cut off. By age six to seven, most children were firm in asserting that a cat would not change its identity in spite of apparent perceptual changes. Similar results have been found by DeVries, using a live cat that is covered by a dog mask within the child's view.

The results of Kohlberg and DeVries's developmental studies of constancy of species and gender identity can be questioned from two points of view. One is the commonsense point of view, which would question purely verbal evidence that young children do not believe in constancy of identity. The other is the psychoanalytic view, which sees the young child's unrealistic thoughts about sexual constancy as largely a product of his wishes and fears. In contrast, the Piaget view assumes, first, that there is a parallelism or correspondence between the cognitive-verbal and affective aspects of the development of reality orientations, and, second, that cognitive-structural changes, rather than affective changes, are the primary sources of development in reality orientations.

In Piaget's view, the infant is from the start motivationally oriented toward contacting, maintaining, and mastering objects rather than toward pure tension discharge. The child's gradual increase in reality orientation, his increased awareness of the constancy of the existence and identity of external objects, is the result of increased cognitive differentiation of the self and the world rather than the result of basic qualitative changes in motivational processes. Like Piaget, Freud also stressed the importance of the child's spontaneous processes in determining his basic reactions to the "reality," and viewed infantile and adult thought processes as structurally or qualitatively different from one another (primary and secondary processes). However, Freud stresses motivational changes as basic to the development of different modes of thought. Infantile thought has the structure of fantasy; it is governed by the pleasure principle and the desire for immediate gratification. Mature thought is governed by the reality principle, by the delay of gratification, and by stable attachments to external objects. In more mundane terms, psychoanalysis holds that the young child's unrealistic thoughts about sexual identity are the result of his wishes and fears. Where emotional preoccupations are strong, fantasy thought predominates over secondary-process thought.

An example suggesting this psychoanalytic interpretation of gender identity is a spontaneous response made by Jimmy, a boy just turned five: "I can be a girl, you know. I can. I can wear a wig and have my throat so I can talk like a girl." It would seem plausible to attribute the immature logic of this statement to the fact that the boy's wishes and conflicts in this area were strong enough to override his interests in being realistic or correct. On another occasion, however, the writer (experimenter) had the following conversation with Jimmy:

> *Experimenter:* Do airplanes get small when they fly away in the sky?
> *Jimmy:* Yes, they get real tiny.
> *Experimenter:* Do they really get small, or do they just look small?
> *Jimmy:* They really get small.
> *Experimenter:* What happens to the people inside?
> *Jimmy:* They shrink.
> *Experimenter:* How can they shrink and get small?
> *Jimmy:* They cut their heads off.

These statements might also be taken as motivationally determined, rather than as a reflection of Jimmy's general level of thinking. Obviously, in the second conversation, Jimmy doesn't care about being correct, and ends up making a "fantasy" response. Sometimes Jimmy may care too much (sex-role), sometimes too little (airplane query), but if his general level of thinking is the same, it is hard to maintain that this level is a product of affective rather than cognitive-structural factors.

In order to compare the cognitive-structural and the affective interpretations of gender-identity beliefs in young children, the Kohlberg study asked the correlational question: "To what extent is level of development of belief in constancy consistent from physical and emotionally neutral types of constancies to social and emotionally charged constancies?"

In addition to the gender-identity task, children aged four to six were given three other conservation tasks: constancy of the species identity of the cat, conservation of mass of a piece of clay under various shape changes, and conservation of length of a piece of gum. The age norms for the gender-identity and species-identity tasks were found to be similar, with constancy on both slightly preceding constancy on conservation of quantitative dimensions of the classical Piaget type. Not only was the age development of the various constancy tasks parallel, but the gender-identity task was found to correlate quite highly ($r = .52$ to $.73$) with the other tasks among children of a given age. Even with mental age partialed out, correlations of gender identity with the other conservation tasks were substantial ($r = .36$ to $.64$). This evidence of consistency clearly indicates the importance of general cognitive-structural features in the child's beliefs about gender identity.

In addition to affective factors, psychoanalytic theory holds that the adult's withholding of anatomical information plays an important role in the child's uncertainties about the constancy of gender identity. In fact, however, the Kohlberg study suggests that young children revealing early exposure to parental anatomical "enlightenment" were no more advanced in sex-role constancy than children who did not reveal such enlightenment. The children of four to seven who indicated anatomical awareness in explaining "how you could tell boys from girls when they had clothes on" and "when they had clothes off" were not more advanced in sex-role constancy than were those who did not indicate such anatomical awareness. In general, even the enlightened younger child does not use genital differences as the basic criterion for sex classification. The writer has recorded questions from enlightened children in their third and fourth year who wanted to know whether they would still be boys if they did not have a penis. These questions indicate that awareness of genital differences does not directly lead to their use as the primary criterion of gender categorization or of gender constancy.

The major implication of the Kohlberg study is that the process of forming a constant gender identity is not a unique process determined by instinctual wishes and identifications, but a part of the general process of conceptual growth. . . .

The Homosexual Role | Mary McIntosh

Recent advances in the sociology of deviant behavior have not yet affected the study of homosexuality, which is still commonly seen as a condition characterizing certain persons in the way that birthplace or deformity might characterize them. The limitations of this view can best be understood if we examine some of its implications. In the first place, if homosexuality is a condition, then people either have it or do not have it. Many scientists and ordinary people assume that there are two kinds of people in the world: homosexuals and heterosexuals. Some of them recognize that homosexual feelings and behavior are not confined to the persons they would like to call "homosexuals" and that some of these persons do not actually engage in homosexual behavior. This should pose a crucial problem; but they evade

From Mary McIntosh, "The Homosexual Role," *Social Problems*, Fall 1968 (Vol. 16, no. 2), pp. 182–192. References cited in the original have been deleted.

the crux by retaining their assumption and puzzling over the question of how to tell whether someone is "really" homosexual or not. Lay people too will discuss whether a certain person is "queer" in much the same way as they might question whether a certain pain indicated cancer. And in much the same way they will often turn to scientists or medical men for a surer diagnosis. The scientists, for their part, feel it incumbent on them to seek criteria for diagnosis.

Thus one psychiatrist, discussing the definition of homosexuality, has written:

> . . . I do not diagnose patients as homosexual unless they have engaged in overt homosexual behavior. Those who also engage in heterosexual activities are diagnosed as bisexual. An isolated experience may not warrant the diagnosis, but repetitive homosexual behavior in adulthood, whether sporadic or continuous, designates a homosexual.

Along with many other writers, he introduces the notion of a third type of person, the "bisexual," to handle the fact that behavior patterns cannot be conveniently dichotomized into heterosexual and homosexual. But this does not solve the conceptual problem, since bisexuality too is seen as a condition (unless as a passing response to unusual situations such as confinement in a one-sex prison). In any case there is no extended discussion of bisexuality; the topic is usually given a brief mention in order to clear the ground for the consideration of "true homosexuality."

To cover the cases where the symptoms of behavior or of felt attractions do not match the diagnosis, other writers have referred to an adolescent homosexual phase or have used such terms as "latent homosexual" or "pseudo homosexual." Indeed one of the earliest studies of the subject, by Krafft-Ebing, was concerned with making a distinction between the "invert" who is congenitally homosexual and others who, although they behave in the same way, are not true inverts.

A second result of the conceptualization of homosexuality as a condition is that the major research task has been seen as the study of its etiology. There has been much debate as to whether the condition is innate or acquired. The first step in such research has commonly been to find a sample of "homosexuals" in the same way that a medical researcher might find a sample of diabetics if he wanted to study that disease. Yet, after a long history of such studies, the results are sadly inconclusive and the answer is still as much a matter of opinion as it was when Havelock Ellis published *Sexual Inversion* seventy years ago. The failure of research to answer the question has not been due to lack of scientific rigor or to any inadequacy of the available evidence; it results rather from the fact that the wrong question has been asked. One might as well try to trace the etiology of "committee chairmanship" or "Seventh Day Adventism" as of "homosexuality."

The vantage point of comparative sociology enables us to see that the conception of homosexuality as a condition is, in itself, a possible object of study. This conception and the behavior it supports operate as a form of social control in a society in which homosexuality is condemned. Furthermore, the uncritical acceptance of the conception by social scientists can be traced to their concern with homosexuality as a social problem. They have tended to accept the popular definition of what the problem is and they have been implicated in the process of social control.

The practice of the social labeling of persons as deviant operates in two ways as a mechanism of social control. In the first place it helps to provide a clear-cut, publicized, and recognizable threshold between permissible and impermissible behavior. This means that people cannot so easily drift into deviant behavior. Their first moves in a deviant direction immediately raise the question of a total move into a deviant role with all the sanctions that this is likely to elicit. Secondly, the labeling serves to segregate the deviants from others and this means that their deviant practices and their self-justifications for these practices are contained within a relatively narrow group. The creation of a specialized, despised, and punished role of homosexual keeps the bulk of society pure in rather the same way that the similar treatment of some kinds of criminals helps keep the rest of society law-abiding.

However, the disadvantage of this practice as a technique of social control is that there may be a tendency for people to become fixed in their deviance once they become labeled. This, too, is a process that has become well recognized in discussions of other forms of deviant behavior such as juvenile delinquency and drug taking and, indeed, of other kinds of social labeling such as streaming in schools and racial distinctions. One might expect social categorizations of this sort to be to some extent self-fulfilling prophecies: if the culture defines people as falling into distinct types—black and white, criminal and noncriminal, homosexual and normal—then these types will tend to become polarized, highly differentiated from each other. Later in this paper I shall discuss whether this is so in the case of homosexuals and "normals" in the United States today.

It is interesting to notice that homosexuals themselves welcome and support the notion that homosexuality is a condition. For just as the rigid categorization deters people from drifting into deviancy, so it appears to foreclose on the possibility of drifting back into normality and thus removes the element of anxious choice. It appears to justify the deviant behavior of the homosexual as being appropriate for him as a member of the homosexual category. The deviancy can thus be seen as legitimate for him and he can continue in it without rejecting the norms of the society.

The way in which people become labeled as homosexual can now be seen as an important social process connected with mechanisms of social control. It is important, therefore, that sociologists should examine this process objectively and not lend themselves to participation in it, particularly since, as we have seen, psychologists and psychiatrists on the whole have not retained their objectivity but become involved as diagnostic agents in the process of social labeling.

It is proposed that the homosexual should be seen as playing a social role rather than as having a condition. The role of "homosexual," however, does not simply describe a sexual behavior pattern. If it did, the idea of a role would be no more useful than that of a condition. For the purpose of introducing the term "role" is to enable us to handle the fact that behavior in this sphere does not match popular beliefs: that sexual behavior patterns cannot be dichotomized in the way that the social roles of homosexual and heterosexual can.

It may seem rather odd to distinguish in this way between role and behavior, but if we accept a definition of role in terms of expectations (which may or may not be fulfilled), then the distinction is both legitimate and useful. In modern societies where a separate homosexual role is recognized, the expectation, on behalf of those who play the role and of others, is that a homosexual will be exclusively or very predominantly homosexual in his feelings and behavior. In addition, there are other expectations that frequently exist, especially on the part of nonhomosexuals, but affecting the self-conception of anyone who sees himself as homosexual. These are: the expectation that he will be effeminate in manner, personality, or preferred sexual activity; the expectation that sexuality will play a part of some kind in all his relations with other men; and the expectation that he will be attracted to boys and very young men and probably willing to seduce them. The existence of a social expectation, of course, commonly helps to produce its own fulfillment. But the question of how far it is fulfilled is a matter for empirical investigation rather than *a priori* pronouncement. Some of the empirical evidence about the chief expectation— that homosexuality precludes heterosexuality—in relation to the homosexual role in America is examined in the final section of this paper.

In order to clarify the nature of the role and demonstrate that it exists only in certain societies, we shall present the cross-cultural and historical evidence available. This raises awkward problems of method because the material has hitherto usually been collected and analyzed in terms of culturally specific modern Western conceptions.

The Homosexual Role in Various Societies

To study homosexuality in the past or in other societies we usually have to rely on secondary evidence rather than on direct observation. The reliability and the validity of such evidence is open to question because what the original observers reported may have been distorted by their disapproval of homosexuality and by their definition of it, which may be different from the one we wish to adopt.

For example, Marc Daniel tries to refute accusations of homosexuality against Pope Julian II by producing four arguments: the Pope had many enemies who might wish to blacken his name; he and his supposed lover, Alidosi, both had mistresses; neither of them was at all effeminate; and the Pope had other men friends about whom no similar accusations were made. In other words Daniel is trying to fit an early sixteenth-century Pope to the modern conception of the homosexual as effeminate, exclusively homosexual, and sexual in relation to all men. The fact that he does not fit is, of course, no evidence, as Daniel would have it, that his relationship with Alidosi was not a sexual one.

Anthropologists too can fall into this trap. Marvin Opler, summarizing anthropological evidence on the subject, says,

> Actually, no society, save perhaps Ancient Greece, pre-Meiji Japan, certain top echelons in Nazi Germany, and the scattered examples of such special status groups as the berdaches, Nata slaves, and one category of Chuckchee shamans, has lent sanction in any real sense to homosexuality.

Yet he goes on to discuss societies in which there are reports of sanctioned adolescent and other occasional "experimentation." Of the Cubeo of the North West Amazon, for instance, he says, *"true* homosexuality among the Cubeo is rare if not absent," giving as evidence the fact that no males with persistent homosexual patterns are reported.

Allowing for such weaknesses, the Human Relations Area Files are the best single source of comparative information. Their evidence on homosexuality has been summarized by Ford and Beach, who identify two broad types of accepted patterns: the institutionalized homosexual role and the liaison between men or boys who are otherwise heterosexual.

The recognition of a distinct role of *berdache* or transvestite is, they say, "the commonest form of institutionalized homosexuality." This form shows a marked similarity to that in our own society, though in some ways it is even more extreme. The Mohave Indians of California and Arizona, for example, recognized both an *alyhā*, a male transvestite who took the role of the woman in sexual intercourse, and a *hwamē,* a female homosexual who took the role of the male. People were believed to be born as *alyhā* or *hwamē,* hints of their future proclivities occurring in their mothers' dreams during pregnancy. If a young boy began to behave like a girl and take an interest in women's things instead of men's, there was an initiation ceremony in which he would become an *alyhā*. After that he would dress and act like a woman, would be referred to as "she" and could take "husbands."

But the Mohave pattern differs from ours in that although the *alyhā* was considered regrettable and amusing, he was not condemned and was given public recognition. The attitude was that "he was an *alyhā*, he could not help it." But the "husband" of an *alyhā* was an ordinary man who happened to have chosen an *alyhā*, perhaps because they were good house-keepers or because they were believed to be "lucky in love," and he would be the butt of endless teasing and joking.

This radical distinction between the feminine passive homosexual and his masculine active partner is one which is not made very much in our own society,* but which is very important in the Middle East. There, however, neither is thought of as being a "born" homosexual, although the passive partner, who demeans himself by his feminine submission, is despised and ridiculed, while the active one is not. In most of the ancient Middle East, including among the Jews until the return from the Babylonian exile, there were male temple prostitutes. Thus even cultures that recognize a separate homosexual role may not define it in the same way as our culture does.

Many other societies accept or approve of homosexual liaisons as part of a variegated sexual pattern. Usually these are confined to a particular stage in the individual's life. Among the Aranda of Central Australia, for instance, there are long-standing relationships of several years' duration, between unmarried men and young boys, starting at the age of ten to twelve. This is rather similar to the well-known situation in classical Greece, but there, of course, the older man could have a wife as well. Sometimes, however, as among the Siwans of North Africa, all men and boys can and are expected to engage in homosexual activities, apparently at every stage of life. In all of these societies there may be much homosexual behavior, but there are no "homosexuals."

The Development of the Homosexual Role in England

The problem of method is even more acute in dealing with historical material than with anthropological, for history is usually concerned with "great events" rather than with recurrent patterns. There are some records of attempts to curb sodomy among minor churchmen during the medieval period, which seem to indicate that it was common. At least they suggest that laymen feared on behalf of their sons that it was common. The term "catamite" meaning "boy kept for immoral purposes," was first used in

---

* The lack of cultural distinction is reflected in behavior; Gordon Westwood found that only a small proportion of his sample of British homosexuals engaged in anal intercourse and many of these had been both active and passive and did not have a clear preference. See *A Minority* (London: Longmans, 1960), pp. 127–134.

1593, again suggesting that this practice was common then. But most of the historical references to homosexuality relate either to great men or to great scandals. However, over the last seventy years or so various scholars have tried to trace the history of sex, and it is possible to glean a good deal from what they have found and also from what they have failed to establish.

Their studies of English history before the seventeenth century consist usually of inconclusive speculation as to whether certain men, such as Edward II, Christopher Marlowe, William Shakespeare, were or were not homosexual. Yet the disputes are inconclusive not because of lack of evidence but because none of these men fits the modern stereotype of the homosexual.

It is not until the end of the seventeenth century that other kinds of information become available and it is possible to move from speculations about individuals to descriptions of homosexual life. At this period references to homosexuals as a type and to a rudimentary homosexual subculture, mainly in London, began to appear. But the earliest descriptions of homosexuals do not coincide exactly with the modern conception. There is much more stress on effeminacy and in particular in transvestism, to such an extent that there seems to be no distinction at first between transvestism and homosexuality.* The terms emerging at this period to describe homosexuals—Molly, Nancy-boy, Madge-cull—emphasize effeminacy. In contrast the modern terms—fag, queer, gay, bent—do not have this implication.†

By the end of the seventeenth century, homosexual transvestites were a distinct enough group to be able to form their own clubs in London. Edward Ward's *History of the London Clubs*, published in 1709, describes one called "The Mollies' Club" which met "in a certain tavern in the City" for "parties and regular gatherings." The members "adopt(ed) all the small vanities natural to the feminine sex to such an extent that they try to speak, walk, chatter, shriek, and scold as women do, aping them as well in other respects." The other respects apparently included the enactment of marriages and childbirth. The club was discovered and broken up by agents of the Reform Society. There were a number of similar scandals during the course of the eighteenth century as various homosexual coteries were exposed.

---

* Dr. Evelyn Hooker has suggested that in a period when homosexual grouping and a homosexual subculture have not yet become institutionalized, homosexuals are likely to behave in a more distinctive and conspicuous manner because other means of making contact are not available. This is confirmed by the fact that lesbians are more conspicuous than male homosexuals in our society, but does not seem to fit the seventeenth century, where the groups are already described as "clubs."

† However, "fairy" and "pansy," the commonest slang terms used by nonhomosexuals, have the same meaning of effeminate as the earlier terms.

A writer in 1729 describes the widespread homosexual life of the period:

> They also have their Walks and Appointments, to meet and pick up one another, and their particular Houses of Resort to go to, because they dare not trust themselves in an open Tavern. About twenty of these sort of Houses have been discovered, besides the Nocturnal Assemblies of great numbers of the like vile Persons, what they call the *Markets,* which are the Royal Exchange, Lincoln's Inn, Bog Houses, the south side of St. James's Park, the Piazzas in Covent Garden, St. Clement's Churchyard, etc.
>
> It would be a pretty scene to behold them in their clubs and cabals, how they assume the air and affect the name of Madam or Miss, Betty or Molly, with a chuck under the chin, and "Oh, you bold pullet, I'll break your eggs," and then frisk and walk away.

The notion of exclusive homosexuality became well established during this period. When "two Englishmen, Leith and Drew, were accused of paederasty. . . . The evidence given by the plaintiffs was, as was generally the case in these trials, very imperfect. On the other hand the defendants denied the accusation, and produced witnesses to prove their predeliction for women. They were in consequence acquitted." This could only have been an effective argument in a society that perceived homosexual behavior as incompatible with heterosexual tastes.

During the nineteenth century there are further reports of raided clubs and homosexual brothels. However, by this time the element of transvestism had diminished in importance. Even the male prostitutes are described as being of masculine build and there is more stress upon sexual license and less upon dressing up and play-acting.

The Homosexual Role and Homosexual Behavior

Thus, a distinct, separate, specialized role of "homosexual" emerged in England at the end of the seventeenth century and the conception of homosexuality as a condition which characterizes certain individuals and not others is now firmly established in our society. The term role is, of course, a form of shorthand. It refers not only to a cultural conception or set of ideas but also to a complex of institutional arrangements which depend upon and reinforce these ideas. These arrangements include all the forms of heterosexual activity, courtship, and marriage as well as the labeling processes—gossip, ridicule, psychiatric diagnosis, criminal conviction—and the groups and networks of the homosexual subculture. For simplicity we shall simply say that a specialized role exists.

How does the existence of this social role affect actual behavior? And, in particular, does the behavior of individuals conform to the cultural conception in the sense that most people are either exclusively heterosexual or exclusively homosexual? It is difficult to answer these questions on the basis of available evidence because so many researchers have worked with the preconception that homosexuality is a condition, so that in order to study the behavior they have first found a group of people who could be identified as "homosexuals." Homosexual behavior should be studied independently of social roles, if the connection between the two is to be revealed.

This may not sound like a particularly novel program to those who are familiar with Kinsey's contribution to the field. He, after all, set out to study "sexual behavior"; he rejected the assumptions of scientists and laymen:

> that there are persons who are "heterosexual" and persons who are "homosexual," that these two types represent antitheses in the sexual world and that there is only an insignificant class of "bisexuals" who occupy an intermediate position between the other groups . . . that every individual is innately—inherently—either heterosexual or homosexual . . . (and) that from the time of birth one is fated to be one thing or the other . . . .

But, although some of Kinsey's ideas are often referred to, particularly in polemical writings, surprisingly little use has been made of his actual data.

Most of Kinsey's chapters on the "Homosexual Outlet" centers on his "heterosexual-homosexual rating scale." His subjects were rated on this scale according to the proportion of their "psychologic reactions and overt experience" that was homosexual in any given period of their lives. It is interesting, and unfortunate for our purposes, that this is one of the few places in the book where Kinsey abandons his behavioristic approach to some extent. However, "psychologic reactions" may well be expected to be affected by the existence of a social role in the same way as overt behavior. Another problem with using Kinsey's material is that although he gives very full information about sexual behavior, the other characteristics of the people he interviewed are only given in a very bald form. But Kinsey's study is undoubtedly the fullest description there is of sexual behavior in any society and as such it is the safest basis for generalizations to other Western societies.

The ideal way to trace the effects on behavior of the existence of a homosexual role would be to compare societies in which the role exists with societies in which it does not. But as there are no adequate descriptions of homosexual behavior in societies where there is no homosexual role, we shall have to substitute comparisons within American society.

1. *Polarization.* If the existence of a social role were reflected in people's behavior, we should expect to find that relatively few people would engage in bisexual behavior. The problem about investigating this empirically is to know what is meant by "relatively few." The categories of Kinsey's rating scale are, of course, completely arbitrary. He has five bisexual categories, but he might just as well have had more or less, in which case the number

Table 1   Heterosexual-Homosexual Rating: Active Incidence by Age*

	(1)	(2)	(3)	(4)	(5)	(6)	(7)	(8)	(9)
Age	X	0	1	2	3	4	5	6	1–6
15	23.6	48.4	3.6	6.0	4.7	3.7	2.6	7.4	28.0
20	3.3	69.3	4.4	7.4	4.4	2.9	3.4	4.9	27.4
25	1.0	79.2	3.9	5.1	3.2	2.4	2.3	2.9	19.8
30	0.5	83.1	4.0	3.4	2.1	3.0	1.3	2.6	16.4
35	0.4	86.7	2.4	3.4	1.9	1.7	0.9	2.6	12.9
40	1.3	86.8	3.0	3.6	2.0	0.7	0.3	2.3	11.9
45	2.7	88.8	2.3	2.0	1.3	0.9	0.2	1.8	8.5

Percent of each age group of male population having each rating

* Based on Kinsey (1948), p. 652, Table 148.

X = unresponsive to either sex; 0 = entirely heterosexual; 1 = largely heterosexual, but with incidental homosexual history; 2 = largely heterosexual but with a distinct homosexual history; 3 = equally heterosexual and homosexual; 4 = largely homosexual but with distinct heterosexual history; 5 = largely homosexual but with incidental heterosexual history; 6 = entirely homosexual.

falling into each would have been smaller or larger. The fact that the distribution of his scale is U-shaped, then, is in itself meaningless. (See Table 1.)

It is impossible to get direct evidence of a polarization between the homosexual and the heterosexual pattern, though we may note the suggestive evidence to the contrary that at every age far more men have bisexual than exclusively homosexual patterns. However, by making comparisons between one age group and another and between men and women, it should be possible to see some of the effects of the role.

2. *Age comparison.* As they grow older, more and more men take up exclusively heterosexual patterns, as Table 1, column 2 shows. The table also shows that *each* of the bisexual and homosexual categories, columns 3–8, contains fewer men as time goes by after the age of 20. The greatest losses are from the fifth bisexual category, column 7, with responses that are "almost entirely homosexual." It is a fairly small group to begin with, but by the age of 45 it has almost entirely disappeared. On the other hand the first bisexual category, column 3, with only "incidental homosexual histories" has its numbers not even halved by the age of 45. Yet at all ages the first bisexual category represents a much smaller proportion of those who are almost entirely homosexual (columns 2 and 3) than the fifth category represents of those who are almost entirely homosexual (columns 7 and 8). In everyday language, it seems that proportionately more "homosexuals" dabble in heterosexual activity than "heterosexuals" dabble in homosexual activity and such dabbling is particularly common in the younger age groups of 20 to 30. This indicates that the existence of the despised role operates at all ages to inhibit people from engaging in occa-

sional homosexual behavior, but does not have the effect of making the behavior of many "homosexuals" exclusively homosexual.

On the other hand, the overall reduction in the amount of homosexual behavior with age can be attributed in part to the fact that more and more men become married. While the active incidence of homosexual behavior is high and increases with age among single men, among married men it is low and decreases only slightly with age. Unfortunately the Kinsey figures do not enable us to compare the incidence of homosexuality among single men who later marry and those who do not.

3. *Comparison of men and women.* The notion of a separate homosexual role is much less well developed for women than it is for men and so too are the attendant techniques of social control and the deviant subculture and organization. So a comparison with women's sexual behavior should tell us something about the effects of the social role on men's behavior.

Fewer women than men engage in homosexual behavior. By the time they are 45, 26 percent of women have had *some* homosexual experience, whereas about 50 percent of men have. But this is probably a cause rather than an effect of the difference in the extent to which the homosexual role is crystalized, for women engage in less nonmarital sexual activity of any kind than men. For instance, by the time they marry 50 percent of women have had some premarital heterosexual experience to orgasm, whereas as many as 90 percent of men have.

The most revealing contrast is between the male and female distributions

Table 2. Comparison of Male and Female Heterosexual-Homosexual Ratings: Active Incidence at Selected Ages*

		Percent of each age group having each rating								
		(1)	(2)	(3)	(4)	(5)	(6)	(7)	(8)	(9)
	Age	X	0	1	2	3	4	5	6	1–6
Male		3.3	69.3	4.4	7.4	4.4	2.9	3.4	4.9	27.4
	20									
Female		15	74	5	2	1	1	1	1	11
Male		0.4	86.7	2.4	3.4	1.9	1.7	0.9	2.6	12.9
	35									
Female		7	80	7	2	1	1	1	1	13

* Based on Kinsey (1948), p. 652, Table 148, and Kinsey (1953), p. 499, Table 142. For explanation of the ratings, see Table 1.

on the Kinsey rating scale, shown in Table 2. The distributions for women follow a smooth J-shaped pattern, while those for men are uneven with an increase in numbers at the exclusively homosexual end. The distributions for women are the shape that one would expect on the assumption that homosexual and heterosexual acts are randomly distributed in a ratio of

1 to 18.* The men are relatively more concentrated in the exclusively homosexual category. This appears to confirm the hypothesis that the existence of the role is reflected in behavior.

Finally, it is interesting to notice that although at the age of 20 far more men than women have homosexual and bisexual patterns (27 percent as against 11 percent), by the age of 35 the figures are both the same (13 percent). Women seem to broaden their sexual experience as they get older whereas more men become narrower and more specialized.

None of this, however, should obscure the fact that, in terms of behavior, the polarization between the heterosexual man and the homosexual man is far from complete in our society. Some polarization does seem to have occurred, but many men manage to follow patterns of sexual behavior that are between the two, in spite of our cultural preconceptions and institutional arrangements.

Conclusion

This paper has dealt with only one small aspect of the sociology of homosexuality. It is, nevertheless, a fundamental one. For it is not until he sees homosexuals as a social category, rather than a medical or psychiatric one, that the sociologist can begin to ask the right questions about the specific content of the homosexual role and about the organizations and functions of homosexual groups. All that has been done here is to indicate that the role does not exist in many societies, that it only emerged in England toward the end of the seventeenth century, and that, although the existence of the role in modern America appears to have some effect on the distribution of homosexual behavior, such behavior is far from being monopolized by persons who play the role of homosexual.

* This cannot be taken in a rigorously statistical sense, since the categories are arbitrary and do not refer to numbers, or even proportions, of actual sexual acts.

Woman's Intellect | *Eleanor E. Maccoby*

Not many years ago, families took it for granted that an intelligent son would be sent to college and an intelligent daughter would not. It is only during a brief span of thirty to forty years that large numbers of women

From Eleanor E. Maccoby, "Woman's Intellect," in S. M. Farber and R. H. L. Wilson (eds.), *The Potential of Women* (New York: McGraw-Hill, 1963), pp. 24–38. References cited in the original have been deleted.

have had opportunities for higher education opened to them, but the period has been long enough so that we are in a position to begin to appraise the results. To those who had hoped that equal educational opportunities for women would yield equal intellectual achievements, an appraisal must be disappointing. A madame Curie is conspicuous by her very rarity. Even in the field of letters, where many of women's special talents are presumed to lie, we have more men than women who are productive, creative writers. When it comes to achievement in science, the imbalance is much greater. Our colleges produce very few women who become intellectually excited by, and immersed in, a scientific research problem or who organize large bodies of diverse data into a new theoretical statement. And even though creative scientists must have moments of almost intuitive insight, woman's famous intuition does not appear to have helped her much in making a contribution to scientific thought.

Taking publication as an index of productivity (and although it is not an entirely satisfactory index, it is difficult to find a better one!) we find, from a study of 400 Radcliffe Ph.D.s (1965) that women published substantially less than men of comparable jobs and rank. Half of these women Ph.D.s had published little or nothing since earning their advanced degrees. So even with first-rate advanced graduate training, the difference between the sexes in intellectual achievement appears not to be erased.

It is evident that women have many other things they often choose to do with their lives, over and beyond pursuit of their intellectual interests. It is reasonable to believe that the other demands upon women are more incompatible with the life of an intellectual than would be the case for men. It is difficult to continue in the single-minded pursuit of a set of ideas while being a competent wife and mother—more difficult than for a man to do so while being a competent husband and father. These matters of conflicting interests and responsibilities will be discussed by others in this conference, and they are not our primary concern today. It is necessary to ask, however, whether they constitute the entire explanation for women's lack of signal accomplishment in the intellectual sphere. I am inclined to think they do not. One bit of evidence comes from the study of Radcliffe Ph.D.s already cited; the ones who had married had published as much as those who had not, and this would appear to indicate that even an unmarried professional woman (who presumably is more comparable to men with respect to the other demands on her time) is either under some special restraints affecting her intellectual productivity or lacks in some degree the positive motivation that would optimally affect her work.

If we examine woman's intellectual performance through a large range of her life cycle, we find other reasons for suspecting that it is not just the conflicting demands upon her time created by marriage and children that interfere with her achievement. There are not very good facts available on the subject, but I suspect careful studies would reveal that the educated woman does not behave as an intellectual during her college years, nor "go underground" during the period of life when she is raising young children and then emerge again as an intellectual when the children are grown and no longer require so much of her time. Rather, it appears that some of the restraints upon her intellectuality make themselves felt long before marriage and continue to be present during those long years from thirty-five to sixty-five when the most demanding phase of child rearing is over—the period when many men are at the peak of their productive careers. It seems possible that there may be some relevant early-formed personality traits, or even some early-established basic qualities of mind, that characterize women and that bear upon intellectual performance, and it is these factors that I would like to explore today.

Let us first review what is known concerning the development of intellectual abilities in girls. In attempting to determine what are the special intellectual qualities of females (if indeed such special qualities exist), we must stress the ways in which girls differ from boys in their performance. In doing so, we may give insufficient attention to the ways in which the two sexes are alike intellectually, or to the great variations among individuals of the same sex. But bearing this danger in mind, let us attempt to draw a quick picture of some of the reliably established sex differences in intellectual functioning.

The Stanford-Binet intelligence test, which was for many years the most widely used individual test, revealed few differences between boys and girls in total "intelligence" as this test measured it. From this fact it was widely assumed that the sexes might differ in interests and in temperament but not in underlying mental abilities. It was not widely known or understood that during the early phases of work on the Stanford-Binet test, when many items were being tried out for possible inclusion in the test, items which consistently revealed sex differences were discarded from the test whenever possible. The test builders hoped in this way to create a test on which the scores for boys and the scores for girls could be evaluated against the same norms. And for the most part they succeeded, although girls did come out slightly ahead in the early years and boys in the middle and later school years. But it is clearly not possible to use a test standardized in this way to investigate the magnitude of the sex differences that do exist or at what ages they make their appearance.

Relying now on test materials which were not standardized so as to eliminate a portion of existing sex differences, we find the following facts: Girls get off to a very good start. Insofar as it is possible to measure abilities which we would be willing to call intellectual abilities during the first three or four years of life, girls seem to be slightly ahead of boys. They articulate more clearly than boys; they say their first word at a slightly younger age on the average; they begin to combine words into sentences slightly sooner; they count accurately sooner. In interpreting these facts we should remember that performance on the sorts of tests we have been able to devise for very young children does not predict very well what intellectual level the individual will ultimately reach. Furthermore, we know that girls are on a somewhat faster developmental timetable than boys from the standpoint of physical growth; this same slightly advanced timetable may apply to the maturation of certain motor and perceptual abilities that underlie intellectual performance, and again, this rate of maturation doesn't necessarily imply anything concerning the ultimate level to be reached.

But to continue with the description of sex differences in abilities. Upon entrance into school, girls learn to read a little more easily, and there are more boys who have reading problems severe enough to call for special remedial reading programs. But the differential between the sexes on some aspects of verbal skill soon begins to disappear. During the school years, there are no consistent differences to be found in vocabulary; and after about the fifth or sixth grade, most studies show the boys to be doing as well as the girls in reading comprehension. The girls do continue to excel in "language" skills such as spelling, punctuation, and diagramming sentences. They also excel in measures of "verbal fluency"; for example, they write longer themes, they can think of more words with certain characteristics in a short time, and they can tell longer stories in response to stimulus pictures. So the stereotype that women talk more than men appears to have some basis in fact, but it does not imply a general superiority of the female in all aspects of verbal skill.

How about mathematical skills? It is commonly supposed that men have a consistent edge over women in this respect. It came as a surprise to us, therefore, when we recently reviewed the test results bearing upon mathematical abilities, to discover that the sexes do not differ consistently in the early and middle school years. Of course, during much of this time, it may be a misnomer to say that we are dealing with *mathematical* abilities. It would be more accurate to say that the skill usually measured between the ages of seven and eleven or twelve is skill at arithmetical computation. Children are also given some of the so-called arithmetical reasoning problems at these ages—questions about how long would it take three men to dig a basement if seven men can do it in 2½ days, or how long it would take a bullet to travel from one train to another if the speeds of the two trains and the time since starting are given—and girls appear to be able to handle these questions about as well as boys. It is not until high school that we begin to get quite consistent sex differences, with the boys forging ahead when they come to analytic geometry, trigonometry, and algebra and doing considerably better in tests involving quantitative reasoning. By the time the Scholastic Aptitude tests are administered for admission to college, we find that boys score on the average as much as 50 points higher on the mathematical portion of the test, while girls are scoring only 8 to 10 points higher on the verbal, or "language," segment. Of course, girls do not as frequently elect to take the more advanced math courses in high school, and it is difficult to know whether this is true because they lack the ability to handle the material or whether their interests lie elsewhere. The career fields which will require training in math—engineering, and the natural sciences—are primarily masculine fields, and girls may stop taking math simply because they are preparing themselves for more feminine occupations. But another possible explanation exists: that girls may indeed more often lack certain abstract or analytical qualities of mind that are not called into play during the learning of square root, decimals, etc., in the earlier grades, and that it is not until mathematics becomes more abstract (as it does in geometry and algebra) that this particular deficiency becomes a handicap to them.

At the moment, we lack definitive data that would make it possible to choose between these alternatives. But girls' characteristic difficulty with geometry does probably relate to a fairly consistent sex difference that may be detected at a considerably earlier age. Throughout the grade-school years, boys do better than girls on tests of "spatial" ability. Some of you may have taken tests which include items for space ability: such tests require the subject, for example, to say how many surfaces there would be on the opposite side of a pile of cubes—the side the viewer cannot see—or to select from an array of jigsaw drawings those that would fit together to form a designated pattern. Another element in spatial ability involves finding a simple figure which is embedded in a more complex one. Newspapers sometimes carry drawings of landscapes in which one can find animals or human faces involving the same lines that are first perceived as parts of clouds, leaves, or tree trunks; the trick in finding these hidden figures is to be able to break away from the set that is established by the entire drawing of the landscape—to respond to only an isolated segment of the drawing and avoid being influenced by the momentarily irrelevant parts. There are formal tests of the ability to perceive parts of a visual field analytically, and the results very consistently show that boys can perceive more analytically, while the girls are more global, more influenced by all the elements of the field together.

The sex differences, to the extent of being bound by the field as a whole, are well illustrated by the performance of the two sexes on the so-called rod-and-frame test, a test used extensively by Witkin in his studies of individual differences in underlying modes of perceiving. In this test, the subject is seated in a darkened room. He looks at an illuminated frame that looks like a picture frame; and within this frame is an illuminated rod, which can be adjusted through various degrees of tilt to an upright position. The subject's task is to adjust the rod so that it looks straight up and down. Sometimes he is required to do this when the frame itself is tilted. Girls are consistently more influenced by the tilt of the frame; if it is tilted, they think the rod is upright when it is tilted to correspond to the tilt of the frame rather than when it is truly upright. Boys, on the other hand, are more able to ignore the frame and adjust the rod to the true upright. It is on the basis of tests of this kind, as well as the embedded-figures test, that girls have been labeled more "field dependent," and it is interesting to note that the greater field dependence of women and girls has been found in studies of people in a variety of cultures, from Western Europe to Hong Kong. It appears entirely possible that some of the difficulty many girls have with the kinds of analytical processes required in high-school math could be traced to this earlier-established difference in their mode of dealing with a stimulus field.

Related to the greater field dependence of women is their greater difficulty in breaking an established set. Let me illustrate what is meant by set. Suppose you were asked to solve some number series—to say what would come next in a series of numbers. We would begin with some easy series. For example, we would ask what comes next after 2, 4, 6, 8—and you could easily say 10. Or what comes next after 2, 4, 8, 16, 32—and you would say 64. Now try this one: 14, 23, 34, 42, 50, 59, 72, 81—. Even if you knew New York very well, you would have difficulty recognizing these as the stops on the Eighth Avenue subway, because you were set for an entirely different kind of number series. If you had not had the other series first, you might recognize this series immediately and be able to continue it. There are special test problems which are designed to test an individual's ability to break away from an established set, to restructure a situation for a fresh attack on it, and men do better on such tests than women.

Another kind of task that illustrates the difference between the sexes in their mode of dealing with problem materials is a task developed by Kagan et al. Subjects are given an array of pictures or drawings showing a variety of objects and people with a variety of postures, modes of dress, and states of activity. The subjects are simply asked to group together the pictures that seem to belong together. Girls are more likely to form what Kagan calls "functional" groupings. For example, they will group together the picture of a doctor, a nurse, and a wheel chair, because they are all associated with the care of sick people. Boys, on the other hand, will be more likely to form groups by selecting out some detail they have in common— they will, for example, group together all the pictures of people who have their right arms raised. This kind of grouping Kagan calls "analytic" grouping, and the fact that boys do this kind of grouping more may be regarded as another instance of their tendency to break down a percept—to deal with detailed elements rather than the whole.

I would like to suggest, then, that the difficulty girls have with doing high-level work in math and science is only partly a result of the fact that these subjects are required for preparation for engineering and other distinctly masculine occupations; I suggest that girls on the average develop a somewhat different way of handling incoming information—that their thinking is less analytic, more global, and more perseverative—and that this kind of thinking may serve them very well for many kinds of functioning but that it is not the kind of thinking most conducive to high-level intellectual productivity, especially in science. Let me hasten to add that in trying to make this point I may have produced an exaggerated impression of the magnitude of the sex differences that exist. There are many women who think analytically, and many men who do not, but there are consistent differences in the average performance of the two sexes, and by concentrating on the differences we may be able to find some clues as to what underlies the development of intellectual processes in women.

Why do some people develop more analytic modes of thought than others? So far, we are only beginning to make a research attack upon this question. But there do seem to be some consistent trends in the work that has been done so far. The key to the matter seems to lie in whether, and how soon, a child is encouraged to assume initiative, to take responsibility for himself, and to solve problems by himself, rather than rely upon others for the direction of his activities. An early study by David Levy was among the first to suggest the importance of independence training for certain intellectual functions. He studied a group of boys whom he labeled "overprotected." The behavior of the mothers of these boys was extreme in the direction of "babying" them at a late age—for example, some of the boys, at age ten or eleven, were still being led to school by the hand of their mothers, and their mothers were still dressing them each morning. These overprotected boys were quite good in their language work at school—they were good readers, for example. But they were notably poor at math.

Recently, Dr. Rau and I at Stanford studied a group of children who were good at verbal tasks but poor at math or space tasks and contrasted them with children who were good at math or space but relatively poor at verbal tasks. Dr. Elizabeth Bing observed these children in interaction with their mothers. She asked the mothers to give the children some problems to work on and noted how much the mother became involved as the child worked on the problems. To speak now only about the girls in the study, it was evident from Dr. Bing's reports that the mothers of the highly verbal girls were intrusive: they offered suggestions, praised the child for performing well, and criticized her for performing poorly. The mothers of the girls who were best at math or spatial tasks, however, more often left their daughters alone to solve the problems by themselves.

Still another piece of evidence comes from some recent exploratory work of Witkin, Dyk, Faterson, Goodenough, and Karp, who wished to discover what conditions of a child's life were associated with his being field-dependent versus field-independent on the rod-and-frame test and the embedded-figures test. Witkin interviewed mothers to ascertain their attitudes about child rearing and the methods they had used to raise the particular child whose modes of perceiving Witkin had measured. The mothers of the children who were analytic in their perceptions had given their children quite a bit of freedom to explore the environment at an early age and had tried to encourage them to do things on their own initiative; by contrast, the mothers of the children who were "field-dependent" in their perceptions had kept their childhood quite closely tied to the maternal apron strings, had talked to them a good deal about the dangerous aspects of the environment, and had been in general unwilling to tolerate self-assertiveness in their children. There were many other things that characterized these two groups of mothers, as well, and it is difficult to sort out the factors that were most crucial in the home lives of the children with different modes of perceiving. But the relationships that I have selected to report here are consistent with our own findings and those of Levy in suggesting that activities of parents which are designed to foster the independence of their children and encourage them to take initiative will be associated with analytic thinking in the children and good ability in the math-science area, while continued close control and restriction of the child will be associated with the more field-dependent, or global, modes of thinking in the child and *poor* ability in math.

If this is true, we must ask ourselves whether girls are allowed less independence, less self-assertiveness in early childhood than is allowed to boys. We have very little evidence indeed on this point. I know of no evidence that would show that boys are allowed to play outside alone or cross streets earlier than girls, for example, but it may very well be true that they are. At the moment we will simply have to consider it an unanswered question whether parents treat daughters differently from sons with respect to training for independence, and whether they do so to a sufficient degree to account for the differences between the sexes in their modes of perceiving and their differential skill at tasks, such as mathematics, which seem to require an especially high degree of analytical thinking.

I think we can begin to see, however, from what has been said so far, that when we begin to try to understand the intellectual performance of women and girls, we cannot understand them by studying these kinds of performance alone; we will find that intellectual development does not occur as a kind of isolated "unfolding" process obeying its own inner laws, but rather that it is responsive, in some degree, to the nature of the network of interpersonal relations in which the child is involved, and that certain modes of thought may depend on the development of certain aspects of the person that we have previously thought of as "personality" rather than as qualities of intellect.

Let me take another approach to illustrate this point. As you may know, the "intelligence" of an individual child as it is measured by standard intelligence tests is not constant over the period of his growth from birth to maturity. Some children show progressive increases in IQ as they grow older; others show a progressive decline. There are a few centers of child-development research in this country which have studied groups of children longitudinally; that is, they have followed the same children from very early childhood into adulthood, and it is possible to determine from their data what some of the factors are which are associated with progressive changes in children's intelligence-test scores. Sontag et al., at Fels Research Institute have selected from their files a group of cases of children whose intelligence-test scores consistently improved from preschool years through age ten and contrasted them with a group whose scores consistently declined during this period. They asked these questions: What kinds of children show increases or decreases in IQ? Can one predict, from knowing something about the personality characteristics of young children, which ones will have rising, and which falling, IQs? The answer to the second question is clearly yes. Here is what a child is like at age six if he or she is among those whose IQs will increase during the next four years: he or she is competitive, self-assertive, independent, and dominant in interaction with other children. And the children who will show declining IQs during the next four years are children who are passive, shy, and dependent.

I'm sure it will already have struck you that the characteristics associated with a rising IQ are not very feminine characteristics. One of the people working on the Fels study I have just described was asked about what kind of developmental history was necessary to make a girl into an intellectual person; he replied, "The simplest way to put it is that she must be a tomboy at some point in her childhood."

Does this seem bizarre? Before we consider the implications for the raising of girls, let us see whether there is any other evidence, beyond the Fels study, for an association between the sorts of analytic thinking we have been discussing and the possession of nonfeminine traits by girls. First of all, if we may consider high ability in arithmetic and math as indicative of analytic skill (and it is known, for example, that skill in math is correlated with ability to find embedded figures while verbal skill is not), then it is relevant to refer to a study of the autobiographies of a few famous women mathematicians, done by Plank and Plank. This study revealed that women mathematicians had one important element in common: they all described an unusually close relationship with their fathers, rather than their mothers, as they were growing up, and they attempted to pattern themselves on their fathers. Related to this is the finding of Bieri and his colleagues, who devised measures to determine the degree to which a group of college women had identified with, or patterned themselves upon, each of their parents. They found that women who were especially good at finding the hidden figures in the embedded-figures test were more strongly identified with their fathers than their mothers, while the reverse was true of the women who were relatively poor at solving embedded figures. The women in this study were also given a test designed to measure their acceptance of authority, and the women who were good at solving the embedded-figures problems tended to be *low* in acceptance of authority—another indication of the importance of autonomy in the development of this particular kind of analytic thinking. In still another study, college students were given problems to solve, many of which required breaking of set, or "restructuring." For both sexes, the students who were most skillful at problem solving were those who scored at the more masculine end of personality tests designed to measure masculine versus feminine traits.

And finally, our own work at Stanford, in which we selected groups of fifth-grade girls who were especially good at arithmetical or spatial tasks, revealed the following characteristics of these girls: The girls who did better on spatial problems than other kinds of problems were somewhat more masculine and aggressive than other girls with similar total IQs, and rather withdrawn from social contact with their age-mates. The girls whose area of greatest competence was numerical tasks were popular with their classmates, largely because they were seen as girls with high competence in planning and organizing. According to their own report, these girls were also less likely than others of similar IQ to ask their parents for help when they encountered difficulty in solving a problem. When the girls were observed in interaction with their mothers, it was the girls who were especially good at verbal tasks who most often asked their mothers for help; the girls who were best at either math or space tasks tended to work on their own. Thus we see that these girls not only were characterized by greater independence while working on problems but also possessed some traits we think of as being more characteristic of boys: aggression in the case of the high-space girls, dominance in the case of the high-number girls.

It would appear, then, that what evidence we have indicates that girls who do well at the various kinds of analytic thinking we have been discussing are not very feminine creatures, at least not according to the standards our present society sets for feminine behavior. It has been repeatedly shown, in studies of girls, that they early develop a greater interest in other people, and in what other people think of them, than do boys;

they tend to be more influenced by the opinions of others, and they are more conforming to what they perceive to be the social demands of the situations they are in. It is probably these conformist tendencies that help them to excel at spelling and punctuation—the kinds of performance for which there is only one socially prescribed, right answer. But for higher-level intellectual productivity, it is independence of mind that is required—the ability to turn one's back on others at least for a time, while working alone on a problem—and it is this which girls, from an early age, appear to find so difficult to do.

But of course, not all girls find it difficult. And it is interesting to consider for a moment the situation of a little girl who at preschool age does have the qualities that could make her into an analytic thinker. She is full of curiosity, likes to explore things, is dominant and independent, probably likes to play with boys and wear blue jeans, and isn't especially interested in dolls. Assuming that her parents have been tolerant of her temperament, what happens when she enters school? One of the first blows is that the boys won't play with her any more—they form their own exclusive play groups, and she must fall back upon the company of girls. In many ways she begins to discover that she is not behaving as girls are expected to behave, and the disapproval she encounters generates a certain amount of anxiety. This may sound like pure speculation, but there is some evidence that this is the course that development does take in girls who start out as tomboys. Sears, in a recent study, traced the development of aggression, and anxiety about aggression, between the ages of five and twelve. The boys who were most anxious about aggression at age twelve were the ones whose parents had not allowed fighting when they were younger, and at the age of five they had already become fairly unaggressive children. The girls who showed most anxiety about aggression at age twelve, however, were the ones who had been fairly aggressive at kindergarten age. But more importantly for our present discussion, the ones who showed the most of this kind of anxiety in middle childhood were the ones who had been trained in ways inappropriate to their sex in preschool years. For example, in most American homes, there is a certain amount of division of labor between the parents such that mothers assume a larger role in the discipline and caretaking of daughters, fathers of sons. But the girls with high aggression anxiety levels in middle childhood had received an unusually high amount of both discipline and caretaking from their *fathers*. Furthermore, they had been encouraged to fight back when attacked by other children in the neighborhood—an encouragement which is more often reserved for boys in our culture. We see, then, that these girls were being to some degree masculinized in early childhood, and we can only assume that it was at least partly the social disapproval they encountered over their unfeminine behavior that produced the anxiety they manifested at a later time.

Let me make a leap from these findings to our present concerns with woman's intellect. Suppose a girl does succeed in maintaining, throughout her childhood years, the qualities of dominance, independence, and active striving that appear to be requisites for good analytic thinking. In so doing, she is defying the conventions concerning what is appropriate behavior for her sex. She may do this successfully, in many ways, but I suggest that it is a rare intellectual woman who will not have paid a price for it: a price in anxiety. And I hazard the guess that it is this anxiety which helps to account for the lack of productivity among those women who do make intellectual careers. We are beginning to know a good deal about the effects of anxiety on thinking: it is especially damaging to creative thinking, for it narrows the range of solution efforts, interferes with breaking set, and prevents scanning of the whole range of elements open to perception. When anxiety facilitates performance, as it sometimes does, it facilitates already well-learned tasks; it does not contribute to breaking new ground.

From the standpoint of those who want women to become intellectuals, this is something of a horror story. It would appear that even when a woman is suitably endowed intellectually and develops the right temperament and habits of thought to make use of her endowment, she must be fleet of foot indeed to scale the hurdles society has erected for her and to remain a whole and happy person while continuing to follow her intellectual bent.

From the standpoint of parents and educators who are charged with the responsibility of raising and training girls, the requisites for intellectual development in girls appear to pose something of a dilemma. Shall mothers encourage whatever tomboy tendencies they find in their young daughters? Shall teachers attempt to free girls from the emotional involvement with others that helps to make them so tractable in the classroom? I do not mean to imply that the concerted efforts of parents and teachers together would necessarily serve to make girls just like boys intellectually. I think it is quite possible that there are genetic factors that differentiate the two sexes and bear upon their intellectual performance other than what we have thought of as innate "intelligence." For example, there is good reason to believe that boys are innately more aggressive than girls—and I mean aggressive in the broader sense, not just as it implies fighting, but as it implies dominance and initiative as well—and if this quality is one which underlies the later growth of analytic thinking, then boys have an advantage which girls who are endowed with more passive qualities will find difficult to overcome. But it also appears likely that the way children are dealt with by the adults responsible for their care, and the social roles girls know they are preparing themselves for, have a bearing also on whether they will develop the characteristics that will be conducive to the growth of higher-level intellectual skills. And insofar as child training does have an influence, parents and educators have some difficult value judgments to make. What kinds of women do they want to produce? Do we want to encourage intellectuality in women if it must be done at the expense of femininity?

As always, when faced with this kind of devil-and-deep-blue-sea dilemma, it is wise to inquire whether there may not be some other alternative. I wonder whether our current social definition of the feminine woman and girl could not undergo some revisions without any damage to the essential functions of woman. Does a woman really need to be passive and dependent in order to be sexually attractive to men, or in order to be a good mother? Could we not accept and encourage the active, dominant, independent qualities of the intellectual girl without labeling her as masculine, and encourage in her whatever aspects of femininity *are* compatible with an analytic quality of mind? I recognize that I am raising some controversial and intricate issues here, for the social and economic role of woman is by very necessity a dependent one during her childbearing years. But these years have become a much smaller segment of her life span than they once were, and I ask whether our whole definition of femininity should be such as to prepare her for this segment of her life and no other. I hope that the remainder of this symposium will help to elucidate this issue.

Family Size and Sex-Role Stereotypes

F. E. Clarkson,
S. R. Vogel,
I. K. and D. M. Broverman,
and P. S. Rosenkrantz

Rising concern about world overpopulation has focused interest on factors that influence family size. Initial optimism about the efficacy of the rapidly developing birth-control technology has now become tempered by recognition of the possibility that social and psychological attitudes affecting the acceptance of the available methods may set limits to effective population control. A number of social factors related to family size have been previously identified and discussed, for example, socioeconomic class, education, and religion.

From F. E. Clarkson et al., "Family Size and Sex-Role Stereotypes," *Science*, January 23, 1970, pp. 390–392. References cited in the original have been deleted.

Davis and Blake have proposed that a critical psychological factor affecting the number of children a woman both desires and achieves is her acceptance or rejection of the feminine stereotypic social role prevalent in our society. Blake has argued that most societies hold "pro-natalistic" attitudes which prescribe for women the role of child-bearer and rearer. Acceptance of alternative feminine roles, such as employment in the work force, could reduce the social and intrapsychic pressure on women to produce children, and thus result in a smaller achieved family size. Several studies have reported that working women do indeed desire and have smaller families than nonworking women. However, to our knowledge, no data exist on relationships between completed family size and the self-concepts of women with respect to alternative sex roles. The present study reports the finding that women who hold relatively masculine self-concepts have significantly smaller completed families than women who hold more stereotypically feminine self-concepts.

Ninety-six Catholic mothers of male college students completed a sex-role stereotype questionnaire. The construction and use of this instrument have been described in detail elsewhere. Briefly, it consists of 122 traits chosen by college students as discriminating between men and women. For each trait there is a bipolar horizontal scale, labeled at intervals with numbers, from "1" on the left to "7" on the right, with nine points between any two numbers. (On one such scale, for example, "1" would mean "not at all aggressive" and "7" would mean "very aggressive.") The responder can place a mark anywhere on the scale, under a variety of instructional conditions.

Each mother filled out the form three times: once as descriptive of adult men (masculinity response), once as descriptive of adult women (femininity response), and finally as descriptive of herself. Approximately half the mothers received "male" instructions first, while half received the "female" instructions first; "self" instructions were always given last so that the self ratings were always made within a masculinity-femininity context.

The male and female poles of each questionnaire item were defined by majority opinion of the mothers. Those items on which the consensus exceeded the .001 level of probability (at least 68 percent agreement) were termed "stereotypic." Fifty-seven items met this criterion.

Social desirability ratings for each item were obtained from a previous study where 48 male and 39 female college-age students were asked to indicate the extent to which each trait would be desirable for a mature, healthy adult, sex unspecified.

To facilitate the present data analysis, the scores of all items on which a low score was judged socially desirable were reflected about the mean such that a high score always indicated social desirability. Items where the male pole was more socially desirable were termed male-valued items, while items where the female pole was more socially desirable were termed female-valued items. Of the 57 stereotypic items, 45 were male-valued and 12 were female-valued. The positive poles of the male-valued stereotypic items describe a rational, competent, active, mature individual who is capable of functioning effectively in our society. These stereotypic items have been termed a "competency" cluster.

The positive poles of the stereotypic female-valued items, on the other hand, describe a gentle, sensitive, expressive individual. Hence, the female-valued stereotypic items have been termed a "warmth and expressiveness" cluster. The description of the typical adult male, then, involves high scores on the competency cluster and low scores on the warmth and expressiveness cluster, while the pattern of responses describing the typical female is the reverse.

Each mother's 366-item responses were converted to sigma scores in order to eliminate any individual response biases which might have been present; for example, a tendency for a particular subject to use only one part of the scale.

Two self-concept scores were computed for each mother by summing and averaging the sigma scores of the "self" responses (1) to the male-valued stereotypic items, that is, the competency cluster, and (2) to the female-valued stereotypic items, that is, the warmth and expressiveness cluster.

A variety of background information was also requested from the subjects; pertinent to this report are (1) the number of children that she has had, (2) years of completed formal education, and (3) the number of years worked subsequent to termination of formal education. Sixty mothers who were between 45 and 59 years old, who were living with their husbands, and who had two or more children were included in the remainder of the study. Women with only one child were excluded to eliminate possible early fertility problems, and younger women were excluded because their families might not yet be completed.

Subjects were divided into two groups based on a median split of the self-concept scores derived from the competency cluster. Mothers with above-median scores, that is, those who tend to incorporate more of the positively valued, masculine stereotypic traits into their self-concepts, were compared to mothers with below-median scores, that is, women whose self-concepts include less of the positively valued male competency cluster. The two groups did not differ significantly in educational level or in the total number of years worked since the completion of formal schooling.

A 2 x 2 x 2 analysis of variance for unequal group size with number of children as the dependent variable was performed. The independent variables were: self-concept score on the competency cluster (above versus below the median); total number of years worked (8 or more years versus 7 or less years); and educational level (13 or more grades versus 12 or less grades).

Mothers with high-competency self-concept scores were found to have significantly fewer children (mean = 3.12) than mothers who perceive themselves to be low on the competency cluster (mean = 3.93). The difference of 0.81 children is significant beyond the .025 level of probability $(F = 6.13, \text{d.f. } 1/52)$.

Number of years worked was related to number of children in the expected direction, but did not reach statistical significance $(P < .10)$. Women who worked for 8 or more years had a mean of 3.20 children, while women who worked 7 or less years had a mean of 3.80 children. This finding, although not significant at the .05 level of probability, replicates findings of earlier studies that extent of work is negatively related to number of children born.

The number of years worked appears most strongly related to family size in women who perceive themselves as having less of the behavioral traits comprising the competency cluster: women with low self-concepts who have worked 8 or more years average 3.30 children, while women with low self-concepts who have worked 7 years or less averaged 4.43 children. Number of years worked did not differentially relate to family size in women with above-median self-concepts. The mean family sizes of these latter groups are 3.12 children for 8 years or more work, versus 3.13 children for 7 years or less. This interaction does not quite reach the 5 percent level of confidence $(F = 3.10, \text{d.f. } 1/52, P < .10)$.

Similar analyses performed with self-concept scores derived from the female-valued warmth-expressiveness cluster did not yield significant results.

The results indicate, then, that women who perceive themselves as possessing to a greater degree the socially desirable traits stereotypically associated with the masculine role have fewer children than women who perceive themselves as more stereotypically feminine on these traits.

Interpretation of these findings is not without ambiguity. It is not clear whether women perceiving themselves as relatively more competent chose to have fewer children, or whether a woman's estimation of her own competency diminishes under the stress of a larger family. A longitudinal study will be required to resolve this question. It would also be useful to examine these variables in a non-Catholic population.

The incorporation of male-valued stereotypic traits into the female self-concept should not be interpreted as a shift away from the positively valued characteristics of femininity. The correlation between the male-valued self-concept scores (competency cluster) and the female-valued self-concept scores (warmth and expressiveness) is low and not significant ($r = .158, P > .10$). Thus the self-concepts of the two groups differ only with respect to the negatively valued aspects of the feminine stereotype.

Although sex-role stereotypes assign greater competency to the masculine role and lesser competency to the feminine role, competency can be conceived more broadly as a developmental attribute toward which healthy adults of both sexes aspire. In fact, the items making up the competency cluster have been judged by psychologists and psychiatrists as attributes of mental health. Incorporation by women of the male-valued stereotypic items, therefore, implies an enhancement of self-concept along a dimension of mental health, maturity, or self-actualization.

The fact that our society tends to prescribe for women a role that entails less competence and maturity than the role prescribed for men has been deemed harmful when viewed from the perspectives of human development and mental health. In addition, it now appears that the prescribed feminine sex role is related to problems in population control. Our finding that women who reject in themselves the traits of the feminine stereotype implying low competence and immaturity have fewer children than women who incorporate these undesirable feminine characteristics provides support for Davis's and Blake's thesis that the stereotypic feminine social role is a critical factor affecting family size in our society.

The Abortion Revolution | Robert Hall

Under the nineteenth-century laws still in force in most of our states, a doctor may legally perform an abortion only to preserve a woman's life. Carried to its illogical extreme, this provision would, today, require the termination of every pregnancy for the simple reason that now a woman is ten times more likely to die from pregnancy or childbirth than from a hospital abortion.

This farfetched interpretation serves to illustrate the absurdity of governing the twentieth-century practice of abortion by laws based on nineteenth-century medical conditions. For in the 1800s, before anesthesia, antibiotics, blood banks, and modern surgical techniques, abortion was a medically hazardous procedure. Indeed, it was this medical hazard, not moral compunction, that originally prompted the passage of these laws.

From Robert Hall, "The Abortion Revolution," *Playboy*, September 1970, pp. 112 ff.

And now that abortion is safe, the argument for the repeal of these laws can be based on one of the oldest principles of common law: *Cessante ratione legis, cessat et ipsa lex* (When the reason for the law ceases to exist, the law itself ceases to exist).

Unfortunately, this basic legal point has been lost in the heated debate about a separate, nonlegal issue: the alleged rights of the fetus. The controversy derives from theological metaphysics—and, in a nation founded on the principle of separation of church and state, should never have been introduced to our courtrooms and legislative chambers.

By the early 1900s, medical science had advanced to the point where hospital abortions were fairly safe. They were performed for such conditions as diabetes, tuberculosis, heart disease, and pernicious vomiting—conditions that did then pose a threat to a pregnant woman's life. The decision to do an abortion for any of these reasons was not easy, however, for usually the patient wanted the baby, and doctors had to weigh her desire against risks that were difficult to determine with accuracy. Such Solomonic wisdom is rarely needed now that most of these diseases can be controlled or cured.

A new dilemma appeared in the early forties, when doctors learned that rubella, or German measles, can cause fetal deformities. Unfortunately, the profession cannot take much pride in its reaction to this discovery. For a time, the danger went unpublicized; only when rubella threatened their wives or nurses would most doctors perform abortions—usually under some psychiatric pretext. When news of the rubella danger eventually reached the public, creating a demand too strong to ignore, the profession timorously refused to press for legislative change. Instead, doctors formed therapeutic-abortion boards to diffuse the responsibility for breaking the laws.

Up to that point, the medical profession was not directly confronted with the problem of premarital or unwanted pregnancies; it could stand behind the shield of laws that were restrictive and explicit, leaving the pregnant teenager and most other women to the traditional fates of forced marriage, illegitimate childbirth or back-alley abortion. "Respectable" doctors had only to grapple with those cases where some extenuating circumstance—the woman's life or possible fetal deformity—required the exercise of legal and ethical judgments. But times were changing; increasing public knowledge of abortion policies in other countries, of the simplicity of the operation, of the loopholes in the law, led more and more women to seek termination of their pregnancies for personal or economic reasons. For some, the solution lay in psychiatry. If a psychiatrist would certify that a patient was suicidal due to her pregnancy, the vagueness of many laws would allow for an abortion to save her life. So this became the ruse for performing most "legal" abortions—on private patients who could afford a psychiatrist who would lie for them. As long as the magic word suicide appeared in his recommendation, the abortion board was satisfied.

These boards were a step backward. They permitted doctors to avoid any exercise of personal conscience by passing the buck to a hospital committee, where bureaucratic protocol usually took precedence over humanitarian considerations. I saw one teenager's request for an abortion approved on psychiatric grounds by a committee that later rejected a second request from the same girl, just because she dared to get pregnant twice. I saw a 13-year-old, impregnated by her mother's lover, turned down because her story could not be officially authenticated—the eyewitness testimony of her half brother having been ruled inadmissible because he was only nine years old. I saw a rubella victim turned down because she lived a few miles across the state line: The hospital would have readily accepted cases of trauma or disease from another continent, but it wouldn't accept an abortion case from a nearby town.

Of course, such laws and policies discriminated heavily against the poor. In the early sixties, New York City's private hospitals aborted one pregnant woman in 250; the municipal hospitals, one in 10,000. The rate for white women was five times that for nonwhites and 30 times that for Puerto Ricans. If a debutante could not find a compliant psychiatrist, for $1000 she could always go to a competent M.D. abortionist or fly to Mexico or Puerto Rico (where abortions are illegal but available), England or Japan (where they are legal). These women almost never suffered medical aftereffects. If, on the other hand, a lower-class woman became unwillingly pregnant, her options were less attractive. She could have the baby (which was often illegitimate and virtually unadoptable if black) or she could, by herself or with the help of a friend, resort to using Lysol or a coat hanger and end up very, very sick—or dead. Over 350,000 clinic patients were admitted to our hospitals every year with complications resulting from abortion. Every year, more than 500 of them died.

Naturally, the illegal-abortion business involves big money and has attracted organized crime. So one of the objectives in legalizing abortion has been the same as the reason for legalizing off-track betting. Since both will go on regardless of the law, the public interest will be better served by legitimizing them.

As I have indicated, the argument for legalizing abortion could stop right here, for it is predicated on legitimate concern for the health and welfare of the pregnant woman—just as were our original abortion laws. As it happened, however, some theologians, particularly Roman Catholics, gradually developed equal concern for the fetus. And it is over this difference in the priority of human values that the abortion battle has been waged.

Curiously enough, this is a recent development. In previous centuries, the Catholic Church had no answer to the conundrum of when the soul enters the embryo. Saint Augustine admitted that he didn't know. Saint Thomas Aquinas thought that it might occur at the time of quickening—about halfway through pregnancy. Not until 1869 did the Church decide that the embryo is ensouled at the moment of conception and that abortion at any time is therefore equivalent to murder.

So while new medical discoveries and new social concepts dictated freedom in abortion, a new religious tenet called for stricture. And virtually the entire legislative debate became mired in this completely tangential issue—tangential because the question is *not* whether the fetus has a soul (which is unanswerable) nor whether fetal life is as sacrosanct as existing human life (which is a uniquely Catholic contention). The question is whether women have a fundamental right to bear or not to bear children and, incidentally, whether a church should be free to impose its beliefs on the state.

Ironically, most Catholics do want reform; one out of three favors total legalization, and among college students, this figure rises to almost 50 percent. Many polls have shown this. It is primarily the celibate Catholic leaders who denounce abortion—just as they denounce contraception, sterilization, and divorce. But the power of this relatively small body of men is disproportionately great, based as it is on such overwhelming dedication, organization, wealth, resources, and access to millions of people. For example, on several occasions during the legislative battle to repeal New York's abortion law, the state's eight Catholic bishops issued a joint pastoral letter that was read from the pulpits of 1700 churches, reaching an audience of 6,500,000. The same tactic was also used in other states, usually with devastating results.

The advocates of abortion reform have had no such power. Two national groups were organized, but they had little money and no pulpits. Local groups sprang up—idealistic and eager but usually unable to raise the money or the manpower to wage an effective campaign. Most people, although admitting privately that they wanted reform, would not readily lend their time, open their purses, or sign their names for a cause so controversial.

Faced with 1000 letters branding him a murderer if he voted for abortion reform and 100 letters demanding female rights, the unknowing legislator of five years ago was led to believe that reform was not wanted—until he polled his constituents, as many eventually did. Then he invariably found that his mail had been misleading.

Whenever a Catholic legislator debated an abortion bill, his oratory typically began with the admission, "I am a Catholic" (which made him seem ingenuous), then proceeded to the qualification, "But I am not speaking as a Catholic" (which was disarming but untrue), and ended with the assertion, "Abortion is murder" (which he learned from his earliest religious training). Constantly referring to the fetus (or even the embryo) as a child, he would then reach the height of his polemic by equating the legalization of abortion with the genocidal atrocities of the Nazis and predicting that easing the abortion laws would lead to infanticide, euthanasia, the eradication of social misfits, and complete disintegration of American morality.

At the end of the New York debate, Senate Majority Leader Earl W. Brydges rose, actually in tears, to recite a pile of doggerel, long known to participants in the abortion battle, titled *The Diary of an Unborn Child.* In it, the "child" proceeds to rhapsodize about the prospect of extrauterine life, until, one day—pause—"My parents killed me!"

Ultimately, these tactics offended even some of the Catholic legislators, who this year rose for the first time to say, "I, too, am a Catholic. And I, too, do not believe in abortion. *But* I also believe my religious convictions should not be imposed, as law, upon those who believe otherwise." And this, of course, is the nub of the issue. Throughout these battles—in New York and elsewhere—it has never been sufficiently stressed that no matter how liberal the law, it can never force a woman to have an abortion against her will. This is what opponents of abortion always seem to imply —that its legalization would somehow make it mandatory. And the silence traditionally surrounding the subject has helped foster the notion that abortion laws somehow have protected society from some sinister urge to cease procreating.

Ten years ago, abortion was not a subject suitable for polite conversation. Women who terminated their unwanted pregnancies did so in fear and silence, often risking their lives and suffering the shame and guilt that surrounds such back-street activity. Society tolerated illegal abortion as a necessary evil, sufficiently costly to individual sinners to leave the public conscience clear. Then a series of events took place that no thinking person could ignore.

First there was the Sherri Finkbine incident, in 1962: the young housewife from Arizona who had taken Thalidomide, a tranquilizer found later to often cause serious birth defects, and who had to go to Sweden for an abortion because no American doctor had the guts to bend the law.

Next came the rubella epidemic of 1963-1965, leaving 30,000 deformed babies in its wake. Hospitals were by this time permitting abortions for rubella—but not often enough.

And in 1965, the momentous decision of the U.S. Supreme Court declared the birth-control laws unconstitutional on the ground that they infringed upon a newly enunciated right—the right to marital privacy.

In addition, the sexual revolution, the population explosion, the decline in religiosity, and the demand for equality of the sexes helped change the climate of thinking about abortion. Finally, in the age of modern contraceptives, women were beginning to regard sex without pregnancy as a natural and personal right. As this concept firmly took hold, the pill could be viewed as a safeguard against unwanted pregnancy and abortion as the simple solution to contraceptive failure.

By the mid-sixties, abortion—like contraception and sex itself—was no longer a taboo subject and the first real efforts at reform were getting into gear. But what could such a movement hope to achieve five years ago? Its leaders, who had wrestled with the problem, professionally and personally, favored outright repeal of the laws; but most laymen and legislators, who had not thought much about it, were not yet ready to go that far.

With foresight, the prestigious American Law Institute (A. L. I.) had proposed a Model Penal Code to update the entire book of criminal law. Its recommendation about abortion, made in 1959: that it be permitted for mental and physical health, fetal deformity, rape, and incest. Although this A. L. I. package would have merely legitimized the hospital abortions already being done by many respectable doctors in reputable hospitals, it provided the thin edge of the wedge on which the movement could begin to hammer.

The first legislative breakthrough occurred in 1967 in Colorado. If this initial victory had happened in Nevada—with its reputation for divorce, gambling, and prostitution—the movement could have been set back ten years. Even a Southern state would have been unfortunate, for some militant blacks might have charged genocide—as, indeed, they did when Georgia changed its law the following year.

Now, 12 states have A. L. I. reform laws—four in the West, one in the Midwest, six in the South, and one in the East. And, as is usually the case with halfway measures, they have solved much less than half the problem. Hospital abortions are up 25 times in Colorado and California, but criminal abortions still abound. In Georgia, the hospital rate hasn't changed at all. Once it became clear that the liberalized statutes were mostly paper reforms, that particular movement died. The states with reform laws can be congratulated for having achieved all that was possible in those times and circumstances, for having helped awaken the country to the inequities of the older laws, and for having proved that "reform" is a futile compromise. Now the movement is calling for outright repeal.

Hawaii led the way. And then New York and Alaska. Ironically, repeal may now be easier to achieve than reform. In a reform bill, legislators must agree on the reasons for which an abortion may be performed. And it has been repeatedly demonstrated that legislators, playing amateur doctors and theologians, can debate these stipulations indefinitely—and then abandon the effort. But with repeal, they pass this responsibility on to the medical profession. Neither legislators nor doctors are willing to concede that this responsibility rightfully rests with the woman herself. This was the real issue in the long and bitter fight to reform, and later to repeal, the 140-year-old New York law that had survived as long as it did through religious and political skulduggery hardly rivaled in American legislative history.

The most recent fight began in 1964. I received a clue to its future course when I testified that year before New York's Temporary State Commission on Revision of the Penal Law and Criminal Code, which was considering reform of the laws pertaining to every crime, from homosexuality to homicide—but not abortion. When I urged the adoption of the A. L. I. proposals, the commission candidly conceded that "it would be most unrealistic for any assemblyman who had dreams of a political future to put a bill vis-à-vis abortion laws [before the legislature] of New York."

Heedless of this admonition, Assemblyman Percy E. Sutton did introduce such a bill. And the following year, when Sutton left Albany to become Manhattan's borough president, Assemblyman Albert H. Blumenthal took over. Every year there were public hearings. Every year the legislators voted according to their religion or their erroneous appraisal of their constituents' will, and the bill was ultimately defeated. This despite the support of Governor Rockefeller, Senators Javits and the late Robert Kennedy, Mayor Lindsay, and virtually every non-Catholic medical, legal, religious, and civic group in the state—and over 80 percent of the New York electorate, according to polls.

In 1969, Blumenthal, a Democrat, finally lined up enough votes to guarantee passage of his reform bill. At the same time, however, he vigorously opposed Governor Rockefeller's budget cuts. Perhaps in retaliation for this unrelated stand—although ostensibly in response to an emotional speech by a polio-crippled Republican assemblyman, whom many assumed to be a victim of a birth defect—13 Republicans switched their votes and the bill died again.

During the five years the New York assembly debated abortion reform, it was never even considered by the senate—largely due to the opposition of Majority Leader Brydges, a Roman Catholic. Then, in 1970, a total repeal bill—one that would leave abortion a matter to be decided only by the woman and her physician—was drafted by none other than Brydges himself. His intent, evidently, was to head off the growing reform movement by proposing a bill so radical that it had no prospects of passage— and whose defeat would, by implication, buttress the existing New York law. He even announced that he would vote against his own bill.

Senator Brydges first scheduled debate on the bill for March 17, Saint

Patrick's Day, until *The New York Times* suggested that his timing might be more than coincidental, whereupon he rescheduled the debate for the following day. Perhaps because the bill's opponents were confident of its defeat, and because the debate lasted only one day, the Catholic leaders did not mobilize their usual campaign before the vote was taken. To the surprise of everyone, and especially Senator Brydges, the repeal bill passed, 31 to 26.

In the assembly, the bill was successfully bottled up in the Codes Committee, whose chairman opposed reform. Momentum was lost and the opposition was able to rally its forces. Amendments were introduced. Easter intervened. The blistering pastoral letters were read from 1700 pulpits and pressure began to mount against Catholic assemblymen—some of whom were denounced by name in their own churches for having indicated their support for the bill. Seventy-six votes were needed for passage. Those present at roll call, on March 30, cast 73 yes votes, and two assemblymen who had left the chamber had instructed the clerk to record their votes in favor of the bill—a routine practice. Speaker Perry B. Duryea had promised to cast the 76th vote for repeal if it was needed; but, instead, he made the unprecedented move of refusing to count the votes recorded by the two absentees. So the bill went down, 73 to 71.

Enraged by this denouement, reformers demanded a revote. Another week elapsed. Catholic pressure intensified. On April eighth, the day before the assembly's second debate, Speaker Duryea, who had been chastised by his colleagues for disallowing the absentee votes, took the unique precaution of refusing to permit a revote unless all members of the assembly were in attendance. Those not present, he announced, would be brought to the chamber "by whatever force necessary," including the state police.

Martial methods were not required, however. All the assemblymen were in their seats the next day. To succeed, of course, the reform group had to hold onto each of its original 75 votes. But as the roll call proceeded, it became apparent that there were defectors. Having been denounced as murderers by their parish priests, three Catholics switched their votes from yes to no. Two votes switched the other way, but this was not enough. And then—only seconds before the clerk was to announce defeat of the bill for want of a single vote—Assemblyman George Michaels stopped the roll call. "The act I take here today may terminate my political career," he said, and then he requested that his no vote be changed to a yes. Duryea then asked that his name be called, so that he could cast the decisive 76th vote. (Assemblyman Michaels was subsequently denied the endorsement of the Democratic Party and defeated in his bid for re-election by his predominately Catholic constituency.)

The senate still had to consider the assembly's amendments to its original bill. These would limit the time of an abortion to the 24th week of pregnancy and require the woman's written consent (both farcical restrictions, since abortion is defined medically as the termination of pregnancy prior to the 20th week, and no one advocates involuntary abortion). Despite frantic last-minute efforts by the bill's opponents, no votes were switched. On April tenth, the measure passed, 31 to 26. The following day, Governor Rockefeller signed the bill. It became law on July first.

The dramatic New York battle has had its counterparts in other states. In Hawaii, a repeal bill sponsored by Senator Vincent Yano—a Catholic and the father of ten children—passed both houses after fierce debate and became law without the signature of Governor John A. Burns, also a Catholic. In Alaska, Governor Keith Miller vetoed the state's abortion-law-repeal bill on the ground that it infringed on the "right of life," but Senator John Rader was able to gather enough votes to override the governor's action. In Maryland, Assemblyman Allen Spector's repeal bill passed both houses, only to be vetoed two months later by Governor Marvin Mandel. One of Mandel's justifications for the veto was that the bill set no time limit. He professed shock that women might have abortions up to the eighth and ninth month of pregnancy. This, of course, was a specious argument, since an operation that late in pregnancy is not, medically speaking, an abortion. In a number of other states, repeal bills either died in committee or were defeated in the legislature.

These stories illustrate the problem of securing abortion reform through legislation. Even when possible, it takes enormous time and effort; and in many states, the obstacles are simply insurmountable. But in one respect, the problems of ultrastrict laws and ultraconservative lawmakers have proved a blessing in disguise. It was the failure of the moderate reform efforts that led the movement's tacticians to try a new and potentially more successful approach: challenging the abortion laws in court. The great advantage of this approach is that a single Supreme Court ruling could nullify the abortion laws of every state that still restricts such operations.

Several lower courts already have handed down favorable decisions. A court in Brooklyn, for example, awarded $100,000 to the child and $10,000 to the mother, a rubella victim, because the hospital had neither informed her of the likelihood that her child would be deformed nor referred her to another hospital where she could have obtained a therapeutic abortion. As in most such cases, a Catholic obstetrician was involved. For the first time, however, a jury found his actions incompatible with those of the general medical community. The judge—who happened also to be a Catholic—sustained the award to the mother but overruled the award to the child (who is partially blind, deaf, retarded, and spastic), on the ground that "a plaintiff has no remedy against a defendant whose offense is that it failed to consign the plaintiff to oblivion." Both sides have appealed.

A Catholic judge in Massachusetts ruled adversely on a motion to dismiss the indictment of Dr. Pierre V. Brunelle, a physician accused of performing an extrahospital abortion. After hearing voluminous expert testimony challenging the constitutionality of the law, Superior Court Judge Cornelius J. Moynihan contended that "the evidence before me clearly establishes that the . . . fetus . . . is not a potential human life, but actual human life" and dismissed all ten of the defense's constitutional arguments with the incredible rationale that "If the law on abortion is not as responsive to felt need as the people believe contemporary life demands, the remedy rests with a democratically elected legislature and not with the courts." His decision, too, is being appealed.

Fortunately, other abortion cases have been judged on their legal merits. In Los Angeles, for example, Dr. Leon Belous was convicted, at the criminal-court level, for having referred a patient to an unlicensed doctor-abortionist. A respected obstetrician active in the abortion-law-reform movement, Belous appealed to the state supreme court, claiming that the law under which he had been charged was unconstitutional. On September 5, 1969, the court agreed with him and, in so doing, struck down the law. The attorney general of California appealed the decision, but, as expected, the U. S. Supreme Court refused to review it—for it is unusual for the High Court to review the decision of a state supreme court that voids one of its own statutes.

Regrettably, Belous had been arrested in 1966, before the California law was liberalized; so the 1967 reform law was left standing on the books. And it is one of the poorest of the new laws, because, thanks to the insistence of Governor Reagan, it does not even permit abortion for fetal deformity. Recently, however, the present California law has been found unconstitutional by municipal-court judges in Hayward and in Orange County, and other cases will probably reach the courts this year.

The Belous case illustrates why attempts at limited legislative reform are now dead—or should be. The old laws, which still exist in 35 states, are vulnerable to constitutional attack; but if these are ruled null and void, the states with reform laws may remain stuck with them. It will then take another round of litigation to get rid of these laws—which seemed so progressive just a few years ago.

In yet another California case, nine San Francisco obstetricians were brought before the State Board of Medical Examiners, at the instigation of a Catholic member, for having performed hospital abortions for rubella during the 1963-1965 epidemic. Disregarding the well-known fact that

The Politics of Sex and Marriage

rubella abortions were accepted medical practice throughout most of the country, the board took it upon itself to discipline these physicians, who, in turn, had the courage to take their case to court. The board's action was overruled. A superior court held that it would be cruel and unusual punishment to deprive a woman of an abortion if she had had rubella during her pregnancy and that the California law violated the Fourteenth Amendment, which provides for due process and equal protection.

It seems evident to me that all of these laws are unconstitutional, though I am not a lawyer. Experts claim that they are unconstitutionally vague, that they deprive the doctor of due process, that they infringe on marital privacy, that they interfere with the doctor-patient relationship, that they prevent physicians from practicing medicine in accordance with modern standards, that they discriminate against the poor, that they violate the guarantee against cruel and unusual punishment, and that they are inconsistent with the separation of church and state.

Several of these allegations were upheld in the Belous case. In reaffirming the married couple's "right to privacy or liberty in matters related to marriage, family, and sex," the court further asserted that the abortion law infringed upon "the fundamental right of the woman to choose whether to bear children." The main point, however, was vagueness.

In November 1969, two months after the California decision, the District of Columbia's abortion law was struck down by Federal District Court Judge Gerhard A. Gesell. Reiterating many of the arguments cited in the West Coast case, Judge Gesell held the District of Columbia law unconstitutionally vague (although it permitted abortions for health as well as life) and ruled that it "improperly limits the physician in carrying out his professional responsibilities." Judge Gesell then called upon the city's public hospitals to liberalize their abortion policies immediately and urged the U. S. District Attorney's office to appeal his ruling directly to the U. S. Supreme Court. The judge in this case is the son of the famous pediatric psychologist, the late Dr. Arnold Gesell, who is sometimes cited by Catholics to prove that the fetus is a human being, because he believed (as all doctors do) that there is neurological growth *in utero*.

Similar rulings have been handed down by a South Dakota circuit court, a district court in Michigan, and Federal courts in Wisconsin and Texas, which have unequivocally struck down state abortion statutes on constitutional grounds.

The Wisconsin case invoked an expeditious new principle in jurisprudential procedure. It seems that now the constitutionality of a given law, if challenged on reasonable grounds, can be tested by requesting the appointment of a three-man federal court. And the decision of this body, if appealed, goes directly to the highest Court in the land. This strategy was first applied to abortion law by a brilliant young constitutional lawyer, Roy Lucas, who prepared the model brief now being used in court actions throughout the country.

But the Wisconsin decision was significant in another respect. It did not void the law on grounds that it was vague or violated due process or otherwise lacked certain legal features that a legislature might easily remedy by enacting a new and more carefully written law just as restrictive as the old one. Instead, the court found that the crucial sections of the statute infringed on the citizen's fundamental right of privacy as implicit under the Ninth Amendment and as protected from state interference by the Fourteenth Amendment. If the Supreme Court should uphold this ruling on such sweeping grounds—the basic right of privacy—state legislatures would have virtually no legal basis for either rewriting their laws to correct legal deficiencies or attempting to impose any new legal restrictions beyond those concerned merely with the practice of medicine by licensed physicians. In short, abortion would be ruled a basic right beyond the reach of any law, liberal or otherwise. Similar court actions are under way in at least 20 states.

These test cases have, of course, had their effect on legislative action, and vice versa. Throughout the debate on New York's repeal bill, for example, its supporters were able to cite the groundswell of judicial as well as public opinion favoring freedom of abortion; and this doubtlessly influenced many otherwise timid legislators to vote in favor of repeal. And now the Supreme Court finds itself asked to rule on not one lower-court decision but several, with more on the way. As things stand now, the Court will grapple with the abortion question sometime this fall. It could elect to sidestep the issue on technical grounds; it could find only certain specific laws unconstitutional on narrow grounds; or it could extend the right-of-privacy doctrine to the termination of pregnancy and take the government out of the picture once and for all. The last course of action would accomplish in one stroke what would otherwise take years of legislative wrangling in state after state.

In my view, repeal through the courts instead of through legislatures is preferable for yet another reason—a subtle one that involves the peculiarities of the medical mind. If the states repeal their laws, the doctors are going to say, "OK, now there is no law against doing an abortion"—but many doctors still won't do them, just as many refuse to do sterilizations. But if the courts declare abortion laws unconstitutional, then doctors will say, "Now it is against the law *not* to do abortions"—and then they will do them, for, in some cases, they may be sued if they don't.

Doctors are confused about abortion. They are disturbed by its sexual connotations. They are atavistically punitive toward pregnant teenagers.

They think that eradicating even problem pregnancies is somehow anti-obstetrics or anti-God.

When I entered the private practice of obstetrics 15 years ago, I thought that I could differentiate the truly desperate woman, overburdened by an urgent psychiatric problem, from the merely inconvenienced woman facing an everyday dilemma—and, further, I thought that only the former deserved an abortion. After listening to a few hundred such women, however, I learned that the distinction between the two types is unimportant and, what's more, that distinction is none of my business.

To determine when to prescribe an antibiotic or when to perform an appendectomy requires a doctor's judgment. Since abortion is a medical procedure, one that once entailed considerable risk, doctors have come to believe that their medical judgment, as well as their surgical skill, is required to decide who should have one. It is not. Now that abortions are actually safer than childbirth, it's no longer within a doctor's purview to decide which women qualify and which do not.

Of course, the doctor still must play a role—three roles, in fact:

1. He must be able to detect the occasional woman whose reason for requesting an abortion is unduly impetuous, self-destructive, or vindictive: the engaged couple, for example, very much in love but inclined toward abortion simply because they are afraid to tell their parents about their predicament; or the man or woman who wants to get rid of a wanted pregnancy in order to punish the spouse. I would say that these irrational motives are responsible for about 1 percent of the abortion requests I receive. In these cases, I think it's the doctor's job to try to dissuade the patient from making a decision she might later regret. But if he fails, he must either do the abortion or send her to someone who will.

2. He must actually suggest abortion as a possibility to the occasional unhappily pregnant woman who is too ignorant or too fearful to ask. This situation will occur more often in hospital clinics, where there are patients who are still unaware, for example, of the dangers of rubella in pregnancy. In these cases, I think it is the doctor's duty to encourage the patient to consider abortion as an alternative to having the baby.

3. And, finally, he must perform the abortion.

If the doctor's roles are limited to these three, he will in most cases serve as a mere technician, which is not quite the aspiration of most physicians but, in the unique area of abortion, exactly what he should be. *Doing* an abortion properly requires medical training, but *deciding* whether to do it, in most cases, does not. The only excuse for a doctor's refusing to do an abortion should be the contrary dictates of his conscience, and then he should be obligated to refer his patient elsewhere.

When doctors realize that their roles are limited in this way, they will balk. They will claim a dearth of hospital beds (although abortions can be done safely on an outpatient basis); they will plead lack of manpower (although they find time to do more than 1,000,000 pelvic operations a year on nonpregnant women); and they will resent being "told" by their patients to do an operation (although, of course, they are no less "told" to deliver babies). A massive educational effort will be required to teach them that in the seventies, their M. D. degree imposes upon them social as well as professional responsibilities.

Some doctors will sense this innately. Some will come around later. Many will hold out in self-righteous disdain of such a change in social values. Others, however, will capitalize on their colleagues' hang-ups by opening abortoria or doing abortions in their offices—and making a fortune. These latter-day pirates are little better than their former criminal counterparts. To stop them, other, more scrupulous doctors are going to have to provide this service in a proper setting at a reasonable cost.

John Adams once said that the American Revolution took place in the minds of the people years before the first shot was fired at Lexington. In the same sense, the abortion revolution has long been anticipated by the American people. Their minds have already changed. Our youth, in particular, have seen the hypocrisy of these laws. Not long ago, a news magazine reported on a girl who went to Mexico City for an abortion, because, in her words, "I feel I don't have to be declared nutty to make up for the fact that my diaphragm didn't work. I refuse to go through this humiliating process." Women, in growing numbers, are insisting that their unwanted pregnancies be terminated right here in the United States, without interference from the law.

Women:
The Longest Revolution

Juliet Mitchell

It is only in the highly developed societies of the West that an authentic liberation of women can be envisaged today. But for this to occur, there must be a transformation of all the structures into which they are integrat-

From Juliet Mitchell, "Women: The Longest Revolution," *New Left Review,* November–December 1969 (no. 40), pp. 19–26. References cited in the original have been deleted.

ed, and an *"unité de rupture."* A revolutionary movement must base its analysis on the uneven development of each, and attack the weakest link in the combination. This may then become the point of departure for a general transformation. What is the situation of the different structures today?

1. *Production*: The long-term development of the forces of production must command any socialist perspective. The hopes which the advent of machine technology raised as early as the nineteenth century have already been discussed. They proved illusory. Today, automation promises the *technical* possibility of abolishing completely the physical differential between man and woman in production, but under capitalist relations of production, the *social* possibility of this abolition is permanently threatened, and can easily be turned into its opposite, the actual diminution of woman's role in production as the labor force contracts.

This concerns the future, for the present the main fact to register is that woman's role in production is virtually stationary, and has been so for a long time now. In England in 1911, 30 percent of the work force were women; in the 1960s, 34 percent. The composition of these jobs has not changed decisively either. The jobs are very rarely "careers." When they are not in the lowest positions on the factory floor, they are normally white-collar auxiliary positions (such as secretaries)—supportive to masculine roles. They are often jobs with a high "expressive" content, such as "service" tasks. Parsons says bluntly: "Within the occupational organization they are analogous to the wife-mother role in the family." The educational system underpins this role structure. Seventy-five percent of 18-year-old girls in England are receiving neither training nor education today. The pattern of "instrumental" father and "expressive" mother is not substantially changed when the woman is gainfully employed, as her job tends to be inferior to that of the man's, to which the family then adapts.

Thus, in all essentials, work as such—of the amount and type effectively available today—has not proved a salvation for women.

2. *Reproduction*: Scientific advance in contraception could, as we have seen, make involuntary reproduction—which accounts for the vast majority of births in the world today, and for a major proportion even in the West—a phenomenon of the past. But oral contraception—which has so far been developed in a form which exactly repeats the sexual inequality of Western society—is only at its beginnings. It is inadequately distributed across classes and countries and awaits further technical improvements. Its main initial impact is, in the advanced countries, likely to be psychological—it will certainly free women's sexual experience from many of the

anxieties and inhibitions which have always afflicted it. It will definitely divorce sexuality from procreation, as necessary complements.

The demographic pattern of reproduction in the West may or may not be widely affected by oral contraception. One of the most striking phenomena of very recent years in the United States has been the sudden increase in the birth rate. In the last decade it has been higher than that of underdeveloped countries such as India, Pakistan, and Burma. In fact, this reflects simply the lesser economic burden of a large family in conditions of economic boom in the richest country in the world. But it also reflects the magnification of familial ideology as a social force. This leads to the next structure.

3. *Socialization*: The changes in the composition of the work force, the size of the family, the structure of education, etc.—however limited from an ideal standpoint—have undoubtedly diminished the societal function and importance of the family. As an organization it is not a significant unit in the political power system, it plays little part in economic production, and it is rarely the sole agency of integration into the larger society; thus at the macroscopic level it serves very little purpose.

The result has been a major displacement of emphasis onto the family's psychosocial function, for the infant and for the couple. Parsons writes:

> The trend of the evidence points to the beginning of the relative stabilization of a *new* type of family structure in a new relation to a general social structure, one in which the family is more specialized than before, but not in any general sense less important, because the society is dependent *more* exclusively on it for the performance of *certain* of its vital functions.

The vital nucleus of truth in the emphasis on socialization of the child has been discussed. It is essential that socialists should acknowledge it and integrate it entirely into any program for the liberation of women. It is noticeable that recent "vanguard" work by French Marxists—Baby, Sullerot, Texier—accords the problem its real importance. However, there is no doubt that the need for permanent, intelligent care of children in the initial three or four years of their lives can (and has been) exploited ideologically to perpetuate the family as a total unit, when its other functions have been visibly declining. Indeed, the attempt to focus women's existence exclusively on bringing up children, is manifestly harmful to children. Socialization as an exceptionally delicate process requires a serene and mature socializer— a type which the frustrations of a *purely* familial role are not liable to produce. Exclusive maternity is often in this sense "counterproductive." The mother discharges her own frustrations and anxieties in a fixation on the child. An increased awareness of the critical importance of socialization, far from leading to a restitution of classical maternal roles, should lead to a reconsideration of them—of what makes a good socializing agent, who can genuinely provide security and stability for the child.

The same arguments apply, *a fortiori,* to the psychosocial role of the family for the couple. The beliefs that the family provides an impregnable enclave of intimacy and security in an atomized and chaotic cosmos assumes the absurd—that the family can be isolated from the community, and that its internal relationships will not reproduce in their own terms the external relationships which dominate the society. The family as refuge in a bourgeois society inevitably becomes a reflection of it.

4. *Sexuality:* It is difficult not to conclude that the major structure which at present is in rapid evolution is sexuality. Production, reproduction, and socialization are all more or less stationary in the West today, in the sense that they have not changed for three or more decades. There is, moreover, no widespread *demand* for changes in them on the part of women themselves—the governing ideology has effectively prevented critical consciousness. By contrast, the dominant sexual ideology is proving less and less successful in regulating spontaneous behavior. Marriage in its classical form is increasingly threatened by the liberalization of relationships before and after it which affects all classes today. In this sense, it is evidently the weak link in the chain—the particular structure that is the site of the most contradictions. The progressive potential of these contradictions has already been emphasized. In a context of juridical equality, the liberation of sexual experience from relations which are extraneous to it—whether procreation or property—could lead to true intersexual freedom. But it could also lead simply to new forms of neocapitalist ideology and practice. For one of the forces behind the current acceleration of sexual freedom has undoubtedly been the conversion of contemporary capitalism from a production-and-work ethos to a consumption-and-fun ethos. Riesman commented on this development early in the 1950s:

> . . . there is not only a growth of leisure, but work itself becomes both less interesting and less demanding for many . . . more than before, as job-mindedness declines, sex permeates the daytime as well as the playtime consciousness. It is viewed as a consumption good not only by the old leisure classes, but by the modern leisure masses.

The gist of Riesman's argument is that in a society bored by work, sex is the only activity, the only reminder of one's energies, the only competitive act; the last defense against *vis inertiae*. The same insight can be found with greater theoretical depth, in Marcuse's notion of "repressive de-sublimation"—the freeing of sexuality for its own frustration in the service of a totally coordinated and drugged social machine. Bourgeois society at present can well afford a play area of premarital *non*procreative sexuality.

Even marriage can save itself by increasing divorce and remarriage rites, signifying the importance of the institution itself. These considerations make it clear that sexuality, while it presently may contain the greatest potential for liberation—can equally well be organized against any increase of its human possibilities. New forms of reification are emerging which may void sexual freedom of any meaning. This is a reminder that while one structure may be the *weak link* in a unity like that of woman's condition, there can never be a solution through it alone. The utopianism of Fourier or Reich was precisely to think that sexuality could inaugurate such a general solution. Lenin's remark to Clara Zetkin is a salutary if overstated corrective:

> However wild and revolutionary (sexual freedom) may be, it is still really quite bourgeois. It is, mainly, a hobby of the intellectuals and of the sections nearest them. There is no place for it in the Party, in the class-conscious, fighting, proletariat.

For a general solution can only be found in a strategy which affects *all* the structures of women's exploitation. This means a rejection of two beliefs prevalent on the left:

Reformism: This now takes the form of limited ameliorative demands: equal pay for women, more nursery schools, better retraining facilities, etc. In its contemporary version it is wholly divorced from any fundamental critique of women's condition or any vision of their real liberation (it was not always so). Insofar as it represents a tepid embellishment of the *status quo,* it has very little progressive content left.

Voluntarism: This takes the form of maximalist demands—the abolition of the family, abrogation of all sexual restrictions, forceful separation of parents from children—which have no chance of winning any wide support at present, and which merely serve as a substitute for the job of theoretical analysis or practical persuasion. By pitching the whole subject in totally intransigent terms, voluntarism objectively helps to maintain it outside the framework of normal political discussion.

What, then, is the responsible revolutionary attitude? It must include both immediate and fundamental demands, in a single critique of the *whole* of women's situation, that does not fetishize any dimension of it. Modern industrial development, as has been seen, tends toward the separating out of the originally unified function of the family—procreation, socialization, sexuality, economic subsistence, etc.—even if this "structural differentiation" (to use a term of Parsons') has been checked and disguised by the maintenance of a powerful family ideology. This differentiation provides the real historical basis for the ideal demands which should be posed: structural differentiation is precisely what distinguishes an advanced from a primitive society (in which all social functions are fused *en bloc*).

In practical terms this means a coherent system of demands. The four elements of women's condition cannot merely be considered each in isolation; they form a structure of specific interrelations. The contemporary bourgeois family can be seen as a triptych of sexual, reproductive, and socializatory functions (the woman's world) embraced by production (the man's world)—precisely a structure which in the final instance is determined by the economy. The exclusion of women from production—social human activity—and their confinement to a monolithic condensation of functions in a unity—the family—which is precisely unified in the *natural part* of each function, is the root cause of the contemporary *social* definition of women as *natural* beings. Hence the main thrust of any emancipation movement must still concentrate on the economic element— the entry of women fully into public industry. The error of the old socialists was to see the other elements as reducible to the economic; hence the call for the entry of women into production was accompanied by the purely abstract slogan of the abolition of the family. Economic demands are still primary, but must be accompanied by coherent policies for the other three elements, policies which at particular junctures may take over the primary role in immediate action.

Economically, the most elementary demand is not the right to work or receive equal pay for work—the two traditional reformist demands—but *the right to equal work itself*. At present, women perform unskilled, uncreative, service jobs that can be regarded as "extensions" of their expressive familial role. They are overwhelmingly waitresses, office cleaners, hairdressers, clerks, typists. In the working class, occupational mobility is thus sometimes easier for girls than boys—they can enter the white-collar sector at a lower level. But only two in a hundred women are in administrative or managerial jobs, and less than five in a thousand are in the professions. Women are poorly unionized (25 percent) and receive less money than men for the manual work they do perform: in 1961 the average industrial wage for women was less than half that for men, which, even setting off part-time work, represents a massive increment of exploitation for the employer.

Education

The whole pyramid of discrimination rests on a solid extra-economic foundation—education. The demand for equal work, in Britain, should above all take the form of a demand for an *equal educational system,* since this is at present the main single filter selecting women for inferior work roles. At present, there is something like equal education for both sexes up to 15. Thereafter three times as many boys continue their education as girls. Only one in three "A"-level entrants, one in four university students, is a girl. There is no evidence whatever of progress. The proportion of girl university students is the same as it was in the 1920s. Until these injustices are ended, there is no chance of equal work for women. It goes without saying that the content of the educational system, which actually instills limitation of aspiration in girls, needs to be changed as much as methods of selection. Education is probably the key area for immediate economic advance at present.

Only if it is founded on equality can production be truly differentiated from reproduction and the family. But this in turn requires a whole set of noneconomic demands as a complement. Reproduction, sexuality, and socialization also need to be free from coercive forms of unification. Traditionally, the socialist movement has called for the "abolition of the bourgeois family." This slogan must be rejected as incorrect today. It is maximalist in the bad sense, posing a demand which is merely a negation without any coherent construction subsequent to it. Its weakness can be seen by comparing it to the call for the abolition of the private ownership of the means of production, whose solution—social ownership—is contained in the negation itself. Marx himself allied the two, and pointed out the equal futility of the two demands: ". . . this tendency to oppose general private property to private property is expressed in animal form; *marriage* . . . is contrasted with the community of women, in which women become communal and common property." The reason for the historic weakness of the notion is that the family was never analyzed structurally—in terms of its different functions. It was a hypostasized entity; the abstraction of its abolition corresponds to the abstraction of its conception. The strategic concern for socialists should be for the equality of the sexes, not the abolition of the family. The consequences of this demand are no less radical, but they are concrete and positive, and can be integrated into the real course of history. The family as it exists at present is, in fact, incompatible with the equality of the sexes. But this equality will not come from its administrative abolition, but from the historical differentiation of its functions. The revolutionary demand should be for the liberation of these functions from a monolithic fusion which oppresses each. Thus dissociation of reproduction from sexuality frees sexuality from alienation in unwanted reproduction (and fear of it), and reproduction from subjugation to chance and uncontrollable causality. It is thus an elementary demand to press for free state provision of oral contraception. The legalization of homosexuality—which is one of the forms of nonreproductive sexuality— should be supported for just the same reason, and regressive campaigns against it in Cuba or elsewhere should be unhesitatingly criticized. The straightforward abolition of illegitimacy as a legal notion as in Sweden and Russia has a similar implication; it would separate marriage civically from parenthood.

From Nature to Culture

The problem of socialization poses more difficult questions, as has been seen. But the need for intensive maternal care in the early years of a child's life does not mean that the present single sanctioned form of socialization—marriage and family—is inevitable. Far from it. The fundamental characteristic of the present system of marriage and family is in our society its *monolithism:* there is only one institutionalized form of intersexual or intergenerational relationship possible. It is that or nothing. This is why it is essentially a denial of life. For all human experience shows that intersexual and intergenerational relationships are infinitely various—indeed, much of our creative literature is a celebration of the fact—while the institutionalized expression of them in our capitalist society is utterly simple and rigid. It is the poverty and simplicity of the institutions in this area of life which are such an oppression. Any society will require some institutionalized and social recognition of personal relationships. But there is absolutely no reason why there should be only one legitimized form—and a multitude of unlegitimized experience. Socialism should properly mean not the abolition of the family, but the diversification of the socially acknowledged relationships which are today forcibly and rigidly compressed into it. This would mean a plural range of institutions—where the family is only one, and its abolition implies none. Couples living together or not living together, long-term unions with children, single parents bringing up children, children socialized by conventional rather than biological parents, extended kin groups, etc.—all these could be encompassed in a range of institutions which matched the free invention and variety of men and women.

Chapter 5

Marriage:
Origins, Patterns, and Prospects

On the Origin of Family, Private Property, and State

Friedrich Engels

We have, then, three chief forms of marriage, which, by and large, conform to the three main stages of human development. For savagery—group marriage; for barbarism—pairing marriage; for civilization—monogamy, supplemented by adultery and prostitution. In the upper stage of barbarism, between pairing marriage and monogamy, there is wedged in the dominion exercised by men over female slaves, and polygamy.

As our whole exposition has shown, the advance to be noted in this sequence is linked with the peculiar fact that while women are more and more deprived of the sexual freedom of group marriage, the men are not. Actually, for men, group marriage exists to this day. What for a woman is a crime entailing dire legal and social consequences, is regarded in the case of a man as being honorable or, at most, as a slight moral stain that one bears with pleasure. The more the old traditional hetaerism is changed in our day by capitalist commodity production and adapted to it, and the more it is transformed into unconcealed prostitution, the more demoralizing are its effects. And it demoralizes the men far more than it does the women. Among women, prostitution degrades only those unfortunates who fall into its clutches; and even these are not degraded to the degree

From Friedrich Engels, "On the Origin of the Family, Private Property, and the State," in Karl Marx and Friedrich Engels, *Selected Works,* Vol. II (Moscow: Foreign Languages Publishing House, 1962). References cited in the original have been deleted.

that is generally believed. On the other hand, it degrades the character of the entire male world. Thus, in nine cases out of ten, a long engagement is practically a preparatory school for conjugal infidelity.

Thus, monogamy does not by any means make its appearance in history as the reconciliation of man and woman, still less as the highest form of such a reconciliation. On the contrary, it appears as the subjection of one sex by the other, as the proclamation of a conflict between the sexes entirely unknown hitherto in prehistoric times. In an old unpublished manuscript, the work of Marx and myself in 1846, I find the following: "The first division of labor is that between man and woman for child breeding." And today I can add: The first class antagonism which appears in history coincides with the development of the antagonism between man and woman in monogamian marriage, and the first class oppression with that of the female sex by the male. Monogamy was a great historical advance, but at the same time it inaugurated, along with slavery and private wealth, that epoch, lasting until today, in which every advance is likewise a relative regression, in which the well-being and development of the one group are attained by the misery and repression of the other. It is the cellular form of civilized society, in which we can already study the nature of the antagonisms and contradictions which develop fully in the latter.

With the rise of property differentiation—that is, as far back as the upper stage of barbarism—wage labor appears sporadically alongside of slave labor; and simultaneously, as its necessary correlate, the professional prostitution of free women appears side by side with the forced surrender of the female slave. Thus, the heritage bequeathed to civilization by group marriage is double-sided, just as everything engendered by civilization is double-sided, double-tongued, self-contradictory, and antagonistic: on the one hand, monogamy, on the other, hetaerism, including its most extreme form, prostitution. Hetaerism is as much a social institution as any other; it is a continuation of the old sexual freedom—in favor of the men. Although, in reality, it is not only tolerated but even practiced with gusto, particularly by the ruling classes, it is condemned in words. In reality, however, this condemnation by no means hits the men who indulge in it, it hits only the women: they are ostracized and cast out in order to proclaim once again the absolute domination of the male over the female sex as the fundamental law of society.

A second contradiction, however, is hereby developed within monogamy itself. By the side of the husband, whose life is embellished by hetaerism, stands the neglected wife. And it is just as impossible to have one side of a contradiction without the other as it is to retain the whole of an apple in one's hand after half has been eaten. Nevertheless, the men appear to have thought differently, until their wives taught them to know better. Two permanent social figures, previously unknown, appear on the scene along with monogamy—the wife's paramour and the cuckold. The men had gained the victory over the women, but the act of crowning the victor was magnanimously undertaken by the vanquished. Adultery—proscribed, severely penalized, but irrepressible—became an unavoidable social institution alongside of monogamy and hetaerism. The assured paternity of children was now, as before, based, at best, on moral conviction; and in order to solve the insoluble contradition, Article 312 of the *Code Napoléon* decreed: *"L'enfant conçu pendant le mariage a pour père le mari,"* "a child conceived during marriage has for its father the husband." This is the final outcome of three thousand years of monogamy.

Thus, in the monogamian family, in those cases that faithfully reflect its historical origin and that clearly bring out the sharp conflict between man and woman resulting from the exclusive domination of the male, we have a picture in miniature of the very antagonisms and contradictions in which society, split up into classes since the commencement of civilization, moves, without being able to resolve and overcome them. Naturally, I refer here only to those cases of monogamy where matrimonial life really takes its course according to the rules governing the original character of the whole institution, but where the wife rebels against the domination of the husband. That this is not the case with all marriages no one knows better than the German Philistine, who is no more capable of ruling in the home than in the state, and whose wife, therefore, with full justification, wears the breeches of which he is unworthy. But in consolation he imagines himself to be far superior to his French companion in misfortune, who, more often than he, fares far worse.

Thus, full freedom in marriage can become generally operative only when the abolition of capitalist production, and of the property relations created by it, has removed all those secondary economic considerations which still exert so powerful an influence on the choice of a partner. Then, no other motive remains than mutual affection.

Since sex love is by its very nature exclusive—although this exclusiveness is fully realized today only in the woman—then marriage based on sex love is by its very nature monogamy. We have seen how right Bachofen was when he regarded the advance from group marriage to individual marriage chiefly as the work of the women; only the advance from pairing marriage to monogamy can be placed to the men's account, and, historically, this consisted essentially in a worsening of the position of women and in facilitating infidelity on the part of the men. With the disappearance of the economic considerations which compelled women to tolerate the customary infidelity of the men—the anxiety about their own livelihood and even more about the future of their children—the equality of woman thus achieved will, judging from all previous experience, result far more effectively in the men becoming really monogamous than in the women becoming polyandrous.

What will most definitely disappear from monogamy, however, is all the characteristics stamped on it in consequence of its having arisen out of property relationships. These are, first, the dominance of the man, and secondly, the indissolubility of marriage. The predominance of the man in marriage is simply a consequence of his economic predominance and will vanish with it automatically. The indissolubility of marriage is partly the result of the economic conditions under which monogamy arose, and partly a tradition from the time when the connection between these economic conditions and monogamy was not yet correctly understood and was exaggerated by religion. Today it has been breached a thousandfold. If only marriages that are based on love are moral, then, also, only those are moral in which love continues. The duration of the urge of individual sex love differs very much according to the individual, particularly among men; and a definite cessation of affection, or its displacement by a new passionate love, makes separation a blessing for both parties as well as for society. People will only be spared the experience of wading through the useless mire of divorce proceedings.

Thus, what we can conjecture at present about the regulation of sex relationships after the impending effacement of capitalist production is, in the main, of a negative character, limited mostly to what will vanish. But what will be added? That will be settled after a new generation has grown up: a generation of men who never in all their lives have had occasion to purchase a woman's surrender either with money or with any other means of social power, and of women who have never been obliged to surrender to any man out of any consideration other than that of real love, or to refrain from giving themselves to their beloved for fear of the economic consequences. Once such people appear, they will not care a rap about what we today think they should do. They will establish their own practice and their own public opinion, conformable therewith, on the practice of each individual—and that's the end of it.

On Marriage

Bertrand Russell

When we look round the world at the present day and ask ourselves what conditions seem on the whole to make for happiness in marriage and what for unhappiness, we are driven to a somewhat curious conclusion, that the more civilized people become the less capable they seem of life-long happiness with one partner. Irish peasants, although until recent times marriages were decided by the parents, were said by those who ought to know them to be on the whole happy and virtuous in their conjugal life. In general, marriage is easiest where people are least differentiated. When a man differs little from other men, and a woman differs little from other women, there is no particular reason to regret not having married someone else. But people with multifarious tastes and pursuits and interests will tend to desire congeniality in their partners, and to feel dissatisfied when they find that they have secured less of it than they might have obtained. The Church, which tends to view marriage solely from the point of view of sex, sees no reason why one partner should not do just as well as another, and can therefore uphold the indissolubility of marriage without realizing the hardship that this often involves.

Another condition which makes for happiness in marriage is paucity of unowned women and absence of social occasions when husbands meet other women. If there is no possibility of sexual relations with any woman other than one's wife, most men will make the best of the situation and, except in abnormally bad cases, will find it quite tolerable. The same thing applies to wives, especially if they never imagine that marriage should bring much happiness. That is to say, a marriage is likely to be what is called happy if neither party ever expected to get much happiness out of it.

Fixity of social custom, for the same reason, tends to prevent what are called unhappy marriages. If the bonds of marriage are recognized as final and irrevocable, there is no stimulus to the imagination to wander outside and consider that a more ecstatic happiness might have been possible. In order to secure domestic peace where this state of mind exists, it is only necessary that neither the husband nor the wife should fall outrageously below the commonly recognized standard of decent behavior, whatever this may be.

Among civilized people in the modern world, none of these conditions

From Bertrand Russell, "Marriage," in *Marriage and Morals* (New York: Liveright, 1929), Ch. 10. References cited in the original have been deleted.

for what is called happiness exist, and accordingly one finds that very few marriages after the first few years are happy. Some of the causes of unhappiness are bound up with civilization, but others would disappear if men and women were more civilized than they are. Let us begin with the latter. Of these the most important is bad sexual education, which is a far commoner thing among the well-to-do than it can ever be among peasants. Peasant children early become accustomed to what are called the facts of life, which they can observe not only among human beings but among animals. They are thus saved from both ignorance and fastidiousness. The carefully educated children of the well-to-do, on the contrary, are shielded from all practical knowledge of sexual matters, and even the most modern parents, who teach children out of books, do not give them that sense of practical familiarity which the peasant child early acquires. The triumph of Christian teaching is when a man and woman marry without either having had previous sexual experience. In nine cases out of ten where this occurs, the results are unfortunate. Sexual behavior among human beings is not instinctive, so that the inexperienced bride and bridegroom, who are probably quite unaware of this fact, find themselves overwhelmed with shame and discomfort. It is little better when the woman alone is innocent but the man has acquired his knowledge from prostitutes. Most men do not realize that a process of wooing is necessary after marriage, and many well-brought-up women do not realize what harm they do to marriage by remaining reserved and physically aloof. All this could be put right by better sexual education, and is in fact very much better with the generation now young than it was with their parents and grandparents. There used to be a widespread belief among women that they were morally superior to men on the ground that they had less pleasure in sex. This attitude made frank companionship between husbands and wives impossible. It was, of course, in itself quite unjustifiable, since failure to enjoy sex, so far from being virtuous, is a mere physiological or psychological deficiency, like a failure to enjoy food, which also a hundred years ago was expected of elegant females.

Other modern causes of unhappiness in marriage are, however, not so easily disposed of. I think that uninhibited civilized people, whether men or women, are generally polygamous in their instincts. They may fall deeply in love and be for some years entirely absorbed in one person, but sooner or later sexual familiarity dulls the edge of passion, and then they begin to look elsewhere for a revival of the old thrill. It is, of course, possible to control this impulse in the interests of morality, but it is very difficult to prevent the impulse from existing. With the growth of women's freedom there has come a much greater opportunity for conjugal infidelity than existed in former times. The opportunity gives rise to the thought, the thought gives rise to the desire, and in the absence of religious scruples the desire gives rise to the act.

Women's emancipation has in various ways made marriage more difficult. In old days the wife had to adapt herself to the husband, but the husband did not have to adapt himself to the wife. Nowadays many wives, on grounds of woman's right to her own individuality and her own career, are unwilling to adapt themselves to their husbands beyond a point, while men who still hanker after the old tradition of masculine domination see no reason why they should do all the adapting. This trouble arises especially in connection with infidelity. In old days the husband was occasionally unfaithful, but as a rule his wife did not know of it. If she did, he confessed that he had sinned and made her believe that he was penitent. She, on the other hand, was usually virtuous. If she was not, and the fact came to her husband's knowledge, the marriage broke up. Where, as happens in many modern marriages, mutual faithfulness is demanded, the instinct of jealousy nevertheless survives, and often proves fatal to the persistence of any deeply rooted intimacy even where no overt quarrels occur.

There is another difficulty in the way of modern marriage, which is felt especially by those who are most conscious of the value of love. Love can flourish only as long as it is free and spontaneous; it tends to be killed by the thought that it is a duty. To say that it is your duty to love so-and-so is the surest way to cause you to hate him or her. Marriage as a combination of love with legal bonds thus falls between two stools. Shelley says:

> *I never was attached to that great sect*
> *Whose doctrine is, that each one should select*
> *Out of the crowd a mistress or a friend,*
> *And all the rest, though fair and wise, commend*
> *To cold oblivion, though it is in the code*
> *Of modern morals, and the beaten road*
> *Which those poor slaves with weary footsteps tread,*
> *Who travel to their home among the dead*
> *By the broad highway of the world, and so*
> *With one chained friend, perhaps a jealous foe,*
> *The dreariest and the longest journey go.*

There can be no doubt that to close one's mind on marriage against all the approaches of love from elsewhere is to diminish receptivity and sympathy and the opportunities of valuable human contacts. It is to do violence to something which, from the most idealistic standpoint, is in itself desirable. And like every kind of restrictive morality it tends to promote what one may call a policeman's outlook upon the whole of human life— the outlook, that is to say, which is always looking for an opportunity to forbid something.

For all these reasons, many of which are bound up with things undoubtedly good, marriage has become difficult, and if it is not to be a barrier to happiness it must be conceived in a somewhat new way. One solution often suggested, and actually tried on a large scale in America, is easy divorce. I hold, of course, as every humane person must, that divorce should be granted on more grounds than are admitted in the English law, but I do not recognize in easy divorce a solution of the troubles of marriage. Where a marriage is childless, divorce may be often the right solution, even when both parties are doing their best to behave decently; but where there are children the stability of marriage is to my mind a matter of considerable importance. (This is a subject to which I shall return in connection with the family.) I think that where a marriage is fruitful and both parties to it are reasonable and decent, the expectation ought to be that it will be lifelong, but not that it will exclude other sex relations. A marriage which begins with passionate love and leads to children who are desired and loved ought to produce so deep a tie between a man and woman that they will feel something infinitely precious in their companionship, even after sexual passion has decayed, and even if either or both feels sexual passion for someone else. This mellowing of marriage has been prevented by jealousy, but jealousy, though it is an instinctive emotion, is one which can be controlled if it is recognized as bad, and not supposed to be the expression of a just moral indignation. A companionship which has lasted for many years and through many deeply felt events has a richness of content which cannot belong to the first days of love, however delightful these may be. And any person who appreciates what time can do to enchance values will not lightly throw away such companionship for the sake of new love.

It is therefore possible for a civilized man and woman to be happy in marriage, although if this is to be the case a number of conditions must be fulfilled. There must be a feeling of complete equality on both sides; there must be no interference with mutual freedom; there must be the most complete physical and mental intimacy; and there must be a certain similarity in regard to standards of values. (It is fatal, for example, if one values only money while the other values only good work.) Given all these conditions, I believe marriage to be the best and most important relation that can exist between two human beings. If it has not often been realized hitherto, that is chiefly because husband and wife have regarded themselves as each other's policeman. If marriage is to achieve its possibilities, husbands and wives must learn to understand that whatever the law may say, in their private lives they must be free.

Five Types of Marriage

John F. Cuber and
Peggy B. Harroff

The qualitative aspects of enduring marital relationships vary enormously. The variations described to us were by no means random or clearly individualized, however. Five distinct life styles showed up repeatedly and the pairs within each of them were remarkably similar in the ways in which they lived together, found sexual expression, reared children, and made their way in the outside world.

The following classification is based on the interview materials of those people whose marriages had already lasted ten years or more and who said that they had never seriously considered divorce or separation. While 360 of the men and women had been married ten or more years to the same spouse, exclusion of those who reported that they had considered divorce reduced the number to 211. The discussion in this chapter is, then, based on 211 interviews: 107 men and 104 women.

The descriptions which our interviewees gave us took into account how they had behaved and also how they felt about their actions past and present. Examination of the important features of their lives revealed five recurring configurations of male-female life, each with a central theme— some prominent distinguishing psychological feature which gave each type its singularity. It is these preeminent characteristics which suggested the names for the relationship: the *Conflict-Habituated,* the *Devitalized,* the *Passive-Congenial,* the *Vital,* and the *Total.*

The Conflict-Habituated

We begin with the conflict-habituated not because it is the most prevalent, but because the overt behavior patterns in it are so readily observed and because it presents some arresting contradictions. In this association there is much tension and conflict—although it is largely controlled. At worst, there is some private quarreling, nagging, and "throwing up the past" of which members of the immediate family, and more rarely close friends and relatives, have some awareness. At best, the couple is discreet and polite, genteel about it in the company of others—but after a few drinks at the cocktail party the verbal barbs begin to fly. The intermittent conflict is rarely concealed from the children, though we were often as-

From John F. Cuber and Peggy B. Harroff, "Five Kinds of Relationship," in *Sex and the Significant Americans* (Baltimore: Penguin, 1965), pp. 43–65.

sured otherwise. "Oh, they're at it again—but they always are," says the high-school son. There is private acknowledgment by both husband and wife as a rule that incompatibility is pervasive, that conflict is ever-potential, and that an atmosphere of tension permeates the togetherness.

An illustrative case concerns a physician of fifty, married for twenty-five years to the same woman, with two college-graduate children promisingly established in their own professions.

> You know, it's funny; we have fought from the time we were in high school together. As I look back at it, I can't remember specific quarrels; it's more like a running guerrilla fight with intermediate periods, sometimes quite long, of pretty good fun and some damn good sex. In fact, if it hadn't been for the sex, we wouldn't have been married so quickly. Well, anyway, this has been going on ever since. . . . It's hard to know what it is we fight about most of the time. You name it and we'll fight about it. It's sometimes something I've said that she remembers differently, sometimes a decision—like what kind of car to buy or what to give the kids for Christmas. With regard to politics, and religion, and morals—oh, boy! You know, outside of the welfare of the kids—and that's just abstract—we don't really agree about anything. . . . At different times we take opposite sides—not deliberately; it just comes out that way.
>
> Now these fights get pretty damned colorful. You called them arguments a little while ago—I have to correct you—they're brawls. There's never a bit of physical violence—at least not directed to each other—but the verbal gunfire gets pretty thick. Why, we've said things to each other that neither of us would think of saying in the hearing of anybody else. . . .
>
> Of course we don't settle any of the issues. It's sort of a matter of principle *not* to. Because somebody would have to give in then and lose face for the next encounter. . . .
>
> When I tell you this in this way, I feel a little foolish about it. I wouldn't tolerate such a condition in any other relationship in my life— and yet here I do and always have. . . .
>
> No—we never have considered divorce or separation or anything so clear-cut. I realize that other people do, and I can't say that it has never occurred to either of us, but we've never considered it seriously.
>
> A number of times there has been a crisis, like the time I was in the automobile accident, and the time she almost died in childbirth, and then I guess we really showed that we do care about each other. But as soon as the crisis is over, it's business as usual.

There is a subtle valence in these conflict-habituated relationships. It is easily missed in casual observation. So central is the necessity for channeling conflict and bridling hostility that these considerations come to preoccupy much of the interaction. Some psychiatrists have gone so far as to suggest that it is precisely the deep need to do psychological battle with one another which constitutes the cohesive factor insuring continuity of the marriage. Possibly so. But even from a surface point of view, the overt and manifest fact of habituated attention to handling tension, keeping it chained, and concealing it, is clearly seen as a dominant life force. And it can, and does for some, last for a whole lifetime.

The Devitalized

The key to the devitalized mode is the clear discrepancy between middle-aged reality and the earlier years. These people usually characterized themselves as having been "deeply in love" during the early years, as having spent a great deal of time together, having enjoyed sex, and most importantly of all, having had a close identification with one another. The present picture, with some variation from case to case, is in clear contrast —little time is spent together, sexual relationships are far less satisfying qualitatively or quantitatively, and interests and activities are not shared, at least not in the deeper and meaningful way they once were. Most of their time together now is "duty time"—entertaining together, planning and sharing activities with children, and participating in various kinds of required community responsibilites. They do as a rule retain, in addition to a genuine and mutual interest in the welfare of their children, a shared attention to their joint property and the husband's career. But even in the latter case the interest is contrasting. Despite a common dependency on his success and the benefits which flow therefrom, there is typically very little sharing of the intrinsic aspects of career—simply an acknowledgment of their mutual dependency on the fruits.

Two rather distinct subtypes of the devitalized take shape by the middle years. The following reflections of two housewives in their late forties illustrate both the common and the distinguishing features:

> Judging by the way it was when we were first married—say the first five years or so—things are pretty matter-of-fact now—even dull. They're dull between us, I mean. The children are a lot of fun, keep us pretty busy, and there are lots of outside things—you know, like Little League and the P.T.A. and the Swim Club, and even the company parties aren't always so bad. But I mean where Bob and I are concerned—if you followed us around, you'd wonder why we ever got *married*. We take each other for granted. We laugh at the same things sometimes, but we don't really laugh together—the way we used to. But, as he said to me the other night—with one or two under the belt, I think—"You know, you're still a little fun now and then." . . .
>
> Now, I don't say this to complain, not in the least. There's a cycle to life. There are things you do in high school. And different things you do in college. Then you're a young adult. And then you're middle-aged. That's where we are now. . . . I'll admit that I do yearn for the old days when sex was a big thing and going out was fun and I hung on to every thing he said about his work and his ideas as if they

were coming from a genius or something. But then you get the children and other responsibilities. I have the home and Bob has a tremendous burden of responsibility at the office. . . . He's completely responsible for setting up the new branch now. . . . You have to adjust to these things and we both try to gracefully. . . . Anniversaries though do sometimes remind you kind of hard. . . .

The other kind of hindsight from a woman in a devitalized relationship is much less accepting and quiescent:

I know I'm fighting it. I ought to accept that it has to be like this, but I don't like it, and I'd do almost anything to bring back the exciting way of living we had at first. Most of my friends think I'm some kind of a sentimental romantic or something—they tell me to act my age—but I do know some people—not very darn many—who are our age and even older, who still have the same kind of excitement about them and each other that we had when we were all in college. I've seen some of them at parties and other places—the way they look at each other, the little touches as they go by. One couple has grandchildren and you'd think they were honeymooners. I don't think it's just sex either—I think they are just part of each other's lives—and then when I think of us and the numb way we sort of stagger through the weekly routine, I could scream. And I've even thought of doing some pretty desperate things to try to build some joy and excitement into my life. I've given up on Phil. He's too content with his balance sheets and the kids' report cards and the new house we're going to build next year. He keeps saying he has everything in life that any man could want. What do you *do?*

Regardless of the gracefulness of the acceptance, or the lack thereof, the common plight prevails: on the subjective, emotional dimension, the relationship has become a void. The original zest is gone. There is typically little overt tension or conflict, but the interplay between the pair has become apathetic, lifeless. No serious threat to the continuity of the marriage is generally acknowledged, however. It is intended, usually by both, that it continue indefinitely despite its numbness. Continuity and relative freedom from open conflict are fostered in part because of the comforts of the "habit cage." Continuity is further insured by the absence of any engaging alternative, "all things considered." It is also reinforced, sometimes rather decisively, by legal and ecclesiastical requirements and expectations. These people quickly explain that "there are other things in life" which are worthy of sustained human effort.

This kind of relationship is exceedingly common. Persons in this circumstance frequently make comparisons with other pairs they know, many of whom are similar to themselves. This fosters the comforting judgment that "marriage is like this—except for a few oddballs or pretenders who claim otherwise."

While these relationships lack visible vitality, the participants assure us that there is "something there." There are occasional periods of sharing at least something—if only memory. Even formalities can have meanings. Anniversaries can be celebrated, if a little grimly, for what they once commemorated. As one man said, "Tomorrow we are celebrating the anniversary of our anniversary." Even clearly substandard sexual expression is said by some to be better than nothing, or better than a clandestine substitute. A "good man" or a "good mother for the kids" may "with a little affection and occasional attention now and then, get you by." Many believe that the devitalized mode is the appropriate mode in which a man and woman should be content to live in the middle years and later.

The Passive-Congenial

The passive-congenial mode has a great deal in common with the devitalized, the essential difference being that the passivity which pervades the association has been there from the start. The devitalized have a more exciting set of memories; the passive-congenials give little evidence that they had ever hoped for anything much different from what they are currently experiencing.

There is therefore little suggestion of disillusionment or compulsion to make believe to anyone. Existing modes of association are comfortably adequate—no stronger words fit the facts as they related them to us. There is little conflict, although some admit that they tiptoe rather gingerly over and around a residue of subtle resentments and frustrations. In their better moods they remind themselves (and each other) that "there are many common interests" which they both enjoy. "We both like classical music." "We agree completely on religious and political matters." "We both love the country and our quaint exurban neighbors." "We are both lawyers."

The wife of a prominent attorney, who has been living in the passive-congenial mode for thirty years, put her description this way:

> We have both always tried to be calm and sensible about major life decisions, to think things out thoroughly and in perspective. Len and I knew each other since high school but didn't start to date until college. When he asked me to marry him, I took a long time to decide whether he was the right man for me and I went into his family background, because I wasn't just marrying him; I was choosing a father for my children. We decided together not to get married until he was established, so that we would not have to live in dingy little apartments like some of our friends who got married right out of college. This prudence has stood us in good stead too. Life has moved ahead for us with remarkable orderliness and we are deeply grateful for the foresight we had. . . .

When the children were little, we scheduled time together with them, although since they're grown, the demands of the office are getting pretty heavy. Len brings home a bulging briefcase almost every night and more often than not the light is still on in his study after I retire. But we've got a lot to show for his devoted effort. . . .

I don't like all this discussion about sex—even in the better magazines. I hope your study will help to put it in its proper perspective. I expected to perform sex in marriage, but both before and since, I'm willing to admit that it's a much overrated activity. Now and then, perhaps it's better. I am fortunate, I guess, because my husband has never been demanding about it, before marriage or since. It's just not that important to either of us. . . .

My time is very full these days, with the chairmanship of the Cancer Drive, and the Executive Board of the (state) P.T.A. I feel a little funny about that with my children already grown, but there are the grandchildren coming along. And besides so many of my friends are in the organizations, and it's so much like a home-coming.

People make their way into the passive-congenial mode by two quite different routes—by default and by intention. Perhaps in most instances they arrive at this way of living and feeling by drift. There is so little which they have cared about deeply in each other that a passive relationship is sufficient to express it all. In other instances the passive-congenial mode is a deliberately intended arrangement for two people whose interests and creative energies are directed elsewhere than toward the pairing—into careers, or in the case of women, into children or community activities. They say they know this and want it this way. These people simply do not wish to invest their total emotional involvement and creative effort in the male-female relationship.

The passive-congenial life style fits societal needs quite well also, and this is an important consideration. The man of practical affairs, in business, government service, or the professions—quite obviously needs "to have things peaceful at home" and to have a minimum of distraction as he pursues his important work. He may feel both love and gratitude toward the wife who fits this mode.

A strong case was made for the passive congenial by a dedicated physician:

I don't know why everyone seems to make so much about men and women and marriage. Of course, I'm married and if anything happened to my wife, I'd get married again. I think it's the proper way to live. It's convenient, orderly, and solves a lot of problems. But there are other things in life. I spent nearly ten years preparing for the practice of my profession. The biggest thing to me is the practice of that profession, to be of assistance to my patients and their families. I spend twelve hours a day at it. And I'll bet if you talked with my wife, you wouldn't get any of that "trapped housewife" stuff from her either. Now that the children are grown, she finds a lot of useful and necessary work to do in this community. She works as hard as I do.

The passive-congenial mode facilitates the achievement of other goals too. It enables people who desire a considerable amount of personal independence and freedom to realize it with a minimum of inconvenience from or to the spouse. And it certainly spares the participants in it from the need to give a great deal of personal attention to "adjusting to the spouse's needs." The passive-congenial ménage is thus a mood as well as a mode.

Our descriptions of the devitalized and the passive-congenials have been similar because these two modes are much alike in their overt characteristics. The participants' evaluations of their *present situations* are likewise largely the same—the accent on "other things," the emphasis on civic and professional responsibilities, the importance of property, children, and reputation. The essential difference lies in their diverse histories and often in their feelings of contentment with their current lives. The passive-congenials had from the start a life pattern and a set of expectations essentially consistent with what they are now experiencing. When the devitalized reflect, however, when they juxtapose history against present reality, they often see the barren gullies in their lives left by the erosions of earlier satisfactions. Some of the devitalized are resentful and disillusioned—their bitterness will appear at various points throughout this book; others, calling themselves "mature about it," have emerged with reasonable acceptance of their existing devitalized modes. Still others are clearly ambivalent, "I wish life would be more exciting, but I should have known it couldn't last. In a way, it's calm and quiet and reassuring this way, but there are times when I get very ill at ease—sometimes downright mad. Does it *have* to be like this?"

The passive-congenials do not find it necessary to speculate in this fashion. Their anticipations were realistic and perhaps even causative of their current marital situation. In any event, their passivity is not jarred when teased by memory.

The Vital

In extreme contrast to the three foregoing is the vital relationship. The vital pair can easily be overlooked as they move through their worlds of work, recreation, and family activities. They do the same things, publicly at least; and when talking for public consumption say the same things— they are proud of their homes, love their children, gripe about their jobs, while being quite proud of their career accomplishments. But when the close, intimate, confidential, empathic look is taken, the essence of the vital relationship becomes clear: the mates are intensely bound together psychologically in important life matters. Their sharing and their togetherness is genuine. It provides the life essence for both man and woman.

> The things we do together aren't fun intrinsically—the ecstasy comes from being *together in the doing.* Take her out of the picture and I wouldn't give a damn for the boat, the lake, or any of the fun that goes on out there.

The presence of the mate is indispensable to the feelings of satisfaction which the activity provides. The activities shared by the vital pairs may involve almost anything: hobbies, careers, community service. Anything—so long as it is closely shared.

It is hard to escape the word *vitality*—exciting mutuality of feelings and participation together in important life segments. The clue that the relationship is vital (rather than merely expressing the joint activity) derives from the feeling that it is important. An activity is flat and uninteresting if the spouse is not a part of it.

Other valued things are readily sacrificed in order to enhance life within the vital relationship.

> I cheerfully, and that's putting it mildly, passed up two good promotions because one of them would have required some traveling and the other would have taken evening and weekend time—and that's when Pat and I *live.* The hours with her (after twenty-two years of marriage) are what I live for. You should meet her. . . .

People in the vital relationship for the most part know that they are a minority and that their life styles are incomprehensible to most of their associates.

> Most of our friends think we moved out to the country for the kids; well—the kids *are* crazy about it, but the fact of the matter is, we moved out for ourselves—just to get away from all the annoyances and interferences of other people—our friends actually. We like this kind of life—where we can have almost all of our time together. . . . We've been married for over twenty years and the most enjoyable thing either of us does—well, outside of the intimate things—is to sit and talk by the hour. That's why we built that imposing fireplace—and the hi-fi here in the corner. . . . Now that Ed is getting older, that twenty-seven-mile drive morning and night from the office is a real burden, but he does it cheerfully so we can have our long uninterrupted hours together. . . . The children respect this too. They don't invade our privacy any more than they can help—the same as we vacate the living room when Ellen brings in a date, she tries not to intrude on us. . . . Being the specialized kind of lawyer he is, I can't share much in his work, but that doesn't bother either of us. The *big* part of our lives is completely mutual. . . .

Her husband's testimony validated hers. And we talked to dozens of other couples like them, too. They find their central satisfaction in the life they live with and through each other. It consumes their interest and dominates their thoughts and actions. All else is subordinate and secondary.

This does not mean that people in vital relationships lose their separate identities, that they may not upon occasion be rivalrous or competitive with one another, or that conflict may not occur. They differ fundamentally from the conflict-habituated, however, in that when conflict does occur, it results from matters that are important to them, such as which college a daughter or son is to attend; it is devoid of the trivial "who said what first and when" and "I can't forget when you. . . ." A further difference is that people to whom the relationship is vital tend to settle disagreements quickly and seek to avoid conflict, whereas the conflict-habituated look forward to conflict and appear to operate by a tacit rule that no conflict is ever to be truly terminated and that the spouse must never be considered right. The two kinds of conflict are thus radically different. To confuse them is to miss an important differentiation.

The Total

The total relationship is like the vital relationship with the important addition that it is more multifaceted. The points of vital meshing are more numerous—in some cases all of the important life foci are vitally shared. In one such marriage the husband is an internationally known scientist. For thirty years his wife has been his "friend, mistress, and partner." He still goes home at noon whenever possible, at considerable inconvenience, to have a quiet lunch and spend a conversational hour or so with his wife. They refer to these conversations as "our little seminars." They feel comfortable with each other and with their four grown children. The children (now in their late twenties) say that they enjoy visits with their parents as much as they do with friends of their own age.

There is practically no pretense between persons in the total relationship or between them and the world outside. There are few areas of tension, because the items of difference which have arisen over the years have been settled as they arose. There often *were* serious differences of opinion but they were handled, sometimes by compromise, sometimes by one or the other yielding; but these outcomes were of secondary importance because the primary consideration was not who was right or who was wrong, only how the problem could be resolved without tarnishing the relationship. When faced with differences, they can and do dispose of the difficulties without losing their feeling of unity or their sense of vitality and centrality of their relationship. This is the mainspring.

The various parts of the total relationship are reinforcing, as we learned from this consulting engineer who is frequently sent abroad by his corporation.

> She keeps my files and scrapbooks up to date. . . . I invariably take
> her with me to conferences around the world. Her femininity, easy
> charm and wit are invaluable assets to me. I know it's conventional to
> say that a man's wife is responsible for his success and I also know
> that it's often not true. But in my case I gladly acknowledge that it's
> not only true, but she's indispensable to me. But she'd go along with
> me even if there was nothing for her to do because we just enjoy each
> other's company—deeply. You know, the best part of a vacation is
> not *what* we do, but that we do it together. We plan it and reminisce
> about it and weave it into our work and other play all the time.

The wife's account is substantially the same except that her testimony
demonstrates more clearly the genuineness of her "help."

> It seems to me that Bert exaggerates my help. It's not so much that
> I only want to help him; it's more that I want to do those things any-
> way. We do them together, even though we may not be in each oth-
> er's presence at the time. I don't really know what I do for him and
> what I do for me.

This kind of relationship is rare, in marriage or out, but it does exist and
can endure. We occasionally found relationships so total that all aspects of
life were mutually shared and enthusiastically participated in. It is as if
neither spouse has, or has had, a truly private existence.

The customary purpose of a classification such as this one is to facilitate
understanding of similarities and differences among the cases classified. In
this instance enduring marriage is the common condition. The differentiating features are the dissimilar forces which make for the integration of
the pair within each of the types. It is not necessarily the purpose of a
classification to make possible a clear-cut sorting of all cases into one or
another of the designated categories. All cannot be so precisely pigeon-
holed; there often are borderline cases. Furthermore, two observers with
equal access to the facts may sometimes disagree on which side of the line
an unclear case should be placed. If the classification is a useful one, however, placement should *as a rule* be clear and relatively easy. The ease is
only relative because making an accurate classification of a given relationship requires the possession of amounts and kinds of information which
one rarely has about persons other than himself. Superficial knowledge of
public or professional behavior is not enough. And even in his own case,
one may, for reasons of ego, find it difficult to be totally forthright.

A further caution. The typology concerns relationships, not personalities.
A clearly vital person may be living in a passive-congenial or devitalized
relationship and expressing his vitality in some other aspect of his life—
career being an important preoccupation for many. Or, possibly either or
both of the spouses may have a vital relationship—sometimes extending
over many years—with someone of the opposite sex outside of the marriage.

Nor are the five types to be interpreted as *degrees* of marital happiness or adjustment. Persons in all five are currently adjusted and most say that they are content, if not happy. Rather, the five types represent *different kinds of adjustment* and *different conceptions of marriage*. This is an important concept which must be emphasized if one is to understand the personal meanings which these people attach to the conditions of their marital experience.

Neither are the five types necessarily stages in a cycle of initial bliss and later disillusionment. Many pairings started in the passive-congenial stage; in fact, quite often people intentionally enter into a marriage for the acknowledged purpose of living this kind of relationship. To many the simple amenities of the "habit cage" are not disillusionments or even disappointments, but rather are sensible life expectations which provide an altogether comfortable and rational way of having a "home base" for their lives. And many of the conflict-habituated told of courtship histories essentially like their marriages.

While each of these types tends to persist, there *may* be movement from one type to another as circumstances and life perspectives change. This movement may go in any direction from any point, and a given couple may change categories more than once. Such changes are relatively *in*frequent however, and the important point is that relationship types tend to persist over relatively long periods.

The fundamental nature of these contexts may be illustrated by examining the impact of some common conditions on persons of each type.

Infidelity, for example, occurs in most of the five types, the total relationship being the exception. But it occurs for quite different reasons. In the conflict-habituated it seems frequently to be only another outlet for hostility. The call girl and the woman picked up in a bar are more than just available women; they are symbols of resentment of the wife. This is not always so, but reported to us often enough to be worth noting. Infidelity among the passive-congenial, on the other hand, is typically in line with the stereotype of the middle-aged man who "strays out of sheer boredom with the uneventful, deadly prose" of his private life. And the devitalized man or woman frequently is trying for an hour or a year to recapture the lost mood. But the vital are sometimes adulterous too; some are simply emancipated—almost bohemian. To some of them sexual aggrandizement is an accepted fact of life. Frequently the infidelity is condoned by the partner and in some instances even provides an indirect (through empathy) kind of gratification. The act of infidelity in such cases is not construed as disloyalty or as a threat to continuity, but rather as a kind of basic human right which the loved one ought to be permitted to have—and which the other perhaps wants also for himself.

Divorce and separation are found in all five of the types, but the reasons, when viewed realistically and outside of the simplitudes of legalistic and ecclesiastical fiction, are highly individual and highly variable. For example, a couple may move from a vital relationship to divorce because for them the alternative of a devitalized relationship is unendurable. They can conceive of marriage only as a vital, meaningful, fulfilling, and preoccupying interaction. The "disvitality" of any other marriage form is abhorrent to them and takes on "the hypocrisy of living a public lie." We have accounts of marriages which were unquestionably vital or total for a period of years but which were dissolved. In some respects relationships of this type are more readily disrupted, because these people have become adjusted to such a rich and deep sharing that evidences of breach, which a person in another type of marriage might consider quite normal, become unbearable.

> I know a lot of close friendships occur between men and women married to someone else, and that they're not always adulterous. But I know Betts—and anyway, I personally believe they eventually do become so, but I can't be sure about that. Anyway, when Betty found her self-expression was furthered by longer and longer meetings and conversations with Joe, and I detected little insincerities, not serious at first, you understand, creeping into the things we did together, it was like the little leak in the great dike. It didn't take very long. We weren't melodramatic about it, but it was soon clear to both of us that we were no longer the kind of pair we once were, so why pretend. The whole thing can go to hell fast—and after almost twenty years!

Husbands in other types of relationships would probably not even have detected any disloyalty on the part of this wife. And even if they had, they would tend to conclude that "you don't break up a home just because she has a passing interest in some glamorous writer."

The divorce which occurs in the passive-congenial marriage follows a different sequence. One of the couple, typically a person capable of more vitality in his or her married life than the existing relationship provides, comes into contact with a person with whom he gradually (or suddenly) unfolds a new dimension to adult living. What he had considered to be a rational and sensible and "adult" relationship can suddenly appear in contrast to be stultifying, shallow, and an altogether disheartening way to live out the remaining years. He is left with "no conceivable alternative but to move out." Typically, he does not do so impulsively or without a more or less stubborn attempt to stifle his "romanticism" and listen to well-documented advice to the effect that he should act maturely and "leave the romantic yearning to the kids for whom it is intended." Very often he is convinced and turns his back on his "new hope"—but not always.

Whether examining marriages for the satisfactions and fulfillments they have brought or for the frustrations and pain, the overriding influence of life style—or as we have here called it, relationship type—is of the essence. Such a viewpoint helps the observer, and probably the participant, to understand some of the apparent enigmas about men and women in marriage—why infidelities destroy some marriages and not others; why conflict plays so large a role for some couples and is so negligible for others; why some seemingly well-suited and harmoniously adjusted spouses seek divorce while others with provocations galore remain solidly together; why affections, sexual expression, recreation, almost everything observable about men and women is so radically different from pair to pair. All of these are not merely different objectively; they are perceived differently by the pairs, are differently reacted to, and differently attended to.

If nothing else, this chapter has demonstrated that realistic understanding of marital relationships requires use of concepts which are carefully based on perceptive factual knowledge. Unfortunately, the language by which relationships between men and women are conventionally expressed tends to lead toward serious and pervasive deceptions which in turn encourage erroneous inferences. Thus, we tend to assume that enduring marriage is somehow synonymous with happy marriage or at least with something comfortably called adjustment. The deception springs from lumping together such dissimilar modes of thought and action as the conflict-habituated, the passive-congenial, and the vital. To know that a marriage has endured, or for that matter has been dissolved, tells one close to nothing about the kinds of experiences, fulfillments, and frustrations which have made up the lives of the people involved. Even to know, for example, that infidelity has occurred, without knowledge of circumstances, feelings, and other essences, results in an illusion of knowledge which masks far more than it describes.

To understand a given marriage, let alone what is called "marriage in general," is realistically possible only in terms of particular sets of experiences, meanings, hopes, and intentions. This chapter has described in broad outline five manifest and recurring configurations among the Significant Americans.

3

The Politics
of Child Rearing

Introduction

A grownup is the man standing next to you in the elevator with the briefcase and the hat; he is not wearing his suit; it is wearing him. You feel that he is, well, *purposeful.* It's not that he's *serious;* children at play are serious. It's just that the grownup seems to do everything, even smile and joke, for reasons that can't be found within his own skin. He goes to work because, reads because, makes friends because, even makes love because. The perfect grownup will someday be replaced by a computer. Meanwhile, he exists as a homunculus inside a role. That's why he rarely really listens to you; he's just waiting for you to cue the next line in that interminable script he mistakes for a life.[1]

The American sociologist, Talcott Parsons, has called the birth of new generations of children a recurrent barbarian invasion.[2]

Physical punishment of children by parents has been accepted down through the ages . . .
Excusable homicide, or murder, is defined in Kansas Statutes Annotated 21-405 and reads in part, "homicide shall be deemed excusable when committed by accident or mistake in lawfully correcting a child, apprentice, or servant."[3]

. . . Every one of these campus disorders is essentially a prison riot. . . .
. . . The purpose of elementary pedagogy, through age 12, should be to delay socialization, to protect children's free growth, since family and community pressure them too much. . . .
. . . the goal of elementary education should be a modest one: it is for a small child, under his own steam, not on a leash, to be able to poke interestedly into whatever goes on and to be able, by observation, questions, and practical imitation, to get something out of it on his own terms. In our society this happens pretty well at home up to age four, but after that it becomes forbiddingly difficult.[4]

The preceding quotations are meant to show why we speak of a politics of child rearing or "socialization." We have seen before with regard to sex roles that any relations based on power may be defined as political. But the politics of socialization involves even more than power. It embraces assumptions and value judgments about reality, human nature, and society;

and about what is valuable and worth preserving in childhood and adulthood.

For the functional sociologist, guided by a vision of society as always in danger of falling apart, children are seen mainly as the agents of social survival:

> It is readily apparent that what will terminate a society will not disintegrate an individual, at least not when he is viewed mainly as a biological organism. It should be evident, however, that the ways in which society meets its imperatives for survival have implications for the individual's socialization and that in actuality the requisites of continuing social life come down to what is largely a set of requirements for individual socialization.[5]

Yet this analysis of the significance of socialization involves a choice of social values. The metaphor of societies as living and dying organisms is, as we have noted earlier, not persuasive to everyone. Those who find such imagery unconvincing often suspect that behind a concern for society's imperatives lurks a preference for a particular social order. Thus, Christopher Lasch observes:

> It is no wonder that the revolt of the intellectuals so often took the form of a rebellion against the traditional family. The family was the agency which transmitted from generation to generation—and not only transmitted but embodied down to the last detail of domestic architecture—the enormous weight of respectable culture; as its defenders would have said, of civilization itself.[6]

Moreover, by stressing the fragility of society and its need for well-adjusted manpower, functionalism downgrades alternative concerns that might be involved in socialization, such as introducing the child to his cultural heritage without sacrificing imagination, ability to love, and the development of selfhood.

Concepts of socialization also imply images of what children are like. Actually, as Aries has argued, the concept of childhood was an invention of the late Middle Ages. In a way, the child is the first "victim" of technological unemployment; children first became childlike in the upper strata of society and only later was the idea of distinctive dress and activities extended to children of the middle and lower classes, as their contributions to the economy of the family came to be unnecessary. As we have noted before, working and "lower-class" children often do not seem to act in the ways we expect children to act—playful, innocent, curious, imaginative.

Nevertheless, two images of the child have prevailed in Western culture. One is the child as angel, all sweetness and innocence, to be protected from the sexuality and workaday concerns of the adult world. This image has always coexisted with actual conditions of great brutality and neglect for children. The opposing image is found in both Calvinistic Protestantism and early psychoanalysis: it is the child as devil, imp of darkness, seething cauldron of murderous and sexual impulses, a beast who must be tamed. This image has been forcefully portrayed in such literary works as *Lord of the Flies, The Bad Seed,* and others.

The Meaning of Socialization

Both images of the child share the assumption that socialization is something done to the child, that he learns to be reasonable, moral, and competent from the outside, as a result of adult guidance. This is also the position of sociological functionalism. It suggests as a model for human socialization the child being weaned or toilet trained—precisely those aspects of child rearing in which child and parent are most likely to be embroiled in a battle for control of the child's impulses. The concept of socialization as the control of impulse overlooks, however, the intellectual aspects of the process, and the active, creative part played by the child himself. The model child for theories of socialization need not be the child on the potty chair, but the child learning his native language and the elementary nature of the physical world.

The creative side of human growth has been most forcefully stated and experimentally documented in the work of Jean Piaget. According to Piaget, the child inherently is neither good nor evil, but is biologically endowed, as part of his mammalian heritage, with the motivation to explore, understand, and master the environment—master it, that is, in the sense of a scientist testing out one hypothesis after another to find the principle behind some effect. According to this view the child is an active participant in the attainment of logical and moral competence, rather than the passive recipient of rules and rewards from the outside. The infant banging his cup, throwing toys out of his crib, or fitting objects into each other is actually performing experiments in physics, learning about the nature of matter. Later, when he learns to communicate in words, he will also learn the rules of logic and morality. As Roger Brown writes:

> The mature persons with whom a child interacts behave in accordance with such systems of norms or rules as are called logic, mathematics, language, morality, aesthetics . . . and so on. For the most part these systems have not been explicitly formulated by the adults whose behavior is governed by them and they will not be explicitly formulated by the child who acquires them. This process is not a simple "passing over" of the systems from one generation to another. What each child extracts at a given age is a function of his idiosyncratic experience and of his present intellectual capabilities. The systems governing the child change as he grows older and they need not, in the end, simply reproduce the rules that prevail in his society. The outcome can be unique and sometimes revolutionary.[7]

The selections by Bruner and Denzin also emphasize these intellectual and active features of learning overlooked in the traditional views of socialization. Bruner deals with a fundamental question: what makes the child learn? The traditional answer to this question in education and psychology is called reinforcement or the law of effect: either reward the child for being right, reprove him for being wrong, or both. Bruner argues that there is no need to resort to such extrinsic methods. The child has a natural will to learn. If the school could learn how to capitalize on this desire, most problems of discipline would disappear.

The will to learn is composed mainly of the child's inherent curiosity, but also of his desire for competence and mastery, his wish to be like a person he admires, and finally his "commitment to the web of social reciprocity"—for example, a group of people trying to accomplish some aim together. In all of these, the reward is intrinsic to the activity. When a person's curiosity is aroused by something puzzling or uncertain and he explores it until his curiosity is satisfied, it would be preposterous, as Bruner puts it, to praise him for this. Thus the main problem for education is to understand how to make learning interesting. Why, for example, does a story hold the child's rapt attention in spite of distractions? What is there about toys, playgrounds, the environment, television, that amuses the child?

Denzin's article argues that adults normally assume children would be reduced to a state of utter boredom without a planned schedule of play activities. But, Denzin argues, children do not really "play"; they work at constructing social orders and understanding the world around them.

Motherhood and Fatherhood

If the prevailing ideology has underestimated children's seriousness and competence, it has, as we pointed out in the introduction to this book, exaggerated the child's dependency on the biological mother. Much of the literature assumes that because the child's emotional growth seems to require an attachment to one mothering figure, who may or may not be his natural mother, that other people cannot or should not play an important part in his life. Presumably, the child cannot form such an attachment unless his mother takes care of him full time. Bowlby, one of the originators of the concept of maternal deprivation, has reconsidered this assumption in a recent work.[8] He suggests three different ways an adult can interact with a young child: as a playmate; as a caretaker attending to the child's routine needs for food and clean clothing; and finally as a sensitive respondent to the signals of the child's emotional needs. Only the latter relationship, argues Bowlby, produces an emotional attachment. Thus, in the Israeli kibbutz, where the child is cared for by a nurse and sees his parents for only an hour or two a day, the child's main attachment is to the parents. In fact, observers have noted that kibbutz children seem even more devoted to their parents than children in our society. Other studies have shown, by way of contrast, that in nuclear family households where the mother cares for the child all day but communicates with him rarely, and the father sees the child only a little but responds to him freely, the child becomes more attached to the father.[9] In sum, it seems to be not the amount but the quality of maternal care that counts.

If the mother's absence need not always be negative, her presence need not always be positive. The prevailing ideology of the family seems to ascribe an almost mystical effect on children to the mother's mere presence. In the introductory essay we challenged the assumption that "all mothers are good mothers." Yet, aside from the gruesome statistics on battered children, we have little reliable information on actual family behavior, since the family is ordinarily a secret institution. Still, the relatively few social scientists who have actually observed parents and children interacting at home have not been greatly impressed by all the mothers they have seen. For example, one of the writers recently spoke to a psychologist carrying out a large, long-term study of about forty young children and their families. When asked how many of these mothers she thought were really competent, who gave her no cause to worry about their effects on the children, physical or emotional, the psychologist thought for a moment and said, "Well, I don't believe in the concept of a 'good mother,' but I'd say about three." Indeed, a number of recent theories of schizophrenia have argued that the isolated nuclear family provides a fertile setting for driving children crazy. In the isolation of the nuclear family, the parent can easily deny some aspect of reality, usually the parents' behavior or motives, thus causing the child to doubt his own perceptions. For example, the parent may act very angry or sexy, yet deny he or she is doing so.

Laing even argues that all parents tend to drive their children crazy, differing only in degree from the schizophrenic's parents. Parents do this in two related ways, according to Laing. First, they make the child conform to demands which, if they were not so socially acceptable, would be patently absurd. And second, in the process of making the child conform, they deny the validity of the child's own experiences and perceptions. Laing goes on to define the key to understanding what goes on between parents and children as the concept of mystification. The term was first used by Marx to describe how ruling classes cloak their exploitations with a rhetoric of benevolence. Thus the exploitations of colonial imperialism were defined as "the white man's burden"—bringing progress and enlightenment to savages.

Laing argues that parents characteristically engage in mystification. We have noted before the example of the bedtime problem: parents need to have their children take naps and go to bed because in the isolated household that provides the simplest method for parental relief from the relentless demands of child rearing. The parent cannot admit this, at least to the child, and tries to persuade the child that the child's own experience of not being sleepy is wrong. Even "permissive" parents may interpose themselves between the child and his natural experience of the world. Thus, Slater writes,

> . . . The old method [of child rearing] was based on the military drill model: you take people who are all basically different and get them to behave outwardly in a uniform manner, regardless of whether they are inwardly committed to this behavior or not. Thus there is a sharp distinction between the inner and outer spheres. The child or recruit is expected to harbor inner feelings of rebellion or contempt, so long as these are not expressed outwardly.
>
> The new method gives much more responsibility to the parents, for they must concern themselves with inner states. . . . The parents under the old method thought they had done their job well if the child was obedient, even if he turned out dull, unimaginative, surly, sadistic, and sexually incapacitated. Spockian parents feel that it is their responsibility to make their child into the most all-around perfect adult possible, which means paying a great deal of attention to his inner states. . . . The consequence of this is what is superficially defined as greater "permissiveness," but from an internal perspective is actually more totalitarian—the child no longer has a private sphere, but has his entire being involved with parental aspirations. What the child is *not* permitted to do is to take his own personality for granted.[10]

But the parent may be a victim as well as villain in the war of the generations; he too was once a child. As Steele and Pollock point out in their article on the battered child, battering parents were battered by their parents, their parents by their grandparents, and so on. Furthermore, as the articles in the section on parenthood argue, the realities of parenthood, especially motherhood, are considerably less idyllic than the myth portrays them to be. Even "good" mothers may be overwhelmed at times by the relentless demands of young children, and be horrified by the rage their children are capable of stirring up in them. For battering parents, the myth that children are supposed to be fulfilling and gratifying has dangerous effects; these parents blame their own children for not living up to the mythical standards they suppose other children meet.

Not only may the transition to the role of parent (as described by Alice Rossi) be felt as a life crisis, but it is also true that the power of the parent is insecure. Thus, Jane Loevinger argues that in spite of the physical power of the parent over the child, no parent can ensure that the child will learn precisely what the parent wants him to learn. Even the professional knowledge of the psychiatrist or the child-development expert does not help; the parent-child relationship inevitably involves a conflict of interest and impulse. Moreover, the effects of motherhood on the mother herself are less than idyllic. The woman who has invested the most in the culturally prescribed maternal role—for example, the classical Jewish mama— is most likely to be devastated by the natural course of the maternal role: the adulthood of her children.

Refusing Socialization

Finally, in modern society there is an increasing tendency for children to refuse socialization, to perceive it as mere conformity. Socialization, besides being based on the model of controls applied from the outside, is based also on assumptions about scarcity and insatiability: the notion that there will never be enough good things in the world to go around. The assumption of scarcity underlies much generational conflict and perception. The new youth culture believes that human needs are easily satisfied and that resources for doing so are plentiful. "The key flaw in the old culture," writes Philip Slater, "is that scarcity is spurious—man-made in the case of bodily gratifications, and man-allowed or man-maintained in the case of material goods." Slater emphasizes that the old culture is terrified of sexuality, but not violence, while in the counterculture these preferences are reversed.

In a rapidly changing world the problem of socialization may be turned on its head. Since the problem is to live with and generate change, not merely to induce conformity, social competency may mean the ability to question tradition. Margaret Mead goes so far as to argue that children must "socialize" parents, rather than the reverse; that society should become based on the model of the child, prefigurative rather than postfigurative, as in traditional society, or cofigurative, based on peer groups, with each generation somewhat different from every other.

It used to be that socialization resulted in a finished product, a person whose character was set by the end of adolescence, and who would change only under the most extreme conditions, such as a religious conversion. Now we live in an age not only of identity crises that may last a lifetime, but, Lifton argues, settled identies may change to other settled identities, and more than once. Thus the conditions of life in the twentieth century have produced a new kind of individual, whom Lifton calls protean man, after the mythological figure who could take the form of any living thing.

We will leave for the reader the task of seeing to what extent these views of the current crisis accord with, or differ from, each other, and the soundness of their analysis of the problem. But we believe that the traditional view of socialization is obsolescent, and must be replaced by a new vision of generational interaction.

References

1. George Leonard, *The Man-Woman Thing* (New York: Delacorte Press, 1970), p. 85.
2. Roger Brown, *Social Psychology* (New York: Free Press of Glencoe, 1965), p. 193.
3. Dan Hopsen, Jr., *Seminar on the Battered Child, Casebook and Proceedings,* January 21, 1965, State Dept. of Social Welfare, Topeka, Kans.
4. Paul Goodman, selections from *New Reformation* (New York: Random House, 1970). Reprinted in *Psychology Today,* October 1970, p. 25.
5. Alex Inkeles, "Society, Social Structure, and Child Socialization," in J. Clausen (ed.), *Socialization and Society* (Boston: Little, Brown, 1968), pp. 75–129.
6. Christopher Lasch, *The New Radicalism in America, 1889–1963: The Intellectual as a Social Type* (New York: Vintage Books, 1967), p. xiii.
7. Brown, *op. cit.,* p. 195.
8. John Bowlby, *Attachment* (New York: Basic Books, 1969).
9. *Ibid.,* p. 317.
10. Philip Slater, *The Pursuit of Loneliness* (Boston: Beacon Press, 1970).

Chapter 6

The Mythology of Childhood

On the Will to Learn | *Jerome S. Bruner*

The single most characteristic thing about human beings is that they learn. Learning is so deeply ingrained in man that it is almost involuntary, and thoughtful students of human behavior have even speculated that our specialization as a species is a specialization for learning. For, by comparison with organisms lower in the animal kingdom, we are ill equipped with prepared reflex mechanisms. As William James put it decades ago, even our instinctive behavior occurs only once, thereafter being modified by experience. With a half century's perspective on the discoveries of Pavlov, we know that a man not only is conditioned by his environment, but may be so conditioned even against his will.

Why then invoke the idea of a "will to learn"? The answer derives from the idea of education, a human invention that takes a learner beyond "mere" learning. Other species begin their learning afresh each generation, but man is born into a culture that has as one of its principal functions the conservation and transmission of past learning. Given man's physical characteristics, indeed, it would be not only wasteful but probably fatal for him to reinvent even the limited range of technique and knowledge required for such a species to survive in the temperate zone. This means that man cannot depend upon a casual process of learning; he must be "educated." The young human must regulate his learning and his attention by reference to external requirements. He must eschew what is vividly right under his nose for what is dimly in a future that is often incomprehensible to him. And he must do so in a strange setting where words and diagrams and other abstractions suddenly become very important.

From Jerome S. Bruner, "The Will to Learn," in *Toward a Theory of Instruction* (Cambridge, Mass.: Belknap Press of Harvard Univ. Press, 1966), pp. 113–128. References cited in the original have been deleted.

School demands an orderliness and neatness beyond what the child has known before; it requires restraint and immobility never asked of him before; and often it puts him in a spot where he does not *know* whether he knows and can get no indication from anybody for minutes at a time as to whether he is on the right track. Perhaps most important of all, school is away from home with all that fact implies in anxiety, or challenge, or relief.

In consequence of all this the problem of "the will to learn" becomes important, indeed exaggerated. Let us not delude ourselves: it is a problem that cannot be avoided, though it can be made manageable, I think. We shall explore what kinds of factors lead to satisfaction in "educated" learning, to pleasure in the practice of learning as it exists in the necessarily artificial atmosphere of the school. Almost all children possess what have come to be called "intrinsic" motives for learning. An intrinsic motive is one that does not depend upon reward that lies outside the activity it impels. Reward inheres in the successful termination of that activity or even in the activity itself.

Curiosity is almost a prototype of the intrinsic motive. Our attention is attracted to something that is unclear, unfinished, or uncertain. We sustain our attention until the matter in hand becomes clear, finished, or certain. The achievement of clarity or merely the search for it is what satisfies. We would think it preposterous if somebody thought to reward us with praise or profit for having satisfied our curiosity. However pleasant such external reward might be, and however much we might come to depend upon it, the external reward is something added. What activates and satisfies curiosity is something inherent in the cycle of activity by which we express curiosity. Surely such activity is biologically relevant, for curiosity is essential to the survival not only of the individual but of the species. There is considerable research that indicates the extent to which even nonhuman primates will put forth effort for a chance to encounter something novel on which to exercise curiosity. But it is clear that unbridled curiosity is little more than unlimited distractibility. To be interested in everything that comes along is to be interested in nothing for long. Studies of the behavior of three-year-olds, for example, indicate the degree to which they are dominated from the outside by the parade of vivid impressions that pass their way. They turn to this bright color, that sharp sound, that new shiny surface. Many ends are beyond their reach, for they cannot sustain a steady course when the winds shift. If anything, they are "too curious." They live by what psychologists have long called the laws of primary attention: attention dominated by vividness and change in the environment. There has been much speculation about the function of this early and exhausting tempo of curiosity. One neuropsychologist, Donald Hebb, has suggested that the child is drinking in the world, better to construct his neural "models" of the environment. And it is plain that a stunted organism is produced by depriving an infant of the rich diet of impressions on which his curiosity normally feeds with such extravagance. Animals raised in homogenized environments show crippling deficits in their later ability to learn and to transfer what they have learned. Children "kept in the attic" by misguided or psychotic parents show the same striking backwardness. Indeed, even the children who have suffered the dull, aseptic environment of backward foundling homes often show a decline in intelligence that can be compensated only by vigorous measures of enrichment. So surely, then, an important early function is served by the child's omnivorous capacity for new impressions. He is sorting the world, storing those things that have some recurrent regularity and require "knowing," discriminating them from the parade of random impressions.

But if attention is to be sustained, directed to some task and held there in spite of temptations that come along, then obviously constraints must be established. The voluntary deployment of curiosity, so slowly and painfully mastered, seems to be supported in part by the young child's new-found capacity to "instruct himself," literally to talk to himself through a sustained sequence. And in part the steadying force seems to be the momentum of concrete overt acts that have a way of sustaining the attention required for their completion by shutting off irrelevant impressions. In time, and with the development of habitual activities, and of language, there emerges more self-directed attention, sometimes called derived primary attention. The child is held steady not so much by vividness as by the habitual round of activity that now demands his attention. Little enough is known about how to help a child become master of his own attention, to sustain it over a long, connected sequence. But while young children are notoriously wandering in their attention, they can be kept in a state of rapt and prolonged attentiveness by being told compelling stories. There may be something to be learned from this observation. What makes the internal sequence of a story even more compelling than the distractions that lie outside it? Are there comparable properties inherent in other activities? Can these be used to train a child to sustain his curiosity beyond the moment's vividness?

Observe a child or group of children building a pile of blocks as high as they can get them. Their attention will be sustained to the flashing point until they reach the climax when the pile comes crashing down. They will return to build still higher. The drama of the task is only its minor virtue. More important is the energizing lure of uncertainty made personal by one's own effort to control it. It is almost the antithesis of the passive attraction of shininess and the vivid. To channel curiosity into more powerful intellectual pursuits requires precisely that there be this transition from the passive, receptive, episodic form of curiosity to the sustained and active form. There are games not only with objects, but with ideas and questions—like Twenty Questions—that provide such a disciplining of the channeling of curiosity. Insofar as one may count on this important human motive—and it seems among the most reliable of the motives—then it seems obvious that our artificial education can in fact be made less artificial from a motivational standpoint by relating it initially to the more surface forms of curiosity and attention, and then cultivating curiosity to more subtle and active expression. I think it is fair to say that most of the success in contemporary curriculum building has been achieved by this route. When success comes, it takes the form of recognition that beyond the few things we know there lies a domain of inference: that putting together the two and two that we have yields astonishing results. But this raises the issue of competence, to which we must turn next.

For curiosity is only one of the intrinsic motives for learning. The drive to achieve competence is another. Professor Robert White puts the issue well:

> According to Webster, competence means fitness or ability, and the suggested synonyms include capability, capacity, efficiency, proficiency, and skill. It is therefore a suitable word to describe such things as grasping and exploring, crawling and walking, attention and perception, all of which promote an effective—a competent—interaction with the environment. It is true, of course, that maturation plays a part in all these developments, but this part is heavily overshadowed by learning in all the more complex accomplishments like speech or skilled manipulation. I shall argue that it is necessary to make competence a motivational concept; there is *competence motivation* as well as competence in its more familiar sense of achieved capacity. The behavior that leads to the building up of effective grasping, handling, and letting go of objects, to take one example, is not random behavior that is produced by an overflow of energy. It is directed, selective, and persistent, and it continues not because it serves primary drives, which indeed it cannot serve until it is almost perfect, but because it satisfies an intrinsic need to deal with the environment.

Observations of young children and of the young of other species suggest that a good deal of their play must be understood as practice in coping with the environment. Primatologists describe, for example, how young female baboons cradle infant baboons in their arms long before they produce their own offspring. In fact, baboon play can be seen almost entirely as the practice of interpersonal skills. Unlike human children, baboons never play with objects, and this, the anthropologists believe, is connected with their inability to use tools when they grow up. And there is evidence that early language mastery, too, depends on such early preparation. One linguist recently has shown how a two-year-old goes on exploring the limits of language use even after the lights are out, parents removed, communication stopped, and sleep imminent.

The child's metalinguistic play is hard to interpret as anything other than pleasure in practicing and developing a new skill. Although competence may not "naturally" be directed toward school learning, it is certainly possible that the great excess of energy that children experience when they "get into a subject they like" is made of the same stuff.

We get interested in what we get good at. In general, it is difficult to sustain interest in an activity unless one achieves some degree of competence. Athletics is the activity par excellence where the young need no prodding to gain pleasure from an increase in skill, save where prematurely adult standards are imposed on little leagues formed too soon to ape the big ones. A custom introduced some years ago at the Gordonstoun School in Scotland has become legendary. In addition to conventionally competitive track and field events within the school, there was established a novel competition in which boys pitted themselves against their own best prior record in the events. Several American schools have picked up the idea and, while there has been no "proper evaluation," it is said that the system creates great excitement and enormous effort on the part of the boys.

To achieve the sense of accomplishment requires a task that has some beginning and some terminus. Perhaps an experiment can serve again as a parable. There is a well-known phenomenon known to psychologists by the forbidding name of the Zeigarnik Effect. In brief, tasks that are interrupted are much more likely to be returned to and completed, and much more likely to be remembered, than comparable tasks that one has completed without interruption. But that puts the matter superficially, for it leaves out of account one factor that is crucial. The effect holds only if the tasks that the subject has been set are ones that have a structure—a beginning, a plan, and a terminus. If the tasks are "silly" in the sense of being meaningless, arbitrary, and without visible means for checking progress, the drive to completion is not stimulated by interruption.

It seems likely that the desire to achieve competence follows the same rule. Unless there is some meaningful unity in what we are doing and some way of telling how we are doing, we are not very likely to strive to excel ourselves. Yet surely this too is only a small part of the story, for everybody does not want to be competent in the same activities, and some competencies might even be a source of embarrassment to their possessors. Boys do not thrill to the challenge of sewing a fine seam (again, in our culture), nor girls to becoming competent street fighters. There are competencies that are appropriate and activating for different ages, the two sexes, different social classes. But there are some things about competence motives that transcend these particulars. One is that an activity (given that it is "approved") must have some meaningful structure to it if it requires skill that is a little bit beyond that now possessed by the person—that it be learned by the exercise of effort. It is probably the combination of the two that is critical.

Experienced teachers who work with the newer curricula in science and mathematics report that they are surprised at the eagerness of students to push ahead to next steps in the course. Several of the teachers have suggested that the eagerness comes from increased confidence in one's ability to understand the material. Some of the students were having their first experience of understanding a topic in some depth, of going somewhere in a subject. It is this that is at the heart of competence motives, and surely our schools have not begun to tap this enormous reservoir of zest.

While we do not know the limits within which competence drives can be shaped and channeled by external reward, it seems quite likely that they are strongly open to external influence. But channelization aside, how can education keep alive and nourish a drive to competence—whether expressed in farming, football, or mathematics? What sustains a sense of pleasure and achievement in mastering things for their own sake—what Thorstein Veblen referred to as a instinct for workmanship? Do competence motives strengthen mainly on their exercise, in whatever context they may be exercised, or do they depend also upon being linked to drives for status, wealth, security, or fame?

There are, to begin with, striking differences among cultures and between strata within any particular society with respect to the encouragement given to competence drives. David McClelland, for example, in writing about the "achieving society," comments upon the fact that in certain times and places one finds a flowering of achievement motivation strongly supported by the society and its institutions and myths alike. Emphasis upon individual responsibility and initiative, upon dependence in decision and action, upon perfectibility of the self—all of these things serve to perpetuate more basic competency motives past childhood.

But cultures vary in their evaluation of *intellectual* mastery as a vehicle for the expression of competence. Fred Bales, for example, in comparing Irish and Jewish immigrant groups in Boston, remarks that the Jewish, much more than the Irish, treat school success and intellectuality as virtues in their own right as well as ways of upward mobility. The reasons can be found in history. Herzog and Zborowski, in their book on eastern European Jewish communities, suggest that the barrier erected against Jews' entering other professions may have helped foster the cultivation of intellectual excellence as a prized expression of competence.

A culture does not "manage" these matters consciously by the applications of rewards and reproofs alone. The son of the rabbi in the eastern

European *shtetl* was not punished if he wished to become a merchant rather than a Talmudic scholar, and, indeed, if he chose to become the latter he typically went through long, extrinsically unrewarding, and arduous training to do so. More subtle forces are at work, all of them fairly familiar but too often overlooked in discussing education. One of them is "approval." The professional man is more "respected" than the manual worker. But that scarcely exhausts the matter. Respected by whom? Contemporary sociologists speak of the approval of one's "reference group"—those to whom one looks for guides to action, for the definition of the possible, for ultimate approbation. But what leads *this* individual to look to *that* particular reference group?

What appears to be operative is a process we cavalierly call identification. The fact of identification is more easily described than explained. It refers to the strong human tendency to model one's "self" and one's aspirations upon some other person. When we feel we have succeeded in "being like" an identification figure, we derive pleasure from the achievement and, conversely, we suffer when we have "let him down." Insofar as the identification figure is also "a certain kind of person"—belongs to some group or category—we extend our loyalties from an individual to a reference group. In effect, then, identification relates one not only to individuals, but to one's society as well.

While this account is oversimplified, it serves to underline one important feature of identification as a process—its self-sustaining nature. For what it accomplishes is to pass over to the learner the control of punishment and reward. Insofar as we now carry our standards with us, we achieve a certain independence from the immediate rewards and punishments meted out by others.

It has been remarked by psychologists that identification figures are most often those who control the scarce psychological resources that we most desire—love, approval, sustenance. Let me skip this issue for a moment and return to it later.

The term identification is usually reserved for those strong attachments where there is a considerable amount of emotional investment. But there are "milder" forms of identification that are also important during the years of childhood and after. Perhaps we should call those who serve in these milder relationships "competence models." They are the "on the job" heroes, the reliable ones with whom we can interact in some way. Indeed, they control a rare resource, some desired competence, but what is important is that the resource is attainable by interaction. The "on the job" model is nowhere better illustrated than in the manner in which the child learns language from a parent. The tryout-correction-revision process continues until the child comes to learn the rules whereby sentences are generated and transformed appropriately. Finally he develops a set of productive habits that enable him to be his own sentence maker and his own corrector. He "learns the rules of the language." The parent is the model who, by interaction, teaches the skill of language.

Finally, a word about one last intrinsic motive that bears closely upon the will to learn. Perhaps it should be called reciprocity. For it involves a deep human need to respond to others and to operate jointly with them toward an objective. One of the important insights of modern zoology is the importance of this intraspecies reciprocity for the survival of individual members of the species. The psychologist Roger Barker has commented that the best way he has found to predict the behavior of the children whom he has been studying in great detail in the midst of their everyday activities is to know their situations. A child in a baseball game behaves baseball; in the drugstore the same child behaves drugstore. Situations have a demand value that appears to have very little to do with the motives that are operative. Surely it is not simply a "motive to conform"; this is too great an abstraction. The man who is regulating his pressure on the back of a car, along with three or four others, trying to "rock it out," is not so much conforming as "fitting his efforts into an enterprise." It is about as primitive an aspect of human behavior as we know.

Like the other activities we have been discussing, its exercise seems to be its sole reward. Probably it is the basis of human society, this response through reciprocity to other members of one's species. Where joint action is needed, where reciprocity is required for the group to attain an objective, then there seem to be processes that carry the individual along into learning, sweep him into a competence that is required in the setting of the group. We know precious little about this primitive motive to reciprocate, but what we do know is that it can furnish a driving force to learn as well. Human beings (and other species as well) fall into a pattern that is required by the goals and activities of the social group in which they find themselves. "Imitation" is not the word for it, since it is usually not plain in most cases what is to be imitated. A much more interesting way of looking at what is involved is provided by the phenomenon of a young child learning to use the pronouns "I" and "you" correctly. The parent says to the child, "You go to bed now." The child says, "No, you no go to bed." We are amused. "Not *me* but *you*," we say. In time, and after a surprisingly brief period of confusion, the child learns that "you" refers to himself when another uses it, and to another person when he uses it—and the reverse with "I." It is a prime example of reciprocal learning. It is by much the same process that children learn the beautifully complicated games they play (adult and child games alike), that they learn their role in the family and in school, and finally that they come to take their role in the greater society.

At the risk of being repetitious, let me restate the argument. It is this. The will to learn is an intrinsic motive, one that finds both its source and its reward in its own exercise. The will to learn becomes a "problem" only under specialized circumstances like those of a school, where a curriculum is set, students confined, and a path fixed. The problem exists not so much in learning itself, but in the fact that what the school imposes often fails to enlist the natural energies that sustain spontaneous learning—curiosity, a desire for competence, aspiration to emulate a model, and a deep-sensed commitment to the web of social reciprocity.

The Work of Little Children | *Norman K. Denzin*

When I was One,
I had just begun.
When I was Two,
I was nearly new.
When I was three,
I was hardly me.
When I was Four,
I was not much more.
When I was Five,
I was just alive.
But now I am Six,
I'm as clever as clever.
So I think I'll be six
Now for ever and ever.
              —Christopher speaking to Winnie-the-Pooh

Societies and people organize themselves into interacting moral orders: families and schools, rich people and poor people, the educated and the uneducated, the child and the adult. Relationships between them are grounded in assumptions which justify the various social evaluations. Thus, it is taken as right and proper that the rich should have more privileges than the poor, or that children cannot engage in adult activities.

From Norman K. Denzin, "The Work of Little Children," *New Society,* July 1970, pp. 13–15.

These assumptions are institutionalized and routinely enforced, so that those people who are judged to be less competent are kept in their place. In this article, I want to look at some of the ideologies that surround the adult-child relationship. I shall present data from an ongoing field study of young children in "preschools," in recreational areas and in families, which challenge the view of children that is taken for granted, at least in America.

Childhood is conventionally seen as a time of carefree, disorganized bliss. Children find themselves under constant surveillance. They are rewarded and punished so that proper standards of conduct can be instilled in their emergent selves. The belief goes that they enjoy nonserious, play-directed activities. They avoid work and serious pursuits at all costs. It is the adult's assignment to make these nonserious selves over into serious actors. In America, this belief lasts at least until the child enters the world of marriage and gainful employment.

There is a paradox in these assumptions. Even if a child or adolescent wants to take part in serious concerns, he may find himself excluded. Thus, when the state of California recently passed a law, along the lines already adopted in Britain, giving the vote to 18-year-olds, members of the assembly refused to accord them drinking privileges, and one argument held that 18-year-olds were not yet competent enough to incur debts and assume other adult responsibilities (like signing contracts).

The paradox extends beyond exclusion. Even when children go so far as to act in adultlike ways, these actions are usually defined as unique, and not likely to occur again unless an adult is there to give guidance and direction. This assumption serves to justify the position of the educator. If children could make it on their own, there would be no place for the teacher. This fact is best seen in American preschools, where instructors assume that little children have short attention or concentration spans. The belief is quite simple. If left to their own ingenuity, little children become bored. Therefore, time structures must be developed, so that the child does not become bored. In California, these timetables typically go as follows:

9–9:15: Hang up coats and say "Good morning" to other children.

9:15–10: Play inside on solitary activities (painting, puzzles, toys).

10–10:30: Go outside for group activities on swings, in sandbox, dancing, making things.

10:30–11: Juice and biscuit time in small groups around tables.

11–11:20: Quiet time; small groups around instructors where instructor reads a story.

11:20–11:30: Get coats and jackets and prepare to be picked up by parents.

11:30: Session over; instructors relax and have coffee and cigarettes.

When there are clashes over timetables—if, for example, a child refuses to come in for juice and biscuits—an instructor will be dispatched to inform him that it is time to come in.

These timetables are revealing and serve several functions. They tell the instructor what he will be doing at any given moment. They give instructors control over the children. They state that children, if left on their own, could not organize their own actions for two and one-half hours.

Another paradox is evident. Although children are systematically informed of their incompetence, and rewarded for the quality of their non-serious conduct, adults appear to assume that something important is happening at these early ages. In fact, it is something so serious that normal, everyday adults cannot assume responsibility for what occurs. As rapidly as possible, the child is taken from the family setting and placed in any number of child-care educational and baby-sitting facilities.

My interviews with, and observation of, 100 American parents, who delivered their children to a cooperative and experimental preschool, revealed two assumptions. First, the school was a cheap and effective babysitter. The parents had no fears for their child's safety when he was there. Second, if the child was an only child, or if the parents lived in a neighborhood where there were no other playmates, the preschool would expand and cultivate the child's skill at getting on with other children. These parents fear that their child would appear later in kindergarten, and not know how to interact with other children. Because preschools do not formally assess how a child is doing, the parent felt fairly safe. They transferred the function of looking after their child's sociability from themselves to a neutral party—the preschool instructor.

The school, then, gave the parents a year to get the child ready for his first encounter with formal education. The task of the preschool was to shape up the child's speech, teach him or her how to be polite and considerate of others. A side function was to give the child different toys and play experiences—finger painting, say, which many parents defined as too messy for their homes. Economically stable families with several children were less likely to send their child to the preschool. The child's brothers and sisters performed the sociability function of the preschool.

Let me now note a final paradox. Observers like Iona and Peter Opie—in their *Lore and Language of Schoolchildren* and their *Children's Games in Street and Playground*—have found that, when left on their own, children produce complex societies and social orders. The fact that children's

games are often spontaneously produced, yet are passed on from generation to generation, and that their songs and stories are made to fit special
selves, must indicate the child's ability to be a serious, accountable actor.

An example from the Opies' study of children's games reveals the
serious character of play. Here the game is "playing school":

"The most favorite game played in school is 'Schools,'" says an Edin-
burgh 9-year-old.

> Tommy is the headmaster, Robin is the schoolteacher, and I am the
> naughty boy. Robin asks us what are two and two. We say they are
> six. He gives us the belt. Sometimes we run away from school and
> what a commotion! Tommy and Robin run after us. When we are
> caught we are taken back and everyone is sorry.

In their analysis of this game, the Opies observe:

> Clearly, playing "Schools" is a way to turn the tables on real
> school: a child can become a teacher, pupils can be naughty, and fun
> can be made of punishments. It is noticeable, too, that the most de-
> mure child in the real classroom is liable to become the most talkative
> when the canes are make-believe.

Urie Bronfenbrenner's recent study of child-rearing practices in the Soviet
Union shows, too, that Russians take the games of their young children quite
seriously. Such games are used to instill self-reliance and collective respect
on the part of the child. Here is one instance:

> Kolya started to pull at the ball Mitya was holding. The action was
> spotted by a junior staff member who quickly scanned the room and
> then called out gaily: "Children, come look! See how Vasya and
> Marusya are swinging their teddy bear together. They are good
> comrades." The two offenders quickly dropped the ball to join the
> others in observing the praised couple, who now swung harder than
> ever.

Bronfenbrenner notes that such cooperation is not left to chance. From
preschool on, Soviet children are encouraged to play cooperatively. Group
games and special toys are designed to heighten this side of self-development.

The point I want to make is that when they are left on their own, young
children do not play, they work at constructing social orders. "Play" is a
fiction from the adult world. Child's work involves such serious matters as
developing languages for communication; presenting and defending their
social selves in difficult situations; defining and processing deviance; and
constructing rules of entry and exit into emergent social groups. Children
see these as serious concerns and often make a clear distinction between
their play and their work. This fact is best grasped by entering those situations where children are naturally thrown together and forced to take
account of one another.

Many specialists have assumed that young children lack well-developed self-conceptions. My observations show, on the contrary, that as early as four, a child can stand outside his own behavior and see himself from another's perspective. I carried out intensive interviews with 15 four-year-olds. These revealed support for the general hypothesis that a person's self-concept reflects the number of people he interacts with. The more friends a child had, or the larger his network of brothers and sisters, the more elaborate his self-conception.

Keith, who was four years seven months old at the time of the interview, described himself as follows:

> 1. My name is Keith—.
> 2. I am a boy who plays at a nursery school.
> 3. If I was asked, "What do you like to play best?" I would say: "I like to dance to my favorite records." [What are your favorite records?] *"Yummy, Yummy; Bonnie and Clyde."*
> 4. If someone asked me, "Where do you live?" I'd say, [Name of street]."
> 5. If someone said, "Do you know how to do cartwheels?" I'd say "No!"
> 6. If someone said, "What kind of picture can you draw?" I'd say, "I can draw my favorite things. I like to draw a man's head." [Why?] "Because so much can be added to it. I'd put hair, a chin, eyes, a forehead, a nose, a mouth, and a chin on it."

Keith was a leader of the boys' group at the preschool, had nine good friends, and was one of the family that had two other children. Nancy, on the other hand, was an isolate, having only four acquaintances at the school. However, her family also had two other children. Her low integration in the social network of the school is reflected in the fact that she could only give two self-descriptions:

> 1. I'm at school.
> 2. I live in [name of city].

As extremes, Keith and Nancy point to a basic feature of life at the preschool. Insofar as a child is a member of the social life of the preschool, the more adultlike will be his, or her, behavior. The social life of the school, then, makes the child into a small adult.

Name games take many forms, and they reveal another side of the child's serious self. Children may reverse or switch names. On a Halloween afternoon, I saw three girls, all aged four, who were sitting around a table mixing pumpkin muffins, systematically assign to themselves and all newcomers the name of the child next to them. The rule was quite simple. Each child was assigned every name in the group but their own. One girl resisted and said: "That's a mistake! My name isn't Kathy, I'm Susan." Kathy replied: "We know your name isn't mine, silly; we're just pretending. We don't mean it."

There was a clear separation of play, fantasy, and serious activity in this episode. Each girl knew her name. The sequence merely solidified their self-identity. Martha Wolfenstein, in a study of children's humor, has observed that inevitably some child will find these games disturbing, refusing to accept the identity that goes with the new name. Probably such children are not yet firmly committed to the identity designated by their proper name.

Name calling is another game. Here, the child's proper name is dropped and replaced by either a variation on that name, or by an approving/disapproving term. Martha Wolfenstein noted names like "Heinie," "Tits," "Freeshow," "Fuckerfaster," and "None-of-your-business." In name-calling games the child's real identity is challenged. He or she is signed out of the group and made a special object of abuse or respect. (Parenthetically, it must be noted that adults also engage in such games. Special names for sports and political figures are examples.)

A more severe game is where the child has his name taken away. The other children simply refuse to interact with him. By taking away his name, they effectively make him a nonperson, or nonself. In name-loss games the child may be referred to as a member of a social category (young child, honkie, brat, dwarf). In those moments his essential self, as a distinct person, is denied.

The Opies have described another name game, called "Names," "Letters in Your Name," or "Alphabet." Here, a child calls out letters in the alphabet, and contestants come forward every time a letter contained in their name is called. All of these name games reflect the importance children assign to their social selves. A name is a person's most important possession simply because it serves to give a special identity.

In preschools, children are continually constructing rules to designate group boundaries. In those schools where sexual lines are publicly drawn, boys and girls may go so far as to set off private territories where members of the opposite sex are excluded. One observer working with me noted boys and girls in a four-year-old group carrying posters stating that they were "Boys" or "Girls." On another occasion I observed the creation of a "Pirate Club" which denied entry to all females and all males who did not have the proper combination of play money for paying the membership dues. This group lasted for one hour. At juice and biscuit time, it was disbanded by the instructor and the boys were made to sweep out their tree house. Adult entry into the club seemed to reduce its interest for the boys.

The study of early childhood conversations reveals several similarities to adult speech. Like adults, young children build up special languages. These languages are silent and gestural. What a child says with his eyes or hands may reveal more than his broken speech. As children develop friendships, "private" terms and meanings will be employed. To grasp the conversations of young children, it is necessary to enter their language communities and learn the network of social relationships that bind them together. Single words have multiple meanings ("baby" can cover a younger brother or sister, all small children, or contemporaries who act inappropriately). To understand what the word "baby" means for the child, it is necessary to (a) understand his relationship to the person called a baby, (b) the situation where he uses the word, and (c) the activity he is engaging in at the moment.

Neologisms are especially crucial in the development of new relationships. The involved children attempt to produce a word that outsiders cannot understand. Its use sets them off from the other children; it serves to give a special designation to the newly formed relationship. I observed two girls, aged three, who had suddenly discovered one another. Within an hour they had developed the word "Buckmanu." With smiles on their faces they came running inside the preschool, holding hands and singing their new word. After several repetitions of "Buckmanu," they came over for juice, and a mother asked them what they were saying. They ignored her and suddenly switched the word to "Manubuck." And then, with precision and correct enunciation, they said, "Manuel bucked us off!" Manuel was the name of a preschool instructor. They had taken one of his actions (playing horseback) and his name, and forged the two into a new word. Once they revealed the name to the mothers, they ceased using it.

Mystification and the Family | *R. D. Laing*

In much contemporary writing on the individual and the family, there is assumed some not-too-unhappy confluence, not to say preestablished harmony, between nature and nurture. Some adjustments may have to be

From R. D. Laing, "The Mystification of Experience," in *The Politics of Experience* (New York: Ballantine, 1967), pp. 63–76. References cited in the original have been deleted.

made on both sides, but all things work together for good to those who
want only security and identity.

Gone is any sense of possible tragedy, of passion. Gone is any language
of joy, delight, passion, sex, violence. The language is that of a board-
room. No more primal scenes, but parental coalitions; no more repression of sexual ties to parents, but the child "rescinds" its Oepidal wishes.
For instance:

> The mother can properly invest her energies in the care of the young
> child when economic support, status, and protection of the family are
> provided by the father. She can also better limit her cathexis of
> the child to maternal feelings when her wifely needs are satisfied
> by her husband.

Here is no nasty talk of sexual intercourse or even "primal scene." The
economic metaphor is aptly employed. The mother "invests" in her child.
What is most revealing is the husband's function. The provision of economic support, status, and protection, in that order.

There is frequent reference to security, the esteem of others. What one
is supposed to want, to live for, is "gaining pleasure from the esteem and
affection of others." If not, one is a psychopath.

Such statements are in a sense true. They describe the frightened,
cowed, abject creature that we are admonished to be, if we are to be normal—offering each other mutual protection from our own violence. The
family as a "protection racket."

Behind this language lurks the terror that is behind all this mutual back-
scratching, this esteem-, status-, support-, protection-, security-giving
and getting. Through its bland urbanity the cracks still show.

In our world we are "victims burning at the stake, signaling through the
flames," but for some, things go blandly on. "Contemporary life requires
adaptability." We require also to "utilize intellect," and we require "an
emotional equilibrium that permits a person to be malleable, to adjust
himself to others without fear of loss of identity with change. It requires a
basic trust in others, and a confidence in the integrity of the self."

Sometimes there is a glimpse of more honesty. For instance, when we
"consider society rather than the individual, each society has a vital interest
in the *indoctrination* of the infants who form its new *recruits*."

What these authors say may be written ironically, but there is no evidence that it is.

Adaptation to what? To society? To a world gone mad?

The family's function is to repress Eros; to induce a false consciousness
of security; to deny death by avoiding life; to cut off transcendence; to
believe in God, not to experience the Void; to create, in short, one-dimen-

sional man; to promote respect, conformity, obedience; to con children out
of play; to induce a fear of failure; to promote a respect for work; to promote a respect for "respectability."

Let me present here two alternative views of the family and human
adaptation:

> Men do not become what by nature they are meant to be, but what
> society makes them. . . . Generous feelings . . . are, as it were, shrunk
> up, seared, violently wrenched, and amputated to fit us for our inter-
> course with the world, something in the manner that beggars maim
> and mutilate their children to make them fit for their future situation
> in life.

and:

> In fact, the world still seems to be inhabited by savages stupid
> enough to see reincarnated ancestors in their newborn children.
> Weapons and jewelry belonging to the dead men are waved under the
> infant's nose; if he makes a movement, there is a great shout—Grand-
> father has come back to life. This "old man" will suckle, dirty his
> straw, and bear the ancestral name; survivors of his ancient generation
> will enjoy seeing their comrade of hunts and battles wave his tiny
> limbs and bawl; as soon as he can speak they will inculcate recollec-
> tions of the deceased. A severe training will "restore" his former
> character, they will remind him that "he" was wrathful, cruel, or mag-
> nanimous, and he will be convinced of it despite all experience to the
> contrary. What barbarism! Take a living child, sew him up in a dead
> man's skin, and he will stifle in such senile childhood with no occupa-
> tion save to reproduce the avuncular gestures, with no hope save to
> poison future childhoods after his own death. No wonder, after that,
> if he speaks of himself with the greatest precautions, half under his
> breath, often in the third person; this miserable creature is well aware
> that he is his own grandfather.
>
> These backward aborigines can be found in the Fiji Islands, in Tahi-
> ti, in New Guinea, in Vienna, in Paris, in Rome, in New York—wher-
> ever there are men. They are called parents. Long before our birth,
> even before we are conceived, our parents have decided who we will be.

In some quarters there is a point of view that science is neutral, and that
all this is a matter of value judgments.

Lidz calls schizophrenia a failure of human adaptation. In that case,
this too is a value judgment. Or is anyone going to say that it is an objective fact? Very well, let us call schizophrenia a successful attempt not to
adapt to pseudosocial realities. Is this also an objective fact? Schizophrenia is a failure of ego functioning. Is this a neutralist definition?
But what is, or who is, the "ego"? In order to get back to what the ego is
and what actual reality it most nearly relates to, we have to desegregate it,
de-depersonalize it, de-extrapolate, de-abstract, de-objectify, de-reify, and

we get back to you and me, to our particular idioms or styles of relating to each other in social context. The ego is by definition an instrument of adaptation, so we are back to all the questions this apparent neutralism is begging. Schizophrenia is a successful avoidance of ego-type adaptation? Schizophrenia is a label affixed by some people to others in situations where an interpersonal disjunction of a particular kind is occurring. This is the nearest one can get at the moment to something like an "objective" statement, so called.

The family is, in the first place, the usual instrument for what is called socialization, that is, getting each new recruit to the human race to behave and experience in substantially the same way as those who have already got here. We are all fallen Sons of Prophecy, who have learned to die in the Spirit and be reborn in the flesh.

This is also known as selling one's birthright for a mess of pottage.

Here are some examples from Jules Henry, an American professor of anthropology and sociology, in his study of the American school system:

> The observer is just entering her fifth-grade classroom for the observation period. The teacher says, "Which one of you nice, polite boys would like to take (the observer's) coat and hang it up?" From the waving hands, it would seem that all would like to claim the honor. The teacher chooses one child, who takes the observer's coat. . . . The teacher conducted the arithmetic lessons mostly by asking, "Who would like to tell the answer to the next problem?" This question was followed by the usual large and agitated forest of hands, with apparently much competition to answer.
>
> What strikes us here are the precision with which the teacher was able to mobilize the potentialities of the boys for the proper social behavior, and the speed with which they responded. The large number of waving hands proves that most of the boys have already become absurd; but they have no choice. Suppose they sat there frozen?
>
> A skilled teacher sets up many situations in such a way that a *negative attitude can be construed only as treason*. The function of questions like, "Which one of you nice, polite boys would like to take (the observer's) coat and hang it up?" is to blind the children into absurdity—to compel them to acknowledge that it is better to exist absurd than not to exist at all. The reader will have observed that the question is not put, "Who *has* the answer to the next problem?" but "Who *would like to tell* it?" What at one time in our culture was phrased as a challenge in skill in arithmetic, becomes an invitation to group participation. The essential is *that nothing is but what it is made to be by the alchemy of the system.*
>
> In a society where competition for the basic cultural goods is a pivot of action, people cannot be taught to love one another. It thus becomes necessary for the school to teach children how to hate, and without appearing to do so, for our culture cannot tolerate the idea that babes should hate each other. How does the school accomplish this ambiguity?

Here is another example given by Henry:

> Boris had trouble reducing 12/16 to the lowest terms, and could
> only get as far as 6/8. The teacher asked him quietly if that was as
> far as he could reduce it. She suggested he "think." Much heaving up
> and down and waving of hands by the other children, all frantic to
> correct him. Boris pretty unhappy, probably mentally paralyzed. The
> teacher quiet, patient, ignores the others and concentrates with look
> and voice on Boris. After a minute or two she turns to the class and
> says, "Well, who can tell Boris what the number is?" A forest of
> hands appears, and the teacher calls Peggy. Peggy says that four may
> be divided into the numerator and the denominator.

Henry comments:

> Boris's failure made it possible for Peggy to succeed; his misery is
> the occasion for her rejoicing. This is a standard condition of the con-
> temporary American elementary school. To a Zuni, Hopi, or Dakota
> Indian, Peggy's performance would seem cruel beyond belief, for com-
> petition, the wringing of success from somebody's failure, is a form of
> torture foreign to those noncompetitive cultures.
> Looked at from Boris's point of view, the nightmare at the black-
> board was, perhaps, a lesson in controlling himself so that he would
> not fly shrieking from the room under enormous public pressure.
> Such experiences force every man reared in our culture, over and over
> again, night in, night out, even at the pinnacle of success, to dream not
> of success, but of failure. In school the external nightmare is internal-
> ized for life. Boris was not learning arithmetic only; he was learning
> the *essential nightmare also. To be successful in our culture one must
> learn to dream of failure.*

It is Henry's contention that in practice education has never been an instrument to free the mind and the spirit of man, but to bind them. We
think we want creative children, but what do we want them to create?

> If all through school the young were provoked to question the Ten
> Commandments, the sanctity of revealed religion, the foundations of
> patriotism, the profit motive, the two-party system, monogamy, the
> laws of incest, and so on . . .

. . . there would be such creativity that society would not know where
to turn.

Children do not give up their innate imagination, curiosity, dreaminess
easily. You have to love them to get them to do that. Love is the path
through permissiveness to discipline; and through discipline, only too
often, to betrayal of self.

What school must do is to induce children to want to think the way
school wants them to think. "What we see," in the American kindergarten
and early schooling process, says Henry, "is the pathetic surrender of
babies." You will, later or sooner, in the school or in the home.

It is the most difficult thing in the world to recognize this in our own culture.

In a London class, average age ten, the girls were given a competition. They had to bake cakes and the boys were to judge them. One girl won. Then her "friend" let out that she had bought her cake instead of baking it herself. She was disgraced in front of the whole class.

Comments:

1. The school is here inducting children into sex-linked roles of a very specific kind.

2. Personally, I find it obscene that girls should be taught that their status depends on the taste they can produce in boys' mouths.

3. Ethical values are brought into play in a situation that is at best a bad joke. If coerced into such game-playing by adults, the best a child can do is to play the system without getting caught. I most admire the girl who won and hope she will choose her "friends" more carefully in future.

What Henry describes in American schools is a strategy that I have observed frequently in British families studied by my colleagues and myself.

The double action of destroying ourselves with one hand, and calling this love with the other, is a sleight of hand one can marvel at. Human beings seem to have an almost unlimited capacity to deceive themselves, and to deceive themselves into taking their own lies for truth. By such mystification, we achieve and sustain our adjustment, adaptation, socialization. But the result of such adjustment to our society is that, having been tricked and having tricked ourselves out of our minds, that is to say, out of our own personal worlds of experience, out of that unique meaning with which potentially we may endow the external world, simultaneously we have been conned into the illusion that we are separate "skin-encapsuled ego." Having at one and the same time lost our *selves* and developed the illusion that we are autonomous *egos*, we are expected to comply by inner consent with external constraints, to an almost unbelievable extent.

We do not live in a world of unambiguous identities and definitions, needs and fears, hopes, disillusions. The tremendous social realities of our time are ghosts, specters of murdered gods and our own humanity returned to haunt and destroy us. The Negroes, the Jews, the Reds. *Them.* Only you and I dressed differently. The texture of the fabric of these socially shared hallucinations is what we call reality, and our collusive madness is what we call sanity.

Let no one suppose that this madness exists only somewhere in the night or day sky where our birds of death hover in the stratosphere. It exists in the interstices of our most intimate and personal moments.

We have all been processed on Procrustean beds. At least some of us have managed to hate what they have made of us. Inevitably we see the other as the reflection of the occasion of our own self-division. . . .

We must be very careful of our selective blindness. The Germans reared children to regard it as their duty to exterminate the Jews, adore their leader, kill and die for the Fatherland. The majority of my own generation did not or do not regard it as stark raving mad to feel it better to be dead than Red. None of us, I take it, has lost too many hours' sleep over the threat of imminent annihilation of the human race and our own responsibility for this state of affairs.

In the last fifty years, we human beings have slaughtered by our own hands coming on for one hundred million of our species. We all live under constant threat of our total annihilation. We seem to seek death and destruction as much as life and happiness. We are as driven to kill and be killed as we are to let live and live. Only by the most outrageous violation of ourselves have we achieved our capacity to live in relative adjustment to a civilization apparently driven to its own destruction. Perhaps men and women were born to love one another, simply and genuinely, rather than to this travesty that we call love. If we can stop destroying ourselves we may stop destroying others. We have to begin by admitting and even accepting our violence, rather than blindly destroying ourselves with it, and therewith we have to realize that we are as deeply afraid to live and to love as we are to die.

Chapter 7

The Mystique of Parenthood

Transition to Parenthood | *Alice S. Rossi*

From Child to Parent: An Example

What is unique about this perspective on parenthood is the focus on the adult parent rather than the child. Until quite recent years, concern in the behavioral sciences with the parent-child relationship has been confined almost exclusively to the child. . . .

The very different order of questions which emerge when the parent replaces the child as the primary focus of analytic attention can best be shown with an illustration. Let us take, as our example, the point Benedek makes that the child's need for mothering is *absolute* while the need of an adult woman to mother is *relative*. From a concern for the child, this discrepancy in need leads to an analysis of the impact on the child of separation from the mother or inadequacy of mothering. Family systems that provide numerous adults to care for the young child can make up for this discrepancy in need between mother and child, which may be why ethnographic accounts give little evidence of postpartum depression following childbirth in simpler societies. Yet our family system of isolated households, increasingly distant from kinswomen to assist in mothering, requires that new mothers shoulder total responsibility for the infant precisely for that stage of the child's life when his need for mothering is far in excess of the mother's need for the child.

From the perspective of the mother, the question has therefore become: what does maternity deprive her of? Are the intrinsic gratifications of maternity sufficient to compensate for shelving or reducing a woman's involve-

Abridged from Alice S. Rossi, "Transition to Parenthood," *Journal of Marriage and the Family,* 30 (1968), pp. 26–39. References cited in the original have been deleted.

ment in nonfamily interests and social roles? The literature on maternal deprivation cannot answer such questions, because the concept, even in the careful specification Yarrow has given it, has never meant anything but the effect on the child of various kinds of insufficient mothering. Yet what has been seen as a failure or inadequacy of individual women may in fact be a failure of the society to provide institutionalized substitutes for the extended kin to assist in the care of infants and young children. It may be that the role requirements of maternity in the American family system extract diversified interests and social expectations concerning adult life. Here, as at several points in the course of this paper, familiar problems take on a new and suggestive research dimension when the focus is on the parent rather than the child. . . .

Parsons' analysis of the experience of parenthood as a step in maturation and personality growth does not allow for negative outcome. In this view either parents show little or no positive impact upon themselves of their parental-role experiences, or they show a new level of maturity. Yet many women, whose interests and values made a congenial combination of wifehood and work role, may find that the addition of maternal responsibilities has the consequence of a fundamental and undesired change in both their relationships to their husbands and their involvements outside the family. Still other women, who might have kept a precarious hold on adequate functioning as adults had they *not* become parents, suffer severe retrogression with pregnancy and childbearing, because the reactivation of older unresolved conflicts with their own mothers is not favorably resolved but in fact leads to personality deterioration and the transmission of pathology to their children.

Where cultural pressure is very great to assume a particular adult role, as it is for American women to bear and rear children, latent desire and psychological readiness for parenthood may often be at odds with manifest desire and actual ability to perform adequately as parents. Clinicians and therapists are aware, as perhaps many sociologists are not, that failure, hostility, and destructiveness are as much a part of the family system and the relationships among family members as success, love, and solidarity are. . . .

Role-Cycle Stages

A discussion of the impact of parenthood upon the parent will be assisted by two analytic devices. One is to follow a comparative approach, by asking in what basic structural ways the parental role differs from other primary adult roles. The marital and occupational roles will be used for this comparison. A second device is to specify the phases in the development of a social role. If the total life span may be said to have a cycle, each stage with its unique tasks, then by analogy a role may be said to have a cycle and each stage in that role cycle to have its unique tasks and problems of adjustment. Four broad stages of a role cycle may be specified:

1. Anticipatory Stage

All major adult roles have a long history of anticipatory training for them, since parental and school socialization of children is dedicated precisely to this task of producing the kind of competent adult valued by the culture. For our present purposes, however, a narrower conception of the anticipatory stage is preferable: the engagement period in the case of the marital role, pregnancy in the case of the parental role, and the last stages of highly vocationally oriented schooling or on-the-job apprenticeship in the case of an occupational role.

2. Honeymoon Stage

This is the time period immediately following the full assumption of the adult role. The inception of this stage is more easily defined than its termination. In the case of the marital role, the honeymoon stage extends from the marriage ceremony itself through the literal honeymoon and on through an unspecified and individually varying period of time. Raush has caught this stage of the marital role in his description of the "psychic honeymoon": that extended postmarital period when, through close intimacy and joint activity, the couple can explore each other's capacities and limitations. I shall arbitrarily consider the onset of pregnancy as marking the end of the honeymoon stage of the marital role. This stage of the parental role may involve an equivalent psychic honeymoon, that post-childbirth period during which, through intimacy and prolonged contact, an attachment between parent and child is laid down. There is a crucial difference, however, from the marital role in this stage. A woman knows her husband as a unique real person when she enters the honeymoon stage of marriage. A good deal of preparatory adjustment on a firm reality base is possible during the engagement period which is not possible in the equivalent pregnancy period. Fantasy is not corrected by the reality of a specific individual child until the birth of the child. The "quickening" is psychologically of special significance to women precisely because it marks the first evidence of a real baby rather than a purely fantasized one. On this basis alone there is greater interpersonal adjustment and learning during the honeymoon stage of the parental role than of the marital role.

3. Plateau Stage

This is the protracted middle period of a role cycle during which the role is fully exercised. Depending on the specific problem under analysis, one would obviously subdivide this large plateau stage further. For my present purposes it is not necessary to do so, since my focus is on the earlier anticipatory and honeymoon stages of the parental role and the overall impact of parenthood on adults.

4. Disengagement-Termination Stage

This period immediately precedes and includes the actual termination of the role. Marriage ends with the death of the spouse or, just as definitively, with separation and divorce. A unique characteristic of parental-role termination is the fact that it is not closely marked by any specific act but is an attenuated process of termination with little cultural prescription about when the authority and obligations of a parent end. Many parents, however, experience the marriage of the child as a psychological termination of the active parental role.

Unique Features of Parental Role

With this role-cycle suggestion as a broader framework, we can narrow our focus to what are the unique and most salient features of the parental role. In doing so, special attention will be given to two further questions: (1) the impact of social changes over the past few decades in facilitating or complicating the transition to and experience of parenthood and (2) the new interpretations or new research suggested by the focus on the parent rather than the child.

1. Cultural Pressure to Assume the Role

On the level of cultural values, men have no freedom of choice where work is concerned: They must work to secure their status as adult men.

The equivalent for women has been maternity. There is considerable pressure upon the growing girl and young woman to consider maternity necessary for a woman's fulfillment as an individual and to secure her status as an adult.*

This is not to say there are no fluctuations over time in the intensity of the cultural pressure to parenthood. During the depression years of the 1930s, there was more widespread awareness of the economic hardships

---

*The greater the cultural pressure to assume a given adult social role, the greater will be the tendency for individual negative feelings toward that role to be expressed covertly. Men may complain about a given job, not about working per se, and hence their work dissatisfactions are often displaced to the nonwork sphere, as psychosomatic complaints or irritation and dominance at home. An equivalent displacement for women of the ambivalence many may feel toward maternity is to dissatisfactions with the homemaker role.

parenthood can entail, and many demographic experts believe there was a great increase in illegal abortions during those years. Bird has discussed the dread with which a suspected pregnancy was viewed by many American women in the 1930s. Quite a different set of pressures were at work during the 1950s, when the general societal tendency was toward withdrawal from active engagement with the issues of the larger society and a turning in to the gratifications of the private sphere of home and family life. Important in the background were the general affluence of the period and the expanded room and ease of child rearing that go with suburban living. For the past five years, there has been a drop in the birth rate in general, fourth and higher-order births in particular. During this same period there has been increased concern and debate about women's participation in politics and work, with more women now returning to work rather than conceiving the third or fourth child.*

2. Inception of the Parental Role

The decision to marry and the choice of a mate are voluntary acts of individuals in our family system. Engagements are therefore consciously considered, freely entered, and freely terminated if increased familiarity decreases, rather than increases, intimacy and commitment to the choice. The inception of a pregnancy, unlike the engagement, is not always a voluntary decision, for it may be the unintended consequence of a sexual act that was recreative in intent rather than procreative. Secondly, and again unlike the engagement, the termination of a pregnancy is not socially sanctioned, as shown by current resistance to abortion-law reform.

The implication of this difference is a much higher probability of unwanted pregnancies than of unwanted marriages in our family system. Coupled with the ample clinical evidence of parental rejection and sometimes cruelty to children, it is all the more surprising that there has not been more consistent research attention to the problem of *parental satisfaction,* as there has for long been on *marital satisfaction or work satisfaction.* Only the extreme iceberg tip of the parental satisfaction continuum is clearly demarcated and researched, as in the growing concern with "battered babies." Cultural and psychological resistance to the image of a nonnurturant woman may afflict social scientists as well as the American public.

---

* When it is realized that a mean family size of 3.5 would double the population in 40 years, while a mean of 2.5 would yield a stable population in the same period, the social importance of withholding praise for procreative prowess is clear. At the same time, a drop in the birth rate may reduce the number of unwanted babies born, for such a drop would mean more efficient contraceptive usage and a closer correspondence between desired and attained family size.

The timing of a first pregnancy is critical to the manner in which parental responsibilities are joined to the marital relationship. The single most important change over the past few decades is extensive and efficient contraceptive usage, since this has meant for a growing proportion of new marriages, the possibility of and increasing preference for some postponement of childbearing after marriage. When pregnancy was likely to follow shortly after marriage, the major transition point in a woman's life was marriage itself. *This transition point is increasingly the first pregnancy rather than marriage.* It is accepted and increasingly expected that women will work after marriage, while household furnishings are acquired and spouses complete their advanced training or gain a foothold in their work. This provides an early marriage period in which the fact of a wife's employment presses for a greater egalitarian relationship between husband and wife in decision-making, commonality of experience, and sharing of household responsibilities.

The balance between individual autonomy and couple mutuality that develops during the honeymoon stage of such a marriage may be important in establishing a pattern that will later affect the quality of the parent-child relationship and the extent of sex-role segregation of duties between the parents.   It is only in the context of a growing egalitarian base to the marital relationship that one could find, as Gavron has, a tendency for parents to establish some barriers between themselves and their children, a marital defense against the institution of parenthood as she describes it. This may eventually replace the typical coalition in more traditional families of mother and children against husband-father. . . .

There is one further significant social change that has important implications for the changed relationship between husband and wife: the increasing departure from an old pattern of role-inception phasing in which the young person first completed his schooling, then established himself in the world of work, then married and began his family. Marriage and parenthood are increasingly taking place *before* the schooling of the husband, and often of the wife, has been completed. An important reason for this trend lies in the fact that, during the same decades in which the average age of physical-sexual maturation has dropped, the average amount of education which young people obtain has been on the increase. Particularly for the college and graduate or professional school population, family roles are often assumed before the degrees needed to enter careers have been obtained. . . .

The major implication of this change is that more men and women are achieving full adult status in family roles while they are still less than fully adult in status terms in the occupational system. Graduate students are, increasingly, men and women with full family responsibilities. Within the family many more husbands and fathers are still students, often quite dependent on the earnings of their wives to see them through their advanced training. No matter what the couple's desires and preferences are, this fact alone presses for more egalitarian relations between husband and wife, just as the adult family status of graduate students presses for more egalitarian relations between students and faculty.

3. Irrevocability

If marriages do not work out, there is now widespread acceptance of divorce and remarriage as a solution. The same point applies to the work world: we are free to leave an unsatisfactory job and seek another. But once a pregnancy occurs, there is little possibility of undoing the commitment to parenthood implicit in conception except in the rare instance of placing children for adoption. We can have ex-spouses and ex-jobs but not ex-children. This being so, it is scarcely surprising to find marked differences between the relationship of a parent and one child and the relationship of the same parent with another child. If the culture does not permit pregnancy termination, the equivalent to giving up a child is psychological withdrawal on the part of the parent.

This taps an important area in which a focus on the parent rather than the child may contribute a new interpretive dimension to an old problem: the long history of interest, in the social sciences, in differences among children associated with their sex-birth-order position in their sibling set. . . .

Some birth-order research stresses the influence of sibs upon other sibs, as in Koch's finding that second-born boys with an older sister are more feminine than second-born boys with an older brother. A similar sib-influence interpretation is offered in the major common finding of birth-order correlates, that sociability is greater among last-borns and achievement among first-borns. It has been suggested that last-borns use social skills to increase acceptance by their older sibs or are more peer-oriented because they receive less adult stimulation from parents. The tendency of first-borns to greater achievement has been interpreted in a corollary way, as a reflection of early assumption of responsibility for younger sibs, greater adult stimulation during the time the oldest was the only child in the family, and the greater significance of the first-born for the larger kinship network of the family.

Sociologists have shown increasing interest in structural family variables in recent years, a primary variable being family size. . . . The question posed is: what is the effect of growing up in a small family, compared with a large family, that is attributable to this group-size variable? Unfortunately, the theoretical point of departure for sociologists' expectations of the effect of the family-size variables is the Durkheim-Simmel tradition of the differential effect of group size or population density upon members or inhabitants. In the case of the family, however, this overlooks the very important fact that family size is determined by the key figures *within* the group, i.e., the parents. To find that children in small families differ from children in large families is not simply due to the impact of group size upon individual members but to the very different involvement of the parent with the children and to relations between the parents themselves in small versus large families.

An important clue to a new interpretation can be gained by examining family size from the perspective of parental motivation toward having children. A small family is small for one of two primary reasons: either the parents wanted a small family and achieved their desired size, or they wanted a large family but were not able to attain it. In either case, there is a low probability of unwanted children. Indeed, in the latter eventuality they may take particularly great interest in the children they do have. Small families are therefore most likely to contain parents with a strong and positive orientation to each of the children they have. A large family, by contrast, is large either because the parents achieved the size they desired or because they have more children than they in fact wanted. Large families therefore have a higher probability than small families of including unwanted unloved children. Consistent with this are Nye's finding that adolescents in small families have better relations with their parents than those in large families, and Sears and Maccoby's finding that mothers of large families are more restrictive toward their children than mothers of small families.

This also means that last-born children are more likely to be unwanted than first- or middle-born children, particularly in large families. This is consistent with what is known of abortion patterns among married women, who typically resort to abortion only when they have achieved the number of children they want or feel they can afford to have. Only a small proportion of women faced with such unwanted pregnancies actually resort to abortion. *This suggests the possibility that the last-born child's reliance on social skills may be his device for securing the attention and loving involvement of a parent less positively predisposed to him than to his older siblings.*

In developing this interpretation, rather extreme cases have been stressed. Closer to the normal range, of families in which even the last-born child was desired and planned for, there is still another element which may contribute to the greater sociability of the last-born child. Most parents are themselves aware of the greater ease with which they face the care of a third fragile newborn than the first; clearly parental skills and confidence are greater with last-born children than with first-born chil-

dren. But this does not mean that the attitude of the parent is more positive toward the care of the third child than the first. There is no necessary
correlation between skills in an area and enjoyment of that area. Searls
found that older homemakers are *more* skillful in domestic tasks but experience *less* enjoyment of them than younger homemakers, pointing to a declining euphoria for a particular role with the passage of time. In the same
way, older people rate their marriages as "very happy" less often than
younger people do. It is perhaps culturally and psychologically more difficult to face the possibility that women may find less enjoyment of the maternal role with the passage of time, though women themselves know the
difference between the romantic expectation concerning child care and the
incorporation of the first baby into the household and the more realistic
expectation and sharper assessment of their own abilities to do an adequate job of mothering as they face a third confinement. Last-born children may experience not only less verbal stimulation from the parents than
first-born children but also less prompt and enthusiastic response to their
demands—from feeding and diaper change as infants to requests for
stories read at three or a college education at eighteen—simply because the
parents experience less intense gratification from the parent role with the
third child than they did with the first. The child's response to this might
well be to cultivate winning, pleasing manners in early childhood that
blossom as charm and sociability in later life, showing both a greater need
to be loved and greater pressure to seek approval.

One last point may be appropriately developed at this juncture. Mention was made earlier that for many women the personal outcome of experience in the parent role is not a higher level of maturation but the negative
outcome of a depressed sense of self-worth, if not actual personality deterioration. There is considerable evidence that this is more prevalent than
we recognize. On a qualitative level, a close reading of the portrait of the
working-class wife in Rainwater, Newsom, Komarovsky, Gavron, or
Zweig gives little suggestion that maternity has provided these women with
opportunities for personal growth and development. So, too, Cohen notes
with some surprise that in her sample of middle-class educated couples, as
in Pavenstadt's study of lower-income women in Boston, there were more
emotional difficulty and lower levels of maturation among multiparous
women than primiparous women. On a more extensive sample basis, in
Gurin's survey of Americans viewing their mental health, as in Bradburn's
reports on happiness, single men are less happy and less active than single
women, but among the married respondents the women are unhappier,
have more problems, feel inadequate as parents, have a more negative and
passive outlook on life, and show a more negative self-image. All of these
characteristics increase with age among married women but show no rela-

tionship to age among men. While it may be true, as Gurin argues, that women are more introspective and hence more attuned to the psychological facets of experience than men are, this point does not account for the fact that the things which the women report are all on the negative side; few are on the positive side, indicative of euphoric sensitivity and pleasure. The possibility must be faced, and at some point researched, that women lose ground in personal development and self-esteem during the early and middle years of adulthood, whereas men gain ground in these respects during the same years. The retention of a high level of self-esteem may depend upon the adequacy of earlier preparation for major adult roles: men's training adequately prepares them for their primary adult roles in the occupational system, as it does for those women who opt to participate significantly in the work world. Training in the qualities and skills needed for family roles in contemporary society may be inadequate for both sexes, but the lowering of self-esteem occurs only among women because their primary adult roles are within the family system.

4. Preparation for Parenthood

Four factors may be given special attention on the question of what preparation American couples bring to parenthood.

(a) *Paucity of Preparation.* Our educational system is dedicated to the cognitive development of the young, and our primary teaching approach is the pragmatic one of learning by doing. How much one knows and how well he can apply what he knows are the standards by which the child is judged in school, as the employee is judged at work. The child can learn by doing in such subjects as science, mathematics, art work, or shop, but not in the subjects most relevant to successful family life: sex, home maintenance, child care, interpersonal competence, and empathy. If the home is deficient in training in these areas, the child is left with no preparation for a major segment of his adult life. A doctor facing his first patient in private practice has treated numerous patients under close supervision during his internship, but probably a majority of American mothers approach maternity with no previous child-care experience beyond sporadic baby-sitting, perhaps a course in child psychology, or occasional care of younger siblings.

(b) *Limited Learning During Pregnancy.* A second important point makes adjustment to parenthood potentially more stressful than marital adjustment. This is the lack of any realistic training for parenthood during the anticipatory stage of pregnancy. By contrast, during the engagement period preceding marriage, an individual has opportunities to develop the skills and make the adjustments which ease the transition to marriage. Through discussions of values and life goals, through sexual experimentation, shared social experiences as an engaged couple with friends and relatives, and planning and furnishing an apartment, the engaged couple can make considerable progress in developing mutuality in advance of the marriage itself. No such headstart is possible in the case of pregnancy. What preparation exists is confined to reading, consultation with friends and parents, discussions between husband and wife, and a minor nesting phase in which a place and the equipment for a baby are prepared in the household.*

(c) Abruptness of Transition. Thirdly, the birth of a child is not followed by any gradual taking on of responsibility, as in the case of a professional work role. It is as if the woman shifted from a graduate student to a full professor with little intervening apprenticeship experience of slowly increasing responsibility. The new mother starts out immediately on 24-hour duty, with responsibility for a fragile and mysterious infant totally dependent on her care.

If marital adjustment is more difficult for very young brides than more mature ones, adjustment to motherhood may be even more difficult. A woman can adapt a passive dependence on a husband and still have a successful marriage, but a young mother with strong dependency needs is in for difficulty in maternal adjustment, because the role precludes such dependency. This situation was well described in Cohen's study in a case of a young wife with a background of coed popularity and a passive dependent relationship to her admired and admiring husband, who collapsed into restricted incapacity when faced with the responsibilities of maintaining a home and caring for a child.

(d) Lack of Guidelines to Successful Parenthood. If the central task of parenthood is the rearing of children to become the kind of competent adults valued by the society, then an important question facing any parent is what he or she specifically can do to create such a competent adult. This is where the parent is left with few or no guidelines from the expert. Parents can readily inform themselves concerning the young infant's nutritional, clothing, and medical needs and follow the general prescription that a child needs loving physical contact and emotional support. Such advice

---

*During the period when marriage was the critical transition in the adult woman's life rather than pregnancy, a good deal of anticipatory "nesting" behavior took place from the time of conception. Now more women work through a considerable portion of the first pregnancy, and such nesting behavior as exists may be confined to a few shopping expeditions or baby showers, thus adding to the abruptness of the transition and the difficulty of adjustment following the birth of a first child.

may be sufficient to produce a healthy, happy, and well-adjusted pre-schooler, but adult competency is quite another matter.

In fact, the adults who do "succeed" in American society show a complex of characteristics as children that current experts in child-care would evaluate as "poor" to "bad." Biographies of leading authors and artists, as well as the more rigorous research inquiries of creativity among architects or scientists, do not portray childhoods with characteristics currently endorsed by mental-health and child-care authorities. Indeed, there is often a predominance of tension in childhood family relations and traumatic loss rather than loving parental support, intense channeling of energy in one area of interest rather than an all-round profile of diverse interests, and social withdrawal and preference for loner activities rather than gregarious sociability. Thus, the stress in current child-rearing advice on a high level of loving support but a low level of discipline or restriction on the behavior of the child—the "developmental" family type as Duvall calls it—is a profile consistent with the focus on mental health, sociability, and adjustment. Yet, the combination of both high support and high authority on the part of parents is most strongly related to the child's sense of responsibility, leadership quality, and achievement level, as found in Bronfenbrenner's studies and that of Mussen and Distler.

Brim points out that we are a long way from being able to say just what parent-role prescriptions have what effect on the adult characteristics of the child. We know even less about how such parental prescriptions should be changed to adapt to changed conceptions of competency in adulthood. In such an ambiguous context, the great interest parents take in school reports on their children or the pediatrician's assessment of the child's developmental progress should be seen as among the few indices parents have of how well *they* are doing as parents.

Patterns of Child Rearing as Theories of Learning

Jane Loevinger

Gerhart Piers (in a talk which I quote from memory) has divided methods of learning into three types: learning by reinforcement, by insight, and

From Jane Loevinger, "Patterns of Child Rearing as Theories of Learning," *Journal of Abnormal and Social Psychology,* 59 (1959), pp. 148–150. References cited in the original have been deleted.

by identification. All three types of learning unquestionably occur, and theories of learning espoused by professional psychologists must account for those facts whatever they take as the prototype of all learning.

Any consistent method of child rearing contains by implication a theory of how children function, particularly how they learn. One can easily set up a correspondence between well-known patterns of parenthood and the three types of learning. Corresponding to any pattern of child rearing there is, then, a "theory of learning," emphasizing one type of learning at the expense of others. Theories of learning held by parents are, of course, far more naive and uncomplicated than similar theories held by psychologists. To avoid confusion, the term "parental theory" may be used to distinguish the implicit learning theory.

The disciplinarian parent apparently believes that any wrong thing a child does will be continued indefinitely if the parent does not see that it is punished. While psychological research has tended to emphasize rewards as more effective than punishments as reinforcing agents, disciplinarian parents emphasize punishments as reinforcers.

Apparently insight learning is assumed to predominate by those parents, once reputed to be numerous, who believe that every demand made on a child must be rationalized and explained.

Finally, the typical permissive parent must surely believe that the socialization of his child takes place by means of the child identifying himself with the well-socialized parent.

Consider the following situation. Five-year-old Johnny is beating on his two-year-old sister Sue. Mother comes in. Let us assume that every mother will want to prevent repetition of such behavior. What will she do?

Mother One believes that if Johnny does not feel pain, he will repeat the behavior at every coincidence of impulse and opportunity. She therefore punishes him sharply, thus demonstrating her adherence to a parental reinforcement theory of learning.

Mother Two believes that Johnny can be shown how wrong his conduct is and sets about to persuade him. She believes in a parental insight theory of learning.

Mother Three believes that Johnny wants to grow up to be like his parents. If she punishes him harshly, he will learn that it is all right for the bigger one to be mean to the littler one if he or she feels like it, so his behavior is less likely to be repeated if reprimanded gently than if dealt with harshly. She believes in a parental identification theory of learning.

There is one fallacy common to all parental learning theories. Kelly points out that we are not victims of our history but only of our construction of that history. Kelly finds in that fact hope for the psychotherapist. But just as it gives hope for the therapist, it generates despair for the parent. A parent can decide to beat his child, but he cannot decide how the child will construe the beating. Nor, if he abstains from punishing, can he decide how the child will construe the abstention.

Rules for rearing children are beyond the scope of this note, indeed, beyond the competence of the writer. But one superordinate rule can safely be stated: Whatever the parent's theory of learning, the child will in fact be learning by an alternative method. Thus the son of Mother One is probably identifying with a punitive, disciplinarian adult; for the son of Mother Two it is being stamped in that beating on sister has no painful consequences; while the son of Mother Three has probably discerned, "Aha! I can get away with it." The explanation of why a child shifts his mode of learning to escape his parents' vigilant efforts at socialization is not difficult. He is attempting to defend the gratification of his impulses, and in this respect he is not altogether different from his parents.

The foregoing formulation helps to solve two riddles. Why is the battle between the generations fought, generation after generation, with such vigor? And why is it that experts on child rearing are not conspicuously more successful at the art than those less expert?

The failure of expertise in child rearing was foreshadowed in 1909 with Freud's publication of *Analysis of a Phobia in a Five-Year-Old Boy,* for little Hans was the child of two of Freud's followers. One should not make too much of the fact. He was not necessarily the most neurotic child in Vienna, merely the one that Freud had opportunity to observe and indirectly to treat. Nonetheless, the occurrence of so severe a phobia in the child was a striking omen.

Reasons have been advanced for the failure of children of experts to be vastly superior to others in their adjustment. Without disputing or discounting these reasons, one can focus on a slightly different one. The experts know what other parents did wrong, and they avoid those errors. But while they avoid the errors of parents in other houses, their children contrive to defend their instinctual gratification against the parents in their own house. In current terms, a shift in parentmanship is countered by a shift in childmanship.

The battle between the generations is commonly accounted for by the fact that parents have need to socialize their children, and the children forever battle against the socializing process. This view is the one being elaborated here. But is it not quite the whole story. A useful way to test a theory is to see what happens in the most extreme cases. Redl and Wineman have depicted extreme cases of "children who hate." Many of the sentiments of those children, such as "Grown-ups don't want kids to have any fun," are echoed occasionally in almost all homes. But the ferocity and implacability of the war with adults is entirely disproportionate to what takes place in an ordinary household. Were their parents, then, so rigorous in their attempts at socialization? On the contrary, the parents of those children presented a picture of impulsivity no less striking than that of the children. The abuses to which the children were subjected could hardly be called punishments; they did not appear to result from any theory of how children learn but rather were crude lashing out on impulse. The picture of parent-child relations in *The Aggressive Child* is a conspicuously undesirable one, both prima facie and in terms of outcome. It serves to demonstrate that not all parents are informed by a parental theory. The battle between the generations is never more vicious than when all pretense of representing the interests of society is dropped and it becomes the parent's impulsivity versus the child's.

A general theory of the battle between generations must account for all of the cases. It must therefore read that the child's impulse gratification conflicts with the needs of society, represented by parents, to socialize him, as well as with the parent's own impulse gratification. The normal parent, to be sure, satisfies many of his desires in and through his children. But moment by moment and day by day the needs which the children gratify are not always uppermost. The presence of an infant or child in the household necessarily imposes delay or surrender on many of the parents' wishes.

The conclusions of this discussion can be stated simply, though they do not exactly simplify life. Every consistent pattern of child rearing embodies a theory of learning, and all those parental theories are substantially wrong. However, any parental theory is better than none.

Is it possible to base one's pattern of child rearing on a more nearly realistic theory of learning? That is an intriguing question. In view of the adaptability of the normal child in shifting his tactics to match those of his parents, such a method would require constant reconsideration and change. Yet inconsistency, so the child-rearing experts tell us, is one of the worst faces a parent can turn to his child. Possibly, however, inconsistency got its bad name not from conscientious parents trying to outwit their children but from the label being applied to such parents as Redl and Wineman have sketched.

If, as the present discussion suggests, parental theories are more wrong than right, how does it happen that it is better to have one than not? The chief value of a parental learning theory may well be in providing a model for the child of curbing one's own impulses out of regard for the future welfare of another. The very oversimplification of parental theories may serve to make accessible to the child that his parent is acting on principle rather than on impulse. To say this is to lay emphasis on learning by identification. But probably most psychologists, whatever their professional theories, act in relation to their own children as if they expect them to learn chiefly by identification.

"All I say is by way of discourse, and nothing by way of advice. . . . I should not speak so boldly, if it were my due to be believed."

Motherhood: Who Needs It? | Betty Rollin

Motherhood is in trouble, and it ought to be. A rude question is long overdue: Who needs it? The answer used to be (1) society and (2) women. But now, with the impending horrors of overpopulation, society desperately *doesn't* need it. And women don't need it either. Thanks to The Motherhood Myth—the idea that having babies is something that all normal women instinctively want and need and will enjoy doing—they just *think* they do.

The notion that the maternal wish and the activity of mothering are instinctive or biologically predestined is baloney. Try asking most sociologists, psychologists, psychoanalysts, biologists—many of whom are mothers—about motherhood being instinctive; it's like asking department-store presidents if their Santa Clauses are real. "Motherhood—instinctive?" shouts distinguished sociologist/author Dr. Jessie Bernard. "Biological destiny? Forget biology! If it were biology, people would die from not doing it."

"Women don't need to be mothers any more than they need spaghetti," says Dr. Richard Rabkin, a New York psychiatrist. "But if you're in a world where everyone is eating spaghetti, thinking they need it and want it, you will think so too. Romance has really contaminated science. So-called instincts have to do with stimulation. They are not things that well up inside of you."

"When a woman says with feeling that she craved her baby from within, she is putting into biological language what is psychological," says University of Michigan psychoanalyst and motherhood-researcher Dr. Frederick Wyatt. "There are no instincts," says Dr. William Goode, president-elect of the American Sociological Association. "There are reflexes, like eye-blinking, and drives, like sex. There is no innate drive for children. Otherwise, the enormous cultural pressures that there are to reproduce wouldn't exist.

From Betty Rollin, "Motherhood: Who Needs It?" *Look,* September 22, 1970 (Vol. 34, No. 19), pp. 15–17.

There are no cultural pressures to sell you on getting your hand out of the fire."

There are, to be sure, biologists and others who go on about biological destiny, that is, the innate or instinctive goal of motherhood. (At the turn of the century, even good old capitalism was explained by a theorist as "the *instinct* of acquisitiveness.") And many psychoanalysts still hold the Freudian view that women feel so rotten about not having a penis that they are necessarily propelled into the child-wish to replace the missing organ. Psychoanalysts also make much of the psychological need to repeat what one's parent of the same sex has done. Since every woman has a mother, it is considered normal to wish to imitate one's mother by being a mother.

There is, surely, a wish to pass on love if one has received it, but to insist women must pass it on in the same way is like insisting that every man whose father is a gardener has to be a gardener. One dissenting psychoanalyst says, simply, "There is a wish to comply with one's biology, yes, but we needn't and sometimes we shouldn't." (Interestingly, the woman who has been the greatest contributor to child therapy and who has probably given more to children than anyone alive is Dr. Anna Freud, Freud's magnificent daughter, who is not a mother.)

Anyway, what an expert cast of hundreds is telling us is, simply, that biological *possibility* and desire are not the same as biological *need*. Women have childbearing equipment. To choose not to use the equipment is no more blocking what is instinctive than it is for a man who, muscles or no, chooses not to be a weight lifter.

So much for the wish. What about the "instinctive" *activity* of mothering? One animal study shows that when a young member of a species is put in a cage, say, with an older member of the same species, the latter will act in a protective, "maternal" way. But that goes for both males and females who have been "mothered" themselves. And studies indicate that a human baby will also respond to whoever is around playing mother—even if it's father. Margaret Mead and many others frequently point out that mothering can be a fine occupation; if you want it, for either sex. Another experiment with monkeys who were brought up without mothers found them lacking in maternal behavior toward their own offspring. A similar study showed that monkeys brought up without other monkeys of the opposite sex had no interest in mating—all of which suggests that both mothering and mating behavior are learned, not instinctual. And, to turn the cart (or the baby carriage) around, baby ducks who lovingly follow their mothers seemed, in the mother's absence, to just as lovingly follow wooden ducks or even vacuum cleaners.

If motherhood isn't instinctive, when and why, then, was The Motherhood Myth born? Until recently, the entire question of maternal motivation was academic. Sex, like it or not, meant babies. Not that there haven't always been a lot of interesting contraceptive tries. But until the creation of the diaphragm in the 1880s, the birth of babies was largely unavoidable. And, generally speaking, nobody really seemed to mind. For one thing, people tend to be sort of good sports about what seems to be inevitable. For another, in the past, the population needed beefing up. Mortality rates were high, and agricultural cultures, particularly, have always needed children to help out. So because it "just happened" and because it was needed, motherhood was assumed to be innate.

Originally, it was the word of God that got the ball rolling with "Be fruitful and multiply," a practical suggestion, since the only people around then were Adam and Eve. But in no time, supermoralists like St. Augustine changed the tone of the message: "Intercourse, even with one's legitimate wife, is unlawful and wicked where the conception of the offspring is prevented," he, we assume, thundered. And the Roman Catholic position was thus cemented. So then and now, procreation took on a curious value among people who viewed (and view) the pleasures of sex as sinful. One could partake in the sinful pleasure, but feel vindicated by the ensuing birth. Motherhood cleaned up sex. Also, it cleaned up women, who have always been considered somewhat evil, because of Eve's transgression ("... but the woman was deceived and became a transgressor. Yet woman will be saved through bearing children ... ," I Timothy, 2:14-15), and somewhat dirty because of menstruation.

And so, based on need, inevitability, and pragmatic fantasy—the Myth *worked,* from society's point of view—the Myth grew like corn in Kansas. And society reinforced it with both laws and propaganda—laws that made woman a chattel, denied her education and personal mobility, and madonna propaganda that she was beautiful and wonderful doing it and it was all beautiful and wonderful to do. (One rarely sees a madonna washing dishes.)

In fact, the Myth persisted—breaking some kind of record for long-lasting fallacies—until something like yesterday. For as the truth about the Myth trickled in—as women's rights increased, as women gradually got the message that it was certainly possible for them to do most things that men did, that they live longer, that their brains were not tinier—then, finally, when the really big news rolled in, that they could *choose* whether or not to be mothers—what happened? The Motherhood Myth soared higher than ever. As Betty Friedan made oh-so-clear in *The Feminine Mystique,* the '40s and '50s produced a group of ladies who not only had babies as if they were going out of style (maybe they were) but, as never before, they turned motherhood into a cult. First, they wallowed in the aesthetics of it all—natural childbirth and nursing became maternal musts. Like heavy-bellied ostriches, they grounded their heads in the sands of motherhood, only coming up for air to say how utterly happy and fulfilled they were. But, as Mrs. Friedan says only too plainly, they weren't. The Myth galloped on, moreover, long after making babies had turned from practical asset to liability for both individual parents *and* society. With the average cost of a middle-class child figured conservatively at $30,000 (not including college), any parent knows that the only people who benefit economically from children are manufacturers of consumer goods. Hence all those gooey motherhood commercials. And the Myth gathered momentum long after sheer numbers, while not yet extinguishing us, have made us intensely uncomfortable. Almost all of our societal problems, from minor discomforts like traffic to major ones like hunger, the population people keep reminding us, have to do with there being too many people. And who suffers most? The kids who have been so mindlessly brought into the world, that's who. They are the ones who have to cope with all of the difficult and dehumanizing conditions brought on by overpopulation. They are the ones who have to cope with the psychological nausea of feeling unneeded by society. That's not the only reason for drugs, but, surely, it's a leading contender.

Unfortunately, the population curbers are tripped up by a romantic, stubborn, ideological hurdle. How can birth-control programs really be effective as long as the concept of glorious motherhood remains unchanged? (Even poor old Planned Parenthood has to euphemize—why not Planned Unparenthood?) Particularly among the poor, motherhood is one of the few inherently positive institutions that are accessible. As Berkeley demographer Judith Blake points out, "Poverty-oriented birth control programs do not make sense as a welfare measure . . . as long as existing pronatalist policies . . . encourage mating, pregnancy, and the care, support, and rearing of children." Or, she might have added, as long as the less-than-idyllic child-rearing part of motherhood remains "in small print."

Sure, motherhood gets dumped on sometimes: Philip Wylie's Momism got going in the '40s and Philip Roth's *Portnoy's Complaint* did its best to turn rancid the chicken-soup concept of Jewish motherhood. But these are viewed as the sour cries of a black humorist here, a malcontent there. Everyone shudders, laughs, but it's like the mouse and the elephant joke. Still, the Myth persists. Last April, a Brooklyn woman was indicted on charges of manslaughter and negligent homicide—11 children died in a fire in a building she owned and criminally neglected—"But," sputtered her lawyer, "my client, Mrs. Breslow, is a mother, a grandmother, and a great-grandmother!"

Most remarkably, The Motherhood Myth persists in the face of the most overwhelming maternal unhappiness and incompetence. If reproduction were merely superfluous and expensive, if the experience were as rich and rewarding as the cliché would have us believe, if it were a predominantly joyous trip for everyone riding—mother, father, child—then the going everybody-should-have-two-children plan would suffice. Certainly, there are a lot of joyous mothers, and their children and (sometimes, not necessarily) their husbands reflect their joy. But a lot of evidence suggests that for more women than anyone wants to admit, motherhood can be miserable. (If it weren't," says one psychiatrist wryly, "the world wouldn't be in the mess it's in.")

There is a remarkable statistical finding from a recent study of Dr. Bernard's, comparing the mental illness and unhappiness of married mothers and single women. The latter group, it turned out, was both markedly less sick and overtly more happy. Of course, it's not easy to measure slippery attitudes like happiness. "Many women have achieved a kind of reconciliation—a conformity," says Dr. Bernard,

> that they interpret as happiness. Since feminine happiness is supposed to lie in devoting one's life to one's husband and children, they do that; so *ipso facto*, they assume they are happy. And for many women, untrained for independence and "processed" for motherhood, they find their state far preferable to the alternatives, which don't really exist.

Also, unhappy mothers are often loath to admit it. For one thing, if in society's view not to be a mother is to be a freak, not to be a *blissful* mother is to be a witch. Besides, unlike a disappointing marriage, disappointing motherhood cannot be terminated by divorce. Of course, none of that stops such a woman from expressing her dissatisfaction in a variety of ways. Again, it is not only she who suffers but her husband and children as well. Enter the harridan housewife, the carping shrew. The realities of motherhood can turn women into terrible people. And, judging from the 50,000 cases of child abuse in the U.S. each year, some are worse than terrible.

In some cases, the unpleasing realities of motherhood begin even before the beginning. In *Her Infinite Variety,* Morton Hunt describes young married women pregnant for the first time as "very likely to be frightened and depressed, masking these feelings in order not to be considered contemptible. The arrival of pregnancy interrupts a pleasant dream of motherhood and awakens them to the realization that they have too little money, or not enough space, or unresolved marital problems. . . ."

The following are random quotes from interviews with some mothers in Ann Arbor, Mich., who described themselves as reasonably happy. They all had positive things to say about their children, although when asked about the best moment of their day, they *all* confessed it was when the children were in bed. Here is the rest:

Suddenly I had to devote myself to the child totally. I was under the illusion that the baby was going to fit into my life, and I found that I had to switch my life and my schedule to fit *him*. You think, "I'm in love, I'll get married, and we'll have a baby." First there's two, then three, it's simple and romantic. You don't even think about the work. . . .

You never get away from the responsibility. Even when you leave the children with a sitter, you are not out from under the pressure of the responsibility. . . .

I hate ironing their pants and doing their underwear, and they never put their clothes in the laundry basket. . . . As they get older, they make less demands on your time because they're in school, but the demands are greater in forming their values. . . . Best moment of the day is when all the children are in bed. . . . The worst time of day is 4 p.m., when you have to get dinner started, the kids are tired, hungry and crabby—everybody wants to talk to you about *their* day . . . your day is only half over.

Once a mother, the responsibility and concern for my children became so encompassing. . . . It took a great deal of will to keep up other parts of my personality. . . . To me, motherhood gets harder as they get older because you have less control. . . . In an abstract sense, I'd have several. . . . In the non-abstract, I would not have any. . . .

I had anticipated that the baby would sleep and eat, sleep and eat. Instead, the experience was overwhelming. I really had not thought particularly about what motherhood would mean in a realistic sense. I want to do *other* things, like to become involved in things that are worthwhile—I don't mean women's clubs—but I don't have the physical energy to go out in the evenings. I feel like I'm missing something . . . the experience of being somewhere with people and having them talking about something—something that's going on in the world.

Every grownup person expects to pay a price for his pleasures, but seldom is the price as vast as the one endured "however happily" by most mothers. We have mentioned the literal cost factor. But what does that mean? For middle-class American women, it means a life style with severe and usually unimagined limitations; i.e., life in the suburbs, because who can afford three bedrooms in the city? And what do suburbs mean? For women, suburbs means other women and children and leftover peanut-butter sandwiches and car pools and seldom-seen husbands. Even the Feminine Mystiqueniks—the housewives who finally admitted that their lives behind brooms (OK, electric brooms) were driving them crazy— were loath to trace their predicament to their children. But it is simply a fact that a childless married woman has no child-work and little housework. She can live in a city, or, if she still chooses the suburbs or the country, she can leave on the commuter train with her husband if she wants to. Even the most ardent job-seeking mother will find little in the way of great opportunities in Scarsdale. Besides, by the time she wakes up, she usually lacks both the preparation for the outside world and the self-confidence to get it. You will say there are plenty of city-dwelling working mothers. But most of those women do additional-funds-for-the-family kind of work, not the interesting career kind that takes plugging during "childbearing years."

Nor is it a bed of petunias for the mother who does make it professionally. Says writer critic Marya Mannes:

> If the creative woman has children, she must pay for this indulgence with a long burden of guilt, for her life will be split three ways between them and her husband and her work. . . . No woman with any heart can compose a paragraph when her child is in trouble. . . . The creative woman has no wife to protect her from intrusion. A man at his desk in a room with closed door is a man at work. A woman at a desk in any room is available.

Speaking of jobs, do remember that mothering, salary or not, is a job. Even those who can afford nursies to handle the nitty-gritty still need to put out emotionally. "Well-cared-for" neurotic rich kids are not exactly unknown in our society. One of the more absurd aspects of the Myth is the underlying assumption that, since most women are biologically equipped to bear children, they are psychologically, mentally, emotionally, and technically equipped (or interested) to rear them. Never mind happiness. To assume that such an exacting, consuming, and important task is something almost all women are equipped to do is far more dangerous and ridiculous than assuming that everyone with vocal chords should seek a career in the opera.

A major expectation of the Myth is that children make a not-so-hot marriage hotter, or a hot marriage, hotter still. Yet almost every available study indicates that childless marriages are far happier. One of the biggest, of 850 couples, was conducted by Dr. Harold Feldman of Cornell University, who states his finding in no uncertain terms: "Those couples with children had a significantly lower level of marital satisfaction than did those without children." Some of the reason are obvious. Even the most adorable children make for additional demands, complications, and hardships in the lives of even the most loving parents. If a woman feels disappointed and trapped in her mother role, it is bound to affect her marriage in any number of ways: she may take out her frustrations directly on her husband, or she may count on him too heavily for what she feels she is missing in her daily life.

". . . You begin to grow away from your husband," says one of the Michigan ladies. "He's working on his career and you're working on your family. But you both must gear your lives to the children. You do things the children enjoy, more than things you might enjoy." More subtle and possibly more serious is what motherhood may do to a woman's sexuality. Often when the stork flies in, sexuality flies out. Both in the emotional minds of some women *and* in the minds of their husbands, when a woman becomes a mother, she stops being a woman. It's not only that motherhood may destroy her physical attractiveness, but its madonna concept may destroy her *feelings* of sexuality.

And what of the payoff? Usually, even the most self-sacrificing maternal self-sacrificers expect a little something back. Gratified parents are not unknown to the Western world, but there are probably at least just as many who feel, to put it crudely, shortchanged. The experiment mentioned earlier—where the baby ducks followed vacuum cleaners instead of their mothers—indicates that what passes for love from baby to mother is merely a rudimentary kind of object attachment. Without necessarily feeling like a Hoover, a lot of women become disheartened because babies and children are not only not interesting to talk to (not everyone thrills at the wonders of da-da-ma-ma talk) but they are generally not empathetic, considerate people. Even the nicest children are not capable of empathy, surely a major ingredient of love, until they are much older. Sometimes they're never capable of it. Dr. Wyatt says that often, in later years particularly, when most of the "returns" are in, it is the "good mother" who suffers most of all. It is then she must face a reality: The child—the appendage with her genes—is not an appendage, but a separate person. What's more, he or she may be a separate person who doesn't even like her—or whom she doesn't really like.

So if the music is lousy, how come everyone's dancing? Because the motherhood minuet is taught freely from birth, and whether or not she has rhythm or likes the music, every woman is expected to do it. Indeed, she *wants* to do it. Little girls start learning what to want—and what to be—when they are still in their cribs. Dr. Miriam Keiffer, a young social psychologist at Bensalem, the Experimental College of Fordham University, points to studies showing that

> at six months of age, mothers are already treating their baby girls and boys quite differently. For instance, mothers have been found to touch, comfort, and talk to their females more. If these differences can be found at such an early stage, it's not surprising that the end product is as different as it is. What is surprising is that men and women, are in so many ways, similar.

Some people point to the way little girls play with dolls as proof of their "innate motherliness." But remember, little girls are *given* dolls. When Margaret Mead presented some dolls to New Guinea children, it was the boys, not the girls, who wanted to play with them, which they did by crooning lullabies and rocking them in the most maternal fasion.

By the time they reach adolescence, most girls, unconsciously or not, have learned enough about role definition to qualify for a master's degree. In general, the lesson has been that no matter what kind of career thoughts one may entertain, one must, first and foremost, be a wife and mother. A girl's mother is usually her first teacher. As Dr. Goode says, "A woman is not only taught by society to have a child; she is taught to have a child who will have a child." A woman who has hung her life on The Motherhood Myth will almost always reinforce her young married daughter's early training by pushing for grandchildren. Prospective grandmothers are not the only ones. Husbands, too, can be effective sellers. After all, they have The Fatherhood Myth to cope with. A married man is *supposed to* have children. Often, particularly among Latins, children are a sign of potency. They help him assure the world—and himself—that he is the big man he is supposed to be. Plus, children give him both immortality (whatever that means) and possibly the chance to become "more" in his lifetime through the accomplishments of his children, particularly his son. (Sometimes it's important, however, for the son to do better, but not *too* much better.)

Friends, too, can be counted on as myth-pushers. Naturally one wants to do what one's friends do. One study, by the way, found a correlation between a woman's fertility and that of her three closest friends. The negative sell comes into play here, too. We have seen what the concept of non-mother means (cold, selfish, unwomanly, abnormal). In practice, particularly in the suburbs, it can mean, simply, exclusion—both from child-centered activities (that is, most activities) and child-centered conversations (that is, most conversations). It can also mean being the butt of a lot of unfunny jokes. ("Whaddya waiting for? An immaculate conception? Ha ha.") Worst of all, it can mean being an object of pity.

In case she's escaped all those pressures (that is, if she was brought up in a cave), a young married woman often wants a baby just so that she'll (1) have something to do (motherhood is better than clerk/typist, which is often the only kind of job she can get, since little more has been expected of her and, besides, her boss also expects her to leave and be a mother); (2) have something to hug and possess, to be needed by and have power over; and (3) have something to *be*—e.g., a baby's mother. Motherhood affords an instant identity. First, through wifehood, you are somebody's wife; then you are somebody's mother. Both give not only identity and activity, but status and stardom of a kind. During pregnancy, a woman can look forward to the kind of attention and pampering she may not ever have gotten or may never otherwise get. Some women consider birth the biggest accomplishment of their lives, which may be interpreted as saying not much for the rest of their lives. As Dr. Goode says, "It's like the gambler who may know the roulette wheel is crooked, but it's the only game in town." Also, with motherhood, the feeling of accomplishment is immediate. It is really much faster and easier to make a baby than paint a painting, or write a book, or get to the point of accomplishment in a job. It is also easier in a way to shift focus from self-development to child development—particularly since, for women, self-development is considered selfish. Even unwed mothers may achieve a feeling of this kind. (As we have seen, little thought is given to the aftermath.) And, again, since so many women are underdeveloped as people, they feel that, besides children, they have little else to give—to themselves, their husbands, to their world.

You may ask why then, when the realities do start pouring in, does a woman want to have a second, third, even fourth child? OK, (1) just because reality is pouring in doesn't mean she wants to *face* it. A new baby can help bring back some of the old illusions. Says psychoanalyst Dr. Natalie Shainess, "She may view each successive child as a knight in armor that will rescue her from being a 'bad unhappy mother.'" (2) Next on the horror list of having no children, is having one. It suffices to say that only children are not only OK, they even have a high rate of exceptionality. (3) Both parents usually want at least one child of each sex. The husband, for reasons discussed earlier, probably wants a son. (4) The more children one has, the more of an excuse one has not to develop in any other way.

What's the point? A world without children? Of course not. Nothing could be worse or more unlikely. No matter what anyone says in *Look* or anywhere else, motherhood isn't about to go out like a blown bulb, and who says it should? Only the Myth must go out, and now it seems to be dimming.

The younger-generation females who have been reared on the Myth have not rejected it totally, but at least they recognize it can be more loving to children not to have them. And at least they speak of adopting children instead of bearing them. Moreover, since the new nonbreeders are "less hung-up" on ownership, they seem to recognize that if you dig loving children, you don't necessarily have to own one. The end of The Motherhood Myth might make available more loving women (and men!) for those children who already exist.

When motherhood is no longer culturally compulsory, there will, certainly, be less of it. Women are now beginning to think and do more about development of self, of their individual resources. Far from being selfish, such development is probably our only hope. That means more alternatives for women. And more alternatives mean more selective, better, happier, motherhood—and childhood and husbandhood (or manhood) and peoplehood. It is not a question of whether or not children are sweet and marvelous to have and rear; the question is, even if that's so, whether or not one wants to pay the price for it. It doesn't make sense any more to pretend that women need babies, when what they really need is themselves. If God were still speaking to us in a voice we could hear, even He would probably say, "Be fruitful. Don't multiply."

The Battered Child's Parents
Brandt F. Steele and Carl B. Pollock

The Project and the Sample Studied

Our study of parental attack on infants began inadvertently several years ago when C. Henry Kempe asked one of us to see the parents of a battered baby on the pediatric ward, hoping we could find out the why and wherefore of this distressing type of behavior. We had refused previous requests because consultations on the pediatric service were not in our domain, but this time out of curiosity we acquiesced and unwittingly were launched on a long-term investigation. This first patient, an effusive, hysterical woman with a vivid, dramatic history and way of life, turned out to be a challenging "gold mine" of psychopathology. Our feelings alternated between horror and disbelief that she had actually fractured the femur and skull of her three-month-old daughter, but these feelings were soon lost and replaced by a wish to know her, to understand her behavior as fully as possible, and to find out if treatment could help. Before long, other attacking parents were seen, and it became apparent that one psychiatrist alone could not possibly handle all the available cases as a part-time "hobby." Hence, a second psychiatrist and a psychiatric social worker were enlisted to work part time on what had come to be a fascinating problem.

During a period of five and one-half years, we studied intensively 60 families in which significant abuse of infants or small children had occurred. In many cases we began our acquaintance with parents referred by

Abridged from Brandt F. Steele and Carl B. Pollock, "A Psychiatric Study of Parents Who Abuse Infants and Small Children," in R. E. Helfer and C. H. Kempe, *The Battered Child* (Chicago: Univ. of Chicago Press, 1968), pp. 103–113. References cited in the original have been deleted.

the pediatric service while the attacked child was in the hospital. Other contacts were established with parents who had not injured their children seriously enough to require hospitalization, some of them referred by other physicians, social agencies, or legal authorities, and some of them coming voluntarily to seek help. Other cases were picked up when the problem of child abuse was discovered during treatment in the psychiatric hospital or outpatient clinic. One couple was first seen in jail after we read newspaper reports of their arrest for child beating.

Our study group of parents is not to be thought of as useful for statistical proof of any concepts. It was not picked by a valid sampling technique nor is it a "total population." It is representative only of a group of parents who had attacked children and who came by rather "accidental" means under our care because we were interested in the problem. We believe, however, that our data have particular significance because our haphazardly selected group provides a spectrum of child-abusing behavior which negates in many respects stereotypes of the "child beater" popularly held in the past.

We began by seeing parents of severely injured children, work which was publicized under the title of "The Battered Child Syndrome." The injuries included serious fractures of the skull and long bones and subdural hematomas, other less serious fractures, lacerations, multiple bruises, and burns. Soon we became aware that we were dealing only with the extreme of a much more widespread phenomenon and began including cases in which the infant was moderately bruised by severe hitting, shaking, yanking, choking, or being thrown about. It is difficult, as all those familiar with the problem can testify, to draw a line separating "real abuse" from the "accidental" signs of appropriate, albeit severe, disciplinary punishment. We feel we have been conservative in our classification of injuries as abuse. . . .

General Characteristics of the Parents in the Study Group

If all the people we studied were gathered together, they would not seem much different from a group picked by stopping the first several dozen people one would meet on a downtown street. They were not a homogenous group, but rather a random cross-section sample of the general population. They were from all socioeconomic strata—laborers, farmers, blue-collar workers, white-collar workers, and top professional people. Some were in poverty, some were relatively wealthy, but most were in-between. They lived in large metropolitan areas, small towns, and in rural communities. Housing varied from substandard hovels to high-class suburban homes. At both extremes they could be either well-kept or messy.

Educational achievement ranged from partial grade school up to advanced post-graduate degrees. In like fashion, determination of intellectual ability ranged from low borderline figures of IQs in the 70s to superior ratings of 130. The employment record of those with scanty education was characterized by many job changes and periods of unemployment. Those with higher IQs and advanced education were steadily employed in their professional roles or in the industrial, business, or financial fields. Several with adequate intelligence and education had poor job histories related to neurotic conflicts and difficult personality traits.

Our study parents ranged from eighteen to forty years of age, the great majority being in the twenties. One exception is an eleven-year-old girl who attacked two children with whom she was baby sitting. The marital situations of our group seemed not significantly different from that of others in their socioeconomic groups in the general population. A few cases were involved in separations or having only a temporary liaison. A few had been divorced and were in a second marriage. A few were in recurrent marital conflict. The great majority, however, were in a relatively stable marriage. The stability of the marriage was not always based on firm grounds of real love and a happy, cooperative relationship. Rather, it was often a desperate, dependent clinging together out of a fear of loneliness and losing everything, which held the partners together despite incompatibilities and friction. This will be discussed more fully later.

Religious affiliations included Catholic, Jewish, and Protestant. Among the latter were Episcopal, Methodist, Presbyterian, Lutheran, Mormon, Mennonite, Baptist, and Christian. Several families had no religious affiliation or only a nominal one without participation. A few were definitely antichurch. It was our impression that among those who were actively involved in their religion, there was a greater than average adherence to a strong, rigid, authoritative "fundamentalist" type of belief.

The ethnic background of most of our families was Anglo-Saxon American. There were also a few whose backgrounds were Scandinavian, Irish, German, Eastern European, and Spanish-American. We saw only one Negro family very briefly, but we draw from a population which is less than 10 percent Negro. There were children of immigrants but no immigrants. True alcoholism was not a problem except in one family, and many were total abstainers. Among those who did use alcohol, drinking was occasionally a source of marital conflict but bore no significant, direct relationship to episodes of child beating.

The actual attack on the infant is usually made by one parent. In our series, the mother was the attacker in 50 instances and the father in 7 instances. We were unable to be sure which parent was involved in two families, and in one family both parents attacked.

These general characteristics of the parents in this study, as described above, are significantly different from those reported by Elmer and others. The incidence of poverty, alcoholism, broken marriages, and prominence of certain racial groups is not significant in our series. We do not believe our data are any more accurate than those of other reporters, but that different reports reflect the inevitable result of using skewed samples. Social agencies, welfare organizations, and municipal hospitals will inevitably draw most of their child beaters from lower socioeconomic strata. Our institution serves a wide range of socioeconomic groups and is closely associated with physicians in private medical practice. Obviously, our sample will be skewed in a quite different way. Our data shows a great majority of women as child beaters. Other reports show a roughly fifty-fifty distribution between male and female, and some a significant predominance of men. We suspect that our low incidence of male attackers is related in part to a low incidence of unemployment among the males in the group. There were less hours of contact between males and infants than between females and infants—therefore, less exposure time for attack to occur by males. In samples in which women are working out of the home and unemployed men spend more time with the infant, the male attack rate would doubtless increase. While the factors of employment and unemployment have some contributing effect on the presence or absence of child attack, they are certainly not crucial. In our small series both employed and unemployed men have attacked their children.

Similar comments may be made concerning the other social, economic, and demographic factors mentioned above. Basically they are somewhat irrelevant to the actual act of child beating. Unquestionably, social and economic difficulties and disasters put added stress in people's lives and contribute to behavior which might otherwise remain dormant. But such factors must be considered as incidental enhancers rather than necessary and sufficient causes. Not all parents who are unemployed and in financial straits, poor housing, shattered marriages, and alcoholic difficulties abuse their children; nor does being an abstaining, devout Christian with a high IQ, stable marriage, fine home, and plenty of money prevent attack on infants. These facts are well recognized by most of those who work in the area of child abuse. We have stressed them, however, because large segments of our culture, including many in the medical profession, are still prone to believe that child abuse occurs only among "bad people" of low socioeconomic status. This is not true.*

---

* It would be hard to find a group more deprived and in more socioeconomic difficulty than the Spanish-American migrant agricultural workers. We spent some time running down rumors of child abuse in this group and were unable to document a single instance. Possibly some cases do occur, but we were unable to find them.

Psychopathology of the Attackers

General Characteristics

As noted in the previous section, the parents in this study were not at all a homogenous group from the standpoint of their general descriptive characteristics. In respect to psychopathology they were equally heterogenous. They do not fall into any single one of our usual psychiatric diagnostic categories. On the contrary, they present the wide spread of emotional disorders seen in any clinic population—hysteria, hysterical psychosis, obsessive-compulsive neurosis, anxiety states, depression, schizoid personality traits, schizophrenia, character neurosis, and so on. It was not possible to make a simple diagnosis in most patients. They presented mixed pictures such as "obsessive-phobic neurosis with marked masochistic features and mild depression." A majority of the patients could be said to be depressed at some time. Psychosomatic illnesses such as asthma, headaches, migraine, colitis, dysmenorrhea, urticaria, and vomiting were significant in several patients. Sociopathic traits such as passing bad checks were quite rare. The diagnosis of sociopathy was entertained in one case but could not be firmly established. We would not agree with the concept that by definition anyone who abuses a child is a sociopath. No doubt sociopaths have attacked children many times, but certainly, sociopathy and child abuse are not closely related.

It is our impression that with few exceptions our patients had emotional problems of sufficient severity to be accepted for treatment had they presented themselves at a clinic or psychiatrist's office. As noted before, a few of our patients were picked up in the clinic or hospital during treatment undertaken for reasons other than child abuse. One patient had been treated for depression during adolescence and again for a mild postpartum psychosis a year before she abused her child and came into our study. Most of our patients had been living for years with a significant amount of emotional difficulty, feeling it was not worthwhile or not possible to look for help from anyone. They had not been able to engender in their environment any useful, sympathetic awareness of their difficulties.

Child abusers have been described as "immature," "impulse ridden," "dependent," "sado-masochistic," "egocentric," "narcissistic," and "demanding." Such adjectives are essentially appropriate when applied to those who abuse children, yet these qualities are so prevalent among people in general that they add little to specific understanding. Categorical psychiatric diagnoses contribute little more, and do not answer the crucial question of why a certain parent abuses children.

Instead of trying to associate child abuse with a specific type of psychiatric disorder or a commonly accepted character-type description, we have searched for a consistent behavior pattern which can exist in combination with, but quite independently of, other psychological disorders. Although we constantly dealt with the whole gamut of emotional turmoil, we persistently focused on the interaction between caretaker and infant. From direct observation of parents with children and the descriptions given by them of how they deal with their offspring, it is obvious that they expect and demand a great deal from their infants and children. Not only is the demand for performance great, but it is premature, clearly beyond the ability of the infant to comprehend what is wanted and to respond appropriately. Parents deal with the child as if he were much older than he really is. Observation of this interaction leads to a clear impression that the parent feels insecure and unsure of being loved, and looks to the child as a source of reassurance, comfort, and loving response. It is hardly an exaggeration to say the parent acts like a frightened, unloved child, looking to his own child as if he were an adult capable of providing comfort and love. This is the phenomenon described as "role reversal" by Morris and Gould. They define this "as a reversal of the dependency role, in which parents turn to their infants and small children for nurturing and protection." We see two basic elements involved—a high expectation and demand by the parent for the infant's performance and a corresponding parental disregard of the infant's own needs, limited abilities, and helplessness—a significant misperception of the infant by the parent. Kaufman has described the same thing in terms of parental distortion of reality and misperception of the infant. He states that "the child is not perceived as a child, but some symbolic or delusional figure" and "may be perceived as the psychotic portion of the parent which the parent wishes to control or destroy." He further describes how "other parents who are extremely infantile and wish to be babied themselves resent the dependency and needs of their child and express this resentment in hostile ways." Kaufman believes parents "project much of their difficulty onto their child and feel that the child is the cause of their troubles" and "they attempt to relieve their anxiety by attacking the child instead of facing their own problems." He conceives of this as "a type of schizophrenic process" because of the strong use of the mechanisms of denial and projection. While agreeing with Kaufman's phenomenological descriptions and his thought that there is an abnormal ego function, we do not believe this is necessarily a schizophrenic process. Our concepts of the particular type of ego function involved will be discussed later.

Examples of this high parental demand combined with disregard of the infant are the following:

Henry J., in speaking of his sixteen-month-old son, Johnny, said, "He knows what I mean and understands it when I say 'come here.' If

he doesn't come immediately, I go and give him a gentle tug on the
ear to remind him of what he's supposed to do." In the hospital it was
found that Johnny's ear was lacerated and partially torn away from
his head.

Kathy made this poignant statement: "I have never felt really loved
all my life. When the baby was born, I thought he would love me; but
when he cried all the time, it meant he didn't love me, so I hit him."
Kenny, age three weeks, was hospitalized with bilateral subdural
hematomas.

Implied in the above vignettes and clearly evident in the tone of voice of
the parents as they told us these stories, is a curious sense of "rightness."
We have often called it a "sense of righteousness" in the parents.   From
early in infancy the children of abusing parents are expected to show ex-
emplary behavior and a respectful, submissive, thoughtful attitude toward
adult authority and society.   Common parental expressions were: "If you
give in to kids, they'll be spoiled rotten."   "You have to teach children to
obey authority."   "I don't want my kids to grow up to be delinquent."
"Children have to be taught proper respect for their parents."   To be sure,
such ideas are extremely prevalent in our culture and are essentially acceptable ideals of child rearing.   Parents feel quite justified in following
such principles.   The difference between the nonabusing and the abusing
parent is that the latter implements such standards with exaggerated intensity, and most importantly, at an inappropriately early age.   Axiomatic to
the child beater are that infants and children exist primarily to satisfy
parental needs, that children's and infants' needs are unimportant and
should be disregarded, and that children who do not fulfill these requirements deserve punishment.

We believe there exists in parents who abuse children this specific pattern of child rearing, quite independently of their other personality traits.
It is not an isolated, rare phenomenon but rather a variant form, extreme
in its intensity, of a pattern of child rearing pervasive in human civilization
all over the world.   Reports of this same type of attack on infants and
young children have come from England, Canada, Australia, Norway,
Sweden, Germany, Italy, Hungary, the Netherlands, South Africa, and
Hawaii.   While we know of no medical reports from Oriental countries describing child abuse in the sense with which we have been dealing with it,
we do not doubt that it occurs there also.   We have heard from a friend
who observed the following: A Chinese mother who had four children
dealt with her two younger ones in very opposite ways.   The youngest, who
had originally been unwanted, turned out to be a very fat, delightful baby
who conformed to all the standards of an ideal Chinese baby.   He was
much loved and well cared for.   The older child, who had originally been

wanted, was terribly skinny, less happy, and less responsive. The mother thought of him as an "unrewarding baby" and often stuck pins and needles into him.

It is this pattern of caretaker-child interaction and style of child rearing with which we will be concerned in the following sections.

Background and Life History of the Parents

In describing the life histories of the parents in our study, we will concentrate on those elements which have the most direct connection with the problem of the parent-child relationship involved in abuse. It is not our purpose to trace development of other facets of the personality, such as the particular form of the Oedipal conflict and its resolution, the source of obsessive-compulsive traits, or psychosomatic illness, and so on. These follow the various patterns which are familiar from the study of patients in general and need not be elaborated here. To be sure, the vicissitudes of early experience in the lives of our patients carried genetic potential for the many variations of their character structures, but we will accent their importance as sources of the particular type of parent-child relationship described in the preceding section.

Without exception in our study group of abusing parents, there is a history of having been raised in the same style which they have recreated in the pattern of rearing their own children. Several had experienced severe abuse in the form of physical beatings from either mother or father; a few reported "never having had a hand laid on them." All had experienced, however, a sense of intense, pervasive, continuous demand from their parents. This demand was in the form of expectations of good, submissive behavior, prompt obedience, never making mistakes, sympathetic comforting of parental distress, and showing approval and help for parental actions. Such parental demands were felt to be excessive, not only in degree but, possibly more importantly, in their prematurity. Performance was expected before the child was able to fully comprehend what was expected or how to accomplish it. Accompanying the parental demand was a sense of constant parental criticism. Performance was pictured as erroneous, inadequate, inept, and ineffectual. No matter what the patient as a child tried to do, it was not enough, it was not right, it was at the wrong time, it bothered the parents, it would disgrace the parents in the eyes of the world, or it failed to enhance the parents' image in society. Inevitably, the growing child felt, with much reason, that he was unloved, that his own needs, desires, and capabilities were disregarded, unheard, unfulfilled, and even wrong. These factors seem to be essential determinants in the early life of the abusing parent: the excessive demand for performance with the criticism of inadequate performance and the disregard of the child as an individual with his own needs and desires. Everything was oriented toward the parent; the child was less important.

From another descriptive standpoint, all of our parents were deprived as infants and children. We are not concerned here with material deprivation. Some were raised in poverty with great material deprivation, others in average circumstances, and a few in the midst of material abundance and wealth. We are referring to deprivation of basic mothering—a lack of the deep sense of being cared for and cared about from the beginning of one's life. When describing this deprivation of mothering, we do not imply that our patients have lacked maternal attention. Usually, they have been the object of great attention. Their mothers have hovered over them, involving themselves in all areas of the patient's life throughout the years. But again, this has been in a pattern of demand, criticism, and disregard designed to suit the mother and leave the patient out.

Our very strong belief in the importance of "the lack of mothering" as a most basic factor in the genesis of parental abuse is based on several things. First, it is based on the recollections given by patients of their unrewarding experiences with their own mothers. They documented their ideas with many reported incidents from early childhood up to the present and felt this type of relationship had been there "all their lives." Even allowing for the inevitable distortions, exaggerations, and omissions in patients' stories of their lives, we could not avoid the great significance of this consistently reported pattern. In addition, we occasionally had the experience, both enlightening and distressing, of talking to the abusing parent and her mother together. On these occasions, it was possible to observe many of the interactions which our patient had previously described. Her mother would "take over," answer questions directed to the daughter, tell the daughter what to answer, indicate in many ways what she expected the daughter to do, and either overtly or implicitly criticize and belittle her, all without paying attention to what the daughter was thinking, feeling, or trying to do. From spouse and sibling we have had further corroboration of the abusing parent's life story.

Of great interest to us has been the scant but suggestive data concerning the childhood experience of some of the abusing parents' parents. From what our patients know of their own parents' lives, from what they (the grandparents of the abused child) themselves told us, and from bits of information from aunts and uncles, it appears that the grandparents, too, were subjected to a constellation of parental attitudes similar to that described above. We believe we have seen this style of child rearing or pattern of parent-child relationship existing in three successive generations. Unwittingly and unfortunately, it is transmitted from parent to child, generation after generation. To a large extent, it has been socially acceptable, although subrosa, and to some extent it is probably culture-bound.

The central issue involved concerns a breakdown in what we referred to earlier as "mothering"—a disruption of the maternal affectional system. In speaking of this we do not mean to sound as if we were joining the popular pastime of glibly blaming everybody's trouble on "bad mothers"; rather, we are trying to explore and understand the process by which the tragic handicaps of parents, resulting from their own unhappy childhood experiences, are unintentionally effective in recreating a similar handicap in their own children's ability to be good parents. We believe our observations are useful in the understanding of child abuse, and may also contribute to knowledge of early psychic development in infants and to general problems of child rearing.

Chapter 8

The Future of Socialization

Selections from
Culture and Commitment

| *Margaret Mead*

Today, suddenly, because all the peoples of the world are part of one electronically based, intercommunicating network, young people everywhere share a kind of experience that none of the elders ever have had or will have. Conversely, the older generation will never see repeated in the lives of young people their own unprecedented experience of sequentially emerging change. This break between generations is wholly new: it is planetary and universal.

Today's children have grown up in a world their elders never knew, but few adults knew that this would be so. Those who did know it were the forerunners of the prefigurative cultures of the future in which the prefigured is the unknown.

Our present crisis has been variously attributed to the overwhelming rapidity of change, the collapse of the family, the decay of capitalism, the triumph of a soulless technology, and, in wholesale repudiation, to the final breakdown of the Establishment. Behind these attributions there is a more basic conflict between those for whom the present represents no more than an intensification of our existing cofigurative culture, in which peers are more than ever replacing parents as the significant models of behavior, and those who contend that we are in fact entering a totally new phase of cultural evolution.

Most commentators, in spite of their differences in viewpoint, still see the future essentially as an extension of the past. Teller can still speak of

Abridged from Margaret Mead, "Prefigurative Cultures and Unknown Children," in *Culture and Commitment* (New York: Natural History Press/Doubleday, 1970), pp. 65–76, 80–85, 87–88.

the outcome of a nuclear war as a state of destruction relatively no more drastic than the ravages wrought by Genghis Khan. Writing about the present crisis, moralists refer to the decay of religious systems in the past and historians point out that time and again civilization has survived the crumbling of empires.

Similarly, most commentators treat as no more than an extreme form of adolescent rebellion the repudiation of present and past by the dissident youth of every persuasion in every kind of society in the world. So Max Lerner can say "Every adolescent must pass through two crucial periods: one when he identifies with a model—a father, an older brother, a teacher —the second when he disassociates himself from his model, rebels against him, reasserts his own selfhood." There is little substantial difference between Lerner's view and that of David Riesman in his delineation of the autonomous man, who emerges from the present without too sharp a break with the past.

Perhaps the most extraordinary response to youthful rebellion has been that of Mao, who has attempted to turn the restive young against their parents as a way of preserving the momentum of the revolution made by the grandparent generation. Little as we understand the details of what has been going on in China, what we do know suggests a tremendous effort to transform the desire to destroy, which characterizes the attitudes of young activists all around the world, into an effective instrument for the preservation of the recently established Chinese Communist regime. If the Maoists succeed in this attempt, they will have made the most dramatic use of the techniques of temporary cofiguration to bring about a return to a postfigurative culture of which we have any record. There are indications that the modern Chinese may treat such new Western technologies as electronics as parallel to processes of assimilation that have occurred many times in the long history of Chinese civilization—no more significant than a new form of metallurgy.

Theorists who emphasize the parallels between past and present in their interpretations of the generation gap ignore the irreversibility of the changes that have taken place since the beginning of the industrial revolution. This is especially striking in their handling of modern technological development, which they treat as comparable in its effects to the changes that occurred as one civilization in the past took over from another such techniques as agriculture, script, navigation, or the organization of labor and law.

It is, of course, possible to discuss both postfigurative and cofigurative cultures in terms of slow or rapid change without specifying the nature of the process. For example, when the children of agricultural and handicraft workers entered the first factories, this marked the beginning of an irreversible change. But the fact that accommodation to this new way of living was slow, since it was spread out over several generations, meant that the changes were not necessarily perceived to be more drastic than those experienced by the peoples who were incorporated by conquest into the Roman Empire. So also, when attention is focused on generation relationships and on the type of modeling through which a culture is transmitted, it is possible to treat as fully comparable a past situation, as when a formerly land-bound people learned the techniques of fishing, and a present situation, as when the children of emigrant Haitians learn computer programming.

It is only when one specifies the nature of the process that the contrast between past and present change becomes clear. One urgent problem, I believe, is the delineation of the nature of change in the modern world, including its speed and dimensions, so that we can better understand the distinctions that must be made between change in the past and that which is now ongoing.

The primary evidence that our present situation is unique, without any parallel in the past, is that the generation gap is worldwide. The particular events taking place in any country—China, England, Pakistan, Japan, the United States, New Guinea, or elsewhere—are not enough to explain the unrest that is stirring modern youth everywhere. Recent technological change or the handicaps imposed by its absence, revolution or the suppression of revolutionary activities, the crumbling of faith in ancient creeds or the attraction of new creeds—all these serve only as partial explanations of the particular forms taken by youth revolt in different countries. Undoubtedly, an upsurge of nationalism is more likely in a country like Japan, which is recovering from a recent defeat, or in countries that have newly broken away from their colonial past, than it is, for example, in the United States. It is easier for the government of a country as isolated as China to order vast changes by edict than it is for the government of the Soviet Union, acting on a European stage, to subdue Czechoslovakian resistance. The breakdown of the family is more apparent in the West than in the East. The speed of change is more conspicuous and more consciously perceived in the least and in the most industrialized countries than it is in countries occupying an intermediate position. But all this is, in a sense, incidental when the focus of attention is on youthful dissidence, which is worldwide in its dimensions.

Concentration on particularities can only hinder the search for an explanatory principle. Instead, it is necessary to strip the occurrences in each country of their superficial, national, and immediately temporal aspects. The desire for a liberated form of communism in Czechoslovakia, the search for "racial" equality in the United States, the desire to liberate

Japan from American military influence, the support given to excessive conservatism in Northern Ireland and Rhodesia or to the excesses of communism in Cuba—all these are particularistic forms. Youthful activism is common to them all.

It was with the hope of turning anthropological analysis to this use that I tried to describe the essential characteristics of the postfigurative model and some of the forms taken by the cofigurative model under certain conditions of rapid change. It is my belief that the delineation of these models, as we have come to understand them through the study of older cultures, can help to clarify what is happening in the contemporary world.

The key question is this: What are the new conditions that have brought about the revolt of youth right around the world?

The first of these is the emergence of a world community. For the first time human beings throughout the world, in their information about one another and responses to one another, have become a community that is united by shared knowledge and danger. We cannot say for certain now that at any period in the past there was a single community made up of many small societies whose members were aware of one another in such a way that consciousness of what differentiated one small society from another heightened the self-consciousness of each constituent group. But as far as we know, no such single, interacting community has existed within archaeological time. The largest clusters of interacting human groups were fragments of a still larger unknown whole. The greatest empires pushed their borders outward into regions where there were peoples whose languages, customs, and very appearance were unknown. In the very partially charted world of the past the idea that all men were, in the same sense, human beings was either unreal or a mystical belief. Men could think about the fatherhood of God and the brotherhood of man and biologists could argue the issue of monogenesis versus polygenesis; but what all men had in common was a matter of continuing speculation and dispute.

The events of the last twenty-five years changed this drastically. Exploration has been complete enough to convince us that there are no humanoid types on the planet except our own species. Worldwide rapid air travel and globe-encircling television satellites have turned us into one community in which events taking place on one side of the earth become immediately and simultaneously available to peoples everywhere else. No artist or political censor has time to intervene and edit as a leader is shot or a flag planted on the moon. The world is a community though it still lacks as yet the forms of organization and the sanctions by which a political community can be governed.

The nineteenth-century industrial revolution replaced the cruder forms of energy. The twentieth-century scientific revolution has made it possible to multiply agricultural production manyfold but also drastically and dangerously to modify the ecology of the entire planet and destroy all living things. Science has made possible, through the use of computers, a new concentration of intellectual efforts that allows men to begin the exploration of the solar system, and opens the way to simulations by means of which men, especially men working in organized groups, can transcend earlier intellectual accomplishments.

The revolution in the development of food resources is on a worldwide scale. Up to the present, in many parts of the world, the medical revolution has so increased the population that the major effect of increased, efficient food production has been to stave off famine. But if we are able to bring the human population into a new balance, all of humanity can be, for the first time, well nourished. The medical revolution by reducing the pressure for population increase has begun, in turn, to release women from the age-old necessity of devoting themselves almost completely to reproductivity and, thus, will profoundly alter women's future and the future rearing of children.

Most importantly, these changes have taken place almost simultaneously—within the lifetime of one generation—and the impact of knowledge of the change is worldwide. Only yesterday, a New Guinea native's only contact with modern civilization may have been a trade knife that was passed from hand to hand into his village or an airplane seen in the sky; today, as soon as he enters the smallest frontier settlement, he meets the transistor radio. Until yesterday, the village dwellers everywhere were cut off from the urban life of their own country; today radio and television bring them sounds and sights of cities all over the world.

Men who are the carriers of vastly different cultural traditions are entering the present at the same point in time. It is as if, all around the world, men were converging on identical immigration posts, each with its identifying sign: "You are now about to enter the post-World War II world at Gate 1 (or Gate 23 or Gate 2003, etc.)." Whoever they are and wherever their particular point of entry may be, all men are equally immigrants into the new era—some come as refugees and some as castaways.

They are like the immigrants who came as pioneers to a new land, lacking all knowledge of what demands the new conditions of life would make upon them. Those who came later could take their peer groups as models. But among the first comers, the young adults had as models only their own tentative adaptations and innovations. Their past, the culture that had shaped their understanding—their thoughts, their feelings, and their conceptions of the world—was no sure guide to the present. And the elders among them, bound to the past, could provide no models for the future.

Today, everyone born and bred before World War II is such an immigrant in time—as his forebears were in space—struggling to grapple with the unfamiliar conditions of life in a new era. Like all immigrants and pioneers, these immigrants in time are the bearers of older cultures. The difference today is that they represent all the cultures of the world. And all of them, whether they are sophisticated French intellectuals or members of a remote New Guinea tribe, land-bound peasants in Haiti or nuclear physicists, have certain characteristics in common.

Whoever they are, these immigrants grew up under skies across which no satellite had ever flashed. Their perception of the past was an edited version of what had happened. Whether they were wholly dependent on oral memory, art, and drama or also had access to print and still photography film, what they could know had been altered by the very act of preservation. Their perception of the immediate present was limited to what they could take in through their own eyes and ears and to the edited versions of other men's sensory experience and memories. Their conception of the future was essentially one in which change was incorporated into a deeper changelessness. The New Guinea native, entering the complex modern world, followed cultural models provided by Europeans and expected in some way to share their future. The industrialist or military planner, envisaging what a computer, not yet constructed, might make possible, treated it as another addition to the repertoire of inventions that have enhanced man's skills. It expanded what men could do, but did not change the future.

It is significant that mid-twentieth-century science fiction, written by young writers with little experience of human life, rang untrue to the sophisticated and experienced ear and was less interesting to most well-educated men than such myths as those of Icarus and Daedalus, which include men and gods as well as the mechanisms of flight. Most scientists shared the lack of prescience of other members of their generation and failed to share the dreams of modern science-fiction writers.

When the first atom bomb was exploded at the end of World War II, only a few individuals realized that all humanity was entering a new age. And to this day the majority of those over twenty-five have failed to grasp emotionally, however well they may grasp intellectually, the difference between any war in which, no matter how terrible the casualties, mankind will survive, and one in which there will be no survivors. They continue to think that a war, fought with more lethal weapons, would just be a worse war; they still do not grasp the implications of scientific weapons of extinction. Even scientists, when they form committees, are apt to have as their goal not the total abolition of war, but the prevention of the particular kinds of warfare for which they themselves feel an uncomfortable special responsibility—such as the use of pesticides in Vietnam.

In this sense, then, of having moved into a present for which none of us was prepared by our understanding of the past, our interpretations of ongoing experience or our expectations about the future, all of us who grew up before World War II are pioneers, immigrants in time who have left behind our familiar worlds to live in a new age under conditions that are different from any we have known. Our thinking still binds us to the past—to the world as it existed in our childhood and youth. Born and bred before the electronic revolution, most of us do not realize what it means.

We still hold the seats of power and command the resources and the skills necessary to keep order and organize the kinds of societies we know about. We control the educational systems, the apprenticeship systems, the career ladders up which the young must climb, step by step. The elders in the advanced countries control the resources needed by the young and less advanced countries for their development. Nevertheless, we have passed the point of no return. We are committed to life in an unfamiliar setting; we are making do with what we know. We are building makeshift dwellings in old patterns with new and better understood materials.

The young generation, however, the articulate young rebels all around the world who are lashing out against the controls to which they are subjected, are like the first generation born into a new country. They are at home in this. Satellites are familiar in their skies. They have never known a time when war did not threaten annihilation. Those who use computers do not anthropomorphize them; they know that they are programmed by human beings. When they are given the facts, they can understand immediately that continued pollution of the air and water and soil will soon make the planet uninhabitable and that it will be impossible to feed an indefinitely expanding world population. They can see that control of conception is feasible and necessary. As members of one species in an underdeveloped world community, they recognize that invidious distinctions based on race and caste are anachronisms. They insist on the vital necessity of some form of world order.

They live in a world in which events are presented to them in all their complex immediacy; they are no longer bound by the simplified linear sequences dictated by the printed word. In their eyes the killing of an enemy is not qualitatively different from the murder of a neighbor. They cannot reconcile our efforts to save our own children by every known means with our readiness to destroy the children of others with napalm. Old distinctions between peacetime and wartime, friend and foe, "my" group and "theirs"—the outsiders, the aliens—have lost their meaning. They know that the people of one nation alone cannot save their own children; each holds the responsibility for the others' children. . . .

In most discussions of the generation gap, the alienation of the young is emphasized, while the alienation of their elders may be wholly overlooked. What the commentators forget is that true communication is a dialogue and that both parties to the dialogue lack a vocabulary.

We are familiar with the problems of communication between speakers of two languages who have been reared in radically different cultures, one, for example, in China and the other in the United States. Not only language, but also the incommensurability of their experience, prevents them from understanding each other. Yet a willingness to learn the other's language and to explore the premises of both cultures can open the way to conversation. It can be done, but it is not often done.

The problem becomes more difficult, because it is more subtle, when speakers from two different cultures share what is regarded as a common tongue, such as English for Americans and Englishmen, Spanish for Spaniards and Latin Americans. Then true communication becomes possible only when both realize that they speak not one, but two languages in which the "same" words have divergent, sometimes radically different meanings. Then, if they are willing to listen and to ask, they can begin to talk and talk with delight.

This is also the problem of the two generations. Once the fact of a deep, new, unprecedented worldwide generation gap is firmly established, in the minds of both the young and the old, communication can be established again. But as long as any adult thinks that he, like the parents and teachers of old, can become introspective, invoke his own youth to understand the youth before him, then he is lost.

But this is what most elders are still doing. The fact that they delegate authority—that the father sends his sons away to school to learn new ideas and the older scientist sends his pupils to other laboratories to work on newer problems—changes nothing. It only means that parents and teachers are continuing to use the mechanisms of cofiguration characteristic of a world in which parents, having given up the right to teach their own children, expect their children to learn from other adults and their more knowledgeable age mates. Even in science, where we have tried to build in the expectation of discovery and innovations, students learn from old models, and normal young scientists work to fill in blank spaces in accepted paradigms. In today's accelerating rate of scientific discovery, the old are outmoded rapidly and replaced by near peers, but still within a framework of authority.

In the deepest sense, now as in the past, the elders are still in control. And partly because they are in control, they do not realize that the conditions for beginning a new dialogue with the young do not yet exist.

Ironically, it is often those who were, as teachers, very close to former generations of students, who now feel that the generation gap cannot be bridged and that their devotion to teaching has been betrayed by the young who cannot learn in the old ways.

From one point of view the situation in which we now find ourselves can be described as a crisis in faith, in which men, having lost their faith not only in religion but also in political ideology and in science, feel they have been deprived of every kind of security. I believe this crisis in faith can be attributed, at least in part, to the fact that there are now no elders who know more than the young themselves about what the young are experiencing. C. H. Waddington has hypothesized that one component of human evolution and the capacity for choice is the ability of the human child to accept on authority from elders the criteria for right and wrong. The acceptance of the distinction between right and wrong by the child is a consequence of his dependence on parental figures who are trusted, feared, and loved, who hold the child's very life in their hands. But today the elders can no longer present with certainty moral imperatives to the young.

True, in many parts of the world the parental generation still lives by a postfigurative set of values. From parents in such cultures children may learn that there have been unquestioned absolutes, and this learning may carry over into later experience as an expectation that absolute values can and should be reestablished. Nativistic cults, dogmatic religious and political movements flourish most vigorously at the point of recent breakdown of postfigurative cultures and least in those cultures in which orderly change is expected to occur within a set of stable values at higher levels of abstraction.

The older industrialized countries of the West have incorporated in their cultural assumptions the idea of change without revolution through the development of new social techniques to deal with the conditions brought about by economic change and technological advances. In these same countries, obsolescence tends to be treated as survival, loved or deprecated as the case may be. In England the messenger who carried a dispatch case to France was retained long after the dispatches were sent by post; there, too, the pageantry of the throne exists side by side with the parliamentary government that has long superseded the throne as the source of power. In Sweden the most modern laws about sex behavior coexist with the most uncompromising orthodox religious support of an absolute morality.

Similarly, in the United States there is both a deep commitment to developmental change, which is interpreted as progress, and a continuing resort to absolutism, which takes many forms. There are the religious sects and minor political groups, the principal appeal of which is their dogmatism with regard to right and wrong. There are the Utopian communities that have been a constant feature of our social, political, and intellectual development. And there is the tacit acceptance of a color caste system that exists in violation of our declared belief in the fundamental equality of all men.

Elsewhere in the world where change has been rapid, abrupt and often violent, where the idea of orderly processes of change has not taken hold, there is a continuing possibility of sudden eruptions that may take the form of revolutions and counterrevolutions—as in most Latin American countries—or may bring about, in sudden reversal—even though in a new form—the reestablishment of an archaic orthodoxy in which nonbelievers may be persecuted, tortured, and burned alive. The young people, today, who turn themselves into living torches mirror in very complex ways both the attitudes of orthodox absolutism and reactions to it. They follow the example of Buddhists who responded to the dogmatisms of communism and reactive anticommunism with an extreme violation of their own permissive and unabsolute religious values. But their acts also represent, implicitly, the treatment accorded heretics and nonbelievers by any absolutist system that allows no appeal from its dogmas.

There are still parents who answer a child's questions—why must I go to bed? or eat my vegetables? or stop sucking my thumb? or learn to read?—with simple assertions: Because it is *right* to do so, because *God* says so, or because *I* say so. These parents are preparing the way for the reestablishment of postfigurative elements in the culture. But these elements will be far more rigid and intractable than in the past because they must be defended in a world in which conflicting points of view, rather than orthodoxies, are prevalent and accessible.

Most parents, however, are too uncertain to assert old dogmatisms. They do not know how to teach these children who are so different from what they themselves once were, and most children are unable to learn from parents and elders they will never resemble. In the past, in the United States, the children of immigrant parents pleaded with them not to speak their foreign language in public and not to wear their outlandish, foreign clothes. They knew the burning shame of being, at the same time, unable to repudiate their parents and unable to accept simply and naturally their way of speaking and doing things. But in time they learned to find new teachers as guides, to model their behavior on that of more adapted age mates, and to slip in, unnoticed, among a group whose parents were more bearable.

Today the dissident young discover very rapidly that this solution is no longer possible. The breach between themselves and their parents also exists between their friends and their friends' parents and between their friends and their teachers. There are no bearable answers in the old books or in the brightly colored, superficially livened-up new textbooks they are asked to study. . . .

These, in brief, are the conditions of our time. These are the two generations—pioneers in a new era and their children, who have as yet to find a way of communicating about the world in which both live, though their perceptions of it are so different. No one knows what the next steps should be. Recognizing that this is so is, I submit, the beginning of an answer.

For I believe we are on the verge of developing a new kind of culture, one that is as much a departure in style from cofigurative cultures, as the institutionalization of cofiguration in orderly—and disorderly—change was a departure from the postfigurative style. I call this new style *prefigurative,* because in this new culture it will be the child—and not the parent and grandparent—that represents what is to come. Instead of the erect, white-haired elder who, in postfigurative cultures, stood for the past and the future in all their grandeur and continuity, the unborn child, already conceived but still in the womb, must become the symbol of what life will be like.

Protean Man | *Robert Jay Lifton*

In the course of studying young (and not so young) Chinese, Japanese, and Americans, I have become convinced that contemporary psychological patterns are creating a new kind of man—a "protean man."

I found that many East Asians I interviewed had experienced an extraordinary number of beliefs and emotional involvements, each of which they could readily abandon in favor of another. Observations I have been able to make in America have also led me to the conviction that a very general process is taking place. I do not mean to suggest that everybody is becoming the same, or that a totally new "world-self" is taking shape. But I am convinced that a new psychological style is emerging everywhere.

As illustration of this protean pattern, I would like to recount the remarkable history of one young Japanese whom I interviewed in Tokyo and Kyoto from 1960 to 1962. Though I mention him as an extreme example, there were many others who in various ways resembled him. This young man was 25 when I first spoke with him.

As the youngest son in a professional family, he was brought up to be a proper middle-class Japanese boy. But when he was evacuated to the

From Robert Jay Lifton, "Protean Man," *Yale Alumni Review,* January 1969, pp. 14–21.

country from the age of eight to eleven during and after the war, his contacts with farmers' and fishermen's sons created in him a lasting attraction to the life and the tastes of the "common man." He was at that time a fiery young patriot who was convinced of the sacredness of Japan's cause, revered her fighting men (especially his oldest brother, a naval pilot saved from a *kamikaze* death only by the war's end), accepted without question the historical myth of the Emperor's divine descent, and "hated the Americans." Japan's surrender came as a great shock and left him temporarily confused in his beliefs, though he felt curious about rather than hostile toward American soldiers. He soon became an eager young exponent of democracy, caught up in the "democracy boom" which then swept Japan and which seemed to most youngsters to promise "freedom" and moral certainty.

During junior high school and high school he was an all-round leader, excelling in his studies, prominent in student government and in social and athletic activities. Yet he also became an outspoken critic of society at large (on the basis of Marxist ideas current in Japanese intellectual circles) and of fellow students for their narrow careerism.

He was an English-speaking student, having concentrated since childhood on learning English, stimulated by his growing interest in America and by the size, wealth, and seemingly relaxed manner of individual Americans he had met and observed. Therefore, when he found himself unaccountably developing what he called a "kind of neurosis" in which he completely lost interest in everything he was doing, he decided to seek a change in mood and took advantage of an opportunity to become an exchange student for one year at an American high school.

During that year he became a convert to many aspects of American life, and was so moved by the direction and example of his American "father" (a Protestant minister and courageous defender of civil rights during McCarthyite controversies) that he made a sudden, emotional decision to be baptized as a Christian. He returned to Japan reluctantly, and there found himself looked upon as something of an oddity—one friend told him he "smelled like butter" (a traditional Japanese phrase for Westerners). Eager to regain acceptance, he re-immersed himself in Japanese experience—sitting on tatami, indulging in quiet, melancholy moods, drinking tea, and so on.

Yet he did not reintegrate himself to Japanese student life quickly enough to organize himself for the desperate all-out struggle to pass the entrance examination for Tokyo University. He failed in his first attempt and thereby became a *ronin* (in feudal days, a *samurai* without a master, now a student without a university) for one year, before passing the examination on his second attempt. Once admitted to the university, he found little to interest him and rarely attended classes until—through the influence of a Marxist professor and bright fellow students in an economics seminar—he became an enthusiastic *Zengakuren* activist. His embrace of the *Zengakuren* ideal of "pure communism" and his participation in student demonstrations and planning sessions gave him a sense of comradeship and fulfillment beyond any he had previously known. But when offered a position of leadership during his third year at the university, he decided that his character was not suited for "the life of a revolutionary" and that the best path for him was a conventional life of economic and social success within the existing society.

He left the *Zengakuren* and drifted into a life of dissipation, devoting his major energies to heavy drinking, marathon *mahjong* games, and affairs with bar girls. But when the time came, he had no difficulty in gaining employment with one of Japan's mammoth business organizations (and one of the *bêtes noires* of his Marxist days) and embarking upon the life of a young executive or *sarariman* (salaried man). In fact he did so with eagerness, careful preparation, and relief, but at the same time had fantasies and dreams of kicking over the traces, sometimes violently, and embarking upon a world tour (largely Hollywood-inspired) of exotic and sophisticated pleasure-seeking.

There are, of course, important differences between the protean life styles of this young man and his American counterparts—differences which have to do with cultural emphases and which contribute to what is generally called national character. But such is the intensity of the shared aspects of historical experience that contemporary Chinese, Japanese, and American self-process turn out to have striking points of convergence.

I use the term "self-process" rather than "character" or "personality" in order to convey the idea of flux and change. Erik Erikson's concept of identity has, among other things, been an effort to get away from the principle of fixity and permanence. My stress is even more specifically on the idea of flow. For it is quite possible that even the image of personal identity, insofar as it suggests inner stability and sameness, is derived from a vision of a traditional culture in which man's relationship to his institutions and symbols are still relatively intact—which is hardly the case today.

While stemming from the interplay of several factors, this new protean self-process is, I am convinced, shaped in large measure by the increasingly important part played in human behavior by those cultural traits related to modern (and particularly contemporary) historical forces. Two historical developments in particular have special importance for creating protean man.

The first is the worldwide sense of what I have called *historical* (or *psychohistorical) dislocation.* We are experiencing a break in the sense of connection which men have long felt with the vital and nourishing symbols of their cultural tradition—symbols revolving around family, idea systems, religions, and the life cycle in general. Today we perceive these traditional symbols as irrelevant, burdensome, or inactivating, and yet we cannot avoid carrying them within us or having our self-process profoundly affected by them.

The second large historical tendency is the *flooding of imagery* produced by the extraordinary flow of postmodern cultural influences over the mass communication networks, which readily cross local and national boundaries. Each individual is touched by everything, but at the same time he is overwhelmed by superficial messages and undigested cultural elements, by headlines and endless partial alternatives in every sphere of life. These alternatives, moreover, are universally and simultaneously shared—if not as courses of action, at least in the form of significant inner imagery.

In Greek mythology Proteus was able to change his shape with relative ease—from wild boar to lion to dragon to fire to flood. But what he found difficult, and would not do unless seized and chained, was to commit himself to a single form, the form most his own, and carry out his function of prophecy. We can say the same of protean man, but we must keep in mind his possibilities as well as his difficulties.

The protean style of self-process is characterized by an interminable series of experiments and explorations—some shallow, some profound— each of which may be readily abandoned in favor of still new psychological quests. The pattern in many ways resembles what Erikson has called "identity diffusion" or "identity confusion," and the impaired psychological functioning which those terms suggest can be very much present. But I would stress that the protean style is by no means pathological as such, and in fact may well be one of the central adaptive patterns of our day. It extends to all areas of human experience—to sexual as well as political behavior, to the holding and promulgating of ideas, and to the general organization of lives.

To illustrate the expression of the protean style in America and Europe, I would like to draw first from my psychotherapeutic work with patients and then from some observations on contemporary Western literature and art.

One patient of mine, a gifted young teacher, spoke of himself this way: "I have an extraordinary number of masks I can put on or take off. The question is: is there, or should there be, one face which should be authentic? I'm not sure that there is one for me. I cannot imagine a single act that I could not commit." He went on to compare himself to an actor on the stage who performs with a "certain kind of polymorphous versatility." And he asked: "Which is the real person, so far as an actor is concerned? Is he more real when performing on stage—or when he is at home? I tend to think that for people who have these many, many masks, there is no home."

My patient was by no means a happy man, but neither was he incapacitated. And although we can see the strain with which he carries his "polymorphous versatility," it could also be said that, as a teacher and a thinker, and in some ways as a man, it served him well.

In contemporary American literature, Saul Bellow is notable for creating protean men. In *The Adventures of Augie March,* one of his earlier novels, we meet a picaresque hero with an exceptional talent for adapting himself to divergent social worlds. Augie himself says: "I touched all sides, and nobody knew where I belonged. I had no good idea of that myself." A perceptive young English critic, Tony Tanner, describes Bellow's more recent protean hero, Herzog, as "a representative of modern intelligence, swamped with ideas, metaphysics, and values, and surrounded by messy facts. He labors to cope with them all."

A distinguished French literary spokesman for the protean style—in his life and in his work—is of course Jean-Paul Sartre. I believe it is precisely because of these protean traits that Sartre strikes us as such an embodiment of twentieth-century man. An American critic, Theodore Solotaroff, characterizes Sartre as "constantly on the go, hurrying from point to point, subject to subject; fiercely intentional, his thought occupies, fills, and distends its material as he endeavors to lose and find himself in his encounters with other lives, disciplines, books, and situations."

This image of repeated, autonomously willed death and rebirth of the self, so central to the protean style, is associated psychoanalytically with the theme of fatherlessness. Sartre writes:

> "There is no good father, that's the rule. Don't lay the blame on men but on the bond of paternity, which is rotten. To beget children, nothing better; *to have* them, what iniquity! Had my father lived, he would have lain on me at full length and would have crushed me. . . . I move from shore to shore, alone and hating those invisible begetters who bestraddle their sons all their life long. I left behind me a young man who did not have time to be my father and who could now be my son. Was it a good thing or bad? I don't know. But I readily subscribed to the verdict of an eminent psychoanalyst: I have no Superego.

We note Sartre's image of interchangeability of father and son, of "a young man who did not have time to be my father and who could now be my son"—which in a literal sense refers to the age at which his father died, but symbolically suggests an extension of the protean style to intimate family relationships.

What has actually disappeared—in Sartre and in protean man generally— is not susceptibility to guilt, but rather the classic superego, the internalization of clearly defined criteria of right and wrong transmitted within a particular culture by parents to their children. Protean man requires freedom from that kind of superego—he requires a symbolic fatherlessness—

in order to carry out his explorations. But rather than being free of guilt, his guilt merely takes on a different form.

In the visual arts, one of the most important postwar movements has been aptly named "action painting" to convey its stress upon process rather than fixed completion. And kinetic art, a more recent and related movement in sculpture, goes further. According to Jean Tinguely, one of its leading practitioners, "artists are putting themselves in rythm with their time, especially with permanent and perpetual movement." I have frequently heard artists, themselves considered radical innovators, complain bitterly of a turnover in art movements so rapid as to discourage holding still long enough to develop a particular style.

John Cage, the composer, is an extreme exponent of the protean style, both in his music and in his sense of all of us as listeners. He concluded a recent letter to the *Village Voice* with the sentence: "Nowadays, everything happens at once and our souls are conveniently electronic, omniattentive." The comment is McLuhan-like, but I wish to stress particularly the idea of omniattention—the sense of contemporary man as having the capacity to receive and take in everything. In attending, as in being, nothing is off limits.

To be sure, one also observes a tendency which seems to be precisely the opposite of the protean style. I refer to the straight-and-narrow specialization in psychological as well as in intellectual life, a closing off and reluctance to let in any "extraneous" influences. But I would emphasize that where this kind of constricted or "one-dimensional" self-process exists, it is essentially reactive and compensatory. Continuous psychological work is required to fend off protean influences which are always abroad.

Just as protean man can readily experiment with and alter elements of his self, he can also embrace, modify, let go of, and reembrace idea systems and ideologies, all with an ease that stands in sharp contrast to the inner struggle we have in the past associated with such shifts. Until relatively recently, no more than one major ideological switch was likely to occur in a lifetime, and that one would be long remembered as a significant individual turning point, accompanied by profound soul-searching and conflict. But today it is not unusual to encounter several such shifts, accomplished relatively painlessly, within a year or even a month; and among many groups, the rarity is a man who has gone through life holding firmly to a single ideological vision.

While protean man is incapable of an unquestioning allegiance to the large ideologies and utopian thought of the nineteenth and early twentieth centuries, one does encounter in him a strong ideological hunger. He is starved for ideas and feelings that give coherence to his world. But here too his leaning is toward new combinations. While he is by no means without yearning for the absolute, he finds fragmentary images more accept-able than the complete ideologies of the past. And these images, although limited and often fleeting, can have great influence upon his psychological life. Thus political and religious movements, as they confront protean man, are likely to experience less difficulty convincing him to alter previous convictions than they do providing him with a set of beliefs which can command his allegiance for more than a brief experimental interlude.

Underlying his flux in emotions and beliefs is a profound inner sense of absurdity which most often finds expression in a tone of mockery. The feeling of absurdity, of course, has a considerable modern tradition, and has been discussed by writers like Camus as a function of man's spiritual homelessness and inability to find meaning in traditional belief systems. But absurdity and mockery have taken much more extreme form in the post-World War II world, and have in fact become a prominent part of a universal life style.

In American life, absurdity and mockery are everywhere. Perhaps their most vivid expression can be found in such areas as pop art and the more general burgeoning of "pop culture." Important here is the complex stance of the pop artist toward the objects he depicts. On the one hand he embraces the materials of the everyday world, celebrates and even exalts them—boldly asserting his creative return to representational art (in active rebellion against the previously reigning nonobjective school), and his psychological return to the "real world" of *things*. On the other hand everything he touches he mocks. "Thingness" is pressed to the point of cari-cature. He is indeed artistically reborn as he moves freely among the physical and symbolic materials of his environment, but mockery is his birth certificate and his passport.

A similar spirit seems to pervade literature and social action alike. What is best termed a "literature of mockery" has come to dominate fic-tion and other forms of writing on an international scale. Günter Grass's *The Tin Drum* comes to mind as probably the greatest single example of this literature—a work, I believe, which will eventually be appreciated as much as a general evocation of contemporary man as of the particular German experience with Nazism. In this country the divergent group of novelists known as "black humorists" also fit into the general category—related as they are to a trend in the American literary consciousness which R. W. B. Lewis has called a "new kind of ironic literary form and disturb-ing vision, the joining of the dark thread of apocalypse with the nervous detonations of satiric laughter." For it is precisely death itself, and particu-larly threats of the contemporary apocalypse, that protean man ultimately mocks.

The relationship of mockery to political action has been less apparent, but is, I would claim, equally significant. There have been signs of craving for mockery in major American expressions of protest such as the Negro movement and the opposition to the war in Vietnam. In the former a certain chord can be struck by the comedian Dick Gregory, and in the latter by the use of satirical skits and parodies, which revives the flagging attention of protestors becoming gradually bored with the repetition of their "straight" slogans and goals. And on an international scale, I would say that, during the past decade, Russian intellectual life has been enriched by a leavening spirit of mockery—against which the Chinese leaders are now, in the extremes of their Cultural Revolution, fighting a vigorous but ultimately losing battle.

Closely related to the sense of absurdity and the spirit of mockery is another characteristic of protean man which I will call "suspicion of counterfeit nurturance." I first began to think of the concept several years ago while working with survivors of the atomic bomb in Hiroshima. In psychological terms, the core problem here is severe conflict over dependency. I found that these survivors both felt themselves in need of special help, and resented whatever help was offered them because they equated it with weakness and inferiority.

Considering the matter more generally, I find this equating of aid or nurturance with a threat to autonomy a major theme of contemporary life. The breakdown of traditional institutions leads to increased dependency needs, and protean man seeks out replacements wherever he can find them. The large organizations to which he turns (government, business, academia, etc.), and which contemporary society more and more holds out as substitutes for traditional institutions, present a threat to his autonomy in one way; and the intense individual relationships in which he seeks to anchor himself threaten him in another. Both are likely, therefore, to be perceived as counterfeit. The obverse of this tendency, however, is an expanding sensitivity to the unauthentic, which may be just beginning to exert its general creative force on man's behalf.

Technology (and technique in general), together with science, have special significance for protean man. Technical achievement of any kind can be strongly embraced to combat inner tendencies toward diffusion, and to transcend feelings of absurdity and conflicts over counterfeit nurturance. The image of science itself, however, as the ultimate power behind technology and, to a considerable extent, behind contemporary thought in general, becomes much more difficult to cope with. Only in certain underdeveloped countries can one find, in relatively pure form, those expectations of scientific-utopian deliverance from all human want and conflict which were characteristic of eighteenth- and nineteenth-century Western thought. Protean man retains much of this utopian imagery, but he finds it increasingly undermined by massive disillusionment. More and more he calls forth the other side of the God-devil polarity generally applied to science, and sees it as a purveyor of total destructiveness. This kind of profound ambivalence creates for him the most extreme psychic paradox: the very force he still feels to be his liberator from the heavy burdens of past irrationality also threatens him with absolute annihilation, even extinction. But this paradox may well be—in fact, I believe, already has been—the source of imaginative efforts to achieve new relationships between science and man, and indeed, new visions of science itself.

I suggested before that protean man was not free of guilt. Indeed he suffers considerably from it, but often without awareness of what is causing his suffering. For his is a form of hidden guilt: a vague but persistent kind of self-condemnation related to an awareness that he has no outlet for his loyalties and no symbolic structure for his achievements. This is the guilt of social breakdown, and it includes various forms of historical and racial guilt experienced by whole nations and peoples, both the privileged and the abused. Rather than a clear feeling of evil or sinfulness, it takes the form of a nagging sense of unworthiness, all the more troublesome for its lack of clear origin.

Vague constellations of anxiety and resentment are particularly tied in with the suspicion of counterfeit nurturance. Often feeling himself uncared for, even abandoned, protean man responds with diffuse fear and anger. But he can neither find a good cause for the former, nor a consistent target for the latter. He nevertheless cultivates his anger because he finds it more serviceable than anxiety—and because there are plenty of targets of one kind or another beckoning. His difficulty is that focused indignation is as hard for him to sustain as any single identification or conviction.

Involved in all of these patterns is a profound internal struggle with the idea of change itself. For here too protean man finds himself ambivalent in the extreme. He is intensely attracted to the idea of making all things, including himself, totally new. But he is equally drawn to the image of a mythical past of perfect harmony and prescientific wholeness. Amidst the extraordinarily rapid change surrounding his own life, nostalgia is pervasive, and can be one of his most explosive and dangerous emotions. This longing for a "Golden Age" not only sets the tone for the restorationism of the politically Rightist antagonists of history: the still-extant emperor-worshipping assassins in Japan, the Colons in France, and the John Birch-ites and Ku Klux Klanners in this country. It also, in more disguised form, energizes that totalistic transformationism of the Left which courts violence, and is even willing to risk nuclear violence, in a similarly elusive quest.

Central to all that I have been discussing are radical impairments to the

symbolism of transition within the life cycle—the *rites de passages* surrounding birth, entry into adulthood, marriage, and death. Whatever rites
remain seem shallow, inappropriate, fragmentary. Protean man cannot
take them seriously, and he often seeks to improvise new ones with whatever contemporary materials he has available, including cars and drugs.

Perhaps the most crucial impairment here is that of symbolic immortality—of the universal need for imagery of connection predating and extending beyond the individual life span, whether the idiom of this symbolism
is biological (living through children and grandchildren), theological
(through a life after death), natural (*in* nature itself which outlasts all), or
creative (through what man makes and does). This sense of immortality
is a fundamental component of ordinary psychic life, and it is now being
profoundly threatened; by simple historical velocity and, of particular importance to protean man, by the existence of nuclear weapons which, even
without being used, call into question all modes of immortality. (Who can
be certain of living on through children or grandchildren, through teachings or kindnesses?)

Protean man is left with two paths to symbolic immortality which he
tries to cultivate, sometimes pleasurably and sometimes desperately. One
is the natural mode we have mentioned. His attraction to nature and
concern at its descration has to do with an unarticulated sense that, in whatever holocaust, at least nature will endure—though such are the dimensions of our present weapons that he cannot be absolutely certain even of
this.

His second path is that of "experiential transcendance"—of seeking a
sense of immortality as mystics always have, through psychic experience of
such intensity that time and death are, in effect, eliminated. This, I believe, is the larger meaning of the "drug revolution," of protean man's
hunger for chemical aids to expanded consciousness. Indeed, all revolutions may be thought of, at bottom, as innovations in the struggle for
immortality.

It is evident that young adults individually, and youth movements collectively, express most vividly the psychological themes of protean man.
However, although it is true that these themes make contact with what we
sometimes call the psychology of adolescence, we err badly if we overlook
their expression in all age groups and dismiss them as mere adolescent
phenomena. On the contrary, protean man's affinity for the young—his
being metaphorically and psychologically so young in spirit—has to do
with this never-ceasing quest for imagery of rebirth. He seeks such imagery
from all sources: from ideas, techniques, religious and political systems,
mass movements, and drugs; or from special individuals whom he sees as
possessing that problematic gift of his namesake, the gift of prophecy.

The dangers inherent in this quest seem hardly to require emphasis. What perhaps needs most to be kept in mind is the general principle that renewal on a large scale is impossible to achieve without forays into danger, destruction, and negativity. The principle of "death and rebirth" is as valid historically as it is mythologically. However misguided many of his forays may be, protean man also carries with him an extraordinary range of possibility for man's betterment, or more important, for his survival.

4

The Politics of Household and Life Style

387

Duane Denfeld and Michael Gordon
Mate Swapping:
The Family That Swings Together Clings Together

Chapter 11   Experimental/Utopian Forms of the Family

Kent Geiger
The Soviet Experiment

William M. Kephart
Oneida: An Early American Commune

David W. Plath and Yoshie Sugihara
A Japanese Commune

Melford Spiro
The Israeli Kibbutz

Bennett Berger, Bruce Hackett, Sherri Cavan,
Gilbert Zickler, Mervyn Millar, Marilyn Noble,
Susan Theiman, Richard Farrell, and Benjamin Rosenbluth
Child-Rearing Practices of the Communal Family

Sara Davidson
The Hippie Alternative: Getting Back to the Communal Garden

Introduction

This last section returns to the most fundamental issue in the field of family sociology, namely, the centrality and necessity of the traditional nuclear family. The first selection is by Talcott Parsons, perhaps the leading establishment American sociologist. His views are both influential and representative. His articles justify the traditional American nuclear family structure in tones of impartiality and scientific objectivity. A careful reading, however, will reveal that his functional analysis is also political in so far as it affirms traditional sex roles, power relations, and conceptions of socialization.

The Nuclear Family

In fact, neither American social life nor American family life is so stable nor traditional as Parsons suggests. The kinship patterns prevailing among different ethnic groups, the prevalence of divorce, the variety of child-rearing patterns among the divorced and among minority groups, the movement for women's liberation, the openness of sexual discussion and even behavior in the suburbs, the new moralities of high-school and college-age youth, the politicization and militancy of homosexuals, and the open search for new forms of family organization all suggest a complexity and diversity in the American family and sex scene which Parsonian functionalism both obscures and ignores. The Parsonian functional view of the family is in many respects the obverse of the early "correctional" approach to deviance. Matza writes:

> A basic difficulty with a correctional perspective is that it systematically interferes with the capacity to empathize and thus comprehend the subject of inquiry. Only through appreciation [trying to see the world from the viewpoint of the deviant person] can the texture of social patterns and the nuances of human engagement with those patterns be understood and analyzed. . . .
> . . . When deviant phenomena are seen and studied from the correctional perspective, the possibility of "losing the phenomenon" . . . is heightened. . . . The phenomenon itself receives only cursory atten-

tion. . . . [There is a] highly disproportionate division of attention between description and explanation.[1]

In the functionalist approach, both the "normal" American family and the "deviant" ones are studied only cursorily, and from the outside. Further, the assumption that the nuclear family is an obvious "good" is as uncritical as was the correctional view of deviance as simply "bad." Concern with normality and pathology obscures how much the actual experience of the people involved may differ from normative models. For example, the functional sociologists try to "normalize" divorce by defining it as a way of perfecting the nuclear family. But to the people experiencing divorce, nuclear family norms may be irrelevant. Morton Hunt writes of a "sex without love" pattern that may prevail among divorced people between marriages: both men and women learn to adapt to a set of sex norms among the formerly married that is quite different from those of single people and the married. Only from a remote and abstract viewpoint can one assert that the nuclear family of remarried spouses is the same kind of nuclear family as any other.

In this section we present readings that offer some indication of the variety and diversity of family life and personal styles in America today. The statistics on parents without partners (as LeMasters points out) are initially almost startling. He shows, for example, that in the United States there were about seven million children in the 1960s living with a stepparent. This suggests that the model of the nuclear family cannot be applied to a considerable and significant proportion of those who are engaged in at least some of the family functions. To exclude consideration of these so-called deviant family patterns because they do not fit the model of what ought to be is to inform one's theory of the family, not with reality, but with ideology. Perhaps the most pernicious outcome of this ideology is the stigmatization of families that do not conform to what is, in effect, a normativist model of the nuclear family decked out in positivist attire. In particular, this ideology stigmatizes the families of the poor, and implies that they are the major cause of their own troubles. As Warren D. TenHouten points out with respect to the black family, the assumption is that its "pathological" characeristics may be located in the so-called matriarchal form of the family. The important insight of TenHouten's article is that the research evidence does not support the notion that the matriarchal form of the family causes social pathology. Surely, there is a high correlation between poverty and matriarchy, yet to assume that matriarchy rather than poverty is causing problems permits the broader society to see itself as relatively unproblematic and to define the family organization within the black community as the source of social pathology. The poor black families described by Liebow are not totally disorganized; and the male role is clearly undermined by the economy's inability to provide meaningful and rewarding work. As Richard Sennett has observed:

> What Moynihan describes occurs wherever unemployment or intermittent employment is a long-term family experience; one therefore finds a much higher rate of female-headed households, with shifting male partners and "illegitimate" children, among persecuted rural Catholics in Northern Ireland than among the blacks of New York City.[2]

Middle-class social scientists often write of the experience of poverty in their own terms, not in terms of the subjective vision of the poor. Accordingly, the poor are sometimes romanticized, sometimes stigmatized, but rarely, as Rodman points out in his selection, understood through their own evaluations and concepts.

The aged constitute another family "problem" in America. When the social and geographical mobility of the small nuclear family unit prevails, older people are often excluded from family life. Increasingly, within the United States, we find that there are paradoxical similarities between the culture of the young and the culture of the aged, although these similarities are not usually perceived. All those not embraced by the nuclear family find themselves in a situation of considerable discomfort. In response, both youth and aged are increasingly developing distinctive peer-group cultures as a substitute for the nuclear family structure.

Deviant Life Styles

Age and color are not the only factors creating life styles at variance with the model of the traditional nuclear family. We have included a series of selections on deviant life styles for people who conceivably, because of their age and social position, could function within a nuclear family structure. Yet because of sexual or emotional preferences they choose to develop a variant life style. Moreover, homosexuals are claiming social legitimacy through such movements as "gay liberation"; and in some cases are even adapting homosexuality to the affectional model of the nuclear family.

Even within the formal structure of the nuclear family, we find people adopting what would traditionally be regarded as a deviation from the nuclear family model. One of the most sensitive and controversial patterns is the regularized extramarital affair, a kind of secret and often anxious polygamy. As Morton Hunt points out, the extramarital affair is an institutionalized feature of American family life. Yet the partial or total separation of sex and marriage evokes a more European vision of attitudes toward the family, perceiving it as an economic and social institution in which sexual gratification may be only partly fulfilled. Still, if the affair is an institutionalized feature of American life, perhaps the double standard has traditionally been even more institutionalized. Indeed, many men who engage in extramarital affairs become indignant when their wives do. Some couples have come to deal with the problem of sexual gratification in marriage by avoiding the affair and adopting the "swinging" pattern. That is, they engage in extramarital sex with both the knowledge and participation of their spouse, feeling that their marriage is strengthened, or its continuation made possible, through open sexual gratification outside of the "one-on-one trip."

Experimental and Utopian Forms of the Family

The final chapter deals with dramatic attempts to alter the forms of the family and the relations of the family to the community. We include the attempt by the Soviet Union to undermine the nuclear family through governmental policy, as well as attempts to change family practices in utopian or intentional communities.

The flowering of communal living experiments in America during the late 1960's was not something new under the sun, but rather the revival of an old American tradition. As Rosabeth M. Kantor writes:

> About a hundred utopian communities were born and died in the nineteenth-century America, most founded before 1850. Some of these lasted as long as 180 years (the Shaker Villages), while others were in existence only six months (Yellow Springs, Ohio). Some were more or less sectarian, some primarily secular; some were celibate, others favored free love. Some utopias derived from immigrant groups and spoke a foreign language. There was a Catholic community, Owenite communes, Fourierite phalanxes (phalansteries), and even one community derived from a literary utopia (Icaria, after Etienne Cabot's *Voyage en Icarie*). While many of the nineteenth-century American utopian communities shared general values, they often implemented them in different ways.

G. R. Taylor argues that the early Christians lived in utopian communal groups, and that the tradition has survived in an underground way for the past two thousand years.

Yet, if the study of deviant forms of the family has been overly preoccupied with the idea of "pathology," the corresponding preoccupation in the study of the utopian family is "viability": can the new community survive and reproduce itself? As we shall see later, to define success and failure is not as easy as some writers make it appear. Moreover, there has been a lack of attention to the conditions necessary for such experiments to succeed, and also to those impeding the success of utopian forms—such factors as the prior social and physical conditioning of the participants, and the attitudes of the larger society, certainly seem salient.

Furthermore, although utopian forms of the family have often been labeled "experimental," the designation is misleading. True, they are experimental in the sense that they are innovative. But they are not scientifically experimental for at least two reasons. First, in a true experiment, the subjects are randomly assigned to the different experimental conditions; they do not assign themselves. Random assignment to varying family forms is, of course, out of the question both practically and ethically. But without random assignment, we really don't know whether any outcome of a family "experiment" (its stability or longevity, the mental health of the children) is due to the design of the community or to the personal characteristics of the people who chose those living arrangements. For example, Rosabeth Kantor concludes from her study of the 19th century communes that those demanding the greatest degree of commitment and sacrifice from their members lasted longer than those that were less strict. But we do not know whether it was demandingness of the communes that resulted in longer community life, or whether the stricter communes attracted people who were more committed to begin with.

The second reason that experimental forms of the family are not truly experimental in a scientific sense is that they usually involve several innovations at once. As a result, it is impossible to assess the effects of a particular innovative feature. For example, all the forms of the family discussed in this part involve at least two innovations: first, the introduction of new family and child-rearing patterns; and second, the founding of a new society from the ground up. In scientific terms, the assessment of these two "variables" is confounded. The problem is similar to that of trying to interpret the effects of a new fertilizer on plant growth while also introducing more sunlight and less water. So, since utopian communities do not "control" for the effects of variables that may significantly influence the outcome of the "experiment," they are not scientifically experimental.

The first selection on utopian forms considers the Soviet experience, often cited as an illustration of the necessity for the nuclear family. In the 1920's, many laws were passed to liberate women and free individuals from the demands of the family: marriage and divorce were free, illegitimacy was abolished, abortion was easily available, etc. Yet the selection by Geiger reveals a set of conditions which made it almost impossible for the Soviet Union to have succeeded in such an "experiment." We learn that the attempt to equalize the woman's role failed for several reasons: first, the government did not provide sufficient retraining to qualify women for skilled positions within the economy; second, few men believed in female equality; third, even those men, such as party members, who professed such beliefs did not always carry them out in practice; fourth, the condition of the Soviet economy in that period did not permit such "luxuries" as good day-care facilities and communal kitchens; and finally, the Soviet economy required a high birth rate. As a result, Stalin, by fiat, revoked the previous laws and restored traditional norms. Thus it is erroneous to cite the Soviet experience as conclusive evidence for the necessity of traditional nuclear family organization.

The case of the Israeli kibbutzim is a bit more complicated. M. E. Spiro has described the Israeli kibbutz as a society where emancipation of women was a major goal, but where the attempt to alter the division of labor by sex proved a tragic failure. This conclusion has filtered through the social-science literature to become a definitive statement on the impossibility of altering the sexual division of labor.

Closer examination of Spiro's own work, plus other data as well, casts doubt on the notion that the kibbutz was actually an experiment in sexual equality, or that it failed miserably. According to Spiro, when the first settlers began to work on the land, there was no sexual division of labor; women worked in the fields and men in the kitchen and laundry. Gradually, however, it emerged that women were not truly the equals of men in doing the hard work in the fields, and furthermore, pregnancy and childbirth restricted them still more, in spite of the communal nurseries.

> . . . Hence, as the Kibbutz grew older and the birth rate increased, more and more women were forced to leave the "productive" branches of the economy and enter its "service" branches. . . . The result was that women found themselves in the same jobs from which they were supposed to have been emancipated—*cooking, cleaning, laundering, teaching, caring for children,* etc.
> . . . Instead of cooking and sewing and baking and cleaning and laundering and caring for children, the woman in Kiryat Yedidim cooks *or* sews *or* launders *or* takes care of children for eight hours a day. . . . This new housekeeping is more boring and less rewarding than the traditional type. It is small wonder, then, given this combination of low prestige, difficult working conditions, and monotony, that the chavera [female member of the Kibbutz] has found little happiness in her domestic activities.[4]

First, let us recall the list of conditions that must be met if women's equality is to prevail. These are (1) economic equality; (2) voluntary reproduction; (3) aid in the socialization of children; (4) sexual equality; (5) a change in the definition of housework as dirty work fit only for women.

It is obvious from Spiro's description of Kiryat Yedidim that the first and last of these conditions were not met. It may well be true that women cannot achieve economic equality when heavy agricultural labor is the major means of subsistence, even if there is an ideological commitment to such equality, although in many primitive societies agriculture is women's work exclusively. The first generation of kibbutz women, however, could provide no test of the "agricultural inferiority" hypothesis because they had been brought up in cities by parents who held to traditional Jewish notions of woman's place. Of course, the whole issue of whether the sexes are equal in the fields has no relevance for sexual equality in an advanced technology.

There is evidence, also, that the commitment of kibbutz men to female equality was less than their devotion to other kibbutz ideals, such as achieving socialism, establishing a Jewish homeland, and overcoming ghetto stereotypes of Jews as weak, pale, bookish types incapable of hard farm work. Women in the peace and civil-rights movements in America have also been disappointed by the values and behavior of radical men toward women. Further, many of the present readings also show there is no necessary correlation between communes and equality for women. But to state that female equality demands a set of conditions that are hard to meet is not to state that such equality is impossible to achieve or is against nature.

In the United States, perhaps the most radical attempt to alter family relations was in the Oneida Community in New York, where the community practiced total economic communism and group sexual access—that is, any man and woman in the community might have relations together if mutually agreeable. The Oneida case highlights several interesting issues pertaining to communes: Is there a human need for "coupling"? How do we define communal stability? And how does a generation of rebels replace itself? On coupling, we find Spiro, based on his observations of the Israeli kibbutz where sex relations are free, suggesting that people seem to have need for psychological intimacy beyond sex alone. Still, the cultural background of kibbutzim is hardly representative of mankind in general, and it is questionable whether basic human needs can be inferred from a limited sample of Jewish radicals. Indeed, Rosabeth Kantor concluded, on the basis of her research on nineteenth-century utopian communities, that communes which forbade pairing, either to implement rules of celibacy or of free love, lasted the longest. There is a sense in which the commitments involved in coupling undermine commitments to the larger community, but not necessarily, as witness the Israeli case. But, of course, in Israel, a special set of conditions prevails, in which the kibbutzim play a central role in defense of the national community.

There is also a question of the parameters of communal stability. Should we compare an experimental form of the family to the duration of the ordinary marriage or to the duration of a society? There is no obvious answer to that question, but it would certainly seem to be as appropriate to think of the experimental form of the family in the same terms as ordinary marriage. Furthermore, there is some question as to how relevant the whole issue of durability is. The commune represents a form of human experience and variation regarding sexual activity, work, reproduction, and socialization. The simple fact that such a community could exist over a period of years may suggest a great deal about variations in family forms whether or not that community continues to exist.

Further, every utopian community has to face a genuine dilemma regarding its second generation. Can such a society actually duplicate itself? Communal organization begins with a first generation that has made a sharp break with its parents. In the second generation, the community of rebels must raise a generation of conformists—children who accept the values and practices of their parents even though these are highly restrictive. Margaret Mead once chided a group of kibbutz leaders for making greater demands on their children to stay put than would any other group of farm villagers. She pointed out that young people raised on farms often yearn to see the world. For kibbutz parents, of course, there is not just the issue of holding onto children, but of seeing lifelong ideals maintained. This dilemma is just an example of how the inevitable conflict of interest between generations translates itself into new terms in utopian communities. Some communards have concluded that it is better for the children to "do their own thing" than to maintain the community. Others have wondered whether a commune should not plan for its own dissolution right from the start, so that its maintenance will not oppress members when the community no longer seems meaningful.

References

1. David Matza, *Becoming Deviant* (Englewood Cliffs, N. J.: Prentice-Hall, 1969), pp. 15–17.

2. Richard Sennett, "The Brutality of Modern Families," *Trans-action,* September 1970 (Vol. 7, no. 11), p. 32.

3. Rosabeth M. Kantor, "Commitment and Social Organization: A Study of Commitment Mechanisms in Utopian Communities," *American Sociological Review,* 33, August 1968, pp. 499–518.

4. M. E. Spiro, *Kibbutz: Venture in Utopia* (Cambridge, Mass.: Harvard Univ. Press, 1956), p. 229.

Chapter 9

Varieties of Family Style

The Normal American Family | *Talcott Parsons*

The most important process of development in American society during the present century, as before, have been continuing differentiation in its structure, a general process of upgrading of expectations and responsibilities, and the related development of new modes of integration of persons and substructures in the increasingly complex society. As a process of very rapid social change, complicated by such external disturbances as hot and cold wars, it is a process marked by much internal disturbance, anxiety, and conflict on many different levels.

The family and its more immediate environment have been centrally involved in the general process, and the end certainly is still far away. Perhaps the best single reference point is to the structural differentiation of the nuclear family, both from other components of the kinship system and from nonkin elements. The most striking case is the performance of occupational roles outside the family in many types of employing organizations. The most massive index of this is the decline of the proportion of the labor force engaged in agriculture, but many other family-operated productive units, like small retail shops and handicraft enterprises, have also been declining in number. With this, of course, has gone dependence of the family household, as consuming unit, on money income, and drastic reduction in its relative self-sufficiency.

The composition of the household has also tended increasingly to be confined to nuclear family members. Thus households with complete nuclear families, i.e., husband, wife, and their own children, increased in proportion of total persons from 80 to 82.7 percent between 1940 and

From Talcott Parsons, "The Normal American Family," in S. M. Farber, P. Mustacchi, and R. H. L. Wilson (eds.), *Man and Civilization: The Family's Search for Survival* (New York: McGraw-Hill, 1965), pp. 31-50.

1960. During the same period, the proportion of household members who were relatives of the head, other than spouse or own children, decreased from 7.7 to 5.5 percent. The categories of nonfamily members, lodgers, and living-in domestic servants decreased from 4.2 to 1.5 percent: the domestic-service figure, though small, is particularly striking in decreasing from 0.8 to 0.2 percent, i.e., being cut to one-fourth in only twenty years. Of course the other side of the picture has been a sharp increase in nonfamilial households, i.e., those composed of single persons or those unrelated, such as two women. The increase in proportions of husbands and wives living together, from 40.5 percent of total household members to 44.1 percent, an increase of nearly 10 percent in twenty years, is particularly striking in the light of the high divorce rate, which remains high though it has tended to decline slowly since the postwar peak. I think the proposition is correct that we now have the largest proportion, in the history of the United States Census, of persons of marriageable age and not widowed living with their spouses and, if the children are not yet too old, with their own children. The broad picture is that of an increasingly specialized but structurally intact family.

This impression of the importance of the family is strengthened by two further facts, namely, the decreasing average age of marriage to a point of near twenty-two for males and twenty for females, and the well-known increased birth rate, which has now been sustained since about 1940—the net reproduction rate for 1959 being a little over 1.7. There have, however, been other crucial changes. One of the most important is the extension of the span of life. Though there has been relatively little change in the last decade or so, since early in the century it has been dramatic. The *average* expectancy of life at birth has reached seventy years, though as of 1959 there was a differential of 6.5 years in favor of women over men. A further particularly interesting change is the compression of the childbearing period. Combined with the trend to early marriage, this meant that by 1957 (Glick) the average American mother had her *last* child when she was twenty-six years old, in spite of the higher birth rates. This, of course, means that most married couples face a much longer period of the "empty nest," when their children are independent and neither is widowed, than has previously been the case. The combination of early marriage for girls and the greater longevity of women also means that there is a considerable excess of widows over widowers.

Another important phenomenon of differentiation in the life cycle has been the enormous growth of formal education. There is, first, the extension of full secondary education to all but a decreasing minority, though the dropouts from high school constitute the core of the juvenile-delinquency problem. Second, there is the rapid increase in the college population, running to about 40 percent beginning some kind of college, and close to 25 percent completing a four-year college course. Finally, postgraduate professional education, though still small in percentage, is by far the most rapidly growing sector of the educational system. This has occasioned important family problems in that a rapidly increasing proportion marry before completing their formal training.

A final notable set of demographic facts in this area concerns the gainful employment of married women. Between 1950 and 1960 the proportion of single women in the labor force actually declined, presumably because more of them were in school or college. The most striking figure, however, is the increase from 24.8 to 30 percent between 1950 and 1960 among those living with their spouse, an increase of more than 25 percent in a decade. The employment of women who were widowed or divorced has, on the other hand, increased much more slowly. Clearly the former increase is associated with the compression of the period of responsibility for the care of small children. It is quite clear, however, that the American woman is more frequently a married woman and probably for a larger fraction of her life than ever before. She is, at the same time, becoming increasingly highly educated and, in spite of the scarcity and expense of domestic service, she is less often "only" a housewife and a volunteer church and community worker than her predecessors. Particularly over the life cycle, her roles have become much more differentiated.

It is of course a commonplace that the American family is predominantly and, in a sense, increasingly an urban middle-class family. There has indeed been, if not a very great equalization of income (though there has been some in the present century), a very substantial homogenization of patterns of life in the population with reference to a number of things. Basic to this are the employment of one or more family members outside the home; the nuclear family household without domestic service except for cleaning and babysitting, and the basic constituents of the standard of living, including in particular the familiar catalogue of consumer durable goods, which constitute the basic capital equipment of the household.*

It can then be said that, in a sense that has probably never existed before, in a society that in most respects has undergone a process of very extensive structural differentiation, there has emerged a remarkably uniform, basic type of family. It is uniform in its kinship and household composition in the sense of confinement of its composition to members of the nuclear family, which is effective at any given stage of the family cycle, and in the outside activities of its members, e.g., jobs for adult men, some par-

---

* Another important set of facts concerns the very large proportion of single-family dwellings in this country, and within this, the high proportion of owner occupancy.

ticipation in the labor force for women, school for children, and various other types of community participation. Indeed it is also highly uniform in the basic components of the standard of living, e.g., the private dwelling, the mechanical aids, the impingement of communications from the outside through the mass media, etc. There is one increasingly conspicuous and distressing exception to the general pattern, namely, the situation of the lowest groups by most of the socioeconomic indices, such as income, education, occupational level, etc. This problem will have to be taken up again later.

The author has, perhaps more than anyone else, been responsible for diffusing the phrase "isolated nuclear family" to describe one aspect of this unit. This concept has recently been challenged notably by two groups of sociologists, Eugene Litwack and Melvin Seeman and their associates, in the name of the importance of the network of extended kinship relations beyond the nuclear family. To my mind the two views are not contradictory but complementary. The concept of isolation applies in the first instance to kinship structure as seen in the perspective of anthropological studies in that field. In this context our system represents an extreme type, which is well described by that term. It does not, however, follow that all relations to kin outside the nuclear family are broken. Indeed the very psychological importance for the individual of the nuclear family in which he was born and brought up would make any such conception impossible.

By and large, however, as our population elements are further removed from peasant or other similar backgrounds, these extended kinship elements do not form firmly structured units of the social system. They are not residential or economic units—in the consuming, to say nothing of the producing, sense—nor are they "corporate groups" in the sense that clans and lineages in so many societies have been. There are above all two significant features of their relations to the nuclear family. First, in the maintenance of going relations, though there seems to be clear precedence of members of the families of orientation of both spouses—parents so long as they live, and siblings, even among siblings as between the two families, and much more so beyond that—there is a marked optional quality of the expectation system. There certainly are some structured preferences on kinship bases, and others on those of geographical propinquity, but still there is a strong tendency for kinship to shade into friendship in the sense of absence from the latter of ascriptive components of membership. Hence, the amount of visiting, of common activity, of telephone and written communication, etc., is highly variable within formal categories of relationship. This suggests that extended kin constitute a resource which may be selectively taken advantage of within considerable limits.

This supposition is greatly strengthened by the second consideration. This is the extent to which extended kin, especially members of the family of orientation but not only they, serve as a "reserve" of expectations of solidarity and willingness to implement them which can be mobilized in case of need. To take one primary context, there is a clear expectation that adult siblings, children, and, increasingly, parents of adults will be economically independent and should not need to be the recipients of direct financial aid from relatives. The extended family is, in this sense, normally not a solitary-operating economic unit. In case of special need, however, the first obligation to help, if there is no organized community provision and sometimes when there is, falls on close relatives who are financially able to bear the burden. Such obligations are not likely to be unlimited, but they are nonetheless real—in cases of sickness, of the dependency of old age, and similar cases.

An interesting case is the one mentioned above. The tendency is for earlier marriage, which, in the most highly educated groups, very frequently occurs before completion of higher education. Not only does this situation give rise to an important part of the employment of younger married women—who thereby earn the fictional degree of P. H. T. ("put hubby through"). There is also a substantial amount of aid from parents and some from older siblings which helps fill the gap. Often this is partially concealed in the form of "gifts," e.g., of a car or a vacation trip, testifying to the importance of the need for "independence." Ritual solidarity on the occasion of weddings, but even more especially funerals, fits in with this pattern.

On this background I may now turn to a few functional and analytical considerations. More than any other influence, psychoanalytic psychology has, during the last generation, made us aware of two crucial things. The first is the fundamental importance for the individual personality of the process of growing up in the intimacies of the family. Not only is mental illness to a large, though by no means exclusive, extent generated in the relations of a child to members of his family,* but normal personality development is highly contingent on the proper combination of influences operating in the family situation. Of course the family stands by no means alone, and as the child grows older, influences from the neighborhood, then the school and beyond become increasingly important. The family, however, lays the essential foundations and continues always to be important.

---

* The psychoanalytic tendency has been to "individualize" these relations by treating a child's relation to each of the other members one at a time—his mother, his father, his rivalry with a particular sibling, etc. More recently, however, there has emerged, particularly in the work of Theodore Lidz and his associates, a tendency to treat the family as a system in such a way that both illness and normality are conceived to be a function of the impact of the system as a whole—not of particular members in isolation—on the individual.

There has been a good deal of discussion of the importance of psychological "security" in this whole context. An individual's sense of security naturally depends on his experience in his family of orientation. It remains, however, an essential problem throughout life.† We have become increasingly aware that for the adult, in psychologically very complex ways, his family of procreation is dynamically most intimately linked with his family of orientation. The experience of parenthood is of course a recapitulation in reverse of that of the child in relation to his parents, and in important ways reactivates the psychological structures belonging to that period. Just as much, marriage is a complex organization of components in the personality which are derived from childhood experience—the common involvement of eroticism in both is the surest clue to the relationship.

For the normal adult, then, his marriage and his role as parent constitute the primary going reinforcement of his psychological security. The family can thus be seen to have two primary functions, not one. On the one hand it is the primary agent of socialization of the child, while on the other it is the primary basis of security for the normal adult. Moreover, the linkage of these two functions is very close. The point may be put by saying that their common responsibility as parents is the most important focus of the solidarity of marriage partners, and that the desire for children is the natural outcome of a solid "romantic" attraction between two persons of opposite sex. The primary link between these two functions in terms of agency is clearly the feminine role in its dual capacity as mother and as wife.

I think it reasonable to suggest that the broad pattern of the contemporary American family, sketched above in statistical terms, fits this functional analysis. It seems to be a case of a process of differentiation through which the central functions of early socialization and giving individuals a psychological security base have become separated out from others to which they have been ascribed in less differentiated societies. The sharing of the common household as the place to "live" with all its implications is the fundamental phenomenon—it is this sharing which makes the normal nuclear family a distinctive unit which cannot be confused with *any* others, based either on kinship or on other criteria. The home, its furnishings, equipment, and the rest constitute the "logistic" base for the performance of this dual set of primary functions.

---

† Erik Erikson has, in his *Childhood and Society,* given an especially clear formulation of this point in his discussion of the importance of what he calls "basic trust" and its relation to personality development.

Parents Without Partners   E. E. LeMasters

In thinking about parents it is easy to assume a model of what might be termed "the biological parent team" of mother and father. In this model two parents act as partners in carrying out the parental functions. Furthermore, both of the parents are biological as well as social parents. It is this parent team model that is analyzed in most of the chapters in this book.

What is not realized by many observers, especially by parent critics, is the fact that a considerable proportion of contemporary American parents do not operate under these ideal conditions. These parents include "parents without partners" (mostly divorced or separated women, but including a few men also); widows and widowers with children; unmarried mothers; adoptive parents; step-parents; and, finally, foster parents.

Some of the groups in the list above are amazingly large—Simon, for example, reports that in the 1960s in the United States there were about *seven million* children living with a step-parent. This means that approximately one out of every nine children in modern America is a stepchild.

Mothers Without Fathers

One of the by now familiar parental types in our society is the mother rearing her children alone. As of 1960 about one household out of ten in the United States was headed by a woman. In an earlier, more innocent America, this mother without father was seen as a heroic figure—a brave woman whose husband had died who was struggling to rear her brood by scrubbing floors, taking in family laundry, and so on. This was the brave little widow of an earlier day.

After the end of World War I, as the divorce rate began to climb, this picture—and this woman—underwent a radical change. With the rapid improvement of American medicine, marriages in the early and middle decades of life were no longer broken primarily by death; now the great destroyers of marriages came to be social and psychological, not biological.

With this shift the public's attitude toward the mother with no father by her side changed drastically—it became ambivalent. In some cases she

From E. E. LeMasters, "Parents Without Partners," in *Parents in Modern America* (Homewood, Ill.: Dorsey, 1970), pp. 157–174. References cited in the original have been deleted.

might be viewed with sympathy and understanding, if she happened to be your sister or a close friend, but more often she was perceived as a woman of questionable character—either the gay divorcee of the upper-social class levels or the ADC mother living off of the taxpayers at the lower social-class levels. In either case the image was a far cry from that of the heroic little widow of the Victorian era.

Statistically, and otherwise, these mothers without fathers fall into five different categories: divorced, separated, deserted, widowed, and never married. All of these categories overlap, so that some mothers might at some point in their lives occupy all five positions in the list.

Our procedure in discussing these mothers in their parental role will be to identify the generic patterns and problems shared by all of these mothers, and then to look at the relatively unique patterns that cluster about any specific position.

Generic Features of Mothers Without Partners

1. *Poverty.* It has been estimated that while households headed by a woman comprise only about 10 percent of all U. S. households, they constitute about 25 percent of the families in the so-called poverty group in American society.

In the best study yet published on divorced women, Goode found financial stress to be a major complaint. At any given time approximately 40 percent of the divorced husbands in this study were delinquent in their support payments, a pattern that seems to be nationwide.

Poverty is extremely relative, as is deprivation. A divorced woman receiving even $1,000 a month in support payments may have to reduce her standard of living from what it was before her divorce.

The reasons for the financial difficulties of these mothers are not mysterious or difficult to identify. Most American men cannot afford to support two living establishments on a high level. This is one reason why some support payments are delinquent. The man usually gets involved with at least one other woman, and this costs money. Often his new woman is not well off financially and the man may find himself contributing to her support also.

Since a considerable proportion of divorced women are apparently employed at the time of their divorce, they had what is commonly called a two-income family. The mother may continue to work after the father has left the home, but with two living establishments to maintain, two cars, and so on, the financial situation tends to be tight.

In a study of ADC mothers in Boston, it was discovered that these women faced financial crises almost monthly. They coped with these difficult situations by accepting aid from members of their family; by pooling their resources with neighbors and women friends in the same plight; and by occasional aid from a boy friend.

In several counseling cases with divorced women, the writer was impressed with the annoying feature of the relative poverty experienced by these women—one woman didn't have the money to get her television set repaired and this created tension between herself and her children. Another woman, who lived in an area with inadequate bus service, could not afford an automobile. Any person in our society can understand how frustrating problems of this nature can be.

2. *Role conflicts.* Since these women have added the father role to their parental responsibilities, they tend to be either overloaded or in conflict over their various role commitments. The presence of a husband-father provides more role flexibility than these women now have—if the mother is ill, or has to work late, the husband may be able to be home with the children.

When these mothers are employed outside of the home, as a sizeable proportion are, the work hours usually conflict with those of the school system. Children leave for school too late, get home too early, and have far too many vacations for the employed mother. There are also childhood illnesses that must be coped with.

It is true that the termination of the marriage has reduced or eliminated the mother's role as wife, but she is still a woman in the early decades of life and men will be in the picture sooner or later. Thus she may not be a wife at the moment but she will soon be a girl friend, and the courtship role may be even more demanding than that of wife.

It is the writer's belief, based on numerous interviews with divorced women, that being the head of a household is, for most women, an 18-hour day, seven days a week, and 365 days a year job. It would seem that only the most capable, and the most fortunate, can perform all of the roles involved effectively.

3. *Role shifts.* Since the vast majority of the mothers being discussed here—80 to 90 percent—will eventually remarry, they face the difficult process of taking over the father role and then relinquishing it. This is not easy for most of us; once we have appropriated a role in a family system, it is often difficult to turn it over to somebody else.

Furthermore, these mothers operate in an unusual family system in that, for an indefinite period, they do not have to worry about what the other parent thinks. They are both mother and father for the time being.

This is not entirely true, of course, in the case of the divorced woman, but it seems to be largely true, even for this group. The departed father starts out with the best intentions of "not forgetting my kids," but a variety of factors tend to reduce his parental influence as time goes on. . . .

4. *Public attitudes.* These mothers are operating in deviant family situa-

tions, and for the most part the community tends to regard them and their children as deviants. Except for the widow, all of these mothers are viewed with some ambivalence in our society. They receive some sympathy, some respect, and some help, but they are also viewed as women who are not "quite right"—they did not sustain their marriage "until death do us part."

The unmarried mother, of course, never had a marriage to sustain and the public has no ambivalence about her; they simply condemn her and that's that.

If these mothers require support from public welfare they will find the community's mixed feelings reflected in their monthly check—the community will not permit them and their children to starve, but it will also not allow them to live at a decent level.

We have now examined some of the generic problems of the one-parent family system, except for the system in which the one parent is a father, which will be looked at later. Now let us analyze the specific features of the subsystems in the one-parent family.

Specific Features of the Subsystems in the One-Parent Family

1. *The divorced mother.* The divorced mother has several advantages over the deserted mother: she at least has had the help of a domestic-relations court in spelling out the financial responsibility of the father, also the legal arrangements for custody. In this sense divorce is a lot less messy than desertion in our society.

The divorced mother is also legally free to associate with other men and to remarry if she finds the right person—advantages the deserted woman does not have.

The divorced father, it seems to us, is not in an enviable position in his role as father. He may be happy not to be married to his children's mother any more but he often hates to be separated from his children. In a sense he still has the responsibility of a father for his minor children but few of the enjoyments of parenthood. To be with his children he has to interact to some degree with his former wife—a process so painful that he was willing to have the marriage terminated.

In an unpublished study of 80 divorced men, one of the most frequent regrets expressed by the men was their frustration and concern about their relationship to their children.

The divorced mother has one parental advantage that she shares with all other parents without partners; she does not have to share the daily parental decisions with a partner who might not agree with her strategy. In the Goode study of divorced women, the mothers seemed to think this was an advantage. The parental partner can be of great help if the two parents can agree on how their children should be reared, but when this is not the case one parent can probably do a better job going it alone.

2. *The deserted mother.* It has already been indicated that desertions in our society are more messy than divorces. There are two reasons: (1) desertion is more apt to be unilateral with the decision to pull out being made by one party alone; and (2) there is no court supervision of the desertion process—it is unplanned from society's point of view.

The deserted mother is likely to have more severe financial problems than the divorced mother because support payments have not been agreed upon.

Psychologically, desertion is probably more traumatic than divorce, partly because it is more unilateral but also because it is less planned. To the extent that this is true—and we recognize that the evidence on this point is not conclusive—then the deserted mother is handicapped in her parental role by her emotional upheaval or trauma.

This woman also has other problems; she is legally not free to remarry and in a sense not even free to go out with other men since she is technically still a married woman. These feelings, of course, will tend to reflect the social class and the moral subculture of the particular woman.

3. *The separated mother.* If we assume that most marital separations in modern America have been arrived at by mutual agreement, then this mother has certain advantages over the deserted mother. One disadvantage is that her courtship status is ambiguous; another is that she is not free to remarry. Psychologically, the separated mother should reflect patterns similar to those of the divorced mother: her marriage has failed but she has done something about it and now has to plan for her future life.

4. *The widowed mother.* The one big advantage of this parent is the favorable attitude of her family, her friends, and the community toward her. This tends to be reflected in her self-image, thus giving her emotional support. Once she emerges from the period of bereavement, however, she has to face about the same problems as the women discussed previously— she probably will have financial problems; she will have to be father as well as mother. . . .

5. *The unmarried mother.* This is not the place to review the status and problems of the unmarried mother in our society—the literature on this woman is quite voluminous. It only needs to be said here that this mother has all of the problems of the women discussed before plus a few of her own. She is more likely to be a member of a racial minority—one of the extra burdens she has to shoulder. She is also more likely to be on public welfare—a major burden in itself in our society. Her chances for marriage are not as gloomy as some people once thought, but her chances for a successful marriage may be more dubious. . . .

Father-Only Families

It has been estimated that approximately 600,000 U. S. families have only a father present in the home at any given time. This figure seems large but is small compared to the 4 to 5 million American families in which only a mother is present.

There seems to be relatively little research data available on these "father-only" families. Since custody of minor children is awarded to the mother in our divorce courts in 90 to 95 percent of the cases, it seems logical to assume that the bulk of these "fathers without mothers" represent either desertion or the death of the mother.

It seems likely that these fathers do not continue indefinitely to rear their children alone, that the majority of them remarry, in which case they would experience the same problems of role shifts discussed earlier for mothers on their own.

It also seems likely that these men experience role conflicts between their jobs, their social life, and their parental responsibility.

It is doubtful that these solo fathers would suffer from poverty to the extent found among solo mothers—but the writer has no data to cite in support of this statement.

The rat race experienced by mothers rearing families without the help of a father would likely be found among these men also; it simply reflects what might be termed "role overload."

Psychologically, . . . these men probably suffer from the same syndrome found among mothers who have lost their husbands—loneliness, sorrow, perhaps bitterness, often a sense of failure, plus a feeling of being overwhelmed by their almost complete responsibility for their children. About the only effective treatment for feelings of this nature is to find a new partner and get married—the solution most adult Americans rely on for whatever ails them. These fathers are no exception to this statement.

It would appear that these men have a few problems that would be less likely to bother mothers: the physical care of preschool children and the tasks of home management, such as shopping for food and clothes, preparing meals, doing the family laundry, and cleaning the house. Some men become quite adept at this women's work after awhile, but for others a stove or an iron remains a mystery forever. . . .

Is the One-Parent Family Pathological?

Most of us probably assume that the one-parent family is inherently pathological—at least for the children involved. It seems only logical to assume that two parents are better than one—the old adage that two heads are better than one.

In his text on the American family, Bell summarizes several studies that question the assumption that two parents are better than one—judging by the adjustment of the children. This, however, does not say anything about the impact of solo child rearing on the parent, which is the major concern of this book.

If one wishes to debate the number of adults required to socialize children properly the question can be raised: who decided that *two* parents was the proper number? Biologically this is natural enough, but this does not prove its social rightness.

As a matter of fact, a good family sociologist, Farber, has asked the question—"Are two parents enough? . . . In almost every human society *more* than two adults are involved in the socialization of the child."

Farber goes on to point out that in many societies a "third parent," outside of the nuclear family, acts as a sort of "social critic" of the child.

In a recent review of the literature on the one-parent family by Kadushin, the data did not seem sufficient to support the hypothesis that the one-parent family is inherently dysfunctional or pathological. It has been demonstrated by Schorr that the one-parent family is considerably overrepresented in the American poverty population and also on our public welfare rolls. This does not prove, however, that these families are inherently dysfunctional; it merely proves that our economic, political, and social welfare systems are not properly organized to provide an adequate standard of living for the one-parent family. A casual drive through many rural areas in America, especially Appalachia and the rural South, will soon demonstrate to an unbiased observer that the mere presence of *two* parents does not assure a decent standard of living for a family in our society.

To prove that the one-parent family is inherently pathological one would have to demonstrate that the system generates a disproportionate amount of personal disorganization. Kadushin's search of the literature did not reveal enough firm research data to support such a conclusion. This, of course, does not prove that one parent in the home is as good as two—it simply says that the research to date is not adequate to answer the question.

It is obvious to any clinician that the two-parent system has its own pathology—the two parents may be in serious conflict as to how their parental roles should be performed; one parent may be competent but have his (or her) efforts undermined by the incompetent partner; the children may be caught in a "double bind" or crossfire between the two parents; both parents may be competent but simply unable to work together as an effective team in rearing their children; one parent may be more competent than the other but be inhibited in using this competence by the team pattern inherent in the two-parent system.

The writer happens to believe that one *good* parent is enough to rear children adequately or better in our society. It seems to us that enough prominent Americans have been reared by widows or other solo parents to prove the point.

It is interesting to note that adoption agencies are taking another look at the one-parent family and that some agencies are now willing to consider single persons as potential adoptive parents.

Lower-Class Family Behavior | *Hyman Rodman*

It is lower-class family behavior that presents the greatest challenge to the person who tries to understand lower-class life. The following have all been considered as characteristic of the lower class: "promiscuous" sexual relationships; "illegitimate" children; "deserting" husbands and fathers; and "unmarried" mothers. These characteristics are frequently viewed in a gross manner as, simply, *problems* of the lower class. My own feeling is that it makes more sense to think of them as *solutions* of the lower class to problems that they face in the social, economic, and perhaps legal and political spheres of life.

How is it that lower-class behavior can so easily be misunderstood? That a cross-eyed, middle-class view of lower-class behavior (uncorrected by lenses designed to eliminate the "crossedness" and the middle-class values) can lead to misunderstanding has already been pointed out. And one of the major ways in which alien values become incorporated into one's view of the lower class is through the use of middle-class terms to describe lower-class behavior. It is little wonder that, if we describe the lower-class family in terms of "promiscuous" sexual relationships, "illegitimate" children, "deserting" men, and "unmarried" mothers, we are going to see the situation as disorganized and chock-full of problems.

We therefore have to stress the fact that words like *promiscuity, illegitimacy,* and *desertion* are not part of the lower-class vocabulary, and that it is inaccurate to describe lower-class behavior in this way. These words have middle-class meanings and imply middle-class judgments, and it is

From Hyman Rodman, "Middle-Class Misconceptions About Lower-Class Families," in A. B. Shostak and W. Gomberg (eds.), *Blue-Collar World* (Englewood Cliffs, N. J.: Prentice-Hall, 1964), pp. 65–68. References cited in the original have been deleted.

precisely because of this that we ought not to use them to describe lower-class behavior—unless, of course, our intention is to judge this behavior in a middle-class manner in order to bolster a sagging middle-class ego.

I am not saying—I want to be clear on this point—that demographers should stop talking about rates of desertion or rates of illegitimacy. In a strictly scientific sense, these rates have a clear enough meaning, and they may be extremely important pieces of information for certain kinds of analyses. What I am saying is that these terms can also be used in a judgmental sense, and it is this judgmental use that I am cautioning against. I am also cautioning against the rather easy way in which a scientific stance on these matters can buckle under the weight of a middle-class morality. Consider the following example, in which the author rushes headlong into a fallacy that she apparently cannot see because of her middle-class blinders:

> In my opinion, it is indefensible to write off as "culturally acceptable" to a certain group poverty and its terrible hardships, personality disturbances and their painful results, or the pervasive effect of impaired relationships. How often we have heard that in a particular cultural group it's acceptable for a teen-age girl to have a baby out of wedlock. Whether or not this is a valid generalization is for the sociologist to study. The social worker, on the other hand, must be concerned about the loneliness a teen-age girl feels when she has no husband with whom to share her parenthood, when she cannot return to school, when her friends go out on dates while she stays at home to care for the baby, or when her friends get their first jobs and she must apply for public assistance.

The social scientist who studies lower-class families should pay more attention to the language of the lower class than he does to the middle-class language. In a practical vein, this means that lower-class family patterns are usually best described in lower-class terms:

> The language problem is . . . involved in the terms used for the different forms of marital or quasi-marital relationships in the different parts of the West Indies. R. T. Smith has discussed some of the difficulties that develop when the observer sets up his own classification scheme for dealing with lower-class marital unions. In addition, the great variety of terms used by different observers for a marital union that is socially but not legally sanctioned, and the reasons they give for a particular usage, also suggest that the observer's terms may not be the most satisfactory ones. Henriques and R. T. Smith use common-law marriage; Clarke rejects the term "common law" because it suggests legal recognition, and uses concubinage; Stycos rejects "concubinage" and uses consensual union; Matthews, more simply and perhaps more sensibly, uses non-legal union. Although all of these writers recognize the distinctions between the legal and social aspects of the union, it seems to me that in using their own particular terms for the union, they may be causing unnecessary confusion. Would it not make better

sense to use the terms that are used by the lower class itself to refer to these unions?

Accordingly, in my own study of lower-class families in Coconut Village, Trinidad, I deal with three different kinds of marital or quasi-marital relationships—"friending," "living," and married. Through a consideration of some of the findings of this study we can come to a better understanding of what I regard as a major middle-class misconception of lower-class families—viewing certain patterns as *problems* when, in reality, they can as easily be viewed as *solutions.*

Although the few details that follow deal with lower-class marital relationships in Coconut Village, I believe that the essence of the description applies to lower-class families generically. The "friending" relationship is one in which a man visits a woman at intervals for sexual intercourse, and in which he has certain limited obligations to the woman and to any children of his that she may bear. Although this relationship is not fully acceptable, it is the most frequent type of relationship, and it usually precedes one of the other relationships. The "living" relationship is one in which the man and woman live together under one roof, but in which they are not legally married. It is an acceptable marital relationship and it occurs more frequently than marriage. A married relationship is similar to a "living" relationship, but it involves a church marriage and a legal bond between the man and woman. It occurs least frequently within the lower class. From one point of view, these data represent a reluctance to take on responsibility, because a greater degree of marital responsibility is involved in the "living" than in the "friending," and in the married than in the "living" relationship.

One man put it this way when I asked him why the people were reluctant to marry: "Matrimony is a money that you can't spend." He explained this to mean that it was something you could not easily get rid of. Another man answered the same question this way: "You can buy a penny milk, so what you want with a cow, na?" Such comments are by no means unique to Coconut Villagers, but they do point out for us the reluctance of the villager to enter a strong marital alliance.

What are the reasons for this reluctance, especially on the man's part, to take on responsibilities within the marital relationship? Also, why is there a good deal of "marital shifting" within Coconut Village, such that most villagers in their lifetime will have gone through a great many "friending" relationships as well as three or more "living" relationships? Part of the answer to these questions must be sought in the relation of family life to the structure of the society as a whole, particularly to its economy.

All Coconut Villagers, with two or three exceptions, are members of the lower class of Trinidad society and face a series of economic deprivations. Although someone in approximately half the households of Coconut Village owns some land, not one household is able to earn its living from the land alone. The land is poor and the hoe and cutlass are the only tools used. Transportation is a severe problem because the lands are practically all at a considerable distance from the main road, so that the meager crops are difficult to market. Wage labor must therefore be relied upon by all households within Coconut Village, and here they share, with other members of the lower class, a situation in which wages are low, unemployment and underemployment are high, and geographical mobility is at times necessary in order simply to find a job.

It is the man who is responsible for the financial support of his wife and children. However, because the economic circumstances faced by the lower-class man often make it difficult or impossible for him to meet these responsibilities, it becomes clear why there is a reluctance to accept such responsibilities in the first place. We can therefore understand why "friending" occurs more frequently than "living," and "living" more frequently than marriage within lower-class communities. We can also understand why a marital relationship such as "living" becomes such an acceptable lower-class pattern, for it provides the lower-class person with a fluid marital bond.

In addition to the greater number of acceptable marital relationships the lower-class person can choose from, there is also a ready acceptance of a separation when economic circumstances make it necessary for the man to move in order to find employment. In this way the man can later set up another marital relationship, when he is in a position to do so, while the woman may be able to set up a new marital relationship with a man who can support her.

Fluidity is therefore the essence of marital life. On the one hand there is fluidity with respect to the type of relationship a person enters into, and on the other hand there is fluidity with respect to the permanence of the marital bond, such that it is possible to shift from one marital partner to another. We can therefore see that the marital relationships that have developed are functional in that they provide the lower-class person with acceptable alternatives that permit him to live with both his conscience and his economic uncertainties.

This fluidity of the marital bond is, I believe, characteristic of lower-class families generally. Within the United States, the higher rates of divorce and desertion within the lower class, as well as of "common-law" unions and illegitimacy, are indicative of such fluidity. If, as I am suggesting, these lower-class patterns are responses to the deprivations of lower-class life, and if they are functional for lower-class individuals, then we can see the sense in which many of the lower-class family patterns that are often regarded as problems are actually solutions to other, more pressing, problems.

Families of Negro Streetcorner Men

Elliot Liebow

Looking at the spectrum as a whole, the modal father-child relationship for these streetcorner men seems to be one in which the father is separated from the child, acknowledges his paternity, admits to financial responsibility but provides financial support irregularly, if at all, and then only on demand or request. His contacts with the child are infrequent, irregular, and of short (minutes or hours) duration.

When we look away from these more formal aspects of father-child relationships and turn to their quality and texture, a seeming paradox emerges. The men who do not live with their own children seem to express more affection for their children and treat them more tenderly than those who do live with them. Moreover, the men are frequently more affectionate toward other men's children than toward their own.

Fathers who live with their children, for example, seem to take no pleasure in their children and give them little of their time and attention. They seldom mention their children in casual conversation and are never seen sitting or playing with them on the steps or in the street. The fathers do not take their children to tag along while they lounge on the street corner or in the Carry-out, nor do they, as they see other fathers in the neighborhood do, promenade with them on Easter Sunday or take them for walks on any other Sunday or holiday. When the father walks into the home, the child may not even look up from what he is doing and the father, for his part, takes no more notice than he receives. If their eyes happen to catch one another's glances, father and child seem to look without seeing until one or the other looks elsewhere.

Perhaps this routine absence of warmth and affection accounts for the way in which an offhand gesture by the father can suddenly deepen the relationship for the child, for however brief a time. John casually distributed some change among his six children. His wife Lorena describes what happened:

> He give Buddy and the others a dime. You'd think Jesus had laid something on them. They went all around the neighborhood bragging their daddy give them a dime. I give them nickels and dimes all day

From Elliot Liebow, *Tally's Corner* (Boston: Little, Brown, 1966), pp. 78–83, 130–136.

long and they don't think anything about it. But John, he can give them a dime and they act like he gave them the whole world.

Since father and child are seldom together outside the home, it is in the home that casual gestures bespeaking paternal warmth and tenderness are most likely to occur. Leroy and two friends are in Leroy's house passing the time. Leroy sits on the bed and absentmindedly strokes the head of his small son lying next to him. In Richard's house, Richard distractedly rolls a ball or marble back and forth across the floor to his four-year-old son, at the same time going on with his drinking and talking; or he casually beckons to his son to come stand between his knees and, with one hand around the child's waist, the other around a can of beer, he goes on talking.

The easy manner with which the fathers manage these intimacies suggests that they have occurred before. But the child does not manage them casually. He is excited by these intimacies, and the clear delight he takes from them suggests that he assigns to them a special quality and that they are by no means routine. Indeed, physical contact between father and son seems generally to be infrequent. When it does take place, it is just as likely to be a slap as a caress.

Compared with fathers who live with their children, separated fathers who remain in touch with their children speak about them more often and show them more warmth when father and child are together. For separated fathers, the short, intermittent contacts with their children are occasions for public display of parental tenderness and affection. When Bess brought the baby along on her money-collecting visits to the Carry-out, she and Tally would sometimes remain on the corner with Tally holding the baby in his arms, cooing at or nuzzling the baby as he and Bess talked. On a Saturday morning, after a visit from his wife, Stoopy stands on the corner with three other men, watching his wife disappear down the street with their two school-age children on either side of her. "There goes my heart," says Stoopy, "those two kids, they're my heart." The other men nod understandingly. They would have felt and said the same thing had they been in his place.

These are fathers whose children are raised by the mothers. Even closer to his child is the father whose child is raised by the father's mother or members of his family. For him, too, the child is "my heart," "my life," or "the apple of my eye." Parental pride and affection are even more in public evidence when father and child are together. When Tonk's daughter arrives for her summer stay, Tonk walks around holding her hand, almost parading, stopping here and there to let bystanders testify that they didn't know Tonk had such a pretty girl, such a smart girl, or a girl who has grown so much so quickly. No, Sweets won't be at the Carry-out tomorrow afternoon, he has to take his daughter shopping for some clothes. He swears he didn't recognize her when his mother first walked up with her. It hadn't even been a year and he almost didn't know his own kid. If she hadn't called him "Daddy" he would still not have known, that's how big she got. And (with pride), she wants to be with him all the time she's here, go everywhere he goes.

But after the brief visit is over, each goes back to his own life, his own world, in which the other plays so small a part that he may be forgotten for long stretches of time. "Out of sight, out of mind" is not far off the mark at all for any of these separated father-child relationships.

There are many ways to explain this paradox in which fathers who live with their children appear to be less warm, tender, and affectionate in their face-to-face relationships with their children than separated fathers.* The most obvious, perhaps, is that the separated father, like the proverbial doting grandfather or favorite uncle, not charged with the day-to-day responsibility for the child, with the routine rearing and disciplining and support of this child, can afford to be attentive and effusive. Since his meetings with the child are widely spaced, he comes to them fresh and rested; since the meetings are brief, he can give freely of himself, secure in the knowledge he will soon go back to his own child-free routine. . . .

The primacy ascribed to financial support derives from two analytically separable sources of value: the simple use value, in and of itself, of supporting and maintaining the lives of one's wife and children; and the expressive or symbolic value associated with providing this support. Men and women both agree that providing financial support has a weightiness that goes beyond its simple use value. One of the men was talking to several others, derogating someone he didn't particularly care for. "But one thing you got to say," he conceded, "when he was living with her, he stone* took care of her and the children."

By itself, the plain fact of supporting one's wife and children defines the principal obligation of a husband. But the expressive value carried by the providing of this support elevates the husband to manliness. He who provides for his wife and children has gone a long way toward meeting his obligations to his family as he sees them. Drinking, gambling, or seeing other women may detract from but cannot, by themselves, nullify his performance. Both as husband and father, he has gone a long way toward proving himself a man.

---

* Since the attempt here is to sort out the different streetcorner father-child relationships rather than to judge them, it is not relevant that the father's willingness to remain with his children and support them, day in, day out, may be a better measure of the man as father than his expressive behavior in his face-to-face contacts with his children.

* An intensive, in this case meaning "really took care . . ."

Few married men, however, do in fact support their families over sustained periods of time. Money is chronically in short supply and chronically a source of dissension in the home. Financial support for herself and her children remains one of the principal unmet expectations of the wife. Moreover, although providing such support would be, so far as the husband is concerned, necessary and sufficient, the wife—who seldom gets even this much—wants more, much more.

She wants him to be a man in her terms, a husband and father according to her lights. It is not enough that he simply give money for her and the children's support, then step away until the next time he shares his pay day with them. She wants him to join them as a full-time member of the family, to participate in their affairs, to take an active interest in her and the children, in their activities, in their development as individuals. She wants his ultimate loyalty to be to her and the children, and she wants this loyalty to be public knowledge. She wants the family to present a united front to the outside world.

Most important of all, perhaps, she wants him to be *head of the family,* not only to take an interest and demonstrate concern but to take responsibility and to make decisions. She wants him to take charge, to "wear the pants," to lay down the rules of their day-to-day life and enforce them. She wants him to take over, to be someone she can lean on. Alas, she ends up standing alone or, even worse perhaps, having to hold him up as well.

Wryly, and with a bitterness born of experience, Shirley smiles to herself and says,

> I used to lean on Richard. Like when I was having the baby, I leaned on him but he wasn't there and I fell down . . . Now, I don't lean on him anymore. I pretend I lean, but I'm not leaning.

Shirley had not always surrendered with quiet resignation. Like Lorena and other women, she too had tried to cajole, tease, shame, encourage, threaten, or otherwise attempt to make her man a man. Lorena said that in the beginning of her marriage, she used to pray to God, "Make John a good husband and father." Then she realized that "that's not God's job, that's my job," and she changed her prayers accordingly: "Lord, this is Lorena Patterson. You know all about me. You know what I need."

So Lorena took on herself the job of making John a good husband and father, but it didn't work. She blames herself for the failure of her marriage but she blames John, too. John was a boy, she said, not a man. He wasn't the "master."

> I want the man to wear the pants but John made me wear the pants, too. His pants had a crease in them, mine had a ruffle, but I was wearing the pants, too.

Lorena's desperate gambits to force John to assert himself as man of the house ended disastrously, leaving her with mixed feelings of contempt, indignation, pity, and failure.

> After we got married, I used to push him to see how far I could go. Once, I told him to kiss my ass. He laid my lip open and I stayed in the room till the scar healed up. For the next two weeks, he didn't do anything, no matter what I did, so I tried again. I called him an s.o.b. His family used to say that those were fighting words to John. They said he couldn't stand to hear anyone say something about his mother. So I called him an s.o.b. You know what he did? He sat down in a chair and cried. He just sat down and cried!

The husband who sometimes responds to this testing and challenging by slapping his wife's face or putting his fist in her mouth is frequently surprised at the satisfactory results. He does not understand—or does not admit to understanding—the woman's motives and may attribute them to some vague impulse to masochism latent in women. Leroy, for example, was getting ready to take his leave from the streetcorner. He said he was going home to see what "Mouth" (Charlene) wanted. She probably wanted a whipping, he said; she seems to beg him to beat her. Afterwards, she's "tame as a baby, sweet as she can be."

Then he told of how, the day before, Charlene beat on him with a broomstick, daring him to slap her, but he simply walked out because he knew this would hurt her more than a whipping. Doubtless, it did. For Charlene, like Lorena, wanted some tangible evidence that her husband cared about her, about them as a family, and that he was willing to fight to establish and protect his (nominal) status as head of the family. She openly envied Shirley who, when things were going tolerably well for her and Richard, took pleasure in boasting to Charlene, Lorena, and other women that Richard pushed her around, insisted she stay off the street, and enforced the rule that she be up early every morning, dress the children, and clean the house. For evidence of this kind of concern, Charlene would gladly pay the price of a slap in the face or a pushing around. All too often, however, Leroy declined to accept the challenge or, accepting it, was himself reduced, like John, to tears of shame, helplessness, and defeat.

Richard and Shirley, whom Leroy and Charlene lived with for several months, were frequent observers—or rather overhearers—of these tearful denouements to Leroy and Charlene's domestic quarrels. Richard was contemptuous of Leroy. No one had ever seen Richard cry. Leroy must be "weak" or "lame" to let Charlene make him cry like that. As for himself, he cried, too, he admitted, but he always cried "on the inside."

Thus, marriage is an occasion of failure. To stay married is to live with your failure, to be confronted by it day in and day out. It is to live in a world whose standards of manliness are forever beyond one's reach, where one is continuously tested and challenged and continually found wanting. In self-defense, the husband retreats to the streetcorner. Here, where the measure of man is considerably smaller, and where weaknesses are somehow turned upside down and almost magically transformed into strengths, he can be, once again, a man among men.

The Black Family: Myth and Reality

Warren D. TenHouten

The view that black families in America are matriarchal was developed by Frazier, who describes four kinds of black families. The first type, from which the stereotype derives, is the *maternal family*. This family form was most often found in the rural South and existed during slavery. The second type is akin to the traditional American white family, with the father having undisputed authority in the family and a high level of involvement in family life. A third type originated in free black communities of mixed black, white, and American Indian origin; this structure was patriarchal. The last type delineated was composed of people who also were of a mixed ancestry, but who defined themselves as a separate, isolated race; this structure, too, was strictly patriarchal.

In the great migration of blacks from the South to the urban North during the early decades of this century, the maternal family was viewed by Frazier as unable to cope with an urban environment, becoming dependent on charity, and having its children run amuck—with sons joining delinquent gangs and daughters bearing illegitimate children. Families of the patriarchal types, on the other hand, were better able to adjust to urbanism and formed the black middle class. Frazier, in sum, argues that there are two cultural traditions in black society: (1) the "folk culture" of the rural blacks; and (2) the genteel tradition of mulattoes and other black groups who assimilated the values and family patterns of the Southern aristocracy. Neither cultural pattern is seen as surviving among poor urban blacks, and disintegration of the folk culture is assumed to have brought about chaos, normlessness, immorality, and family pathology.

From Warren D. TenHouten, "The Black Family: Myth and Reality," *Psychiatry,* May 1970 (Vol. 33, no. 2), pp. 145–155. References cited in the original have been deleted.

The explanations offered for the development of matriarchal black families are *historical* and *socioeconomic*. The historical argument describes the black female as traditionally the most permanent and dependable member of black society. Burgess and Locke write:

> Under slavery the mother remained the important figure in the family. The affectional relations of mother and child developed deep and permanent attachment. Frequently, also, the father was a member of the family group, but often the relationship was casual and easily broken. . . . Then, too, Negro husbands were sold more often. These and other factors contributed to the development of a matricentric form of the family during slavery.

It is not the intention of this paper to examine the proposition that the black family in American society was at one time matriarchal. However, the assumptions and empirical evidence used in support of the foregoing historical account of matriarchy merit critical reevaluation. Frazier's use of census data, social-work case histories, and public records is at best marginal in meeting the standards of evidence in present-day social science.

In modern urban society the subdominance of the black husband to the wife is attributed to employment behavior. The female in the black home has a better chance to find work than does her husband, who is at an extreme disadvantage in economic competition. Since the husband is defined as having low economic "value" in society relative to his wife, the black woman has greater control of economic resources (money, economic security, and occupational status), and brings more resources *into* the family unit. As a result of (1) the wife's contribution to the family, and (2) the husband's lack of contribution—so the argument goes—the wife wields *power* in the family and plays the dominant role. Rainwater, in elaborating this argument, writes that in such a circumstance, the wife (and the husband) may "turn to others," and the husband is more apt to drink and become involved with his peers at the family's expense. The result of this behavior is seen as desertion and divorce.

The link between control of the economic function and power in the family is also assumed by Parson and Bales. But the empirical evidence supporting this relationship is, as Aldous points out, "scanty." Research by Blood and Hamblin, for instance, shows that the occupational status of the *husband* is not very predictive of family power, relative to other social factors. There is a limited amount of empirical evidence that employment by the *wife* decreases the relative power of her husband. Middleton and Putney report that wives increase in dominance of *minor* decisions if they do *not* work.

The stereotype of the matriarchal black family has been given recent attention by a Department of Labor publication, *The Negro Family: The Case for National Action,* whose major author is Moynihan and which is widely known as the Moynihan Report. His description of the black family draws on both "causal" arguments—the supposed historical tradition of matriarchy, and the economic dependence of black males. Moynihan hypothesizes that:

> At the heart of the deterioration of the fabric of Negro society is the deterioration of the Negro family.
>
> The white family has achieved a high degree of stability and is maintaining that stability.
>
> By contrast, the family structure of lower-class Negroes is highly unstable, and in many centers is approaching complete breakdown.

He goes on:

> . . . the Negro community has been forced into a matriarchal structure which, because it is so out of line with the rest of American society, seriously retards the progress of the group as a whole, and imposes a crushing burden on the Negro male.

And on:

> It was by destroying the Negro family under slavery that white America broke the will of the Negro people. Although that will has reasserted itself in our time, it is a resurgence that is doomed to frustration unless the viability of the Negro family is restored.*

Moynihan's position thus reiterates Frazier's conceptualization of the maternal family in the black community. But it also implies that the black family's adverse position has become self-sustaining, by its own internal dynamics of *family role deviancy*. Parker and Kleiner state that Moynihan's writings carry such an implication, and cite the following statement:

> The cumulative result of unemployment and low income, and probably also of excessive dependence upon the income of women, has produced an unmistakable crisis in the Negro family, and raises the serious question of whether this crisis is beginning to create conditions which tend to reinforce the cycle that produced it in the first instance.

The Moynihan Report contains even more explicit statements on this topic:

> . . . the circumstances of the Negro American community in recent years probably have been getting worse, not better. . . . The fundamental problem, in which this is most clearly the case, is that of family

---

* It is in all probability an overstatement to say that the black family was "destroyed" by enslavement. Frazier himself notes that blacks lived in the United States for 43 years prior to the legalization of slavery, and his research suggests that there may be African cultural survivals in black-family power structures.

structure. . . . So long as this situation persists, the cycle of poverty
and disadvantage will continue to repeat itself. . . . [The] present tangle of pathology is capable of perpetuating itself without assistance
from the white world.

Parker and Kleiner conclude that there are indeed problems in the black
family, but that these problems appear to be created and maintained not
by a deviant subculture, but by the social and psychological consequences
of unemployment and discrimination. As a result of being unable to attain
socioeconomic success because of social and economic discrimination,
blacks may be apt to feel that they are not successful in family role
performances.

Thus Moynihan contends that emasculation and family disorganization
are basic weaknesses in the black community. To "help" the black community, it may not be sufficient to directly assault institutional and informal racism in *white* society, as it also seems necessary to directly intervene
in the family in *black* society. Because family roles are deviant from the
white norms, black families need to be rehabilitated to overcome the family role deviancy which perpetuates the "tangle of pathology" in the black
community. This is the political consequence implied by the Moynihan
Thesis. It in part explains the apprehension and adverse reaction by the
black community in response to the proposed "national action."

Certainly an empirical generalization used as a rationale for government
intervention in the black family merits most careful scrutiny. It is the purpose of this paper to provide such an evaluation. The evaluation will be
carried out in two ways. First, empirical evidence used by Moynihan in
defense of his Thesis will be critically evaluated. Second, an empirical
study of black and white families carried out to test the general thesis of
male subdominance and female dominance in the black family will be
described and reported on.

The Moynihan Thesis: An Evaluation

The Moynihan Thesis can be evaluated both as an *analytic concept* and
as an *empirical generalization*. First, there exists some lack of conceptual
clarity about the meaning of matriarchy. A family can be defined as matriarchal if the wife is dominant and the husband subdominant. To say the
sex roles are *reversed* in black families means that the husband plays a role
that a white wife would play, and the wife plays a role that a white husband would play. That is, the roles of the husband and wife are reversed
vis-à-vis the "normal" pattern in white society. But it is not always clear
which roles are reversed. Role reversal could occur for domination of the
conjugal role, or the *parental* role. Conjugal role reversal would mean that

the wife is dominant and the husband subdominant in their relations with each other. Parental role reversal would mean that the wife plays a dominant role in parent-child relations (control and socialization). It may be that conjugal roles are reversed in black families, but that parental roles are not; or, the obverse could be the case.

As Parker and Kleiner point out, Moynihan implicitly used family role deviancy as an *intervening variable* between socioeconomic discrimination and the "pathology" of the black community. They argue that the relationship between socioeconomic discrimination and community pathology is *direct,* and that family role deviancy is not involved in the explanation of the continuing poverty of the black community.

The idea that pathology in poor and black communities is sustained through the socialization process in the family derives from a traditional mode of social science theorizing about the lower strata of society. According to this conception, poor youth learn from their parents a value system that devalues motivation to succeed. This lack of motivation—so it is argued—explains why the poor are unsuccessful and are not upwardly mobile. In short, the poor perpetuate their own poverty from generation to generation. This lack of desire for success, according to Hyman, "creates a *self-imposed* barrier to an improved position." This view has also been advanced by Aldous,* Lewis, Matza, and Walter Miller. Lewis writes that lower classes have developed a "culture of poverty," in which the poor have "a high incidence of maternal deprivation, of orality, of weak ego structure, confusion of sexual identity, a lack of impulse control, [and] a strong present-time orientation with little ability to defer gratification and to plan for the future. . . ."

Although Lewis's view of the "culture of poverty" differs from Moynihan's in that he views "male supremacy" as a part of this culture, Lewis does locate pathology in sex-role identification and child socialization.

This conception of the poor has been criticized by Underhill on the grounds that: (1) The aspirations of poor youth are higher than their attainments; (2) experimental research shows that aspirations are reduced by the denial of opportunity to succeed (he cites Lewin et al.); and (3) the positive *correlation* between aspirations and social class is well known, but social research has yet to demonstrate that high aspirations *cause* suc-

---

* Aldous states that employment may be necessary to black husbands' "adequate performance" of their role but is not sufficient, because of "lack of motivation, previous rebuffs, inability to conform to work requirements, and personal indulgence, . . . [and] abdication from family responsibility." This "makes their probability of being good family men . . . low . . . and their families are probably better off without them."

cess, and suggests instead that both aspirations to success and success itself may be caused by inequality of opportunity. Ireland, Moles, and O'Shey, in a comparative study of Mexican-Americans, blacks, and Anglos (non-Mexican-American whites), find little overall support for the "culture of poverty" as a characteristic of poor people. They find minimal evidence for this among Mexican-Americans, and find blacks to be closer to Anglos than to Mexican-Americans. Liebow, in a participant-observation study of lower-class black males in Washington, D. C., found no evidence showing that these men were deviant from white middle-class norms, and found no evidence that family role deviancy is perpetuated intergenerationally. He finds the relationship between socioeconomic discrimination and family instability to be *direct*. Parker and Kleiner's data show no such family role deviancy among blacks. Thus there exists substantial negative evidence for the view of family role deviancy and a culture of poverty in the black family.

Presumably the *pathology* attributed to low success motivation, as described by Hyman and Lewis, derives from the fact that this motivation *deviates* from the nonpoor's high motivation to succeed. Similarly, female dominance in black families is seen as pathological *because* it differs from the male dominance of the white and middle-class black family. Such an inference that *statistical* deviancy (deviation from the modal type) is pathological is stated explicitly by Moynihan in his statement that matriarchal structure retards the progress of blacks "because it is so out of line with the rest of American society." The *causal* connection between the plight of black communities and the assumed matriarchy is not given. Certainly it cannot be assumed.

There are other factors related to the hypothesis of matriarchy which must be considered in any empirical evaluation. Differences between blacks and whites may reflect differences in socioeconomic level (roughly, "lower class" as contrasted with "middle class") as much as or more than race. Thus, social class represents an important specification of the thesis of matriarchy in the black family. As mentioned, Frazier claims that lower-class black families are matriarchal and middle-class black families patriarchal. Moynihan's view of the black family is consistent with this. He is explicit in stating that the deterioration of the black family is most intense in lower-class black families. He contends that the family structure of lower-class black families is highly unstable, and in many urban centers is approaching complete breakdown. He feels at the same time that the middle-class black family "is steadily growing stronger and more successful," and "puts a higher premium on family stability and the conserving of family resources than does the white middle-class family." It is not entirely clear if this statement means that middle-class black families are more patriarchal than are middle-class white families. Since blacks are disproportionately represented in the lower strata of society, it follows from the specified Thesis that, for an overall black-white comparison, black families are more unstable and more matriarchal than are white families. Thus the specification of the Thesis is consistent with its general formulation, that matriarchy is more predominant in black families than in white families.

In the data presented later in this paper, explicit control is given to race and class variables, allowing separation of the independent effects of each from their statistical interaction. Such control is necessitated by Moynihan's implication that there exists interaction between these variables as they affect family roles.

As a final analytic comment, female dominance in *any* role cannot be *assumed* to be dysfunctional for the particular group to which it refers. Since groups differ in their relations to important systems in society, especially the economy, it may be that different family role patterns are appropriate to different social contexts.

The Moynihan Thesis can also be evaluated as an empirical generalization. A general review of studies pertaining to the black family is beyond the scope of this paper. In the balance of this section, major empirical indicators of family "instability" and "pathology" used in the Report are critically examined. The variables to be considered are illegitimacy rates, percentages of female-headed families, and unemployment rates. Moynihan also employs statistics on participation in the Aid to Dependent Children program, failure to pass armed forces entrance examinations,* delinquency,† and crime to describe the "tangle of pathology" in the black community.

---

* Moynihan states, "The ultimate mark of the inadequate preparation for life is the failure rate on the Armed Forces Mental Test." He also writes: "There is another special quality about military service for Negro men: it is an utterly masculine world. Given the strains of the disorganization and matrifocal family life in which so many Negro youth come of age, the Armed Forces are a dramatic and desperately needed change: a world away from women, a world run by strong men of unquestioned authority, where discipline, if hard, is nonetheless orderly and predictable, and where rewards, if limited, are granted on the basis of performance."

† References to certain of these studies are given in Parker and Kleiner. The reader is also referred to Gould's study of a sample of 104 white and 220 black males from a junior high school in central Seattle. He finds that the usual race difference in official delinquency records (with blacks more delinquent than whites) does not hold for self-reported delinquency. This suggests that the "pathology" of black delinquency may result from black youth being apt to be caught and convicted. In addition, for two kinds of delinquency related to family pathology, the percentages of blacks reporting delinquency are *lower* than the corresponding percentages for whites. The percentages "defying parents" are blacks 20 and whites 44; the percentages "running away," blacks 9 and whites 15.

Illegitimacy Rates

Illegitimacy rates can be defined in a number of ways. In the Moynihan Report, illegitimacy rates are defined as *1000 times the ratio of illegitimate births to all live births.* Moynihan uses these rates as indicative of family pathology. This interpretation can be questioned on a number of grounds: the statistical properties of the data, including the definition of illegitimacy; the validity of the government figures; the substantive explanation of illegitimate births; the relevance of data on illegitimacy for the measurement of family pathology; and the lack of control of the variable family socio-economic status.

The illegitimacy rates in 1940 were, by Moynihan's definition, 20 for whites and 168 for nonwhites. (Since over 90 percent of nonwhites are blacks, the nonwhite rates are used to estimate the black rates.) By 1963, the rates for whites had increased to 31, and the rates for nonwhites to 236. Thus there has been an increase in both groups. As Moynihan observes, the total increase for whites is 11, as compared to 68 for nonwhites. But these increases can be given a second interpretation, which takes into account the differences in the 1940 base figures. As a proportion of this base, the rate has increased 55 percent among whites, as compared to 40 percent among blacks. The nonwhite figure rises more rapidly in absolute terms in part because its initial level is higher.

Thus, the claim that the black family is *increasingly* disorganized in comparison to white families is supported if the absolute increase is used as the empirical indicator of family disorganization. But, if the ratio of the later rate to the earlier rate is used as the indicator of disorganization, the data show that white families may be increasingly disorganized in comparison to black families. Herzog states, however, that given the uneven quality of these data—with many states submitting estimates and others no data at all—such slight differences in rates should not be regarded as significant.

In addition, there are two difficulties with the definition of illegitimacy used in the Moynihan Report, both of which create biases toward higher rates for nonwhites. First, black women have absolutely higher birth rates, whether married or not. Second, the proportion of women who are unmarried and of child-bearing age (15 through 44) is higher for blacks than for whites. If the illegitimacy rate is defined as *1000 times the number of illegitimate births per unmarried woman 15-44 years of age,* illegitimacy is related to the population of women at risk, and nonwhite-white comparisons are more meaningful. By this measure the 1940 rates were 36 for nonwhites and 3.6 for whites, a nonwhite-white ratio of 10 to 1. This rate increased until 1950, at which time it was 12 to 1. But since

1950 the ratio of nonwhite to white illegitimacy rates has declined, so that by 1960 the rates were nonwhites 92 and whites 12, a ratio of less than 8 to 1. Ventura also reports that "since 1960 the illegitimacy rate for non-white women has declined 6 percent while the rate for whites has risen 30 percent. . . ." *If these rates could be defined as valid empirical indicators of family pathology, one would conclude that the* white *family is becoming more pathological and the* black *family less pathological.*

With regard to the second criticism of illegitimacy rates as an indicator of family pathology, Moynihan concurs with Herzog that the data on illegitimacy have limited dependability. He writes:

> There are almost certainly a considerable number of Negro children who, although technically illegitimate, are in fact the offspring of stable unions. On the other hand, it may be assumed that many births that are in fact illegitimate are recorded otherwise. Probably the two effects cancel each other.

There is some basis for believing that illegitimate black births are more apt to be recorded as such than are similar births for whites. Ventura points out that ". . . it is probable . . . that variations in reporting accuracy exist among different segments of the population. For example, it is likely that women in higher socioeconomic groups have more opportunity to under-report the incidence of illegitimate births." Since blacks are less apt to have high socioeconomic status than are whites, this socioeconomic effect also leads to more probable reporting of black illegitimate births as opposed to white illegitimate births. In sum, the data that *are* available are of questionable validity; and the data that *are not* available (as of 1966) represent 16 states and 30 percent of the population. The data do not constitute a random sample of the entire nation.

Third, the substantive explanation of nonwhite illegitimacy is apparently not, as is sometimes suggested, related to the availability of Aid to Dependent Children. Two factors that may be important to an explanation of the nonwhite-white difference in illegitimacy are *poverty* and *access to birth control.*

As Herzog points out, comparisons between poor and nonpoor census tracts show a strong relationship between higher illegitimacy rates and poorer tracts. There is variation within races according to income. Pakter et al., for example, find the illegitimacy rates of blacks to be 38 in Central Harlem (poor black) but only 9 in Pelham Bay (nonpoor black). Poverty contributes to illegitimacy in at least two ways. First, poor persons are apt to be on welfare, and hence reluctant to risk eligibility by admitting that a man is living in the home. Second, poor persons and black persons are less able to afford, less likely to define as necessary, legal divorce or legal separation.

In considering other possible explanations of the illegitimacy rates, one finds that there are no reliable data indicating that unmarried black women have more interesting sex lives than do unmarried white women: there is no evidence for a "morality gap" in the black community. Since extramarital sex is frequent in both groups, any difference in illegitimacy may depend on the greater access to birth control by white women (and men). Whites are more apt to know what birth control *is,* are better able to afford and use it,* and have greater access to abortion as a means of birth control. It is this writer's opinion that much of the race difference in illegitimacy results from this factor, and that the decline in nonwhite illegitimacy will be greater as birth control becomes more available in the black community.

Fourth, the higher rate of illegitimacy reported in the black community may reflect the greater extent to which illegitimate black babies are incorporated into the family unit, rather than being expelled and concealed from the family and community. Black people in the United States are apparently far more accepting of illegitimate children and are more apt to care for them than whites. Perhaps it is a *pathology of white values* that lowers the frequency of illegitimate births accepted as members of the family. At any rate, there is an ethnocentric bias in regarding black acceptance of illegitimate babies as pathological *because* this is not done in the white family and is deviant from white "normality."

The word "legitimate," after all, means only that a certificate of legitimation of a birth is registered with some municipal officer for a fixed fee. This, per se, says nothing about a commitment to take responsibility for, and care for, and express loyalty to a child. In the black community, there are norms that the *entire family* will take responsibility for a child. In the white community, this is somewhat less apt to be the case if a child is illegitimate.

Fifth, Ventura indicates that socioeconomic level is itself an important factor contributing to nonwhite-white differences in illegitimacy. He writes: "It is likely that if it were possible to control for social class, much of the difference between the two groups would disappear." That is, blacks are more apt to be in a lower class than whites, and lower-class people are more apt to have illegitimate children, and these factors, per se, may constitute an explanation for the higher illegitimacy rates in the black group. The data on illegitimacy rates collected before 1968 contain no information on the parents' socioeconomic status. Thus, until the later data

---

* Ventura uses research by Whelpton, Campbell, and Patterson to conclude that it is likely that white couples involved in premarital sex relations are more apt to use contraceptives than are black couples.

are analyzed, there is no way to know that black-white differentials in illegitimacy rates are not a spurious result of social-class differences.

For all these reasons, data on illegitimacy are inappropriate for testing the Moynihan Thesis of pathology among *lower-class* blacks.

Female-Headed Families

The percentage of women with husbands absent has been stable among whites from 1950 to 1960 but has increased somewhat for blacks. Controlling for women of child-bearing age, in the decade from 1950 to 1960, the percentages of female-headed homes for nonwhites and whites, respectively, are 33 and 8 for urban areas, 15 and 6 for rural nonfarm areas, and 10 and 3 for rural farm areas. Overall, the 1960 rates are 21 percent for nonwhite and 9 for white families. Thus in both urban and rural areas, female-headed families are more prevalent among blacks than among whites.

. The percentage of female-headed families among blacks (as distinct from nonwhites) gradually rose from 19 in 1940 to 24 in 1959. The overall rise from 1949 to 1965 for blacks is about one-third of one percent per year. But from 1959 through 1965, there has been no rise, and the 1965 percentage is 24 (as compared to 9 for whites). Thus the Census data show that the level of female-headed families is not rising for blacks. If the percentage of female-headed families could be defined as a valid indicator of family pathology, one would not conclude that the black family is becoming more pathological. As with illegitimacy rates (by Ventura's definition), this empirical outcome does not contribute directional support for the Moynihan Thesis of increasing deterioration in the black family.

The most common family structure among blacks is one in which there are both a husband and a wife present in the home. In urban areas, where the black family is alleged to be rapidly deteriorating, the percentage of such families is 65. Of the remaining 35 percent, only 18 are headed by the wife. The increase in female-headed homes for blacks may in part be a statistical artifact of urban migration, rather than family disorganization. For, as Moynihan points out, (1) blacks are more urban than whites, and (2) black families in cities are more apt to be headed by a woman than are black families in the country.

Since the Moynihan Thesis states that matriarchy is characteristic of lower-class urban black families, data comparing urban blacks and whites are necessary. If the percentage of female-headed families is a valid indicator of family pathology and matriarchy, the percentage for the lower-class black group should be higher than that for other groups. The 1960

Census data show the following: for families with children that have annual incomes under $3,000, the percentages are blacks 47 and whites 38; for families with incomes of $3,000 or more, blacks 8 and whites 4. Thus blacks at both levels are more apt to have female-headed families, but the black-white differences within income groups are only 9 and 4 percent. Further, percentage of female-headed families is far more closely related to income level than to race; among blacks, the low-income families are 39 percent more apt to have female-headed families; among whites, 34 percent. The effects of income level are about five times as strong as the effects of race. Female-headed families are five times more characteristic of poor families than of black families.

One reason why black women (both poor and nonpoor) are more apt to head families is a differential access to adoption. Most white women that have illegitimate babies are able to have them adopted. But since the demand for black babies is so low, black women have comparatively limited opportunities to have their illegitimate babies adopted, and thus are apt to keep them.

The data on female-headed homes in black and poor communities undoubtedly exaggerate the extent to which the fathers are not present. Substitute father laws and welfare requirements often make financial aid contingent on there being no father in the home. This of course creates a strong economic incentive to conceal the presence of the husband, and also contributes to husbands' motivation to leave the family unit. It has been estimated that the decennial U. S. Census undercounts urban blacks by as much as 20 percent.

The Moynihan Thesis implies that black men are emasculated and subdominant in their homes. There is, however, no empirical evidence showing that black men who leave their wives do so *because* they were unable to play a dominant role in the family. To say a man is subdominant because he is *absent* reduces the meaning of dominance to that of triviality. Further, as regards the approximately 60 percent of black homes with a husband present, there is no convincing evidence that these husbands are, in comparison to white husbands, emasculated and subdominant. Evidence in support of this view would require comparative analysis of *complete* families in the black and white race groups. The study to be reported in this paper is designed to provide such a comparison. Thus, it is most important to make a conceptual distinction between female-headed families and matriarchal families. In female-headed families there is no husband. In matriarchal families, there is a husband present, who plays subdominant conjugal and/or parental roles. For this reason, the data on female-headed families may not be valid for the measurement of family pathology.

As a final point, there is little if any justification for defining black families, or any families, as pathological on the ground that there is no husband present. Family units in which the husband is present may be unhappy and disorganized, and family units in which the husband is absent may be happy and well organized. Duncan and Duncan have analyzed data from the Current Population Survey conducted by the U. S. Bureau of the Census in 1962. The data show that for neither black men nor white men does an intergenerational transmission of family instability (absence of a parent) appear to operate. They conclude:

> There is, then, no sound basis for postulating a cycle of broken family relations, such as the failure of the parents to share a home with one another and their offspring predispose their sons to live without a spouse.

This study, then, does not provide positive support for Moynihan's position that family role deviance perpetuates family pathology from generation to generation. The Duncan and Duncan data do show, however, that an intact family background facilitates the occupational success of sons.

Unemployment Rates

Moynihan writes that ". . . unemployment among Negroes outside the South has persisted at a catastrophic level since the first statistics were gathered in 1930." The high level of unemployment among blacks is certainly a sad commentary on American society and the performance of the American economy. But black unemployment has *not* increased. The data presented for the years 1930, 1940, 1950, and 1960 indicate that 1960 is the year of least unemployment for blacks. Unemployment among blacks also has declined slightly from 1960 to 1964. Unemployment among both whites and blacks has decreased, and further, the decrease has been more rapid among blacks than among whites.

It is argued that unemployment causes instability in the home (a study of white families by Bakke is cited by Moynihan). It is further argued that unemployment has more deleterious effects on the black home than on the white home. But the two conclusions imply that the decrease in black unemployment levels should *increase* family stability, just as decreased white unemployment should stabilize white families. Since unemployment has decreased faster for blacks than for whites, black homes should be increasingly stable vis-à-vis white homes. To support his Thesis, Moynihan relies on data showing that between 1960 and 1964 the number of new ADC cases rose. But the other data used in the Report as measures of family instability did not show such a rise. Marital separation, for example, continued to parallel employment. Valentine points out that Moynihan ignores other evidence in the Report, such as the *decline* of family income relative to white income. Valentine concludes that *there is in the Report more evidence to support the interpretation that family structure measures are caused by economic factors than to support the opposite interpretation.* It may be too strong a statement to say that these data contradict Moynihan's argument, but any support they give to the Thesis is, at best, equivocal.

A *methodological* weakness in the use of such census data for inferences about individuals and families is that it assumes that variables correlated for groups are correlated for persons or families *within* groups. Robinson shows that this dependence on ecological correlations makes such inferences unsound. For instance, in a given time period, the unemployment rate and the percent of female-headed families may both rise in the black community. But there is no way to know, from *this,* that the husbands who left their wives are the same husbands who had become unemployed. Further, much of the family research consistent with Frazier's and Moynihan's conclusions was carried out in the 1930s, a time when many factors were at work which could cause both unemployment and family instability.

Further, the instability of employment of blacks as opposed to whites reflects social class as well as race. Lower-class persons work at jobs that are unstable in comparison to the jobs of the middle class. Thus part of the instability of employment behavior for blacks derives from the fact that they are more apt to be lower-class than whites. When social class is controlled, much of the race difference in employment behavior is removed.

In summary, the evidence for deterioration of the black family (1) is derived from sociodemographic data rather than from data on family dynamics, and (2) does not support the conclusion drawn from it. As Geismar and Gerhart write, "The act of inferring functioning patterns from such structural and official, recorded behavioral characteristics, is not so much the articulation of a theoretical position as it is a form of research which grasps at available straws."

The Old in the Country of the Young

Time Magazine

Edward Albee once wrote a play about a middle-aged couple who, before putting Grandma permanently in the sandbox with a toy shovel, gave her a nice place to live under the stove, with an Army blanket and her very own dish. The play contains more truth than allegory. One of the poignant trends of U. S. life is the gradual devaluation of older people, along with their spectacular growth in numbers. Twenty million Americans are 65 or over. They have also increased proportionately, from 2.5 percent of the nation's population in 1850 to 10 percent today.

While the subculture of youth has been examined, psychoanalyzed, photographed, deplored, and envied, few have wanted even to admit the existence of a subculture of the aged, with its implications of segregation and alienation. Strangely enough, the aged have a lot in common with youth: they are largely unemployed, introspective, and often depressed; their bodies and psyches are in the process of change, and they are heavy users of drugs. If they want to marry, their families tend to disapprove. Both groups are obsessed with time. Youth, though, figures its passage from birth; the aged calculate backward from their death day. They sometimes shorten the wait: the suicide rate among elderly men is far higher than that of any other age group.

The two subcultures seldom intersect, for the young largely ignore the old or treat them with what novelist Saul Bellow calls "a kind of totalitarian cruelty, like Hitler's attitude toward Jews." It is as though the aged were an alien race to which the young will never belong. Indeed, there is a distinct discrimination against the old that has been called age-ism. In its simplest form, says psychiatrist Robert Butler of Washington, D.C., age-ism is just "not wanting to have all these ugly old people around." Butler believes that in 25 or 30 years, age-ism will be a problem equal to racism.

We have time to grow old—the air is full of our cries.
—Samuel Beckett

It is not just cruelty and indifference that cause age-ism and underscore the obsolescence of the old. It is also the nature of modern Western culture. In some societies, explains anthropologist Margaret Mead, "the past of the adults is the future of each new generation," and therefore is taught and respected. Thus, primitive families stay together and cherish their elders. But in the modern U.S., family units are small, the generations live apart, and social changes are so rapid that to learn about the past is considered irrelevant. In this situation, new in history, says Miss Mead, the aged are "a strangely isolated generation," the carriers of a dying culture. Ironically, millions of these shunted-aside old people are remarkably able: medicine has kept them young at the same time that technology has made them obsolete.

Many are glad to end their working days. For people with money, good health, careful plans, and lively interests, retirement can be a welcome time

From "The Old in the Country of the Young," *Time,* August 3, 1970, pp. 49ff.

to do the things they always dreamed of doing. But for too many others, the harvest of "the golden years" is neglect, isolation, anomie, and despair. One of every four Americans 65 or over lives at or below "the poverty line." Some of these 5,000,000 old people were poor to begin with, but most are bewildered and bitter *nouveaux pauvres,* their savings and fixed incomes devoured by spiraling property taxes and other forms of inflation. More than 2,000,000 of them subsist on Social Security alone.

Job discrimination against the aged, and increasingly against the middle-aged, is already a fact of U. S. life. While nearly 40 percent of the long-term unemployed are over 45, only 10 percent of federal retraining programs are devoted to men of that age. It is often difficult for older people to get bank loans, home mortgages, or automobile insurance. When the car of a 68-year-old Brooklyn grocer was stolen last winter, he was unable to rent a substitute. Though his driving record was faultless and he needed a car for work, he was told falsely by two companies that to rent him one was "against the law."

> *Youth is everywhere in place;*
> *Age, like woman, requires fit*
> *surroundings.*
> —Ralph Waldo Emerson

Treated like outsiders, the aged have increasingly clustered together for mutual support or simply to enjoy themselves. A now familiar but still amazing phenomenon has sprung up in the past decade: dozens of good-sized new towns that exclude people under 65. Built on cheap, outlying land, such communities offer two-bedroom houses starting at $18,000, plus a refuge from urban violence, the black problem (and in fact blacks), as well as generational pressures. "I'm glad to see my children come and I'm glad to see the back of their heads," is a commonly expressed sentiment. Says Dr. James Birren of the University of Southern Cailfornia: "The older you get the more you want to live with people like yourself. You want, to put it bluntly, to die with your own."

Most important, friendships are easy to make. One relative newcomer to Laguna Hills Leisure World, Calif., received more than 200 get-well cards from her new neighbors when she went to a hospital in Los Angeles. There is an emphasis on good times: dancing, shuffleboard, outings on oversized tricycles, and bowling (the Keen Agers *v.* the Hits and Mrs.). Clubs abound, including Bell Ringing, Stitch and Knit, Lapidary, and "tepees" of the International Order of Old Bastards. The I.O.O.B. motto: "Anything for fun." There is, in a sense, a chance for a new start. "It doesn't matter what you used to be; all that counts is what you do here," said a resident of Sun City, Ariz.

To some residents the communities seem too homogeneous and confining. A 74-year-old Californian found that life was flavorless at his retirement village; he was just waiting for "the little black wagon." Having begun to paint seascapes and landscapes at 68, he moved near an artists' colony, where he now sells his landscapes and lives happily with a lady friend of 77.

> *In silent synods, they play chess or cribbage . . .*
> —W.H. Auden

In fact, less than 1 percent of the elderly leave their own states. The highest proportion of the aged outside Florida is in Arkansas, Iowa, Maine, Missouri, Nebraska, and South Dakota—on farms and in communities from which youth has fled. In small towns, the able elderly turn abandoned buildings into "senior centers" for cards, pool, slide shows, lectures, and pie socials. In Hebron, N. Dak. (pop. 1,137), grandmothers use the balcony of the former J. C. Penney store for their quilting. But there is little socializing among the rural aged, who often subsist on pittances of $60 a month, and become even more isolated as public buses disappear from the highways, cutting off their lifelines to clinics, stores, and friends.

A third of the nation's aged live in the deteriorating cores of the big cities. On Manhattan's Upper West Side, thousands of penniless widows in dingy single-room-occupancy hotels bar their doors against the alcoholics and dope addicts with whom they share the bathroom, the padlocked refrigerator, and the telephone down the hall. "Nine out of ten around here, there's something wrong with them," says a 72-year-old ex-housekeeper living on welfare in a hotel on West 94th Street. "I get disgusted and just sleep every afternoon. Everybody dying around you makes you kind of nervous." Terrified of muggings and speeding cars, the disabled and disoriented do not leave their blocks for years on end, tipping anyone they can find to get groceries for them when their welfare checks arrive.

Close to a million old people live in nursing homes or convalescent facilities provided by Medicare. A new growth industry, nursing homes now provide more beds than hospitals. They are badly needed. But in many of the "homes," the food and care are atrocious. Patients have even been confined to their beds merely because bed care entitles the owners to $2 or $3 more a day. Mrs. Ruby Elliott, 74, recalls her year in a California nursing home with fear and bitterness: "It's pitiful, but people are just out for the money. That whole time I was among the living dead."

Fewer than half of the country's 25,000 nursing homes actually offer skilled nursing. Arkansas Congressman David Pryor recently visited twelve nursing homes near Washington, D.C. "I found two where I would be willing to put my mother," he said. "But I don't think I could afford either one on my $42,500 congressional salary." Pryor is trying to set up a congressional committee to investigate long-term care for the aged.

> *How terrible strange to be seventy.*
> —Simon and Garfunkel

Almost everyone hates to think about aging. Doctors and social scientists are no exception. "They think one shouldn't look at it too closely, as though it were the head of Medusa. It is considered a morbid preoccupation," says one anthropologist. But the acute problems and swelling ranks of the American aged have lately stimulated a number of new behavioral studies that are more scientific than any ever done before. They show, among other things, that people age at very different speeds and that many changes formerly attributed to age are actually caused by other factors. The cliché that a man is as old as his arteries, for example, has been found to be misleading. It is probably more accurate to say that a man is as sick as his arteries, and that such sickness is caused by diet and stress rather than by age.

The ability of elderly people to memorize and recall new information has been exhaustively tested at the Duke University Center for the Study of Aging and Human Development. They can do it, but they need more time than younger people. Their responses are apparently slowed down by anxiety; an older person's goal is less to achieve success than to avoid failure. Changes in the blood of elderly pupils showed that they were undergoing the physiological equivalent of anxiety without being aware of it. Drugs that changed this physiological happening helped them, and their performances improved. Dr. Carl Eisdorfer, who conducted the experiments, suggests that what initially slowed down his subjects was not so much their age as their attitude toward their age.

Old people may be ridiculed when they try to act young, but according to San Francisco psychologist Frances Carp, it is better to fight age than to accept it. In America today, "acceptance of old age holds out few if any rewards," she says. Those who surrender often become debilitated by a devastating "elderly mystique"—and victims of self-fulfilling prophecies. For example, doctors at the University of Illinois studied 900 old people living at home and found many so sick that they could not walk to the door. They had lived for months without medical attention because they felt that they were old and therefore were supposed to be sick.

Actually, the overwhelming majority of the aged can fend very well for themselves. Only 5 percent of aged Americans live in institutions; perhaps another 5 percent remain bedridden at home. True, four out of five older people have a chronic condition. "But chronic diseases must be redefined," says Duke's Dr. Eisdorfer.

I've seen too many depressed people leaving their doctor's office saying, "My God, I've got an incurable disease." Chronic illness gets confused with fatal illness. Life itself is fatal, of course, but as far as most chronic illnesses go, we simply don't know what they do to advance death. The role of the doctor has to change. Now that infectious diseases are on their way out, the doctor must stop thinking about cures and start teaching people how to live with what they have.

New findings show that hypochondria, or "high body concern," one of the most common neuroses of the elderly, can often be cured. According to Dr. Ewald Busse, director of the Duke study center, if a man's family

keeps criticizing him unjustly, makes him feel uncomfortable, unwanted, he may retreat into an imaginary illness as a way of saying, "Don't make things harder for me. I'm sick and you should respect me and take care of me." It is clear from our studies that if the older hypochondriac's environment changes for the better, he will too. He will again become a reasonable, normal person. This is quite different from the reaction of the younger hypochondriac, who is much sicker psychologically and much less likely to respond to a favorable change in environment.

Recent studies bear out sex researchers Masters and Johnson's findings that men who enjoyed sex earlier in life can, if all else goes well, continue to enjoy it. Questionnaires over a ten-year period at Duke showed that the same men's interest in sex changed little from age 67 to 77, although there was a slight drop in activity. Result: a gradual widening in what the researchers coolly call the "interest-activity gap." A much lower proportion of women continued to be interested in sex after 67, but they managed to keep their interest-activity graph lines close together. "It depends on the individual," an elderly San Franciscan points out. "All ages have sexy people."

> People expect old men to die,
> They . . . look
> At them with eyes that wonder when.
> —Ogden Nash

A common and unfortunate diagnosis of many aged people is that they are senile, a catchword for a number of conditions. There may be organic brain damage—for example, the brain may run short of oxygen because of impaired blood flow. But many of the "senile" actually have psychological problems. One 70-year-old retired financier, who insisted on calling his successor at the company all the time and had all sorts of paranoid suspicions, was diagnosed as having organic brain disease. A combination of psychotherapy and a new job as treasurer of a charitable organization helped the man to recover completely. Other "senile" patients actually suffer from malnutrition, or have simply broken down out of loneliness, perhaps caused by a temporary overload. As one old man put it: "There is no one still alive who can call me John." Explains Harvard psychoanalyst Martin Berezin: "The one thing which neither grows old nor diminishes is the need for love and affection. These drives, these wishes never change."

Actually, senile traits are not peculiar to the aged. A group of college students and a group of the elderly were recently rated according to the characteristics of senility, and the students were found to be the more neurotic, negative, dissatisfied, socially inept, and unrealistic. The students, in sum, were more senile than their elders. Other studies have shown that the percentage of psychiatric impairment of old persons is no greater than that for younger groups.

But younger people are usually treated if their psychological problems are severe. Says New York psychologist Muriel Oberleder:

> If we encounter unusual nervousness, irritability, depression, unaccountable anger, personality change, apathy, or withdrawal in a young person, we make sure that he is seen by a physician. But when those symptoms appear in elderly people, they are considered par for the course of old age. We rarely consider the possibility that elderly people who have had a breakdown can recover.

Dr. Berezin successfully treated a 70-year-old woman who had a severe breakdown, her first. She had been picked up for drinking, setting fire to her home, and other bizarre behavior, including chalking off a section of the sidewalk and claiming it as her own. In therapy, she revealed that she had yearned all her life for marriage and children. Eventually, she mastered her grief and regrets, settled down, and began to enjoy the people around her.

Psychotherapy has never been easily available to the aged. Since it demands so much time and effort, it is considered better to expend it on those who have a long life ahead. There is also the still-powerful influence of Freud. If one's behavior is believed to be programmed in the first years of life, one cannot hope to change that program substantially during old age. (Freud, who contributed to age-ism, was also its victim. At 81, discussing "the many free hours with which my dwindling analytical practice has presented me," he added: "It is understandable that patients don't surge toward an analyst of such an unreliable age.")

> *. . . I reach my center,*
> *my algebra and my key,*
> *my mirror.*
> *Soon I shall know who I am.*
> —Jorge Luis Borges

Most psychologists have simply ignored the process of aging. Says Harvard's Erik Erikson:

It is astonishing to behold how (until quite recently and with a few notable exceptions) Western psychology has avoided looking at the whole of life. As our world image is a one-way street to never-ending progress, interrupted only by small and big catastrophes, our lives are to be one-way streets to success—and sudden oblivion.

But lately Erikson and other psychiatrists have become interested in all stages of man's development, and the "aging" that goes on at every stage.

One practitioner of "life-cycle psychiatry," Washington's 43-year-old Dr. Butler, believes that the possibilities for psychic change may be greater in old age than at any other period of life. "Little attention has been paid to the wish to change identity, to preserve and exercise the sense of possibility and incompleteness against a sense of closure and completeness." When a person's identity is maintained throughout old age, "I find it an ominous sign rather than the other way around. If the term needs to be used at all, I suggest that a continuing, lifelong identity crisis is a sign of good health."

Though many believe that age accentuates personality characteristics, Dr. Butler notes that "certain personality features mellow or entirely disappear. Others prove insulating and protective, although they might formerly have been impairing, such as a schizoid disposition." Some doctors suggest that neuroses and some psychoses burn themselves out with age, and note that the rate of mental disorders declines after the age of 70.

Carl Jung, who lived with great vigor until the age of 85, saw aging as a process of continuous inward development ("individuation"), with important psychic changes occurring right up to the time of death. "Anyone who fails to go along with life remains suspended, stiff, and rigid in mid-air," Jung wrote.

That is why so many people get wooden in old age; they look back and cling to the past with a secret fear of death in their hearts. From the middle of life onward, only he remains vitally alive who is ready to die with life, for in the secret hour of life's midday the parabola is reversed, death is born. We grant goal and purpose to the ascent of life, why not to the descent?

Erik Erikson agrees: "Any span of the cycle lived without vigorous meaning, at the beginning, in the middle, or at the end, endangers the sense of life and the meaning of death in all whose life stages are intertwined."

> *Better to go down dignified*
> *With boughten friendship at your side*
> *Than none at all. Provide, provide!*
> —Robert Frost

The problems of the aged are not their concern alone. Since reaching the age of 70 or 80 is becoming the norm rather than the exception, more and more of the middle-aged—even when they retire—have elderly parents and other relatives to care for. For the "command generation" there are two generation gaps, and the decisions to be made about their parents are often more difficult than those concerning their children. Various community agencies sometimes help, and in Manhattan a private referral service is kept busy helping distraught people find the right place for parents who can no longer live at home. One 81-year-old woman was persuaded to go to a nursing home when her daughter, with whom she had always lived, married late in life. To her own surprise, she is happier than she was before, taking great pride in reading to and helping her older roommate. A difficult decision of the middle-aged is how to allot their resources between children and parents and still provide for their own years of retirement, which may well extend for two decades.

The next generation of the aged may be healthier, certainly better educated, and perhaps more politically aware. Those over 65 are now a rather silent minority, but in number they are almost exactly equal to the nation's blacks. Since none are below voting age, the aged control a high percentage of the vote—15 percent. More and more are banding together. The American Association of Retired Persons, for example, helps its nearly 2,000,000 members get automobile insurance, cheaper drugs, and cut-rate travel. A more politically oriented group, the 2,500,000-member National Council of Senior Citizens, played a major role in pushing through Medicare. Now the group is lobbying to improve Medicare, which helps the sick but does not provide checkups, by including some sort of Preventicare.

Aside from health, money is the most pervasive worry of the aged; income maintenance is a major need. Private pension plans need attention too. According to one informed estimate, only 10 percent of the people who work under pension plans actually receive any benefits, usually because they do not stay long enough to qualify. As presently arranged, pensions also tend to lock older workers into their jobs and, if they become unemployed, to lock them out. They are then denied jobs because it is too expensive to let them join a pension plan.

> Come, my friends,
> 'Tis not too late to seek a newer
> world.
> —Tennyson

Will able 70-year-olds have more opportunities to work in the future? Probably not. Instead of raising the age of mandatory retirement, business and labor may lower it, perhaps to 50 or below—making workers eligible even earlier for social insecurity. Aside from those fortunate few in the professions—law, medicine, dentistry, architecture—most of the people over 65 who are still at work today are farmers, craftsmen, and self-employed tradesmen, all categories whose numbers are shrinking. Of course, people cannot work hard forever. Each man ages according to his own clock, but at long last he is likely to lose much of his strength, his drive, and adaptability. Witness the gerontocracy that slows down Congress and the businesses that have failed because of rigid leadership. But there are still many areas where the aged can serve and should, for aside from humane consideration, they can provide skill and wisdom that otherwise would be wasted.

New plans to recruit, train, and deploy older workers to provide much needed help in hospitals, special schools, and elsewhere will be discussed at the White House Conference on Aging scheduled for November 1971. Meanwhile, a few small-scale programs point the way. One is Operation Green Thumb, which hires retired farmers for landscaping and gardening. Another is the International Executive Service Corps, which arranges for retired executives to lend their management skills to developing countries. Hastings College of Law in San Francisco is staffed by law professors who have retired from other schools. A federally financed program called Foster Grandparents pays 4,000 low-income "grandparents" to care for 8,000 underprivileged youngsters. Although they have numbered only in the hundreds, most elderly volunteers in Vista and the Peace Corps have been great assets. "We know about outhouses and can remember when there weren't any refrigerators," says Nora Hodges, 71, who spent two years in Tunisia and is now associate Peace Corps director in the Ivory Coast. "People in underdeveloped countries rate age very highly. When we meet with this appreciative attitude, we outdo ourselves."

> *Begin the preparation for your death*
> *And from the fortieth winter by that*
> *   thought*
> *Test every work of intellect or faith.*
> —W.B. Yeats

Life would be richer, students of aging agree, if a wider repertory of activities were encouraged throughout life. Almost everyone now marches together in a sort of lockstep. They spend years in school, years at work, and years in retirement. Youth might well work more, the middle-aged play more, and the older person go back to school. Former HEW Secretary John Gardner wants to see "mid-career clinics to which men and women can go to re-examine the goals of their working lives and consider changes of direction. I would like to see people visit such clinics with as little self-consciousness as they visit their dentist." As psychiatrist Robert Butler puts it: "Perhaps the greatest danger in life is being frozen into a role that limits one's self-expression and development. We need Middle Starts and Late Starts as well as Head Starts."

To get a late start does not necessarily require a federal program. Many an enterprising individual has done it on his own. Mrs. Florida Scott-Maxwell, who at the age of 50 began training to become a psychotherapist, recently wrote down her reflections about aging in *The Measure of My Days*. "My seventies were interesting and fairly serene," she noted, "but my eighties are passionate. I am so disturbed by the outer world, and by human quality in general, that I want to put things right as though I still owed a debt to life. I must calm down."

> *Old age should burn and rave at close of day.*
> —Dylan Thomas

How socially involved older people should be is a question in hot dispute among students of aging. Some believe in the "theory of disengagement," which holds that aging is accompanied by an inner process that makes the loosening of social ties a natural process, and a desirable one. Others disagree. Says Harvard sociologist Chad Gordon: "Disengagement theory is a rationale for the fact that old people haven't a damn thing to do and nothing to do it with."

After analyzing lengthy interviews with 600 aged San Franciscans, anthropologist Margaret Clark found that engagement with life, rather than disengagement, contributed most to their psychological well-being. But not when that engagement included acquisitiveness, aggressiveness, or a drive to achievement, supercompetence, and control. To cling to these stereotypical traits of the successful American seems to invite trouble, even geriatric psychiatry. The healthiest and happiest of the aged people in the survey were interested in conserving and enjoying rather than acquiring and exploiting, in concern for others rather than control of others, in "just being" rather than doing. They embraced, Dr. Clark points out, many of the values of today's saner hippies. Similarly, religion often teaches the aged, in spite of their physical diminishment, to accept each day as a gift.

The ranker injustices of age-ism can be alleviated by governmental action and familial concern, but the basic problem can be solved only by a fundamental and unlikely reordering of the values of society. Social obsolescence will probably be the chronic condition of the aged, like the other deficits and disabilities they learn to live with. But even in a society that has no role for them, aging individuals can try to carve out their own various niches. The noblest role, of course, is an affirmative one—quite simply to demonstrate how to live and how to die. If the aged have any responsibility, it is to show the next generation how to face the ultimate concerns. As octogenarian Scott-Maxwell puts it: "Age is an intense and varied experience, almost beyond our capacity at times, but something to be carried high. If it is a long defeat, it is also a victory, meaningful for the initiates of time, if not for those who have come less far."

Chapter 10

"Deviant" Life Styles

The Gay World | *Martin Hoffman*

I am going to use the term "homosexual" in this book to refer to those individuals who have a sexual attraction toward partners of the same sex, over at least a few years of their lives. It should, however, be made clear that there is no definition of "homosexual" or "homosexuality" which is going to be agreed to by 100 percent of the scientists working in this field. Kinsey, for example, objects to using the term "homosexual" or "heterosexual" even as an adjective to describe persons, and prefers to reserve these words to describe the nature of the overt sexual relations or of the stimulae to which the individual erotically responds. Yet, a few pages later in this same book, he sets up a heterosexual-homosexual rating scale, which includes both psychological reactions and overt experience and in which individuals are rated, for example, as "predominantly homosexual, but more than incidentally heterosexual." So we see that Kinsey himself is forced into using the term as an adjective to describe persons. I think that there is no way that we can talk intelligently about the subject without speaking of individuals as homosexuals. To avoid doing so would be to sacrifice any attempt at a common understanding of the subject to a merely quantified study of overt behavior. Even Kinsey, who was himself most sympathetic to a taxonomic approach to sexuality, does not quite do this. It would certainly behoove those of us who wish to arrive at a broad sociopsychological understanding of the phenomenon to adhere to the commonsense use of the terms, at least insofar as they can be made serviceable.

When I use the term "homosexual" to describe a man, by this I do not mean that he may not also be heterosexual, for I think there are a signifi-

From Martin Hoffman, "What Is Homosexuality?" in *The Gay World* (New York: Basic Books, 1968), Chapter 2. References cited in the original have been deleted.

cant number of people, such as Tom, who are sexually attracted to and seek out sexual partners of both sexes. These people we could very conveniently call bisexual, and I will do so, providing only that it is understood that the nature of the sexual attraction to men may not be the same as the sexual attraction to women. In other words, just because we say that Tom is sexually attracted to both men and women does not imply that his feelings on seeing a man and his feelings on seeing a woman are the same. In both cases he may be sexually stimulated, but his entire perception of the situation may be quite different, and his behavior with men— both in bed and out—may be of an altogether different kind than his behavior with women. We saw in the last chapter how Tom's sexual interest in men was almost entirely directed toward performing fellatio and that he engaged in foreplay and other sexual acts with his partner simply in order to satisfy the partner. When Tom goes to bed with his wife, on the other hand, he *is* interested in extensive foreplay and *is* interested in having conventional sexual intercourse with her. His feeling toward women is much more of a warm and enveloping kind in which he ultimately (in fantasy) wants to mingle his body with that of his partner. With men, on the other hand, he feels as if sucking his partner's penis will be very exciting and he can somehow derive a peculiar kind of satisfaction from this activity, the nature of which is not entirely clear to him. I think, therefore, that when we use the term "homosexual" to describe Tom, we must be clear that he is also heterosexual, and when we use the term "bisexual" to describe him, we must be completely clear, as many writers are not, that we are talking about two very different kinds of feeling and behavioral states.

What I am saying here, in effect, is that there are many different kinds of homosexuals and many different kinds of bisexuals. We might also add that there are many different kinds of heterosexuals. This will hopefully become clearer when we come to the discussion of the genesis of homosexuality. In asking the question "Why is a man homosexual?" we do not wish to imply by any means that this is to be regarded as a basically different kind of question from "Why is a man heterosexual?" Virtually all the literature on homosexuality is marred by the failure of its authors to take account of the fact that heterosexuality is just as much a problematic situation for the student of human behavior as is homosexuality. The only reason it does not seem to us a problem is because we take its existence for granted. However, we should know enough about science by now to realize that it is just those questions we take for granted that are the ones, when properly asked, which would open up new areas of scientific exploration. The question should really be put as follows: "Why does a person become sexually excited (i.e., in the case of a man, why does he get an erection) when confronted with a particular kind of stimulus?" If the question is asked in this way it can be seen that heterosexuality is just as much of a problem as homosexuality, in the scientific if not in the social sense.

The fact is that there are almost as many different kinds of homosexual, bisexual, and heterosexual responses as there are individuals. On the other hand, there *are* a number of common features which characterize large groups of individuals, so that we *can* make generalizations about particular kinds of response. Obviously, Tom's wish for fellatio and David's wish to hold another man close to him are not unique, but are shared by a sufficient number of other men so that in fact they have already been described and very convincing explanations of them have already been given in the psychiatric literature. We will come to these explanations in a later chapter.

Incidence

In the Introduction, in order to make the point that homosexuality is a social problem of enormous proportions, I discussed the incidence figures on male homosexual behavior from the 1948 Kinsey report. The figures that I think are particularly significant are the following: "four percent of the white males are exclusively homosexual throughout their lives, after the onset of adolescence." This figure, which refers to at least 4,000,000 American males, tells us that there is a very significant number of men who are exclusively homosexual, both in regard to their overt experience and their psychic reactions. These are people like David, who never have any interest in having sexual relations with a woman. They constitute a considerable part of those individuals who make up the most visible portion of the gay world. However, because 10 percent of the American male population is more or less exclusively homosexual for *at least* three years between the ages of 16 and 55, a significant number of those men who are to be seen in the visible sector of the gay world, e.g., in the bars, are not exclusively homosexual for their whole lives. This added 6 percent includes those individuals who, at the very least, have three years during their late adolescent or adult lives in which, although they may have incidental experience with the opposite sex, and sometimes react psychically to members of the opposite sex, are almost entirely homosexual in their overt activities and/or their reactions. This 6 percent includes a substantial number of men who have had some trial heterosexual experience but who have then become exclusively gay. It is probably this figure which deserves the most emphasis, because it indicates how very widespread male homosexuality is. Kinsey pointed out that those who are more or less exclusively gay for at least three years represent approximately one male in ten in the white male population. The journalist Jess Stearn once wrote a book called *The Sixth Man,* which gave the idea that one out of every six American men was gay. This, of course, was pooh-poohed and I remember that when I first saw the book's title I reacted very skeptically. But, as a matter of fact, if one looks at Kinsey's figures, one finds that 18 percent of the males have at least as much homosexual as heterosexual experience in their lives for at least three years between the ages of sixteen and fifty-five. This is more than one in six of the white male population.

Individual Types

What kind of men are these homosexuals? What do they look like? How do they act? To these questions one can only give the most general (and unsatisfactory) answer, namely, that these people run the entire gamut from the swishy faggot who can be identified a block away, to the husband, son, or brother whom even the fairly sophisticated person would not suspect of any homosexual interest. They include people who are handsome, clever, and rich, those who are ugly, stupid, and poor, and all combinations and gradations in between. Homosexuality penetrates into every conceivable socioeconomic, religious, and geographical classification. There *are* some slight differences, however. For example, Kinsey found that the highest rate of homosexual behavior occurs among those males who go to high school but not beyond. It is also quite true that homosexuals migrate to large urban centers, so that there is probably a higher percentage of practicing homosexuals in Los Angeles than in Bakersfield, California. But these minor differences do not obviate the more significant fact that homosexuals are to be found throughout the entire nation in all social strata.

A great deal of nonsense has been written in the scientific literature about "active" and "passive," "masculine" and "feminine" homosexuals. The implication is often made that there is a sharp difference between these two kinds of individuals. It is certainly true that there is a minority of homosexual men who can be classified both from the point of view of their own conscious definition of themselves as masculine or feminine and from the point of view of what they will do or not do in bed. But this is true only for a minority. The fact is that most homosexuals cannot be so classified and, in fact, will generally take a great variety of roles in sexual performance. Evelyn Hooker has arrived at the same conclusion from her detailed study of 30 predominantly or exclusively homosexual males whom she has intensively interviewed over a period of eight years. She found that the consciousness of masculinity or femininity on the part of her research subjects appeared to bear no clear relation to particular sexual patterns, and that for the majority of individuals in her sample, there was no apparent correspondence between a conscious sense of identity as masculine or feminine and a preferred or predominant role during the sexual act. This does not mean that these men don't have preferred sexual patterns. They do. But these patterns do not, with a very few exceptions, bear any relationship to their conscious sense of themselves as "masculine" or "feminine."

Granted, then, that homosexuals do a lot of different things in bed, just what exactly do they do? Most American investigators have found that there are four "classic" positions in which an individual might find himself engaged when he is in bed with another male. These can be divided into oral and anal and then again into insertor or receptor roles, so that an individual may be an oral inserter, an anal inserter, an oral receptor, or an anal receptor. He can also engage in mutual fellatio (69) and can engage in a great deal of alternation among these roles.

Curiously enough, the English social psychologist, Michael Schofield, found that the largest proportion of homosexuals who were members of the English homosexual community which he studied (using roughly the same kind of ethnographic methods which Hooker and I have used) prefer "genital apposition," or very close body contact without penetration of a body orifice as the means to ejaculation. The term "rub-off" is sometimes used to refer to this method of achieving orgasm. The individual simply rubs his penis against his partner's body, for example, against his belly or his leg. Schofield's finding is in quite sharp contrast to what all investigators would agree is the sexual preference of American male homosexuals, who by and large think of this technique as rather adolescent and generally prefer one or more variations of either oral or anal insertion. Why this curious national contrast exists has never been explained, and, as a matter of fact, it has not really even been noticed. I am not going to attempt an explanation of it here, but I think it is certainly something which is at least very curious and might even be an indicator, especially if it can be verified by other English investigators, of a quite different attitude toward sexuality across the ocean.

In classifying homosexual sex behavior in this way, we cannot, of course, really give the reader a feeling for the immense variation that exists in sexual practices, both among individuals and, to a lesser but significant extent, within the *same* individual over a period of time. It must be emphasized that people *learn* sexual behavior just as they learn any other form of complex activity. Thus, the sexual preferences and sexual repertory of an individual who has been "out" for five years is going to be quite different from that which he had at the time of his first experience. Or perhaps this statement might be qualified: these factors may very well be quite different, but they are not necessarily different. For some people stick to the very same preference that they began with. Some people find out right away what they "really" like, but with others it takes much more time. Some of them are never sure. Both Bieber and Hooker have reported that there is a substantial number of homosexuals who express no sexual preference. That is, they do not prefer one sexual act to another. My own interviews have yielded a different result and I have been somewhat at a loss to explain this. I have never encountered a male homosexual who did not express a preference for a particular kind of sexual act. It seems to me that this discrepancy can be explained in the following way: Hooker and Bieber, in classifying sexual behavior, have stuck pretty close to the four "classic" types of sexual activity, i.e., oral and anal insertion, and they have not included as objects of preference those kinds of activities which fall outside these four types. In other words, because the four "classic" types are so standard among American male homosexuals, some men have been at a loss to explain what they really like to do in terms of them, since they really do not like to do one of those four things best of all. I would guess that when Hooker or Bieber asked them about this they were somewhat unsure of what to say, so they said that they didn't know what they liked to do or said that they really had no preference—that anything would do. My own interviews indicate that they actually do have a specific preference but they don't know how to express it. When they say that they will do anything or that they like to do anything, what they really mean is that they are quite willing to go along with their partner's desires, and thus they will engage in one or more of these four "classic" kinds of sexual activity. Very often, however, such individuals might actually prefer simply to go to bed with another man, engage in necking and petting and close body contact, and might not really be interested in either achieving orgasm themselves or in inducing their partner's orgasm. One might say that, for these individuals, *simply going to bed with another male* is the thing they really want. Obviously, this can be described as sexual, provided it is understood that an ejaculation is not the thing that is most desired. Among these people, one would probably find a number of those whom Schofield has described in his English studies to which we have referred above. Although this does not explain the discrepancy in numbers between the English and American homosexual populations, it does serve, to some extent, to include these individuals in the American figures. In other words, it may be that the American investigators have simply included as "expressing no preference" those whom Schofield would have classified as preferring "genital opposition."

Two Roommates

The story of Bob and Danny, who have been living together for about nine months, is a good example of the varied (and sometimes nonpreferred) sexual roles homosexuals will utilize in order to achieve different kinds of sexual and nonsexual goals. Bob is 26 years old. He first began engaging in homosexual behavior when he was in college, at the age of 20. He had had substantial heterosexual experience and considered himself a heterosexual, but he was willing to go along with homosexual behavior for reasons which he did not entirely understand. He was willing to do anything in bed in order to please his partner. But he didn't particularly like any form of sexual activity in any special sense. He said that he liked a close relationship with another man, especially an older one, and he was willing to go to bed with him in order to get this kind of relationship. He had a number of affairs with older men, and then he became a male prostitute. By the time he was 22, after he had been hustling for about a year, he realized that he actually liked having fellatio performed on him and he definitely enjoyed the experience of having another man's mouth on his penis. His hustling has continued off and on until the present time. During all this time he has engaged in considerable heterosexual experience and it would appear that in a strictly sexual sense his interest has always been more directed toward women than toward men. However, for psychological reasons, he has had great difficulty in his relationships with women. He is more emotionally comfortable with men, so that he has been continually attracted into homosexual practices, until the point was reached at which he actually began to enjoy them. He really only enjoys the insertor role and prefers being fellated, although if his partner enjoys being screwed, he can work up a certain amount of enthusiasm for this activity as well.

Danny is one of those individuals who always knew what he liked. He began having homosexual experiences at the age of 24. He is now 28. For about ten years prior to his first homosexual experience he had the fantasy, which was especially clear during masturbation, that he wanted to be screwed by another man and he has always adhered to this desire. He found that the practice of this activity was at least as satisfying as the fantasy and he has made no secret of his preference to all his sexual partners. When he and Bob have sex together, which is about once every two weeks, there is no question about what they are going to do in bed. They do not engage in very many preliminaries.

It should be added that by no means do these two men limit their sexual relationships to each other. Bob is still having heterosexual relations and Danny has numerous other homosexual partners. Danny is quite willing to do other things in bed besides taking the receptor role in anal intercourse, but it is clear what his real preference is. As a matter of fact, he feels that he has become more interested in this kind of activity and less interested in any other type in the four years since he has been out. It should probably be added here that Bob has had a great deal of difficulty in coming to terms with the self-concept of himself as homosexual, a problem which we will want to discuss at some length later on in the book. Danny has not really shown much conscious guilt about his homosexual interests, nor has he let considerations of prudence interfere with his very vigorous search for sexual partners. He has been known to engage in his favorite form of sexual activity in public places, especially parks. It remains to be asked, however, why Danny waited a full ten years after he knew he was gay and knew what he wanted sexually before he engaged in his first homosexual experience. And while this is a question that cannot definitely be answered, it is our opinion that he has in fact been struggling with some of the same kinds of problems on an unconscious level that Bob has been struggling with consciously. Just why he was finally able to throw off what he described as "hesitancy" in approaching other men and develop instead what psychiatrists might call a counterphobic attitude toward homosexuality, i.e., an overreaction to his previous shyness, is not at all clear. This is, however, a not uncommon thing to find in the biographies of male homosexuals, for quite a considerable number of them have waited a very long time before they engaged in their first sexual act.

Also, for a remarkable number of individuals, including many people who have gone into professions concerned with the study of human behavior, and who are both bright and sensitive, a number of years have elapsed between puberty and the time when they began to become *aware* of their homosexual interests. Although Danny was aware of his homosexual feelings practically since puberty, other individuals who have shown the same overt pattern of behavior, that is, who have not engaged in their first homosexual act until they were well into their 20s, have gone those ten years without ever realizing that they had any interest in other men. A lot of them simply did not feel that they had any interest in girls, but they were never able to feel an active sexual interest in their male schoolmates, nor were they able to define themselves in any way as sexually deviant.

The Female Homosexual | *Lynn Lilliston*

Female homosexuals feel they are members of two underprivileged groups.

"The lesbian minority in America, which may run as high as 10 million women, is probably the least understood of all minorities and the most downtrodden," two young women wrote in a church publication.

"She has two strikes on her from the start: She is a woman and she is a homosexual, a minority scorned by the vast majority of the people in our country."

In keeping with the revolutionary spirit of the times, female homosexuals are beginning to organize and speak out against forms of repression they believe are directed at them. They would like to see the removal of employment restrictions for homosexuals and they would like to see laws against sex acts between consenting adults taken off the books.

"Lesbians Are People"

They have a sort of "lesbians are people" campaign going: They would like to be accepted as members of a community rather than regarded with the fastidious horror that often greets them, and they would like to see an end to the discussion of whether they are "sick."

"I'm not sick; I feel fine," declared a young lesbian secretary.

The disagreements begin at the beginning. Many female homosexuals, for instance, dislike being called lesbians.

"I am not a citizen of Lesbos, therefore I am not a Lesbian," another girl said. (The island of Lesbos in the Aegean Sea, since renamed, was the legendary home of the poetess Sappho, who supposedly had a female lover named Bilitis.)

Many others, however, find the term acceptable.

A female homosexual is generally understood to be a woman whose romantic or erotic preference is the same sex, although she may never express it physically. She is not to be confused with a female transsexual, a woman who feels she is a man trapped in a woman's body. These are the women who sometimes seek sex-changing operations.

Lesbians are anatomically normal women and they come in all shapes

From Lynn Lilliston, "A Minority with New Visibility," *Los Angeles Times,* June 21, 1970.

and sizes, all degrees of prettiness or ugliness, just as do heterosexuals or "straight" women. The stereotype of a female homosexual as a tough, masculine, aggressive person is just that—a stereotype. There are as many femmes, as feminine lesbians are sometimes called, as there are butches, a term for mannish types.

A lesbian population places exactly the same importance on sex as a heterosexual population, studies have shown. In other words, some settle into long-term relationships, while others are promiscuous and conduct restless searches for new partners.

Explaining why she would not change her sex preference if she could, a female homosexual said, "Women are more gentle and just plain nicer. Also, it takes another woman to fully understand a woman's sexual needs."

Medical science does not know whether homosexuals are born or formed by experience; although most of the research has been in the area of environment or earliest upbringing, some students believe biology or genetics may some day provide a key.

Even as society in general has stopped calling homosexuality a sin and now calls it a sickness, the scientific community is asking whether it is even the latter.

Dr. Evelyn G. Hooker of UCLA and two colleagues reported: "Some homosexuals, like some heterosexuals, are ill; some homosexuals, like some heterosexuals, are preoccupied with sex as a way of life. But probably for a majority of adults, their sexual orientation constitutes only one component of a much more complicated life-style."

According to one way of thinking, "Psychiatrists who say homosexuals are sick only see sick homosexuals."

A woman psychiatrist said that she does not consider homosexuality an out-and-out sickness. But it may be a way of life dictated by a certain kind of pathology (related to disease), she said.

A male psychiatrist declined to answer the question. "There are too many layers of definition involved," he said.

Rita Laporte of San Francisco, president of the Daughters of Bilitis, a national organization of lesbians, said, "There are lesbians who swallow the sickness theory just as there are many heterosexual women who believe in the inferiority of the female."

Miss Laporte, who makes frequent speeches in an effort to secure better understanding for lesbians, added:

> Five to 10 million lesbians daily pass as "just women" in our society, functioning efficiently in the labor force at all levels open to women, studying seriously in colleges and graduate schools (including Harvard), or raising their children.

> The psychologists must write all of us lesbians off as sick, or where would their theories be? If being a first-rate teacher, for instance, and living happily with another gainfully employed woman is sick, well, that's psychology.

Positive Attitude

The Rev. Edward Hansen of Chollas View United Methodist Church in San Diego, who has opened his meeting rooms to the San Diego chapter of Daughters of Bilitis, said he believes

> it is quite evident that homosexuals—male or female—may relate to each other out of a deep feeling of love. The relationship may be positive and constructive.
>
> There is a need for more understanding and acceptance. A homosexual person ought to be able to fulfill all the potentials of his or her life.
>
> If it is a sickness, it is only one by definition. I don't happen to believe that it is. They can be just as healthy as a heterosexual can, and they are not sick in terms of their ability to contribute to society.

Laws against sexual practices between consenting adults are still on the books in many states, including California, despite occasional efforts to have them stricken. The California Bar Association and the American Civil Liberties Union are two organizations which have supported reform.

Illinois became the first state, almost ten years ago, to remove the penalty for homosexual relations between consenting adults in private. Connecticut will follow suit with a law which goes into effect in 1971.

A panel of experts assembled by the National Institute of Mental Health in 1969 asserted, "The extreme opprobrium that our society has attached to homosexual behavior, by way of criminal statutes and restrictive employment practices, has done more harm than good and goes beyond what is necessary for the maintenance of public order and human decency."

Bitter Amusement

Great Britain struck its old homosexual law several years ago. Lesbians in America take a rather bitter amusement at the fact that women were never mentioned in the old English law because Queen Victoria did not believe that females were capable of such a thing.

Why does society in general feel so threatened by the subject of homosexuality?

Dr. Hooker's belief is that "some people have a fear of homosexuality which some psychiatrists attribute to latent homosexuality. Also, there is a general fear of departure from known standards. And there's the unwillingness to grant other individuals the right to live as they see fit."

Apparently many people associate homosexuality with child molesta-tion, but the record does not bear this out. Homosexuals are no more likely to be sex criminals than heterosexuals, and women homosexuals are far less likely to be arrested than males. One ACLU study showed that women (of all persuasions) were involved in 11 percent of felony arrests overall, but only 2 percent of sexual offenses, and most of those concerned prostitution and pandering.

"Sexual offenses by women against either male or female children are practically nonexistent," the Sex Information and Education Council of the United States reported. The study continued, "The man who is sexually interested in children is rarely a homosexual with well-developed interests in adult males and he seldom is a member of the 'gay' community."

"I am sure that many people connect homosexuality with child molesta-tion, but it is a false connection," Mr. Hansen said. "The homosexuals I know would not condone it any more than the heterosexuals I know."

According to an article in the UCLA *Law Review,* "Lesbians are de-scribed by the police as less aggressive and promiscuous than males; they do not constantly seek new partners and contacts.

". . . Female activity is much less conspicuous than that of males and less likely to offend the public. Thus, there are a minimal number of complaints concerning female activity."

Many employers remain nervous about hiring homosexuals, and lesbians are not exempt from sudden firings. An officer of the Daughters of Bilitis was sacked recently from her office job because she invited a fellow worker to attend a meeting of the Bilitis organization.

She was reinstated after her union and minister appealed in her behalf.

Many female homosexuals consulted for this series of articles said they were reluctant to give their names only because they were afraid to do so for fear of losing their jobs.

Homosexual organizations are trying to build an atmosphere in which these fears can be dissipated. They also want homosexuals to stop auto-matically accepting society's verdict.

According to the *Ladder,* the Daughters of Bilitis magazine, "The tradi-tional anonymity of the majority of homosexuals, their tendency to assess themselves in society's terms and almost masochistic acceptance of preju-dice against them" will be challenged from now on.

Homosexuals agree that accepting themselves often is the hardest battle.

"I knew I was different when I was 10 or 11," a clerk said. "Eventually you learn to accept yourself but it is hard because your parents have told you how terrible these queers are." Apparently typically, she said she would not change her sex orientation if she could.

A boy told a Gay Liberation Front meeting at a Southland university:

"I grew up feeling like a freak in New York. Until I came out here I had no idea there were this many people my age who were homosexuals."

(There are no figures on female homosexuality. The Kinsey report estimated that 2 percent of the adult female population might practice it at some time. Sex researchers Masters and Johnson are just beginning a study of the subject.)

If it is hard for a homosexual to accept himself, it is equally hard for parents. A mother who regularly attends Metropolitan Community Church, a homosexually oriented church, says, "They welcomed me with open arms. They said they had been treated as if they were diseased. They often tell me, 'I wish my mother were like you.'"

This woman—call her Mrs. Rose—has a grown son whose homosexuality emerged when he was 14.

"I have heard of some homosexuals being kicked out of the house when their parents found out, but what's a mother for?" she asked. "There are a lot of things worse than homosexuality, for instance having a child turn out to be a criminal.

"I do not think it is a sickness, although some are sick."

Mrs. Rose often is called to the church to consult with another parent.

"A lady last night was upset because she said she'd never have any grandchildren by her son. I told her just to think about how lucky she is that her daughter has children." (Mrs. Rose also has grandchildren by her daughters.)

Mrs. Rose said she has been to two marriage ceremonies at the church uniting homosexuals (but without benefit of a county license—the county refuses to grant such licenses, despite a large increase in requests).

"It's a beautiful ceremony, and they say, 'Do you take this spouse' rather than husband or wife," Mrs. Rose added. "I think the church and Rev. Troy (the Rev. Troy Perry, pastor) are going to do a lot of good."

Equally a part of the homosexual scene in Los Angeles—and perhaps performing a similar function—are the gay bars. They fall into four categories, generally: bars strictly for lesbians, with male visitors of any kind discouraged; bars for homosexual men only; bars for homosexuals of both sexes, and "open" bars where straight visitors may be charged inflated prices for the extra titillation of watching the gay life in action.

One popular hangout in North Hollywood is operated by Del Pace, a former nurse who came here from New York City. Miss Pace considers her establishment open, although the clientele is mostly female homosexual, but it is open because she hopes it will foster understanding.

It looks like any other neighborhood bar in a less than affluent area: a sign over the mirror jokes "Now Showing," other signs invite, "We Serve Hot Sandwiches," or warn "Please Don't Ask for Credit." There's an illuminated forest waterfall, courtesy of Coors, a jukebox, a pool table, television set, potato chips for sale, and free pretzels in a dish.

The gossip ebbs and flows around the bar:

> ". . . she's an interesting person until she has one drink and then she loses her cool."
> "You know how she pulls out her cigar and waits for you to light it?"
> "Hey, you must be having your femme day (as a long-haired girl dances a solo)."
> "It's my fall," she replies.

Only one house rule is much different from comparable straight bars: The ladies' room is off-limits except to one customer at a time.

"It might cause a fight if somebody's girlfriend went in there with another girl," Miss Pace explained. "This is an open bar, open to the public," she said,

> although it does happen to have 90 percent female homosexuals coming to it. It is like a club, a home away from home, and a kid can come here and spend the evening even if all she has is a dollar.
> I feel the place serves the same purpose in the community as a club. The police are aware of us and we have a good rapport with them.
> I think there's a lot of discussion of homosexuality going on now, and it's healthy. All we ask is the same consideration you would give any neighbor.
> Not all homosexuals are good; they are just everyday people.

Miss Pace said she had consulted professional help, but not because she wanted to change her sex life. "I've been to psychologists and psychiatrists in an effort to understand myself. My big hangup was that I had to live behind a facade, had to live in a world that said 'wrong' and called me 'bad.' So I went, and it was a good experience."

She is cooperating with a group of college students who are doing a study on homosexuality, but she thinks the questions are silly:

When were you first aware?
Did you feel guilty?

"I liked girls when I was three years old," Miss Pace said, making a mock confession. "I liked boys, too."

The Affair | *Morton Hunt*

To date there is still only one major source of sound statistical information on extramarital sexual activity in the United States—the first and second volumes written by Alfred Kinsey and his associates, of the Institute for Sex Research at Indiana University. Despite the limitations of Kinsey's methodology and sampling procedures—his sample, critics have said, is overweighted with the too-willing; it is more a group of the self-selected than the randomly selected—these reports do say how many men and women in a very large, more-or-less national, sample have ever experienced sexual relations outside their marriage. In brief the findings are these: In each five-year age group of married men, somewhere around a third (27 percent to 37 percent) had at least some—that is, at least one—extramarital experience, while the cumulative figure—the total percentage of men who had extramarital experience at any time during their married lives—was a good deal larger. As the authors wrote, in their celebrated estimate, "On the basis of these active data, and allowing for the cover-up that has been involved, it is probably safe to suggest that about half of all the married males have intercourse with women other than their wives, at some time while they are married." For women, in each five-year age group between the ages of 26 and 50, somewhere between one in six and one in ten had at least some extramarital experience; the cumulative incidence was calculated at about one in four, although it is possible, according to the authors, that the true figures might be still higher due to cover-up.

These are the best, and almost the only credible, figures available. But since *Sexual Behavior in the Human Male* was published in 1948 and *Sexual Behavior in the Human Female* in 1953, I returned to the same source to ask what the figures might be today. Dr. Paul Gebhard, successor to Kinsey and present director of the Institute, said that he and his staff, on the basis of their recent work and their general impressions, feel there has been a continuation of previous trends. To quote Dr. Gebhard:

> If I were to make an educated guess as to the cumulative incidence figures for 1968, they'd be about 60 percent for males and 35 to 40 percent for females. This is change, but not revolution. The idea that there has been a sexual revolution in the past decade or two comes from the fact that we have so rapidly become permissive about what you can say and print. That isn't the same as actual change in behav-

From Morton Hunt, *The Affair* (Cleveland: World, 1969), pp. 10–17.

ior; still, all this talk *is* going to change the overt behavior of the next generation.

But how much it will do so, and whether men, women, and marriage will prosper or suffer from the changes, is not scientifically predictable; perhaps, though, we will feel entitled to make some reasonable guesses about the future after we have looked at the present more closely.

The ambiguity of the term "extramarital affair" is part of the general American ambivalence toward such relationships. Despite the immense change in what it is permissible to say and to print, the United States still has a dominant sexual code which disapproves of premarital sex and condemns common-law marriage, illegitimacy, abortion, sexual variations and deviations of most sorts, and, of course, adultery. We hear a great deal today about those growing minorities that openly flaunt the code—the undergraduates who openly sleep together and even room together, the show-business celebrities who freely speak of their love affairs, the homosexuals who publicly indicate their bent through clothing, speech, and the companions they are seen with. What is much more significant, there continues to exist a vast underground of good middle-class citizens who overtly accept the code but in fact secretly disagree with, and violate, one or more parts of it.

In *The Significant Americans,* a study of the sexual mores of upper-middle-class people, sociologist John F. Cuber and his co-author, Peggy B. Harroff, term the traditional code a "colossal unreality" based on "collective pretense" and on the systematic misrepresentation, by most people, of what they think and do sexually. They are not alone in this finding: Virginia Satir, a leading family therapist and co-founder of the Esalen Institute at Big Sur, told the 1967 convention of the American Psychological Association that "almost any study of sexual practices of married people done today reports that many marital partners do not live completely monogamously. . . . The myth is monogamy. The fact is frequently polygamy."

There are widespread indications of this schism between code and reality. Christian and particularly Calvinist tradition continues to make adultery a punishable offense in the criminal codes of 45 of the 50 states; maximum penalties range from a $10 fine in Maryland to a five-year jail term, plus substantial fines, in Maine, Vermont, South Dakota, and Oklahoma— yet these laws are almost never enforced except when, as very rarely happens, some aggrieved third party introduces a complaint on which the state must act. Prior to 1967 the only ground for divorce in New York was adultery, and accordingly the State granted some 7,000 to 8,000 divorces annually on this ground (the law has since been liberalized), but even though all the defendants were shown in divorce court to have done something that constituted a criminal act, the county district attorneys prosecuted none of them. Legislators, however, continue to reflect the hypocrisy of their constituents: During New York's penal code revision of 1965, it was proposed that the unenforced and outmoded criminal statute against adultery be removed, but the legislators rejected the suggestion by a three-to-one vote. Even in Illinois, a state which has modernized some of its sex statutes, adultery continues to be a crime if "open and notorious"; in other words, it is criminal if made public knowledge, but noncriminal if kept quiet.

Whatever disapproval most Americans exhibit toward infidelity, their fascination with it is evidenced by the ubiquitousness of the subject in movies, television, novels, and drama; significantly, in these media it is often presented as an exciting and beautiful experience, and even in the movies is no longer required invariably to end in disaster. A story like Elia Kazan's *The Arrangement,* in which adulterous lovers eventually find happiness together in marriage, might have pleased the bohemians and radicals of thirty or forty years ago, but could hardly have been a national best-seller. Yet when the kind of people who read and enjoy this novel today are asked to state how they feel about adultery—even by professional pollsters guaranteeing them anonymity—they tend to give lip service to the traditional code. Are they deliberately lying? Probably not; more likely, they are of two minds about it all, and can find justifications or excuses for it in some cases (including their own, if they have been unfaithful), while condemning it on principle.

A large majority of the respondents to my own questionnaire said they always or usually disapprove of adultery; those who had had affairs themselves were somewhat more tolerant, although even in this group over half were generally disapproving. Other and larger attitude surveys have shown the same thing. As recently as 1958, sociologist Harold Christensen reported that only 6 to 12 percent of a sample of midwestern college students thought adultery ever justifiable for men; the figures may have grown in the past eleven years, but not much, if we may judge by other sex-attitude surveys. A national poll conducted for *McCall's* magazine in 1966 showed somewhat larger percentages tolerant of adultery where home life was miserable, the marriage sexless, and the like, but a large majority still condemned it under almost all circumstances. Half of all the *McCall's* respondents, in fact, said they had *never* felt any sympathy with, or tendency to condone, the extramarital affairs even of friends or acquaintances. Where then, we must ask ourselves, do all those avid movie-goers and TV-watchers, never tired of infidelity as a theme, come from? One can only suppose that what people say they feel about the matter, or even what they think they feel, is only part of what they actually feel.

The most common American attitude toward extramarital affairs is somewhat like the American attitude toward paying one's income tax: Many people cheat—some a little, some a lot; most who don't would like to, but are afraid; neither the actual nor the would-be cheaters admit the truth or defend their views except to a few confidants; and practically all of them teach their children the accepted traditional code though they neither believe in it themselves nor expect that their children will do so when they have grown up.

This is what the disjunction between code and reality looks like, when one penetrates the facade:

—On a Saturday night, in a meagerly furnished apartment in a large Southern city, a young man and woman sit in stony silence watching television. They had been separated and now are attempting a reconciliation, largely because they have a one-year-old son; it is not going well, however, and despite the effort to live with him again, she is still secretly seeing a man she had had a relationship with during the separation and avoiding her husband's sexual advances whenever possible. Toward midnight they go to bed; he makes a feeble try, she pleads weariness, and he turns his back on her in anger and eventually falls asleep without another word. She lies awake, watching the hands of the luminous clock on the night table. At about 1:30 A.M. a car drives up and stops almost under their window; she recognizes the sound, and swiftly slips out of bed, throws on a coat, and hurries downstairs. The man at the wheel drives off to Lovers' Lane, where the two of them feverishly make love in the cramped back seat. At 4 A.M. she slides herself back between the sheets of the bed, sleeps until the clock goes off at 7:30, and then rises, dresses, and makes breakfast. At 9:30 A.M. she is sitting in front of a classroom full of eight-year-old children at the Methodist church, and beginning the lesson on the meaning of communion.

—In a well-to-do suburb of Philadelphia, a slender, somewhat over-dressed and over-coiffed woman of thirty-eight speaks of some new facts she has learned about life since her separation from her husband:

> You could ask all these married couples around here and they'd lie in their teeth denying that anything happens except for a little fooling around at parties. But I learned the truth when my husband and I broke up. The first couple of months, about ten of my friends' husbands called me with one excuse or another—some didn't even bother with an excuse—and wanted to take me to dinner, or openly told me what they were after. It shook me up—I didn't know what to believe in any more. Since then, I've noticed things I never used to notice—I've seen Frank's car parked at the Marriott Motel in the afternoon, and Joe Goodbody's car a half block from Lynn's house one night when Lynn's husband was on an out-of-town trip. God! Sometimes I

feel so bitter and cynical. I lived in the middle of this for years and never knew what was going on; it was all a lie around me.

—A salesman who represents several small manufacturers tells how he began his infidelities at thirty, after nine years of happy marriage:

It never occurred to me to fool around; I didn't know any different, and none of my friends in our town were doing anything, as far as I knew. Then I started in for myself as a freelance sales representative in New York, and I saw for the first time how things really were. Everybody was screwing anything they could, whenever they had the chance. People I was doing business with would come to town and expect me to fix them up, or they'd want me to go cruising the bars with them and help them find something. I learned about human nature; I saw it the way you don't see it until you're behind the scenes. And it seemed like everybody was having fun and not getting hurt. So I was *ready*. One night I was having a drink with one of the out-of-town manufacturers I represented, and he sent a note over to two girls in the far corner, and first thing you know we were with them, and it was great fun. Later, I took mine home in a cab and put an arm around her, and the next thing I knew I was making it with her three or four times a week, and really living it up. It was tremendous. I never wanted any of that originally—all I wanted was to be a small-town boy and love my wife.

—In Washington, D.C., a forty-four-year-old woman sums up the effects of the dozen affairs she has had during her very happy marriage to a man she has never thought of leaving, and who is unaware of her way of life:

When I compare my life to the lives of women I know who haven't had affairs, I feel I'm happier than most of them and my marriage is better than most of theirs. Not that I would ever dare admit it, or urge anyone else to do the same thing. Besides, to tell you the truth, I don't even approve of affairs, on the whole. I feel that most people can't handle them and still have a good solid marriage. But I can, and I don't regret a single one.

—A late-night disc jockey on a southwestern radio station, plump, boyish, and thirty-seven:

One day my wife told me she was going to have dinner and spend the night with some friends who live forty miles away; the maid would sleep in and take care of the kids. So I went to see this girl I was making it with, and because my wife wasn't home and I didn't have to get back any special time that night, I forgot to wake up until early the next morning. When I did, I thought, "Oh God, if Deirdre gets home first, she'll see that I haven't been there and the fat will be in the fire." So even though this eager girl is lying next to me naked and waiting, I'm dialing the phone, sweating and trembling and praying I reach Deirdre at her friends' house before she starts home. But when

I get the number at last, her friends sound puzzled and say she isn't there and hasn't been, and they hadn't been expecting her.

So then I knew. I'd wondered for weeks whether she might not be having an affair with my best friend, and now I knew. I left that naked girl right where she was, and threw on my clothes and rushed out to beat Deirdre home and establish my own innocence while confronting her with her lies and her cheating. I was boiling with rage. I drove home like a maniac and she wasn't there, so I mussed up the bed, talked to the maid and the kids for a minute, and then cleared out. In the afternoon she called me at the studio and I told her not to tell me any lies because I knew she hadn't been where she was supposed to have been; I sounded like a hellfire-and-brimstone preacher when I said it. She was quiet for a while and then just said, "I guess there's nothing to say," and hung up. Before dark, she and the kids had moved to her parents' house; I came home to an empty house that night and walked around looking at everything and seeing my whole life in ruins. She had been cheating on me with one of my closest friends and didn't even want to be forgiven! That night I woke up with what felt like an immense stone crushing my chest and I grabbed the phone; half an hour later I was in the hospital under an oxygen tent. The attack kept me flat on my back for three weeks. By the time I got out, she had seen a divorce lawyer—she didn't want to come back and didn't give a damn what I thought or felt about it. She actually married that bastard after a while.

It may well be that within a generation or so, the schism between code and reality will greatly narrow and the ambivalence felt by so many Americans about the matter will diminish. The theoretical liberalism of one generation is often absorbed into the feelings of the next one, and what had been permissible only in thought becomes so in action. Yet revolutions, sexual as well as political, change the outward appearance and structure of things more quickly than they do the deeply internalized emotions and habits that constitute much of the stuff of each culture. Fifty years of socialism in Russia have transformed the economy and the power structure of that nation, but most Western observers find the Russians still rather puritanical, submissive, dogged, and given to alternating between moodiness and gaiety. Similarly, the so-called sexual revolution in America will produce certain outward changes—particularly in the direction of greater tolerance of whatever other people do—but much smaller changes in how most people feel about their own behavior; the ambivalence is deep-seated in our character. Significantly, the considerable increase in premarital sexual freedom has not radically altered the basically monogamous nature of the male-female relationship: Young men and women today expect and require fidelity of each other in their premarital love affairs, and infidelity among them remains, by and large, concealed and guilt-producing. Although it does seem likely that there will be some increase in the incidence and openness of extramarital activity in the next few decades, most Americans will probably continue to keep their unfaithful longings and acts secret, and to profess personal allegiance to the ideal of fidelity.

Mate Swapping: The Family That Swings Together Clings Together

Duane Denfeld and Michael Gordon

In the early decades of this century, and to a certain extent still today, social scientists equated deviant behavior with disease and set about to find the cures. The tone of this early perspective is nicely illustrated by the following excerpt:

> The study of social pathology is undertaken not to breed pessimism but to furnish a rational ground for faith in the future of the world. The diseases of society, like the diseases of the human body, are to be studied so that remedies may be found for them where they exist, but most of all, that by a larger wisdom the number of diseases may be reduced to the lowest terms and we may set ourselves to social tasks with the ideal of conquering them altogether.

So firm a commitment to the extirpation of "social pathology" obviously precluded consideration of any contributions its phenomena might make to the social order.

More recently there has been a reappraisal of the role of deviant behavior in society. Albert Cohen, for one, has admonished his colleagues for equating deviance with social disorganization, and other sociologists have begun to focus their attention on deviance as a societal process rather than as a social disease. Howard Becker, a leading proponent of this new position, has argued:

> We ought not to view it [deviant behavior] as something special, as depraved or in some magical way better than other kinds of behavior. We ought to see it simply as a kind of behavior some disapprove of and others value, studying the processes by which either or both perspectives are built up and maintained.

From Duane Denfeld and Michael Gordon, "The Sociology of Mate Swapping: The Family That Swings Together Clings Together," *Journal of Sex Research,* May 1970 (Vol. 7, no. 2), pp. 85–99. References cited in the original have been deleted.

Perhaps of greater significance for the viewpoint of this paper are the opinions of the students of deviance who claim that deviance may support, not undermine, social order; among the most eloquent of these is Kai Erikson:

> . . . Deviant behavior is not a simple kind of leakage which occurs when the machinery of society is in poor working order, but may be, in controlled quantities, an important condition for preserving the stability of social life. Deviant forms of behavior, by marking the outer edges of group life, give the inner structure its special character and thus supply the framework within which the people of the group develop an orderly sense of their own cultural identity.

We shall maintain that only from the perspectives found in the writings of Becker, Erikson, and their associates can the social scientist understand mate swapping and the role it plays in American society.

In this country there has been a tradition of great ideological commitment to the importance of confining sexual behavior in general, but sexual intercourse in particular, to the sanctity of the marital bed. Concomitantly there has also been a rich history of institutionalized nonmarital sex. One of the foremost historians of colonial family life has noted that "the cases of premarital fornication [in colonial New England] by husband and wife were evidently numerous." Further, prostitution never appears to have been completely absent from these shores. However, it was not until the second half of the nineteenth century that sexual morality and prostitution especially became a national concern. David Pivar, in his history of the Social Purity Movement in the United States, claims that

> during the nineteenth century many social evils existed, but *the* Social Evil was prostitution.
>
> Prostitution, its development and spread, constituted the primary element in the moral crisis that shook Western civilization in the latter decades of the nineteenth century. A premonition that traditional morality was failing permeated the fabric of American life, and reformers increasingly expressed alarm over a general decay in morality. Religionists and moralists found decay manifestly evident in official life, but most strikingly in the man-woman relationship.

Attention to the destructive effects of prostitution did not cease with the coming of the new century, or even with the moral revolutions supposedly wrought by World War I; in a very much milder form it is present still.

Nevertheless, in 1937 Kingsley Davis published a paper that was to cause many social scientists, at least, to reappraise this great "Social Evil." He advanced what has since come to be known as the "safety-valve" model of deviance, developing with great insight and much cogency the idea that

> . . . the attempt of society to control sexual expression, to tie it to so-
> cial requirements, especially the attempt to tie it to the durable relation
> of marriage and the rearing of children, or to attach men to a celibate
> order, or to base sexual expression on love, creates the opportunity for
> prostitution. It is analogous to the black market, which is the illegal
> but inevitable response to an attempt to fully control the economy.
> The craving for sexual variety, for perverse satisfaction, for novel and
> provocative surroundings, for ready and cheap release, for intercourse
> free from entangling cares and civilized pretense—all can be demand-
> ed from the women whose interest lies solely in price.

A further point implicit in Davis' argument is that since the prostitute by "virtue" of her profession is, for the most part, excluded from the ranks of potential spouses, the risk of romantic involvement which may threaten a man's marriage is greatly reduced.

Let us stop at this point to look more closely at the underlying assumption of this "safety-valve" model of deviance: a society may provide certain institutionalized outlets for forms of behavior which are condemned by the prevailing legal and/or moral system. This is not to say that in every society all deviants will find some structured way of satisfying their proclivities with minimal danger of running afoul of the law. A good case in point here would be pedophilia. With the virtual disappearance of child brothels, the pedophile must, if he wishes to gratify his need, engage in acts which almost certainly will result in a confrontation with the police; in contrast is the man who frequents houses of prostitution for some unusual form of sexual activity. Therefore, the "safety-valve" model does not assume that *all* forms of deviant behavior will be provided with outlets; but rather that *some* of those forms for which "frustration and discontent may lead to an attack on the rules themselves and on the social institutions they support" will be provided with outlets. So, then, in the case of prostitution (or any other form of deviance), the "safety-valve" model does not explain why it exists, but why it is tolerated: presumably it is supportive of monogamous marriage. It should be emphasized that this idea is best thought of as an hypothesis, not as a law. Interestingly enough, one of the few other convincing applications of the "safety-valve" model also applies to sexual behavior.

Ned Polsky recently applied Davis' ideas concerning prostitution to pornography, and claimed that the latter was a functional alternative to the former:

> In saying that prostitution and pornography are, at least in modern
> societies, functional alternatives, I mean that they are different roads
> to the same desired social ends. Both provide for the discharge of
> what the society labels antisocial sex, i.e., impersonal, nonmarital sex:

prostitution provides this via real intercourse with a real sex object, and pornography provides it via masturbatory, imagined intercourse with a fantasy object.

He places particular emphasis on a point which Davis mentions but does not elaborate, *viz.*, that prostitution and pornography cater to a considerable amount of what, in the parlance of the prostitute, is known as "kinky" sex—oral, anal, masochistic, fetishistic, etc. To this extent pornography, more than prostitution, provides a safety valve for those sexual inclinations for which no institutionalized behavioral outlets exist, e.g., pedophilia, which we have already mentioned.

In both the Davis and Polsky papers the focus is almost exclusively, if not exclusively, on *male* nonmarital sex. Males prostituting themselves for females has never been common, perhaps merely because, apart from their economic positions, males are constitutionally less suited for frequent and prolonged intercourse. Drawing largely on the Kinsey studies, Polsky argues that pornography is largely produced for, and consumed by, males. Kinsey found that relatively few women are aroused by pornography, and even fewer use it as grist for the masturbatory fantasy mill. While no reliable systematic data are available, there is some indication that at least one form of pornography, the "stag" film, is migrating from the fraternity house and VFW lodges—though not abandoning them altogether—to the suburban home, i.e., it is now being viewed by heterosexual audiences. A replication now of the section of the Kinsey study dealing with female response to pornography might yield some surprising results.

If, in fact, pornography is now becoming more of a heterosexual item—and we must emphasize again that this is by no means documented—it provides support for the main argument of this paper: mate swapping (we will use the terms "mate swapping" and "swinging" synonymously) is an outgrowth of the dramatic changes that have taken place in this century in the position of women in American society and, more crucially, changes that have taken place in the conceptions of female sexuality and female sexual rights. While the contention that women are now seeing and enjoying pornography more than was so previously cannot be proved, there is no lack of documentation for the larger changes noted above. Evidence can be found both in the realm of sexual ideology and behavior.

One of the most vivid indicators of the degree to which American women have come into their own sexually since 1900 is the marriage manual. Michael Gordon has recently completed an extensive study of American marital education literature for the period 1830 to 1940. Perhaps the most striking finding to emerge from his work is that the transformation in the prevailing conception of female sexuality, and marital sex in general, took place in the first four decades of this century. The following passage is based on the Gordon article.

Throughout most of the nineteenth century the commonly held attitude toward sexual intercourse was that it was, unhappily, required for the perpetuation of the species. Not only was it an unfortunate necessity, but also a dangerous one at that. Frequent indulgence by the male in the pleasures of the flesh could lead to an enervating loss of the "vital fluids" contained in the sperm; for the female it could result in nervous and constitutional disorders. In short, sex was a seriously debilitating business. As the century drew to a close we begin to get rumblings of acceptance of marital sex as something which, apart from its procreative function, was beneficial to the marriage, but such views are very much in the minority even in the 1890s.

With the first decade of the twentieth century, however, and reaching—if the reader will pardon the expression—its climax in the 1930s, there is a growing belief not only in the fact that women experience sexual desire (which in its own way is held to be as strong as that of men), but also that this desire should be satisfied, most appropriately in intercourse resulting in simultaneous orgasm. What we observe in these decades, then, is sex moving, ideologically, from an act whose prime purpose is procreation to one whose prime purpose is recreation, a shift which has been commented on by others. Because this development has been extensively documented in the article by Gordon, there is no need to explore it further. Let it suffice to say that by 1930 the concern with marital sex, its "artistry" and technique, has reached such proportions as to allow characterization of the authors of marriage manuals of the time as proponents of a "cult of mutual orgasm."

The increasing acceptance of the pleasures of marital sex seems to have had an impact on a number of areas relevant to the theme of this paper; possibly the most important of these is prostitution. To the best of our knowledge there are no data available which support the contention that since 1900 prostitution has been a declining profession. However, it has been claimed that there has been a reduction in the number of brothels in American cities; furthermore, there is good evidence on which to base the opinion that premarital intercourse with prostitutes is declining:

> The frequencies of premarital sexual relations with prostitutes are more or less constantly lower in the younger generations of all educational levels. . . . In most cases the average frequencies of intercourse with prostitutes are down to two-thirds or even one-half of what they were in the generation that was most active 22 years ago.

This, it could be reasoned, may well be related to a finding reported in the second Kinsey volume:

> Among the females in the sample who were born before 1900, less than half as many had had premarital coitus as among the females born in any subsequent decade. . . . For instance, among those who

were still unmarried by age twenty-five, 14 percent of the older generation had had coitus, and 36 percent of those born in the next decade. This increase in the incidence of premarital coitus, and the similar increase in the incidence of premarital petting, constitute the greatest changes which we have found between the patterns of sexual behavior in the older and younger generations of American females.

It should be noted, by way of qualification, that Kinsey also found that most women who did have premarital intercourse had it exclusively with the men they eventually married. These two phenomena—the decreasing amount of premarital contact with prostitutes for males and the increasing amount of premarital sex for women—give credence to our argument that the acceptance of female sexuality and the pleasures of marital sex has grown in this century. It is unusual now to find a man saying he has intercourse with prostitutes because his idealized wife-mother image of his spouse prevents him from carrying out the act with her. Furthermore, there are also attitudinal data on the breakdown of the double standard in this country.

It is implicit in our thesis that shifts in attitudes toward female sexuality, premarital sex, and, especially, marital sex, which we have been discussing, are crucial to the understanding of mate swapping as an institutionalized form of extramarital sex. Another factor which has undoubtedly also made a contribution to the development of mate swapping, or at least has facilitated its growth, is the revolution in contraceptive techniques that has occurred in the past decade. A study done in 1960, based on a national probability sample, found the following order of frequency for contraceptive techniques: condom, 50 percent; diaphragm, 38 percent; rhythm, 35 percent; douche, 24 percent; withdrawal, 17 percent; and others in small percentages. (The total exceeds 100 percent because many couples used more than one method.) Similar studies are yet to be made for the last years of the 1960s, but some comparative data are available. Tietze estimated that as of mid-1967 there were 6½ million women in this country on the pill, and somewhere between one and two million using the IUD. A recent Gallup poll estimated that 8½ million American women were on the pill *(Newsweek,* February 9, 1970). Figures such as these allow us to estimate that about 10 percent of the fecund American women take the pill and another 1 percent use the IUD.

The emergence of chemical and intrauterine birth-control methods is of significance on several counts. One, they are considerably more reliable than the previously available techniques, and thus, one would assume, dramatically reduce anxiety over unwanted pregnancy. Two, and the importance of this cannot be minimized, they separate the act of prevention from the act of sex. While the new methods insure against pregnancy resulting from failure to take contraceptive measures in the heat of spontaneous passion, they also improve what could be termed the aesthetics of sex, i.e., there need be no hasty retreat to insert a diaphram or roll on a "safe" (to use an antiquated but charming term). All in all, then, the new contraceptives allow sex to be indulged in with less apprehension and more pleasure.

We shall now try to summarize and more explicitly state the argument contained in what we have written up to this point. The current conception of female sexuality as legitimate and gratifying, coupled with enlarged opportunities for women to pursue sex without unwanted pregnancies, is likely to have greatly increased the incentive for women to seek—as men have always done—sexual variety outside marriage. Among the available ways for both husbands *and* wives to find such variety, mate swapping is the least threatening and the one most compatible with monogamy.

Of the alternatives to mate swapping, the one which comes to mind immediately is what might be called "bilateral prostitution" (a term suggested to us by Albert Cohen). We have already pointed out that constitutionally males seem less suited than females for prostitution, although there may be some homosexual hustlers who can turn "tricks" at a surprising rate, but nothing that compares with that of their female counterparts. There are, however, economic problems associated with bilateral prostitution. It might place a greater drain on the family's financial resources than swinging, and, more significantly, create conflict over budgeting for the extramarital sexual expression of the husband and wife, i.e., how is the decision on allotment of funds to be made? Perhaps of greater concern is that it would separate the husband and wife for recreation at a time when a great deal of emphasis is placed on "familistic" activity, especially of the recreational variety, e.g., couples play bridge together, bowl together, boat together, and so on. That is to say, bilateral prostitution would enlarge their private worlds at the expense of their common world.

Given such considerations, the advantages of mate swapping as a solution to the problem of marital sexual monotony become obvious, though in all fairness we must note that many of the points we are going to make cannot be fully appreciated until the reader has completed our description of mate swapping himself. To begin with, the cost is probably less than that of bilateral prostitution, and is much more easily integrated into the normal recreational or entertainment budget. Second, it keeps the couple together, or at least in the same house. But further, it is an activity which involves common planning and preparation, and provides subject matter for conversation before and after; thus it could further consolidate the marriage. Finally, the sexual activity that takes place is, to a greater or lesser extent, under the surveillance of each; this means that each exercises control over the extramarital activity of the other, and the danger that the sexual relationship will become a romantic relationship is minimized. This, of course, is also facilitated by the brief and segmented nature of the relationship.

In summary, then, for the couple committed to the marital relationship and for whom it still performs important functions for which no other relationship exists, mate swapping may relieve sexual monotony without undermining the marriage.

The Study of Swinging

Swinging, or mate swapping, has been a subject that sells "adult reading" paperbacks, but few social scientists have analyzed it. Fortunately, there are a handful of serious studies of the swinging scene. This is not to maintain that we know all we need to know; the analyses available must be viewed as tentative. The findings of the research are problematic because designs have not been employed which allow generalization. Furthermore, some crucial aspects of the phenomenon have been neglected, e.g., what are the characteristics of those who drop out of swinging? We say this not by way of criticism of the research of our colleagues; they are pioneering in an area that involves great technical as well as ethical problems. Our statements are merely intended to qualify what we have to say in the rest of the paper.

Despite the problems cited above, there are studies, some of which are included in this issue, which provide excellent descriptive data based on participant observation and interviewing. We will use these ground-breaking papers to test the model presented earlier. It is hoped that the important contributions of Symonds, Bartell, the Smiths, and the Breedloves will encourage further research in this area. Before evaluating our model it is necessary to specify the term "swinging," to discuss the emergence and extent of swinging, and the swingers themselves.

Swinging

One definition of "swinging" is "having sexual relations (as a couple) with at least one other individual." Another definition, and more appropriate for our purposes, is that "swinging" is a husband and wife's "willingness to swap sexual partners with a couple with whom they are not acquainted and/or to go a swinging party and be willing for both he and his mate to have sexual intercourse with strangers." The latter definition directs our attention to swinging as a husband-wife activity. The accepted term among mate-sharing couples is "swinging"; the term "wife swapping" is objectionable, as it implies sexual inequality, i.e., that wives are the property of husbands.

Swingers, according to Symonds, are not of one mold; she distinguishes "recreational" from "utopian" swingers. The recreational swinger is someone "who uses swinging as a form of recreation"; he does not want to change the social order or to fight the Establishment. He is, in Merton's typology of deviance, an "aberrant." The recreational swinger violates norms but accepts them as legitimate. The utopian swinger is "nonconformist," publicizing his opposition to societal norms.

> He also tries to change them. He is generally acknowledged by the general society to be doing this for a cause rather than for personal gain.

Swinging, for the utopian, is part of a new life style that emphasizes communal living. The proportion of utopians within the swinging scene has not been determined. Symonds feels that their number is small. She found the utopians more interesting

> because of their more deviant and encompassing view concerning the life that they desire to live if it ever becomes possible. In some respects, they fall close to the philosophy of some hippies in that they would like to retreat from the society at large and live in a community of their own kind.

In societal terms, the recreational swinger is a defender of the status quo; the utopian swinger is one who wants to build a new order.

We are most interested in the recreational swingers, because their deviation is limited to the sharing of partners; in other areas they adhere to societal norms. Couples who engage in recreational swinging say they do so in order to support or improve their marriage. They favor monogamy and want to maintain it.

The Swinger

The swingers who advertise and attend swinging parties do not conform to the stereotypical image of the deviant. They have higher levels of education than the general population; 80 percent of one study attended college, 50 percent were graduates, and 12 percent were still students. They are disproportionately found in professional and white-collar occupations. They tend to be conservative and very straight.

> They do not represent a high order of deviance. In fact, this is the single area of deviation from the norms of contemporary society. The

mores, the fears, that plague our generation are evidenced as strongly in swingers as in any random sampling from suburbia.

Every study we looked at emphasized the overall normality, conventionality, and respectability of recreational swingers.

Extent of Swinging

The number of couples engaged in swinging can at best be roughly estimated. The Breedloves developed, on the basis of their research, an estimate of eight million couples. Their figure was based on a sample of 407 couples. They found that less than 4 percent of them placed or replied to advertisements in swinging publications, and in the year prior to publication (1962-1963) of their study, "almost 70,000 couples either replied to, or placed, ads as swinging couples." With this figure as a base they arrived at their estimate of the number of couples who have at one time or another sexually exchanged partners. They further concluded that, conservatively, 2½ million couples exchange partners on a somewhat *regular* basis (three or more times a year).

Getting Together

The "swap" or swingers club is an institutionalized route to other swingers, but it is not the only method of locating potential partners. Bartell suggests four ways: (1) swingers' bars, (2) personal reference, (3) personal recruitment, and (4) advertisement. The last method deserves special attention.

Advertisements are placed in underground papers and more frequently in swingers' magazines. The swingers' publications, it has been claimed, emerged following an article in *MR.* magazine in 1956.

> Everett Meyers, the editor of *MR.*, later claimed that it was this article which touched off a flood of similar articles on wife-swapping, or mate-swapping. In any event, *MR.* followed up its original article with a regular monthly correspondence column filled with alleged letters from readers reporting their own mate-swapping accounts.

Publications began to appear with advertisements from "modern marrieds" or swingers who wished to meet other swingers. *La Plume,* established about 1955, has boasted in print that it was the first swingers' magazine. A recent issue of *Select,* probably the largest swingers' publication, had 3,500 advertisements, over 40 percent from married couples. *Select* and *Kindred Spirits* co-sponsored "Super Bash '70'" on April 11, 1970. It was advertised to be "the BIGGEST SWINGDING yet," and featured dancing, buffet dinner, go-go girls, and a luxurious intimate ballroom. Clubs such as Select, Kindred Spirits, Mixers, and Swingers Life have moved beyond the swingers' party to hayrides and vacation trips.

> There are at least a couple of hundred organizations like Select throughout the country. Many of them are very small, some with only a few members, and many of them are fly-by-night rackets run by schlock guys less interested in providing a service than in making a quick buck. Most, however, are legitimate and, as such, very successful. They have been a major factor influencing the acceleration of the swapping scene.

Our review of the swinging club and magazine market located approximately fifty nationally sold publications. The "couple of hundred" figure reported above may include some lonely hearts, nudist directories, homosexual, and transvestite organizations, some of which serve the same purpose as swingers' publications. They bring together persons with the same sociosexual interests.

A person's first attendance at a swingers' party can be a difficult situation. He must learn the ideologies, rationalizations, and rules of swinging. These rules place swinging in a context that enables it to support the institution of the family. We turn to these rules in the next section.

Rules of the Game

Our model views swinging as a strategy to revitalize marriage, to bolster a sagging partnership. This strategy can be seen in the following findings of the empirical research. Evidence to support the model is divided into four parts: (1) the perception of limitation of sex to the marital bond, (2) paternity, (3) discretion, and (4) marital supportive rules.

1. *"Consensual adultery": the perception that sex is limited to the marital bond.* Swingers have developed rules that serve to define the sexual relationship of marriage as one of love, of emotion. Some of the Smiths' respondents would answer "no" to questions pertaining to "extramarital sexual experience," but would answer "yes" to questions pertaining to "mate-sharing or comarital relations." Sharing, for the swingers, means that the marriage partners are not "cheating." Swingers believe that the damaging aspect in extramarital sex is the lying and cheating, and if this is removed extramarital sex is beneficial to the marital bond. In other words, "those who swing together stay together." Swingers establish rules such as not allowing one of a couple to attend a group meeting without the other. Unmarried couples are kept out of some groups, because they "have less regard for the marital responsibilities." Guests who fail to conform to rules are asked "to leave a party when their behavior is not appropriate."

For one group of recreational swingers, it is important that there be no telephone contact with the opposite sex between functions. Another group of recreational swingers always has telephone contact with people they swing with, although they have no sexual contact between functions.

2. *Swinging and children.* "Recreational swingers are occasionally known to drop out of swinging, at least temporarily, while the wife gets pregnant." By not swinging, the couple can be assured that the husband is the father of the child; unknown or other parentage is considered taboo. This reflects a traditional, middle-class view about the conception and rearing of children.

Swinging couples consider themselves to be sexually avant-garde, but many retain their puritan attitudes with respect to sex socialization. They hide from their children their swinging publications. Swingers lock their children's bedrooms during parties or send them to relatives.

3. *Discretion.* A common word in the swingers' vocabulary is discretion. Swingers desire to keep their sexual play a secret from their non-swinging or "square" friends. They want to protect their position in the community, and an effort is made to limit participation to couples of similar status or "respectability."

> Parties in suburbia include evenly numbered couples only. In the area of our research, singles, male or female, are discriminated against. Blacks are universally excluded. If the party is a closed party, there are rules, very definitely established and generally reinforced by the organizer as well as other swingers . . . Stag films are generally not shown. Music is low key fox trot, not infrequently Glenn Miller, and lighting is definitely not psychedelic. Usually nothing more than a few red or blue lightbulbs. Marijuana and speed are not permitted.

The swinging suburban party differs, then, from the conventional cocktail party only in that it revolves around the sexual exchange of mates.

4. *Swingers' rules.* We suggest that the above rules on sex and paternity are strategies to make swinging an adjunct to marriage rather than an alternative. Another set of rules or strategies that is relevant is that dealing with jealousy. Swingers recognize the potentially disruptive consequences of jealousy, and are surprisingly successful in minimizing it. The Smiths found that only 34 percent of the females and 27 percent of the males reported feelings of jealousy. Some of the controls on jealousy are: (1) that the marriage commands paramount loyalty, (2) that there is physical but not emotional interest in other partners, (3) that single persons are avoided, and (4) that there be no concealment of sexual activities. The sharing couples

> reassure one another on this score by means of verbal statements and by actively demonstrating in large ways and small that the marriage still does command their paramount loyalty. Willingness to forego an

attractive swinging opportunity because the spouse or lover is uninterested or opposed is one example of such a demonstration.

Developing a set of rules to control potential jealousies demonstrates the swingers' commitment to marriage.

Conclusion

In this paper we have attempted to account for a new form of extra-marital sexual behavior in terms of a sociological model of deviance. We have contended that swinging may support rather than disrupt monogamous marriage as it exists in this society. A review of the volumes of the *Reader's Guide to Periodical Literature* and *The New York Times Index* failed to reveal any articles dealing with this phenomenon in the United States. This would suggest that swinging has not as yet been defined as a social problem in the traditional sense of the word. Thus swinging, like prostitution, despite its violation of the social and, in many cases, legal norms, is permitted a degree of tolerance which would appear to demonstrate the appropriateness of our model.

Finally, it should be said that we make no pretense to having touched upon all the changes that have played a role in the emergence of swinging. Restrictions of space prevented our looking at the larger societal trends that may have been at work here, e.g., feminism, the changing occupational position of women, suburbanization, and so on. Nevertheless, we do feel that we have delineated those issues which are most directly related to it. The validity of our model will be tested by time.

Chapter 11

Experimental/Utopian
Forms of the Family

The Soviet Experiment | *Kent Geiger*

The equalitarian reformist zeal of the early years must not be under-estimated. After all, the traditional form of the parent-child tie was considered unsatisfactory by the bolsheviks not only because parents were apt to be conservative or reactionary toward the new regime, but also because it epitomized the old moral system—based on blood ties and sympathy for relatives. Hence, just as in capitalist society, this tie bred further inequality by virtue of the differential capacities of parents to give their children education and a suitable general upbringing. But the epicenter of communist equalitarian aspirations was in the relation between the sexes. After the abolition of private property ownership, the assumption of family functions by the state, and the engagement of all women in social production, a situation was to arise in which "marriage will no longer have the appearance of a family as its obligatory consequence." The author of this phrase went so far as to allege that the separation of the kitchen from marriage is "a more significant historical event than the separation of church from state." In fact, as we have seen, there was not a little sentiment in favor of residential separation of husband from wife. As one radical young woman wrote in an "open letter," "It is precisely a separate life [of husband and wife] which creates full 'equality of rights' for both parties, guarantees spiritual growth, liberates the woman."

Many were in disagreement with this, but all were willing to vote for the desirability of economic independence for women. In countless pamphlets, posters, and speeches, Russian women were urged to enter the factory and

From Kent Geiger, *The Family in Soviet Russia* (Cambridge, Mass.: Harvard Univ. Press, 1968), pp. 55–60. References cited in the original have been deleted.

office. Since this goal could obviously be achieved only gradually, it soon became clear that an additional measure was needed: motherhood deserved special economic support. As Kollontai, the most enthusiastic proponent of independence for women, had written even before the Revolution, only with "all around security of motherhood" could marriage be cleansed of that "bourgeois scum," that calculated self-interest which had nothing in common with love. A later writer, with a fine flair for phrasing, carried on the Kollontai tradition by referring to the need of a "social correction factor for the biological inequality of the sexes."

In addition to its programs, proclamations, and exhortations, the new regime did actually take some important legal measures. It repudiated the conservative, patriarchal Church, decreeing that henceforth only civil marriages were to be legal. It granted substantial freedom of marriage and divorce to all except near relatives. Mutual consent was the main requirement for marriage, and for divorce the desire of either of the spouses was deemed sufficient cause. The new freedoms were taken with sufficient seriousness by enough people so that in a few years the divorce rate began to rise, and the complaint could be made that the courts were "buried under alimony cases." Actually, even the party itself played a role in the trend, since from time to time members were encouraged to look closely after the political education of their wives and to divorce those who were hopeless laggards.

In addition, full equality of legal and political rights was accorded to women in the marriage relationship. Alongside those securing freedom of choice in marriage and divorce, several provisions attracted considerable attention at the time because of their symbolic importance, especially those providing that the wife "need not follow the husband" in case of change of residence and concerning the surname to be taken by the woman after marriage. The former is best interpreted as an expression of resentment against an explicit provision of tsarist law which did require the wife to follow the husband if he should for any reason change his residence; it was easy for communist thinkers to see this as intentional and unjust interference with the right of the wife to pursue an occupational career independently, and hence as constituting the real underpinning of inequality. The article on surnames gave three possible choices: husband's, wife's, or joint surnames. For some reason, in the first code of laws on marriage and family, permission was not given to allow each party to retain his or her premarital name. This lack aroused some criticism at the time and was suitably amended in 1926.

Once women had also been accorded full rights to vote, to participate in public associations and activities, and, of course, to enter into occupational life, or social production, on a basis of full equality with men, the problem was then seen as one of persuading women to seize their new opportunities. A special section of the party, the Women's Section (*Zhenotdel*), occupied itself mainly with the task of drawing women into broader public activities. However, no special rights were accorded at this time to women for those "biological infirmities," pregnancy and childbirth.

In addition to such positive measures as these, the fight was carried on against "survivals of the old regime." The chief targets relevant to sex equality were the Church, the Islamic tradition with institutions perpetuating the inferior status of women such as the bride price, and those basic attitudes of the population, especially among the peasantry, which were so strongly linked to the old patriarchal mores. The prevailing communist attitude toward sexual jealousy was particularly revealing. It was seen as an extension of the private property spirit: "Nowadays it is one of the worst crimes to kill a woman for jealousy, because we are trying to free our women, not regard them as the property of man any more. If a man kills his wife or lover out of jealousy, he is given the maximum penalty—ten years—and in Central Asia he is shot."

But good marxists regarded such details as minor, for their central verbal commitment was to the development of facilities which would accord *de facto* release from kitchen and children. Virtually every public utterance on family and women from the time of the Revolution forward was to be permeated with this thought. Unfortunately, with the exception of the period known as War Communism, when ration cards were issued on the basis of employment, the drift of women into social production was very slow. It was no secret that for many there were no opportunities. During the New Economic Policy (NEP) period, and in glaring contradiction with the goal and intention of the party, unemployment was widespread, and those women who could find work often faced the unsolved question of providing for children and maintaining the household.

In spite of repeated assertions of the intention to establish communal kitchens, dining halls, laundries, and a network of children's homes and crèches, it was hard to accomplish much. The extensive communal institutions of War Communism could not be continued for financial reasons, and owners and managers of private enterprise during the NEP period were reluctant to invest in such uneconomic ventures as crèches and public restaurants. In the press, side by side with the stated intention of doing better, there were constant complaints about the insignificant extent of communal feeding. For example, the party's leading publicist on such affairs, Emelian M. Iaroslavski, counted "public dinners" served on November 1, 1925: 20,000 in Moscow, 50,000 in Leningrad, and 67,000 in the provinces, a total of 137,000. At the same time he noted that only three out of 100 children were coming to the crèches. All the rest were being reared entirely by individual families. With the end of the NEP period further efforts were made in the direction of socializing the family's functions, but as resources and personnel were committed to the "harder" part of the Five Year Plan, the claim of establishing crèches and public dining rooms began to sound more and more hollow.

This problem concerned quality as well as quantity. In the early communal facilities the food was bad and poorly served, often in crude, unpleasant surroundings. The children's crèches were dirty and understaffed and, as one writer put it, "the public laundries tear and steal more than they wash." Reactions were understandably negative, and the tendency of some of the party theorists to identify the institutions of War Communism as a first step toward the achievement of the idealized classless society could hardly have been more ill conceived. All in all, it was a poor beginning, and the population was skeptical about such communal activities for years afterward.

Apparently there was little improvement in later years. Various expert estimates and surveys established in the early 1930s that few in the population were interested in communal housing, and that Russian women did not care about communal dining halls and were avoiding the crèches, while the "better-placed workers" who ate in the public dining halls were glad to return to their family dining tables as soon as rationing was abolished (in 1935).

Within the family nobody could be certain whether women were becoming more nearly equal, but many opinions were expressed. Some pointed to greater sex equality in everyday life as an accomplished achievement of the Revolution. More writers stressed the slowness of change in everyday living and complained about the continued presence of prostitution, "calculation in marriage," and the fact that "men remain superior and continue to exploit the women." An especially bitter pill was the discovery of a new social type, the party member who was reactionary in domestic life. One woman wrote to the newspaper about her husband, an important activist, who had forbidden her to work or engage in political activity:

> And in those very meetings which he forbids me to attend because he is afraid I will become a real person—what he needs is a cook and mistress wife—in those very meetings where I have to slip in secretly, he makes thunderous speeches about the role of women in the revolution, calls women to a more active role.

A widely recommended proposal for correction of the "temporary" inability of the state to take over the family's functions was that men share women's household work. In 1920 Lenin, in commiseration with the much pitied housewife of marxist theory, had complained to Zetkin:

> So few men—even among the proletariat—realize how much effort and trouble they could save women, even quite do away with, if they

were to lend a hand in "woman's work." But no, that is contrary to the "right and dignity of a man."

A few years later E. O. Preobrazhenski, noting that there was as yet no socialist child rearing available, called for an "elementary equality" between man and woman in discharging this responsibility, asserting that in no case should the burden lie fully upon the woman. In later years others carried on the theme: Lunacharski wrote that he would shake the hand of a comrade—an "honest Leninist"—who would rock the baby's cradle so his wife could go out to a meeting or to study. And Krupskaia, lamenting in 1928 that the rationalization of daily life was still not complete, urged that all members of the family share the housework. She was glad to report that: "The new is already starting to break into the pattern of daily life; even now one sees a grown worker take a child out for a walk, a husband help a wife at home." One suspects, however, that the Soviet husbandly masses were as a rule little inclined to take over duties that in other bolshevik speeches were described as trivial and properly social rather than familial functions. Possibly the problem is best epitomized by the experience with the new freedom about surnames. As of 1928 nine-tenths of the women marrying were still taking the name of the husband, and cases in which the man would take the wife's name could "be counted absent."

Probably closer to reality was the view held by some that the first decade or two of Soviet history saw a worsening rather than an improvement in the status of Soviet women. The great mass of women, illiterate and submissive, were little interested in their new freedoms and equality. Legal rights were often completely unappreciated. Peasant women, for example, rarely sought alimony in the event of divorce. In urban families the right to work, if it existed in the form of a concrete opportunity, was more often seen as a financial necessity than as a new freedom.

Without replacing child rearing, food purchase and preparation, and the like by the family, the Revolution simply brought an additional burden to women. They remained tied to the family and home and often, in addition, had to work in a factory or office. Studies made in these years showed that women were on a day-to-day basis generally busier than men. Since they could spend less time in public or political work, study, and even sleep, they were less able to develop themselves and become the equals of their husbands. Trotsky wrote in 1937:

> One of the very dramatic chapters of the great book of the Soviets, will be the tale of the disintegration and breaking up of these Soviet families where the husband as a party member, trade unionist, military commander or administrator, grew and developed and acquired new tastes in life, and the wife, crushed by the family, remained on the old level. The road of the two generations of the Soviet bureaucracy is sown thick with the tragedies of wives rejected and left behind.

All in all, it was the men who profited most surely and immediately by the new freedoms intended to bring equality to women. The women who remained tied to the family often seemed more liable to exploitation after the Revolution than they were before. Perhaps the most spectacular, if relatively rare, variety of male who exploited the situation was the crafty peasant who married a peasant girl in the spring to get himself an extra harvest hand and divorced her in the fall to save the expense of feeding her over the winter. Much more common was sexual exploitation.

Oneida: An Early American Commune

William M. Kephart

Origins

The story begins in Putney, Vermont, in 1831, where a religious revival was in process. One of the converts was John Humphrey Noyes, a twenty-year-old graduate of Dartmouth College, who had been serving his apprenticeship in a local law office. Warfield states that "the great revival of 1831 seems fairly to have rushed him off his feet. He took his conversion hard, yielding with difficulty; but when he yielded he yielded altogether." Forsaking the practice of law, Noyes entered the ministry and, upon graduation from Yale Theological Seminary in 1833, he was licensed to preach.

Although he was an avid reader of the Bible, and held to what he termed a literal translation, Noyes could not bring himself to accept the orthodox religious teachings of his day. Rejecting the Calvinistic interpretation of the Bible, and opposing the "miserable sinner" philosophy, John Humphrey Noyes preached that man was not depraved but was capable of living a sinless life. Basing his belief on certain scriptural passages, Noyes was convinced that Christ, whose second coming was awaited by so many, *had already returned to earth,* so that redemption or liberation from sin was an accomplished fact. The Kingdom of God was here on earth, and not only was it unnecessary for man alternately to "sin and repent," but once having accepted Christ, man could live as a sinless being. The doctrine itself—the attainability of the sinless or perfect state—Noyes called

From William M. Kephart, "The Oneida Community," in *The Family, Society, and the Individual,* 2nd ed. (Boston: Houghton Mifflin, 1966), pp. 166–178. References cited in the original have been deleted.

"Perfectionism," and for the spreading of this alleged heresy, his license to preach was revoked.

A small group had already begun to be attracted to the Perfectionist doctrine, however, in spite of its heterodox nature. Starting as a Bible class in 1839 with Noyes as the pivotal member, this small group of Perfectionists grew both in number and in scope. Their discussions centered on the idea of spiritual equality, a belief which eventually came to embrace both the economic and sexual spheres. In the Kingdom of God, all beings were to love one another equally. The accepted monogamous pattern of one man being married to one woman was looked upon by the Perfectionists as a sign of selfishness.

In 1846 their ideas were put into practice, and the Putney Community was formed. Individual members followed a "share the wealth" type of economy in which private ownership was taboo. Paralleling their collectivist economy, adult members practiced sexual communism; that is, every adult male has marital privileges with every adult female, and vice versa. As Noyes explained it to outsiders, the Putneyites were simply following the example set by members of the Primitive Church between the time of Christ's ascension and his second appearance, which occurred in the year 70 A.D. Thus, the radical practice of *complex marriage* had its real beginning in New England—an area that had once been the heart of Puritanism!

As the Putney Community grew, Noyes kept busy spreading the Perfectionist gospel elsewhere, through both the printed and the spoken word. In many quarters he was looked upon as a fanatic and a heretic, and rumors soon spread concerning the "sexual promiscuity" of the Putneyites. There were, nevertheless, some converts to Noyes's brand of Perfectionism. As might be imagined, the citizens of Vermont were literally up in arms, and in 1847 Noyes was arrested and charged with adultery.

Released under bond, he did not wait to stand trial but fled southward. Had he chosen to fight the case in court, the outcome would doubtless have been of sociohistorical interest. As it turned out, neither Noyes nor any of his Perfectionist followers were ever to stand trial for their marital practices. They were much better off, in this respect, than the Mormons, whose legal involvements ultimately led to their abandonment of polygyny.

Even as the Putney Community was being broken up, however, Noyes was reassembling his flock in central New York State. The new Community took shape in 1848 on the old Indian lands along Oneida Creek, and henceforth the Perfectionists were known as the Oneida Community. It was here that the most revolutionary of all American marriage systems took root and, for several decades, flourished.

Starting again as a small group—no more than twenty or thirty persons in all—the Oneida Colony was barely able to survive the first few winters.

The original members were primarily farmers and mechanics, and while their collectivist economy had certain advantages, they found it difficult to support a growing community solely from their land yields. Fortunately, one of their members, Sewell Newhouse, invented a steel trap, which turned out to be the best of its kind in America. Demand for the product grew, and soon the major part of the Oneida economy came to be based on the manufacture of the now-famous traps. Thereafter, the group was without financial worry.

As the membership increased, three basic principles of Noyes's teaching combined to become the very heart of Perfectionist philosophy: (*a*) economic communism, (*b*) mutual criticism, and (*c*) complex marriage. Although there were other facets to the Oneida brand of Perfectionism, it was these three principles which served more or less as the trademark of the Colony.

Economic Communism

Members of the Oneida Community held equal ownership of all property, their avowed aim being to eliminate competition for the posssesion of material things. Needs of individual members were taken care of, but there was simply no concept of private ownership, even in the realm of personal belongings such as clothes, trinkets, and children's toys. Writing of his boyhood, Pierrepont Noyes, a son of John Humphrey, states that:

> Throughout my childhood the private ownership of anything seemed to me a crude artificiality to which an unenlightened Outside still clung. . . . For instance, we were keen for our favorite sleds, but it never occurred, to me at least, that I could possess a sled to the exclusion of the other boys. So it was with all Children's House property.

With respect to clothing, the same author writes that " 'going-away clothes' for grown folks, as for children, were common property. Any man or woman preparing for a trip . . . was fitted out with one of the suits kept in stock for that purpose."

In addition to the manufacture of traps, the Oneidans found a ready market for their crops, which they put up in glass jars and cans, and which became known for their uniform quality. The Community also engaged in silk-spinning on a large scale, and in 1877 they began the manufacture of silverware. The latter venture proved so profitable that when the Community disbanded, the silverware component was perpetuated as a joint-stock company (Oneida Ltd.), whose product is still widely used today.

How much the economic success of the group was due to its communistic methods and how much was due to fortuitous circumstances (e.g., Sewell Newhouse's invention) is difficult to say. On the one hand, collectivist methods probably had certain advantages over competing private enterprise. In tracing the economic history of the Oneida Community, for example, Edmonds notes that "to meet the deadline on an order, the whole Community—including the children—turned out."

On the other hand, the fact remains that the Perfectionists were fast becoming bankrupt until Newhouse's trap, figuratively and literally, "caught on." Pierrepont Noyes states that:

> By 1860 the Newhouse trap had become the standard of the United States and Canada. Professional trappers would accept no other brand, and for nearly seventy years all the steel traps used by the Hudson's Bay Company were made at Oneida. Later, Community traps caught sable and ermine in Russia, rabbits in Australia, and nutria along the rivers Parana and Uruguay. Thus an industrious community became, by force of circumstances, an industrial community.

It is problematical whether the subsequent Oneida industries—including that of silverware—would ever have developed had it not been for the financial windfall brought about by Sewell Newhouse's timely invention. The economic health of the Colony has been mentioned here somewhat in detail since most of the other sixty-odd communistic experiments then under way in America became defunct either partly or largely because of economic difficulties.

Insofar as possible, the various jobs within the Oneida Community were rotated from year to year in order to eliminate feelings of discrimination. Members were quick to point out that at one time or another almost everyone took his turn at the necessary menial tasks. Nevertheless, while the jobs were generally rotated, individual variations in ability were recognized, and men were not placed in positions beyond their innate capacities. At the same time, social differentiation by occupational status was played down. If a man did his work well, he presumably had equal status whether he was a farm laborer or a plant superintendent. It was work rather than a specific type of job which was held in high regard, and from all accounts the system worked rather well. Seldes maintains that

> There was never any trouble with idlers, and Noyes' chief difficulty was to keep people from attaching themselves to Oneida. Few members were admitted, the period of probation was long, the terms intentionally made harsh.

As a further effort in promoting equality, all Community members ate the same food, wore the same kind of clothing, and, quite literally, lived in the same home. For both sexes, dress was uniformly simple, with jewelry tabooed. The women, incidentally, bobbed their hair and wore short, knee-length skirts with loose trousers (pantalettes) down to the shoes. In an era where women were noted for their long hair and long dresses, it is little wonder that to "outsiders" the Oneida ladies created quite a figure.

From the beginning, Noyes had planned to house the group under one roof, and by 1849 the first communal home was ready for occupancy. Over the years, however, the Community grew in size—at one time there were several hundred members—and it became necessary to build a larger home. The new building, a spacious brick residence called the Mansion House, was finished in the 1860s and still stands today, inhabited by some of the descendants of the original Community members.

Mutual Criticism

The Oneida Colony had neither laws nor law-enforcing officers, and there was little need for them, major infractions being all but unknown. In any community, however, no matter how closely knit, conduct problems are bound to occur, and while the Oneidans considered themselves, as a group, to be Perfectionists, they acknowledged that individual foibles did exist. "Mutual criticism" was the method by which such problems were handled. The system had its inception at Putney, where the original followers of Noyes would subject themselves periodically to a searching criticism by the rest of the group. At Oneida the system was perpetuated— with remarkably successful results.

Whenever a member was found to be deviating from group norms, or whenever a personality or character weakness manifested itself, a committee of peers would meet with the "offender" to discuss the matter. "The criticisms," according to Edmonds,

> were administered in a purely clinical spirit. The subject sat in complete silence while each member of the committee in turn assessed his good points as well as his bad. In cases of unusual seriousness, perhaps involving the violation of a fundamental tenet of their common philosophy, the committee would be expanded to include the entire Community.

From the accounts of the individuals who had undergone criticism, it is evident that while the experience itself was often an ordeal, the end result was that of a catharsis or spiritual cleansing. The success of the system probably hinged on the willingness of the subjects to accept the analysis, and also on the fact that though the criticisms were penetrating, they were offered in a frank, impersonal manner.

Some of those who underwent criticism issued public statements about their experiences. The following comments appeared during 1871–1872 in the *Oneida Circular,* the Community's weekly newspaper:

> I feel as though I had been washed; felt clean through the advice and criticism given. I would call the truth the soap; the critics the scrubbers; Christ's spirit the water.

> Criticism is administered in faithfulness and love without respect to persons. I look upon the criticisms I have received since I came here as the greatest blessings that have been conferred upon me.

Although the Perfectionists had their share of internal strife, as we shall see, the conflict was over policy, and had nothing to do with what would normally be regarded as deviant behavior. The harmonious living enjoyed by the group, and the virtual lack of pernicious behavior, attests to the effectiveness of mutual criticism as an instrument of social control. In fact, as the Colony grew in membership, the technique of mutual criticism came to be employed not so much with errant members but with those who volunteered for purposes of self-improvement.

Complex Marriage

The world does not remember the Oneida Community for its economic communism nor for its practice of mutual criticism, but for its system of complex marriage. Rightly or wrongly, just as the term "Mormon" signifies polygyny, so the term "Oneida" conjures up thoughts about the unique sex practices of the Colony. Noyes, himself, coined the term "free love," although he seems to have preferred the phrase "complex marriage" or, occasionally, "pantogamy." Realistically, the Oneida marital system can best be characterized as a combination of group marriage and community living.

From the Putney days, Noyes had no time for romantic love nor for monogamous marriage. Such practices were, to him, manifestations of selfishness, exclusiveness, and personal possession. Romantic love, or "special love" as it was called in the Community, was believed to give rise to jealousy and hypocrisy, and, according to Perfectionist doctrine, made spiritual love impossible to attain. Accordingly, Noyes promulgated the idea of complex marriage: since it was natural for all men to love all women and all women to love all men, it followed that every adult should consider himself married to every other adult of the opposite sex. This collective spiritual union of men and women also included the rights to sexual intercourse.

Noyes felt strongly that

> Men and women find universally that their susceptibility to love is not burnt out by one honeymoon, or satisfied by one lover. On the contrary, the secret history of the human heart will bear out the assertion that it is capable of loving any number of times and any number of persons. . . . Variety is, in the nature of things, as beautiful and as use-

ful in love as in eating and drinking. . . . We need love as much as we need food and clothing, and God knows it; and if we trust him for those things, why not for love? . . .

John Humphrey Noyes was a devout man, and the Oneida Community was a deeply religious group; and any assessment of their sexual practices must take these factors into consideration. Insofar as the records indicate, the Colony abided by the doctrine of complex marriage not for reasons of lust, as was sometimes charged, but because of the conviction that they were following God's word.

In practice, since most of the adult men and women lived in the Mansion House, sex relations were easy to arrange. There was, however, one requirement which was adhered to: a man could not have sexual intercourse with a woman unless the latter gave her consent. Procedurally, if a man desired sex relations he would make his request known to a Central Committee, who would thereupon convey his request to the woman in question. The actual go-between was usually an older female member of the Committee.

The system was inaugurated, as Parker points out, in order that

> women members might, without embarrassment or restraint, decline proposals that did not appeal to them. No member should be obliged to receive . . . at any time, under any circumstances, the attention of those they had not learned to love. . . . Every woman was to be free to refuse any, or every, man's attention.

If the Central Committee granted approval, and if the woman in question assented, then, Carmer states, "the man presented himself at the woman's door at bedtime and spent an hour or two in her room before returning to his own room for the night."

Although rumors a-plenty were carried by the outsiders, there is unfortunately no published record of the extent to which requested sexual liaisons were vetoed by the Central Committee or refused by the women themselves. That there was some rejection might be inferred from Parker's statement that

> This entire freedom of the women to accept or reject the advances of their lovers kept men as alert as during more conventional courtships. Men sought, as always, to prove themselves worthy of the favor of their sweethearts; and that made their life, they confessed, one continuous courtship.

It must be admitted, apropos of complex marriage, that many of the operational details were never revealed, and that some writers—both past and present—have taken a more cynical view toward the sex practices of the Oneidans. Webber, for example, writes as follows:

It was commonly declared that a committee of men and women received applications from those desiring certain persons; that if they considered the pairing suitable they arranged the meetings or obtained a refusal which was relayed to the applicant. . . . Thus if there was a refusal there was less embarrassment than if the proposal were made directly.

So much for the rule. One may suspect that it was honored largely, as it were, in the breach. Men and women constantly associated and were free to visit in each other's rooms. It seems unlikely that a burst of romantic feeling might be interrupted while someone trotted off to find a go-between.

Whether, in fact, the Central Committee or the go-between were frequently by-passed must remain a matter of conjecture. One should remember that the Oneidans were a devout group, and that their sexual practices were part of an overall religious system. It is difficult, therefore, for outsiders to assess the sexual motivations of individual Community members.

It is known that Oneidans were presumed to act like ladies and gentlemen at all times. Inappropriate behavior, suggestive language, overt displays of sexuality—such actions were not tolerated. As a matter of fact, sexual behavior was not openly discussed within the Community, and it is doubtful whether the subject of "Who was having relations with whom?" ever became common knowledge. One male member who became too inquisitive on this score was literally thrown out of the Community, an act which represented the only expulsion in the group's history.

Stirpiculture

Child rearing occupied a special place in the Perfectionist scheme of things. Having familiarized himself with the principles of Charles Darwin and Francis Galton, Noyes was convinced of the feasibility of applying scientific methods to the propagation of the race. He felt that the only people who should have children were those who possessed superior physical and mental abilities. Although the term "eugenics" had not yet been coined, a eugenics program in which specially chosen adults would be utilized for breeding purposes was exactly what Noyes had in mind. And, of course, what more logical group to put eugenic principles into actual practice than the Oneida Community? Noyes called his program "stirpiculture," and it was not long before the scientific world was discussing the implications of the unique experiment being conducted in central New York State.

For twenty years after its founding, the Oneidans had deliberately refrained from bearing children. They reasoned that procreation should be delayed until such time as the group had the facilities for proper child care. The first two decades, so to speak, merely served the purpose of laying the groundwork for the future growth of the Colony. The birth-control technique advocated by Noyes was *coitus reservatus;* i.e., sexual intercourse up to but not including ejaculation on the part of the male. Until they had learned the necessary coital control, younger males in the Community were required to limit their sex relations to women who had passed the menopause. Although the technique was claimed by many writers of the period to be incapable of attainment, the record apparently contradicts the claim.

In any case, by 1869 the group was ready to embark upon its pioneer eugenics program. Couples desirous of becoming parents (stirps) made formal application before a cabinet composed of key members of the Community, Noyes apparently holding the deciding vote. The cabinet, after assessing the physical and mental qualities of the applicants, proceeded either to approve or disapprove the requests.* The stirpiculture program was in effect for about a decade before the Community disbanded, and during this ten-year period 58 children were born. Noyes, himself, fathered a dozen children, so that evidently he was not averse to self-selection.

Children remained in their mothers' care up to the age of fifteen months, whereupon they were gradually transferred to a special section of the Mansion House. Henceforth they would spend most of their childhood in age-graded classes. Although the children were treated with kindness by their parents, sentimentalizing was frowned upon in the Colony, the feeling being that under Perfectionism all adults should love all children and vice versa.

By their own reports, the children were evidently well adjusted. Recreation, schooling, medical care—all were provided in keeping with accepted child-rearing practices. As a group, the children were remarkably healthy. Mortality comparisons indicated that the products of Stirpiculture had a significantly lower death rate than children born outside the Community. Interestingly enough, thirteen of the Oneida children—all in their eighties and nineties—are still living. The writer recently had the privilege of talking with several of them, and, as the following comments indicate, their childhood seems to have been a happy one:

> I was born in the old Community, and the times we used to have! I don't think kids today have the kind of fun we did. There was a ready-made play group all the time, with something always going on. There was some activity in the Big Hall almost every night—plays,

---

* The specific criteria and methods for selecting the stirps have never been revealed. It is known that a cabinet was set up to make the selection, but what system they used remains a mystery.

musical concerts, entertainment of all kinds. As children, there was always something to look forward to.

Well, I remember one little girl always wanted her mother. She'd stand outside her window and call to her, even though the mother wasn't supposed to answer. Other than that particular case, all the children seemed happy enough. Everybody was good to us. You knew you were loved because it was like a big family. Also, there were so many activities for the youngsters, so many things to do, well—believe me—we were happy children. Everybody around here will give you the same answer on that!

We were happy youngsters, and we lived in a remarkable group. Unfortunately, they broke up when I was quite young. I wish I could have lived my whole life with them. . . .

The Breakup

As was true in the case of Mormon polygymy, outside pressures against the Oneida Community were becoming irresistible. Rumblings grew louder against such practices as "free love," "incest," "lust," and "animal breeding." Although many of the surrounding townspeople knew the Perfectionists as hard-working, devout individuals, professional crusaders such as Anthony Comstock, self-appointed watchdog of American morals, were successful in creating a storm of adverse public criticism. As Ditzion points out, the Oneidans gave up their practice of complex marriage "in response to one of the greatest pressure campaigns that has been waged against any religious group in history."

Then, too, in the later years all was not well within the Community itself. John Humphrey Noyes was growing old, and in 1877 he resigned as leader. One of his sons, Dr. Theodore R. Noyes, took over the headship, but he was in no sense the leader his father was, and factionalism within the Community became rife. Some of the younger men voiced open dissatisfaction at being permitted to cohabit only with older women, and some of the mothers were reportedly dissatisfied at being separated from their children. Whereas effective leadership might have overcome or reconciled the difficulties, such leadership was nowhere to be found; in fact, for some inexplicable reason John Humphrey Noyes left the Colony in June 1879 for Canada, never to return.

A few months later, after fearlessly defying public opinion for almost half a century, Noyes sent a message to the Community proposing that they abolish complex marriage and revert to the accepted marital patterns of society. Soon afterward the group disbanded, many of the members becoming formally married. Economically, a joint-stock company was organized with the money that had been made (around $600,000), and the stock was then divided among the members. Last-ditch efforts to salvage some communal type of family organization failed, thus ending—in rather pathetic fashion—what was probably the most radical social experiment in America.

In Retrospect

Any attempt to explain either the success or the failure of the Oneida Colony must take into consideration the character of its leader, John Humphrey Noyes. By all accounts, he was an original thinker with a remarkable sense of dedication, perseverance, and courage. He had tremendous vigor, a vigor which manifested itself in the spiritual, the mental— and the physical. It can be no coincidence that his utopian community included relative freedom of sex expression. At the same time, he strove to keep the behavior of the group on a consistently high plane. The most striking comment on John Humphrey Noyes was the following, made to the writer by a woman whose mother had known the Perfectionist leader quite well:

> I've often wondered about the traits that made him what he was. I just don't know. You might have got an answer 100 years ago. Now, maybe it's too late. I remember asking my mother the same question when I was a young girl. "Why did you live that way? What was there about him?" and I remember her saying, "Don't ask me to explain it. I can't. All I know is that when you were in his presence you knew you were with someone who was not an ordinary man."

Utterly frank in the expression of his innermost thoughts, Noyes wrote a voluminous amount of material dealing with his own particular brand of Perfectionism. He believed that the power of the printed word was stronger than that of the spoken word, and he was the guiding hand for a variety of publications: *The Perfectionist, The Witness, The Spiritual Magazine, The Free Church Circular, The American Socialist, The Oneida Circular,* and so on. By the time of his death in 1886, Noyes had penned enough material to keep historians busy for generations. And while it lasted, the Community itself must objectively be described as successful. Not only were the Oneidans satisfied with their way of life, but the usual social problems—poverty, crime, alcoholism, divorce, and desertion—were virtually nonexistent.

On the other side of the ledger, Noyes was often unpredictable, a trait shared by many zealots. He not only left the group for protracted periods of time, but twice—once at Putney and once at Oneida—deserted when the end appeared imminent. During his reign as leader, moreover, he apparently made no provision for the succession of authority. Had able young men been trained as potential leaders, the factionalism which developed in later years might have been avoided.

While he inspired tremendous personal loyalty as head of the Perfectionists, Noyes permitted the group to follow the fate of other dictatorships—
which tend to founder when the helmsman becomes irreplaceable. And
although the Oneida Community seemed to work well enough while it was
in being, the inexorable fact remains that it did not last. Noyes's personal
attributes aside, the forces which held the group together and which fo-
mented group loyalty were not strong enough to make for survival. It is
true that the Colony lacked the usual social problems, and that on the surface, at least, there was a measure of group cohesion; nevertheless, the existing sentiments, values, and traditions were not sufficiently durable to
bring about an integrated, permanent type of social organization.

Perhaps, under the circumstances, it would have been rather surprising
if the Oneida Community had endured, for Noyes was attempting to create
a society *without marriage and the family* as these terms are commonly
understood. The human family seems to be based on sex attraction, male
exclusiveness, parental child rearing, and the need for primary-group association, all of which operate as powerful systematizing forces. It is quite
possible, in modern society, that some other sort of marital-sexual arrangement could be worked out, but it is difficult to conceive of an Oneida-
type endeavor as filling the bill. The wonder of it may well be that
Noyes's experiment lasted as long as it did.

A Japanese Commune

*David W. Plath and
Yoshie Sugihara*

Shinkyō, in the village of Kasama about 35 miles from Osaka, Japan,
has become widely known in recent years. For it is a communal society
that has been successful, one that has—despite enormous hostility—endured
and prospered.

Communal living—the sharing of resources, produce, and living experiences in a closely knit community—has been engaged in by many groups,
for many reasons, all over the world and throughout history. Examples
are the early Christian communities and the modern Communist collec-
tives. What makes Shinkyō so unusual is that this communal society is
nonideological and nonmissionary; in fact, its establishment was not even

From David W. Plath and Yoshie Sugihara, "A Case of Ostracism—and Its Unusual
Aftermath," *Trans-action,* January-February 1968, pp. 31–36.

premeditated. Shinkyō began for negative reasons—because its founding members were ostracized.

In village Japan, organized ostracism is called *mura-hachibu,* or "village eight-parts." According to tradition, neighborly village social interaction consists of ten parts, including the right to such near-necessities as disaster relief and the use of common land. When a family is ostracized, it will be deprived (at least in theory) of eight of these ten parts.

To have them restored, the head of the household must repent, persuade a village influential to stand as guarantor, and then make appropriate restitution. In Shinkyō, the offenders would not repent.

Shinkyō, and its success, were due in major part to the personality and work of its founder and dominant figure, Masutarō Ozaki.

The ostracism fell on four families at once, and they gave one another support; one alone would hardly have been able to stand up against its force. And they held together because of their trust, respect, and affection for Ozaki, who came to be called their *Sensei,* or revered leader.

Ozaki Sensei was born in 1900, at Kasama, the second son of a fairly prosperous farmer. Like most Kasama families, the Ozakis were ardent supporters of the Tenri church, one of the oldest and strongest of the more than 250 modern-era "new religions" of Japan. For several years, Ozaki himself served as a missionary, but then grew discouraged about Tenri's claims to healing powers—and disgusted by what he saw as the religion's milking of contributions from the poor and credulous. Eventually he refused to accept contributions for Tenri. Not long after, he destroyed the altar of his Osaka mission and persuaded four Kasama families (including his elder brother's) to do the same.

This was the official reason why Ozaki Sensei and the families were ostracized. Below the surface, however, was a covert power struggle between Ozaki and his childhood friend Iwazō Seki, then (1937) the foremost leader in Kasama. Seki reported Ozaki and the four families to the rural police—for criminal irreverence (the smashed altar) and abandoning a corpse (they had buried a man without religious rites, as directed in his will).

The police would not file charges. Thereupon the Seki faction called for *mura-hachibu.*

What happened next is best described by Mrs. Yoshie Sugihara, who joined Ozaki Sensei in the Shinkyō venture and later became his second wife. The following is translated and condensed from the fifth chapter of her book on the history of Shinkyō (Shunjusha Press, Tokyo, 1962):

> On August 10, the Seki faction, having talked with the people of the Eastern section (which included Sensei's home), assembled them in

the Mission, and summoned Sensei there. As they had planned, one after another the Seki faction roundly denounced him.

"You're a troublemaker who's disturbing the peace of the village."

"Have you managed to do anything but disrespectful work like burning up the gods?"

"Didn't you cheat an old man and hold a funeral that as much as threw away the corpse?"

"If these things are going to keep on and on we've got to consider what'll happen to the village. What in hell are you thinking of?"

In short they meant to close in on him, count up and review his "crimes" to date. They probably calculated that once he was faced by the power of the majority even the obstinate Ozaki would humble himself.

But Sensei wasn't bothered a bit. "If you mean the altar affair or that about Kunimatsu's burial," he said, "weren't they done only after everybody had talked them over and agreed to them? You talk about disrupting the village, but aren't those who go crying to the cops and secretly pull strings the real disturbers of the 'peace of the village'? They're right here among us. Do you want me to name names, or let it go at that?"

As Sensei spoke out so sharply and glared around, the gabbling assembly fell silent. Everybody had a guilty conscience. They hadn't foreseen that "Poke in the brush and the snakes come out"; they were completely flustered and didn't say another word.

Sensei said, "Well then, it's better that I hold off naming names for this meeting. I have nothing more to say, so it's best for you all to discuss it by yourselves." He hurried out, and not a single man tried to stop him.

But the gang was as persistent as could be. The next day, the 11th, a summons came for Hisajirō Yamanaka and Sei'ichi Mitani [members of the offending families]. First the gang surrounded Yamanaka and made him sit alone in the center.

"Break off with Ozaki!"

"If a good farmer like you tags along with a dangerous drifter like Ozaki," they said, "what do you think's going to happen in the future? We don't say you've done wrong, but break off with Ozaki today at this meeting and we'll see that you get a voice in village affairs." Such was their carrot-and-stick strategy. Knowing what had happened the day before with Ozaki Sensei, Yamanaka perceived the danger in the situation and was, as he put it, "scared silly." If he refused their demands here, what would come next? Considering how the gang operated, he could expect the worst.

But as Yamanaka himself told me later, "Before I thought about being hurt or helped or anything else I lost my temper at Seki and the rest of that gang, with their stinking proud attitude and their trying to force things their way; and I couldn't help what I did."

Yamanaka lifted his face and said to them, "He hasn't done a thing wrong. What he says is right. I won't leave him even if it kills me."

Next Mitani was called in and given exactly the same grilling. But Mitani also refused then and there and said firmly that he would go along with Ozaki.

"We can't put up with people who've got the mad idea that they'll stick together to the death"—this was their reason for village ostracism. Of course we didn't have any way of knowing when and how it was decided; and there was no formal announcement. Nobody, not even a relative, was permitted to speak to any member of the four families; and a stiff rule was made that anybody who spoke even once would be fined 100 yen [equal to $100 at that time].

Becoming Nonpersons

The members of the four families were treated as if they didn't exist. They were stripped of all human rights. City people can't even imagine what a painful position you're put in when you suffer village ostracism.

Hemmed in by the ostracism, the four families had to resort to any means they could find in order just to keep alive during the war. [The war with China began on July 7, 1937.]

The influence of the China war gradually reached out. Recruits began to leave.

Saying farewell to a recruit was held to be a citizen's duty; neglecting it would be the same as treason. Eventually, unable to stand it, [members of the ostracised families] slipped out to discuss the situation with Sensei in Osaka.

"Out of respect for the red sash the right thing to do is to see off the recruit. Just go ahead and join the farewell party."

At a signal from firecrackers, the recruit, his family and kin, and the villagers assemble in the grounds of the community guardian shrine. The people just pass coldly by the four families, nobody says a word.

"This . . . it's a going-away present for the soldier. Couldn't you hand it to him for us?"

With a sour face Teijirō says. "We can't accept anything like this from people who've been ousted from the village."

Recruits continued to leave one after another, but eventually we couldn't take any more of it and we quit with the eighth one.

Instead we all eagerly poured our energy into our farm work.

The Eve. In Kasama this is the greatest event of the whole year, and a day for rest and relaxation.

Almost two months had passed in ostracism by the first of November 1937, when the Eve came around. By then all contact between the four families and the villagers had been completely cut off, starting with the farewell parties and extending to weddings, death-day anniversaries, and all other celebrations.

That day at Sensei's home we pounded ricecakes and prepared a feast just like anybody else. And the following day all the members of the four families, old and young, male and female, carried the feast and the ricecakes and fled to Hirao Saime. Hirao Saime is the boundary between Kasama and a place in Uda county called Hirao. The Yamanakas have a field there. In that field the families held their festival and "relaxation."

We had brought hoes and spades and rakes along with the feast.

The innocent children had a good time eating the feast and the rice-cakes; the old folks complained and sobbed regrets about "such an Eve"; and the men gritted their teeth, said nothing, and swung their hoes. We didn't care how much fun the villagers were having. We sowed radishes. Then we clasped hands firmly and vowed to each other that we would work together with all our might. And it was this that happened to become the first step toward our communal production and communal living.

Actually, having been ostracized, their ties with the villagers broken, freed from various rights and duties, the four families couldn't avoid strengthening their own bonds, like it or not, in order to make a living. For example they helped each other weed paddy, going from one's fields to another's. From time to time relatives of the four families came to us on the sly and asked us to tell them the reason for the ostracism. But we refused to discuss it, telling them as Sensei had instructed, "If that's what you want to know, instead of asking us you'd better go ask the village big shots."

When the Eve was past we entered the November harvest season. However, in the village they were saying they would not lend the community-owned ricehuller to the four families. The four families went right out, pooled their money in equal shares, and bought a huller and a thresher.

Once they had been refused the use of the huller even though they were members of the association, the four families requested repayment of their capital shares in the farmers' cooperative. The village went into an uproar. People came to offer compromises. The mayor came, the police came, and the head of the neighborhood association came. Finally even Iwazō Seki himself came. Sensei refused bluntly, telling them: "This isn't the kind of dispute you 'compromise.' We didn't start any fight so there's no issue over which we have to come to terms. We've simply been ostracized, and we're content to accept that. Instead of coming here you should go see those poor people in the village who are following the ostracism resolution without knowing anything about it, and ask them to tell you the origins of the reason for our being ostracized."

The Seki faction wouldn't agree to make public the reason for the ostracism. So the deliberate attempts to compromise and reconcile the parties could only end in separating them again. Sensei and the four families grew all the more strong in their desire to take up communal production.

When the autumn collective harvest was done, in December the four families turned to baking charcoal. At first each family dug its own oven, cut its own wood, and made it into charcoal. We helped each other only with the baking. But efficiency was rotten this way. So from the second firing onward we collectivized thoroughly. That is, we baked everything in one oven on one hill.

Beginning the Communal Life

As the new year dawned we had a suggestion—from nobody in particular—that we build a meeting place where all of us could gather at ease. For one thing, we also could get Ozaki Sensei to live there. The site we chose was "Obatake," one of the Ozaki family's fields. It was one of those lonely edge-of-the-village places where at night the foxes and badgers come and go.

The house was not finished until November. Sensei's family and mine were already living communally in Osaka, and because of matters connected with my husband's job Sensei's wife and I decided to take turns for a while coming to the Obatake House. People gossiped about it viciously as "wife-swapping," but by that time we no longer were paying attention to what they said about us.

Once we had the Obatake House, everybody would come gather and talk things over both before going out on communal labor and again after the work was done. Not long after that we began to eat together, each of us bringing food from his home. Next we began to use the bath together.

Once we had a communal kitchen, the women and children also began to take their meals there. Eight of us already were living in the house—Sensei, his wife (or myself), his wife's parents and their two children, my child, and Ritarō's child. At meals we were joined by four Yamanakas (husband, wife, and two children); four Mitanis (same); and two Imanishis. We managed the meals by pooling our money and our own produce.

My job was to cook and to take care of clothing for the eight children. One day when I planned to wash the eight nemaki [sleeping kimono], my hand reached out and grabbed my own child's nemaki first. Once I noticed, I blinked in surprise. I'd had no bad intentions. Without thinking about it at all, sometime or another I'd gotten into the habit of doing it that way. But if somebody else were to see it, well, it would look like selfish concern for my own child. If they said I lack impartiality, what could I say? Warning myself that anything like this is absolutely out when you're working and living communally, I let go of my child's nemaki and began washing them in order from the end of the rack. Much ado about nothing, maybe, but after all we didn't have a single pattern to follow then for the communal way of life we were starting. Only after we hit against various problems in reality would we begin to catch on. We always had to remember to be on the alert for the chance that what seemed to be a trifle might turn into a major issue that could rock the whole basis of our common life. For me this was a great discovery.

Again, when I passed out the children's snacks, I was thinking to myself: "It would be good if my child got the best-looking piece." The children had no way of knowing what I had in mind; innocent beings that they are, they were just yelling for joy. I came to my senses, and once again I felt that a mother's instinct was actually repulsive and could lead to mistakes here.

All we had been thinking of was: what can we do to make communal labor more efficient and economical? and what can we do to make an effective comeback from ostracism? That was the goal of our daily struggles, though no doubt deep in everybody's heart there was a feeling all along that if we were to work communally we ought to be together as much as possible. Then we wouldn't be lonely and it would be equally convenient for all. That's why it wasn't unnatural at all that we began planning together to move and rebuild all the homes in a way that would be convenient for everybody and at the same time suitable for communal life.

As each wife set aside her field clothes and tied on a white apron, and tried her hand at cooking for a group without the meddlesome interference of a mother-in-law, she found a change, gain, and excitement that she hadn't expected. Once you tried it, it could even be fun.

As we were doing these things we definitely gave birth to what I'd call a new style of life. Slowly we had begun to change—especially the women—and to feel that we'd be far better off finding satisfaction in our daily communal life than fretting about family wealth, and so on, in a future that we couldn't count on anyway.

But surely there was no reason to expect that everything would go smoothly. I have to admit that the others could not (any more easily than I could) break away from bonds to dependents or from the instinctive selfishness you feel for kinsmen; and that there was an unseen suspiciousness and sense of competition at work among us. For example, the duty cook would bring her own child to stay with her in the kitchen, and even if she didn't go so far as to make anything special for the child she might leave her own serving untouched and give it to the child. We hadn't particularly talked about it, but it turned out that every one of us was doing the same thing. And we were jealously suspicious about the partiality that other mothers might be showing toward their children. The children themselves caught on too, and each of them began to wait impatiently for his mother to take the kitchen duty. Under these conditions communal life would not work. Ignore them and we probably would end up separating again.

At this point Sensei suggested that the children trade off and sleep with somebody else's parents. At first glance it looked like a bright idea, but in fact a child who happened to wake in the night and realize that the person sleeping next to him was not his mother but "some auntie or other" would start bawling out loud and wouldn't quit. The temporary mother-for-the-night was really in a fix. But no matter how angry it made her, when she realized that her child probably was annoying some other mother too, she just had to set aside her feelings and do something to quiet the one with her. As these experiences accumulated, the idea of playing favorite with your child disappeared of its own accord.

In the early stages the men on cattle duty were just like the women on kitchen duty. Each favored his own pet ox, giving it extra feed or being more careful about cleaning its pen. But he couldn't avoid having a guilty conscience as he did it. The men say that one day when one of them spoke out about it and they realized that they all were worried about it, they had mixed feelings of strangeness and shame.

The Sensei suggested that we sell off the four oxen in order to do away with these feelings. The four families agreed, sold the oxen and bought different ones in their place. That way the notion of which ox was whose no longer applied. For good or bad all of them had to be treated with equal care. This was how the oxen came to be our first common property.

Except for rice we brought everything under communal control, without partitions, and everybody was free to carry home as much as he needed. The need for anyone to carry food home gradually decreased as our communal cooking gradually was done on a more complete scale.

Sharing the Rice

But rice remained the exception. Since rice is the one thing you can readily change into cash it can't be pooled, we thought. Sensei said again and again: "If you all haven't the guts to go on helping each other in any and every way, then how about apologizing to the village right now and getting the ostracism removed?"

The four families said they'd die before they'd do that now anymore. "Well then," Sensei told them, "if you feel that way about apologizing to the village, a little thing like putting all your rice into one bin isn't anything at all, is it?" This took place a number of times, and in the end we eventually were able to bring rice, too, under communal control.

After that came the question of communal bathing. By farm village custom, the women would not enter the bath until all the men were finished. But it wasted time and was uneconomical on fuel, so we revised it and let anybody who was free, man or woman, use the bath. Before long the men also began to enter without embarrassment while women were in the tub, and in a very natural way we developed a practice of group bathing.

Common use of the chests and the clothing also began spontaneously. It wasn't that we had figured out how sensible it might be to rationalize our clothing habits. We merely set out with the idea that by putting things together it would be handy and there'd be no waste. For example, in the first chest we would put all the men's dress over-kimono, in the second chest the women's going-out kimono, in the third all of our everyday clothes—so it was easy to use them in common.

On New Year's Day of 1940 we moved into our new building while its walls were still only rough-plastered. We called it the Cookhouse.

The Cookhouse had four bedrooms on the second floor, and four bedrooms and two guest rooms downstairs. In addition it had a bath, washroom, pantry, kitchen, 20-by-30-foot wood-floored dining room, and a dirt-floored dining room. We even ran pipes to the kitchen, bath, and washroom. We heard that the villagers were spreading rumors that "if they could put in facilities like that, they must've gotten money from Russia."

But in fact the only reason why we had enough labor to build it was that we didn't celebrate Midsummer or New Year's, and we didn't take any days off.

And this was how from 1939 into 1940 we completed laying the main foundations for our communal life.

Ostracism as a technique of social control is not peculiar to Japan, although Japanese villages and small groups are notorious for favoring it. Well-documented cases are rare, however, and even more rare are cases in which the people ostracized proved capable of fighting back.

Shinkyō's development under Masutarō Ozaki calls up many parallels with American "backwoods utopias" of the nineteenth century, particularly with the Oneida community under John Humphrey Noyes. At the same time, its step-by-step collectivization process in the late 1930s is surprisingly similar to what was carried out in rural China in the early years of the Peoples' Republic.

In 1943 the Shinkyō people decided to move to Manchukuo. In August of 1945, the loss of the war obliged them to return to Kasama.

In the reconstruction years they took in some destitute acquaintances from Manchukuo, one of whom was skilled in making *tatami*, the rice-straw mats that carpet Japanese dwellings. Gradually Shinkyō turned from farming to tatami-manufacturing, and within a decade became one of the largest and most mechanized establishments in the country. Part of the profits have been put back into improving the plant, another part into creating a collective standard of living well above that of the ordinary Japanese villager. (For example, in 1965 eight of the founders went on a jet holiday to Taiwan and Hong Kong.) Still another part of the profits are given to various kinds of public service. Shinkyō has made massive donations for improving schools, roads, and other public facilities in Kasama—Seki is dead, and the ostracism has long been ended. For several years the Shinkyō people have regularly cared for two or three juvenile parolees, and this year they expect to open a center for the care of feeble-minded children.

Ozaki refuses to proselytize or propagandize, although the mass media frequently publicize him as a sort of peasant sage. He receives an average of three letters a day from people all over Japan wanting to join the community, but he responds to each by urging the sender to strive harder in his own situation. "People say it's utopia or Communism or a lot of other things," he said to me once. "But for us it's just the way of life we happened to develop together. If people can learn from it to get rid of some stupid old customs, well and good. But the lesson in Shinkyō is that if they really want reform, they need to start at home."

Another lesson is that *mura-hachibu* in village Japan is dying. Under postwar human-rights codes, it is illegal. Today discrimination must take a more subtle course. But even when *mura-hachibu* was strong, the history of Shinkyō indicates that it was not necessarily fatal. Confronted with proper leadership and enough people willing to work together and determined not to submit, it actually provided a spur to new cooperative forms, and a better life. Without *mura-hachibu*, there would have been no Shinkyō.

The Israeli Kibbutz

| *Melford Spiro*

A *kibbutz* (plural, *kibbutzim*) is an agricultural collective in Israel, whose main features include communal living, collective ownership of all property (and, hence, the absence of "free enterprise" and the "profit motive"), and the communal rearing of children. *Kibbutz* culture is informed by its explicit, guiding principle of: "from each according to his ability, to each according to his needs." The "family," as that term is defined in *Social Structure,* does not exist in the *kibbutz,* in either its nuclear, polygamous, or extended forms. It should be emphasized, however, that the *kibbutzim* are organized into three separate national federations, and though the basic structure of *kibbutz* society is similar in all three, there are important differences among them. Hence, the term *kibbutz,* as used in this paper, refers exclusively to those *kibbutzim* that are members of the federation studied by the author.

As Murdock defines it, the "family":

> is a social group characterized by common residence, economic cooperation, and reproduction. It includes adults of both sexes, at least two of whom maintain a socially approved sexual relationship, and one or more children, own or adopted, of the sexually cohabiting adults.

The social group in the *kibbutz* that includes adults of both sexes and their children, although characterized by reproduction, is not characterized by common residence or by economic cooperation. Before examining this entire social group, however, we shall first analyze the relationship between the two adults in the group who maintain a "socially approved sexual relationship," in order to determine whether their relationship constitutes a "marriage."

Murdock's findings reveal that marriage entails an interaction of persons of opposite sex such that a relatively permanent sexual relationship is maintained and an economic division of labor is practiced. Where either of these behavior patterns is absent, there is no marriage. As Murdock puts it:

> Sexual unions without economic cooperation are common, and there are relationships between men and women involving a division

From Melford Spiro, "Is the Family Universal?" *American Anthropologist,* Vol. 56, 1954, pp. 840–846. References cited in the original have been deleted.

of labor without sexual gratification . . . but marriage exists only when the economic and the sexual are united in one relationship, and this combination occurs only in marriage.

In examining the relationship of the couple in the *kibbutz* who share a common marriage, and whose sexual union is socially sanctioned, it is discovered that only one of these two criteria—the sexual—applies. Their relationship does not entail economic cooperation. If this be so—and the facts will be examined in a moment—there is no marriage in the *kibbutz,* if by "marriage" is meant a relationship between adults of opposite sex, characterized by sexual and economic activities. Hence, the generalization that, "marriage, thus defined, exists in every known society," has found an exception.

A *kibbutz* couple lives in a single room, which serves as a combined bedroom-living room. Their meals are eaten in a communal dining room, and their children are reared in a communal children's dormitory. Both the man and the woman work in the *kibbutz,* and either one may work in one of its agricultural branches or in one of the "service" branches. The latter include clerical work, education, work in the kitchen, laundry, etc. In actual fact, however, men preponderate in the agricultural branches, and women, in the service branches of the economy. There are no men, for example, in that part of the educational system which extends from infancy to the junior-high level. Nor do women work in those agricultural branches that require the use of heavy machinery, such as trucks, tractors, or combines. It should be noted, however, that some women play major roles in agricultural branches, such as the vegetable garden and the fruit orchards; and some men are indispensable in service branches such as the high school. Nevertheless, it is accurate to state that a division of labor based on sex is characteristic of the *kibbutz* society as a whole. This division of labor, however, does not characterize the relationship that exists between couples. Each mate works in some branch of the *kibbutz* economy and each, as a member (*chaver*) of the *kibbutz* receives his equal share of the goods and services that the *kibbutz* distributes. Neither, however, engages in economic activities that are exclusively directed to the satisfaction of the needs of his mate. Women cook, sew, launder, etc., for the entire *kibbutz,* and not for their mates exclusively. Men produce goods, but the economic returns from their labor go to the *kibbutz,* not to their mates and themselves, although they, like all members of the *kibbutz,* share in these economic returns. Hence, though there is economic cooperation between the sexes within the community as a whole, this cooperation does not take place between mates because the social structure of this society precludes the necessity for such cooperation.

What then is the nature of the relationship of the *kibbutz* couple? What are the motives for their union? What functions, other than sex, does it serve? What distinguishes such a union from an ordinary love affair?

In attempting to answer these questions it should first be noted that pre-marital sexual relations are not taboo. It is expected, however, that youth of high-school age refrain from sexual activity; sexual intercourse between high-school students is strongly discouraged. After graduation from high school, however, and their election to membership in the *kibbutz,* there are no sanctions against sexual relations among these young people. While still single, *kibbutz* members live in small private rooms, and their sexual activities may take place in the room of either the male or the female, or in any other convenient location. Lovers do not ask the *kibbutz* for permission to move into a (larger) common room, nor, if they did, would this permission be granted if it were assumed that their relationship was merely that of lovers. When a couple asks for permission to share a room, they do so—and the *kibbutz* assumes that they do so—not because they are lovers, but because they are in love. The request for a room, then, is the sign that they wish to become a "couple" *(zug),* the term the *kibbutz* has substituted for the traditional "marriage." This union does not require the sanction of a marriage ceremony, or of any other event. When a couple requests a room, and the *kibbutz* grants the request, their union is *ipso facto* sanctioned by society. It should be noted, however, that all *kibbutz* "couples" eventually "get married" in accordance with the marriage laws of the state—usually just before, or soon after, their first child is born—because children born out of wedlock have no legal rights, according to state law.

But becoming a "couple" affects neither the status nor the responsibilities of either the male or the female in the *kibbutz.* Both continue to work in whichever branch of the economy they had worked in before their union. The legal and social status of both the male and the female remain the same. The female retains her maiden name. She not only is viewed as a member of the *kibbutz* in her own right, but her official registration card in the *kibbutz* files remains separate from that of her "friend" *(chaver)*—the term used to designate spouses.*

But if sexual satisfaction may be obtained outside of this union, and if the union does not entail economic cooperation, what motivates people to become "couples"? It means that the motivation is the desire to satisfy certain needs for intimacy, using that term in both its physical and psycho-

---

* Other terms, "young man" *(bachur)* and "young woman" *(bachura),* are also used in place of "husband" and "wife." If more than one person in the *kibbutz* has the same proper name, and there is some question as to who is being referred to when the name is mentioned in conversation, the person is identified by adding, "the *bachur* of so-and-so," or "the *bachura* of so-and-so."

logical meanings. In the first place, from the sexual point of view, the average *chaver* is not content to engage in a constant series of casual affairs. After a certain period of sexual experimentation, he desires to establish a relatively permanent relationship with one person. But in addition to the physical intimacy of sex, the union also provides a psychological intimacy that may be expressed by notions such as "comradeship," "security," "dependency," "succorance," etc. And it is this pyschological intimacy, primarily, that distinguishes "couples" from lovers. The criterion of the "couple" relationship, then, that which distinguishes it from a relationship between adults of the same sex who enjoy psychological intimacy, or from that of adults of opposite sex who enjoy physical intimacy, is love. A "couple" comes into being when these two kinds of intimacy are united in one relationship.

Since the *kibbutz* "couple" does not constitute a marriage because it does not satisfy the economic criterion of "marriage," it follows that the "couple" and their children do not constitute a family, economic cooperation being part of the definition of the "family." Furthermore, as has already been indicated, this group of adults and children does not satisfy the criterion of "common residence." For though the children visit their parents in the latter's room every day, their residence is in one of the "children's houses" *(bet yeladim),* where they sleep, eat, and spend most of their time.

More important, however, in determining whether or not the family exists in the *kibbutz* is the fact that the "physical care" and the "social rearing" of the children are not the responsibilities of their own parents. But these responsibilities, according to Murdock's findings, are the most important functions that the adults in the "family" have with respect to the children.

Before entering into a discussion of the *kibbutz* system of "collective education" *(chinuch meshutaf),* it should be emphasized that the *kibbutz* is a child-centered society, *par excellence.* The importance of children, characteristic of traditional Jewish culture, has been retained as one of the primary values in this avowedly antitraditional society. "The Parents' Crown" is the title given to the chapter on children in an ethnography of the Eastern European Jewish village. The authors of this ethnography write:

> Aside from the scriptural and social reasons, children are welcomed for the joy they bring beyond the gratification due to the parents—the pleasure of having a child in the house. A baby is a toy, the treasure, and the pride of the house.

This description, except for the scriptural reference, applies without qualification to the *kibbutz.*

But the *kibbutz* has still another reason for cherishing its children. The *kibbutz* views itself as an attempt to revolutionize the structure of human society and its basic social relations. Its faith in its ability to achieve this end can be vindicated only if it can raise a generation that will choose to live in this communal society, and will, thus, carry on the work that was initiated by the founders of this society—their parents.

For both these reasons the child is king. Children are lavished with attention and with care to the point where many adults admit that the children are "spoiled." Adult housing may be poor, but the children live in good houses; adult food may be meager and monotonous, but the children enjoy a variety of excellent food; there may be a shortage of clothes for adults, but the children's clothing is both good and plentiful.

Despite this emphasis on children, however, it is not their own parents who provide directly for their physical care. Indeed, the latter have no responsibility in this regard. The *kibbutz* as a whole assumes this responsibility for all its children. The latter sleep and eat in special "children's houses"; they obtain their clothes from a communal store; when ill, they are taken care of by their "nurses." This does not mean that parents are not concerned about the physical welfare of their own children. On the contrary, this is one of their primary concerns. But it does mean that the active responsibility for their care has been delegated to a community institution. Nor does it mean that parents do not work for the physical care of their children, for this is one of their strongest drives. But the fruits of their labor are not given directly to their children: they are given instead to the community which, in turn, provides for all the children. A bachelor or a "couple" without children contribute as much to the children's physical care as a "couple" with children of their own.

The family's responsibility for the socialization of children, Murdock reports, is "no less important than the physical care of the children."

> The burden of education and socialization everywhere falls primarily upon the nuclear family. . . . Perhaps more than any other single factor collective responsibility for education and socialization welds the various relationships of the family firmly together.

But the education and socialization of *kibbutz* children are the function of their "nurses" and teachers, and not of their parents. The infant is placed in the "infants' house" upon the mother's return from the hospital, where it remains in the care of nurses. Both parents see the infant there; the mother when she feeds it, the father upon return from work. The infant is not taken to its parents' room until its sixth month, after which it stays with them for an hour. As the child grows older, the amount of time he spends with his parents increases, and he may go to their room whenever he chooses during the day, though he must return to his "children's house" before lights-out. Since the children are in school most of the day, however, and since both parents work during the day, the children—even during their school vacations—are with their parents for a (approximately) two-hour period in the evening—from the time that the parents return from work until they go to eat their evening meal. The children may also be with their parents all day Sunday—the day of rest—if they desire.

As the child grows older he advances through a succession of "children's houses" with children of his own age, where he is supervised by a "nurse." The "nurse" institutes most of the disciplines, teaches the child his basic social skills, and is responsible for the "socialization of the instincts." The child also learns from his parents, to be sure, and they too are agents in the socialization process. But the bulk of his socialization is both entrusted, and deliberately delegated, to the "nurses" and teachers. There is little doubt but that a *kibbutz* child, bereft of the contributions of his parents to his socialization, would know his culture; deprived of the contributions of his "nurses" and teachers, however, he would remain an unsocialized individual.

As they enter the juvenile period, preadolescence, and adolescence, the children are gradually inducted into the economic life of the *kibbutz*. They work from an hour (grade-school students) to three hours (high-school seniors) a day in one of the economic branches under the supervision of adults. Thus, their economic skills, like most of their early social skills, are taught them by adults other than their parents. This generalization applies to the learning of values, as well. In the early ages, the *kibbutz* values are inculcated by "nurses," and later by teachers. When the children enter junior high, this function, which the *kibbutz* views as paramount in importance, is delegated to the "homeroom teacher," known as the "educator" *(mechanech)*, and to a "leader" *(madrich)* of the inter-*kibbutz* youth movement. The parents, of course, are also influential in the teaching of values, but the formal division of labor in the *kibbutz* has delegated this responsibility to other authorities.

Although the parents do not play an outstanding role in the socialization of their children, or in providing for their physical needs, it would be erroneous to conclude that they are unimportant figures in their children's lives. Parents are of crucial importance in the *psychological* development of the child. They serve as the objects of his most important identifications and they provide him with a certain security and love that he obtains from no one else. If anything, the attachment of the young children to their parents is greater than it is in our own society. But this is irrelevant to the main consideration of this paper. Its purpose is to call attention to the fact that those functions of parents that constitute the *conditio sine qua non* for the existence of the "family"—the physical care and socialization of children—are not the functions of the *kibbutz* parents. It can only be concluded that in the absence of the economic and educational functions of the typical family, as well as of its characteristic of common residence, the family does not exist in the *kibbutz*.

Interpretation

It is apparent from this brief description of the *kibbutz* that most of the functions characteristic of the typical nuclear family have become the functions of the entire *kibbutz* society. This is so much the case that the *kibbutz* as a whole can almost satisfy the criteria by which Murdock defines the "family." This observation is not meant to imply that the *kibbutz* is a nuclear family. Its structure and that of the nuclear family are dissimilar. This observation does suggest, however, that the *kibbutz* can function without the family because it functions as if it, itself, were a family; and it can so function because its members perceive each other as kin, in the psychological implications of that term. The latter statement requires some explanation.

The members of the *kibbutz* do not view each other merely as fellow citizens, or as coresidents in a village, or as cooperators of an agricultural economy. Rather do they view each other as *chaverim,* or comrades, who comprise a group in which each is intimately related to the other, and in which the welfare of the one is bound up with the welfare of the other. This is a society in which the principle, "from each according to his ability, to each according to his needs," can be practiced not because its members are more altruistic than the members of other societies, but because each member views his fellow as a kinsman, psychologically speaking. And just as a father in the family does not complain because he works much harder than his children, and yet he may receive no more, or even less, of the family income than they, so the *kibbutz* member whose economic productivity is high does not complain because he receives no more, and sometimes less, than a member whose productivity is low. This "principle" is taken for granted as the normal way of doing things. Since they are all *chaverim,* "it's all in the family," psychologically speaking.

In short, the *kibbutz* constitutes a *gemeinschaft.* Its patterns of interaction are interpersonal patterns; its ties are kin ties, without the biological tie of kinship. In this one respect it is the "folk society," in almost its pure form. The following quotation from Redfield could have been written with the *kibbutz* in mind, so accurately does it describe the social-psychological basis of *kibbutz* culture.

> The members of the folk society have a strong sense of belonging together. The group . . . see their own resemblances and feel corre-

spondingly united. Communicating intimately with each other, each
has a strong claim on the sympathies of the other. . . . The personal and
intimate life of the child in the family is extended, in the folk society,
into the social world of the adults. . . . It is not merely that relations in
such a society are personal; it is also that they are familial. . . . The result is a group of people among whom prevail the personal and categorized relationships that characterize families as we know them, and
in which the patterns of kinship tend to be extended outward from the
group of genealogically connected individuals into the whole society.
The kin are the type persons for all experience.

Hence it is that the bachelor and the childless "couple" do not feel that
an injustice is being done them when they contribute to the support of the
children of others. The children *in* the *kibbutz* are viewed as the children
of the *kibbutz*. Parents (who are much more attached to their own children than they are to the children of others) and bachelors, alike, refer to
all the *kibbutz* children as "our children."

The social perception of one's fellows as kin, psychologically speaking,
is reflected in another important aspect of *kibbutz* behavior. It is a striking
and significant fact that those individuals who were born and raised in the
kibbutz tend to practice group exogamy, although there are no rules that
either compel or encourage them to do so. Indeed, in the *kibbutz* in which
our field work was carried out, all such individuals married outside their
own *kibbutz*. When they are asked for an explanation of this behavior,
these individuals reply that they cannot marry those persons with whom
they have been raised and whom they, consequently, view as siblings. This
suggests, as Murdock has pointed out, that "the *kibbutz* to its members *is*
viewed psychologically as a family to the extent that it generates the same
sort of unconscious incest-avoidance tendencies" (private communication).

What is suggested by this discussion is the following proposition: although the *kibbutz* constitutes an exception to the generalization concerning
the universality of the family, structurally viewed, it serves to confirm
this generalization, functionally and psychologically viewed. In the absence of a specific social group—the family—to whom society delegates
the functions of socialization, reproduction, etc., it has become necessary
for the entire society to become a large extended family. But only in a society whose members perceive each other psychologically as kin can it
function as a family. And there would seem to be a population limit
beyond which point individuals are no longer perceived as kin. That point
is probably reached when the interaction of its members is no longer face-
to-face; in short, when it ceases to be a primary group. It would seem
probable, therefore, that only in a "familial" society, such as the *kibbutz,* is
it possible to dispense with the family.

Child-Rearing Practices of the Communal Family

Bennett Berger,
Bruce Hackett,
Sherri Cavan,
Gilbert Zickler,
Mervyn Millar,
Marilyn Noble,
Susan Theiman,
Richard Farrell, and
Benjamin Rosenbluth

During the first eight months of our study of child rearing in communal families, we have done the following:

1. Located and maintained residence of at least a month in seven communes in northern California.

2. Visited and studied less intensively at least a dozen other communes.

3. Held many research-group seminars on clarifying the major research problem in operational terms and on other basic issues of theory and method.

4. Initiated a community study of a small rural town in the heart of a dense cluster of rural communes to study the impact of the influx of "hippies" on local institutions.

5. Attended two major conferences on subjects related to our study: the nature of drug subcultures and the development of "free schools."

6. Studied the "underground press" up close by placing one of our staff members (a former newsman) on the Berkeley *Barb,* where he rose from reporter to managing editor (during the illness of the editor and publisher). A separate report will be made of this study.

7. Conducted a small sample survey of attitudes toward communal living.

8. Compiled and examined a substantial bibliography.

A major focus of the research is on the nature of community-building: on the creation of institutions capable of sustaining and carrying the subculture of hippies and thus provide for the socialization of children. Our initial decision was to study these developments primarily—or at least at the outset—in rural or quasi-rural settings rather than looking at urban networks of hippies. Our rationale was simple: the relative absence of or

From Bennett Berger et al., "Child-Rearing Practices of the Communal Family," excerpts from a progress report to the National Institute of Mental Health, Grant No. 1-RO1-MH 16570-O1A1-SP to Scientific Analysis Corporation, San Francisco. References cited in the original have been deleted.

insulation from "straight" institutions provided by land ownership or rental would permit fuller institutional implementation of hippie ideology in rural areas. Our desire was to gain information and make observations from relatively "pure" communal settings, even if problems of access to data were thus enlarged—as they were. It also meant that we clearly undersampled certain types of communes, for example, the "political" communes which are primarily urban and "crash pads" which serve primarily "drifting" hippies who have not (yet) made a genuine commitment to communal living.

Once this research decision was made, it became necessary to determine what, for the purposes of the study, constituted a commune. We decided against paying great initial attention to crash pads and similar urban places where turnover is high, anticipation of future needs minimal, and a conscious "family" orientation absent. In order to eliminate the less stable living arrangements that have proliferated within the hip scene, our minimum definition of a working commune was at least five adults and at least two children sharing resources and facilities in a common household or domestic establishment, and having been together for at least six months.

Our initial access to existing communes came from two sources primarily. On our research team are two part-time employees of the Haight-Ashbury Medical Clinic. They were able to supply us with very valuable information concerning the character and location of several communes, and they enabled us to make initial contacts. The other source was through our own "regular" assistants who had either done previous commune research or who utilized previous personal contacts with a wide variety of hippies in the Bay Area to locate other communes. Other sources included underground publications, advertisements, bulletin boards, and other scholars doing research in related fields.

In order to gain and maintain access to these communes, special strategies were sometimes necessary to meet the exigencies of each different situation. Access has been a recurrent problem because there are no self-evident reasons why communes should allow themselves to be studied, to say nothing of actually welcoming researchers. In one commune with a substantial number of school-age children, we were able to gain access through a research assistant who happens to have a teaching credential. Although her own research commitment was made clear, she was allowed in to observe the commune in "exchange" for teaching services she is performing. Access to the Berkeley *Barb* was gained through its owner who is an old acquaintance of the project director and through the presence among our assistants of an experienced newsman. In another case we gained access to a commune on the "coattails" of a Medical Clinic team whose good reputation in the hip commune brushed off on us through our association with them. In every case but one, however, our research intent was made clear to the hippies, and misrepresentation or incognito roles avoided. This would have been impossible without the *personal* qualities of our staff who have been able to elicit apparent trust and acceptance from people normally quite skeptical (to put the matter mildly) of the aims of researchers. This "up-front" posture of the research staff enabled us to participate fully in the ongoing life of the communes for long periods without being subject to the sanctions possible against unwanted or ambiguously identified guests or transients. Once inside the communal settlements as participant observers, it was possible to obtain other leads and introductions to other communal settlements by conversations with people there and by visitors who happen by from other communes. The one exception to our candid identity as researchers is the staff member doing the community study of a small town with an influx of large numbers of hippies—most of whom are not living in communal families. She is living and participating in town life in the incognito role of a writer doing a book on children's lore.

During these early months we have been continually concerned with "clearing" our credentials as participant observers within the communes themselves. We knew that the project was being widely discussed both in the hip community and in scholarly circles concerned with related matters, and that communes (fresh from their disastrous experience of the Haight-Ashbury community with researchers and journalists) were formulating very guarded attitudes toward "research" before we ever arrived in their presence. And we worried lest our federal sponsorship create levels of anxiety—even paranoia—too high to overcome. We had continually to face the question of "Why is NIMH interested in supporting a study of us?" We have devoted great care to answering this and similar questions, and by this time our skills at allaying such anxieties have grown enormously. But the problem may be expected to recur continually as we enlarge our samples, and the anxieties rise and fall depending to a considerable extent on a commune's relations with the "straight" institutional world (Has there been a pot bust recently? Have FBI men been around looking for draft evaders? Have county health and housing code officials been harassing them lately?), so that our acceptance may never be completely unreserved or established without question. But so far this issue has not obstructed our work. Actually, the successful confrontation of it has helped to establish our trustworthiness. We have at the same time helped validate our credentials by exercising great discretion in maintaining confidences and in limiting access to our seminars and now-voluminous field notes. And our staff is under instructions to politely turn away all requests (there have been several) from newspaper and television journalists for interviews, which, we feel, cannot do the research any good now, and may do it great harm. While in the field, we have taken great care not to be "intrusive"—notes are taken only in private or after the fact, children are not "interviewed," and access to "private" quarters of nuclear family units (a very important part of the research) is not sought before it happens "naturally." As our assistants move back and forth between their research sites and our seminars, their skills at observing and at retaining information and their ability to systematize their observations have increased greatly, so that our seminars have developed into highly rewarding settings for comparative analysis. . . .

As we emphasized in our research proposal, this has been a period for generating basic ideas and hypotheses, rather than for testing hypotheses already extant in the literature. The following section presents examples of some of our initial observations and of some of the ideas that our preliminary findings and observations have generated.

We have organized this brief discussion of our preliminary findings under four headings: child rearing itself, and three related matters which are both relevant to the viability of all communes (hence relevant to child rearing) and depending upon which child rearing itself is likely to vary somewhat. At this point in the research, these four headings are to some extent arbitrary; they have been selected as convenient ways of presenting in an organized manner illustrations of the kinds of observations we have been making, and the problems of commune viability they reveal. All our conclusions thus far must, of course, be regarded as tentative and subject to further study, particularly with respect to their impact upon the children of the communes.

Child Rearing and the Family

At the outset it must be recognized that such "child rearing" that goes on in communes is in general highly deliberate and self-conscious (hence the quotation marks) because commune members themselves, having rejected much of their own upbringing and having faced (indeed, continually facing) the problems of "getting their heads together," are generally painfully aware of the lasting impact of childhood socialization.

The children of the communes are raised in a variety of family settings. Most of the communes regard themselves as extended families, not only consciously using the term but in one case actually adopting a common surname. And a typical mode of trying to settle disputes among children is through the appeal by adults to the children's sense of kinship, that is, "Janey is your sister, don't abuse her." But over and above the commune-as-family, a variety of nuclear units exist—everything from legally married spouses-plus-their-children, to unmarried couples with and without children, to couples in which the male partner is not the father of the female's child, and even to one case in which the female partner is not the mother of the male's child. We mention this because the character of the nuclear unit seems to affect the intensity of the obligation of "parents" toward "their" children in ways we intend to study more closely. Whereas our studies thus far indicate a rejection of the commonly held stereotype of communes as places of random and unrestricted sexual promiscuity, the *ways* in which couples pair off, the stability of such liaisons, and the consequences of them remain to be intensively investigated. Some general observations, however, can be made at this point in the research. We have, for example, seen a range of variation in child-family relations from an emphasis on the solidarity of the traditional nuclear unit within the communal family to the practice of regarding the child as "belonging" to the commune as a whole—with each adult member sharing responsibility for the child's welfare and upbringing. At this point, however, we have not yet determined whether this is a structural variation in different *types* of communes or a sequential (or developmental) change that occurs as the child becomes less physically dependent on its mother. While infants are nursing they are, of course, literally connected to their mothers and to that extent dependent. But at the same time that there seem to be informal consensuses that biological mothers are primarily responsible for their nursing infants, there is also general agreement that mothers need to "get away" now and then (although how frequently and for what lengths "now and then" may be is a source of argument), and infants left around the communal house will be looked after by the adults there regardless of whether "arrangements" have been made. The situation with older children is more ambiguous still. One observation was made of an argument between the mother of a four-year-old girl and an adult-male commune member (neither the father of the child nor the mother's "old man") who was holding the child on his lap at the dinner table feeding her. The man was berating the mother for interfering with him and the child "doing a dinner thing" together—suggesting that the "mother" in this instance had no special rights over her child.

This ambiguity about the relationship of a child to its parents and to the commune is manifest also in the ritual celebration of childbirth common to many communes. On the one hand, the entire commune is frequently present at the birth (including the children), chanting and offering encouragement in other ways to the mother in labor. On the other hand, the father of the child is encouraged to assist directly in delivery, his actual participation in the birth of his own child being assumed to symbolically establish paternal connection far more profoundly than the impersonal, antiseptic practices of hospitals. This emphasis on "natural" childbirth is significant to communards not only for the obvious ideological rejection of the idea of childbirth as an "illness" requiring doctors and hospitals; far more important, it seems to us, is the significance for the identity of the child and the commune. For when "officials" are not present at the birth, the child "belongs" to the family rather than to the State whose certified representatives preside at hospital births. Or so it seems to seem to the communards. In one instance, the childbirth was not only ritually celebrated by the entire extended family, but a photographic record made of the entire process and an invocational poem in praise of life composed by the father. The father and the photographer are presently engaged in publishing the poem and the photographs as a book which they intend to distribute free to interested communes and others.

Within the range of nuclear family types, stability and fidelity among couples is encouraged as a general pattern in the relatively durable (two to three years) communes we have studied most closely. Although a biological father may be absent in many of these nuclear units, and although children may refer to having had many "fathers," nuclear units generally have a male figure (father) who is *regarded as stable,* even if he and the mother have been together only a short time and are still working out the degree of their commitment to each other. In spite of the approval of couple stability and fidelity as a general pattern, there is a negative attitude toward the idea of sexual property. At the same time, the possibility of sexual freedom may threaten the affectional stability of nuclear units. We have seen instances in which couples remain "together" in spite of the fact that each may occasionally have sexual relations with another—the general feeling being that if one spouse wants to, it's better that he (or she) satisfies that want than if he (or she) doesn't. Exclusive sexual access is, however, a norm that runs deep, and its violation (in spite of ideology) may cause deep tensions. These matters are difficult to study closely because they are generally legitimate areas of privacy in communal life, and we will get more deeply into them the longer our assistants remain with a particular commune, and when we begin formal interviewing next year. These observations have been made in the communes we have studied ourselves, which are mostly quite stable and with a conscious "family" orientation. We have, however, *heard* of other communes in which sexual liaisons and nuclear units are not much less stable, but in which the notion of "incest" among the extended kin group is encouraged. In one group we heard about, several men had sexual relations with a woman during her fertile period so that no one could be sure who the father of the expected child was. We expect to make further efforts to locate some of these "deviant" (from our present perspective) communes.

Parents of communal children face a persistent dilemma regarding discipline and guidance. Their dominant ideology is to let the child "do his own thing," to allow maximum expression of his "individuality" and "creativity." But in implementing their beliefs in the natural creativity of children and their (the children's) rights to choose the activities they want, communal parents find it necessary to circumvent their own ideology to some extent in order to handle necessary discipline, to encourage conformity to valued practices in communes (such as meditation in yoga-based—and other—communes), and to guide the children toward parental goals— goals that intensify the dilemma by including the generally accepted objective of raising the child to be free to "do his own thing." But life has a habit of resolving everything, even dilemmas, and the communards cope with their problem in *ad hoc* ways every day, sometimes preferring to impale themselves on their dilemma rather than applying severe sanctions to recalcitrant children as a matter of principle, and sometimes making efforts toward creating a model of child rearing which encourages the child's desire to "do his own thing," even if such socialization undermines the sources of recruitment to the commune's next generation. Most communes, it seems at this point, if faced with a choice between training the next generation of communards and training children to be free, would opt for the latter. In the terminology of the communes, there are strong pressures on adults not "to lay their own heavy trip" on the children, and only light pressures toward conformity are exercised, as exemplified by the appeal to kinship in settling aggression among children, or by refusal of a father to forcibly take an adult's smoking pipe away from his sixteen-month-old son, who insisted upon smoking it, and would not give it up even after he was coughing on the smoke. The father applied only the gentlest pressure, under the apparent assumption that the child would willingly give it up after a little while (an assumption that turned out to be correct). We are currently paying special attention to the ways in which accommodations occur between the day-to-day pressures of child rearing and what the communards believe with respect to children. The universality of the problem and the highly conscious attempt to cope with it, makes this one of the most fascinating dimensions of the study, and of enormous potential importance.

Economic Support

Members of communes also face a dilemma with respect to economic activities. On the one hand they ideally seek economic self-sufficiency either at the communal level, the tribal (several communes with specially close relations) level, or the regional level (communes tend to cluster regionally). On the other hand, welfare continues to be a principal source of income in most of the communes we studied. The communes tend to be aware of this dilemma but to have no solution for it, and a common topic of discussion at commune meetings is what they will do when "the Man" ceases to support them through welfare. A related dilemma is the desire for subcultural exclusiveness in all economic arrangements, but a reluctance to engage in the kinds of regular commerce which might provide the economic strength they need eventually to achieve the institutional completeness they envision. An example of this is the refusal by the two men producing the book on the baby's birth to accept the several offers they have had from commercial publishers; they prefer instead to go through the difficult process of raising the necessary funds from sources within the subculture, and do the publishing (and the distribution) themselves.

In general, intercommunal or tribal bartering, subsistence farming, and small craft industries do not provide sufficient funds for necessary expenses (machinery, foods, utilities, mortgage, or rent payments) so that they are forced to continue relying on welfare, benefactors, and occasional windfalls from commune members (generous parents, inheritances, etc.). Pressures are also thereby generated to seek economic arrangements with institutions outside the subculture, thus creating other problems for communes. First of all, it contradicts some of their major objectives—about fleeing polluted cities, about engaging in alienated work—and threatens their hope of "living off the land" in harmony with nature. There are no visible solutions to this problem.

Moreover, even when commune members have specially salable skills as craftsmen, too great an involvement in his skills is likely to be regarded as an individual's "side trip," not *directly* connected with solidarity of the commune-as-family. This suggests that *some* work is regarded as more central to the collective welfare of the commune than others (for example, gardening, knowledge of care of domestic animals, plumbing and electrical skills, and so on), and problems develop when a craftsman is so "into" his craft or art that it begins to be perceived by others as distracting from the "family trip," which is the major goal of communal living.

This distrust of "side trips" exists alongside of the aim of most communes to reestablish work as a kind of "holy" or natural activity through which the worker may experience personal growth, satisfaction, and serenity. This is most clear in the tender care and religious feeling with which gardens are sometimes decorated with religious objects. In addition, there is much talk, sometimes in quasi-religious terms, about how the crops are growing. People with "green thumbs" may be heard observing that it's not a good idea for many people to be in the garden at the same time because "too many vibes freak out the plants."

Although communards tend to work hard (subsistence farming is hard work, and the insight that a hard life produces the severity of mien common in communes is contradicted only by the frequent and recurrent festive atmosphere, particularly after family dinners), work tends not be organized except for those tasks that require regularity (preparation of meals, care of animals). Other work is regarded as a "trip" which, if someone is into it, he will ask for help on if he needs or wants it. But most of the work is not scheduled, there are no deadlines, and with few exceptions the "need" for something to be done does not take precedence over the desire or willingness of people to do it.

Communes are not places likely to be praised by serious women's liberationists, since women seem to fall naturally into doing most of the traditional "women's work." But this is less a matter of traditionalism than of natural functionality and available skill. If a woman is in possession of special skills, she will generally not spend a great deal of time in the kitchen or milking goats. If she isn't, she's likely to cook rather than haul lumber or do other heavy work which men are better equipped for.

Leadership and Authority

In the communes we have observed there is a general tendency to have no formal provisions for leadership roles. Nevertheless, in most communes, individuals assume positions of commune-wide influence and leadership, the basis for which and the occasion of which varied from commune to commune. In some, the oldest members had an age-based influence, while in others masters of ideology (or religious practice) central to the commune's self-image maintained a higher status. Seniority of commune membership was another characteristic of influential members, and still another was commitment to communal goals as measured by the amount of communal work one did. On the whole, however, leadership fluctuates among several "strong" figures in a given commune depending on what they call the "flow of energy." Leadership of whatever sort tends to correlate with a talent for serene rhetoric enabling the leader to appeal to the sense of love and fraternity in resolving intracommunal disputes or hostilities, and these talents are often exercised at family meetings where grievances will be aired and disputes over policy discussed.

Decisions affecting the welfare of the community as a whole (such as admission of new members, child welfare, health and hygiene, relations with outsiders) seemed to us to require commune-wide acceptance (at least the withholding of opposition). When meetings are called they are generally in response to particular issues and events. Meetings can be serious, solidarity-shaking occurrences because there is a presumed consensus about issues affecting the routine maintenance of social organization, gaps in which can easily be revealed in the meetings.

There is one other source of leadership which has ambiguous status. Where one person either owns the land or a substantial piece of it, he or she is likely to be prominent by virtue of this fact. But ownership by itself is not regarded as a *legitimate* source of authority, and, in the cases we know of, ownership is correlated either with age, seniority, or commitment. But that individual ownership may be a problem is indicated by the high value placed upon communal or other collective ownership of the land. In any case, we have seen no instances of the kind of leadership that has become notorious through the publicity given to the "Manson Family."

Recruitment

As participant observers we have investigated communal recruitment processes from practical as well as theoretical perspectives. In practical terms, we have sought to identify the processes by which prospective members gain information about and access to communes, and the processes by which prospective membership becomes full membership. By identifying these processes we have also helped to solve our own very practical problems of finding the subjects of our research and of becoming participant observers in the communes. In theoretical terms we have tried to identify types of communes in terms of the active or passive character of their recruitment practices and the population from which they draw their membership.

Those who are seeking communal living arrangements tend to use the same sources we ourselves have used in locating the places we studied: friends, public meetings or benefits presented by communes, crash pads or more stable communal houses in the Bay Area, "underground" information media, and "hip" establishments such as health-food stores, cafes, boutiques, free clinics, and random conversations with "street people" and hitchhikers. First contacts with rural communes tend to be with the "open" places, whose very openness have gained them wide publicity since all are welcome, including journalists who write about them: most prominently places like Wheeler's Ranch and Morningstar. The communes we have studied most closely are primarily "closed" communes, open only to members, to guests invited by members, and for short periods to visitors only if their motives are legitimate or if they otherwise pass the scrutiny of the group.

From a more theoretical perspective, we have recognized that implicit in all recruitment practices is the commune's image of the "ideal" member, a model toward which the already established communes strive. But this image, along with the activity or passivity of recruitment, varies in terms of what Zablocki has called "consensus" or "solidarity" types of communes. Consensus communes are those which are organized around a common religious or ideological (including political) creed which gives the commune its *raison d'etre* and provides a basis for cohesion. Such communes tend to actively recruit new members by advertising the creed and its promise of a new life, and by inviting adherence at least for a trial period. There is often a fee or regular payments of one kind or another involved. For obvious reasons these are the communes for which there is much publicity and to which access is easiest—although our investigations indicate the emergence of a new creedal type of commune in which general dedication to communal living constitutes the creed and in which recruitment has become selective in terms of the skills that the commune needs at the moment to make it more viable.

Access to communes with passive recruitment policies is far more difficult, and is what we have spent most of our time studying. These are the communes Zablocki calls "solidarity" communes, ones in which cohesion is provided by friendship or similar nonconsensual ties, and whose emphasis is on individual and family development rather than on conversion experiences of a basically religious sort. Such groups typically feel that they already have enough or more people than the land can support, and discussion is common on whether and how to acquire more land (to support more people) and whether to admit to membership people who want to join—for example, guests who may have been living at the commune for some time without actually being members of the family.

Communes of this type not only do not actively seek new members but may carefully guard their anonymity and value their insulation from publicity. At the same time they tend to be seriously concerned with the influx of young people into rural areas looking for communal living arrangements, and though they may be unable or unwilling to accommodate these people themselves, they are much concerned with the spread of the communal movement and encourage the development of new communes and the acquisition of additional land to sustain them. A recurrent question to our researchers, for example, is why we don't spend our money to start new communes.

We are currently using this typology and developing others in order to pay closer attention to their impact on the children. One of the first things one learns from field experience with communes is that it is very difficult to make general statements that are true of "communes"; and most of our subsequent findings and assertions will be carefully limited to types of communes.

Methodological Issues and New Directions

Our research design presumes the existence of communes as relatively distinct or discrete entities; it presumes as well the existence of communards with identifiable personal histories or biographies, the understanding of which helps to explain the communard's present situation. The design also assumes the value of gathering information on life in the commune primarily from the commune itself—that is, from observation and interviewing done primarily "on location." It also tends—though this is hardly a necessity—to deemphasize the "historical" quality of daily life. We are inclined to be more interested in "types" of communes and commune experiences than we are in the "stages of growth" of communards, particular communes, or the commune movement as a whole. Finally, we presume a relatively insignificant impact of the study or the individual researcher on the research site. These are not our only assumptions, of course, but they are important ones that have caused some repeated difficulty and should be discussed briefly here.

The assumption that communes can be studied as relatively discrete entities raises the traditional "unit of analysis" question common to most sociology and perhaps the study of socialization most particularly. Studies focusing initially on communities, families, institutions, or similar entities have a tendency to expand their focus as forces generating behavior within the unit being studied are traced to "outside" institutions. Thus our own field work made it apparent early in the study that many communes are integral to larger "tribes" or regional associations and raised the question to what extent these larger networks are the source of ideas or practices that bear directly or indirectly on socialization. Evidence that they are important in this regard raises the question whether we wish to focus primarily on the family or primarily on socialization—these overlap considerably, of course, but are not the same. A rigorously psychological or psychiatric orientation might incline us to limit the focus to the basics of parent- or adult-child interaction, but our view has been that the child may realistically "belong" to more than this primordial association and his growth substantially altered or conditioned by this fact. In practice, we are trying to avoid having to choose between narrower and broader foci; we are examining parent-child interaction in detail, but one of our research assistants is studying the lives of commune children not only within the commune but especially in their interaction with (and comparison to) the lives of children from the larger "straight" community, and another research assistant is studying the commune network in what amounts to an entire county.

In a similar vein, we are moving to include within our research the study of relations between communes and the often substantial panoply of officials with whom they have regular contact, including especially police, welfare, health, and school officials. Government agencies are a rich source of information about commune developments; more importantly, perhaps, the views of officials regarding these developments not only condition the development and implementation of public policy but often have a more direct impact on the behavior of communards. It is especially significant, too, that the "intervention of the state" seems so often to follow or be legitimated by official concern for the welfare or treatment of children—concerns that run directly parallel to our research interests.

This is, of course, especially the case with schools—public agencies of socialization. We have, accordingly, begun to examine in some greater detail a number of the many "free schools" that have recently been springing up in profusion in California and elsewhere. In many respects, examining how communes handle the "school problem" may be one of the best strategies for studying communal child rearing in general; as at least minimally formal and quasi-public institutions, they are relatively open to study—they straddle, as it were, the fence that stands between the commune and the larger society. It may be, too, that having to face the issue of what to do with the school-age children—in terms of their education—typically forces communes to begin formulating child-rearing strategies and ideas with a dedication that can be foregone (relatively and formally) as long as most of the children are not yet old enough for school in conventional terms. Interestingly, too, it has seemed to us that only recently, in the past year or two, have the second-generation school-age communards begun to be a significant population within the larger population of the communes.

The latter point is an example of the kind of information that is probably important but tends to be lost by our tendency, in drafting the original research design, to deemphasize the importance of history or stages of development. Significantly, communards typically do not move into or raise their children in "established" settlements—indeed, the creation of the settlement is one of the dominant themes of commune life. This means, however, that many behaviors might better be related to stages of development than to basic commune or family "types." The development of quasi-"professional" child care, for example, may not be absent in communes: it may come faster in communes that are based on creedal commitments rather than friendship alone, but it may owe its existence primarily to the demographic fact of an enlarging school-age population. This is probably the single most important reason why a longitudinal design is important, and led us to the decision to sample not only communes themselves, but the times at which we visited them over the three-year period of the study.

Another methodological issue of some importance to our study is the problem of gathering "biographical" information. Our design calls for the study of communards over three generations; biographies, however, are not highly visible (except, perhaps, those of the third generation) and information on them must thus be gathered through semistructured interviews. This is a difficult feat; communards are often very reserved about offering information of any kind to social scientists and, in our experience, exceptionally reticent about offering information regarding personal histories. At the outset this seemed to us simply to reflect the fact that building relationships of trust takes time, that biographical details would come naturally as our research team became accepted in the communes. A somewhat more subtle and perhaps more interesting possibility has been suggested, however—that there exists on the communes and perhaps among hippies in general a kind of taboo on "biography." Discourse on one's personal history is rare; the meaning of this, if it turns out to be as distinctive as it now seems, is as yet obscure to us, but it may serve to heighten participation in and commitment to the present setting, just as religious conversion often involves the idea of rebirth and the attempt to diminish the importance of the past. It may, too, make it easy to *leave* the present setting, since one has not selectively reconstructed his past so that it "points to" the decision to join a commune. In either case, however, biographical information may be either very hard to come by or very distorted in its presentation. One consultant has suggested that we attempt to do individual in-depth case histories of particular communards—that if we make our biographical work a more distinctive set of events it may be more acceptable to the subjects. This is a possibility, but it may also be necessary to at least supplement our study of the three generations within particular families with small sample survey (interview) studies of separate adult and youth populations. One pilot study of this sort has already been undertaken—a study of attitudes toward communes and interest in communal living among approximately 300 students at the University of California at Davis; this study is currently approaching the analysis stage.

One final methodological concern deserves mention, namely, the degree to which our field work may operate to alter the situation being studied and hence "contaminate" the data to a greater or lesser degree. In general, our field workers have been accepted into their research sites—after some initial difficulties—to a gratifying degree, and have had no significant sense that the communards were "performing" for them. Such performing, however, is difficult to detect, and it is altogether reasonable to expect that communards being studied will behave more like ideal communards than would otherwise be the case. Moreover, in at least one case discussion of whether or not to admit a sociologist to the commune triggered the elaboration of an extensive set of rules regarding the treatment of outsiders—sociologists, guests, and visitors—that probably "defined" the commune to a greater degree than had previously been the case. In another situation, inquiries about schooling for the children appeared to have stimulated a considerable degree of semiformal "schooling" activity. The research team has been working to increase its sensitivity to issues of this sort and to develop appropriate strategies for handling them, including the use of "unobtrusive measures," interviews with ex-communards and commune visitors, use of field workers with different interests and perspectives in the same site, and, above all, comparison of the apparent consequences of approaching communes in different ways. In any case, we have no reason to believe at the present that the "up-front" identity of our staff as participant-observer researchers has "contaminated" the data in ways that compromise our efforts. And our sensitivity to the possibilities of this may in fact produce important methodological insights for future field work of this sort.

The Hippie Alternative: Getting Back to the Communal Garden

Sara Davidson

The front wheels drop and the car thuds down a wet, muddy ravine. Thick night fog, raining hard. The car squishes to a stop, front end buried in clay and the right rear wheel spinning. I get out and sink to my ankles. No flashlight. No waterproof gear. Utter blackness, except for the car's dulled lights under the dirt. I climb back in, but because of the 45-degree angle, I'm pitched forward against the dashboard. Turn on the radio. Only eight o'clock—a long wait until daylight. Am I anywhere near Wheeler Ranch? Haven't seen another car or a light anywhere on this road. I start honking the horn. Cows bellow back from what seems very close range. I imagine angry ranchers with shotguns. Tomorrow is Sunday—eight miles back to the nearest town, and nothing will be open. Is there an AAA out here? Good God, I'll pay anybody anything! If they'll just get me out of this.

I had started north from San Francisco in late afternoon, having heard vague descriptions of a commune called Wheeler's that was much beloved by those who had passed through it. The commune had had trouble with

From Sara Davidson, "Open Land: Getting Back to the Communal Garden," *Harper's,* June 1970, pp. 91–102.

local police, and no one was sure whether the buildings were still standing or who was there. At sunset, a storm came up, and rather than turn back, I continued slowly along narrow, unlit country roads, my headlights occasionally picking up messages like "Stop War," painted on the side of a barn, and "Drive slowly, no M. D. around," on a fence post. When I reached the woodsy, frontier town I knew to be near Wheeler's, I stopped in a bar to ask directions. Heads turned. People froze, glasses in hand. A woman with an expressionless, milky face said, "Honey, there isn't any sign. You just go up the road six miles and there's a gate on the left. Then you have to drive a ways to git to it. From where I live, you can see their shacks and what have you. But you can't see anything from the road."

After six miles, there was a gate and a sign, "Beware of cattle." I opened it and drove down to a fork, picked the left road, went around in a circle and came back to the fork, took the right and bumped against two logs in the road. I got out and moved them. Nothing could stop me now. Another fork. To the left the road was impassable—deep ruts and rocks; to the right, a barbed-wire fence. Raining harder, darker. This is enough. Get out of here fast. Try to turn the car around, struggling to see . . . then the sickening dip.

I got into my sleeping bag and tried to find a comfortable position in the crazily tilted car. My mood swung between panic and forced calm. At about 5:00 A.M., I heard rustling noises, and could make out the silhouettes of six horses which walked around the car, snorting. An hour later, the rain let up, and a few feet from the car I found a crude sign with an arrow, "Wheeler's." I walked a mile, then another mile, through rolling green hills, thinking, "If I can just get out of here." At last, around a bend were two tents and a sign, "Welcome, God, love." The first tent had a light burning inside, and turned out to be a greenhouse filled with boxes of seedlings. At the second tent, I pushed open the door and bells tinkled. Someone with streaked brown hair was curled in a real bed on two mattresses. There was linoleum on the floor, a small stove, a table, and books and clothes neatly arranged on shelves. The young man lifted his head and smiled. "Come in."

I was covered with mud, my hair was wild and my eyes red and twitching. "I tried to drive in last night, my car went down a ravine and got stuck in the mud, and I've been sleeping in it all night."

"Far out," he said.

"I was terrified."

The young man, who had gray eyes set close together and one gold earring, said, "Of what?"

"There were horses."

He laughed. "Far out. One of the horses walked into Nancy's house and made a hole in the floor. Now she just sweeps her dirt and garbage down the hole."

My throat was burning. "Could we make some coffee?"

He looked at me sideways. "I don't have any." He handed me a clump of green weeds. "Here's some yerba buena. You can make tea." I stared at the weeds.

"What's your name?" I asked.

"Shoshone."

"Mine's Sara."

"Far out."

He got dressed, watered the plants in the greenhouse, and started down a path into the bushes, motioning for me to follow. Every few feet, he would stop to pick yerba buena, listen to birds, watch a trio of pheasants take off, and admire trees that were recently planted—almond, Elberta peach, cherry, plum. They were all in blossom, but I was in no mood to appreciate them. After every ten minutes of walking, we would come to a clearing with a tent or wooden shack, wake up the people in their soggy sleeping bags and ask them to help push the car out. The dwellings at Wheeler's are straight out of Dogpatch—old boards nailed unevenly together, odd pieces of plastic strung across poles to make wobbly igloos, with round stovepipes poking out the side. Most have dirt floors, though the better ones have wood. In one tent, we found a young man who had shaved his head except for one stripe of hair down the center, like a Mohican. He grinned with his eyes closed. "In an hour or so, I might feel like helping you." We came to a crooked green shack with a peace sign on the door and the inside papered with paintings of Krishna. Nancy, a blond former social worker, was sleeping on the floor with her children, Gregory, eight, and Michelle, nine. Both have blond hair of the same length and it is impossible to tell at first which is the girl and which the boy. At communities like this, it is common for children to ask each other when they meet, "What are you?" Nancy said, "Don't waste your energy trying to push the car. Get Bill Wheeler to pull you out with his jeep. What's your hurry now? Sunday's the best day here. You've got to stay for the steam bath and the feast. There'll be lots of visitors." She yawned. "Lots of food, lots of dope. It never rains for the feast."

Shoshone and I walked back to the main road that cuts across the 320-acre ranch. The sun had burned through the fog, highlighting streaks of yellow wild flowers in the fields. Black Angus cows were grazing by the road. People in hillbilly clothes, with funny hats and sashes, were coming out of the bushes carrying musical instruments and sacks of rice and beans. About a mile from the front gate we came to the community garden, with a scarecrow made of rusty metal in the shape of a nude girl. Two children were chasing each other from row to row, shrieking with laughter, as their mother picked cabbage. A sign read, "Permit not required to settle here."

Bill Wheeler was working in his studio, an airy, wood-and-glass building with large skylights, set on a hill. When Bill bought the ranch in 1963, looking for a place to paint and live quietly, he built the studio for his family. Four years later, when he opened the land to anyone who wanted to settle there, the county condemned his studio as living quarters because it lacked the required amount of concrete under one side. Bill moved into a tent and used the studio for his painting and for community meetings.

Bill is a tall, lean man of thirty with an aristocratic forehead, straight nose, deep-set blue eyes, and a full beard and flowing hair streaked yellow by the sun. His voice is gentle with a constant hint of mirth, yet it projects, like his clear gaze, a strength, which is understood in this community as divine grace. Quiet, unhurried, he progresses with steady confidence toward a goal or solution of a problem. He is also a voluptuary who takes Rabelaisian delight in the community's lack of sexual inhibitions and in the sight of young girls walking nude through the grass. He lives at the center of the ranch with his third wife, Gay, twenty-two, and their infant daughter, Raspberry. His humor and self-assurance make it easy for those around him to submit to the hippie credo that "God will provide," because they know that what God does not, Bill Wheeler will.

Bill promises to rescue my car after he has chopped wood and started a fire for the steam bath. "Don't worry," a friend says, patting me on the back. "Bill's saved people who've given up hope, lost all confidence." A grizzly blond called Damian says, "Why don't you let me pull her out?" Bill says, "Damian, I love you, but I wouldn't trust you with any of my vehicles." Later, we pass Damian on the road, into which he is blissfully urinating. "Ha," Bill says, "the first time I met Damian he was peeing."

With the jeep and a chain, Bill pulls out the car in less than two minutes, and as it slides back onto secure road, I feel my tension drain away. Maybe I should stay for the feast. Maybe it really is beautiful here. I park the car at the county road, outside the first gate, and walk the three miles back to Wheeler's. The access road cuts across property owned by James G. Kelly, a breeder of show cattle and horses, who is enraged at the presence of up to a hundred itinerant hippies on the ranch adjacent to his. He has started court action to block Wheeler from using the access road, and his hired hands walk around with guns slung over their shoulders and their faces pinched with bilious hate.

On a bluff behind Wheeler's garden, the steam bath is set to go. Red-hot rocks are taken from the fire into a plastic tent that can be sealed on all sides. Shifts of eight or nine people undress and sit on the mud floor, letting out whoops, chanting and singing. Gallon wine jugs filled with water are poured on the rocks, and the tent fills up with steam so hot and thick that the children start coughing and no one can see anyone else. After a few minutes, they step out, covered with sweat, and wash off in a cold shower. The women shampoo their hair and soap up the children. The men dig out ticks from under the skin. Much gaiety and good-natured ogling, and then, as the last shift is coming out, a teen-age visitor carrying the underground *Berkeley Tribe* wanders in and stops, dumbfounded, staring with holy-fool eyes, his mouth open and drooling, at all that flesh and hair and sweat.

The garden, like a jigsaw puzzle whose pieces have floated together, presents the image of a nineteenth-century tableau: women in long skirts and shawls, men in lace-up boots, coveralls, and patched jeans tied with pieces of rope, sitting on the grass playing banjos, guitars, lyres, wood flutes, dulcimers, and an accordian. In a field to the right are the community animals—chickens, cows, goats, donkeys, and horses. As far as the eye can see, there are no houses, no traffic, nothing but verdant hills, a stream, and the ocean with whitecaps rising in the distance. Nine-year-old Michelle is prancing about in a pink shawl and a floppy hat warbling, "It's time for the feast!" Nancy says, "The pickin's are sort of spare, because tomorrow is welfare day and everybody's broke." She carries from the outdoor wood stove pots of brown rice—plain, she says, "for the purists who are on Georges Ohsawa's ten-day brown-rice diet"—and rice with fruit and nuts for everyone else; beans, red and white; oranges and apples; yoghurt; hash; pot; acid; mescaline. A girl says there are worms in the green apples. Another, with a studious voice and glasses, says, "That's cool, it means they were organically grown. I'd rather eat a worm than a chemical any day." They eat with their fingers from paper plates, and when the plates are gone, directly from the pot. A man in his forties with red-spotted cheeks asks me if I have any pills. "I'll take anything. I'm on acid now." I offer him aspirin. He swallows eight.

Everyone who lives at Wheeler's ranch is a vegetarian. By some strange inversion, they feel that by eating meat they are hastening their own death. Vegetarianism is, ironically, the aspect of their life style that aggravates even the most liberal parents. ("What? You won't eat meat? That's ridiculous!") Bill Wheeler says that diet is "very very central to the revolution. It's a freeing process which people go through, from living on processed foods and eating gluttonous portions of meat and potatoes, to natural foods and a simple diet that is kinder to your body. A lot has to do with economics. It's much cheaper to live on grains and vegetables you can grow in your garden. When Gay and I moved here, we had to decide whether to raise animals to slaughter. Gay said she couldn't do it. Every

Thanksgiving, there's a movement to raise money to buy turkeys, because some people think the holiday isn't complete without them. But an amazing thing happens when carrion is consumed. People are really greedy, and it's messy. The stench and the grease stay with us for days."

Gravy, roast beef, mashed potatoes, Parker House rolls, buttered peas— the weekly fare when Bill was growing up in Bridgeport, Connecticut. His father, a lawyer who speculated famously in real estate, told Bill he could do anything with his life as long as he got an education. So Bill, self-reliant, introspective, who loved the outdoors, went to Yale and studied painting. After graduating, he came to San Francisco to find a farmhouse where he could work. When he saw the 320-acre ranch which was then a sheep and Christmas tree farm, he felt, "I've got to have it. This is my land." He bought it with his inheritance, and still has enough money to live comfortably the rest of his life. "My parents would be shocked out of their gourds if they saw the land now," Bill says. "They died before I opened it."

The idea of open land, or free land, was introduced to Bill by Lou Gottlieb, a singer with the pop folk group, "The Limelighters," who, in 1962, bought a 32-acre piece of land called Morning Star about ten miles from Wheeler's Ranch. Gottlieb visits Wheeler's every Sunday for the feast; when I met him, he was walking barefoot with a pink blanket wrapped around him like a poncho and fastened with a giant safety pin. A man of soaring height with crow eyes and a dark, silky beard, he talks in sermonettes, rising on his toes with enthusiasm. Gottlieb and a friend, Ramon Sender, decided in 1966 to start a community at Morning Star with one governing precept: access to the land would be denied to no one. With no rules, no organization, they felt, hostilities would not arise, and people could be reborn by living in harmony with the earth. Gottlieb deeded the land to God, and, shortly, a woman sued God because her home had been struck by lightning. "Now that God owns property," her lawyer argued, "He can be sued for natural disasters." It was not until 1967, Gottlieb says, that hippies began to patronize open land.

"From the first, the land selected the people. Those who couldn't work hard didn't survive. When the land got crowded, people split. The vibrations of the land will always protect the community." Gottlieb points to the sky. "With open land, *He* is the casting director." What happens, I ask, if someone behaves violently or destructively? Gottlieb frowns. "There have been a few cases where we've had to ask people to go, but it's at terrible, terrible cost to everyone's soul that this is done. When the land begins to throw off people, everyone suffers." He shakes his body, as if he were the land, rejecting a germ. "Open land has no historical precedent. When you give free land, not free food or money, you pull the carpet out from under the capitalist system. Once a piece of land is freed, 'no trespassing' signs pop up all along the adjoining roads."

Bill Wheeler refers to his ranch as "the land," and talks about people who live on the land, babies that are born on the land, music played on the land. He "opened the land," as he phrases it, in the winter of 1967, after Sonoma County officials tried to close Morning Star by bulldozing trees and all the buildings except Gottlieb's house. Some Morning Star people moved to Wheeler's, but others traveled to New Mexico, where they founded Morning Star East on a mesa near Taos owned by another wealthy hippie. The Southwest, particularly northern New Mexico and Colorado, has more communes on open land than any other region. The communes there are all crowded, and Taos is becoming a Haight-Ashbury in the desert. More land continues to be opened in New Mexico, as well as in California, Oregon, and Washington. Gottlieb plans to buy land and deed it to God in Holland, Sweden, Mexico, and Spain. "We're fighting against the territorial imperative," he says. "The hippies should get the Nobel Prize for creating this simple idea. Why did no one think of it before the hippies? Because hippies don't work, so they have time to dream up truly creative ideas."

It was surprising to hear people refer to themselves as "hippies"; I thought the term had been rendered meaningless by overuse. Our culture has absorbed so much of the style of hip—clothes, hair, language, drugs, music—that it has obscured the substance of the movement with which people at Morning Star and Wheeler's still strongly identify. Being a hippie, to them, means dropping out completely, and finding another way to live, to support oneself physically and spiritually. It does not mean being a company freak, working nine to five in a straight job and roaming the East Village on weekends. It means saying no to competition, no to the work ethic, no to consumption of technology's products, no to political systems and games. Lou Gottlieb, who was once a Communist party member, says, "The entire Left is a dead end." The hippie alternative is to turn inward and reach backward for roots, simplicity, and the tribal experience. In the first bloom of the movement, people flowed into slums where housing would be cheap and many things could be obtained free—food scraps from restaurants, second-hand clothes, free clinics and services. But the slums proved inhospitable. The hippies did nothing to improve the dilapidated neighborhoods, and they were preyed upon by criminals, pushers, and the desperate. In late 1967, they began trekking to rural land where there would be few people and life would be hard. They took up what Ramon Sender calls "voluntary primitivism," building houses out of mud and trees, planting and harvesting crops by hand, rolling loose tobacco into cigarettes, grinding their own wheat, baking bread, canning vegetables, delivering their own babies, and educating their own children. They gave up electricity, the telephone, running water, gas stoves, even rock music, which, of all things, is supposed to be the cornerstone of hip culture. They started to sing and play their own music—folky and quiet.

Getting close to the earth meant conditioning their bodies to cold, discomfort, and strenuous exercise. At Wheeler's, people walk twenty miles a day, carrying water and wood, gardening, and visiting each other. Only four-wheel-drive vehicles can cross the ranch, and ultimately Bill wants all cars banned. "We would rather live without machines. And the fact that we have no good roads protects us from tourists. People are carbound, even police. They would never come in here without their vehicles." Although it rains a good part of the year, most of the huts do not have stoves and are not waterproof. "Houses shouldn't be designed to keep out the weather," Bill says. "We want to get in touch with it." He installed six chemical toilets on the ranch to comply with county sanitation requirements, but, he says, "I wouldn't go in one of those toilets if you paid me. It's very important for us to be able to use the ground, because we are completing a cycle, returning to Mother Earth what she's given us." Garbage is also returned to the ground. Food scraps are buried in a compost pile of sawdust and hay until they decompose and mix with the soil. Paper is burned, and metal buried. But not everyone is conscientious; there are piles of trash on various parts of the ranch.

Because of the haphazard sanitation system, the water at Wheeler's is contaminated, and until people adjust to it, they suffer dysentery, just as tourists do who drink the water in Mexico. There are periodic waves of hepatitis, clap, crabs, scabies, and streptococcic throat infections. No one brushes his teeth more than once a week, and they often use "organic toothpaste," made from eggplant cooked in tinfoil. They are experimenting with herbs and Indian healing remedies to become free of manufactured medicinal drugs, but see no contradiction in continuing to swallow any mind-altering chemical they are offered. The delivery of babies on the land has become an important ritual. With friends, children, and animals keeping watch, chanting, and getting collectively stoned, women have given birth to babies they have named Morning Star, Psyche, Joy, Covelo Vishnu God, Rainbow Canyon King, and Raspberry Sundown Hummingbird Wheeler.

The childbirth ritual and the weekly feasts are conscious attempts at what is called "retribalization." But Wheeler's Ranch, like many hippie settlements, has rejected communal living in favor of a loose community of individuals. People live alone or in monogamous units, cook for themselves, and build their own houses and sometimes gardens. "There should not be a main lodge, because you get too many people trying to live under one roof and it doesn't work," Bill says. As a result, there are cliques who eat together, share resources, and rarely mix with others on the ranch. There was one group marriage between two teen-age girls, a forty-year-old man, and two married couples, which ended when one of the husbands saw his wife with another man in the group, pulled a knife, and dragged her off, yelling, "Forget this shit. She belongs to me."

With couples, the double standard is an unwritten rule: the men can roam but the women must be faithful. There are many more men than women, and when a new girl arrives, she is pounced upon, claimed, and made the subject of wide gossip. Mary Cordelia Stevens, or Corky, a handsome eighteen-year-old from a Chicago suburb, hiked into the ranch one afternoon last October and sat down by the front gate to eat a can of Spam. The first young man who came by invited her to a party where everyone took TCP, a tranquilizer for horses. It was a strange trip—people rolling around the floor of the tipi, moaning, retching, laughing, hallucinating. Corky went home with one guy and stayed with him for three weeks, during which time she was almost constantly stoned. "You sort of have to be stoned to get through the first days here," she says. "Then you know the trip." Corky is a strapping, well-proportioned, large-boned girl with a milkmaid's face and long blond hair. She talks softly, with many giggles: "I love to go around naked. There's so much sexual energy here, it's great. Everybody's turned on to each other's bodies." Corky left the ranch to go home for Christmas and to officially drop out of Antioch College; she hitchhiked back, built her own house and chicken coop, learned to plant, do laundry in a tin tub with a washboard, and milk the cows. "I love dealing with things that are simple and direct."

Bill Wheeler admires Corky for making it on her own, which few of the women do. Bill is torn between his desire to be the benefactor-protector and his intolerance of people who aren't self-reliant. "I'm contemptuous of people who can't pull their own weight," he says. Yet he constantly worries about the welfare of others. He also feels conflict between wanting a tribe, indeed wanting to be chieftain, and wanting privacy. "Open land requires a leap of faith," he says, "but it's worth it, because it guarantees there will always be change, and stagnation is death." Because of the fluidity of the community, it is almost impossible for it to become economically self-sufficient. None of the communes have been able to live entirely off the land. Most are unwilling to go into cash crops or light industry because in an open community with no rules, there are not enough people who can be counted on to work regularly. The women with children receive welfare, some of the men collect unemployment and food stamps, and others get money from home. They spend very little—perhaps $600 a year per person. "We're not up here to make money," Bill says, "or to live like country squires."

When darkness falls, the ranch becomes eerily quiet and mobility stops. No one uses flashlights. Those who have lived there some time can feel their way along the paths by memory. Others stay in their huts, have dinner, go to sleep, and get up with the sun. Around 7:00 P.M., people gather at the barn with bottles for the late milking. During the week, the night milking is the main social event. Corky says, "It's the only time you know you're going to see people. Otherwise you could wander around for days and not see anyone." A girl from Holland and two boys have gathered mussels at a nearby beach during the day, and invite everyone to the tipi to eat them. We sit for some time in silence, watching the mussels steam open in a pot over the grate. A boy with glassy blue eyes whose lids seem weighted down starts to pick out the orange flesh with his dirt-caked hands and drops them in a pan greased with Spry. A mangy cat snaps every third mussel out of the pan. No one stops it. . . .

Nancy, in her shack about a mile from the tipi, is fixing a green stew of onions, cabbage, kale, leeks, and potatoes; she calls to three people who live nearby to come share it. Nancy has a seventeen-year-old, all-American-girl face—straight blond hair and pink cheeks—on a plump, saggy-stomached mother's body. She has been married twice, gone to graduate school, worked as a social worker and a prostitute, joined the Sexual Freedom League, and taken many overdoses of drugs. Her children have been on more acid trips than most adults at the ranch. "They get very quiet on acid," she says. "The experience is less staggering for kids than for adults, because acid returns you to the consciousness of childhood." Nancy says the children have not been sick since they moved to Wheeler's two years ago. "I can see divine guidance leading us here. This place has been touched by God." She had a vision of planting trees on the land, and ordered fifty of exotic variety, like strawberry guava, camellia, and loquat. Stirring the green stew, she smiles vacuously. "I feel anticipant of a very happy future."

With morning comes a hailstorm, and Bill Wheeler must go to court in Santa Rosa for trial on charges of assaulting a policeman when a squad came to the ranch looking for juvenile runaways and Army deserters. Bill, Gay, Gay's brother Peter, Nancy, Shoshone, and Corky spread out through the courthouse, peeling off mildewed clothes and piling them on benches. Peter, a gigantic, muscular fellow of twenty-three, rips his pants all the way up the back, and, like most people at Wheeler's, he is not wearing underwear. Gay changes Raspberry's diapers on the floor of the ladies' room. Nancy takes off her rain-soaked long johns and leaves them in one of the stalls.

It is a tedious day. Witnesses give conflicting testimony, but all corroborate that one of the officers struck Wheeler first, leading to a shoving, running, tackling, pot-throwing skirmish which also involved Peter. The defendants spend the night in a motel, going over testimony with their lawyer. Bill and Corky go to a supermarket to buy dinner, and wheel down the aisle checking labels for chemicals, opening jars to take a taste with the finger, uhmmm, laughing at the "obsolete consciousness" of the place. They buy greens, Roquefort dressing, peanut butter, organic honey, and two Sara Lee cakes. The next morning, Nancy says she couldn't sleep with the radiator and all the trucks. Gay says, "I had a dream in which I saw death. It was a blond man with no facial hair, and he looked at me with this all-concealing expression." Bill, outside, staring at the Kodak blue swimming pool: "I dreamed last night that Gay and I got separated somehow and I was stuck with Raspberry." He shudders. "You know, I feel love for other people, but Gay is the only one I want to spend my life with."

The jury goes out at 3:00 P.M. and deliberates until 9:00. In the courtroom, a mottled group in pioneer clothes, mud-spattered and frizzy-wet, are chanting, "Om." The jury cannot agree on four counts, and finds Bill and Peter not guilty on three counts. The judge declares a mistrial. The county fathers are not finished, though. They are still attempting to close the access road to Wheeler's and to get an injunction to raze all buildings on the ranch as health hazards. Bill Wheeler is not worried, nor are his charges, climbing in the jeep and singing, "Any day now . . ." God will provide.

> We must do away with the absolutely specious notion that everybody has to earn a living. . . . We keep inventing jobs because of this false idea that everybody has to be employed at some kind of drudgery because, according to Malthusian-Darwinian theory, he must justify his right to exist. . . . The true business of people should be to . . . think about whatever it was they were thinking about before somebody came along and told them they had to earn a living.
> —R. Buckminister Fuller

> No society racing through the turbulence of the next several decades will be able to do without [some] form of future-shock absorber: specialized centers in which the rate of change is artificially depressed. . . . In such slow-paced communities, individuals who needed or wanted a more relaxed, less stimulating existence could find it.
> —Alvin Toffler, *Coping with Future Shock*

Roads across the upper Northwest are flat and ruler-straight, snow-bound for long months, turning arid and dusty in the summer. At an empty crossing in a poor, wheat-growing county, the road suddenly dips and winds down to a valley filled with tall pines and primitive log cabins. The community hidden in this natural canyon is Freedom Farm, founded in 1963. It is one of the oldest communes to be started on open land. The residents—about twenty-four adults and almost as many children—are serious, straightforward people who, with calculated bluntness, say they are dropouts, social misfits, unable or unwilling to cope with the world "outside." The community has no rules, except that no one can be asked to leave. Because it predates the hippie movement, there is an absence of mystical claptrap and jargon like "far out." Only a few are vegetarians. Members do not want the location of the farm published for fear of being inundated with "psychedelic beggars."

I drove to the canyon in the morning and, having learned my lesson, left the car at the top and walked down the steep, icy road. The farm is divided into two parts—80 acres at the north end of the canyon and 120 acres at the south. The families live separately, as they do at Wheeler's, but their homes are more elaborate and solidly built. The first house in the north end is a hexagonal log cabin built by Huw Williams, who started the farm when he was nineteen. Huw is slight, soft-spoken, with a wispy blond beard. His face and voice are expressionless, but when he speaks, he is likely to say something startling, humorous, or indicative of deep feeling. When I arrived, he was cutting out pieces of leather, wearing a green-and-brown lumberman's shirt and a knife strapped to his waist. His wife, Sylvia, was nursing their youngest son, while their two-year-old, Sennett, wearing nothing but a T-shirt, was playing on the floor with a half-breed Norwegian elkhound. The cabin was snugly warm, but smelled faintly of urine from Sennett peeing repeatedly on the rug. There was a cast-iron stove, tables and benches built from logs, a crib, an old-fashioned cradle, and a large bed raised off the floor for warmth and storage space. On the wall there was a calendar opened to January, although it was March.

I asked Huw how the community had stayed together for seven years. He said, deadpan, "The secret is not to try. We've got a lot of rugged individualists here, and everyone is into a different thing. In reflection, it feels good that we survived. A lot of us were from wealthy backgrounds, and the idea of giving it all up and living off the land was a challenge." Huw grew up on a ranch 40 miles from the canyon. "I had everything. When I was fourteen, I had my own car, a half-dozen cows, and $600 in the bank." When he was fifteen, his house burned down and he saw his elaborate collections—stamps, models, books—disappear. He vowed not to become attached to possessions after that, and took to sleeping outdoors. He remembers being terrified of violence, and idolized Gandhi, Christ, and Tolstoy. At seventeen, he became a conscientious objector and began to work in draft resistance. While on a peace walk from New Hampshire to Washington, D.C., he decided to drop out of the University of Washington and start a nonviolent training center, a community where people could live by sharing rather than competing. He persuaded his mother to give him 80 acres in the canyon for the project, rented a house, called the Hart House, and advertised in peace papers for people to come and share it with him.

The first summer, more than fifty came and went and they all lived in the Hart House. One of the visitors was Sylvia, a fair-skinned girl with long chestnut hair and warm wistful eyes that hint of sadness. They were married, and Huw stopped talking about a peace center and started studying intentional communities. He decided he wanted a community that would be open to anyone, flexible, with no prescribed rules to live by. Work would get done, Huw felt, because people would want to do it to achieve certain ends. "It's a Western idea. You inspire people by giving them a goal, making it seem important; then they'll do anything to get there." If people did not want to work, Huw felt, forcing them would not be the answer.

The results were chaotic. "Emotional crises, fights over everything. A constant battle to get things done. A typical scene would be for one guy to spend two hours fixing a meal. He had to make three separate dishes— one for vegetarians, one for nonvegetarians, and one for people who wouldn't eat government-surplus food. He would put them on the table, everybody would grab, and if you stood back you got nothing. When people live that close together, they become less sensitive, and manners go right out the window. It was educational, but we knew it wasn't suitable for raising children." The group pooled resources and bought another 120 acres two miles away. Huw and Sylvia built their own cabin and moved out of the Hart House; another couple followed. Then around 1966, the drug scene exploded and the farm was swamped with speed freaks, runaways, addicts, and crazies. A schism grew between the permanent people and the transients. The transients thought the permanents were uptight and stingy. The permanents said the transients were abusing the land. When most of the permanents had built their own cabins, they began talking about burning down the Hart House. I heard many versions of the incident. Some say a man, whom I shall call George, burned it. Some say everyone did it. Some said they watched and were against it but felt they should not stop it. Afterwards, most of the transients left, and the farm settled into its present pattern of individual families tending their own gardens, buying their own supplies, and raising their own animals. Each family has at least two vehicles—a car and a tractor, or a motorcycle or truck. Huw says, "We do our share of polluting."

The majority at Freedom live on welfare, unemployment compensation, and food stamps. A few take part-time jobs picking apples or wheat, one does free-lance writing, and some do crafts. Huw makes about $50 a month on his leather work, Ken Meister makes wall hangings, Rico and

Pat sell jewelry to psychedelic shops, and Steve raises rabbits. Huw believes the farm could support itself by growing organic grains and selling them by mail order, but he hasn't been able to get enough cooperation to do this. "It's impossible to have both a commune, where everyone lives and works collectively, and free land, where anyone can settle," he says. "Some day we might have a commune on the land, but not everyone who lived on the land would have to join it."

The only communal rituals are Thanksgiving at the schoolhouse and the corn dance, held on the first full moon of May. Huw devised the corn dance from a Hopi Indian ceremony, and each year it gets wilder. Huw builds a drum, and at sundown everyone gathers on a hillside with food, wine, the children in costumes, animals, and musical instruments. They take turns beating the drum but must keep it beating until dawn. They roast potatoes, and sometimes a kid, a pig, or a turkey, get stoned, dance, howl, and drop to sleep. "But that's only once a year," one of the men says. "We could have one every month, and it would hold the community together." Not everyone wants this solidarity, however. Some are like hermits and have staked out corners of the canyon where they want to be left alone. The families who live nearby get together for dinners, chores, and baby-sitting. At the north end, the Williamses, the Swansons, and the Goldens pop in and out constantly. On the day I arrive, they are having a garden meeting at the Swansons' to decide what to order for spring planting.

The Swansons, who have three children, moved into the canyon this year after buying, for $1,000, the two-story house a man called Steve had built for his own family. Steve had had a falling out with Huw and wanted to move to the south acres. The Swansons needed a place they could move into right away. The house has the best equipment at the farm, with a flush toilet (sectioned off by a blanket hung from the ceiling), running water, and electricity that drives a stove, refrigerator, and freezer. Jack Swanson, an outgoing, ruddy-faced man of thirty-five, with short hair and a moustache, works on a newspaper 150 miles away and commutes to the farm for weekends. His wife, Barbara, twenty-four, is the image of a Midwestern college girl: jeans cut off to Bermuda length, blouses with Peter Pan collars, and a daisy-printed scarf around her short brown hair. But it is quickly apparent that she is a strong-willed nonconformist. "I've always been a black sheep," she says. "I hate supermarkets—everything's been chemically preserved. You might as well be in a morgue." Barbara is gifted at baking, pickling, and canning, and wants to raise sheep to weave and dye the wool herself. She and Jack tried living in various cities, then a suburb, then a farm in Idaho, where they found they lacked the skills to make it work. "We were so ill-equipped by society to live off the earth," Jack says. "We thought about moving to Freedom Farm for three or four years, but when times were good, we put it off." Last year their third child was born with a lung disease which required months of hospitalization and left them deep in debt. Moving to the farm seemed a way out. "If we had stayed in the suburbs, we found we were spending everything we made, with rent and car payments, and could never pay off the debts. I had to make more and more just to stay even. The price was too high for what we wanted in life," Jack says. "Here, because I don't pay rent and because we can raise food ourselves, I don't have to make as much money. We get help in farming, and have good company. In two or three months, this house is all mine—no interest, no taxes. Outside it would cost me $20,000 and 8 percent interest."

A rainstorm hits at midnight and by morning the snow has washed off the canyon walls, the stream has flooded over, and the roads are slushy mud ruts. Sylvia saddles two horses and we ride down to the south 120. There are seven cabins on the valley floor, and three hidden by trees on the cliff. Outside one of the houses, Steve is feeding his rabbits; the mute, wiggling animals are clustering around the cage doors. Steve breeds the rabbits to sell to a processor and hopes to earn $100 a month from the business. He also kills them to eat. "It's tough to do," he says, "but if people are going to eat meat, they should be willing to kill the animal." While Steve is building his new house, he has moved with his wife and four children into the cabin of a couple I shall call George and Liz Snow. George is a hefty, porcine man of thirty-nine, a drifter who earned a doctorate in statistics, headed an advertising agency, ran guns to Cuba, worked as a civil servant, a mason, a dishwasher, and rode the freights. He can calculate the angles of a geodesic dome and quote Boccaccio and Shakespeare. He has had three wives, and does not want his name known because "there are a lot of people I don't want to find me."

Steve, a hard-lived thirty-four, has a past that rivals George's for tumult: nine years as an Army engineer, AWOL, running a coffee house in El Paso, six months in a Mexican jail on a marijuana charge, working nine-to-five as chief engineer in a fire-alarm factory in New Haven, Connecticut, then cross-country to Spokane. Steve has great dynamism and charm that are both appealing and abrasive. His assertiveness inevitably led to friction in every situation, until, tired of bucking the system, he moved to the farm. "I liked the structure of this community," he says. "Up there, I can't get along with one out of a thousand people. Here I make it with one out of two." He adds, "We're in the business of survival while the world goes crazy. It's good to know how to build a fire, or a waterwheel, because if the world ends, you're there now."

Everyone at Freedom seems to share this sense of imminent doomsday. Huw says, "When the country is wiped out, electricity will stop coming through the wires, so you might as well do without it now. I don't believe you should use any machine you can't fix yourself." Steve says, "Technology can't feed all the world's people." Stash, a young man who lives alone at the farm, asks, "Am I going to start starving in twenty years?"

Steve: "Not if you have a plot to garden."

Stash: "What if the ravaging hordes come through?"

Steve: "Be prepared for the end, or get yourself a gun."

There is an impulse to dismiss this talk as a projection of people's sense of their own private doom, except for the fact that the fear is widespread. Stewart Brand writes in the *Whole Earth Catalog*: "One barometer of people's social-confidence level is the sales of books on survival. I can report that sales on *The Survival Book* are booming; it's one of our fastest moving items."

Several times a week, Steve, Stash, and Steve's daughter Laura, fourteen, drive to the small town nearby to buy groceries, visit a friend, and, if the hot water holds out, take showers. They stop at Joe's Bar for beer and hamburgers—40 cents "with all the trimmings." Laura, a graceful, quiet girl, walks across the deserted street to buy *Mad* magazine and look at rock record albums. There are three teenagers at the farm—all girls—and all have tried running away to the city. One was arrested for shoplifting, another was picked up in a crash pad with seven men. Steve says, "We have just as much trouble with our kids as straight, middle-class parents do. I'd like to talk to people in other communities and find out how they handle their teen-agers. Maybe we could send ours there." Stash says, "Or bring teen-age boys here." The women at the farm have started to joke uneasily that their sons will become uptight businessmen and their daughters will be suburban housewives. The history of utopian communities in this country has been that the second generation leaves. It is easy to imagine commune-raised children having their first haute-cuisine meal, or sleeping in silk pajamas in a luxury hotel, or taking a jet plane. Are they not bound to be dazzled? Sylvia says, "Our way of life is an overreaction to something, and our kids will probably overreact to us. It's absurd. Kids run away from this, and all the runaways from the city come here."

In theory, the farm is an expanded family, and children can move around and live with different people or build houses of their own. In the summer, they take blankets and sleeping bags up in the cliffs to sleep in a noisy, laughing bunch. When I visited, all the children except one were staying in their parents' houses. Low-key tension seemed to be running through the community, with Steve and Huw Williams at opposite poles. Steve's wife, Ann, told me, "We don't go along with Huw's philosophy of anarchy. We don't think it works. You need some authority and discipline in any social situation." Huw says, "The thing about anarchy is that I'm willing to do a job myself, if I have to, rather than start imposing rules on others. Steve and George want things to be done efficiently with someone giving orders, like the Army."

At dinner when the sun goes down, Steve's and George's house throbs with good will and festivity. The cabin, like most at the farm, is not divided into separate rooms. All nine people—Steve, Ann, and their four children, the Snows and their baby—sleep on the upstairs level, while the downstairs serves as kitchen, dining and living room. "The teen-agers wish there were more privacy," Steve says, "but for us and the younger children, it feels really close." Most couples at the farm are untroubled about making love in front of the children. "We don't make a point of it," one man says, "but if they happen to see it, and it's done in love and with good vibrations, they won't be afraid or embarrassed."

While Ann and Liz cook hasenpfeffer, Steve's daughters, Laura and Karen, ten, improvise making gingerbread with vinegar and brown sugar as a substitute for molasses. A blue jay chatters in a cage hung from the ceiling. Geese honk outside, and five dogs chase each other around the room. Steve plays the guitar and sings. The hasenpfeffer is superb. The rabbits have been pickled for two days, cooked in red wine, herbs, and sour cream. There are large bowls of beets, potatoes, jello, and the gingerbread, which tastes perfect, with homemade apple sauce. Afterwards, we all got toothpicks. Liz, an uninhibited, roly-poly girl of twenty-three, is describing how she hitchhiked to the farm, met George, stayed, and got married. "I like it here," she says, pursing her lips, "because I can stand nude on my front porch and yell, fuck! Also, I think I like it here because I'm fat, and there aren't many mirrors around. Clothes don't matter, and people don't judge you by your appearance like they do out there." She adds, "I've always been different from others. I think most of the people here are misfits—they have problems in communicating, relating to one another." Ann says, "Communication is ridiculous. We've begun to feel gossip is much better. It gradually gets around to the person it's about, and that's okay. Most people here can't say things to each other's face."

I walk home—I'm staying in a vacant cabin—across a field, with the stars standing out in brilliant relief from the black sky. Lights flicker in the cabins sprinkled through the valley. Ken Meister is milking late in the barn. The fire is still going in my cabin; I add two logs, light the kerosene lamps, and climb under the blankets on the high bed. Stream water sweeps by the cabin in low whooshes, the fire sputters. The rhythm of the canyon, after a few days, seems to have entered my body. I fall asleep around ten, wake up at six, and can feel the time even though there are no clocks around. In the morning light, though, I find two dead mice on the floor, and must walk a mile to get water, then build a fire to heat it. It becomes clear why, in a community like this, the sex roles are so well-defined and satisfying. When men actually do heavy physical labor like chopping trees, baling hay, and digging irrigation ditches, it feels very fulfilling for the woman to tend the cabin, grind wheat, put up fruit, and sew or knit. Each depends on the other for basic needs—shelter, warmth, food. With no intermediaries, such as supermarkets and banks, there is a direct relationship between work and survival. It is thus possible, according to Huw, for even the most repetitive jobs such as washing dishes or sawing wood to be spiritually rewarding. "Sawing puts my head in a good place," he says. "It's like a yogic exercise."

In addition to his farming and leather work, Huw has assumed the job of teacher for the four children of school age. Huw believes school should be a free, anarchic experience, and that the students should set their own learning programs. Suddenly given this freedom, the children, who were accustomed to public school, said they wanted to play and ride the horses. Huw finally told them they must be at the school house every day for at least one hour. They float in and out, and Huw stays half the day. He walks home for lunch and passes Karen and another girl on the road. Karen taunts him, "Did you see the mess we made at the school?"

"Yes," Huw says.

"Did you see our note?"

Huw walks on, staring at the ground. "It makes me feel you don't have much respect for the tools or the school."

She laughs. "Course we don't have any respect!"

"Well, it's your school," Huw says softly.

Karen shouts, "You said it was your school the other day. You're an Indian giver."

Huw: "I never said it was my school. Your parents said that." Aside to me, he says, "They're getting better at arguing every day. Still not very good, though." I tell Huw they seem to enjoy tormenting him. "I know. I'm the only adult around here they can do that to without getting clobbered. It gives them a sense of power. It's ironic, because I keep saying they're mature and responsible, and their parents say they need strict authority and discipline. So who do they rebel against? Me. I'm going to call a school meeting tonight. Maybe we can talk some of this out."

In the afternoon I visit Rico and Pat, whose A-frame house is the most beautiful and imaginative at the farm. It has three levels—a basement, where they work on jewelry and have stored a year's supply of food; a kitchen-living-room floor; and a high sleeping porch reached by a ladder. The second story is carpeted, with harem-like cushions, furs, and wall hangings. There are low tables, one of which lifts to reveal a sunken white porcelain bathtub with running water heated by the wood stove. Rico, twenty-five, designed the house so efficiently that even in winter, when the temperature drops to 20 below zero, it is warm enough for him to lounge about wearing nothing but a black cape. Pat and Rico have talked about living with six adults in some form of group marriage, but, Pat says, "there's no one here we could really do it with. The sexual experiments that have gone on have been rather compulsive and desperate. Some of us think jealousy is innate." Rico says, "I think it's cultural." Pat says, "Hopefully our kids will be able to grow up without it. I think the children who are born here will really have a chance to develop freely. The older children who've come here recently are too far gone to appreciate the environment."

In the evening, ten parents and five children show up at the school, a one-room house built with eighteen sides, so that a geodesic dome can be constructed on top. The room has a furnace, bookshelves and work tables, rugs and cushions on the floor. Sylvia is sitting on a stool in the center nursing her son. Two boys in yellow pajamas are running in circles, squealing, "Ba-ba-ba!" Karen is drawing on the blackboard—of all things, a city skyscape. Rico is doing a yoga headstand. Steve and Huw begin arguing about whether the children should have to come to the school every day. Steve says, in a booming voice, "I think the whole can-yon should be a learning community, a total educational environment. The kids can learn something from everyone. If you want to teach them, why don't you come to our house?" Huw, standing with a clipboard against his hip, says, "They have to come here to satisfy the county school superintendent. But it seems futile when they come in and say I'm not qualified to teach them. Where do they get that?"

Steve says, "From me. I don't think you're qualified." Huw: "Well, I'm prepared to quit and give you the option of doing something else, or send-ing them to public school."

Steve says, "Don't quit. I know your motives are pure as the driven snow. . . ."

Huw says, "I'm doing it for myself as well, to prove I can do it. But it all fits together."

They reach an understanding without speaking further.

Steve then says, "I'd like to propose that we go door-to-door in this community and get everyone enthused about the school as a center for adult learning and cultural activity first, and for the kiddies second. Be-cause when you turn on the adults, the kids will follow. The school build-ing needs finishing—the dome should be built this summer. Unless there's more enthusiasm in this community, I'm not going to contribute a thing. But if we get everybody to boost this, by God I'll be the first one out to dig."

Huw says, "You don't think the people who took the time to come tonight is enough interest? I may be cynical, but I think the only way to get some of the others here would be to have pot and dope."

Steve: "Get them interested in the idea of guest speakers, musicians, from India, all over. We can build bunk dorms to accommodate them."

Huw: "Okay. I think we should get together every Sunday night to discuss ideas, hash things over. In the meantime, why don't we buy materials to finish the building?"

On the morning I leave, sunlight washes down the valley from a cloudless sky. Huw, in his green lumberman's shirt, rides with me to the top road. "My dream is to see this canyon filled with families who live here all the time, with lots of children." He continues in a lulling rhythm: "We could export some kind of food or product. The school is very important—it should be integrated in the whole community. Children from all over could come to work, learn, and live with different families. I'd like to have doctors here and a clinic where people could be healed naturally. Eventually there should be a ham radio system set up between all the communities in the country, and a blimp, so we could make field trips back and forth. I don't think one community is enough to meet our needs. We need a world culture."

Huw stands, with hands on hips, the weight set back on his heels—a small figure against the umber field. "Some day I'm going to inherit six hundred more acres down there, and it'll all be free. Land should be available for anybody to use like it was with the Indians." He smiles with the right corner of his mouth. "The Indians could no more understand owning land than they could owning the sky."